A Practical Approach to Company Accounting

Glynis D Morris BA, FCA

First Edition

LexisNexis™ UK

Members of the LexisNexis Group worldwide

United Kingdom	LexisNexis UK, a Division of Reed Elsevier (UK) Ltd, Halsbury House, 35 Chancery Lane, London, WC2A 1EL, and 4 Hill Street, EDINBURGH EH2 3JZ
Argentina	LexisNexis Argentina, BUENOS AIRES
Australia	LexisNexis Butterworths, CHATSWOOD, New South Wales
Austria	LexisNexis Verlag ARD Orac GmbH & Co KG, VIENNA
Canada	LexisNexis Butterworths, MARKHAM, Ontario
Chile	LexisNexis Chile Ltda, SANTIAGO DE CHILE
Czech Republic	Nakladatelství Orac sro, PRAGUE
France	Editions du Juris-Classeur SA, PARIS
Germany	LexisNexis Deutschland GmbH, FRANKFURT, MUNSTER
Hong Kong	LexisNexis Butterworths, HONG KONG
Hungary	HVG-Orac, BUDAPEST
India	LexisNexis Butterworths, NEW DELHI
Ireland	Butterworths (Ireland) Ltd, DUBLIN
Italy	Giuffrè Editore, MILAN
Malaysia	Malayan Law Journal Sdn Bhd, KUALA LUMPUR
New Zealand	LexisNexis Butterworths, WELLINGTON
Poland	Wydawnictwo Prawnicze LexisNexis, WARSAW
Singapore	LexisNexis Butterworths, SINGAPORE
South Africa	LexisNexis Butterworths, DURBAN
Switzerland	Stämpfli Verlag AG, BERNE
USA	LexisNexis, DAYTON, Ohio

First published in 2003

A CIP Catalogue record for this book is available from the British Library.

ISBN 07545 1992 9

Typeset by Action Publishing Technology Ltd, Gloucester GL1 5SR
Printed and bound in Great Britain by Butler and Tanner Ltd, Frome and London

Visit **LexisNexis UK** at **www.lexisnexis.co.uk**

Preface

My work over the last twenty-five years or so has brought me into contact with a variety of public companies and public sector bodies, but a large part of my time has been spent in working with smaller private companies and I am well aware of the problems that an accountancy practitioner or in-house company accountant can face when trying to research a technical issue in the context of such a business. Many accountancy reference works devote considerable space to the detailed requirements applying to listed companies and other larger businesses and the illustrations and practical examples are drawn from the accounts of such entities.

'A Practical Approach to Company Accounting' aims to provide small and medium-sized companies and their advisors with up to date information on the accounting requirements that apply to private companies, together with detailed guidance on their implementation in practice and brief details of any changes that are expected to come into effect in the near future. Practical illustrations and disclosure examples suitable for the accounts of private companies are also provided.

Throughout the book, attention is drawn to any exemptions that may be available to companies that qualify as small or medium-sized under the Companies Act 1985. Chapter 7 explains in detail how the Companies Act 1985 qualification and eligibility provisions apply, and also sets out detailed information on the content of the Financial Reporting Standard for Smaller Entities.

Accounting remains an art, despite the increasing volume and complexity of company law requirements and accounting standards. In fact, most recent accounting standards are based firmly on underlying concepts rather than detailed prescriptive rules. Inevitably, this can result in grey areas where there is no obviously right or wrong answer – so much depends on the specific circumstances of each individual case. Much of the detailed guidance in this book is based on the interpretations currently being applied and my own opinions, drawn from my experience as an accountant and auditor. However, professional judgement and interpretation always evolve over time. What is accepted as best practice now may well not be acceptable in the future and the importance of keeping up to date with current developments, and of seeking legal or other professional advice where appropriate, should not be underestimated.

The practical issues dealt with in this book are based very much on technical queries and difficulties that have been raised and discussed with me by other practising accountants. I hope that users will find that the information helps to answer many of the questions that arise from day to day and that the general discussion and reasoning in the text will provide a useful basis for solving any problems not specifically dealt with.

Glynis D Morris
Chartered Accountant
28 February 2003

Contents

Chapter 1

Accounting Standards, Accounting Principles and Accounting Rules

ACCOUNTING STANDARDS

The present regime

1.1 Accounting standards are currently developed in the UK by the Accounting Standards Board (ASB) under the auspices of the Financial Reporting Council (FRC). Both bodies were established in 1990, together with the Financial Reporting Review Panel (FRRP) and the Urgent Issues Task Force (UITF). The structure of these bodies can be summarised as follows:

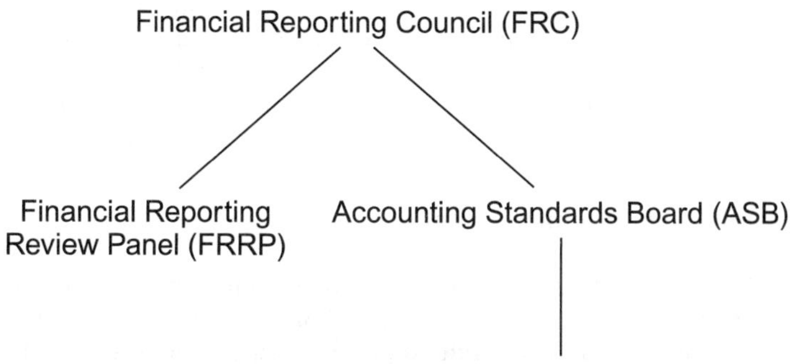

Prior to 1990, standards were developed by the Accounting Standards Committee (ASC). At its first meeting, the ASB formally adopted all existing accounting standards (22 at the time) developed by the ASC, but many of these have now been revised or superseded by new standards issued by the ASB. Standards issued by the ASC were described as Statements of Standard Accounting Practice (SSAPs) and those issued by the ASB are described as Financial Reporting Standards (FRSs). Some of the present accounting standards are therefore in the form of SSAPs whilst others are FRSs, but all have the same status for practical purposes.

Development of accounting standards

1.2 Potential topics for accounting standards are identified by the ASB from its own research and also from external sources, and ASB staff then undertake a programme of consultation and research, considering conceptual issues, existing practice in the UK, any existing pronouncements (both in the UK and abroad), and the practical implications of introducing new requirements in the UK. A Discussion Paper is usually prepared setting out the main issues and inviting comments on the ASB's initial proposals. Following this initial consultation, a Financial Reporting Exposure Draft (FRED) is published to give those who are interested a chance to comment on the proposals and to enable the ASB to assess the likely level of acceptance. The draft document may be amended in the light of the comments received, but the final decision on the content of an FRS rests with the ASB.

Scope and application of accounting standards

1.3 Accounting standards apply to all accounts that are required to show a true and fair view of the profit or loss for the financial period and of the state of affairs of an entity at its balance sheet date. Consequently they apply not only to companies and groups, but also to unincorporated entities if these are required to prepare accounts that show a true and fair view. However, the requirements of accounting standards need not be applied to items that are considered immaterial in the context of the accounts as a whole. They also do not override any exemption from disclosure that is available by law. In its guidance, the ASB emphasises that, when applying accounting standards, preparers of accounts should follow the spirit and reasoning behind the requirements as explained in the standards themselves and in the ASB's *Statement of Principles for Financial Reporting*.

Effective date of accounting standards

1.4 Each accounting standard is effective from a specific date set out in the standard. The date chosen by the ASB will take into account the fact that companies may need time to put detailed procedures into place in order to comply with the new accounting requirements. However, the effective date set by the ASB is the latest date by which compliance must be achieved, and early adoption of new accounting standards is usually encouraged. The question sometimes arises as to whether new requirements apply to all transactions or only to those arising after the effective date of the standard. The ASB's general view is that the requirements of accounting standards should be regarded as applying to all transactions, regardless of when they took place, unless a particular accounting standard specifies a different approach. Care is also required over the early adoption of accounting treatments proposed in Discussion Papers and FREDs. If the subject matter of a Discussion Paper or FRED is not covered by an existing accounting standard, the exposure document may be regarded as indicative of best practice and it may therefore be acceptable to adopt the accounting treatment proposed, bearing in mind that the the final FRS may impose slightly different requirements. If the subject matter of the Discussion Paper or FRED is already covered in an accounting standard, the existing standard remains in force until it is replaced and accounts must therefore be prepared in accordance with the existing standard, even if it is expected that the standard will be superseded by new requirements. In these circumstances, it may be appropriate to explain the effect of the new proposals in a note to the accounts.

Disclosure of compliance with accounting standards

1.5 CA 1985 Sch 4 para 36(a) requires the directors to state whether the company's accounts have been prepared in accordance with applicable accounting standards. There is an exemption from the disclosure requirement (but not from the requirement to follow applicable standards) for companies that qualify as small or medium-sized under the legislation. If there has been a departure from applicable accounting standards, particulars must be given, together with the reasons for the departure. The *Foreword to Accounting Standards* and FRS 18 *Accounting Policies* also require disclosure of the financial effect of a material departure from accounting standards.

Applicable accounting standards

1.6 CA 1985 s 256 defines accounting standards as 'statements of standard accounting practice issued by such body or bodies as may be prescribed by regulations'. Applicable accounting standards are those that are relevant to the company's circumstances and to the accounts. For the purposes of UK company law, FRSs and SSAPs constitute 'accounting standards'.

Role of the UITF

1.7 The role of the Urgent Issues Task Force (UITF) is to help the ASB to fulfil its aim of responding promptly on urgent matters as they arise. The UITF considers issues that are covered by an existing accounting standard or a provision in company law but where conflicting or unacceptable interpretations have developed, or seem likely to develop. Having considered the issue and reached a conclusion, the UITF issues its consensus in the form of an Abstract, which usually becomes effective shortly after publication. Once it is in force, a UITF Abstract has the same authority, scope and application as an accounting standard and therefore forms part of standard accounting practice.

Role of the FRRP

1.8 The Financial Reporting Review Panel (FRRP) enquires into accounts that appear to depart from the requirements of company law, accounting standards and UITF Abstracts, including the requirement to show a true and fair view. To date, reviews have concentrated on the accounts of public companies and larger private companies, but technically all companies come within the remit of the FRRP unless they qualify as small or medium-sized under CA 1985. The FRRP does not review accounts on a routine basis but acts on matters drawn to its attention, either directly or indirectly. Qualified audit reports, press comment and referrals by individuals or companies can all result in an enquiry. Where revision of the accounts is considered necessary, the FRRP usually tries to reach voluntary arrangement with the directors, but it can seek a court order for revision of the accounts under CA 1985 s 245B if it is unable to reach a satisfactory agreement with the directors.

The report of the DTI Co-ordinating Group on Audit and Accounting Issues (CGAAI), issued in January 2003 as part of the post-Enron review, includes the following recommendations in respect of the work of the FRRP:

— a financial reporting regime is only credible if accounting standards are applied in a consistent and rigorous way – effective arrangements for the enforcement of accounting standards are therefore essential;
— the FRRP should develop a pro-active element to its work – the proposal is that this should involve a risk-based selection of accounts for review and should encompass all published information issued by listed companies, including interim reports and preliminary announcements;
— the Financial Services Authority (FSA) should have a greater role in the enforcement process and in particular in identifying the risks to be investigated and the selection of accounts for review by the FRRP - the FRRP and FSA are asked to develop and agree a memorandum of understanding to clarify their respective roles and responsibilities in this process; and
— the Government should explore the scope for opening a legal gateway to enable information to be passed between the Inland Revenue and the FSA, FRRP and DTI to help in the identification of high-risk accounts.

Some changes to the current powers of the FRRP may be needed in order to implement these proposals.

European regulation of quoted groups

1.9 In June 2002, European Ministers ratified a Regulation that will require quoted companies to prepare group accounts in accordance with international accounting standards. This will come into effect in January 2005. The International Accounting Standards Board (IASB) is in the process of revising a number of its existing standards and proposals for 12 revised standards were issued in May 2002. At the same time, the ASB issued a series of exposure drafts of proposed new UK accounting standards, based on the IASB's improved standards. These represent the first major step towards aligning the text of UK accounting standards with international accounting standards in preparation for 2005. The ASB plans to introduce the new standards in the UK at the same time as the IASB issues the final versions of its own revised standards. This is expected to be in the first quarter of 2003.

Government proposals for change

1.10 Following the recent company law review, the Government White Paper *Modernising Company Law* published in July 2002 proposes some changes to the way in which requirements on the form and content of accounts will be developed in future. As noted above, quoted companies preparing group accounts will have to comply with the requirements of international accounting standards from 2005. For other companies, the company law review proposed that most of the detailed requirements on accounts should be removed from company law and that the power to prescribe detailed rules on accounting and financial reporting in its widest sense should be devolved to a new Standards Board, developed from the ASB but with a suitably adapted membership and constitution. The review also recommended the creation of a successor body to the FRRP to enforce compliance with accounting and other disclosure requirements, with an extended remit covering all the documents associated with annual financial reporting. However, the DTI has subsequently published a consultation document on the possible extension of the EU Regulation on the adoption of international accounting standards. Member states have the option of extending the application of the Regulation by:

- permitting or requiring quoted companies to prepare individual accounts in accordance with IASs; and
- permitting or requiring some or all unquoted companies to prepare their group and/or individual accounts in accordance with IASs.

The consultation document notes that the Government does not currently have a preferred option on these issues, but expects to come to a decision early in 2003, based on the results of the consultation. The proposals for a new institutional framework for the development of UK accounting standards could consequently prove to be superfluous.

Financial Reporting Standard for Smaller Entities (FRSSE)

1.11 *A Financial Reporting Standard for Smaller Entities* (FRSSE) was first published in November 1997 and came into immediate effect. A number of revised versions have been published, the latest one becoming effective in June 2002. The FRSSE may be adopted in financial statements that are intended to give a true and fair view of the financial performance and financial position of companies that qualify as small under CA 1985 and of other entities that would qualify if they were incorporated under CA 1985. If the FRSSE is adopted, this fact must be stated in the accounts. The contents of the FRSSE are based on other accounting standards, but definitions and accounting requirements are set out in a more straightforward manner, and more complex issues that are not expected to arise in smaller entities are excluded. The document is reviewed on an annual basis so that its requirements are kept up to date with developments in accounting practice. An appendix to the FRSSE links its requirements with those in accounting standards, and where issues arise that are not specifically covered in the FRSSE, those preparing the accounts are required to have regard to other standards and UITF Abstracts as a means of establishing current practice. The FRSSE includes a specific additional requirement for the accounts to disclose any personal guarantees given by the directors in respect of company borrowings.

SORPs

1.12 Statements of Recommended Practice (SORPs) set out recommended accounting practice for specialised sectors or industries. They are developed by bodies representing the appropriate sector or industry and are supplementary to accounting standards, legislation and other regulations affecting the business. Bodies wishing to develop a SORP are expected to meet criteria laid down by the ASB and to develop the SORP in accordance with the ASB's Code of Practice. The ASB will review the proposed SORP and, where appropriate, issue a 'negative assurance' statement for publication in the document, confirming that:

- the SORP does not appear to contain any fundamental points of principle that are unacceptable in the context of current accounting practice; and
- the SORP does not conflict with an accounting standard or with the ASB's plans for future accounting standards.

The contents of a SORP do not override the requirements of accounting standards, UITF Abstracts or relevant legislation. The ASB Code of Practice specifically notes that the fact that a SORP has not been updated does not exempt relevant entities from complying with more recent accounting standards and UITF Abstracts. If new standards and Abstracts conflict with the provisions of a SORP, those provisions cease to have effect. FRS 18 *Accounting Policies* requires specific disclosures to be given in the accounts when an entity comes with the scope of a SORP.

ACCOUNTING PRINCIPLES

CA 1985 requirements

1.13 CA 1985 Sch 4 requires the preparation of company accounts to be based on the principles of:

- going concern;
- consistency;

— accruals; and

— prudence.

The Act also requires the individual components of assets and liabilities to be considered separately when calculating the aggregate value of the asset or liability.

ASB Statement of Principles and FRS 18 'Accounting Policies'

1.14 SSAP 2 'Disclosure of Accounting Policies' was published in November 1971. At that time, there was no formal framework of accounting principles in the UK and SSAP 2 therefore set out and defined four fundamental accounting concepts - going concern, accruals, consistency and prudence - which were considered to underlie the periodic financial statements of a business enterprise and which were subsequently incorporated into company law. However, the standard made clear that these concepts represented a practical approach based on generally accepted assumptions at the time that the standard was issued, and it was envisaged that more theoretical ideals would evolve over the years as accounting thought and practice developed.

A lengthy ASB project on the development of a conceptual framework culminated in the publication of the 'Statement of Principles for Financial Reporting' in December 1999. This Statement took into account the developments in accounting practice in the long period since the publication of SSAP 2 and the impact of those developments on the fundamental accounting concepts identified in the standard. Going concern, accruals, consistency and prudence all feature in the Statement of Principles but they are no longer referred to as fundamental accounting concepts and the roles attributed to them in the Statement differ from those set out in SSAP 2. In particular, the relative importance attached to each of the concepts varies in the Statement, whereas under SSAP 2 they were accorded similar weight, albeit with the proviso that in any conflict between the accruals concept and the prudence concept, the prudence concept should always prevail.

During the exposure period of the draft 'Statement of Principles for Financial Reporting', it was clear that the requirements of SSAP 2 would need to be updated to remove conflicts between the Statement and the accounting standard and a new accounting standard, FRS 18 'Accounting Policies' was issued in December 2000 and superseded SSAP 2 for accounting periods ending on or after 22 June 2001.

Going concern

1.15 CA 1985 specifies that, for accounts purposes, a company is presumed to be carrying on business as a going concern [*CA 1985, Sch 4 para 10*] but does not provide any further guidance on this issue. Under

FRS 18, financial statements should be prepared on a going concern basis unless the entity is being liquidated or has ceased trading, or the directors have no realistic alternative but to liquidate the entity or to cease trading. In these circumstances, a different basis of preparation may be appropriate. The standard defines the going concern assumption as 'the hypothesis that the entity is to continue in operational existence for the foreseeable future' and notes that financial information will usually be most relevant if it is prepared on this hypothesis.

Significance of the going concern assumption

1.16 The use of the going concern basis for the preparation of accounts is of particular significance in assessing the appropriateness of the accounting policies to be adopted. Some items in the accounts would be unchanged if the entity was not considered to be a going concern, but other items might be significantly affected by this. For instance, fixed assets are usually included in the balance sheet at cost or valuation, depreciated to reflect the proportion of the life of the asset that has been used up in the business to date. The balance sheet value of the fixed assets essentially represents the value of those assets to the business as a going concern. It will not necessarily represent the amount that would be realised if the individual assets had to be sold. If an entity is being liquidated or has ceased trading, a different accounting treatment may be needed for fixed assets (e.g. they may need to be valued on a break-up basis). Other costs and liabilities may also need to be included in the accounts – for instance, redundancy payments and penalties for the breach or early termination of contracts such as leases and other rental agreements.

Directors' assessment

1.17 FRS 18 requires the directors to assess, at the time that the accounts are prepared, whether there are any significant doubts about the entity's ability to continue as a going concern. In making this assessment, the directors must take into account all available information about the foreseeable future. The guidance in the standard emphasises that the degree of consideration needed to make this assessment will vary depending on the circumstances of the entity. If there is a history of profitable operations with ready access to financial resources, and this situation is expected to continue, detailed consideration of the going concern issue may not be necessary. In other situations the directors may need to consider factors such as expected profitability, debt repayment schedules and alternative sources of finance.

Additional guidance

1.18 Additional detailed guidance on the consideration of going concern issues can be found in Statement of Auditing Standards 130 (SAS

130) 'The Going Concern Basis in Financial Statements' and the document 'Going Concern and Financial Reporting' published in November 1994 under the auspices of the Cadbury Committee. Although the latter was developed to provide guidance for directors of UK listed companies reporting under the Cadbury Code (and now the Combined Code), many of the points included in the document are equally relevant to other entities. The key points raised in these two documents are summarised in Appendices 3A and 3B.

Foreseeable future

1.19 FRS 18 does not define the foreseeable future in the context of going concern, nor does it specify the period that should be considered by the directors in their assessment of whether there are any significant doubts over the entity's ability to continue as a going concern. The guidance emphasises that this will once again depend on the circumstances of each case. However, the minimum period for the assessment is usually considered to be a period of twelve months from the date on which the financial statements are approved by the directors. This is reinforced by the fact that, where the directors' assessment has been limited to a shorter period, FRS 18 requires this fact to be disclosed in the notes to the accounts.

Material uncertainties

1.20 Where the directors are aware of material uncertainties that may cast significant doubt on the entity's ability to continue as a going concern, FRS 18 requires those uncertainties to be disclosed in the accounts. Such a situation might arise where loan covenants have been breached so that the loan has technically become repayable on demand, and the loan facility is in the course of being renegotiated but the outcome is still unknown at the time that the financial statements are approved by the directors.

Example 1.1 – Breached covenants: Explaining the use of the going concern basis

At the balance sheet date, the company has breached certain covenants relating to the bank loan of £100,000 and the lender is therefore entitled to recall the loan. The directors are in the process of renegotiating this facility and as yet repayment of the loan has not been requested. The directors are optimistic about the outcome of the negotiations, but these are still at an early stage and it is not possible to predict with any certainty what the outcome will be.

Having considered all the information available to them up to the date on which the financial statements were approved, the directors consider that it is appropriate to prepare the financial statements on a going concern basis. Consequently the financial statements do not include any adjustments that may be necessary if the loan facility is not successfully renegotiated.

Other situations that may need explanation

1.21 It is not usually considered necessary to disclose the fact that the going concern basis has been adopted and users are entitled to presume that this is the case in the absence of any disclosure to the contrary. However, where it is not apparent from the financial statements themselves that the entity is a going concern (e.g. where the entity has made a loss during the year and the balance sheet shows net liabilities) it is good practice to confirm that the going concern basis has been used and to explain why the directors consider this to be appropriate. For instance, it may be that a parent undertaking has formally guaranteed ongoing financial support to the reporting entity and that the directors have taken this into account in making their going concern assessment.

Example 1.2 – Going concern disclosure: Subordination of balance due to parent undertaking

The company's parent undertaking has confirmed that it will not seek repayment of the amount owed to it until the company's other liabilities have been met in full. Having considered this and all other information available to them up to the date on which the financial statements were approved, the directors consider that it is appropriate to prepare the financial statements on a going concern basis.

Example 1.3 – Going concern disclosure: Ongoing financial support from parent undertaking

The company's parent company has confirmed that it will continue to make available such financial support as is required to enable the company to continue to trade for the foreseeable future. Having considered this and all other information available to them up to the date on which the financial statements were approved, the directors consider that it is appropriate to prepare the financial statements on a going concern basis.

Directors' statement of responsibilities

1.22 Because the use of the going concern basis is so fundamental to the accounts, the directors are specifically required to refer to it in the formal statement of their responsibilities in respect of the accounts. This statement is considered in more detail in **Chapter 36**.

Where the going concern basis is not appropriate

1.23 Where an entity is being liquidated or has ceased trading, or the directors have no realistic alternative but to liquidate the entity or to cease trading, the financial statements may (if appropriate) be prepared on a different basis. In this case, the financial statements must disclose:

— the fact that they are not prepared on a going concern basis;

— the basis on which they have been prepared; and

— the reason why the entity is not considered to be a going concern.

Accruals

1.24 CA 1985 requires all income and charges in respect of the financial year to which the accounts relate to be taken into account, regardless of the date of receipt or payment, [*CA 1985, Sch 4 para 13*]. As with the going concern concept, no further guidance on this is provided in the legislation. FRS 18 specifically requires financial statements (other than cash flow information) to be prepared on the accruals basis of accounting. It defines this as requiring the non-cash effects of transactions and events to be reflected, as far as is possible, in the financial statements for the accounting period in which they occur, and not in the period in which any related cash is received or paid. The standard makes a clear link with the definitions of assets and liabilities set out in FRS 5 'Reporting the Substance of Transactions' (and also in the Statement of Principles) and notes that the use of those definitions to determine which items should be recognised as assets and liabilities in the balance sheet is consistent with the accruals concept.

Practical effect

1.25 The practical effect of FRS 18 is that accruals must be made for expenses and losses that relate to the reporting period, and for income and profits relating to that period, subject to the *Companies Act 1985* requirement that only profits realised at the balance sheet date should be included in the profit and loss account. For instance, overhead expenses such as electricity and telephone charges which have been incurred during the year must be included in the accounts, even if they are not paid for until after the balance sheet date. Similarly, expenses that have been paid in advance (e.g. rental costs, insurance, service and maintenance contracts covering an extended period) must be apportioned over the period to which they relate and a prepayment included in the accounts where necessary. However, the 'matching' of income and expenditure that was required under SSAP 2 has now been superseded in FRS 18 by the need to consider which items need to be reflected as assets and liabilities in the balance sheet at the end of the financial reporting period as a result of past transactions and events.

Realisation issues

1.26 FRS 18 also includes a reference to the CA 1985 requirement that only profits realised at the balance sheet date should be included in the profit and loss account and the following definition of realised profits and losses set out in the legislation:

> 'such profits and losses as fall to be treated as realised in accordance with principles generally accepted, at the time when the accounts are prepared,

with respect to the determination for accounting purposes of realised profits and losses.' [*CA 1985, s 262(3)*]

The guidance in FRS 18 notes that profits are to be treated as realised, for these purposes, only when they have been realised in the form of cash or of other assets the ultimate cash realisation of which can be assessed with reasonable certainty. These requirements are to apply unless there are special reasons for departing from them, in which case two additional rules come into effect:

- such 'special reasons' will not exist unless, as a minimum, it is possible to be reasonably certain that an unrealised gain exists and can be measured with sufficient reliability; and
- due consideration must be given to whether a departure from the requirements would result in the use of valuation bases or accounting treatments not permitted by companies' legislation and which could therefore only be used if the true and fair override was justified.

Consistency and comparability

1.27 CA 1985 requires accounting policies to be applied consistently within the same set of accounts and from one financial year to the next. [*CA 1985, Sch 4 para 11*]. There is also a separate requirement for the corresponding figures for the previous financial period to be comparable for those with the current year. This is considered in more detail in Chapter 5. FRS 18 does not specifically discuss consistency, but concentrates instead on comparability as one of the four objectives against which the appropriateness of accounting policies should be judged. Comparability is important to enable users to identify and evaluate similarities in, and differences between, the nature and effects of transactions and events taking place over time and in different reporting entities. The usefulness of financial information is therefore enhanced if it can be compared with similar information about the entity for another period or point in time, or with similar information about other entities. Comparability is usually achieved through a combination of consistency and disclosure, but the guidance in the standard emphasises that consistency is not an end in itself, and there will inevitably be circumstances in which it needs to be sacrificed. In particular, consistency should not be used to prevent improvements in accounting, and where the introduction of a new accounting policy would be of overall benefit to users, the need for consistency should not be used to justify not making the change.

Changes in accounting policy

1.28 Situations will inevitably arise from time to time which make it appropriate for an entity to change one of its accounting policies. For instance, a new accounting standard may have been introduced which requires a different accounting treatment to the one adopted by the entity in previous years. Similarly, the nature or scale of an entity's activities or transactions may change, so that an accounting policy previously adopted is no longer acceptable (i.e. because items that were previously immaterial have now become material). Examples of this might include:

- an entity which had previously only entered into minor finance leases entering into a finance lease agreement in respect of a substantial asset or assets;
- an entity that had previously only carried out an insignificant level of research and development expanding its activities in this field by becoming involved in a major product development project.

Where it is necessary to implement a new accounting policy, or to change an existing policy, the guidance in FRS 18 notes that the entity should ensure wherever possible that the new policy adopted is in accordance with recently issued accounting standards.

Regular review of accounting policies

1.29 FRS 18 requires accounting policies to be regularly reviewed to ensure that they remain the most appropriate in the particular circumstances of the entity, but also notes that in considering whether a new policy is more appropriate, due weight should be given to the potential impact on comparability. The guidance in the standard explains that frequent changes to accounting policies could be detrimental to comparability over the longer term, and the impact of past and expected future changes should therefore be taken into account when assessing whether a change in accounting policy is appropriate. Accounting policies should generally only be changed when the benefits to users will outweigh the disadvantages. Unless other accounting standards or UITF Abstracts require a different treatment, FRS 18 notes that a material adjustment to earlier years as a result of a change in accounting policy should be accounted for as a prior period adjustment in accordance with FRS 3 'Reporting Financial Performance'.

Estimation techniques

1.30 FRS 18 makes a clear distinction between changes in accounting policy and changes in estimation techniques. A change in an estimation technique should not be accounted for as a prior period adjustment unless it:

- represents the correction of a fundamental error; or
- is required by another accounting standard, UITF Abstract or companies' legislation to be accounted for as a prior period adjustment.

Prudence

1.31 CA 1985 includes the following requirements [*CA 1985, Sch 4 para 12*]:

- the amount of any item must be determined on a prudent basis;
- only profits realised at the balance sheet date should be included in the profit and loss account; and
- all liabilities and losses which have arisen, or are likely to arise, in respect of the current financial year or any previous financial year must be taken into account – this should include any liabilities or losses that only become apparent between the balance sheet date and the date on which the accounts are approved and signed by the directors.

SSAP 2 defined the prudence concept in the context of the realisation of profits, on the basis that, at the time that the standard was developed, the main concern was to prevent profits from being overstated. Subsequently, concern began to centre around the need to prevent the smoothing of profits through the deliberate understatement of assets or the deliberate overstatement of liabilities. In particular, the ASB frequently expressed concern at the nature and extent of provisions that were sometimes included in accounts, usually on the grounds that it was prudent to do so, since these could both distort trends in the profit and loss account and also result in substantial amounts of expenditure being 'hidden', in that costs were subsequently charged against the provision rather than as expenses in the profit and loss account. Specific rules were therefore set out in FRS 3 'Reporting Financial Performance' on the timing and content of provisions relating to the sale or termination of an operation, and these were developed further in FRS 12 'Provisions, Contingent Liabilities and Contingent Assets'. Broadly, a provision can now only be recognised when an entity has a legal or constructive obligation at the balance sheet date, and it is probable that this will result in the transfer of economic benefits. The guidance in FRS 12 states unequivocally that:

- uncertainty should not be used to justify excessive provisions or a deliberate overstatement of liabilities; and
- a board or management decision before the balance sheet date will not usually result in a constructive obligation at that date, unless the decision has already been put into effect or has been communicated to those affected in a way that raises a valid expectation that it will be carried out.

Current definition of prudence

1.32 Prudence is defined in the ASB's 'Statement of Principles for Financial Reporting' as:

> 'the inclusion of a degree of caution in the exercise of the judgements needed in making the estimates required under conditions of uncertainty, such that gains or assets are not overstated and losses or liabilities are not understated. In particular, under such conditions it requires more confirmatory evidence about the existence of, and a greater reliability of measurement for, assets and gains than is required for liabilities and losses.'

FRS 18 discusses prudence in the context of the reliability of financial information – reliability being one of the objectives against which the appropriateness of accounting policies should be measured. The standard notes that there will often be uncertainty about the existence of assets, liabilities, gains, losses and changes to shareholders' funds, or about the amount at which they should be measured. Prudence therefore requires that the accounting policies adopted should take account of such uncertainty in recognising and measuring items in the financial statements. The standard also emphasises that more confirmatory evidence is required about the existence of an asset or gain than for a liability or loss, and that greater reliability of measurement is needed for assets and gains than for liabilities and losses.

Inappropriate use of prudence

1.33 The standard makes two specific additional points in respect of prudence, both of which are also included in the 'Statement of Principles':

— it is not necessary to exercise prudence when there is no uncertainty; and

— it is not appropriate to use prudence as a reason for creating hidden reserves or excessive provisions, deliberately understating assets or gains, or deliberately overstating liabilities or losses – to do this would impair the reliability of the financial statements as they would no longer be free from bias.

Relevance, reliability and understandability

1.34 FRS 18 identifies four objectives against which the appropriateness of accounting policies should be assessed – relevance, reliability, comparability and understandability. The objective of financial statements is to provide information about an entity's financial performance and financial position that is useful to users in assessing the stewardship of management and making economic decisions. The guidance in FRS 18 notes that financial information is relevant if it has the ability to influence the economic decisions of users and is provided in time to influence those decisions. Financial information is considered to be reliable if:

— it can be depended upon to represent faithfully what it purports to represent or could reasonably be expected to represent – in other words, if the way in which transactions and events are recognised, measured and presented in the financial statements corresponds closely to their substance and practical effect;

- it is free from deliberate or systematic bias;
- it is free from material error;
- it is complete within the bounds of materiality; and
- under conditions of uncertainty, a degree of caution has been applied in making the necessary judgements and estimates – in other words, it has been prudently prepared.

Under FRS 18, financial information is understandable if it can be understood by users who have a reasonable knowledge of business and economic activities and who are willing to study the information provided with reasonable diligence. The adoption of appropriate accounting policies should result in the presentation of financial information that is relevant, reliable and understandable to users of the accounts.

Off-setting

1.35 The off-setting of assets and liabilities and income and expenditure in annual accounts is prohibited by CA 1985 Sch 4 para 5. Paragraph 14 of Sch 4 also requires individual assets and liabilities to be considered separately when calculating aggregate amounts. Paragraph 29 of FRS 5 'Reporting the Substance of Transactions' reinforces the requirements of CA 1985 by stating that:

- assets and liabilities should not be off-set; and
- debit and credit balances should only be aggregated into a single net item where they do not constitute separate assets and liabilities – specific conditions set out in the standard must be met for this to apply.

Similarly, the ASB's 'Statement of Principles for Financial Reporting' notes that:

- gains and losses should not normally be offset in the financial performance statement, except where they relate to the same event or circumstance and disclosing the gross components is not likely to provide useful information for the assessment of either future results or the effects of past transactions and events; and
- assets should not be offset against liabilities when reporting an entity's financial position.

Departure from accounting principles set out in CA 1985

1.36 CA 1985 permits the directors to depart from the accounting principles set out in the Act where there are special reasons for doing so, provided that the accounts disclose:

- particulars of the departure;
- the reasons for the departure; and
- the effect of the departure.

FRS 18 states unequivocally that, where companies' legislation frames the disclosure of a departure from a specific statutory requirement in these terms, the details given must include:

- a clear and unambiguous statement that there has been a departure from the requirements of an accounting standard, a UITF Abstract or companies' legislation (as appropriate) and that the departure is necessary to give a true and fair view;
- a statement of the treatment that accounting standards, UITF Abstracts or companies' legislation would normally require and a description of the treatment actually adopted;
- a statement of why the usual treatment would not give a true and fair view; and
- a description of how the position shown in the financial statements is different as a result of the departure – this should include quantification of the effect except where:
  - this is already evident in the financial statements themselves; or
  - the effect cannot be quantified, in which case the circumstances should be explained.

This information must be given in the note on compliance with applicable accounting standards (see **1.5** above) or cross-referenced to that note. If the departure continues in subsequent years, the disclosures must be given in each year, with comparatives. Where only the comparatives are affected, the disclosures must still be given in respect of those figures. The disclosure requirements are considered in more detail in **Chapter 2**.

Examples of departures from the CA 1985 accounting principles

1.37 The following examples illustrate some of the situations where departure from the accounting principles set out in the *Companies Act 1985* will usually be required:

- where an entity is not considered to be a going concern – in this case the accounts may need to be prepared on a different basis;
- the inclusion of certain unrealised exchange gains and losses in the profit and loss account in accordance with the accounting requirements of SSAP 20 'Foreign Currency Translation' – this is considered in more detail in **Chapter 6** and also referred to in **Chapter 2**;
- a change of accounting policy as discussed in **1.28** above – this is considered in more detail in **Chapter 4** along with the related accounts disclosures.

ACCOUNTING RULES

Alternative sets of accounting rules

1.38 CA 1985 sets out two alternative sets of accounting rules:

(i) the historical cost accounting rules [*CA 1985, Sch 4 para 16–28*];

(ii) the alternative accounting rules [*CA 1985, Sch 4 para 29–34*].

The two sets of rules are given equal status in the Act and companies are free to choose which they adopt in their accounts. The alternative accounting rules can be applied to all aspects of the accounts to achieve full current cost accounting, or only to selected items. The most common practice in the UK is to adopt the historical cost accounting rules, but often with selective adoption of the alternative accounting rules, most commonly to allow land and buildings to be shown at valuation rather than original cost. The notes to the accounts should state which accounting convention has been adopted.

Example 1.4 – Accounting convention adopted

Basis of preparation

The financial statements have been prepared under the historical cost accounting convention.

or

Basis of preparation

The financial statements have been prepared under the historical cost accounting convention, modified to include the revaluation of land and buildings.

Chapter 6 of the ASB 'Statement of Principles' deals with measurement in financial statements. Under the principles set out in the Statement, the most appropriate measurement basis (either historical cost or current value) should be selected for each category of assets and liabilities – this should be the basis that best meets the objective of financial statements and the demands of the qualitative characteristics of financial information, taking into account the nature of the items concerned and the circumstances involved. At present, this approach might conflict with companies' legislation in the case of certain current assets. FRS 18 'Accounting Policies' defines measurement bases, accounting policies and estimation techniques and sets out requirements on the selection of appropriate accounting policies and estimation techniques. Determining amounts under the historical cost accounting rules

1.39 Paragraphs 16–28 of Sch 4 to the Act set out detailed rules on determining the amount to be shown in the accounts under the historical cost accounting rules for:

— tangible fixed assets;

— development costs;

— goodwill;

— current assets;

— an excess of money owed over value received.

The rules on tangible fixed assets, development costs and goodwill are discussed in detail in the relevant chapters. The general rules on the other items are discussed in **1.39** and **1.40** below. The Act also includes detailed guidance on determining the purchase price or production cost of an asset and this is considered at **1.42-1.45** below.

Current assets

1.40 Current assets are defined in CA 1985 s 262(1) as assets that are not intended for use on a continuing basis in the company's activities. They normally include stocks, debtors, cash and short-term investments. Current assets must be stated at the lower of net realisable value and purchase price or production cost (see below). Where a provision has been made to write down a current asset to its net realisable value and the reasons for the write-down have ceased to apply, either fully or in part, the provision should be written back accordingly. For example, under these rules, the value of debtors should be reduced by appropriate provisions for bad and doubtful debts. However, if circumstances change and a debt previously provided for becomes fully or partially recoverable, the provision should be written back to the extent necessary to state the debt at its expected recoverable amount.

Excess of money owed over value received

1.41 The legislation considers a situation where the amount owed by a company exceeds the value of the consideration received in the transaction giving rise to the liability. For instance, this will arise where debentures issued by the company are issued at a discount, or are redeemable at a premium at a future date. In these circumstances the Act permits (but does not require) the difference in value to be treated as an asset, provided that:

— it is written off by annual instalments of a 'reasonable' amount;

— it is completely written off before the amount owed by the company is repaid;

— the unamortised amount is shown separately in the accounts, either on the balance sheet or in a note to the accounts.

The provisions of the Act are considered in detail in **Chapter 13**, in conjunction with the related requirements of accounting standards.

Determining purchase price or production cost

1.42 There is also detailed guidance on determining the purchase price or production cost of an asset. The rules cover both fixed and current assets. The purchase price of an asset is the actual price paid, plus any expenses incidental to its acquisition. Such expenses would include the cost of getting the asset to its present location and into its present condition. The purchase price of an asset also includes any attributable VAT where this is not recoverable by the purchaser. Any VAT that is recoverable should be excluded from the cost of the asset. The production cost of an asset is to be calculated by adding together the purchase price of the raw materials and consumables used and the direct costs of production. In addition, the following may be included in production cost under CA 1985:

- a reasonable proportion of indirect production costs, but only to the extent that they relate to the period of production;
- interest on capital borrowed to finance the production of the asset, but again only to the extent that it relates to the period of production.

In the case of current assets, the Act specifically prohibits the inclusion of distribution costs in 'production cost'. The interaction of these provisions with the requirements of SSAP 9 'Stocks and Long Term Contracts' is considered in **Chapter 22**. The inclusion of relevant indirect costs in production cost will often involve the use of estimation techniques and the requirements of FRS 18 'Accounting Policies' on the selection of appropriate estimation techniques are covered in Chapter 4. Where interest is included in the production cost of an asset, the notes to the accounts must disclose:

- the fact that interest has been included in the production cost of the asset;
- the amount of interest included.

The inclusion of interest in asset values is considered further in **Chapters 20** and **22**.

Unknown purchase price or production cost

1.43 Where there is no record of the purchase price or production cost of an asset, or any of the amounts needed to calculate purchase price or production cost as set out in CA 1985, or where these details cannot be obtained without unreasonable expense or delay, the value given to the asset in the earliest available record on or after its acquisition or production by the company is to be treated as the purchase price or production cost. Where a company takes advantage of this provision, the first accounts to include the asset on the basis of its earliest recorded value must include a note explaining this.

Stocks and fungible assets

1.44 The Act allows a company to apply special rules in the case of stocks and fungible assets, including investments. Fungible assets are assets of any description that are substantially indistinguishable one from another. For instance, many small consumables (e.g. screws, nuts and bolts, pens and pencils etc.) which are generally interchangeable, would come within this definition. FRS 18 'Accounting Policies' notes that specific accounting requirements for fungible assets may be set out in accounting standards, UITF Abstracts and companies' legislation. Where fungible assets are recorded at historical cost, the accounting policy may require cost to be determined on an asset-by-asset basis or may consider the assets in aggregate by using a measurement basis such as weighted average historical cost, or historical cost measured on a first in, first out (FIFO) basis. The guidance in FRS 18 notes that an accounting policy that considers fungible assets in aggregate will be more consistent with the underlying objective of comparability.

The Act allows stocks and fungible assets to be valued for accounts purposes by one of the following methods, rather than requiring them to be included at actual purchase price or production cost:

- first in, first out (FIFO);
- last in, first out (LIFO);
- a weighted average price;
- any other method similar to the above methods.

Not all of these methods are generally acceptable under SSAP 9 'Stocks and Long Term Contracts' – this is considered further in **Chapter 22**. The method chosen must be one which the directors consider appropriate to the circumstances of the company. This is reinforced by FRS 18 'Accounting Policies' which requires an entity to adopt accounting policies (and, where appropriate, estimation techniques) that enable its financial statements to give a true and fair view and that are consistent with the requirements of accounting standards, UITF Abstracts and companies' legislation. Where more than one policy or technique satisfies these conditions, and it is therefore necessary to choose between them, the standard requires the entity to select whichever policy or technique is considered most appropriate to its particular circumstances for the purpose of giving a true and fair view. The requirements of FRS 18 are considered in detail in **Chapter 4**.

If the value included in the accounts for stocks and fungible assets differs materially from the replacement cost of the assets at the balance sheet date, the difference must be disclosed in a note to the accounts. The comparison can be with the most recent actual purchase price or production cost before the balance sheet date where the directors consider this to be more appropriate. The disclosure requirement is considered further in **Chapter 22**.

Raw materials and consumables

1.45 CA 1985 permits raw materials and consumables to be included in the accounts at a fixed quantity and value provided that:

- the assets are constantly being replaced;
- their overall value is not material to an assessment of the company's state of affairs;
- their quantity, value and composition do not vary materially.

The interaction of this provision with SSAP 9 'Stocks and Long Term Contracts' is considered in **Chapter 22**.

Determining amounts under the alternative accounting rules

1.46 The alternative accounting rules set out in paras 29–34 of Sch 4 to the Act cover the following assets:

- intangible assets, other than goodwill;
- tangible fixed assets;
- investments shown as fixed assets;
- investments shown as current assets;
- stocks.

Each of these is considered briefly below. More detailed consideration of the practical implications of applying the alternative accounting rules to these assets can be found in the chapters dealing with the relevant assets.

Accounting for asset valuations

1.47 The subject of valuations in financial reporting has been considered in various ASB documents, culminating in the publication of FRS 15 'Tangible Fixed Assets' in February 1999. One of the objectives of this standard is to ensure that, where an entity chooses to revalue tangible fixed assets, the valuation is performed on a consistent basis and kept up to date, and that gains and losses on revaluation are recognised in the accounts on a consistent basis. The requirements of FRS 15 on valuation are considered in detail in **Chapter 20**.

Current cost

1.48 The alternative accounting rules allow certain assets to be shown at current cost. The term 'current cost' is not defined in the Act and there is not yet any formal guidance on 'current cost' within accounting standards. In the absence of formal guidance, valuation on the basis of current cost usually follows the guidelines set out in *Accounting for the Effects of*

Changing Prices: a Handbook published by the Accounting Standards Committee in 1986. This defines current cost as the lower of:

— the asset's net current replacement cost; and

— its recoverable amount.

An asset's recoverable amount is defined as the higher of:

— its net realisable value; and

— the amount recoverable from its future use.

This is developed further in FRS 11 'Impairment of Fixed Assets and Goodwill', which is considered in more detail in **Chapter 20**. Chapter 6 of the ASB 'Statement of Principles' also considers how the current value of assets might be determined.

1.49 Intangible fixed assets, other than goodwill, may be included in the accounts at their current cost. Goodwill can never be carried at more than its historical cost, less any amounts by which it has already been amortised. The accounting treatment of goodwill is considered further in **Chapter 19**.

Tangible fixed assets

1.50 Tangible fixed assets may be included in the accounts at either:

— market value as at the date of their last valuation; or

— current cost.

There is no requirement under the Act for market values to be kept up to date. However, FRS 15 'Tangible Fixed Assets' now sets out stringent requirements to ensure that, once assets have been included in the accounts at valuation, their value is kept up to date, and also that all items within an individual class of assets are treated consistently. These requirements are considered in detail in **Chapter 20**. Where an asset is included in the accounts under one of the valuation bases permitted by the alternative accounting rules, this value becomes the basis for the depreciation charge. This point is considered in more detail in **Chapter 12**.

Investments

1.51 Investments shown as fixed assets may be included in the accounts at:

— market value as at the date of their last valuation; or

— at a value determined on any basis which the directors consider to be appropriate in the company's circumstances.

For example, the second approach could be used to establish a value for unlisted investments, for accounts purposes, using either an earnings basis or a net asset basis. Where the second approach is adopted, a note to the accounts must disclose details of the method of valuation adopted and the reasons for choosing this method. It is not sufficient simply to state that the investments have been valued by the directors. Investments shown in the accounts as current assets may be included at their current cost.

Stocks

1.52 Under CA 1985, stocks may be included in the accounts at their current cost. However, this is generally not an acceptable accounting treatment under SSAP 9 'Stocks and Long Term Contracts'.

Disclosure of use of the alternative accounting rules

1.53 Whenever a company adopts the alternative accounting rules, the notes to the accounts must include:

- a note of each item accounted for under the alternative accounting rules; and
- the basis of valuation used for each of those items.

For each balance sheet item, other than stocks, which has been accounted for under the alternative accounting rules, the accounts must show, either separately on the balance sheet or in a note to the accounts:

- the amount at which the item would have been included in the accounts under the historical cost accounting rules, or the difference between this and the amount actually shown in the accounts; and
- the cumulative figures for depreciation or diminutions in value that would have been included in the accounts under the historical cost accounting rules.

The first disclosure must also be given for each of the main balance sheet headings affected (i.e. items given a letter or Roman numeral in the balance sheet formats set out in the Act) as well as for the individual items concerned. Where any assets are included in the accounts at valuation and this affects the profit and loss account (for instance, in terms of the amount of depreciation charged), FRS 3 'Reporting Financial Performance' requires disclosure of what the profit or loss for the year would have been under the historical cost accounting rules. This additional disclosure is considered in **Chapter 35**.

Revaluation reserve

1.54 Where any asset is revalued under the alternative accounting rules, the difference between the previous accounts value and the revalued amount must be credited or debited to a revaluation reserve. Each asset that is revalued must be considered individually. The revaluation reserve must be shown:

- separately in the balance sheet;
- in the prescribed place for the revaluation reserve within the standard balance sheet format.

However, the reserve need not be called a revaluation reserve in the accounts. The treatment for taxation purposes of any amount credited or debited to the revaluation reserve must also be disclosed in a note to the accounts. If any amount transferred to the revaluation reserve is no longer necessary for the purpose of the valuation method used, the amount must be removed from the revaluation reserve. For instance, if a company sells an asset that has previously been revalued, any amount in the revaluation reserve in respect of that asset must be removed as it is no longer needed under the alternative accounting rules. It will normally be transferred to the profit and loss account reserve as a reserves movement during the year in which the asset is sold. The rules relating to the revaluation reserve are considered in more detail in **Chapter 31.**

Appendix 1

SUMMARY OF THE KEY POINTS ON THE APPROPRIATENESS OF THE GOING CONCERN BASIS RAISED IN STATEMENT OF AUDITING STANDARDS 130 (SAS 130) 'THE GOING CONCERN BASIS IN FINANCIAL STATEMENTS'

Foreseeable future

In its definition of the going concern assumption, FRS 18 'Accounting Policies' refers to the ability of the entity to continue in operational existence for the foreseeable future. Neither the accounting standard nor the auditing standard attempts to specify any minimum period that should be covered in the going concern review. SAS 130 emphasises that the directors will need to look forward for a period of time, but that the exact period covered may vary, depending on factors such as:

- the size and complexity of the entity;
- the nature of its operations and the associated risks;
- the quality of its budgeting and reporting systems, particularly its cash flow;
- the systems (both formal and informal) used to identify warnings of future risks and uncertainties on a timely basis;
- the sensitivity of the budgets to variable factors;
- obligations or guarantees arranged with other entities;
- the existence and adequacy of borrowing facilities;
- where relevant, the plans to resolve any issue giving cause for concern in respect of the appropriateness of the going concern basis.

However, in most cases it is usually accepted that the review should cover a period of at least one year from the date of approval of the accounts.

Financial indicators of potential going concern difficulties

The following list illustrates some of the financial issues that may give rise to concern over an entity's ability to continue as a going concern:

- an excess of liabilities over assets;
- net current liabilities;
- adequate borrowing facilities not yet agreed;
- default on terms, or potential breaches of covenants, in respect of loan agreements;
- significant liquidity or cash flow problems;
- major losses or cash flow problems since the balance sheet date;
- substantial sales of fixed assets which are not to be replaced;
- major restructuring of debt;

- major debt repayment falling due without adequate facilities to cover this;
- inability to pay debts as they fall due;
- reductions in terms of trade credit and other difficulties with suppliers.

Operational and other indicators of potential going concern difficulties

The following list illustrates some of the operational and other issues that may give rise to concern over the entity's ability to continue as a going concern:

- fundamental changes in the market, or in technology, to which the entity is unable to adapt;
- forced reductions in operations (e.g. as a result of new legislation);
- loss of key management or staff;
- labour difficulties;
- high level of dependence on limited product lines in a depressed market;
- loss of key customers;
- loss of key suppliers;
- major litigation, where an adverse judgment may threaten the entity's existence.

Appendix 2

SUMMARY OF THE KEY POINTS ON THE APPROPRIATENESS OF THE GOING CONCERN BASIS RAISED IN THE JOINT WORKING GROUP GUIDANCE (JWG) 'GOING CONCERN AND FINANCIAL REPORTING'

Contents of the document

The Cadbury Code of Best Practice (now the Combined Code) recommends that the directors state in the accounts that the business is a going concern (with supporting assumptions or qualifications where necessary) primarily to ensure that directors take appropriate steps to satisfy themselves that it is reasonable to prepare the accounts on a going concern basis. The Joint Working Group Guidance was developed to help directors comply with the recommendation.

The document comprises the following sections.

- Introduction - which sets out the scope of the document and the background to the going concern concept.
- Procedures - which indicates the procedures that the directors should follow in assessing the appropriateness of the going concern basis. Additional detail is given in an Appendix to the document.
- Disclosure - which considers the accounts disclosures that should be given in different situations.
- Other - which includes consideration of the issue of going concern in the context of a group.

Guidance on procedures

The guidance on procedures includes the following points.

- As a minimum, budgets and forecasts should be prepared for the period to the next balance sheet date; further periods will normally be covered by medium or long-term plans which will give a general indication of how the directors expect the business to fare.
- Borrowing facilities should be reviewed and compared to detailed cash flow forecasts for the period to the next balance sheet date (as a minimum) to confirm that there are no expected:
  - shortfalls in facilities against requirements,
  - arrears of interest,
  - breaches of covenants.

Any potential difficulties should be discussed with the company's bankers, as this may prevent potential problems crystallising.

- Sensitivity analyses should be used on all critical assumptions and care should be taken to include all known cash outflows (e.g. loan repayments, payment of tax liabilities).

- The directors should consider the company's exposure to contingent liabilities such as:
  - legal proceedings,
  - guarantees and warranties,
  - product liability not covered by insurance,
  - environmental clean-up costs.
- The directors should assess the major aspects of the economic market in which the company operates and in particular assess for each main product:
  - the size and strength of the market,
  - the company's market share,
  - any economic, political or other factors that may cause the market to change.
- The directors should assess the company's exposure to financial risks such as fixed price contracts and movements in exchange rates.
- The directors should also assess the company's financial adaptability (i.e. its ability to alter the amount or timing of cash flows to respond to unexpected needs or opportunities) - this may help to mitigate some of the other factors referred to above.

Chapter 2

The True and Fair View

COMPANY LAW

Company law requirements

2.1 CA 1985 requires a company's balance sheet to give a true and fair view of the state of affairs of the company at the end of the financial period and the profit and loss account to give a true and fair view of the profit or loss of the company for the financial period. There can be no precise definition of what constitutes a true and fair view. This is essentially a question of judgement and, as a legal concept, it can only be interpreted by the court, although such an interpretation will usually be governed by generally accepted accounting practice and the requirements of accounting standards in particular. The true and fair view is a dynamic concept and the interpretation of it will vary over time, as a result of developments in accounting practice and the introduction of new accounting standards, many of which come about as a result of changes in business practice and general economic development. An accounting treatment that was accepted as achieving a true and fair view ten years ago will not necessarily be acceptable today. The ASB 'Statement of Principles for Financial Reporting' emphasises that the true and fair view lies at the heart of financial reporting in the UK and that, in order to give a true and fair view, financial statements must present information that is sufficient in both quantity and quality to satisfy the reasonable expectations of users.

Small companies

2.2 The requirement for the accounts to give a true and fair view of the state of affairs of the company and of its profit or loss for the period, applies to all companies, irrespective of their size. The true and fair requirement therefore continues to apply in the case of shorter form accounts prepared by a small company. Shorter form and abbreviated accounts for small companies are considered in more detail in **Chapter 7**. Small companies can choose to adopt the *Financial Reporting Standard for Smaller Entities* (FRSSE) in which case they need not follow the requirements of other accounting standards. The detailed requirements of the FRSSE in respect of the true and fair view and disclosure of the use of the true and fair override are also considered in **Chapter 7**. If the FRSSE is not adopted, the requirements of all other accounting standards apply to the accounts of a small company.

Overriding requirement for accounts to give a true and fair view

2.3 Under CA 1985, the requirement for accounts to give a true and fair view is of paramount importance and *s 226* therefore provides for those situations where following the detailed requirements set out in the Act does not achieve this:

(i) if the requirements of the Act are not sufficient for the accounts to show a true and fair view of the company's results or financial position, the additional information necessary to achieve this should be given in the accounts, or in a note to the accounts;

(ii) if compliance with the requirements of CA 1985 is inconsistent with the overriding requirement for the accounts to show a true and fair view, the directors must depart from the provisions of the Act and the following must be given in a note to the accounts:

- particulars of the departure;
- the reasons for the departure; and
- the effect of the departure.

Departure from the requirements of the Act

2.4 A departure from the requirements of the Act can arise in two ways:

- some accounting standards require departure from certain provisions of the Act for the accounts to show a true and fair view – examples include:
  - the non-depreciation of investment property under SSAP 19 'Accounting for Investment Properties';
  - the treatment of certain exchange gains and losses under SSAP 20 'Foreign Currency Translation';
- in rare circumstances, a departure from accounting standards may be required for the accounts to show a true and fair view – as the Act normally requires accounts to be prepared in accordance with applicable accounting standards, such a departure may in effect also require use of the true and fair override.

Departure from the requirements of the Act in order to achieve compliance with individual accounting standards will arise from time to time in practice. Departure from accounting standards should only arise in very exceptional circumstances (see **2.6 below**).

The relationship between accounting standards and the true and fair requirement

2.5 The 'Foreword to Accounting Standards' considers the status of accounting standards within UK companies' legislation and includes as an appendix an opinion by Miss Mary Arden QC (now Dame Mary Arden) entitled 'The True and Fair Requirement'. This considers in detail the relationship between accounting standards and the requirement of the Act for accounts to give a true and fair view and makes the following points:

— Although the true and fair requirement is a question of law and the interpretation of the requirement must therefore be dealt with by the court, this cannot be carried out without evidence of the practice and views of accountants. The more authoritative the practices and views, the more ready the court will be to follow them.

— Amendments to the Act through the *Companies Act 1989* have given statutory recognition to accounting standards.

— As the Act requires disclosure of non-compliance with accounting standards, rather than compliance with them, the court is likely to infer that accounts will usually follow accounting standards in meeting the true and fair requirement and that any departure from an accounting standard needs therefore to be explained and justified.

— Once an accounting standard has been issued, the court is likely to hold that compliance with the standard will be necessary for accounts to show a true and fair view. This is likely to be strengthened by the extent to which the standard is subsequently accepted in practice.

— However, the converse will not necessarily apply. A lack of support for a standard will not automatically lead the court to conclude that compliance with the standard is not necessary for the accounts to show a true and fair view.

— The fact that a departure from an accounting standard is disclosed in accordance with the Act does not mean that the departure is necessarily permitted under the Act.

The full Opinion should be read in any cases where it is intended to depart from the requirements of an accounting standard on the basis that the departure is required in order for the accounts to give a true and fair view. Legal advice may also need to be taken.

Departure from accounting standards

2.6 FRS 18 'Accounting Policies' requires an entity to adopt accounting policies that will enable its financial statements to give a true and fair view, and requires those policies to be consistent with the requirements of accounting standards, UITF Abstracts and companies' legislation. Departures from the requirements of accounting standards and UITF Abstracts should be rare in practice as they are only permissible to the extent that compliance with a standard or Abstract would be inconsistent with the overriding requirement for the accounts to give a true and fair view. In particular, the requirements of accounting standards and UITF Abstracts will not be inconsistent with the true and fair view requirement if such a view can be achieved through additional disclosure in the accounts. It is therefore not acceptable to depart from accounting standards and UITF Abstracts in these circumstances.

Use of the true and fair override

2.7 The most common use of the true and fair override in practice is in order to comply with those accounting standards which require a departure from the requirements of the Act (e.g. SSAP 19 'Accounting for Investment Properties' and SSAP 20 'Foreign Currency translation'). Where the true and fair override is invoked, *CA 1985* requires disclosure of the following in a note to the accounts:

(i) particulars of the departure;

(ii) the reasons for the departure; and

(iii) the effect of the departure.

However, the Act does not provide any further guidance on the details that should be included in these disclosures.

Disclosure requirements under FRS 18

2.8 FRS 18 'Accounting Policies' now specifies that the following details should be given whenever CA 1985 requires disclosure of the particulars of a departure from a specific statutory requirement, the reasons for it and the effect:

— a clear and unambiguous statement that there has been a departure from the requirements of an accounting standard, a UITF Abstract or companies' legislation (as appropriate) and that the departure is necessary to give a true and fair view;

— a statement of the treatment that accounting standards, UITF Abstracts or companies' legislation would normally require and a description of the treatment actually adopted;

— a statement of why the usual treatment would not give a true and fair view; and

— a description of how the position shown in the financial statements is different as a result of the departure – this should include quantification of the effect except where:

— this is already evident in the financial statements themselves; or

— the effect cannot be quantified, in which case the circumstances should be explained.

Examples of how these requirements might be met in the case of the more common departures from the requirements of the Act are set out in the appendix to this chapter. If the departure from *CA 1985* continues in subsequent years, the full disclosures required by FRS 18 must continue to be given each year. If there is no departure in the current year but there was a departure in the previous accounting period (e.g. the company previously held an investment property but this has been disposed of) details must continue to be shown for the comparative figures. FRS 18 also requires the disclosures to be given:

- as part of the note on compliance with applicable accounting standards required by para 36A Sch 4 (see **1.5** above); or
- elsewhere in the notes to the accounts, but cross-referenced to the note on compliance with applicable accounting standards.

This should help to ensure that the departure receives the appropriate degree of prominence in the accounts.

Appendix

EXAMPLE WORDINGS FOR THE USE OF THE TRUE AND FAIR OVERRIDE

1. Non-depreciation of investment properties under SSAP 19 – 'Accounting for Investment Properties'

As the Act does not distinguish between investment properties and other properties, and thus requires an investment property to be included in the accounts at either cost or valuation and to be depreciated over its useful life in the same way as any other tangible fixed asset, compliance with the requirements of SSAP 19 in respect of investment properties will usually constitute a departure from the requirements of the Act. Compliance with SSAP 19 will therefore usually require the use of the true and fair override, unless:

— the estimated residual value of the property (calculated in accordance with FRS 15) is at least equal to its carrying value; or

— the estimated residual value of the property is so close to its carrying value that any depreciation would be immaterial.

Further consideration of both of these issues is set out in **Chapter 12**.

The following is an example of wording that might be appropriate to explain the use of the true and fair override where investment properties are accounted for under SSAP 19.

Example 2.1 – Non-depreciation of investment properties: true and fair override

In accordance with SSAP 19:

— investment properties are revalued annually and the aggregate surplus or deficit is transferred to a revaluation reserve, and

— no depreciation or amortisation is provided in respect of freehold investment properties and leasehold investment properties with over 20 years to run.

The *Companies Act 1985* requires tangible fixed assets to be depreciated systematically over their estimated useful economic lives. However, investment properties are held for investment rather than consumption. The directors therefore consider that depreciation on a systematic basis would not be appropriate in this case and that the accounting policy adopted is necessary for the accounts to give a true and fair view. Depreciation or amortisation is only one of the many factors reflected in the annual valuation and the amount which might otherwise have been shown cannot be separately identified or quantified.

In this case, it is usually accepted that the effect of not depreciating the properties does not require disclosure. This is considered in more detail in **Chapter 20**.

2. Inclusion of unrealised exchange gains and losses in the profit and loss account under SSAP 20 — 'Foreign Currency Translation'

The accounting treatment required by SSAP 20 in respect of unsettled long-term monetary transactions means that unrealised exchange gains and losses will usually be included in the profit and loss account when a company has long-term assets and liabilities denominated in a foreign currency. Under the Act, only profits realised at the balance sheet date may be included in the profit and loss account. [*CA 1985, Sch 4 para 12(a)*]. Compliance with SSAP 20 in these circumstances may therefore constitute a departure from the accounting requirements of the Act under the true and fair override.

The following is an example of wording that might be appropriate to explain the use of the true and fair override where exchange gains relating to long-term monetary transactions are accounted for in accordance with SSAP 20.

Example 2.2 – Inclusion of unrealised exchange gains and losses in the profit and loss account: true and fair override

In accordance with SSAP 20, exchange gains and losses on the translation of monetary items are taken to the profit and loss account for the year. In the case of unrealised exchange gains arising on the translation of unsettled long-term monetary transactions, this treatment represents a departure from the requirement under the *Companies Act 1985* that only profits realised at the balance sheet date should be included in the profit and loss account. However, as explained in paragraph 10 of SSAP 20, exchange gains on unsettled transactions can be determined at the balance sheet date no less objectively than exchange losses; deferring the gains whilst recognising the losses would in effect deny that any favourable movement in exchange rates had occurred and would also inhibit fair measurement of the performance of the company in the year. The directors therefore consider that recognition of such unrealised exchange gains is necessary in order for the accounts to show a true and fair view. The effect of this departure is to increase the profit before taxation by £ ... (200X: £ ...) and to increase the value of ... (asset/liability) ... by £ ... (200X: £ ...).

Further details of the requirements of SSAP 20 are given in **Chapter 6**.

Chapter 3

Substance Over Form

BACKGROUND TO FRS 5 'REPORTING THE SUBSTANCE OF TRANSACTIONS'

Off balance sheet financing

3.1 The publication of FRS 5 'Reporting the Substance of Transactions' in April 1994 marked the end of a long process of developing an accounting standard to deal with the problem of off balance sheet financing. The first step in tackling this issue was the introduction of SSAP 21 'Accounting for Leases and Hire Purchase Contracts', which attempted to ensure that assets held under finance leases were brought onto the balance sheet, together with the related financing liabilities. However, companies were still able to find ways of structuring lease agreements so that they did not meet the SSAP 21 definition of a finance lease and thus avoided disclosure on the balance sheet. Similarly, increasingly complex financing arrangements have been developed over the years, many with the aim of keeping the financing off the borrower's balance sheet.

Conceptual nature of FRS 5

3.2 FRS 5 is deliberately conceptual rather than factual in nature, on the basis that there is little point in laying down stringent rules (as was done in SSAP 21) if subsequent transactions are simply structured to avoid those rules. As FRS 5 sets out the underlying concepts, and then illustrates their application to specific types of transaction, it is inevitably wide in scope and companies are required to apply its spirit rather than being required to follow a prescriptive set of rules.

Transactions covered by the standard

3.3 FRS 5 applies to all transactions, irrespective of when they took place. When FRS 5 was first introduced, companies were therefore required to review the accounting treatment that they had adopted for transactions that took place in earlier years and consider whether this was still appropriate under the requirements of FRS 5. However, the vast majority of commercial transactions will not be affected by the detailed requirements of FRS 5. The main aim of FRS 5 is to ensure that appropriate accounting treatments are adopted for more complex transactions and arrangements, where the commercial substance of the transaction is not always easily identifiable. This will often be the case where:

- the principal benefits of an item are separated in some way from its legal ownership;
- the overall commercial effect of a series of transactions differs from the apparent effect of the individual transactions;
- the transaction includes options or conditions which are not commercially realistic (e.g. the terms of an option mean that it will almost certainly be exercised).

Excluded transactions

3.4 The following transactions are specifically excluded from the requirements of FRS 5 'Reporting the Substance of Transactions', unless they form part of a transaction that does fall within the scope of the standard:

- forward contracts;
- futures;
- contracts for differences;
- purchase commitments and orders (i.e. before payment or delivery has taken place);
- employment contracts.

Application of FRS 5 in practice

3.5 As FRS 5 requires the application of concepts rather than detailed rules, it can be a difficult standard to apply in practice. This is exacerbated by the fact that it is particularly designed to cover transactions whose commercial substance is not readily apparent, and in some cases it may be genuinely difficult to agree on what the true substance of the transaction really is.

Impact of FRS 18 'Accounting Policies'

3.6 FRS 18 'Accounting Policies' sets out four objectives – relevance, reliability, comparability and understandability – against which an entity should judge the appropriateness of its accounting policies and the constraints that should be taken into account in making such an assessment. The guidance on the reliability of financial information emphasises that one of the key factors is that the information can be depended upon by users to represent faithfully what it purports to represent or could reasonably be expected to represent – in other words, that the way in which a transaction or event is recognised, measured and presented in the financial statements corresponds closely to its substance and practical effect.

DETAILED REQUIREMENTS OF FRS 5

Assessing commercial substance

3.7 Under FRS 5, financial statements should report the commercial substance of the transactions entered into by an entity. In assessing the substance of a transaction, greater emphasis should be given to those aspects that are likely to have a practical commercial effect. Where an overall commercial effect is achieved by a series of transactions, the series should be considered as a whole rather than as individual transactions.

Relationship with other accounting standards and with company law

3.8 Where the treatment of a transaction, asset or liability is covered more specifically in another accounting standard or in company (or other) law, the more specific provisions should be followed. However, the requirements of FRS 5 will still have an impact, as the explanatory notes to FRS 5 emphasise that the provisions of other standards or law should be applied to the substance of a transaction rather than to its legal form. Where the requirements of FRS 5 are more specific than those in another accounting standard or in company (or other) law, the requirements of FRS 5 should be followed.

Identifying and recognising assets and liabilities

3.9 Assessing the substance of a transaction involves identifying whether it has given rise to new assets and liabilities for the reporting entity, or has changed the entity's existing assets and liabilities.

Assets are defined as rights or access to future economic benefits, and liabilities are defined as obligations to transfer economic benefits. These definitions are consistent with those set out in the ASB Draft 'Statement of Principles'. An asset or liability should be recognised in the financial statements if there is sufficient evidence of its existence and the monetary amount can be measured with sufficient reliability. The recognition of assets and liabilities is considered in more detail at **3.17–3.20** below.

Options and guarantees

3.10 Where a transaction includes an option, guarantee or conditional provision, the assessment of the commercial effect of the transaction should take into account the likely practical effect of the option, guarantee or condition.

Subsequent transactions in respect of recognised assets

3.11 Depending on the circumstances, a subsequent transaction in respect of a recognised asset may result in:

— the entire asset continuing to be recognised in the accounts;

— the entire asset ceasing to be recognised in the accounts;

— a change to the description or monetary amount of the asset and the recognition of a liability for any obligation to transfer economic benefits.

Non-recourse finance arrangements

3.12 Under certain circumstances, a linked presentation is required in respect of non-recourse finance. In this case, the gross amount of the asset and the deduction for the related finance must both be shown on the face of the balance sheet. This treatment can only be adopted where all of the conditions laid down in FRS 5 are satisfied. This aspect of FRS 5 is considered in detail in the context of factored debts in **Chapter 24** which includes an example of linked presentation under the standard.

Additional disclosures

3.13 The disclosure of a transaction in the accounts should be sufficient to enable a user of the accounts to understand its commercial effect. Where assets and liabilities are recognised which are different in nature from those usually included under the relevant balance sheet heading, the differences should be explained in the accounts. Transactions which do not result in assets and liabilities being recognised in the accounts may nevertheless require disclosure in the notes to the accounts if they give rise to guarantees, commitments, rights or obligations.

Off-setting

3.14 Assets and liabilities should not be off-set and debit and credit balances should only be aggregated into a single item where they do not constitute separate assets and liabilities. A particular problem area, and a cause of much debate over the years, has been the question of whether bank overdrafts can, or should, be off-set against credit balances on other bank accounts. This is not necessarily precluded either by CA 1985 or by FRS 5, but whether it is permissible, or indeed required under FRS 5, will depend very much on the circumstances of each individual case and in particular on:

— whether there is a right of set-off between the accounts;

— if so, whether the right of set-off is legally enforceable; and

— whether any net liability that results from the set-off represents the company's true liability to the bank.

It is unlikely that the off-set of overdrafts and credit balances with different banks could be justified under the present requirements. FRS 5 currently requires credit and debit balances to be aggregated into a single net item where **all** of the following conditions are met:

— the amounts owed to and by the reporting entity are determinable monetary amounts, which are denominated in the same currency or in freely convertible currencies (i.e. currencies for which quoted market rates are available and for which there is an active market);

— the reporting entity can insist on a net settlement of the outstanding balances - in particular, there must be no possibility that the reporting entity could be required to make payment of the creditor balance in its accounting records without first being able to recover payment of the debtor balance; and

— the reporting entity's ability to insist on a net settlement of the balances must be assured beyond all doubt and in particular must be capable of surviving the insolvency of the other party.

Legal advice may need to be taken to confirm some of these points. If all of the conditions are met, the balances are not regarded as separate assets and liabilities under the standard, and they are therefore required to be off-set for accounting purposes.

Quasi-subsidiaries

3.15 Where the reporting entity controls another entity that is in substance no different from a subsidiary (i.e. it is a quasi-subsidiary), the assets, liabilities, profits, losses and cash flows of the quasi-subsidiary should normally be included in the group accounts of the reporting entity. If the reporting entity does not have subsidiaries, consolidated accounts for the reporting entity and the quasi-subsidiary should be prepared in accordance with FRS 2 'Accounting for Subsidiary Undertakings' and should be presented as part of the reporting entity's financial statements, with equal prominence to its own individual accounts. The impact of FRS 5 in the context of group accounts is not considered further in this book, which deals only with company accounts.

Application Notes

3.16 FRS 5 includes six detailed Application Notes which explain how its requirements should be applied to the following transactions.

— Consignment stock (A1–A12).

— Sale and repurchase agreements (B1–B21).

— Factoring of debts (C1–C20).

— Securitised assets (D1–D26).

— Loan transfers (E1–E24).

— Private Finance Initiative and similar contracts (F1–F60).

The Application Notes 'Consignment stocks' and 'Sale and repurchase agreements' are considered in **Chapter 22** and the Application Note 'Factoring of debts' is considered in **Chapter 24**. The other Application Notes relate to more specialised transactions and have therefore not been covered in detail here.

THE RECOGNITION OF ASSETS AND LIABILITIES

Identification of assets and liabilities

3.17 The first step in evaluating the substance of a transaction is to identify the new assets and liabilities that arise as a result of the transaction, or the effect that the transaction has on the entity's existing assets and liabilities. Assets are defined in FRS 5 as 'Rights or other access to future economic benefits controlled by an entity as a result of past transactions or events'. Access to benefits will often, but not always, be associated with legal rights. Control is defined as 'The ability to obtain the future economic benefits relating to an asset and to restrict the access of others to those benefits'. Therefore, the ability to prevent others gaining access to the benefits must also be taken into account.

Impact of risk

3.18 The impact of risk is seen as a key element in identifying an asset under FRS 5. The inherent future economic benefits of an asset are rarely certain. For instance:

— the actual benefits may be greater than expected;

— the actual benefits may be lower than expected;

— the benefits may arise sooner than expected;

— the benefits may arise later than expected.

For example, an amount due from an overseas debtor may:

— result in an exchange gain;

— result in an exchange loss;

— be paid in advance of the due date;

— be paid after the due date.

These aspects are identified in FRS 5 as the risks involved in holding the asset. It can therefore be seen that, in this context, risk encompasses both the potential to gain as a result of holding the asset (i.e. realising an exchange gain or achieving early payment in the above example) and the possible exposure to loss (i.e. realising an exchange loss or suffering poor cash flow, or even a bad debt, in the above example). The entity that has access to the benefits of an asset will in most cases also gain or lose if the actual benefits are different to the expected benefits. Identifying who gains or loses in these circumstances therefore helps to identify who controls access to the benefits of an asset.

Definition of liabilities

3.19 Liabilities are defined in FRS 5 as 'an entity's obligations to transfer economic benefits as a result of past transactions or events'. In many cases, a liability will represent a legal obligation, but this need not necessarily be the case. FRS 5 quotes the example of an entity being commercially obliged to adopt a particular course of action because, in the long term, it is in its best interest to do so. The key issue in identifying a liability is that the entity is not free to avoid an outflow of resources at some point in the future. However, the standard emphasises that it will not always be necessary to recognise a liability in the accounts even though it is possible that a future outflow of resources may not be avoided. For instance, in the case of a contingent liability, an accounting treatment in accordance with FRS 12 'Provisions, Contingent Liabilities and Contingent Assets' will be sufficient.

Recognising assets and liabilities

3.20 The general criteria for recognising assets and liabilities are consistent with those set out in the ASB 'Statement of Principles'. Recognition should only take place where:

— there is sufficient evidence that the asset or liability exists; and

— the monetary amount can be measured with sufficient reliability.

However, the application of prudence will usually mean that the interpretation of 'sufficient reliability' will vary depending on whether the item in question is an asset or a liability (i.e. a lower degree of reliability will usually be acceptable when recognising a liability than when recognising an asset).

THE COMMERCIAL EFFECT OF TRANSACTIONS

Linked transactions

3.21 In considering the commercial effect of a transaction, it is important to take into account any associated transactions, as consideration of the arrangement as a whole may indicate a different commercial effect. For instance, if an entity sells an asset, but is committed to repurchasing the item after a number of years, the overall effect may be that the 'seller' retains the main benefits and risks associated with the asset (depending on the detailed terms of the arrangement). In this case, the 'seller' has not in fact sold the asset and should not record the transaction as a sale. The asset should be retained on the balance sheet, along with the corresponding liability to the other party (i.e. in respect of the 'repurchase' commitment).

Options

3.22 The assessment of the commercial effect of options included in an agreement can be a particularly difficult issue. For instance, a transaction such as that described in **3.21** above, may include an option for the 'seller' to repurchase the asset, rather than a commitment for him to do so. This may seem to indicate that the 'seller' does not have an unavoidable obligation to repurchase the asset and that the transaction can therefore be recorded as a sale. However, the terms of the option will usually need to be carefully reviewed to ensure that it is a genuine option. For instance, there may be a substantial penalty if the option is not exercised, which will have the effect of ensuring that the 'seller' will always choose to exercise the option. There may also be commercial reasons why the 'seller' will inevitably choose to exercise the option to repurchase. For instance, the asset may be essential to the future operation of the business. Particular caution is needed where the arrangement includes both an option for the 'seller' to repurchase and an option for the 'purchaser' to resell. In this situation it will be virtually certain that one of the parties will exercise the option. FRS 5 emphasises that all aspects and implications of a transaction must be identified but that greater weight should be given to those that will have a practical commercial effect. It should also be assumed that all parties to the transaction will act in their own best interest.

Importance of commercial logic

3.23 It is particularly important that the commercial logic of each party in entering into a transaction should be fully understood. If there appears to be no commercial logic to the transaction for one of the parties, this may suggest that there are other aspects to the arrangement that have not yet been identified and which may be important in establishing the substance of the transactions and hence the appropriate accounting treatment. The position of all parties must therefore be considered, not just the position of the reporting entity.

The lender's return

3.24 Where one party to a transaction receives no more than a lender's return, the substance of the transaction will usually be that of a financing arrangement (e.g. a loan that is in effect secured on the asset that is supposedly 'sold' as part of the arrangement). This aspect of FRS 5 will often be particularly relevant in assessing the substance of sale and repurchase arrangements or leasing transactions. A lender's return is described in FRS 5 as interest on the investment (i.e. the 'loan'), and perhaps a relatively small fee, but no more than this. The implication of an arrangement being made on this basis is that:

— if the 'lender' is satisfied with a lender's return, he must be satisfied that he is not taking on any significant risk of loss by entering into the arrangement (other than the normal commercial risk of the 'borrower' failing to repay the amount of the 'loan'); and

— if the 'borrower' is satisfied with the arrangement, he must be satisfied that he is not relinquishing any substantial benefits attached to the asset that has supposedly been 'sold'.

For instance, if A Ltd sells an asset to B Ltd with an option to repurchase it in ten years' time at original cost, plus an amount that in effect represents interest on 'cost' for a period of ten years, B Ltd will not receive more than a lender's return. The transaction should therefore be accounted for as a loan repayable in ten years' time, and the interest cost should be accrued over the period of the loan. The asset will remain on A Ltd's balance sheet throughout the ten-year period.

Subsequent transactions in assets previously recognised

3.25 Depending on the circumstances, a subsequent transaction in respect of an asset that has already been recognised in the accounts may result in:

— the entire asset continuing to be recognised in the accounts;

— the entire asset ceasing to be recognised in the accounts;

— a change to the description or monetary amount of the asset and the recognition of a liability for any obligation to transfer economic benefits.

Continued recognition

3.26 Where the transaction does not result in any significant change in the entity's:

— rights to the benefits relating to the asset; or

— risks in relation to the asset (i.e. both the potential for gain and the exposure to loss);

there will be no change to the recognition of the asset in the accounts. For instance, if a company sells its debtors to another party but:

— the other party has recourse to the company for all bad debts; and

— the level of the finance charges paid varies depending on the speed of payment by the debtors;

there is no change to the company's rights or risks in respect of the debts and they should continue to be shown in the accounts. Depending on the terms of the arrangement (e.g. whether legal title is transferred or not), additional details of the arrangements may need to be disclosed.

Derecognition

3.27 Derecognition of the asset will be required where a transaction transfers all the significant rights to benefits, and all the significant risks relating to the asset to another party. For instance, if a company sells its debtors for a single, non-refundable cash payment and there is no recourse to the company in respect of bad debts or slow payment, the debtors should be removed from the company's balance sheet.

Special cases

3.28 Most transactions will result in either continued recognition or derecognition of an asset. In certain circumstances, a transaction may result in significant changes to the benefits and risks associated with a previously recognised asset, but not transfer them completely to another party. In these cases, it may be necessary to:

— change the description of the asset;

— change the monetary amount of the asset; or

— recognise a new liability for any obligations assumed or risks retained.

These special circumstances will arise where:

— only part of the asset is transferred;

— the whole of the asset is transferred, but for only part of its life (e.g. under a sale and repurchase agreement); or

— the whole of the asset is transferred for all of its life, but the entity retains some right to significant benefits, or some exposure to significant risk, in respect of the asset.

A common example of the transfer of an asset with the retention of some risk by the seller is the sale of an item of equipment with either a related warranty in respect of the standard of the equipment, usually for a specified period of time, or with a guaranteed residual value. The buyer therefore acquires the rights to the benefits relating to the equipment and assumes most of the risks associated with it, but the seller retains an element of risk in the form of liability to bear the cost of any repair work necessary if the equipment does not meet the standard specified, or to make good any deficit in the residual value of the asset. The seller may need to recognise these liabilities in the accounts, depending on the likelihood of a liability crystallising.

Significant benefits and risks

3.29 FRS 5 considers the interpretation of significant in relation to benefits and risks and once again places the emphasis on the likely commercial effect in practice. For instance, a company has debtors totalling £50,000 and expects bad debts to amount to no more than £1,000. If it sells the debtors for £45,000 but the purchaser has recourse to the company for bad debts up to £3,000, the company has in effect retained all the risk relating to the debtors (i.e. in practice, the company has all the risk in respect of the expected bad debts of £1,000). The debtors would therefore normally remain on the balance sheet, with the payment of £45,000 being recognised as a financing liability.

LEASING TRANSACTIONS

The interaction of FRS 5 with SSAP 21

3.30 FRS 5 is clear that it does not supersede the requirements of other accounting standards or company law, and that transactions, assets and liabilities that are dealt with in more detail elsewhere should continue to be accounted for in accordance with those requirements. The only proviso is that the requirements of other accounting standards and company law should always be applied to the substance of transactions, rather than to their legal form, if this is different.

Where the requirements of FRS 5 may be relevant

3.31 There is inevitably a close relationship between FRS 5 and SSAP 21 'Accounting for Leases and Hire Purchase Contracts', as both standards are attempting to deal with a similar accounting issue. In the case of leasing arrangements, the provisions of SSAP 21 are generally more detailed than those set out in FRS 5. However, the requirements of FRS 5 will be relevant for the following:

— the classification of individual leases as finance leases or operating leases – a lease which fails to meet the value criteria (such as the '90% test') set out in SSAP 21 for classification as a finance lease may nevertheless need to be accounted for as a finance lease under the requirements of FRS 5; and

— leasing arrangements that form part of a larger transaction, or a series of transactions, which must be considered together under the requirements of FRS 5.

The requirements of SSAP 21 are considered in more detail in **Chapters 20** and **Chapter 27.**

Guidance in Application Note B to FRS 5

3.32 The guidance in Application Note B to FRS 5 ('Sale and repurchase agreements') will also often be relevant in evaluating a sale and leaseback arrangement, and is generally more detailed than the guidance provided in SSAP 21. It should also be noted that Application Note B specifically states that it covers any arrangement where one party holds an asset on behalf of another. Any leased asset will generally fall within this definition, and consequently the guidance in Application Note B will generally be relevant in assessing the substance of any leasing arrangement.

ACCOUNTING FOR ESOP TRUSTS

Usual features of ESOPs

3.33 Employee Share Ownership Plans operate in a variety of ways but often include the following features:

— a trust provides a means of purchasing and holding shares to be transferred to employees;

— share purchases are often funded by interest-free finance from the sponsoring company or by bank loans guaranteed by the company – the company may also assume responsibility for funding interest payments in respect of a bank loan;

— shares are distributed to employees through some form of employee share scheme – there are many different arrangements that can be put in place;

— although the trustees must act in the interests of the beneficiaries, in practice the company will often have *de facto* control of the shares held by the trust.

Accounting treatment

3.34 The consensus reached in UITF 13 'Accounting for ESOP Trusts' is that certain assets and liabilities of such a trust should be recognised on the balance sheet of the sponsoring company where it has *de facto* control of the shares held by the trust, and therefore bears the benefits and risks relating to those shares. In this case:

— the shares held by the trust should normally be recognised as assets until they vest unconditionally in the employees – shares that have been gifted unconditionally to individual employees should not be recognised as assets, even if they continue to be held by the trust;

— if the shares are held for the continuing benefit of the company's business (as will usually be the case), they should be classified as 'own shares' within fixed assets - otherwise they should be classified as 'own shares' within current assets;

— any permanent diminution in the value of shares held as fixed assets must be recognised immediately;

— where shares are conditionally gifted to employees or put under option at a value below book value, the difference in value should be charged to operating costs over the period of service of the relevant employees;

— any borrowings that are guaranteed, formally or informally, by the sponsoring company should be recognised as a liability;

— finance costs and administrative expenses should be charged as they accrue;

— if dividend income on the shares held by the trust is not waived, it should be included in profit before tax.

The appendix to the Abstract sets out a number of illustrative examples of how the requirements might be applied in practice.

In March 1999, the UITF issued the draft of a revised Abstract proposing changes to this accounting treatment, but it has subsequently indicated that any amendments will be dealt with as part of a future ASB project on equity rather than by revision of Abstract 13.

Disclosure

3.35 UITF 13 also requires disclosure of sufficient information for a user of the company's accounts to be able to understand the significance of the ESOP trust. This should include:

— the main features of the trust, including arrangements for distributing shares;

— details of how costs are dealt with in the profit and loss account;

— the number and market value of shares held by the trust;

— whether dividends have been waived on shares held by the trust;

— the extent to which the shares are under option to employees or have been conditionally gifted to them.

EMPLOYEE BENEFIT TRUSTS AND OTHER INTERMEDIATE PAYMENT ARRANGEMENTS

UITF Abstract 32

3.36 The requirements of UITF Abstract 32 'Employee benefit trusts and other intermediate payment arrangements' apply for accounting periods ending on or after 23 December 2001. The Abstract applies where an entity sets up and provides funds to an employee benefit trust or other intermediary and the trust's or intermediary's accumulated assets are used to remunerate the entity's employees or other service providers. The Abstract is drafted in the context of payments to employees through an intermediary, but emphasises that the requirements apply equally to intermediate payment arrangements used to compensate other suppliers of goods and services. Employee share ownership plans (ESOPs) and pension funds are specifically excluded from the scope of the Abstract as they are already dealt with in UITF Abstract 13 'Accounting for ESOP trusts' and FRS 17 'Retirement Benefits' respectively.

Structure of the intermediary

3.37 The Abstract notes that the relationship between the intermediary and the sponsoring entity may take a variety of forms. In many cases the intermediary will be structured as a trust and the sponsoring entity will not have a right to direct its activities. However, the sponsoring entity may still give advice to the intermediary, or the intermediary may rely on the sponsoring entity to provide the information that it needs to carry out its activities. Also, the sponsoring entity will often have the right to appoint, or veto the appointment of, the trustees (or equivalent) of the intermediary. Payments to the intermediary will usually be in cash, but may take the form of the transfer of other assets.

Employee benefit trusts

3.38 The usual arrangement in an employee benefit trust is that the sponsoring employer makes payments to the trust and the trust uses assets accumulated from those payments to pay the employees, as beneficiaries of the trust, for some or all of their services to the sponsoring employer. The intermediary is usually constituted as a trust but may take a different form and the employees may not be the only beneficiaries – for instance, past employees and their dependants may also benefit from the arrangements, or the intermediary may be authorised to make charitable donations. The precise identity of those who will receive payments from the trust, and the amounts that they will receive, will not usually be known at the outset.

Whether a payment represents an immediate expense

3.39 The main issue considered in the Abstract is whether a payment from the sponsoring employer to the intermediary represents an immediate expense. The Abstract notes that most expenses are incurred when a liability arises rather than at the time of payment. For instance, an entity's liability for services provided to it is incurred as those services are received, not when they are paid for. The same principle applies when the services are paid for through an intermediary - in other words, the liability for employee costs arises when the employee services are provided. The payment to the intermediary will often be made either in advance of the liability arising or in order to settle a liability that has already arisen - only rarely will it be made as the services are actually received.

Creation of an asset

3.40 An asset is defined in the ASB's 'Statement of Principles for Financial Reporting' as a right or other access to future economic benefits that is controlled by the entity as a result of a past transaction or event. UITF Abstract 32 concludes that, in the case of intermediate payment arrangements, the benefit to the sponsoring entity takes the form of meeting some or all of the cost of goods or services provided to the entity. Such a benefit can constitute an asset even though it is not capable of being turned into cash or of being distributed in a liquidation. Control is defined as the ability to direct and the ability to benefit from that direction, and the Abstract notes that control can be exercised by means other than intervention and instruction on an ongoing day-to-day basis. A sponsoring employer may therefore have *de facto* control of an intermediate's assets and liabilities as explained in UITF Abstract 13 'Accounting for ESOP Trusts'.

Impact of FRS 5

3.41 The Abstract also considers the requirements of FRS 5 'Reporting the Substance of Transactions' and, in particular, the need to consider the underlying practical commercial effect of each transaction. The UITF concludes that it would be highly unusual for an entity to pay a significant amount to a third party without receiving something in return, and therefore takes the view that, where an entity transfers funds to an intermediary, there should be a rebuttable presumption that the entity will receive future economic benefits from the amount transferred and that it has the control of the rights or other access to those benefits. This presumption can only be rebutted where:

— the sponsoring entity will not obtain future economic benefit from the amounts transferred (e.g. the only beneficiaries are registered charities or a benevolent fund that is in no way linked to amounts otherwise due from the entity); or

- the sponsoring entity does not have control of the rights or other access to the future economic benefits it is expected to receive (i.e. there is evidence that payments by the intermediary are not habitually made in a way that is in accordance with the wishes of the sponsoring entity).

The Abstract notes that the presumption would not be rebutted where payments by the intermediary relieve the sponsoring entity from paying for items such as retirement benefit increases or benefits in kind, such as medical insurance cover. The presumption of control is rebutted if, at the time that payment is made to the intermediary, the amount transferred vests unconditionally in identified beneficiaries.

Accounting for the asset

3.42 Where the presumption cannot be rebutted, the payment involves the exchange of one asset for another and no immediate expense is incurred. This applies regardless of whether the intermediary changes some or all of the amount transferred for other assets. The UITF therefore takes the view that the sponsoring entity has *de facto* control of the intermediary's assets and liabilities and should account for the intermediary as an extension of its own business. The intermediary's assets and liabilities should therefore be recognised as assets and liabilities of the sponsoring entity. Once recognised, the accounting treatment of those assets and liabilities should follow normal accounting rules. An asset held by the intermediary will therefore usually cease to recognised as an asset of the sponsoring entity once it vests unconditionally in identified beneficiaries.

Disclosure

3.43 Where the assets and liabilities of an intermediary are recognised in the accounts of the sponsoring entity in accordance with UITF Abstract 32, sufficient information should be disclosed in the notes to the accounts to enable readers to understand any restrictions relating to those assets and liabilities.

HEDGE ACCOUNTING

Publication of FRED 23

3.44 The ASB published FRED 23 'Financial instruments: Hedge accounting' in May 2002. In effect, this introduces a new subject into UK accounting standards, although SSAP 20 and UITF Abstract 19 currently deal with accounting for hedges of net investments in foreign operations. However, FRED 23 still forms part of the convergence project with international accounting standards, as much of the material is drawn from IAS 39 'Financial instruments: Recognition and measurement'. Hedge accounting results in gains and losses on hedging instruments being deferred and matched with those arising on the hedged item, and it can therefore have a significant effect on reported financial performance. The new standard will apply to all financial statements that are intended to show a true and fair view, except that smaller entities adopting the Financial Reporting Standard for Smaller Entities (FRSSE) will be exempt from its requirements. FRED 23 deals specifically with hedge accounting in the context of financial instruments - other hedging transactions are therefore outside its scope.

When hedge accounting can be used

3.45 Under the proposals, a financial instrument will qualify for hedge accounting only if it is held as a hedging instrument in a hedge that meets both the hedging relationship criteria and the hedge effectiveness criteria set out in the standard. The proposed hedging relationship criteria are:

- at the inception of the hedge, there is formal documentation of the hedging relationship and the entity's risk management objective and strategy for undertaking the hedge – the documentation should include:
  - identification of the hedging instrument and the related hedged item;
  - the nature of the risk being hedged; and
  - how the entity will assess the hedging instrument's effectiveness in offsetting the exposure to changes in the hedged item's fair value or cash flows;
- the effectiveness of the hedge can be measured reliably (ie the fair value or cash flows of both the hedged item and the hedging instrument can be measured reliably); and
- if a forecast transaction is being hedged, it is highly probable and presents an exposure to variations in cash flows that could ultimately affect the reported net profit or loss.

The guidance notes that it is acceptable for a portion of a financial instrument to be a hedging instrument, or for a financial instrument to hedge just a portion of a hedged item, and for different portions of a hedged item to be designated as hedging different exposures. Similarly, two or more financial instruments may be viewed together as a hedging instrument and a hedged item may be a combination of two or more items.

Hedge effectiveness criteria

3.46 The proposed hedge effectiveness criteria are that:

- the hedge was expected at the outset to be highly effective in offsetting changes in the fair value or cash flows attributable to the hedged item (consistent with the originally documented risk management strategy); and

— the hedge has been assessed on an ongoing basis since commencement, and this assessment has shown the hedge to have been highly effective throughout the financial reporting period.

For a hedge to be highly effective, the actual results should be within a range of 80% to 125%. There is additional guidance on the methods that may be used to assess hedge effectiveness. In particular, a hedge must relate to a specific identified risk, and not merely to overall business risk, in order to be effective.

Accounting treatment

3.47 The proposals set out the following requirements in respect of accounting for hedges:

- if a hedge of a net investment in a foreign operation is involved:
  - the portion of the gain or loss on the hedging instrument that is determined to be an effective hedge should be recognised immediately in the statement of total recognised gains and losses and should thereafter be treated in the same way as gains and losses on the hedged item; and
  - any ineffective portion should be reported immediately in the profit and loss account;
- in the case of other hedges, any ineffective portion of the gain or loss on the hedging instrument that would have been recognised if hedge accounting had not been adopted should be recognised immediately in the profit and loss account.

Changes in circumstances

3.48 A hedging instrument will cease to qualify for hedge accounting only if it no longer meets the hedge accounting criteria or is sold, terminated or exercised. In these circumstances, the use of hedge accounting should be discontinued prospectively as follows:

- if a forecast transaction that was being hedged is no longer expected to occur, the net cumulative gain or loss on the hedging instrument that has not already been recognised in the profit and loss account should be recognised immediately in that statement;
- in other cases, the net cumulative gain or loss on the hedging instrument that has not already been recognised in the profit and loss account or (where appropriate) in the statement of total recognised gains and losses should be recognised in the relevant statement so as to offset the gains and losses arising on the hedged item.

The guidance notes that this treatment does not apply on the replacement or rollover of one hedging instrument into another hedging instrument, provided that this is part of the entity's documented hedging strategy.

Chapter 4

Accounting Policies

BACKGROUND TO ACCOUNTING POLICIES

Definition of accounting policy

4.1 Accounting policies are defined in FRS 18 'Accounting Policies' as:

> 'Those principles, bases, conventions, rules and practices applied by an entity that specify how the effects of transactions and other events are to be reflected in its financial statements through:
>
> (i) recognising;
>
> (ii) selecting measurement bases for; and
>
> (iii) presenting;
>
> assets, liabilities, gains, losses and changes to shareholders' funds.'

In other words, accounting policies provide the framework within which the elements of financial statements are measured. The standard goes on to note that accounting policies do not include estimation techniques.

Measurement bases

4.2 Measurement bases are defined in FRS 18 as the monetary attributes of the elements of financial statements (i.e. assets, liabilities, gains, losses and shareholders' funds) that are reflected in financial statements. The qualities of an individual asset might be expressed in a number of different 'values' (for instance, original cost, current net realisable value and current replacement cost) and these values are all examples of the asset's monetary attributes. Monetary attributes may also be combined into a formula – for instance, the lower of cost and net realisable value. They fall into two broad categories: attributes reflecting historical values and attributes reflecting current values. Not all monetary attributes will be suitable for use in financial statements and the term 'measurement basis' is restricted to those monetary attributes that are suitable for such use.

Purpose of accounting policies

4.3 It is impossible for financial statements to present all of the available information about the monetary attributes of the underlying assets, liabilities, gains, losses and changes in shareholders' funds. For instance, although an asset may have both a historical cost and a current value, it is not possible to reflect both of these in the entity's balance sheet. Accounting policies are therefore used to determine which attribute of the asset is to be measured and how it is to be presented.

Change of measurement basis

4.4 The measurement bases to be used in financial statements will often be prescribed by accounting standards or companies' legislation. However, measurement bases are always a matter of accounting policy, irrespective of whether they are selected or prescribed. Therefore, if an entity has previously reported an asset on a historical cost basis but changes to a current value basis, this will constitute a change of accounting policy and must be accounted for as such.

Fungible assets

4.5 Fungible assets are assets that are substantially indistinguishable from one another in economic terms. Specific accounting requirements for fungible assets may be set out in accounting standards, UITF Abstracts and companies' legislation. Where fungible assets are recorded at historical cost, the accounting policy may require cost to be determined on an asset-by-asset basis or may consider such assets in aggregate by using a measurement basis such as weighted average historical cost, or historical cost measured on a first in, first out (FIFO) basis. The guidance in FRS 18 notes that an accounting policy that considers fungible assets in aggregate will be more consistent with the objective of comparability.

Alternative treatments

4.6 Occasionally, accounting standards allow a choice of what can be recognised in financial statements in respect of a particular transaction. For instance, FRS 15 'Tangible Fixed Assets' allows interest costs that are directly attributable to the construction of a tangible fixed asset to be accounted for as part of the cost of the asset or as an expense. In these circumstances, the choice of which treatment to adopt is a matter of accounting policy.

Presentational changes

4.7 A change in the way in which a particular item is presented in the financial statements is a change of accounting policy. Therefore, if certain overheads have previously been shown as part of cost of sales, but it is in future considered more appropriate to include them within administrative expenses, this change in presentation will constitute a change of accounting policy. However, the guidance in FRS 18 makes clear that the presentation of additional information does not constitute a change of accounting policy, although any corresponding figures should be reanalysed so that they are presented in the same amount of detail. Particular care is needed when an accounting change involves both a change in presentation and a change in estimation techniques – the former is a change of accounting policy but the latter is not, and the two elements of the change must therefore be accounted for separately.

SELECTION OF ACCOUNTING POLICIES

Requirement for a true and fair view

4.8 FRS 18 requires the adoption of accounting policies that enable financial statements to give a true and fair view and that are consistent with the requirements of accounting standards, UITF Abstracts and companies' legislation. In exceptional circumstances, it may be necessary to depart from the requirements of accounting standards and UITF Abstracts. This will only be appropriate when compliance with standards or Abstracts would be inconsistent with the overriding requirement for the financial statements to give a true and fair view. The guidance in FRS 18 emphasises that departure will not be appropriate when a true and fair view can be achieved by additional disclosure in the accounts. These issues are considered in more detail in **Chapter 2**. FRS 18 also identifies two concepts that are considered to play a pervasive role in financial statements and therefore in the selection of appropriate accounting policies – the going concern concept and the accruals concept. These two concepts are considered in more detail in **Chapter 1**.

Choice of accounting policies

4.9 Where more than one accounting policy would satisfy the requirements set out in **4.8**, the entity should select whichever of those policies is judged the most appropriate to its particular circumstances for the purpose of giving a true and fair view. The appropriateness of a policy should be judged against the objectives of relevance, reliability, comparability and understandability and taking into account:

— the need to balance these objectives; and

— the need to balance the cost of providing information against its likely benefit to users of the financial statements (although cost/benefit considerations will never justify the adoption of an accounting policy that is inconsistent with the requirements of accounting standards, UITF Abstracts and companies' legislation).

Balancing objectives

4.10 Tensions will sometimes arise between the four objectives identified in the standard. For instance, the accounting policy that is most relevant might not be the most reliable, and vice versa. In this situation, the entity should select the most relevant of the accounting policies that are reliable. The guidance also discusses the potential conflict between neutrality (i.e. freedom from bias) and prudence, which by definition includes a degree of judgement and is therefore potentially biased. A balance that prevents the deliberate and systematic understatement of assets and gains, and the overstatement of liabilities and losses, should resolve any potential conflict between neutrality and prudence.

Use of additional disclosures

4.11 The guidance in FRS 18 emphasises that the disclosure of additional information in the financial statements will not justify or remedy the adoption of an accounting policy that is not judged to be the most appropriate to the circumstances of the entity.

Industry practices

4.12 In selecting accounting policies, due consideration should be given to industry practices and whether these are appropriate to the particular circumstances of the entity. The guidance in FRS 18 notes that industry practices will be particularly persuasive if they are set out in a SORP that has been generally accepted by the industry or sector.

REVIEW OF ACCOUNTING POLICIES

The need for regular review

4.13 FRS 18 requires accounting policies to be regularly reviewed to ensure that they remain the most appropriate in the circumstances of the entity for the purpose of giving a true and fair view. Accounting policies may need to be changed to take account of changes and developments in the business or to implement the requirements of a new accounting standard. The guidance in FRS 18 emphasises that such a review of accounting policies does not require the early adoption of new accounting standards (although this is usually encouraged in each standard) – the effective date for each new standard is set to allow sufficient time for entities to consider the issues surrounding implementation, and make any necessary changes to the underlying management and reporting processes. However, where it is considered necessary to implement a new accounting policy, or to change an existing policy, the entity should ensure wherever possible that the new policy is in accordance with any recently issued accounting standards.

Accounting for a change in accounting policy

4.14 Unless accounting standards, UITF Abstracts or companies' legislation require otherwise, a material adjustment to prior periods as a result of a change in accounting policy should be accounted for as a prior period adjustment in accordance with the requirements of FRS 3 'Reporting Financial Performance'. Accounting for prior period adjustments is considered in more detail in **Chapter 5**.

Impact on comparability

4.15 Frequent changes to accounting policies may be detrimental to comparability – one of the objectives against which the appropriateness of accounting policies should be judged. The impact of past and expected future changes should therefore be taken into account when assessing whether a change in accounting policy is appropriate and accounting policies should generally only be changed when the benefits to users will outweigh the disadvantages. However, the standard emphasises that consistency is not an end in itself, and it should not be used to prevent improvements in accounting. Where the introduction of a new accounting policy would be of overall benefit to users, the need for consistency should not be used to justify not making the change.

DISCLOSURE OF ACCOUNTING POLICIES

Requirements under the Companies Act 1985

4.16 CA 1985 Sch 4 requires disclosure of the accounting policies adopted by the company in determining amounts to be included in the balance sheet and the profit or loss for the year. The Act specifically requires disclosure of the policies in respect of the depreciation and diminution in value of assets and the translation of amounts denominated in foreign currencies.

Requirements under FRS 18

4.17 FRS 18 requires the following disclosures to be given in respect of accounting policies:

- a description of each of the accounting policies that is material in the context of the entity's financial statements – where a policy is prescribed in detail in an accounting standard, UITF Abstract or companies' legislation, a brief description will suffice but where there is no such prescription, or where there are optional treatments, fuller details should be provided;
- details of any changes to the accounting policies followed in the previous financial period, including:
  - a brief explanation of why each new policy is considered more appropriate;
  - where practicable, the effect of a prior period adjustment on the

results of the preceding financial period, in accordance with the requirements of FRS 3 'Reporting Financial Performance' - if this is not practicable, this fact must be stated and the reasons explained;

— where practicable, an indication of the effect of the change in accounting policy on the results for the current period - if this is not practicable, this fact must be stated and the reasons explained.

The objective is that users with a reasonable knowledge of business and economic activities who are willing to study the information provided with reasonable diligence should understand the accounting policies adopted. The standard also requires specific disclosures in relation to going concern and departures from accounting standards, UITF Abstracts or companies legislation - these are considered in **Chapters 1** and **2** respectively. The disclosure requirements in respect of estimation techniques and SORPs are considered below.

Disclosure requirements under other accounting standards

4.18 A number of other accounting standards require disclosure of the accounting policy adopted in respect of the subject covered in the standard. The following standards specifically require disclosure of an accounting policy:

— SSAP 4 'Accounting for government grants'

— SSAP 9 'Stocks and Long Term Contracts'

— SSAP 13 'Accounting for Research and Development'

— SSAP 20 'Foreign Currency Translation'

— SSAP 21 'Accounting for Leases and Hire Purchase Contracts'

— FRS 10 'Goodwill and Intangible Assets'

— FRS 15 'Tangible Fixed Assets'.

Location of disclosures

4.19 It is normal practice to disclose all accounting policies in a single statement, usually as the first note to the financial statements. This helps to ensure that presentation of the detailed policies is clear and receives the appropriate level of prominence in the accounts. However, neither the Act nor accounting standards specify the form of the disclosure, requiring only that the details are given in the notes to the accounts. Some companies therefore choose to give each accounting policy as part of a relevant note to the accounts (e.g. by explaining the depreciation policy as part of the note on fixed assets). This may be acceptable where the accounts are basic and therefore straightforward to follow, but where more complex transactions arise, it can be difficult to decide where to give the disclosures (e.g.

in the accounts of a lessee, leasing transactions may involve disclosures in notes to the profit and loss account, fixed assets and creditors). This approach can also result in the accounting policies becoming obscured by the other details that are required to be given in the notes to the accounts. A separate statement of the accounting policies adopted is therefore the preferred form of presentation.

Accounting convention adopted

4.20 The accounts will also usually need to state the accounting convention that has been followed, as this will have a material effect on the measurement bases used for items included in the profit and loss account and balance sheet. Accounting conventions are considered in more detail in **Chapter 1**.

ESTIMATION TECHNIQUES

Definition of estimation techniques

4.21 Estimation techniques are defined in FRS 18 as 'the methods adopted by an entity to arrive at estimated monetary amounts, corresponding to the measurement bases selected for assets, liabilities, gains, losses and changes to shareholders' funds'. An accounting policy will therefore specify the basis on which an item is to be measured, and an estimation technique may be needed to arrive at the amount at which the item is to be reflected in the financial statements. Examples of estimation techniques include:

- depreciation methods (e.g. straight line, reducing balance) used to estimate the proportion of the economic benefits of asset that have been consumed during an accounting period;
- methods used to estimate the proportion of trade debts that will not be recovered, where these are based on the population as a whole rather than individual balances;
- methods used to calculate the proportion of indirect costs attributable to production.

Selection of estimation techniques

4.22 Where estimation techniques need to be used to enable the chosen accounting policies to be applied, FRS 18 requires the entity to select estimation techniques that:

- enable the financial statements to give a true and fair view; and
- are consistent with the requirements of accounting standards, UITF Abstracts and companies' legislation.

Where more than one estimation technique would satisfy these conditions, the entity should choose the technique that is most appropriate to its particular circumstances for the purpose of giving a true and fair view.

Factors to be taken into account

4.23 It is important for any estimation technique used in the preparation of financial information to be reliable and the technique chosen should usually be the one that gives the best approximation to the monetary amount of the asset, liability, gain, loss or change in shareholders' funds. There will always be a degree of uncertainty, as estimation techniques only need to be used when the actual amount is unknown. Materiality and cost/benefit considerations may come into play as well – there will often be situations where the time and cost involved in calculating a more accurate estimate will outweigh the benefits to be achieved by doing so. Once the improvement in the accuracy of the estimates ceases to be material, the cost of achieving the higher degree of accuracy will no longer be justified. Where disclosure of an estimation technique is required by FRS 18, the guidance also suggests that the understandability of each technique to users, and the extent to which it will facilitate comparison with other entities, should also be taken into account when deciding which technique is most appropriate.

Disclosure of techniques adopted

4.24 The standard requires the financial statements to include a description of any estimation techniques adopted that are considered significant. An estimation technique will be significant only if the range of reasonable monetary amounts is so large that the use of a different amount from within that range could materially affect the view shown by the financial statements. Consideration of whether or not an estimation technique is significant will usually involve assessing the impact of the various assumptions underlying the technique. Most estimation techniques will result in monetary amounts that fall within a relatively narrow range, and disclosure under FRS 18 is therefore expected to be rare in practice. Where disclosure is required, the description should include details of the underlying assumptions to which the monetary amount is particularly sensitive.

Changes in estimation techniques

4.25 A change in estimation techniques should not be accounted for as a change in accounting policy, unless accounting standards, UITF Abstracts or companies' legislation specifically require this treatment. A change in estimation techniques will therefore not usually result in a prior period adjustment unless it results from the correction of a fundamental error in previous years. The distinction between a change in estimation techniques and a change in accounting policy is considered in more detail in **Chapter 5**. Where the effect of a change in an estimation technique is material, FRS 18 requires the financial statements to include a description of the change and, where practicable, the effect on the results for the current period. There is no requirement to disclose the effect on the results for the previous year.

STATEMENTS OF RECOMMENDED PRACTICE (SORPs)

Definition of SORP

4.26 FRS 18 defines a Statement of Recommended Practice (SORP) as an existing SORP developed either:

- in accordance with the ASB statement 'SORPs: Policy and Code of Practice' and including a statement by the Board in accordance with that Statement; or
- franked by the former Accounting Standards Committee under its process for the approval of SORPs.

Further details on SORPs and the ASB's Code of Practice are given in **Chapter 1**.

Disclosure of adoption

4.27 Where an entity's financial statements come within the scope of a SORP, FRS 18 'Accounting Policies' requires the accounts to disclose:

- the title of the SORP;
- whether the accounts have been prepared in accordance with the current provisions of the SORP;
- in the event of a departure from the SORP, a description of the departure including:
  - the reasons why the treatment adopted is considered more appropriate to the entity's particular circumstances; and
  - details of any disclosures recommended by the SORP which have not been given, together with the reasons for non-disclosure.

The ASB believes that these disclosures will enhance comparability between the financial statements of entities in the specific industries and sectors for which SORPs have been developed. Quantification of the effect of the departure is not required unless this is necessary for the financial statements to give a true and fair view (this is expected to arise only rarely in practice).

Entities who voluntarily comply with a SORP

4.28 Entities whose accounts do not fall within the scope of a SORP but who nevertheless choose to comply with its recommendations are encouraged to disclose the fact that the accounts have been prepared in accordance with the relevant SORP.

Chapter 5

Comparative Figures and Prior Period Adjustments

COMPARATIVE FIGURES

Company law requirements

5.1 CA 1985 Sch 4 para 4(1) requires corresponding amounts for the previous financial period to be given for each item in the profit and loss account and balance sheet. In general, corresponding amounts must also be given for each item that has to be disclosed in the notes to the accounts, although CA 1985 Sch 4 para 58(3) specifically exempts the following disclosures from this requirement:

- detailed opening and closing balances and movements during the year in respect of fixed assets;
- movements on provisions for liabilities and charges;
- movements on reserves;
- detailed information on loans and other transactions involving directors;
- detailed information on shareholdings in other undertakings;
- detailed information on acquisitions.

CA 1985 Sch 4 para 57(1) also requires separate disclosure of any amount relating to the preceding year which is included in any item in the profit and loss account for the current year.

Comparative figures where there is no current year item

5.2 CA 1985 generally allows a company to exclude a heading or sub-heading normally required by the standard profit or loss account and balance sheet formats if there is no amount to be shown for that heading. However, if an amount was shown under that heading in the accounts for the previous financial period, the heading must be repeated in the current year's accounts so that the comparative figure can be correctly shown, with a nil figure for the current year.

Adjustment of comparative figures

5.3 If the corresponding figure previously reported for any item is not comparable with the figure disclosed in the current year, the corresponding figure must be adjusted and a note to the accounts must disclose:

— particulars of the adjustment - this will usually require both the original and the adjusted figures to be stated; and

— the reasons for making the adjustment.

This allows prior period adjustments to be made in accordance with FRS 3 'Reporting Financial Performance'. Where comparative figures have been adjusted for any reason, it is good practice to include the word 'restated' under the previous year heading on each of the primary statements and any relevant notes to the accounts. This helps to draw the attention of the reader to the fact that the figures have been adjusted. The reason for the restatement should be explained in the notes to the accounts.

Requirements of accounting standards

5.4 FRS 3 'Reporting Financial Performance' requires comparative figures to be given for all items included in the primary statements (i.e. the profit and loss account, balance sheet, cash flow statement and statement of total recognised gains and losses) and all related notes. Comparative figures should also be given for the reconciliation of movements in shareholders' funds and the note of historical cost profits and losses. Where there are both continuing and discontinued activities, FRS 3 requires the comparative figures in the profit and loss account to be adjusted so that the 'continuing' category includes only the results of operations that are classified as continuing in the current year. The detailed requirements of FRS 3 on the disclosure of continuing, acquired and discontinued activities are considered in **Chapter 8**.

PRIOR PERIOD ADJUSTMENTS

Definition of prior period adjustment

5.5 FRS 3 'Reporting Financial Performance' defines prior period adjustments as material adjustments relating to previous accounting periods as a result of changes in accounting policy or the correction of fundamental errors. They do not include normal recurring adjustments or corrections of accounting estimates made in prior periods.

Changes in accounting estimates

5.6 Many items in a set of accounts will require a degree of estimation and it is natural that some correction and adjustment to these estimates will be required as time passes and more accurate details become available. For instance, it is often necessary to estimate amounts to be included in accruals in respect of expenses relating to the year (e.g. electricity and telephone costs) but which have not yet been charged to the company. When the actual charges become known, some adjustment to the original estimates may be necessary. These adjustments should be dealt with in the profit and loss account for the period in which they are identified. In most cases, separate disclosure will not be required. The adjustments should not be considered exceptional or extraordinary simply because they relate to an earlier year. Where the effect of any under or over-estimation in earlier years is material, the effect should be separately disclosed in the notes to the accounts.

Reassessment of provisions

5.7 In some cases, changes may need to be made to original estimates as more experience is acquired or additional information is obtained. Examples of this are provisions for claims relating to faulty products and provisions for future claims against warranties given by a company in respect of its products. As time progresses the company will be able to maintain records of the claims actually received and should therefore be able to predict more accurately what the overall level of claims is likely to be. The provisions can then be reassessed each year in the light of the information received during that year. Any changes made to the provisions will arise from new information received during the year and should therefore be reflected in the profit and loss account for that year. If the provision made at the end of the previous period was the best estimate that could be made at the time, based on the information then available, there is not a fundamental error in the calculations simply because more recent information has resulted in the estimate being revised.

Use of estimation techniques

5.8 FRS 18 'Accounting Policies' considers the use of estimation techniques, which are defined as 'the methods adopted by an entity to arrive at estimated monetary amounts, corresponding to the measurement bases selected for assets, liabilities, gains, losses and changes to shareholders' funds'. An accounting policy will therefore specify the basis on which an item is to be measured, and an estimation technique may be needed to arrive at the amount at which the item is to be reflected in the financial statements. Examples of estimation techniques include:

- depreciation methods (e.g. straight line, reducing balance) used to estimate the proportion of the economic benefits of asset that have been consumed during an accounting period;
- methods used to estimate the proportion of trade debts that will not be recovered, where these are based on the population as a whole rather than individual balances;

— methods used to calculate the proportion of indirect costs attributable to production.

The requirements of the standard on the selection of appropriate estimation techniques, the need for regular review of the techniques adopted and the disclosure of the estimation techniques are covered in **Chapter 4**.

Distinction between estimation techniques and accounting policies

5.9 FRS 18 includes detailed discussion on the distinction between estimation techniques and accounting policies. Whilst accounting policies will usually prescribe the measurement bases to be used for particular assets and liabilities, they do not usually specify the method to be used to arrive at the required monetary amount. In some cases this amount will be known and there will be no uncertainty over its measurement. In other cases some form of estimate may need to be made. For example, an accounting policy may involve the current disposal value of a particular asset. This value may be estimated by reference to recent disposals of similar assets or by reference to prices quoted in advertisements for similar assets. Either method should arrive at a reasonable estimate of the monetary amount required. A change from one method of estimation to the other would be a change in estimation techniques, not a change in accounting policy. An appendix to FRS 18 gives practical examples of the distinction between changes in estimation techniques and changes in accounting policies. These include:

— interest relating to the construction of fixed assets has previously been charged to the profit and loss account but is now to be capitalised - this is a change of accounting policy;

— an entity reassesses the proportion of indirect costs attributable to production - this is a change of estimation technique;

— overheads previously classified as cost of sales are now to be shown within administrative expenses - this is a change of accounting policy;

— an asset previously depreciated using the reducing balance method is now to be depreciated using the straight line method - this is a change of estimation technique (i.e. the accounting policy is still to depreciate the asset over its useful economic life - the change is in the estimation technique used to measure the unexpired portion of the asset's economic benefits);

— deferred tax is to be reported on a discounted basis for the first time - this is a change in measurement basis and is therefore a change of accounting policy (i.e. FRS 19 allows an option of reporting deferred tax on a discounted or undiscounted basis);

— a provision has previously been measured on an undiscounted basis because the effect of discounting was not material, but the estimates of future cash flows have now changed with the result that the effect of discounting is material and the provision must therefore be reported at a discounted amount under the requirements of FRS 12 – this is a change of estimation technique (i.e. the policy is still to report the provision at the best estimate of the expenditure required to settle the obligation, but the method of arriving at that 'best estimate' has changed).

As can be seen from the above, the circumstances of each case must be considered very carefully to establish whether the change affects the measurement basis, and therefore the accounting policy, or simply the technique used to arrive at the amount required by the accounting policy. Particular care is needed when an accounting change involves both a change in presentation and a change in estimation techniques – the former is a change of accounting policy but the latter is not, and the two elements of the change must therefore be accounted for separately.

Changes in estimation techniques

5.10 A change in estimation techniques should not be accounted for as a change in accounting policy, unless accounting standards, UITF Abstracts or companies' legislation specifically require this treatment. A change in estimation techniques will therefore not usually result in a prior period adjustment unless it results from the correction of a fundamental error in previous years. Where the effect of a change in an estimation technique is material, FRS 18 requires the financial statements to include:

(i) a description of the change; and

(ii) where practicable, the effect on the results for the current period.

There is no requirement to disclose the effect on results for the previous year.

Change of accounting policy

5.11 Consistency of accounting treatment is one of the accounting principles identified in CA 1985. FRS 18 'Accounting Policies' also considers consistency but in the context of the need for comparability in the presentation of financial information. The standard notes that consistency is not an end in itself and should not be allowed to impede improvements in accounting. FRS 18 requires accounting policies to be regularly reviewed to ensure that they remain the most appropriate in the particular circumstances of the entity for the purpose of giving a true and fair view. They should generally only be changed when the benefits to users will outweigh the disadvantages.

Reasons for changing an accounting policy

5.12 Situations will inevitably arise from time to time which make it appropriate for an entity to change one of its accounting policies. For instance, a new accounting standard may have been introduced which requires a different accounting treatment to the one adopted by the entity in previous years – as an example, the introduction of FRS 12 'Provisions, Contingent Liabilities and Contingent Assets' required many companies to reassess whether provisions already included in their accounts were still justified under the new rules. Similarly, the nature or scale of an entity's activities or transactions may change, so that an accounting policy previously adopted is no longer acceptable (i.e. because items that were previously immaterial have now become material). Examples of this might include:

- an entity which had previously only entered into minor finance leases entering into a finance lease agreement in respect of a substantial asset or assets;
- an entity that had previously only carried out an insignificant level of research and development expanding its activities in this field by becoming involved in a major product development project.

Where it is necessary to implement a new accounting policy, or to change an existing policy, the guidance in FRS 18 notes that the entity should ensure wherever possible that the new policy adopted is in accordance with recently issued accounting standards.

Change in the method of applying an accounting policy

5.13 It is important to distinguish a change in the way an accounting policy is applied from a change in the accounting policy itself. For instance, in the case of depreciation, the underlying policy is to depreciate assets over their useful economic lives. If a company reassesses the economic lives of its assets and this results in the rate of depreciation being changed, this is simply a change in the way that the accounting policy is applied, rather than a change in the policy itself. Alternatively, where a company has a policy of not depreciating land and buildings and decides that, in future, buildings will be depreciated, this may constitute a change in accounting policy. However, the findings of the Financial Reporting Review Panel, published in September 2001 following a review of the accounts of Groupe Chez Gerard plc for the period ended 25 June 2000, emphasised that this will depend on the reasons for non-depreciation in previous years. For instance, if the assets were not previously depreciated on the grounds of immateriality but revisions to useful economic lives and residual values result in a depreciation charge being introduced, this would not constitute a change in accounting policy. The carrying amounts of the relevant assets would therefore be depreciated prospectively over their remaining useful economic lives in accordance with the normal requirements of FRS 15.

Accounting treatment on change of accounting policy

5.14 Where an accounting policy is changed, the figures for the current and the previous financial period should be stated on the basis of the new policy. This will result in a prior period adjustment which, under FRS 3, should be accounted for by:

— restating the relevant corresponding amounts in each of the primary statements;

— restating the relevant corresponding amounts in the notes to the accounts, including the note of historical cost profits and losses;

— adjusting the opening balance on reserves by the cumulative effect of all the necessary adjustments to the figures for previous periods;

— noting the cumulative effect of the adjustments at the foot of the statement of total recognised gains and losses for the current period – this is because the adjustment represents a gain or loss that has been recognised in the period, even though it actually relates to previous periods;

— adjusting the opening balance on the reconciliation of shareholders' funds for the previous year for the cumulative effect of adjustments to that date.

A worked example showing the presentation of a prior period adjustment in the accounts is given in the Appendix to this chapter.

Disclosure of change in accounting policy

5.15 On a change of accounting policy, the notes to the accounts should explain:

— the new accounting policy;

— the previous accounting policy;

— the reasons for the change; and

— the effect of the change in accounting policy on the results for the current financial period and the previous financial period.

In setting out the reasons for the change in accounting policy it is not sufficient simply to state that the new accounting policy is more appropriate. The notes must explain briefly why this is the case. If it is not practicable to disclose the effect of the change on the results for the current or preceding financial period, this fact must be stated and the reasons why disclosure is not practicable must also be given.

Correction of fundamental error

5.16 In certain circumstances, it is possible that the accounts for earlier years included errors that were so significant that they destroyed the true and fair view and thus the validity of those accounts. However, such errors should be very rare in practice. Where they do arise, they should be accounted for by restating the results for earlier years and adjusting the opening balance on the profit and loss reserve. In effect, this results in a prior period adjustment as discussed in **5.14** above. In practice, it may sometimes be difficult to make the distinction between the normal revision of an accounting estimate and a fundamental error. The emphasis in FRS 3 on the 'exceptional circumstances' of a fundamental error suggests that most items should be classified as normal revisions to accounting estimates, with separate disclosure where the effect is material. Where the accounts include a prior period adjustment to correct a fundamental error, the notes to the accounts should explain the reason for the adjustment and the amounts involved.

Appendix

WORKED EXAMPLE OF A PRIOR PERIOD ADJUSTMENT

The draft accounts of X Ltd for the year ended 31 December 2002 and the comparatives from the statutory accounts for 2001 are as follows.

Profit and loss account

	2002	*2001*
	£	*£*
	(Draft)	*(Actual)*
Turnover	541,960	487,732
Cost of sales	(375,998)	(331,750)
	165,962	155,982
Distribution costs	(85,670)	(74,669)
Administrative expenses	(50,443)	(43,771)
Operating profit	29,849	37,542
Interest receivable and similar income	10,976	8,751
Interest payable and similar charges	(8,779)	(11,772)
Profit on ordinary activities before taxation	32,046	34,521
Taxation	(9,550)	(8,750)
Profit on ordinary activities after taxation and for the financial year	22,496	25,771
Dividends paid and proposed	(15,000)	(15,000)
Retained profit for the year	7,496	10,771

Statement of total recognised gains and losses

	2002	*2001*
	£	*£*
Profit for the financial year	22,496	25,771
Unrealised surplus on revaluation of leasehold property	15,650	—
	38,146	25,771

Balance sheet

	2002	2001
	£	£
	(Draft)	(Actual)
Fixed assets:		
Tangible assets	175,690	145,788
Current assets:		
Stocks	195,678	185,743
Debtors	90,665	85,721
Cash at bank and in hand	10,250	7,564
	296,593	279,028
Creditors: amounts falling due within one year	(175,673)	(160,309)
Net current assets	120,920	118,719
Total assets less current liabilities	296,610	264,507
Creditors: amounts falling due after more than one year	(145,575)	(130,875)
Provisions for liabilities and charges	(51,784)	(57,527)
	99,251	76,105
Called up share capital	30,000	30,000
Revaluation reserve	15,650	—
Profit and loss account	53,601	46,105
	99,251	76,105

Reconciliation of movements in shareholders' funds

	2002	2001
	£	£
Profit for the financial year	22,496	25,771
Dividends	(15,000)	(15,000)
	7,496	10,771
Other gains and losses relating to the year	15,650	—
Net addition to shareholders funds	23,146	10,771
Opening shareholders funds	76,105	65,334
Closing shareholders funds	99,251	76,105

Movements on reserves

	Profit and loss account	*Revaluation reserve*
At 1 January 2002	46,105	—
Retained profit for the year transferred from the profit and loss account	7,496	—
Surplus on revaluation of leasehold property	—	15,650
At 31 December 2002	53,601	15,650

In previous years, X Ltd has not depreciated its freehold property. Following a review of the accounting policies, the directors have decided that the freehold building should be depreciated over its expected useful economic life. The building was acquired on 1 January 1997 at a cost of £75,000 and its estimated useful life is 50 years from the date of acquisition. The freehold building is used only for administration purposes. All manufacturing is carried out in the leasehold property. The building is currently included in the draft accounts for 1996 and the accounts for 1995 at its original cost of £75,000. If it had been depreciated since acquisition, its value would be:

	£
Cost 1 January 1997	75,000
Depreciation 1997 75,000 x 2%	(1,500)
NBV at 31 December 1997	73,500
Depreciation 1998 75,000 x 2%	(1,500)
NBV at 31 December 1998	72,000
Depreciation 1999 75,000 x 2%	(1,500)
NBV at 31 December 1999	70,500
Depreciation 2000 75,000 x 2%	(1,500)
NBV at 31 December 2000	69,000
Depreciation 2001 75,000 x 2%	(1,500)
NBV at 31 December 2001	67,500
Depreciation 2002 75,000 x 2%	(1,500)
NBV at 31 December 2002	66,000

Fixed assets at 31 December 2001 therefore need to be reduced by £7,500 (i.e. £75,000 – £67,500) and fixed assets in the draft accounts at 31 December 2002 need to be reduced by £9,000 (i.e. £75,000 – £66,000).

The profit and loss account for both years needs to include a depreciation charge of £1,500, and opening reserves at 1 January 2001 need to be reduced by £6,000 to reflect the depreciation that should have been charged in 1997 to 2000 inclusive (i.e. four years at £1,500 each year). The depreciation charge is treated as an additional administrative expense, as the freehold building is only used for administration. After the prior period adjustment, the accounts will be presented as follows.

Profit and loss account for the year ended 31 December 2002

	2002	*2001*
	£	*£*
		Restated
Turnover	541,960	487,732
Cost of sales	(375,998)	(331,750)
	165,962	155,982
Distribution costs	(85,670)	(74,669)
Administrative expenses*	(51,943)	(45,271)
Operating profit	28,349	36,042
Interest receivable and similar income	10,976	8,751
Interest payable and similar charges	(8,779)	(11,772)
Profit on ordinary activities before taxation	30,546	33,021
Taxation	(9,550)	(8,750)
Profit on ordinary activities after taxation and for the financial year	20,996	24,271
Dividends paid and proposed	(15,000)	(15,000)
Retained profit for the year	5,996	9,271

** £50,443 + £1,500 = £51,943 in 2002*
£43,771 + £1,500 = £45,271 in 2001

Statement of total recognised gains and losses

	2002	*2001*
	£	*£*
		Restated
Profit for the financial year	20,996	24,271
Unrealised surplus on revaluation of leasehold property	15,650	—
Total gains and losses recognised relating to the year	36,646	24,271
Prior year adjustment (as explained in note)*	(7,500)	
Total gains and losses recognised since the last annual report	29,146	

**£1,500 relating to 2001 + £6,000 relating to 1997 – 2000*

The figure disclosed as the total gains and losses recognised since the last report can be reconciled as follows:

	£
Total gains and losses recognised in the year	29,146
Dividends paid and proposed	(15,000)
	14,146
Shareholders funds at 31 December 2001 as reported in 2001 statutory accounts	76,105
Shareholders funds at 31 December 2002 as reported in final accounts for 2002	90,251
	14,146

BALANCE SHEET AS AT 31 DECEMBER 2002

	2002	*2001*
	£	£
		Restated
Fixed assets:		
Tangible assets*	166,690	138,288
Current assets:		
Stocks	195,678	185,743
Debtors	90,665	85,721
Cash at bank and in hand	10,250	7,564
	296,593	279,028
Creditors: amounts falling due within one year	(175,673)	(160,309)
Net current assets	120,920	118,719
Total assets less current liabilities	287,610	257,007
Creditors: amounts falling due after more than one year	(145,575)	(130,875)
Provisions for liabilities and charges	(51,784)	(57,527)
	90,251	68,605
Called up share capital	30,000	30,000
Revaluation reserve	15,650	—
Profit and loss account	44,601	38,605
	90,251	68,605

** Reduced by £9,000 in 2002 and £7,500 in 2001 to reflect the depreciation charged to date under the new accounting policy*

RECONCILIATION OF MOVEMENTS IN SHAREHOLDERS' FUNDS

		2002		*2001*
		£		£
				Restated
Profit for the financial year		20,996		24,271
Dividends		(15,000)		(15,000)
		5,996		9,271
Other gains and losses relating to the year		15,650		—
Net addition to shareholders funds		21,646		9,271
Opening shareholders funds:				
As previously reported	76,105		65,334	
Prior period adjustment	(7,500)		(6,000)	
		68,605		59,334
Closing shareholders funds		90,251		68,605

MOVEMENTS ON RESERVES

	Profit and loss account	*Revaluation reserve*
	£	£
At 1 January 2002 as previously reported	46,105	—
Prior period adjustment	(7,500)	—
At 1 January 2002 as restated	38,605	—
Retained profit for the year transferred from the profit and loss account	5,996	—
Surplus on revaluation of leasehold property	—	15,650
At 31 December 2002	44,601	15,650

CHANGE OF ACCOUNTING POLICY

Freehold buildings were not depreciated in previous years as their estimated future residual value was considered to be at least equal to their book value. In the light of current best practice, the directors now consider it more appropriate to provide for the depreciation of freehold buildings on a straight-line basis over the expected useful economic life of the building. The effect of this change in accounting policy has been to increase the depreciation charge within administrative expenses by £1,500 in both 2002 and 2001, and to reduce reserves at 1 January 2001 by £6,000 in respect of the depreciation that would have been charged in earlier years. In the balance sheet, the value of tangible fixed assets has been reduced by £9,000 at 31 December 2002 and by £7,500 at 31 December 2001.

Chapter 6

Foreign Currency Translation

GENERAL BACKGROUND TO FOREIGN CURRENCY TRANSLATION

Objectives of foreign currency translation

6.1 In the case of individual transactions denominated in other currencies, the explanatory note to SSAP 20 defines the objectives of foreign currency translation as follows:

— to produce results which are generally compatible with the effect of rate changes on a company's cash flows and its equity; and

— to ensure that the accounts present a true and fair view of the results of management actions.

Although SSAP 20 has been in issue since 1983, foreign currency translation remains a problematic area, although most of the difficulties arise from translation for consolidation purposes rather than the translation of transactions for inclusion in an individual company's accounts.

Need for consistency

6.2 A particular concern is the fact that, in some cases, differing treatments are equally acceptable under the present standard, so that two sets of accounts reflecting similar foreign currency transactions may show substantially different results. This makes understanding the figures and comparison between companies more difficult and is one reason why a clear description of the accounting policy adopted in respect of foreign currency translation is so important. The other important point is the need for consistency from year to year within an individual company. Although different treatments may be acceptable under SSAP 20, this does not mean that a company is free to choose which treatment to adopt each year. Where a choice is available, the decision on which treatment to adopt must be taken when foreign currency translation first affects the accounts, and the treatment chosen should be adopted each year from then on unless there are good reasons for making a change.

Formal documentation of policies

6.3 To help ensure consistency between years, companies may find it helpful to document the detailed policies adopted in respect of foreign currency translation. Although the basic policy requires disclosure in the annual accounts, additional detail will usually be necessary to ensure that there is complete consistency year by year. Formal documentation of the detail behind the policy can be particularly useful where there are changes in the personnel responsible for preparing the company's accounts.

Basis of invoicing

6.4 The need for foreign currency translation in respect of trading items only arises if the company invoices customers in a foreign currency and/or commits itself to making payments in another currency for goods and services that it has received. For instance, if the company reaches agreement with its customers that all sales invoices will be raised in sterling, it is the sterling values that will be recorded in the accounting records and there will be no need for translation. In this case, the customer will bear any potential exchange loss and benefit from any potential exchange gain. Similarly, if the company is able to agree with its overseas suppliers that all invoices will be raised in sterling, there is no need to record any foreign currency amounts in the accounting records and hence no requirement for translation. Here the supplier will bear any potential exchange loss and benefit from any potential exchange gain. The following guidance, therefore, relates only to situations where a company is either receiving or making payment in a foreign currency.

DEFINITIONS IN SSAP 20

Separate aspects of SSAP 20

6.5 SSAP 20 'Foreign Currency Translation' deals with two separate aspects of dealing with foreign currency items in the context of annual accounts:

(i) the translation of business transactions in other currencies entered into by an individual company;

(ii) the translation of the results and net assets of foreign operations conducted through entities which maintain their accounting records in another currency.

This chapter deals only with the first aspect of SSAP 20. Group accounts are not covered in this book and the translation of the accounts of foreign operations for consolidation purposes is therefore not considered further.

Translation

6.6 Translation is defined in SSAP 20 as 'the process whereby financial data denominated in one currency are expressed in terms of another currency'. The definition emphasises that translation applies both to individual transactions and also to a full set of accounts.

Local currency

6.7 Local currency is defined as 'the currency of the primary economic environment in which [the company] operates and generates net cash flow'. For UK accounting purposes, therefore, foreign currency translation usually refers to the conversion of amounts denominated in other currencies into sterling.

Exchange rate and closing rate

6.8 An exchange rate is defined as 'a rate at which two currencies may be exchanged for each other at a particular point in time'. The closing rate is defined as 'the exchange rate for spot transactions ruling at the balance sheet date'. The closing rate is also defined in more detail as the average of buying and selling rates at the close of business on the day for which the rate is to be ascertained. Therefore, if the balance sheet date is 31 March, the closing rate will be the average of the buying and selling rate at the close of business on 31 March. If there is no trading on the balance sheet date, the equivalent rate on the last previous trading day is usually used as the best approximation.

Forward contract

6.9 A forward contract is defined as 'an agreement to exchange different currencies at a specified future date and at a specified rate'. Forward contracts are a useful way of hedging against exposure to potentially significant exchange losses. For instance, if a company is due to receive a payment in a foreign currency, by taking out a forward contract it can guarantee that it will be able to exchange the currency for a specific sterling value. However, by removing the potential risk attached to the foreign currency receipt, the company will usually also lose the potential benefit of realising an exchange gain.

Monetary items

6.10 Monetary items are defined as 'money held and amounts to be received or paid in money'. Monetary items will usually comprise cash, bank balances, loans, debtors and creditors. SSAP 20 also requires each monetary item to be classified as short-term or long-term, as different accounting treatments may be necessary in the case of some long-term items. A short-term item is defined as one which falls due within one year of the balance sheet date.

TRANSLATION OF FOREIGN CURRENCY TRANSACTIONS

Basic requirement

6.11 The basic accounting treatment under the standard is that each individual foreign currency transaction should be translated into local currency (which in most cases will be sterling) at the exchange rate ruling when the transaction occurred. If a company has only one or two foreign currency transactions a year, translation on this basis should be relatively straightforward. However, where a company regularly enters into such transactions (e.g. it makes significant purchases from overseas suppliers or sells regularly to overseas customers), this approach is clearly impractical. The standard therefore permits the use of an average rate for a period, as an approximation to the actual rate, provided that rates do not fluctuate widely.

Date when the transaction occurs

6.12 SSAP 20 requires translation to be at the rate ruling when the transaction occurred but does not provide any guidance on how this date should be established. For instance it might be the date when:

— a contract was signed;

— a formal order was placed; or

— the goods or services were delivered.

If exchange rates are fluctuating, the amount of exchange gain or loss recorded on the transaction could be substantially different, depending on which date is used. The most straightforward approach, and the most common approach in practice, is to use the date when the transaction is first recorded in the accounting records (assuming that the accounting records are properly prepared and kept up to date). This will often be the date of delivery as this is when:

— in the case of purchases, the receipt of the goods or services, and the company's liability to pay for them, will first be recorded in the accounting records in some way;

— in the case of sales, the company will record the sale and the fact that the customer has a liability to pay for the goods or services that he has received.

At the time of invoicing the company needs to record either a creditor or a debtor in its accounting records, based on the actual exchange rate on the delivery date or the average rate that the company is using for that period.

Contracted rate

6.13 If the terms of the transaction specify that it is to be settled at a contracted rate, this rate should be used to translate the transaction when it is recorded in the company's accounting records. This situation is almost equivalent to the company buying or selling in sterling as the company knows how much it must pay, or how much it will receive, and as a result it does not bear any exchange risk in relation to the transaction.

Calculation of exchange gains and losses

6.14 The exchange gain or loss in respect of each transaction will be the difference between the amount recorded in the accounting records (i.e. based on the translation procedure outlined above) and the exchange rate ruling on the date that payment is actually received or made.

Example 6.1 – Calculation of exchange gains and losses

On 1 April 200X, A Ltd delivered goods to a German company, the value of the sale being 7,500 Euros. The customer paid for the goods on 15 May 200X.

The relevant £: Euro exchange rates were:

1 April 200X £1: 1.64 Euros

15 May 200X £1: 1.57 Euros

Therefore:

— at the time the goods were delivered, A Ltd should have recorded a sale (and an equivalent debtor) of £4,573.17 (i.e. 7,500 Euros at an exchange rate of £1: 1.64 Euros);

— when payment is made, the company will in effect receive £4,777.07 (i.e. 7,500 Euros at an exchange rate of £1: 1.57 Euros).

The company will therefore record an exchange gain of £203.90 on this transaction.

Use of a forward contract

6.15 Where a company takes out a matching or related forward contract to hedge against any exposure to exchange risk, the exchange rate specified in the forward contract may be used to translate the transaction. This is expressed in SSAP 20 as an option rather than a requirement. Using the contract rate means that the transaction is recorded from the outset at the value that it will eventually realise and that no exchange gain or loss will be recorded. If a company wishes to adopt this treatment, it must adopt it for all foreign currency transactions which have related or matching forward contracts. UITF Abstract 21 clarifies that the introduction of the euro should not have any impact on the accounting treatment used by entities that adopt this policy.

Options

6.16 A company may also hedge against the potential exposure to exchange losses by taking out an option to buy or sell currency at a specified rate (as opposed to a forward contract, where the company is committed to buy or sell at the specified rate). Where the company takes out an option rather than a forward contract, the option can be exercised to prevent an exchange loss arising (i.e. if exchange rates at the time of payment are unfavourable). If exchange rates at the time of payment are favourable, the company can ignore the option and buy or sell at the prevailing rate to realise an exchange gain. In other words, taking out an option enables a company to hedge against a potential risk of an exchange loss without forfeiting the potential benefit of an exchange gain. Although options are not specifically discussed in SSAP 20, there seems to be no reason why they should not be treated in the same way as forward contracts, because the company has taken the decision to guarantee a minimum level of income in each case. If the transaction is recorded at the rate specified in the option and the option is exercised, there will be no exchange gain or loss to record. If the option is not exercised (i.e. because prevailing exchange rates at the time of payment are more favourable), the company will record an exchange gain representing the effect of the difference between the exchange rate in the option and the prevailing rate at the time of payment.

Example 6.2 – Using options

On 1 April 200X A Ltd delivered goods to a German company, the value of the sale being 7,500 Euros.

The relevant £ : Euro exchange rates were:

1 April 200X	£1: 1.64 Euros
15 May 200X	£1: 1.70 Euros
16 June 200X	£1: 1.50 Euros

A Ltd had also taken out a related option at £1: 1.60 Euros.

(i) The customer pays on 15 May 200X.

- A Ltd can record the sale at the exchange rate at the date of delivery as in Example 6.1 (i.e. £4,573.17). As a result of taking out the related option, A Ltd will eventually receive £4,687.50 (i.e. 7,500 Euros at an exchange rate of £1: 1.60 Euros) in respect of the transaction, and will therefore record an exchange gain of £150.33.

- Alternatively, A Ltd can use the exchange rate in the related option to record the sale at the date of delivery, as this is the minimum amount that it is guaranteed to receive in respect of the sale; in this case the sale would be recorded at £4,687.50 and no exchange gain or loss will arise when payment is received.

(ii) The customer pays on 16 June 200X.

- A Ltd can record the sale at the exchange rate at the date of delivery as in Example 6.1 (i.e. £4,573.17). As the exchange rate at the date of payment is £1: 1.50 Euros, A Ltd will choose not to exercise the option that it holds. It will therefore receive £5,000.00 at the date of payment and record an exchange gain of £426.83.
- Alternatively, A Ltd can use the exchange rate in the related option to record the sale at the date of delivery as this is the minimum amount that it is guaranteed to receive in respect of the sale; in this case the sale would be recorded at £4,687.50 (i.e. 7,500 Euros at an exchange rate of £1: 1.60 Euros). As the exchange rate at the date of payment is £1: 1.50 Euros, A Ltd will choose not to exercise the option that it holds. It will therefore receive £5,000.00 at the date of payment and record an exchange gain of £312.50.

Impact on the profit and loss account

6.17 The above examples illustrate how the amounts shown as turnover and exchange gains or losses in the accounts can vary depending on which approach is adopted. The same applies to items of expenditure denominated in a foreign currency. This reinforces the need for a consistent approach to be taken year by year. However, it should be noted that the net profit or loss in respect of an individual transaction reflected in the profit and loss account will be the same, regardless of which approach is used – it is just the analysis between individual profit and loss account headings that will differ. The treatment of exchange gains and losses in the profit and loss account is considered below (see **6.21–6.29**).

TRANSLATION OF ASSETS AND LIABILITIES

Non-monetary assets

6.18 Non-monetary assets comprise assets such as:

- property;
- plant and machinery;
- investments;
- intangible fixed assets;
- stocks.

These assets should be translated on the basis described above, at the date when they are acquired and no further exchange adjustment should generally be necessary.

Example 6.3 – Non-monetary assets

A Ltd buys a machine costing DM 100,000 from a supplier in Germany. The machine is delivered on 1 September 199X and A Ltd pays for the machine on 15 October 199X.

The exchange rates are:

1 September 199X	£1: DM 2.20
15 October 199X	£1: DM 2.23

When the machine is delivered A Ltd should record it in fixed assets at £45,455 (i.e. DM 100,000 at an exchange rate of £1 : DM 2.20). This will be the cost of the asset for depreciation purposes and no further currency adjustments will need to be made to the value of the plant.

When A Ltd pays for the machine on 15 October it will actually pay £44,843 (i.e. DM 100,000 at an exchange rate of £1 : DM 2.23). It should therefore record an exchange gain of £612 in the profit and loss account for the year.

An alternative to the above treatment for non-monetary assets may be adopted in the case of foreign equity investments (see **6.31**)

Monetary assets and liabilities

6.19 At the balance sheet date, a company may hold monetary assets and liabilities denominated in a foreign currency, for instance foreign currency loans, foreign currency bank balances or overdrafts, overseas debtors and/or overseas creditors. For accounts purposes, these assets and liabilities should be translated at the closing rate of exchange unless they are due to be settled at a contracted rate, in which case this rate should be used. If the company has taken out matching or related forward contracts, the rates in these contracts may be used instead.

Overseas debtors and creditors

6.20 Sales and purchases will usually have been translated at the exchange rate prevailing at the date of the transaction and the related debtor or creditor will have been recorded at the same amount. At the balance sheet date, therefore, any outstanding overseas debtors or creditors will be stated in the accounting records at a sterling value, but if exchange rates have varied, this will not be the same as the original currency value translated at the closing exchange rate. The balances in the accounting records will therefore need to be adjusted and an exchange gain or loss recorded. If the company has taken out a matching or related forward contract to limit the potential exposure to an exchange loss, the rate specified in the contract may be used to translate the year-end balance for accounts purposes. However, for consistency, this should only be done if the company has used the contract rate to translate the original transaction.

RECORDING EXCHANGE GAINS AND LOSSES

Settled transactions

6.21 Exchange gains and losses on transactions that have been settled during the year should be included in the profit and loss account for the year. Where exchange gains and losses arise on transactions between members of a group, the gains and losses should be included in the profit and loss account of each individual company in exactly the same way as those arising on transactions with third parties.

Unsettled short-term monetary transactions

6.22 Exchange gains and losses on short-term monetary transactions that are still outstanding at the balance sheet date should also be included in the profit and loss account for the year. This is on the basis that it is reasonably certain that the gains or losses in respect of these transactions will be reflected in the company's cash flows in the near future, even though they are not actually realised at the balance sheet date (e.g. balances appearing in trade debtors and creditors will usually be paid within a few weeks of the balance sheet date).

Unsettled long-term monetary transactions

6.23 In most cases, exchange gains and losses on unsettled long-term monetary transactions (i.e. those that are due more than one year after the balance sheet date) should also be recognised in the profit and loss account for the year. Paragraph 10 of SSAP 20 discusses the rationale behind this requirement. However, in exceptional circumstances, it may be necessary, on the grounds of prudence, to restrict the amount of the exchange gain that is recognised in the profit and loss account, or the amount by which an exchange gain exceeds exchange losses recorded in previous years in respect of the same asset or liability. Such restrictions are rare in practice and should arise only where there are concerns over whether the currency in question is convertible or marketable.

Impact on distributable reserves

6.24 The accounting treatment generally required by SSAP 20 in respect of long-term monetary assets and liabilities means that unrealised gains and losses may be included in the profit and loss account. Where a company has such long-term assets and liabilities it is helpful to maintain a separate record of the unrealised gains and losses credited or charged to the profit and loss account in respect of each item. If a company with unsettled foreign currency long-term monetary transactions wishes to make a distribution, particular care will be needed in establishing the amount of reserves that are available for distribution, and legal advice may need to be taken.

True and fair override

6.25 The accounting treatment required by SSAP 20 in respect of unsettled long-term monetary transactions means that unrealised exchange gains and losses will usually be included in the profit and loss account whenever a company has long-term assets and liabilities denominated in a foreign currency. Under CA 1985, only profits realised at the balance sheet date may be included in the profit and loss account. Compliance with SSAP 20 in these circumstances therefore constitutes a departure from the accounting requirements of the Act under the true and fair override and requires disclosure in the accounts. A suggested disclosure is given in the **Appendix to Chapter 2**.

Post balance sheet events

6.26 SSAP 20 requires monetary assets to be translated at the closing rate for inclusion in the company's balance sheet. If significant fluctuations take place between the balance sheet date and the date of settlement of the transaction, and this gives rise to a material exchange difference in the subsequent accounting period, this may require disclosure in the notes to the accounts as a non-adjusting post balance sheet event.

PROFIT AND LOSS ACCOUNT DISCLOSURE

Gains and losses on ordinary activities

6.27 Exchange gains and losses will arise in respect of the translation of:

— foreign currency transactions during the year; and

— monetary assets and liabilities at the balance sheet date.

Gains and losses on exchange recognised during the year should normally be included as part of the profit or loss for the year on ordinary activities. The only exception to this is where an exchange gain or loss relates to an item that is itself classified as extraordinary. In this case the exchange gain or loss should be included as part of the extraordinary item. Extraordinary items are extremely rare under the requirements of FRS 3 and it is therefore unlikely that this situation will arise in practice.

Inclusion under statutory headings

6.28 The appropriate statutory heading in the profit and loss account for each exchange gain or loss will depend on the nature of the underlying transaction. The usual practice is:

- exchange gains and losses relating to trading transactions are included in other operating income or other operating expenses; this would include, for instance, gains and losses arising on:
  - sales to overseas customers,
  - purchases from overseas suppliers,
  - purchases of plant and equipment from overseas suppliers;
- exchange gains and losses relating to financing transactions are included in 'interest receivable and similar income', or 'interest payable and similar charges' as appropriate.

In each case, the amount included in respect of exchange gains and losses should be separately disclosed. SSAP 20 includes specific disclosure requirements in respect of exchange gains and losses on foreign currency borrowings and deposits.

Exceptional items

6.29 Exceptional items are required by FRS 3 'Reporting Financial Performance' to be included under the relevant statutory heading or, in specific cases, shown under one of the additional headings introduced by FRS 3. Where appropriate, exchange gains and losses relating to exceptional items should be separately disclosed as part of the exceptional item.

Cash flow statement

6.30 The cash flow impact of movements in exchange rates must also be reflected in the cash flow statement. **Chapter 34** includes guidance on dealing with foreign currency items in the cash flow statement.

FOREIGN EQUITY INVESTMENTS

Alternative accounting treatment

6.31 The usual method of accounting for foreign currency non-monetary assets under SSAP 20 is considered in **6.18** above. The standard recognises one situation where this treatment may not be appropriate and where an alternative accounting treatment is offered. Where a company has taken out foreign currency borrowings to finance or hedge against a foreign equity investment, it may adopt the following accounting treatment, but only where the conditions set out in **6.32** apply:

- carry the equity investments at their foreign currency value and translate this value at the closing rate at each balance sheet date;
- take any exchange differences arising on this translation directly to reserves (i.e. in this case, the exchange gain or loss is not credited or charged to the profit and loss account);
- off-set exchange gains and losses arising on the translation of the related foreign currency borrowings against the gains or losses on the investment, also as a reserves movement.

There is no specific requirement for the investments and the borrowings to be in the same currency. In cases where the gain or loss on retranslation of the borrowings is taxable (e.g. where a matching election is not made for tax purposes), UITF Abstract 19 'Tax on gains and losses on foreign currency borrowings that hedge an investment in a foreign enterprise' requires any tax charges or credits that are directly and solely attributable to the exchange differences to be similarly taken to reserves and reported in the statement of total recognised gains and losses.

Conditions to be satisfied

6.32 The following conditions must be satisfied for the above treatment to be adopted:

- in any accounting period, exchange gains and losses arising on the borrowings may only be off-set to the extent of the exchange gains and losses arising on the equity investments (i.e. any gain or loss on the borrowings in excess of that on the investments will have to be charged or credited to the profit and loss account);
- the foreign currency borrowings in respect of which gains and losses are off-set should not exceed, in aggregate, the total amount of cash that the investments are expected to be able to generate, from profits or otherwise;
- if a company chooses to adopt this treatment, it must be applied consistently from year to year; where relevant, this would include the year in which the investment is sold.

Under UITF Abstract 19, the first restriction must be applied after taking into account any tax charges or credits that are directly and solely attributable to the borrowings, and the comparison in the second restriction should also be considered in after-tax terms. If both the investment and the loan show a gain for the year, the gain on the loan must be credited in full to the profit and loss account. Similarly, if both show a loss for the year, the loss on the loan must be charged in full to the profit and loss account. The gain or loss on the investment will always be taken directly to reserves.

Disclosure of adoption

6.33 The fact that this treatment has been adopted should be disclosed in the accounting policy on foreign currency translation (see **6.34** below). UITF Abstract 19 specifically requires disclosure of the amount of tax charges or credits taken directly to reserves and reported in the statement of total recognised gains and losses, in addition to the gross amount of the exchange differences.

ACCOUNTS DISCLOSURE REQUIREMENTS

General disclosure requirement

6.34 The following information must be given in the notes to the accounts:

- the methods used for translating foreign currency transactions;
- the treatment adopted for exchange differences arising on the translation of foreign currency transactions;
- the net amount of exchange gains and losses on foreign currency borrowings less foreign currency deposits, showing separately:
  - the amount off-set in reserves, with separate disclosure of any tax charges or credits;
  - the amount credited or charged to the profit and loss account; and
- the net movement on reserves relating to exchange differences.

Compliance with the requirements of SSAP 20 will usually satisfy the CA 1985 disclosure requirement in respect of foreign currency translation.

Accounting policy

6.35 The first two disclosure requirements will usually be met by a detailed note on the accounting policy adopted in respect of foreign currency translation. The wording of the policy will clearly depend on the company's circumstances, but the following might be suitable in a straightforward case.

Example 6.4 — Accounting policy disclosure

Transactions in foreign currencies are translated into sterling at the rate of exchange ruling on the date when the transaction occurred.

Monetary assets and liabilities are translated into sterling at the rate ruling at the balance sheet date, except where:

(i) they are to be settled at a contracted rate, in which case the contracted rate is used,

(ii) they are covered by a matching forward contract, in which case the rate specified in the contract is used.

Gains and losses arising on translation are included in the profit and loss account.

Where a company chooses to adopt the alternative treatment in respect of foreign equity investments, this will also need to be explained in the accounting policy note.

Example 6.5 — Alternative treatment for foreign equity investments

Where foreign equity investments are financed or hedged by foreign currency borrowings, the investments are denominated in the appropriate foreign currency and translated into sterling at the closing rate at each balance sheet date. Gains and losses arising on this translation are taken directly to reserves and are off-set by gains and losses on translation of the related borrowings. Any gains and losses on translation of the borrowings which are in excess of the gains or losses on the investments are included in the profit and loss account.

Other disclosure requirements

6.36 The remaining disclosure requirements will usually be dealt with in:

- the reserves note; and
- the notes to the profit and loss account detailing:
  - specific amounts charged against or credited to operating profit,
  - other interest receivable and similar income, and
  - interest payable and similar charges.

Gains and losses taken directly to reserves will also be included in the statement of total recognised gains and losses.

LIKELY FUTURE DEVELOPMENTS

FRED 23 'Financial instruments: Hedge accounting'

6.37 The ASB published FRED 23 'Financial instruments: Hedge accounting' in May 2002. In effect, this introduces a new subject into UK accounting standards, although SSAP 20 and UITF Abstract 19 currently deal with accounting for hedges of net investments in foreign operations. However, FRED 23 still forms part of the convergence project with international accounting standards, as much of the material is drawn from IAS 39 'Financial instruments: Recognition and measurement'. Hedge accounting results in gains and losses on hedging instruments being deferred and matched with those arising on the hedged item, and it can therefore have a significant effect on reported financial performance. The main aspects of the current proposals are:

- hedge accounting can only be used where the hedge relationship has been pre-designated and formally documented, and meets certain effectiveness criteria; and
- where hedge accounting is adopted, it should not be applied to any ineffective portion of the hedge.

FRED 23 prescribes the form of hedge accounting to be used for hedges of net investments in foreign operations and also includes specific provisions on dealing with the discontinuance of a hedge. The proposals are considered in more detail in **Chapter 3**.

FRED 24 'The effects of changes in foreign currency exchange rates; Reporting in hyperinflationary economies'

6.38 The ASB published FRED 24 'The effects of changes in foreign exchange rates; Financial reporting in hyperinflationary economies' in May 2002 as part of its project to achieve convergence between UK accounting standards and international accounting standards. This proposes the replacement of SSAP 20 and UITF Abstract 9 with new requirements based on a proposed revision of IAS 21 'The effects of changes in foreign exchange rates' and the existing IAS 29 'Financial reporting in hyperinflationary economies' which does not form part of the IASB's current improvement project. However, there are some differences in the text, the most significant being a proposed prohibition on the recycling of exchange gains and losses between the statement of total recognised gains and losses and the profit and loss account. The ASB hopes that the current IASB project on reporting financial performance will result in such recycling being prohibited internationally as well.

Principal changes proposed

6.39 The main changes from current UK requirements are:

- FRED 24 sets out definitions of functional currency and presentation currency and requires each entity to determine its functional currency and measure its results in that currency. However, it then permits the entity to report its results in any currency that it chooses (the presentation currency). SSAP 20 does not specifically cover the issue of presentation in a currency other than the 'local' currency (ie that of the primary economic market in which the entity operates).
- In the preparation of consolidated accounts, SSAP 20 requires the use of different translation methods (the closing rate/net investment method and the temporal method) depending on the relationship between the investor and the foreign entity. FRED 24 no longer

makes such a distinction, but the requirement to identify and use the functional currency should mean that the effect of the new standard will be the same in situations where SSAP 20 requires use of the temporal method.

- FRED 24 no longer permits use of the closing rate to translate the profit and loss account for consolidation purposes.
- SSAP 20 permits the use of a contracted rate to record a transaction and translate any related assets and liabilities. FRED 24 requires a transaction to measured initially at the spot rate on the date of the transaction, unless hedge accounting techniques can be applied under the proposals in FRED 23.
- FRED 24 requires all exchange gains and losses on monetary items to be recognised in the profit and loss account. SSAP 20 permits gains on long-term monetary items to be deferred if there is concern over whether the currency is convertible or marketable.

FRED 24 also gives specific consideration to the treatment of goodwill and fair value adjustments in respect of a foreign entity. UITF Abstract 9 currently allows a choice of methods for eliminating the distortions that arise in hyperinflationary economies. FRED 24 requires the financial statements of an entity whose functional currency is that of a hyperinflationary economy to be restated to reflect the impact of price changes and does not allow the adoption of a stable currency as the functional currency. The scope of FRED 24 is also wider, in that it covers the accounting treatment to be adopted in the individual financial statements of an entity whose functional currency is that of a hyperinflationary economy, as well as the incorporation of such an entity in consolidated accounts.

FRED 24 also proposes disclosure of:

- the amount of exchange differences included in the net profit or loss for the period;
- any changes to the functional currency;
- where relevant, the fact that the presentation currency differs from the functional currency and the reason for using a different presentation currency.

Chapter 7

Small and Medium-sized Companies

QUALIFICATION AS A SMALL COMPANY

Company qualifying as small

7.1 The general rule is that a company qualifies as small in relation to a specific financial year if it meets the criteria set out in CA 1985 in:

— the financial year under consideration, and

— the previous financial year.

If a company meets the criteria in its first financial year, it qualifies as a small company for that year. However, a parent company cannot qualify as a small company unless the group which it heads qualifies as a small group (see **7.6–7.8** below).

Company treated as qualifying as small

7.2 A company is also treated as qualifying as small in relation to a specific financial year if:

(i) it qualified as small in the previous financial year or was treated as qualifying as small in the previous year under (ii) below; or

(ii) if it qualifies as small in the current financial year and was treated as qualifying as small in the previous year.

Practical effect

7.3 This sounds extremely complicated, but the purpose is to enable a company to continue to qualify as small even if it exceeds the qualifying criteria in one year. If it exceeds the criteria in two consecutive years, then it can no longer be treated as a small company. The effect is illustrated below.

Example 7.1 – Meeting the criteria as a small company

The position of Company A is as follows:

1998	Meets the criteria for a small company
1999	Exceeds the criteria for a small company
2000	Meets the criteria for a small company
2001	Exceeds the criteria for a small company
2002	Exceeds the criteria for a small company

In 1998, it meets the criteria in its first year and therefore qualifies as a small company.

In 1999, it is treated as qualifying as a small company because it qualified as small in the previous year.

In 2000 it is treated as qualifying as small because it meets the criteria in the current year and was treated as qualifying as small in the previous year.

In 2001 it is treated as qualifying as small because it met the criteria in the previous year and was treated as qualifying as small in that year.

In 2002 it does not qualify as small because it fails to meet the criteria in the current year and was only treated as qualifying as small in the previous year (i.e. it did not actually meet the criteria in that year).

Qualifying conditions

7.4 The criteria that must be met are termed 'qualifying conditions' and are set out in CA 1985 s 247(3). The financial limits that form part of these conditions have been updated on a number of occasions since the small company provisions were first introduced. The present criteria are:

- turnover of not more than £2.8 million (if the accounting period is less than or more than a year, this limit must be adjusted proportionately);
- balance sheet total of not more than £1.4 million;
- number of employees not more than 50.

A company must meet two or more of these conditions in order to qualify as small. The DTI document *Modern Company Law for a Competitive Economy: Final Report* issued in July 2001 recommended increasing the qualifying criteria to the maximum permitted under EC Directives and the Government White Paper *Modernising Company Law* issued in July 2002 confirms the intention to proceed with this. The turnover threshold will therefore be raised in due course to £4.2 million and the balance sheet total to £2.4 million.

Definitions

7.5 The term 'balance sheet total' is defined as the aggregate of the amounts shown as assets in the balance sheet, i.e. *before* making any deductions for liabilities. The term 'number of employees' is defined as the average number of persons employed by the company in the year, determined on a monthly basis. The figure should therefore be calculated by adding together the number of persons employed under contracts of service each month (regardless of whether they were employed for the full month) and dividing this by the number of months in the financial year.

Qualification as a small group

7.6 The rules under which a parent company and its subsidiaries qualify as a small group are similar to those for qualification as a small company. A group, which in this instance means a parent company and its subsidiary undertakings, qualifies as small if it meets the criteria set out in the Act in:

— the financial year under consideration; and

— the previous financial year.

If a group meets the criteria in the parent company's first financial year, it qualifies as a small group for that year. A group is also treated as qualifying as small in relation to a specific financial year if:

(i) it qualified as small in the previous financial year or was treated as qualifying as small in the previous year under (ii) below; or

(ii) it qualifies as small in the current financial year and was treated as qualifying as small in the previous year.

These rules apply in exactly the same way as for an individual company as described in **7.3** above and have the same effect (i.e. that a group may continue to qualify as small if it exceeds the qualifying criteria in one year, but if it exceeds them in two consecutive years, it will no longer qualify as a small group).

Qualifying conditions

7.7 The present criteria for a small group are:

— aggregate turnover of not more than £2.8 million net or not more than £3.36 million gross (if the accounting period is less or more than a year, these limits must be adjusted proportionately);

— aggregate balance sheet total of not more than £1.4 million net or not more than £1.68 million gross;

— aggregate number of employees not more than 50.

The same definitions apply as in the case of an individual company (see **7.5** above). A group must meet two or more of the conditions in order to qualify as small. As with the small company criteria (see **7.4** above), the Government has indicated that it intends to increase the current thresholds for a small group to the maximum permitted under EC Directives. The turnover threshold will therefore be raised in due course to £4.8 million net or £5.76 million gross, and the balance sheet total to £2.4 million net or £2.88 million gross.

'Gross' and 'net'

7.8 'Gross' figures within the criteria are those before the adjustments required by CA 1985 Sch 4A (i.e. the set-offs and other adjustments normally made in preparing consolidated accounts) and 'net' figures are after those adjustments have been made. Being able to use 'gross' figures means that a group does not have to go through the mechanics of consolidation in order to demonstrate that it is not required to prepare group accounts. There is no requirement in the Act for the turnover and balance sheet criteria to be considered on the same basis. It is therefore possible to look at (say) net figures when considering turnover and gross figures when considering the balance sheet total, and vice versa. The figures to be used for each subsidiary in the aggregation are those shown in the subsidiary's accounts for:

- the financial year that ends with that of the parent company, if it makes up its accounts to the same date as the parent company; or
- the last financial year ending before the financial year end of the parent company.

The latest available figures may be used if the above details cannot be obtained without undue delay or disproportionate expense.

ACCOUNTS EXEMPTIONS AVAILABLE TO SMALL COMPANIES AND GROUPS

Accounts exemptions for small companies

7.9 Two main accounts exemptions are available to most companies that qualify as small under the Act:

- a small company can prepare its annual accounts in accordance with the requirements set out in CA 1985 Sch 8 (which are less detailed than those in Sch 4) and can file these accounts with the registrar;
- a small company can file abbreviated accounts with the registrar – however, full or shorter form accounts must still be prepared for presentation to the members of the company.

A small company does not have to take advantage of either exemption and can prepare and file full accounts if it wishes.

Ineligible companies

7.10 The above exemptions are not available to the following companies, even if they meet the qualifying conditions:

- a public company;
- a person who has permission under Part 4 of the Financial Services and Markets Act 2000 (FSMA 2000) to carry on one or more regulated activities;
- a person who carries on an insurance market activity; or
- a member of an ineligible group.

An ineligible group is defined as a group where any of the members is:

- a public company;
- a body corporate that has the power to issue shares or debentures to the public;
- a person who has permission under Part 4 of FSMA 2000 to carry on one or more regulated activities; or
- a person who carries on an insurance market activity.

In the case of an intermediate parent company, it is necessary to consider the wider group and not just the one headed by the intermediate parent. The second category here does not need to be a British institution, so the UK subsidiary of a foreign undertaking will not be entitled to the exemptions if the parent has the power to issue shares or debentures to the public. It should also be noted that it is the power to issue shares and debentures, rather than their actual issue, that is the deciding factor.

Shorter form accounts

7.11 Under CA 1985 s 246(2), a small company is permitted to prepare shorter form accounts, provided that there is a statement in a prominent position on the balance sheet, above the director's signature, that the accounts are prepared in accordance with the special provisions of Part VII of CA 1985 relating to small companies (see **7.14** below). Small companies can also adopt the requirements of the Financial Reporting Standard for Smaller Entities (FRSSE) (see **7.26** below). If a small company decides not to adopt the FRSSE, all of the measurement and disclosure requirements set out in other accounting standards must be followed, except where specific exemption is granted. The position of small companies in relation to accounting standards generally is considered in **7.21** below.

Additional disclosure exemptions

7.12 A small number of additional exemptions are set out in CA 1985 s 246(3). Under these provisions, the accounts of a small company need not give:

(i) financial years of subsidiary undertakings (normally required by Sch 5 para 4);

(ii) the number of directors exercising share options or receiving shares under long term incentive schemes (normally required by Sch 6 para 1(2)(b);

(iii) the emoluments of the highest paid director (normally required by Sch 6 para 2); or

(iv) details of any excess retirement benefits to directors and past directors (normally required by Sch 6 para 7).

In addition, only the total of the aggregates for directors' emoluments and other benefits needs to be given in the accounts of a small company, rather than the aggregate for each individual item. However, any compensation for loss of office must continue to be shown separately. A company that qualifies as small need not disclose the fact that its accounts have been prepared in accordance with applicable accounting standards (although this does not alter its obligation to apply appropriate standards) – this exemption applies irrespective of whether the company takes advantage of the other accounts exemptions that are available to it.

Modified directors' report

7.13 A small company need not give all the disclosures that are normally required to be given in the directors' report. Under CA 1985 s 246(4), the directors' report of a small company need not include:

(i) a fair review of the business (normally required by s 234(1)(a));

(ii) the amount recommended to be paid as dividend (normally required by s 234(1)(b));

(iii) a statement of the market values of certain fixed assets where these are substantially different from the amounts included in the balance sheet (normally required by Sch 7 para 1(2));

(iv) important events since the balance sheet date (normally required by Sch 7 para 6(a));

(v) an indication of likely future developments in the business (normally required by Sch 7 para 6(b));

(vi) details of research and development activities (normally required by Sch 7 para 6(c));

(vii) an indication of the existence of branches outside the UK (normally required by Sch 7 para 6(d));

(viii) details of employee involvement (normally required by Sch 7 para 11).

The disclosure requirements of Sch 7 relating to payment of creditors only apply to public companies and members of a group headed by a public company – they therefore do not apply to a company that qualifies as small. If advantage is taken of any of the exemptions listed above, the report must include a statement in a prominent position, above the signature of the director or secretary, that it is prepared in accordance with the special provisions of Part VII of CA 1985 relating to small companies (see **7.14** below). The exemptions in respect of the accounts and directors' report operate entirely independently, but in practice a small company will usually take advantage of both or neither.

Directors' statement

7.14 The directors' statement in respect of shorter form accounts must be given in a prominent position on the face of the balance sheet, immediately above the signature of the director. Where a modified directors' report is prepared, a statement must also be given in the report, immediately above the signature of the director or secretary.

Example 7.2 – Directors' statement – shorter form accounts

Balance sheet

These accounts are prepared in accordance with the special provisions of Part VII of the Companies Act 1985 relating to small companies.

Approved by the board of directors on [date] and signed on its behalf by:

....

[Typed name] Director

Directors' report

This report is prepared in accordance with the special provisions of Part VII of the Companies Act 1985 relating to small companies.

Approved by the board of directors on [date] and signed on its behalf by:

....

[Typed name] Secretary/Director

In the case of a dormant company, neither statement is required if the directors take advantage of the audit exemption conferred by CA 1985 (see **7.122–7.127**).

True and fair view

7.15 Shorter form accounts prepared by a small company are still required to show a true and fair view, even though they are not required by CA 1985 to give all of the detailed disclosures set out for other companies, and the auditors are required to express their opinion on whether the accounts show a true and fair view (unless the company qualifies for audit exemption). In certain circumstances, additional disclosure may need to be given in the shorter form accounts to achieve a true and fair view. For instance, although CA 1985 may permit certain items of income or expenditure to be grouped together for disclosure purposes, separate disclosure may be considered necessary for the accounts to show a true and fair view. Also, the exemptions granted under CA 1985 relate only to disclosure requirements imposed by that Act, and so shorter form accounts must still give any additional disclosures required by applicable accounting standards or the FRSSE.

Abbreviated accounts

7.16 CA 1985 s 246(5) permits a small company to file abbreviated accounts with the registrar. Abbreviated accounts can only be used for filing purposes and full accounts, or shorter form accounts, must still be prepared each year for presentation to the members. Filing abbreviated accounts enables a small company to preserve some degree of confidentiality about its activities, but against this must be weighed the disadvantage of having to prepare two sets of accounts each year. The Company Law Review has recommended that the abbreviated accounts regime is abolished and the Government White Paper '*Modernising Company Law* issued in July 2002 confirms the intention to proceed with this. The provisions in respect of abbreviated accounts are set out in s 246(5) and Sch 8A and the following exemptions apply for small companies:

- there is no requirement for the directors' report to be filed;
- there is no requirement for the profit and loss account to be filed;
- the balance sheet only needs to show those items that are assigned a letter or a Roman number in the standard balance sheet formats – therefore only total figures need to be given for the main asset and liability headings, rather than the detailed analyses required in full accounts, except that the following details must still be given, either on the balance sheet or in a note to the accounts:
  - the aggregate of debtors due after more than one year;
  - the aggregate of creditors due within one year; and

- the aggregate of creditors due after more than one year;
- the notes to the accounts only need to cover the following disclosures [CA 1985, Sch 8A references given in brackets]:
  - the accounting policies adopted [para 4],
  - details of share capital [para 5],
  - details of share allotments during the year [para 6],
  - movements in fixed assets, including depreciation, but only for main headings (i.e. those assigned a letter or Roman number) [para 7],
  - details of borrowings [para 8],
  - the basis of foreign currency conversion [para 9(1)],
  - corresponding amounts [para 9(2)];
  - in the case of a dormant company which has acted as an agent for another party, a statement of that fact (para 9A).
- CA 1985 s 246(6) gives specific exemption from the following disclosures:
  - financial years of subsidiary undertakings and details of shares in the company held by subsidiary undertakings (normally required by Sch 5 paras 4 and 6);
  - directors' emoluments, pensions and compensation for loss of office (normally required by Part I of Sch 6);
  - auditors' remuneration (normally required by s 390A(3)).

If the directors of a small company wish to take advantage of the option to prepare abbreviated accounts for filing purposes, the balance sheet must include a statement that the accounts are prepared in accordance with the special provisions of Part VII of CA 1985 relating to small companies (see **7.14** above)

Special auditors' report

7.17 Where abbreviated accounts are delivered to the registrar, they must be accompanied by a special report from the auditors stating whether, in their opinion:

- the company is entitled to deliver abbreviated accounts prepared in accordance with section 246(5) and (6) of CA 1985 ss 246(5) and (6); and
- the abbreviated accounts have been properly prepared in accordance with those sections.

The report is not required if the company is eligible for audit exemption and the directors have taken advantage of this. The complete text of the auditors' report on the company's full or shorter form accounts must also be included where that report:

- was qualified, in which case additional details may also need to be given to enable the qualification to be understood; or
- included a statement under CA 1985 s 237(2) (inadequate accounts, records or returns, or accounts not in agreement with the records and returns); or
- included a statement under CA 1985 s 237(3) (failure to obtain all the information and explanations that the auditors considered necessary).

Accounts exemptions for small groups

7.18 Two main exemptions are available to most small groups:

- a group that qualifies as small may be exempt from the requirement to prepare group accounts;
- a small company that prepares shorter form individual accounts under the special provisions of CA 1985 and is preparing group accounts for the same financial year may prepare the group accounts in accordance with Sch 8.

However, there is no provision in CA 1985 enabling a small group to file abbreviated group accounts.

Exemption from preparing group accounts

7.19 A parent company is not required to prepare group accounts for a financial year in which the group which it heads qualifies as a small group and is not an ineligible group. An ineligible group is defined in CA 1985 s 248(2) as a group where any of the members is:

- a public company;
- a body corporate that has the power to issue shares or debentures to the public;
- a person who has permission under Part 4 of FSMA 2000 to carry on one or more regulated activities; or
- a person who carries on an insurance market activity.

There was previously a requirement for the auditors to provide the directors with a special report confirming that, in their opinion, the company was entitled to the exemption. This is no longer required. However, if the directors take advantage of the exemption and, in the opinion of the auditors, they are not entitled to do so, the auditors are required to state this in their report on the accounts. FRS 2 'Accounting for Subsidiary Undertakings' repeats the exemption set out in the Act for small groups, but requires disclosure of:

- the fact that the accounts present information about the parent as an individual undertaking and not about the group; and
- the grounds on which the parent is exempt from preparing consolidated accounts for the group.

Shorter form group accounts

7.20 A small company that prepares shorter form individual accounts under the Act and is preparing group accounts for the same financial year can prepare the group accounts in accordance with Schedule 8, except that under the balance sheet heading 'Investments' it must show separately:

- shares in group undertakings;
- shares in associated undertakings; and
- other participating interests.

This is in addition to the analysis required by Sch 8. The exemptions set out in s 246(3) and the requirement to include a directors' statement also continue to apply to shorter form group accounts (see **7.12** and **7.14** above).

ACCOUNTING STANDARDS AND THE SMALL COMPANY

Compliance with accounting standards

7.21 In general, the requirements of accounting standards apply to all accounts that are required to show a true and fair view, irrespective of the size of the entity. In preparing their annual accounts, small companies must therefore comply either with the FRSSE (see **7.26** below) or with all other applicable accounting standards and UITF Abstracts, except in the few cases where an individual standard specifically exempts smaller entities from compliance with some or all of the detailed requirements. At present, these exceptions comprise:

- SSAP 13 *Accounting for research and development* – small companies need not disclose the amount charged to the profit and loss account in respect of research and development, although the other requirements of SSAP 13 (both measurement and disclosure) continue to apply.
- SSAP 25 *Segmental reporting* – small companies need not comply with the additional disclosure requirements set out in this accounting standard.
- FRS 1 *Cash Flow Statements* – small companies are exempt from the requirement to include a cash flow statement in their accounts (see **5.7** below).
- FRS 13 *Derivatives and other financial instruments: Disclosures* – this

standard applies only to listed companies, banks and other financial institutions.

— FRS 14 *Earnings per share* – this standard applies only to companies whose shares are publicly traded and any others who opt voluntarily to disclose earnings per share (which is rare in practice).

Compliance with UITF Abstracts

7.22 At present, UITF Abstract 17 and all subsequent Abstracts grant exemption from their requirements to entities adopting the Financial Reporting Standard for Smaller Entities (FRSSE). However, in its Information Sheet No 43, published in November 2000, the UITF issued a clarification of the position of smaller entities in relation to UITF Abstracts. The exemption note in each UITF Abstract reflects the ASB's policy of including all the requirements applying to smaller entities in a single document. The FRSSE is regularly reviewed and updated, and at each review the ASB considers whether the requirements of recent UITF Abstracts should be incorporated into the document. The exemption note should therefore not be read as implying that the requirements of the Abstract are not appropriate to a smaller entity. When accounting for transactions and events not dealt with in the FRSSE, smaller entities are expected to have regard to other accounting standards and UITF Abstracts, not as mandatory documents in this case, but as a means of establishing current practice.

Disclosure of compliance with accounting standards

7.23 Small companies are specifically exempt from the requirement to state whether the accounts have been prepared in accordance with applicable accounting standards. This exemption relates only to the disclosure requirement. It does not grant any exemption from compliance with the requirements of accounting standards or the FRSSE.

Abbreviated accounts and accounting standards

7.24 Abbreviated accounts (see **7.16** above) are essentially an extract of the full accounts or shorter form accounts that the company is required to prepare for the members. They are not required to show a true and fair view and, in practice, will not do so because of the reduced disclosures. As explained above, both full accounts and shorter form accounts must comply with the requirements of accounting standards and UITF Abstracts or with the FRSSE. In the case of abbreviated accounts, a distinction is effectively made between the measurement requirements of accounting standards (or the FRSSE) and the additional disclosure requirements:

— Measurement requirements – the abbreviated accounts are extracts of the full or shorter form accounts and they must therefore follow all of the measurement requirements set out in applicable accounting standards or in the FRSSE (e.g. assets held under finance leases must be accounted for in accordance with the FRSSE or with SSAP 21 *Accounting for leases and hire purchase contracts*).

— Disclosure requirements - abbreviated accounts are not required to show a true and fair view and the additional disclosures required by accounting standards or the FRSSE need not be given (e.g. the additional disclosures in respect of leased assets required by the FRSSE or by SSAP 21 need not be given in abbreviated accounts but must be given in full or shorter form accounts in order to show a true and fair view).

DTI consultation on possible extension of IASs

7.25 In August 2002, the DTI published a consultation document on the possible extension of the recent EU Regulation on the adoption of International Accounting Standards (IASs) which requires quoted companies to prepare their group accounts in accordance with IASs from January 2005. Member states have the option of extending the application of the Regulation by:

— permitting or requiring quoted companies to prepare individual accounts in accordance with IASs; and

— permitting or requiring some or all unquoted companies to prepare their group and/or individual accounts in accordance with IASs.

The consultation document notes that the Government does not currently have a preferred option on these issues, but expects to come to a decision early in 2003, based on the results of the consultation. Initially, extending the Regulation to small companies may appear to impose a significant and unnecessary burden on them, but this will depend largely on how UK accounting standards develop and how closely they converge with international accounting standards. The consultation document also notes that the IASB has recently added to its work programme the development of an IAS for smaller entities (equivalent to the FRSSE). The document concludes that the operation of a single reporting regime in the UK would undoubtedly bring benefits in terms of comparability, clarity and ease of enforcement.

FINANCIAL REPORTING STANDARD FOR SMALLER ENTITIES (FRSSE): AN OVERVIEW

Background to the FRSSE

7.26 As accounting standards became increasingly complex, and in many cases required more detailed disclosures in the accounts, concern was expressed over the merit of applying these standards to smaller companies. The Consultative Committee of Accountancy Bodies (CCAB), in conjunction with the Accounting Standards Board (ASB), therefore set up a working party to examine the issue of how smaller entities might be granted exemption from compliance with accounting standards, and their work resulted in the publication of the Financial Reporting Standard for Smaller Entities (FRSSE). This was first issued in November 1997 and came into immediate effect. Three revised versions have been issued. The latest version was issued in December 2001 and is generally effective for accounting periods ending on or after 22 June 2002, although the new requirements in respect of defined benefit retirement schemes are only fully effective for accounting periods ending on or after 22 June 2006. Regular revision of the FRSSE is necessary to ensure that it is kept up to date with current accounting practice, and the document is therefore reviewed at not less than yearly intervals. An overview of the FRSSE is set out in this section and the detailed requirements of the latest version are explained in **7.38–7.106** below.

Scope and objective of the FRSSE

7.27 The FRSSE may be applied to financial statements that are intended to give a true and fair view of the results and financial position of small companies or groups (as defined in CA 1985) and entities that would qualify as small if they were incorporated under the Act. As eligibility rests on the CA 1985 criteria, the FRSSE cannot be adopted in the accounts of:

- public companies, or any member of a group which includes a public company; or
- entities that are regulated under Part 4 of the FSMA 2000, or which carry on an insurance market activity; or
- any entity that does not meet the relevant size criteria (see **7.4** and **7.7** above).

The objective of the FRSSE is to ensure that entities falling within its scope provide financial information that is useful in assessing the stewardship of management and for making economic decisions.

Disclosure of adoption

7.28 Adoption of the FRSSE is optional for reporting entities that come within its scope. If it is not adopted, the requirements of all other accounting standards and UITF Abstracts must be followed. If the FRSSE is adopted, this fact must be stated in the accounts. The disclosure can be combined with the directors' statement required under CA 1985 where the small company provisions of the Act have been applied (see **7.14** above) or can be given separately in the notes to the accounts. Early adoption of the latest version of FRSSE is always encouraged but is not required.

Relationship with SORPs

7.29 The FRSSE notes that Statements of Recommended Practice (SORPs) that were already in issue when the FRSSE was first published were prepared on the basis that the financial statements would comply with the requirements of SSAPs, FRSs and UITF Abstracts. Accounts that refer to compliance with such a SORP should therefore observe the requirements of those standards, even though the reporting entity may technically come within the scope of the FRSSE. However, SORPs and other equivalent guidance published since November 1997 may specify when the FRSSE can be adopted. For instance, the revised SORP 'Accounting and Reporting by Charities', which applies for accounting periods beginning on or after 1 January 2001, specifically states that a charity which qualifies as small may prepare its accounts in accordance with the FRSSE.

Definitions

7.30 The FRSSE includes a separate definitions section. All definitions are the same as those in other accounting standards, or a simplified version of them, and items included in the definitions section are identified by bold text in the FRSSE.

Items not specifically covered in the FRSSE

7.31 The issues covered in the FRSSE are restricted to those expected to arise most frequently in smaller entities. The more complex issues covered in many accounting standards are therefore excluded from the FRSSE on the basis that they will not usually be relevant to a smaller entity. Where transactions or events arise that are not specifically covered in the FRSSE, preparers of accounts are required to have regard to other accounting standards and UITF Abstracts, not as mandatory documents in this case, but as a means of establishing current practice.

Voluntary presentation of cash flow statement

7.32 Under FRS 1 *Cash flow statements* companies which meet the CA 1985 criteria for a small company are exempt from the requirement to include a cash flow statement in their accounts. In a separate 'Voluntary disclosure' section, the FRSSE encourages the inclusion of a cash flow statement in the accounts of a smaller entity on the grounds that management of cash is fundamental to the success of a small business, and a cash flow statement can provide a useful focus for discussion and a reference point for more detailed analysis. However, the FRSSE does not require such a statement to be presented as part of the accounts. If a cash flow statement is prepared, the FRSSE sets out the following guidance:

- the statement should be presented using the indirect method (i.e. starting with operating profit and adjusting for non-cash items to arrive at the figure for cash generated from operations);
- cash should be cash at bank and in hand, less overdrafts repayable on demand, and these figures should be reconciled to those shown in the balance sheet;
- cash flows should be net of any attributable VAT (or other sales tax) except where the reporting entity cannot recover the tax;
- material transactions not resulting in cash movements should be disclosed in the notes if this is necessary for the underlying transactions to be properly understood.

An illustrative example of a cash flow statement prepared on this basis is set out in Appendix III to the FRSSE.

Statement of total recognised gains and losses

7.33 Appendix III to the FRSSE also sets out an example of a statement of total recognised gains and losses, but emphasises that the individual circumstances of each entity will indicate the best approach to this disclosure. The example uses the following form of presentation:

Example 7.3 – Statement of total recognised gains and losses

	2002	*2001*
	£	*£*
		(restated)
Profit for the financial year	25,000	13,000
Unrealised surplus on revaluation of property in the year	7,000	4,500
Total recognised gains and losses relating to the year	32,000	17,500
Prior year adjustment (see note x)	(13,000)	
Total gains and losses recognised since the last annual report	19,000	

Link with accounting standards

7.34 Appendix V to the FRSSE provides details of the source of each requirement set out in the FRSSE and shows whether the source requirement has been adopted in full, with minor amendment or with major changes.

Principal relaxations in requirements

7.35 Generally, the measurement requirements of accounting standards are retained in the FRSSE (sometimes in simplified form) but many of the more detailed disclosure requirements are excluded, especially those that relate to events and circumstances that generally do not arise in smaller entities. The principle relaxations can be summarised as follows:

Profit and loss account

- the profit and loss account section makes no reference to continuing and discontinued operations;
- where all the recognised gains and losses are included in the profit and loss account, no separate statement to this effect is required;
- there is no requirement for a reconciliation of movements in shareholders' funds;
- there is no requirement to disclose special circumstances affecting tax on exceptional items;
- there is no requirement for a note of historical cost profits and losses;

Intangible assets and goodwill

- the FRSSE does not allow the useful economic lives of goodwill and intangible assets to exceed 20 years;
- internally generated intangible assets cannot be capitalised, even if they have a readily ascertainable market value;
- intangible assets cannot be revalued;
- the FRSSE does not require the fair values of intangible assets purchased with a business to be restricted to an amount that does not create or increase negative goodwill;
- the FRSSE does not specify how negative goodwill should be disclosed on the balance sheet - FRS 10 requires it to be shown immediately below positive goodwill, with a sub-total of the two amounts;
- none of the detailed disclosure requirements on goodwill are included;

Tangible fixed assets

- there is no reference to:
  - the start up or commissioning period of a tangible fixed asset;
  - when capitalisation of finance costs should begin;
  - the construction of a fixed asset in parts;

  - accounting for a major inspection or overhaul of a tangible fixed asset;
  - renewals accounting;
- the bases for revaluation of tangible fixed assets are simplified:
- the treatment of revaluation losses is simplified;
- there is no specific requirement for an annual impairment review where depreciation is omitted as immaterial or where the remaining useful economic life of a tangible fixed asset exceeds 50 years;
- residual values and useful economic lives are required to be reviewed regularly (rather than annually) and revised when necessary;
- disclosure requirements for tangible fixed assets are limited to the following for (i) land and buildings and (ii) other assets in aggregate:

  - depreciation methods;
  - useful economic lives or depreciation rates;
  - where material, the financial effects of changes in useful economic lives and residual values;

  (NB: certain additional disclosures are required by company law, particularly in the case of revalued assets);
- the FRSSE allows more flexibility in the calculation of value in use;
- the sum recorded as an asset and liability at the inception of a finance lease should normally be the fair value (rather than the present value of the minimum lease payments);
- the FRSSE emphasises that the straight-line method of allocating finance charges to accounting periods may provide a reasonable approximation to a constant periodic rate of charge;
- operating lease commitments do not need to be analysed by type of lease;

Taxation

- the detailed disclosure requirements of FRS 16 and FRS 19 are omitted from the FRSSE and replaced with a more flexible requirement to disclose:

  - material components of the current and deferred tax charges or credits;
  - material components of the deferred tax balance; and
  - material components of the movement in the deferred tax balance;

Provisions, contingent liabilities and contingent assets

- there is no reference to:
  - financial instruments, executory contracts, future operating losses, onerous contracts, restructuring, or the sale of an operation;
  - cases where it is not clear whether there is a present obligation;
  - the need to take account of risks, uncertainties and future events when measuring a provision;
  - capitalisation of related assets;
- the detailed rules on discounting are omitted (although discounting is still required where the effect is material);
- there is no restriction on the amount that may be recognised as reimbursements;
- disclosure requirements are limited to the nature and effect of contingent liabilities (unless remote) and probable contingent assets (although additional disclosures may be required by company law);

Other

- only related party transactions that are considered material to the reporting entity need to be disclosed (i.e. there is no need to consider the materiality of the transaction to the related party);
- there is an overall requirement to disclose the accounting policies followed for items judged material or critical in determining the profit or loss for the period and in stating the entity's financial position – the FRSSE emphasises that this disclosure should be clear, fair and as brief as possible.

The specific requirements of the FRSSE are considered in more detail at **7.38** below.

Disclosure of directors' personal guarantees

7.36 The FRSSE includes a specific additional requirement for the accounts of a smaller entity to disclose any personal guarantees given by the directors in respect of company borrowings.

Group accounts

7.37 Small groups that come within the scope of the FRSSE are not required to prepare group accounts under UK company law. However, the ASB recognises that where a small group prepares group accounts voluntarily, it is appropriate to allow it to take advantage of the FRSSE. To avoid making the FRSSE over-complicated, small groups are simply required to follow those accounting standards and UITF Abstracts that deal with consolidated financial statements, in addition to the FRSSE, if they choose to prepare group accounts.

THE FINANCIAL REPORTING STANDARD FOR SMALLER ENTITIES (FRSSE): DETAILED REQUIREMENTS

True and fair view

7.38 The financial statements of a smaller entity should show a true and fair view of the results of the period and the state of affairs at the period end. In achieving this, the substance of any arrangement or transaction, or series of arrangements or transactions, entered into by the entity during the period should be taken into account. This will involve determining whether the transaction has given rise to any new assets or liabilities, or has changed any of the entity's existing assets and liabilities. The transaction and the accounting treatment adopted should be adequately explained in the notes to the accounts where this is necessary for a true and fair view.

True and fair override disclosures

7.39 Where the true and fair override is applied, the following disclosures should be given:

- a clear and unambiguous statement that the override has been applied;
- a statement of the treatment normally required and a description of the treatment actually adopted;
- an explanation of why the normal treatment would not give a true and fair view; and
- quantification of the effect, unless this is already evident from the financial statements – if the effect cannot be quantified, the circumstances should be explained.

If the override is applied for more than one year, these disclosures should be given each year, with comparatives for the previous year.

Disclosure of adoption

7.40 The financial statements should state that they have been prepared in accordance with the Financial Reporting Standard for Smaller Entities (effective June 2002).

Accounting policies and estimation techniques

7.41 The following requirements apply in respect of accounting policies and estimation techniques:

- accounting policies and estimation techniques should be consistent with the requirements of the FRSSE and of company law (or the equivalent);
- where a choice of policy or technique is permitted, the entity should select the policies and techniques that are most appropriate to its particular circumstances for the purpose of giving a true and fair view, taking into account the objectives of relevance, reliability, comparability and understandability;
- accounting policies should be regularly reviewed to ensure they remain the most appropriate - however, in judging whether to adopt a new policy, due consideration should be given to the impact on comparability;
- where an accounting policy is changed, the amounts for the current and corresponding periods should be restated on the basis of the new policy;
- when preparing financial statements, directors should assess whether there are significant doubts about the entity's ability to continue as a going concern - any material uncertainties of which the directors are aware should be disclosed;
- where the period considered by the directors is less than one year from the date of approval of the financial statements, this fact should be stated;
- the financial statements should include:
  - a description of each material accounting policy followed;
  - details of any changes to the accounting policies followed in the preceding period, a brief explanation of why each new policy is considered to be more appropriate and, where practicable, an indication of the effect of the change on the results for the current period (NB this is in addition to the normal prior period adjustment disclosures); and
  - where the effect of a change in estimation techniques is material, a description of the change and, where practicable, the effect on the results for the current period.

Prior period adjustments

7.42 Prior period adjustments should be accounted for by:

- restating comparative figures for the previous year in the primary statements and the notes to the accounts;

— adjusting opening reserves for the cumulative effect;

— noting the cumulative effect at the foot of the statement of total recognised gains and losses; and

— disclosing the effect on the results of the previous period where this is material.

Gains and losses

7.43 All gains and losses recognised during the year must be included in the profit and loss account or in the statement of total recognised gains and losses. Individual gains and losses may only be excluded from the profit and loss account where this is permitted or required by CA 1985.

Exceptional items

7.44 The following items (including provisions) should be shown separately on the face of the profit and loss account after operating profit and before interest:

— profits and losses on the sale or termination of an operation;

— costs of a fundamental reorganisation or restructuring that has a material effect on the nature and focus of the entity's operations;

— profits and losses on the disposal of fixed assets.

Other exceptional items should be included under the relevant statutory format heading and disclosed on the face of the profit and loss account (if sufficiently material) or in the notes to the accounts. Sufficient detail should be given to enable a user of the accounts to understand the nature of the item.

Profit or loss on disposal

7.45 The profit or loss on disposal of an asset should be calculated as the difference between the net sales proceeds and the net carrying value of the asset. Where a previously acquired business is disposed of, any attributable purchased goodwill that has not already been charged in the profit and loss account should be included in the profit or loss on disposal.

Extraordinary items

7.46 Extraordinary items should be extremely rare, but where they do arise they should be shown separately on the face of the profit and loss account, after the profit or loss on ordinary activities and before dividends and other appropriations.

The euro

7.47 Costs relating to the introduction of the euro should be written off to the profit and loss account and should be disclosed as exceptional items if material. Costs that meet the conditions for capitalisation as a fixed asset may be capitalised:

- where the entity already has an accounting policy to capitalise assets of the relevant type; and
- to the extent that the expenditure clearly enhances the asset rather than merely maintaining it.

Statement of total recognised gains and losses

7.48 A statement of total recognised gains and losses should be presented as a primary statement, with the same degree of prominence as the profit and loss account. Transactions with shareholders should be excluded from this statement. An example of a statement of total recognised gains and losses is given in Appendix III to the FRSSE and is also illustrated in **7.33** above. If all the recognised gains and losses are included in the profit and loss account, no separate statement to this effect needs to be given.

Expenditure on research and development

7.49 The cost of fixed assets acquired or constructed for use in research and development activities over a number of years should be capitalised and written off through the profit and loss account over their useful lives. The costs of pure and applied research should be written off in the profit and loss account as they are incurred. Development expenditure should be written off in the profit and loss account as it is incurred, except that it may be deferred to future periods where all of the following apply:

- there is a clearly defined project; and
- the related expenditure is clearly identifiable; and
- the outcome of the project has been assessed with reasonable certainty as regards both its technical feasibility and its ultimate commercial viability (taking into account likely market conditions, public opinion, consumer and environmental legislation etc); and
- the aggregate of:
  - deferred development costs; and
  - any further development costs; and
  - any related production, selling and administration costs

  is reasonably expected to be exceeded by related future sales and other revenues; and

— adequate resources exist, or are reasonably expected to be available, to complete the project and to provide any necessary increases in working capital.

Where an entity adopts a policy of deferring development expenditure, the policy should be applied to all projects that meet the above criteria. Deferred development costs should be amortised, commencing on the commercial production or application of the product or service, by allocating the costs on a systematic basis to each accounting period by reference to either the sale or use of the product or service, or the period over which it is expected to be used or sold. The deferred expenditure for each project should be reviewed at the end of each accounting period and written off immediately where the circumstances that justified deferral no longer apply. The amount of development expenditure carried forward at the beginning and end of each year should be disclosed on the face of the balance sheet or in the notes to the accounts.

Goodwill and intangible assets

7.50 Positive purchased goodwill and purchased intangible assets should be capitalised. Internally generated goodwill and intangible assets should not be capitalised. An intangible asset purchased with a business should be recognised separately from the purchased goodwill if its value can be measured reliably. It is important to note that purchased goodwill in this context means goodwill arising in the accounts of an individual entity. If an entity adopting the FRSSE also prepares group accounts, any goodwill arising on consolidation must be accounted for in accordance with FRS 10 'Goodwill and Intangible Assets'. Once capitalised, goodwill and intangible assets should not be revalued.

Depreciation of goodwill and intangible assets

7.51 Capitalised goodwill and intangible assets should be depreciated on a straight-line (or more appropriate) basis over their useful economic lives, which must not exceed 20 years. A residual value may be assigned to an intangible asset if this value can be established reliably (e.g. where it has been agreed contractually). No residual value can be assigned to goodwill. The useful economic lives of goodwill and intangible assets should be reviewed at the end of each reporting period and should be revised where necessary. However, the revised life should not exceed 20 years from the date of acquisition. The carrying amount of the asset at the date of the revision should be depreciated over the revised estimate of the remaining useful economic life.

Negative goodwil

7.52 Where an acquisition appears to give rise to negative goodwill, fair values should be checked to ensure that the assets acquired have not been overstated and that the liabilities acquired have not been understated. Negative goodwill up to the fair values of the non-monetary assets acquired should be released to the profit and loss account over the lives of those assets. Any additional negative goodwill should be recognised in the profit and loss account over the period expected to benefit from it. The accounts should disclose the amount of the negative goodwill and the period(s) over which it is being recognised.

Transitional arrangements

7.53 All goodwill that was eliminated against reserves in accordance with an accounting policy permitted until 23 March 1999 may remain eliminated against reserves. Alternatively, an entity may reinstate all such goodwill by prior period adjustment in its first accounting period beginning on or after 31 March 1999.

Tangible fixed assets

7.54 The requirements of this section of the FRSSE apply to all tangible fixed assets except investment properties (see **7.66** below). A tangible fixed asset should initially be measured at cost, and then written down to recoverable amount if necessary. In the case of an asset received by a charity as a gift or donation, the initial carrying amount should be the asset's current value on the date of receipt (i.e. the lower of replacement cost and recoverable amount). Only costs that are directly attributable to bringing the asset into working condition for its intended use should be included in its measurement. Where an entity adopts an accounting policy of capitalising finance costs, finance costs directly attributable to the construction of the asset should be capitalised as part of the cost of the asset. The total finance costs capitalised during an accounting period should not exceed the total finance costs incurred during that period. Capitalisation of costs (including finance costs) should be suspended during extended periods when active development is interrupted. Capitalisation should cease when substantially all the activities necessary to get the asset ready for use have been completed, even if the asset has not yet been brought into use.

Subsequent expenditure on tangible fixed assets

7.55 Subsequent expenditure on a tangible fixed asset should only be capitalised if it enhances the economic benefits of the asset beyond those previously assessed (i.e. it represents an improvement), or if it replaces or restores a component that has been separately depreciated. Other expenditure should be recognised in the profit and loss account as it is incurred.

Revaluation of tangible fixed assets

7.56 Where an entity adopts an accounting policy of revaluing tangible fixed assets, all assets of the same class (i.e. having a similar nature, function or use in the business) should be revalued, but it is not necessary to apply a policy of revaluation to all classes of asset. The carrying amount of a revalued asset should be its market value (or the best estimate thereof) at the balance sheet date. Where the directors consider that market value is not an appropriate basis for valuation, current value (i.e. the lower of replacement cost and recoverable amount) may be used instead. It may be possible to establish values for certain tangible fixed assets by reference to active second-hand markets or appropriate indices where these are publicly available. Properties and other assets should be valued by an experienced valuer (i.e. one with recognised and relevant recent professional experience, and sufficient knowledge of the market and location) at least every five years. The valuation should be updated by an experienced valuer in the intervening years where it is likely that there has been a material change in value. Where relevant, alternative approaches set out in sector-specific guidance and SORPs may be followed instead.

Revaluation gains and losses

7.57 Revaluation losses caused only by changing prices should be recognised in the statement of total recognised gains and losses until the carrying amount of the asset reaches its depreciated historical cost. Other revaluation losses should be recognised in the profit and loss account. Revaluation gains should be recognised in the statement of total recognised gains and losses except to the extent that, after adjusting for subsequent depreciation, they reverse revaluation losses on the same asset that were previously recognised in the profit and loss account. Such gains should be recognised in the profit and loss account. The adjustment for subsequent depreciation achieves the same result as if the downward revaluation had not taken place.

Transitional arrangements

7.58 Where an entity does not adopt an accounting policy of revaluing tangible fixed assets for its first accounting period ending on or after 23 March 2000, but the carrying amount of tangible fixed assets reflects previous revaluations, it may:

- retain the book amounts of the assets and disclose:
  - the fact that the transitional provisions of the FRSSE are being followed;
  - the date of the last revaluation; and
  - the fact that the valuation has not been updated; or

— as a change in accounting policy, restate the carrying amount of the assets to historical cost less restated accumulated depreciation.

Depreciation of tangible fixed assets

7.59 The cost (or revalued amount) of a tangible fixed asset, less its estimated residual value, should be depreciated on a systematic basis over the useful economic life of the asset. The depreciation method used should reflect as fairly as possible the pattern in which the asset's economic benefits are consumed by the entity. The depreciation charged should be recognised as an expense in the profit and loss account unless it is permitted to be included in the carrying amount of another asset. With certain exceptions (e.g. land used for extractive purposes), land has an unlimited life and is not depreciated. Where an asset comprises two or more major components with substantially different useful economic lives, each component should be accounted for separately for depreciation purposes and depreciated over its useful economic life. Where, for its first accounting period ending on or after 23 March 2000, an entity separates tangible fixed assets into separate components in this way for the first time, the changes should be dealt with as a change in accounting policy.

Review of useful economic lives and residual values

7.60 The useful economic lives and residual values of tangible fixed assets should be regularly reviewed and revised where necessary. The carrying amount of the asset at the date of revision, less its revised residual value, should be depreciated over its revised remaining useful economic life.

Change in depreciation method

7.61 A change in the method of depreciation is only permissible on the grounds that the new method will give a fairer presentation of the entity's financial position and results. A change in method does not constitute a change in accounting policy. The carrying amount of the asset should be depreciated using the revised method over its remaining useful economic life, beginning in the accounting period in which the change is made. The reasons for the change and the effect (where material) should be disclosed in the financial statements.

Depreciation disclosures

7.62 The following should be disclosed for (i) land and buildings and (ii) other tangible fixed assets in aggregate:

— depreciation methods used;

— useful economic lives or depreciation rates used;

– where material, the financial effect of a change during the period in the estimate of useful economic lives or residual values.

Additional disclosures are required where the method of depreciation is changed (see **7.61** above).

Write-downs to recoverable amount

7.63 The requirements of the FRSSE on write-downs to recoverable amount apply to capitalised goodwill and all categories of fixed assets except investment properties (see **7.66** below) and financial instruments. Investments in subsidiaries, associates and joint ventures are specifically covered by the requirements. Fixed assets and goodwill should be carried in the balance sheet at no more than recoverable amount, which is defined as the higher of the amounts that can be obtained from selling the asset (i.e. net realisable value) or continuing to use the asset in the business (i.e. value in use). Value in use is calculated as the present value of the future cash flows obtainable as a result of the asset's continued use (and ultimate disposal), or a reasonable estimate thereof. If the net book amount of a fixed asset or of goodwill is considered not to be fully recoverable at the balance sheet date, it should be written down to the estimated recoverable amount, and this should then be written off over the remaining useful economic life of the asset or goodwill.

Reversal of write-down

7.64 In the case of tangible fixed assets and investments, if the recoverable amount subsequently increases as a result of a change in economic conditions or in the expected use of the asset, the net book amount should be written back to the lower of recoverable amount and the amount at which the asset would have been recorded if the original write-down had not been made. In the case of intangible assets and goodwill, the net book amount should only be written back if an external event caused the original write-down and subsequent external events clearly and demonstrably reverse the effects of the first event in a way that was not foreseen when the original write-down was calculated.

Recognition of write-downs and reversals

7.65 Write-downs should normally be charged (and any reversals credited) to the profit and loss account for the period. However, write-downs of revalued assets that reverse previous revaluation gains simply as a result of changing market prices should be recognised in the statement of total recognised gains and losses to the extent that the carrying amount of the asset is greater than its depreciated historical cost.

Investment properties

7.66 Leased investment properties should be depreciated, at least over the period when the unexpired term of the lease is 20 years or less. Other investment properties should be included in the balance sheet at open market value, with their carrying value displayed prominently on the face of the balance sheet or in the notes to the accounts, and the following disclosures should be given:

— names of those carrying out the valuation, or details of their qualifications - if the valuer is an employee or officer of the company or group, this fact must be disclosed;

— the bases of valuation used.

Changes in market value should be taken to the statement of total recognised gains and losses except where a deficit on an individual investment property is expected to be permanent, in which case it should be charged to the profit and loss account of the period. Where such a deficit reverses in a future period, the reversal should be credited to the profit and loss account of that period.

Government grants

7.67 Government grants should be recognised in the profit and loss account so that they are matched with the expenditure towards which they are expected to contribute. Where a grant is given towards the cost of a fixed asset, UK companies legislation does not permit the cost of the asset to be reduced and the grant should therefore be accounted for as deferred income. A grant should not be recognised in the profit and loss account until all conditions relating to its receipt have been met and receipt of the grant is reasonably assured. Potential liabilities to repay grants should be provided for only to the extent that repayment is probable. The repayment of a grant should be set against any unamortised deferred income relating to the grant and any excess should be charged immediately to the profit and loss account. The following details should be disclosed in the accounts:

— the effects of government grants on the results of the period and/or the financial position of the entity; and

— where the results of the period are materially affected by the receipt of government assistance other than grants, the nature of the assistance and, where practicable, an estimate of the effect.

Hire purchase contracts

7.68 Hire purchase contracts of a financing nature should be accounted for on the same basis as finance leases and the asset should be depreciated over its useful economic life. Other hire purchase contracts should be accounted for on the same basis as operating leases.

Lessees: Accounting for finance leases

7.69 A finance lease should be recorded in the lessee's balance sheet as an asset and as an obligation to pay future rentals. The amount recorded as an asset and a liability at the inception of the lease should normally be the fair value of the asset. If this does not give a realistic estimate of the cost to the lessee (for instance, where the lessee is able to benefit from grants and capital allowances that reduce the minimum lease payments to a total that is less than the fair value of the asset) a better estimate should be used, based on an approximation of the present value of the minimum lease payments (e.g. by discounting them at the interest rate implicit in the lease). The total finance charge under a finance lease should be allocated to accounting periods during the lease term in a way that produces a constant periodic rate of charge on the outstanding obligation, or a reasonable approximation to this. The straight-line method may provide such an approximation. The lease term is the period for which the lessee has contracted to lease the asset, plus any further terms where the lessee has an option to lease, with or without payment, and it is reasonably certain at the inception of the lease that the option will be exercised. An asset leased under a finance lease should be depreciated over the shorter of the lease term or the useful life of the asset.

Lessees: Accounting for operating leases

7.70 Operating lease rentals should be charged to the profit and loss account on a straight-line basis over the lease term, even if payments are made on a different basis. Another systematic and rational basis may be used if this is more appropriate. The lease term is as defined in **7.69** above.

Lessees: Accounting for lease incentives

7.71 Incentives to sign a lease, whatever their form, should be allocated on a straight-line basis over the shorter of:

— the lease term; or

— the period to the review date when the rental is first expected to be adjusted to prevailing market rates.

Lessors: Accounting for finance leases

7.72 The amount due from the lessee under a finance lease should be recorded as a debtor in the lessor's balance sheet at the amount of the net investment in the lease, after making provision for bad and doubtful items where necessary. The net investment in a lease is the gross investment in the lease less gross earnings allocated to future periods. Total gross earnings under a finance lease should be recognised on a systematic and rational basis. This will usually give a constant periodic rate of return on the net investment in the lease. Where the lessor is a manufacturer or dealer, the selling profit should be restricted to the excess of the fair value of the asset over the manufacturer's or dealer's cost, less any grants receivable.

Lessors: Accounting for operating leases

7.73 An asset held for use in an operating lease should be recorded as a fixed asset and depreciated over its useful life. Rental income under an operating lease should be recognised on a straight-line basis over the period of the lease, even if payments are made on a different basis. Another systematic and rational basis may be used if this is more representative of the time pattern in which the benefit from the lease is received. A manufacturer or dealer lessor should not recognise a selling profit in respect of an operating lease.

Sale and leaseback transactions

7.74 Where a sale and leaseback transaction results in a finance lease, any apparent profit or loss should be deferred by the seller/lessee and amortised over the shorter of the lease term or the useful life of the asset. Where the transaction results in an operating lease, any profit or loss should be recognised immediately, except where:

- the selling price is below fair value and the apparent loss is compensated for by future rentals below market value - the loss should be deferred to that extent and amortised over the shorter of the lease term and the period during which reduced rentals are charged;
- the selling price is above fair value - the excess over fair value should be deferred and amortised over the shorter of the lease term and the period to the next rent review (if any).

A buyer/lessor should account for sale and leaseback transactions in the same way as other leases (i.e. as described in **7.72–7.73** above).

Disclosure by lessees

7.75 A lessee should include the following disclosures in the accounts:

- the gross amount of assets held under finance leases and the related accumulated depreciation, analysed into the following categories:
  - land and buildings; and
  - other fixed assets (in aggregate).

  As an alternative, details for leased assets may be aggregated with those for owned assets provided that there is separate disclosure (in the two categories described above) of:

  - the net amount of assets held under finance leases; and
  - depreciation in the period in respect of those assets;
- obligations relating to finance leases, net of finance charges allocated to future periods (i.e. separately from other liabilities) – this may be given on the face of the balance sheet or in the notes to the accounts;
- the amount of any commitments under finance leases entered into at the balance sheet date but where inception occurs after the year-end; and
- the commitments in the next twelve months under operating leases, analysed into amounts relating to leases which expire:
  - in the next year;
  - in 2 to 5 years inclusive; and
  - more than 5 years from the balance sheet date.

Disclosure by lessors

7.76 A lessor should include the following disclosures in the accounts:

- the gross amount of assets held for use in operating leases and the related accumulated depreciation;
- the cost of assets acquired (by purchase or under finance leases) for letting under finance leases;
- the net investment in (i) finance leases and (ii) hire purchase contracts at each balance sheet date.

Stocks

7.77 Stocks should be included in the financial statements at the lower of the cost and net realisable value of the separate items or groups of similar items. Appendix III to the FRSSE provides additional guidance on the allocation of overheads, methods of costing, determining net realisable value and the application of net realisable value. The key points included in this guidance are as follows:

- any abnormal conversion costs (e.g. exceptional spoilage, idle capacity) should be excluded in calculating the cost of stock and long-term contracts;
- where firm sales contracts are in place, overheads relating to design, and to marketing and selling costs incurred before manufacture, may be included in arriving at cost;
- the costs of general management, as distinct from functional management, should be excluded from the cost of stock and long-term contracts – however in a smaller business where management may be

involved in more than one function it will usually be appropriate to allocate management costs to the various functions (e.g. production, marketing, selling and administration) on a suitable basis;

— the costs of central service departments (e.g. the accounts department) should be allocated to the functions that the department serves on a suitable basis;

— the allocation of overheads to stocks and long-term contracts should be based on the entity's normal level of activity, taking one year with another, and giving due consideration to:

  — the volume of production that the facilities are designed to achieve under the working conditions prevailing during the year (e.g. single shift, double shift etc);

  — the budgeted level of activity for the current year and the following year; and

  — the level of activity achieved in the current year and in previous years.

— where management accounts are prepared on a marginal cost basis, any production overheads not included in marginal cost will need to be added in for valuation purposes;

— the accounting principle of prudence should not be used to justify the exclusion of certain overheads from the valuation – it should instead be taken into account when determining net realisable value;

— the method of costing chosen should provide the fairest possible approximation to cost;

— where standard costs are used, they should be regularly reviewed and updated where necessary;

— methods such as 'base stock' and 'LIFO' will not usually be appropriate as they result in stock valuations that bear little relationship to recent cost levels;

— in certain circumstances it may be appropriate to arrive at cost by valuing stock at selling price less an estimated margin, but only if it can be shown that this gives a reasonable approximation to actual cost;

— where the cost of minor by-products cannot be separated from the cost of the principal products, it may be appropriate to include stocks of the by-products at net realisable value – in this case, the costs of the main products should be calculated after deducting the net realisable value of the by-products;

— initial provisions to reduce cost to net realisable value will often be based on the use of formulae (for instance, to take account of age, past movements, expected future movements etc) but the results should always be reviewed in the light of other available information (e.g. the current order book);

- where provision needs to be made to reduce the value of finished goods below cost, the stock of parts and assemblies held for the production of those goods should also be reviewed to establish whether additional provision is required against these items;
- where stocks of spares are held for sale, the determination of net realisable value should take into account:
  - the number of units sold to which they relate;
  - the estimated frequency with which a spare part is required; and
  - the expected useful life of the unit to which they relate.
- events between the balance sheet date and completion of the financial statements need to be taken into account in assessing net realisable value (e.g. changes in prices) - however it will not usually be necessary to write down the purchase price of raw materials provided that the goods into which they will be incorporated can still be sold at a profit (i.e. after taking account of the materials at actual cost);
- net realisable value is most likely to be less than cost where there have been:
  - increases in costs or reductions in selling prices;
  - physical deterioration of the items in stock;
  - obsolescence of the products (e.g. due to technological change);
  - a strategic decision to sell certain products at a loss;
  - errors in purchasing or production.

Long-term contracts

7.78 Long-term contracts should be assessed on an individual basis and should be reflected in the profit and loss account by recording turnover and the related costs as the contract progresses. The calculation of turnover should be appropriate to the stage of completion of the contract and to the type of business undertaken. Where the outcome of a long-term contract can be assessed with reasonable certainty before its conclusion, the attributable profit, calculated on a prudent basis, should be recognised in the profit and loss account as the difference between turnover and related costs for that contract. Appendix III to the FRSSE sets out additional guidance on long-term contracts, including:

- it is not usually appropriate to include interest on borrowings in the costs of a long-term contract - however, this may be acceptable where specific borrowings can be identified as financing specific contracts, in which case the accounts should disclose both the fact that interest is included and the amount involved;
- where contract prices are determined and invoiced as separate parts of a contract, it will usually be appropriate to match revenue and costs

for each separable part and to reflect the profit accordingly - however future revenues and costs should also be reviewed to establish whether any provision is required for expected future losses;

- only profit that prudently reflects the amount of work performed to date should be recognised in the accounts, and the method used for taking up such profit should be consistently applied;
- in calculating total estimated profit on a contract, the total sales value of the contract should be compared with:
  - total costs to date;
  - total estimated future costs to completion;
  - the estimated future costs of rectification and guarantee work; and
  - the estimated future costs of any further work to be undertaken under the terms of the contract;
- in considering future costs, the following should be taken into account to the extent that they are not recoverable from the customer:
  - likely increases in wages and salaries;
  - likely increases in raw material prices; and
  - likely increases in general overheads;
- where approved variations have been made to a contract but the amount to be received has not yet been settled and is likely to be a material factor in the outcome of the contract, the total sales value should include a conservative estimate of the amount likely to be received - allowance should also be made for expected claims or penalties arising from delays or other factors;
- the settlement of claims is generally subject to a high degree of uncertainty and it is generally prudent to recognise receipts in respect of claims only when negotiations have reached an advanced stage and there is sufficient evidence both that the claim has been accepted and that adequate resources are available to meet it.

Disclosure of long-term contracts

7.79 Long-term contracts should be disclosed in the balance sheet as follows:

- an excess of turnover over payments on account should be shown separately within debtors as 'amounts recoverable on contracts';
- an excess of payments on account over the amount matched with turnover and the amount offset against long-term contract balances should be shown separately within creditors as 'payments on account';
- the amount of long-term contracts at cost, less amounts transferred to cost of sales and after deducting foreseeable losses and payments on

account not matched with turnover, should be shown separately within the balance sheet heading 'stocks' and classified as 'long-term contract balances' – the notes to the accounts should show separately:

- net cost less foreseeable losses; and
- related payments on account;

- where the accrual or provision for foreseeable losses exceeds cost (after transfers to cost of sales), the excess should be shown within 'creditors' or 'provisions for liabilities and charges' as appropriate.

Consignment stocks

7.80 Where consignment stock is in substance an asset of the dealer, both the stock and the corresponding liability to the manufacturer should be shown on the dealer's balance sheet. Any deposit paid by the dealer should be deducted from the liability and the remaining balance should be classified as a trade creditor. Where the consignment stock is not an asset of the dealer it should be excluded from the dealer's balance sheet until title has transferred. Any deposit paid by the dealer should be shown under 'other debtors'. Appendix III to the FRSSE sets out a table to help identify whether the substance of the agreement is that the stock is an asset of the dealer (i.e. whether the dealer has access to the benefits of the stock and is exposed to the inherent risks).

Debt factoring

7.81 Where all significant benefits (i.e. future cash flows) and all significant risks (i.e. slow payment and non-payment) relating to the factored debts have been transferred to the factor, and the entity has no obligation to repay the factor, the debts should be removed from the reporting entity's balance sheet. A profit or loss should be recognised, calculated as the difference between the carrying value of the debts and the proceeds received. A linked presentation should be adopted where significant benefits and risks relating to the debts have been retained by the reporting entity and all of the following conditions are met:

- there is no doubt whatsoever that the entity's exposure to loss is limited to a fixed monetary amount;
- amounts received from the factor are secured only on the debts factored;
- the debts factored can be separately identified;
- the factor has no recourse to other debts or assets;
- the entity has no right to reacquire the debts at some point in the future; and
- the factor has no right to return the debts, even if the factoring agreement ceases.

The linked presentation involves separate disclosure on the face of the balance sheet of the gross amount of the factored debts (after providing for bad debts, credit protection charges and accrued interest where relevant) and amounts received from the factor:

Example 7.4 – Linked presentation of factored debts

	£	£
Stocks		233
Debtors:		
Gross debtors factored without recourse	100	
Less: Non-returnable proceeds	(75)	
	25	
Other debtors	124	
		149
Cash at bank and in hand		50
Current assets		432

A note to the accounts should disclose the fact that the entity is not required to support bad debts in respect of factored debts and that the factor has given a written undertaking not to seek recourse other than out of factored debts. Interest charged by the factor should be recognised as it accrues and should be included with other interest in the profit and loss account. In all other cases where significant benefits and risks relating to the debts have been retained by the reporting entity, the following accounting treatment (separate presentation) should be adopted:

- the gross amount of the debts should be shown as an asset on the balance sheet;
- a corresponding liability in respect of the proceeds received from the factor should be shown within liabilities; and
- interest charged by the factor should be recognised as it accrues and should be included with other interest in the profit and loss account.

Appendix III to the FRSSE sets out a table of terms commonly included in factoring agreements with guidance on whether these indicate that derecognition, a linked presentation or separate presentation is appropriate.

Start-up costs

7.82 Start-up costs should be accounted for on a basis consistent with the accounting treatment of similar costs incurred as part of the entity's ongoing activities. Where there are no similar costs, start-up costs that do not meet the criteria for recognition as an asset under other specific requirements of the FRSSE should be recognised as an expense when they are incurred.

Taxation

7.83 Current and deferred tax should be recognised in the profit and loss account, except to the extent that it is attributable to a gain or loss recognised directly in the statement of total recognised gains and losses, in which case the tax should also be recognised in that statement. The material components of the current and deferred tax charge or credit for the period should be disclosed separately. Any special circumstances affecting the overall tax charge or credit for the period, or which may affect those of future periods, should be disclosed in the notes to the accounts, with quantification of their individual effects. The effects of a fundamental change in the basis of taxation should be included in the tax charge for the year and should be disclosed separately on the face of the profit and loss account.

Recognition of deferred tax

7.84 Deferred tax should be recognised in respect of all timing differences that have originated but not reversed by the balance sheet date, except that it should not be recognised on:

- revaluation gains and losses unless, at the balance sheet date, the entity has entered into a binding agreement to sell the asset and has revalued it to selling price; or
- taxable gains arising on revaluation or sale, if it is more likely than not that the gain will be rolled over into a replacement asset.

Deferred tax should not be recognised on permanent differences. Deferred tax should be recognised when tax allowances for the cost of a fixed asset are received before or after the recognition of the related depreciation in the profit and loss account. However, once any conditions for retaining the tax allowances have been met, the deferred tax should be reversed. Unrelieved tax losses and other deferred tax assets should be recognised only to the extent that it is more likely than not that they will be recovered against the reversal of deferred tax liabilities or against future taxable profits. The FRSSE warns that the very existence of unrelieved tax losses is strong evidence that there may not be any future taxable profits available for such recovery.

Measurement of deferred tax

7.85 Deferred tax should be measured at the average tax rates that are expected to apply when the timing differences reverse, based on tax rates and laws enacted by the balance sheet date. Deferred tax assets and liabilities do not need to be discounted. If an entity adopts a policy of discounting, it should discount all deferred tax balances that have been measured by reference to undiscounted cash flows and for which the impact of discounting is material. The unwinding of the discount should be disclosed separately as part of the tax charge.

Disclosure of deferred tax

7.86 The following items should be disclosed:

- the deferred tax balance and its material components;
- the movement between the opening and closing deferred tax balances, and the material components of that movement; and
- if assets have been revalued, or if their market values are disclosed, the amount of tax that would be payable or recoverable if the assets were sold at those values.

Tax on dividends

7.87 Outgoing dividends and similar amounts payable, and incoming dividends and similar income, should be recognised at an amount that includes any withholding tax but excludes other taxes, such as attributable tax credits. Any withholding tax suffered should be shown as part of the tax charge.

VAT

7.88 Turnover should exclude output VAT. Any irrecoverable input VAT should be included in the cost of the relevant item where practicable and material.

Defined contribution retirement schemes

7.89 The cost of a defined contribution scheme is equivalent to the amount of the contributions payable to the scheme for the accounting period. This cost should be recognised within operating profit in the profit and loss account. The following should be disclosed:

- the nature of the scheme (i.e. defined contribution);
- the cost for the period; and
- any outstanding or prepaid contributions at the balance sheet date.

Defined benefit retirement schemes

7.90 As few smaller entities participate in defined benefit schemes, the requirements on accounting for such schemes are set out in Appendix II to the FRSSE rather than in the main document. The Appendix sets out requirements based on those in FRS 17 *Retirement Benefits* and applies these for accounting periods ending on or after 22 June 2006, although earlier adoption is encouraged. Separate requirements are set out for accounting periods ending before 22 June 2006 where the new requirements are not adopted early.

Accounting periods ending before 22 June 2006

7.91 Where the requirements for accounting periods ending on or after 22 June 2006 are not adopted early, the following accounting treatment should be applied:

- the employer should recognise the expected cost of providing pensions and other post-retirement benefits on a systematic and rational basis over the period during which it derives benefit from the employees' services;
- the pension cost should be calculated using actuarial valuation methods - the actuarial assumptions and method should be compatible and should result in the actuary's best estimate of the cost of providing the promised pension benefits;
- the method of providing for pension costs over the service lives of the employees should result in the regular pension cost being a substantially level percentage of the current and expected future pensionable payroll, in the light of the current actuarial assumptions;
- variations from regular cost should be allocated over the expected remaining service lives of the current employees in the scheme (a period representing average service lives may be used);
- to the extent that the capital cost of ex gratia pensions is not covered by a surplus, it should be recognised in the profit and loss account in the accounting period in which they are granted;
- where the actuarial assumptions do not allow for discretionary or ex gratia increases in pensions, the capital cost of such increases should be recognised in the profit and loss account for the period in which they are initially granted, to the extent that they are not covered by a surplus;
- where the cumulative pension cost recognised in the profit and loss account has not been completely discharged by the payment of contributions or directly paid pensions, the excess should be shown as a net pension provision, and any excess of contributions or directly paid pensions over the cumulative pension cost should be shown as a prepayment;
- the following disclosures should be given:
  - the nature of the scheme (i.e. defined benefit);
  - whether it is funded or unfunded;

- whether the pension cost and pension provision are assessed with the advice of a professionally qualified actuary and, if so, the date of the last formal valuation (or later formal review);
- the pension cost charge for the period;
- any provision or prepayment in the accounts resulting from a difference between the amount recognised as the cumulative pension cost and the amount funded or paid directly;
- the amount of any deficiency on a current funding level basis and an indication of the action being taken to deal with this;
- an outline of the result of the latest formal actuarial valuation (or later formal review) of the scheme on an ongoing basis;
- any commitment to make additional payments over a limited number of years;
- details of the expected effect on future costs of any material changes in the company's (or group's) pension arrangements;
- the fair value of scheme assets, the present value of scheme liabilities and the resulting surplus or deficit determined in accordance with the requirements on accounting for defined benefit schemes for accounting periods ending on or after 22 June 2006;
- where the surplus or deficit in the scheme differs from the amount that would be recognised under those requirements, an explanation of the difference;
- for accounting periods ending on or after 22 June 2003, comparative figures must be given for the two previous disclosures, together with an analysis of the movements in the surplus or deficit in the scheme during the current period ;
- for accounting periods ending on or after 22 June 2004, comparative figures must also be given for the analysis of the movement in the surplus or deficit.

A subsidiary that is a member of a group scheme should disclose this fact and the nature of the group scheme, indicating where appropriate that contributions are based on pension costs for the group as a whole. Such a company is exempt from the detailed disclosures on funding levels and the results of the most recent actuarial valuation (or later review), provided that:

- the notes to the accounts give the name of the holding company in whose financial statements this information can be found; and
- that holding company is registered in the UK or Republic of Ireland.

Accounting periods ending on or after 22 June 2006

7.92 The following requirements apply to defined benefit schemes for accounting periods ending on or after 22 June 2006:

- scheme assets should be measured at fair value at the balance sheet date;
- scheme liabilities (which comprise benefits promised under the scheme and any constructive obligations for further benefits) should be measured on an actuarial basis using the projected unit method;
- the assumptions underlying the valuation should be mutually compatible and should result in the best estimate of the future cash flows that will arise – the directors have ultimate responsibility for the assumptions but should seek appropriate advice from an actuary;
- any assumptions that are affected by economic conditions should reflect market expectations at the balance sheet date;
- scheme liabilities should be discounted at the current rate of return on a high quality corporate bond of equivalent currency and term;
- full actuarial valuations by a professionally qualified actuary should be obtained at least every three years and the actuary should review and update the latest valuation at each intervening balance sheet date;
- the excess or shortfall of the value of scheme assets over the present value of scheme liabilities represents the surplus or deficit in the scheme – the employer should:
  - recognise an asset to the extent that it can recover a surplus through reduced contributions or a refund from the scheme; and
  - recognise a liability to the extent that it reflects a legal or constructive obligation;
- any unpaid contributions to the scheme should be shown as creditors due within one year;
- the defined benefit asset or liability should be shown separately on the face of the balance sheet as follows:
  - in a balance sheet prepared under Format 1 under CA 1985 Sch 8, after item J (Accruals) but before item K (Capital and reserves); and
  - in a balance sheet prepared under Format 2 under CA 1985 Sch 8, an asset should be shown after Assets item D (Prepayments and accrued income) and a liability should be shown after Liabilities item D (Accruals and deferred income);
- any deferred tax relating to the defined benefit asset or liability should be offset against that asset or liability (i.e. it should not be included with other deferred tax assets or liabilities);
- the individual components of the change in the defined benefit asset or liability (other than contributions to the scheme) should be shown as follows:
  - the current service cost should be included in operating profit in the profit and loss account;

  - the net of interest cost and the expected return on assets should be shown as other finance costs (or income) adjacent to interest;
  - actuarial gains and losses should be recognised in the statement of total recognised gains and losses;
  - past service costs should be recognised in the profit and loss account in the period in which the increased benefits vest;
  - losses arising on a settlement or curtailment should be recognised in the profit and loss account when the employer becomes demonstrably committed to the transaction – gains should be recognised only when all parties whose consent is required are irrevocably committed;
- the following disclosures should be given:
  - the nature of the scheme (i.e. defined benefit);
  - the date of the latest full actuarial valuation on which amounts included in the accounts are based – if the actuary is an employee or officer of the reporting entity (or of another member of the group), this fact should be disclosed;
  - the contributions made in respect of the accounting period and any agreed contribution rates for future years;
  - for closed schemes and those in which the age profile of the active membership is rising significantly, the fact that, under the projected unit method, the current service cost will increase as members approach retirement;
  - the fair value of scheme assets, the present value of scheme liabilities and the resulting surplus or deficit in the scheme;
  - where the defined benefit asset or liability in the balance sheet differs from the surplus or deficit in the scheme, an explanation of the difference; and
  - an analysis of movements in the surplus or deficit during the period.

Provisions

7.93 The section of the FRSSE on provisions, contingent liabilities and contingent assets does not apply to retirement benefits, deferred tax or leases, as these are dealt with in separate, more specific sections. A provision should be recognised only when it is probable (i.e. more likely than not) that a present obligation exists as a result of a past event and that a transfer of economic benefits will be required to settle the obligation, and when the amount of the transfer can be estimated reliably. The amount recognised as a provision should be the best estimate of the expenditure required to settle the obligation at the balance sheet date. Where the effect of the time value of money is material, the amount of a provision should be the present value of the expenditures required to settle the obligation.

There are a number of acceptable discounting methods, and the appropriate discount rate will depend on the method used. If cash flows have already been adjusted for risk, it will usually be appropriate to use a risk-free discount rate. Where discounting is used, the unwinding of the discount should be shown as other finance costs adjacent to interest. An illustrative example of discounting a provision is given in Appendix III to the FRSSE. Where some or all of the expenditure needed to settle the obligation may be reimbursed by a third party (e.g. an insurer), the reimbursement should be recognised (as a separate asset) only when it is virtually certain to be received if the entity settles the obligation. A net presentation of the provision and the reimbursement may be given in the profit and loss account. Gains from the expected disposal of assets should be excluded from the measurement of a provision. Provisions should be reviewed at each balance sheet date and adjusted to reflect the current best estimate of the amount required to settle the obligation at that date and a provision should only be used for the purpose for which it was originally recognised.

Contingent liabilities and contingent assets

7.94 Contingent liabilities and contingent assets should not be recognised. The following details should be disclosed for contingent liabilities (except where they are remote), and for probable contingent assets:

- brief description of the nature of the contingent item; and
- where practicable, an estimate of its financial effect.

Capital instruments

7.95 Capital instruments other than shares should be classified as liabilities if they include any obligation to transfer economic benefits. Shares and capital instruments that do not include any obligation to transfer economic benefits should be reported as part of shareholders' funds. Borrowings (i.e. capital instruments that are classified as liabilities) should be stated initially at the fair value of the consideration given and should then be:

- increased by the finance costs charged in respect of the period; and
- reduced by any payments made in respect of the borrowings during the period.

Finance costs in respect of borrowings should be allocated to accounting periods over the term of the borrowings at a constant rate on the carrying amount and should be charged in the profit and loss account. Finance costs are the difference between the net proceeds of the instrument and the total payments (or other transfer of economic benefits) that the issuer may be required to make (other than arrangement fees). If an arrangement fee represents a significant additional cost of finance (e.g. when compared with the total interest charge over the life of the instrument), it should be accounted for in the same way as finance costs. In other cases the arrangement fee should be charged in the profit and loss account when it is incurred.

Dividends

7.96 All dividends should be reported as appropriations in the profit and loss account. Where the entitlement to a dividend is calculated by reference to time, the dividend should be accounted for on an accruals basis except where ultimate payment is remote (e.g. where reserves are insufficient and dividends are not cumulative). The excess of amounts accrued over dividends paid or payable should be shown separately within shareholders' funds.

Translation of foreign currency transactions, assets and liabilities

7.97 Assets, liabilities, revenues and costs relating to transactions denominated in a foreign currency should be translated into local currency at the exchange rate ruling on the date of the transaction. An average rate over a period may be used as an approximation of the actual rate, provided that rates do not fluctuate significantly. There are two exceptions to this general rule:

- where the transaction is to be settled at a contracted rate, that rate should be used for the conversion; and
- where a trading transaction is covered by a matching or related forward contract, the rate specified in that contract may be used.

Once non-monetary assets have been translated and recorded, no subsequent translations should normally be made, except in the case of foreign equity investments financed by foreign currency borrowings (see **7.98** below). At the balance sheet date, monetary assets and liabilities denominated in a foreign currency should be translated into local currency using the closing rate, except in the following circumstances:

- where the transaction is to be settled at a contracted rate, that rate should be used for the conversion; and
- where a trading transaction is covered by a matching or related forward contract, the rate specified in that contract may be used.

Exchange gains and losses on settled transactions and unsettled monetary items should be reported in the profit and loss account as part of the profit or loss on ordinary activities for the year.

Foreign equity investments financed by foreign currency borrowings

7.98 Where foreign equity investments are financed or hedged by foreign currency borrowings the following accounting treatment may be adopted:

- the equity investments may be denominated in the relevant foreign currency and translated at the closing rate of exchange at each balance sheet date for inclusion in the reporting entity's financial statements;
- any exchange differences arising should be taken to reserves; and
- exchange gains or losses arising on translation of the related foreign currency borrowings should be offset, as a reserves movement, against those exchange differences, subject to the following rules:
  - in any accounting period, exchange gains and losses on foreign currency borrowings can only be offset to the extent of exchange differences arising on the related investments;
  - those foreign currency borrowings should not exceed, in aggregate, the total amount of cash that the investments are expected to generate, from profits or otherwise.

Where this accounting treatment is adopted, it must be applied consistently from year to year.

Incorporating the accounts of foreign entities

7.99 The accounts of foreign entities (including associated companies and branches) should normally be incorporated into the accounts of the reporting entity using the closing rate/net investment method of translation. Exchange differences arising on translation should be recorded as a movement on reserves. The profit and loss account of a foreign entity should be translated at the closing rate, or at an average rate for the period, calculated in the most appropriate way taking into account the circumstances of the entity. If an average rate is used, the difference between the translation of the profit and loss account at the closing rate and at the average rate should be treated as a movement on reserves. Where the trade of the foreign entity depends more on the economic environment of the investing entity's currency than on that of its own currency, transactions recorded by the foreign entity should be translated as if they were undertaken by the investing entity (i.e. as set out in **7.97**). The method of translation adopted for the accounts of a foreign entity should be applied consistently from year to year, unless there is a change in the financial and other operational relationships with the investing entity.

Investments in foreign entities financed by foreign currency borrowings

7.100 Where investments in foreign entities have been financed or hedged by foreign currency borrowings, exchange gains and losses on the borrowings may be offset as a reserves movement against exchange differences arising on retranslation of the investments, subject to the following rules:

— the relationship between the foreign entity and investor must justify the use of the closing rate method for consolidation purposes;

— in any accounting period, exchange gains and losses on foreign currency borrowings can only be offset to the extent of exchange differences arising on the net investments in foreign entities;

— those foreign currency borrowings should not exceed, in aggregate, the total amount of cash that the net investments are expected to generate, from profits or otherwise.

Where this accounting treatment is adopted, it must be applied consistently from year to year. Where an investor prepares group accounts and in its individual accounts has applied the accounting treatment set out in **7.98** to investments in foreign entities that are not subsidiaries or associates, it may adopt the same treatment in its consolidated financial statements.

Post balance sheet events

7.101 Financial statements should be prepared on the basis of the conditions that exist at the balance sheet date. The financial statements should be changed to reflect a material post balance sheet event that is an adjusting event or that indicates that the going concern concept is not applicable to the whole or a material part of the entity. An adjusting event is one that provides additional evidence of a condition that existed at the balance sheet date. The financial statements should disclose the following:

— non-adjusting events that are so material that non-disclosure would result in a user of the accounts being unable to reach a proper understanding of the financial position of the entity; and

— the reversal or maturity after the year end of a transaction entered into before that date, primarily to alter the appearance of the entity's balance sheet.

Where disclosure is necessary, the following details should be given:

— the nature of the event; and

— an estimate of the financial effect or, where appropriate, a statement that this is not practicable – the financial effect should be stated before taxation and the taxation implications should be explained if this is necessary for a proper understanding of the financial position.

Date of approval of financial statements

7.102 The date on which the board of directors approves the financial statements should be disclosed.

Related party disclosures

7.103 Where the reporting entity enters into a transaction with or on behalf of a related party, irrespective of whether a price is charged, and the transaction is material to the reporting entity, the following details should be disclosed in the financial statements:

- the names of the related parties entering into the transaction;
- a description of the relationship between them;
- a description of the transaction;
- the amounts involved;
- any other elements of the transaction that are necessary for a proper understanding of the financial statements;
- the amounts due to or from related parties at the balance sheet date;
- any provisions for doubtful debts due from related parties at the balance sheet date; and
- amounts written off during the period in respect of debts due to or from related parties.

Purchases, sales, transfers of goods or other assets or liabilities, services rendered or received, and the provision or receipt of finance or financial support are all covered by the disclosure requirements. However, the following items do not require disclosure as related party transactions:

- pension contributions paid to a pension fund;
- emoluments in respect of services as an employee of the reporting entity;
- transactions with the following parties simply as a result of their role:
  - providers of finance (in the course of that business);
  - utility companies;
  - government departments and sponsored bodies;
  - a customer, supplier, franchis or, distributor or general agent.

Transactions may be disclosed in aggregate (i.e. the aggregation of similar transactions by type of related party) unless disclosure of individual transactions (or connected transactions) is necessary for a proper understanding of the impact of the transactions on the financial statements or is required by law. Also, where the reporting entity is part of a group that prepares publicly available consolidated financial statements, it is entitled to the exemption in paragraph 3(a)–(c) of FRS 8 *Related Party Disclosures*.

Personal guarantees given by directors

7.104 The financial statements should disclose any personal guarantees given by the directors in respect of the reporting entity's borrowings.

Disclosure of controlling party

7.105 Where the reporting entity is controlled by another party, the following disclosures should be given, regardless of whether there have been any transactions between the parties:

— the related party relationship and the name of that party; and

— the name of the ultimate controlling party, if different.

If the controlling party or ultimate controlling party is not known, this fact should be explained in the financial statements.

Consolidated financial statements

7.106 Where the reporting entity prepares consolidated financial statements, the detailed requirements (including disclosure requirements) set out in the following accounting standards should be applied:

— FRS 2 – 'Accounting for Subsidiary Undertakings'

— FRS 6 – 'Acquisitions and Mergers'

— FRS 7 – 'Fair Values in Acquisition Accounting'

The FRSSE also requires compliance with the relevant sections of the following:

— FRS 5 'Reporting the Substance of Transactions';

— FRS 9 'Associates and Joint Ventures';

— FRS 10 'Goodwill and Intangible Assets'; and

— FRS 11 'Impairment of Fixed Assets and Goodwill'.

However, the requirements of FRS 10 and FRS 11 apply only in respect of any goodwill arising on consolidation.

MEDIUM-SIZED COMPANIES AND GROUPS

Qualification as a medium-sized company

7.107 The rules on qualification as a medium-sized company and their practical effect are identical to those described in **7.1** to **7.8** above in relation to small companies, except that the qualifying conditions are increased to:

- turnover of not more than £11.2 million (if the accounting period is less than or more than a year, this limit must be adjusted proportionately);
- balance sheet total of not more than £5.6 million;
- number of employees not more than 250.

A parent company cannot qualify as a medium-sized company unless the group which it heads qualifies as a medium-sized group. The rules on qualifying as a medium-sized group are as described in **7.6** to **7.8** above, with the following qualifying conditions.

- aggregate turnover of not more than £11.2 million net or not more than £13.44 million gross (if the accounting period is less than or more than a year, these limits must be adjusted proportionately);
- aggregate balance sheet total of not more than £5.6 million net or not more than £6.72 million gross;
- aggregate number of employees of not more than 250.

Accounts exemptions available to medium sized companies

7.108 Most companies that qualify as medium-sized can file abbreviated accounts with the registrar but the permitted abbreviations are very limited compared with those available to small companies. The exemption relates only to the filing requirement and full accounts must still be prepared each year for presentation to the members. A medium-sized company does not have to take advantage of the exemption and can therefore file a copy of the full accounts if it wishes. Medium-sized companies are also exempt from the requirement to state whether the accounts have been prepared in accordance with applicable accounting standards. This exemption relates only to the disclosure requirement and does not grant any exemption from compliance with the requirements of accounting standards

Ineligible companies

7.109 As with small companies, the exemptions are not available to the following companies, even if they meet the qualifying conditions for a medium-sized company:

- a public company;
- a person who has permission under Part 4 of the Financial Services and Markets Act 2000 (FSMA 2000) to carry on one or more regulated activities;
- a person who carries on an insurance market activity; or
- a member of an ineligible group.

An ineligible group is defined as a group where any of the members is:

- a public company;
- a body corporate that has the power to issue shares or debentures to the public;
- a person who has permission under Part 4 of FSMA 2000 to carry on one or more regulated activities; or
- a person who carries on an insurance market activity.

In the case of an intermediate parent company, it is necessary to consider the wider group and not just the one headed by the intermediate parent. The second category here does not need to be a British institution, so the UK subsidiary of a foreign undertaking will not be entitled to the exemptions if the parent has the power to issue shares or debentures to the public. It should also be noted that it is the power to issue shares and debentures, rather than their actual issue, that is the deciding factor.

Abbreviated accounts for medium-sized companies

7.110 Under CA 1985 s 246(3), the following exemptions apply for medium-sized companies:

- the company may file a profit and loss account that begins with 'gross profit or loss' where this figure combines the figures for:
  - turnover, cost of sales, and other operating income; or
  - turnover, change in stocks of finished goods and work in progress, own work capitalised, other operating income, raw materials and consumables, and other operating charges

  depending on which standard format is used for the profit and loss account;
- the notes to the accounts need not give the analysis of turnover by class of business and by geographical market normally required by CA 1985 Sch 4 para 55.

There are no exemptions in respect of disclosures in the balance sheet and directors' report. The recent company law review concluded that the abbreviated accounts regime should be abolished and the Government White Paper *Modernising Company Law* issued in July 2002 confirms the intention to proceed with this.

Directors' statement

7.111 If the directors of a medium-sized company wish to take advantage of the option to prepare abbreviated accounts for filing purposes, the balance sheet in the abbreviated accounts must include a statement that the accounts are prepared in accordance with the special provisions of Part VII of CA 1985 relating to medium-sized companies. This statement must be given in a prominent position immediately above the director's signature.

Special auditors' report

7.112 Where abbreviated accounts are delivered to the registrar, they must be accompanied by a special report from the auditors stating whether, in their opinion:

— the company is entitled to deliver abbreviated accounts prepared in accordance with CA 1985 s 246(3); and

— the abbreviated accounts have been properly prepared in accordance with that sections.

The complete text of the auditors' report on the company's full accounts must also be included where that report:

— was qualified, in which case additional details may also need to be given to enable the qualification to be understood; or

— included a statement under CA 1985 s 237(2) (inadequate accounts, records or returns, or accounts not in agreement with the records and returns); or

— included a statement under CA 1985 s 237(3) (failure to obtain all the information and explanations that the auditors considered necessary).

Exemption from preparing group accounts

7.113 A parent company is not required to prepare group accounts for a financial year in which the group which it heads qualifies as a medium-sized group and is not an ineligible group. An ineligible group is defined in CA 1985 s 248(2) as a group where any of the members is:

— a public company;

— a body corporate that has the power to issue shares or debentures to the public;

— a person who has permission under Part 4 of FSMA 2000 to carry on one or more regulated activities; or

— a person who carries on an insurance market activity.

There was previously a requirement for the auditors to provide the directors with a special report confirming that, in their opinion, the company was entitled to the exemption. This is no longer required. However, if the directors take advantage of the exemption and, in the opinion of the auditors, they are not entitled to do so, the auditors are required to state this in their report on the accounts. FRS 2 'Accounting for Subsidiary Undertakings' repeats the exemption set out in the Act for medium sized groups, but requires disclosure of:

— the fact that the accounts present information about the parent as an individual undertaking and not about the group; and

— the grounds on which the parent is exempt from preparing consolidated accounts for the group.

The recent company law review recommended that the category of medium-sized group should be abolished on the grounds that the exemptions currently granted are difficult to justify and add complexity to the law, but the Government White Paper *Modernising Company Law* issued in July 2002 notes that the review did not consult specifically on this issue and therefore invites comments on whether medium-sized companies should continue to be exempt from the preparation of group accounts.

AUDIT EXEMPTION

Categories of audit exemption

7.114 CA 1985 s 249A identifies two categories of conditions for audit exemption: total exemption conditions and report conditions. A company that meets the total exemption conditions in respect of a financial year is not required to have an audit for that year. A company that meets the report conditions in respect of a financial year is exempt from an audit for that year, provided that the directors arrange for a special report on the company's accounts to be made to the members by a reporting accountant. Regulations that came into force on 15 April 1997 mean that the report conditions now only apply in the case of a company that is a charity. Separate audit exemption arrangements also apply in the case of a dormant company (see **7.122** below).

Total exemption conditions

7.115 A company will usually meet the total exemption conditions for a financial year if:

— it qualifies as a small company for that year under CA 1985 s 246 (see **7.1**–**7.8** above);

— if it is a charity, its gross income for the year is not more than £90,000 or, if it is not a charity, its turnover for the year is not more than £1.0 million; and

— its balance sheet total for the year is not more than £1.4 million.

All three conditions must be met for the company to qualify for the exemption. In the case of a charity, gross income is defined as income from all sources, as shown in the company's income and expenditure account. If the accounting period is more than a year or less than a year, the turnover (or gross income) limit is adjusted proportionately but there is no change to the other criteria. Balance sheet total has the same definition as for the small company qualification criteria (see **7.5** above).

Report conditions

7.116 The report conditions are now only relevant for a company that is a charity. A charitable company will usually meet the report conditions for a financial year if:

— it qualifies as a small company for that year under CA 1985 s 246;

— its gross income for the year is more than £90,000 but not more than £250,000; and

— its balance sheet total for the year is not more than £1.4 million.

All three conditions must be met to qualify for the exemption. Gross income is as defined in **7.115** above. If the accounting period is more than a year or less than a year, the gross income limit is adjusted proportionately but there is no change to the other criteria.

Ineligible companies

7.117 The exemptions are not available to the following companies, even if they meet the specified conditions:

— a public company;

— a parent company or a subsidiary undertaking (except in the specific circumstances described in **7.118** below);

— a person with permission under Part 4 of FSMA 2000 to carry on one or more regulated activities;

— a person who carries on an insurance market activity;

— an appointed representative, within the meaning of s 39 of FSMA 2000; or

— a special registered body as defined in the Trade Union and Labour Relations (Consolidation) Act 1992 s 117(1) or an employers' association as defined in s 122 of that Act.

Special provisions for dormant subsidiaries and small groups

7.118 The exemptions are not generally available to parent and subsidiary undertakings, but the legislation includes specific provisions to cater for the following:

- a subsidiary that has been dormant under CA 1985 s 249AA throughout the financial year is specifically granted the exemption by s 249B(1A); and
- a parent or subsidiary undertaking will not be regarded as ineligible if, throughout the period that it was a parent or subsidiary, it was a member of a group that:
  - qualifies as a small group (see **7.6** above) for the financial year covering that period (or would so qualify if all bodies corporate in the group were companies) and was not at any time within that year an ineligible group (see **7.10** above);
  - in the case of a company that is not a charity, has an aggregate turnover in that year of not more than £1.0 million net or £1.2 million gross;
  - in the case of a company that is a charity, has an aggregate turnover in that year of not more than £350,000 net or £420,000 gross; and
  - has an aggregate balance sheet total for that year of not more than £1.4 million net or £1.68 million gross.

The definition of 'balance sheet total' and the use of 'gross' and 'net' figures apply in the same way as for qualification as a small group (see **7.7** and **7.8** above)

Members requiring an audit to be carried out

7.119 Any member or members of a company who hold not less than 10% (in nominal value) of the issued share capital or any class of share capital may require an audit for any year by depositing a written notice at the company's registered office no later than one month before the end of that financial year. If the company does not have a share capital, the minimum becomes not less than 10% of the members of the company in number terms.

Directors' statement

7.120 The exemptions are only available if the balance sheet includes a statement by the directors to the effect that:

- for the year in question, the company is entitled to the exemption in CA 1985 s 249A(1) or (2);
- no notice has been deposited under CA 1985 s 249B(2) requiring an audit for that year; and
- the directors acknowledge their responsibilities for:
  - ensuring that the company maintains accounting records which comply with CA 1985 s 221; and

— preparing accounts which give a true and fair view of the state of affairs of the company at the end of the financial year and of the profit or loss for that year in accordance with CA 1985 s 226 of , and which comply with the relevant accounting requirements of the Act.

This statement must be positioned above the director's signature on the balance sheet. Where the company also prepares shorter form accounts, the statement is usually combined with the directors' statement on the shorter form accounts (see **7.14** above). A suitable wording to meet these requirements might be:

Example 7.5 – Directors' statement – audit exemption

In the case of total exemption:

The company is entitled to exemption under Companies Act 1985 s 249A(1) from the requirement to have its accounts for the financial year ended [date] audited.

No notice has been deposited under s 249B(2) of that Act requiring the accounts of the company for that financial year to be audited.

The directors acknowledge their responsibilities for:

(i) ensuring that the company keeps accounting records which comply with Companies Act 1985 s 221; and

(ii) preparing accounts which give a true and fair view of the state of affairs of the company at the end of the financial year and of its profit or loss for that year in accordance with the requirements of s 226 of that Act, and which otherwise comply with the requirements of that Act relating to accounts, so far as these are applicable to the company.

In the case of report exemption:

The company is entitled to exemption under Companies Act 1985 s 249A(2) from the requirement to have its accounts for the financial year ended [date] audited, provided that the accounts are subject to a limited review by a reporting accountant.

No notice has been deposited under s 249B(2) of that Act requiring the accounts of the company for that financial year to be audited.

The directors acknowledge their responsibilities for:

(i) ensuring that the company keeps accounting records which comply with Companies Act 1985 s 221; and

(ii) preparing accounts which give a true and fair view of the state of affairs of the company at the end of the financial year and of its profit or loss for that year in accordance with the requirements of s 226 of that Act, and which otherwise comply with the requirements of that Act relating to accounts, so far as these are applicable to the company.

Special report by reporting accountants

7.121 A charitable company that meets the report conditions in respect of a financial year is exempt from an audit for that year, provided that the directors arrange for a special report on the company's accounts to be made to the members by a reporting accountant. CA 1985 s 249D specifies who is eligible to act as a reporting accountant. The requirements are similar to those applying to the appointment of auditors. The reporting accountant must be:

— a member of one of the recognised bodies specified in s 249D(3) (i.e. one of the principal UK accountancy bodies); and

— entitled to engage in public practice.

The same rules on independence apply as in the case of auditors. The reporting accountant must express an opinion on whether:

— the accounts are in agreement with the company's accounting records;

— the accounts are drawn up in a manner consistent with the relevant provisions of the Act;

— the company satisfied the report conditions set out in s 249A;

— the company did not at any time during the year fall within any categories not entitled to the exemption.

The Act clarifies that the last three opinions above are to be given on the basis of the information in the accounting records. Detailed guidance on the work required to support this report and example wordings for the report are given in 'Audit Exemption Reports', a Statement of Standards for Reporting Accountants issued by the Auditing Practices Board in October 1994. If the directors wish to take advantage of the option to file abbreviated accounts, there is no requirement for a separate report by the reporting accountant on the abbreviated accounts. However, the reporting accountant's report on the full accounts must be delivered to the registrar with the abbreviated accounts. To avoid any confusion, the APB Statement recommends that some explanatory wording is attached, along the following lines.

Example 7.6 – Explanatory note to report filed with abbreviated accounts

The following reproduces the text of the report prepared for the purposes of Companies Act 1985 s 249A(2) in respect of the company's annual accounts, from which the abbreviated accounts (set out on pages ... to ...) have been prepared.

Dormant companies

7.122 A company that is dormant, as defined in CA 1985, is usually entitled to exemption from an annual audit under s 249AA of the Act. The exemption is automatically available to companies that meet the conditions set out in the legislation. A company is classed as dormant for any accounting period during which it does not have a 'significant accounting transaction'. This is defined in the legislation as any transaction which requires an entry to be made in the accounting records, other than:

- the taking up of shares by a subscriber in pursuance of an undertaking given by him in the Memorandum of Association;
- a fee payable to the registrar on a change of the company's name;
- a fee payable to the registrar on the re-registration of the company (i.e. on a change in status from private to public, or vice versa);
- a penalty under CA 1985 s 242A for failure to deliver accounts; and
- a fee payable to the registrar for the registration of the company's annual return.

Entries such as transfers between inter-company accounts will count as significant accounting transactions and will prevent a company from being classified as dormant. A company that is dormant ceases to be so as soon as a significant accounting transaction takes place.

Conditions for dormant company audit exemption

7.123 A company is eligible to take advantage of the exemption from audit granted by CA 1985 s 249AA for a financial year if it has been:

- dormant since its formation; or
- dormant since the end of the previous financial year, and is:
  - entitled to prepare its individual accounts in accordance with CA 1985 s 246 (see 7.9 above) or would have been so entitled if it had not been a member of an ineligible group; and
  - not required to prepare group accounts for that year.

The directors are also required to make a formal statement in the accounts that the company is entitled to the exemption (see **7.126** below) and the members can require an audit to be carried out in the same way as for other small companies (see **7.119** above).

Ineligible companies

7.124 A company is not entitled to audit exemption as a dormant company if it is:

— a person who has permission under Part 4 of FSMA 2000 to carry on one or more regulated activities; or

— a person who carries on an insurance market activity.

Accounts requirements for dormant companies

7.125 The exemption relates only to the audit requirements of CA 1985 and a dormant company must therefore continue to prepare and file annual accounts in the normal manner. The Act requires all companies to prepare a profit and loss account and this applies equally to dormant companies. In the year following the year in which a company becomes dormant, a full profit and loss account will need to be prepared in order to show the detailed comparative figures. Where a company has been dormant for two consecutive years, there will be no detailed figures to disclose in the profit and loss account. In this case it will usually be appropriate to present a narrative profit and loss account.

Example 7.7 — Narrative profit and loss account for dormant company

Profit and loss account for the year ended 31 December 20X2

During the financial year and the preceding financial year, the company did not trade, received no income and incurred no expenditure. Consequently the company made neither a profit nor a loss in either year.

This is usually given immediately before the detailed notes to the accounts.

Directors' statement

7.126

— The exemption from audit is only available if the balance sheet in the company's accounts includes a statement by the directors to the effect that:

— for the year in question, the company is entitled to the exemption in CA 1985 s 249AA (1);

— no notice has been deposited under CA 1985 s 249B(2) requiring an audit for that year;

— the directors acknowledge their responsibilities for:

  — ensuring that the company maintains accounting records which comply with CA 1985 s 221; and

  — preparing accounts which give a true and fair view of the state of affairs of the company at the end of the financial year and of the profit or loss for that year in accordance with CA 1985 s 226, and which comply with the relevant accounting requirements of the Act.

The statement must be given on the balance sheet, immediately above the directors' signature required by CA 1985 s 233. A suitable wording to meet the requirements of the Act might be:

Example 7.8 – Directors' statement – dormant company audit exemption

The company is entitled to exemption under Companies Act 1985 s 249AA(1) from the requirement to have its accounts for the year ended [date] audited.

No notice has been deposited under s 249B(2) of that Act requiring the accounts of the company for that financial year to be audited.

The directors acknowledge their responsibilities for:

(i) ensuring that the company maintains accounting records which comply with Companies Act 1985 s 221; and

(ii) preparing accounts which give a true and fair view of the state of affairs of the company at the end of the financial year and of the profit or loss for that year in accordance with s 226 of the Act, and which otherwise comply with the requirements of that Act relating to accounts, so far as these are applicable to the company.

Dormant companies acting as agents

7.127 Where the directors take advantage of the exemption from audit conferred by CA 1985 s 249AA and the company has acted as agent for another party during the year, the accounts are required to disclose this fact. CA 1985 Sch 4, Sch 8 and Sch 8A all incorporate this disclosure requirement and the information must therefore also be given in abbreviated accounts where the company chooses to prepare these for filing purposes.

Chapter 8

Profit and Loss Account Formats

COMPANY LAW REQUIREMENTS

CA 1985 Prescribed formats

8.1 CA 1985 prescribes standard formats for the profit and loss account and the balance sheet which must be followed by both individual companies and by groups when preparing their annual accounts. The Act provides a choice of four formats for the profit and loss account - these are set out in the Appendix to this chapter. The directors are free to decide which format to use, but once a particular format has been chosen it must be used consistently year by year unless there are good reasons for changing (see **8.4** below). The major differences between the formats relate to the presentation of operating costs. Other items in the profit and loss account (e.g. turnover, income from fixed asset investments, interest payable) are generally presented in the same way, although the order of presentation varies between formats.

Presentation of operating costs

8.2 The formats follow two basic approaches to presenting operating costs. Formats 1 and 3 are centred around the nature or purpose of the various items of expenditure (eg costs of sales, distribution costs, administrative costs). Formats 2 and 4 are centred around the categories or type of expenditure (e.g. raw materials and consumables, staff costs). Formats 1 and 2 present the information vertically and combine income and expenditure, whilst Formats 3 and 4 present it horizontally, grouping together the various types of income and the various charges. In practice, companies usually choose to adopt Format 1 or Format 2 (ie the vertical form of presentation). The nature of the company's activities may indicate which of the formats is more appropriate. For instance, a sales and distribution company is more likely to choose Format 1 because this includes separate headings for cost of sales, distribution and administrative expenses, which will be key features of the business. A construction company is more likely to use Format 2 because this highlights changes in stocks and work in progress, any of the company's own work that has been capitalised, and the charges for raw materials and consumables and staff costs, all of which may be important features in understanding a construction company's results.

Potential sensitivity of information

8.3 In choosing the format for the profit and loss account, companies may also wish to bear in mind the potential sensitivity of some of the information in a commercial context. For instance, Format 1 requires the disclosure of the gross profit or loss for the period and this figure can also be calculated from the details given in Format 3. The gross profit or loss for the period is not evident from the information required under Formats 2 and 4. If a company wishes to avoid disclosing its gross profit or loss, it can therefore do so by choosing Format 2 (or Format 4) rather than Format 1 (or Format 3). Similarly some of the details that are required to be disclosed under Formats 2 and 4 are not disclosed under Formats 1 and 3.

Change of format

8.4 The directors may only change the format of the profit and loss account if, in their opinion, there are special reasons for doing so (for instance, if the nature of the company's activities changes significantly, and as a result a different profit and loss account format would provide a more appropriate way of presenting the company's results). If the format of the profit and loss account is changed, the accounts must disclose:

— the fact that a different format has been used;

— the reasons for changing to a different format.

In practice, changing the format of the profit and loss account can lead to a considerable amount of work as the previous year's figures need to be restated and presented under the new format so that the details are comparable with those for the current year.

Order of headings and sub-headings

8.5 The profit and loss account formats are set out using a hierarchy of letters and Arabic numerals to prescribe the order in which the individual headings and sub-headings must appear. The letters and numerals do not have to be reproduced in the accounts but are provided so that other sections of the Act can refer to the headings by category. Although the headings and sub-headings should normally follow the order prescribed in the formats, the Act requires the directors to adapt or rearrange the items identified by Arabic numerals if the special nature of the company's business requires this. Items may be shown in greater detail than required by the formats and additional items may be shown, provided that they are not already covered elsewhere in the standard format. Items identified by Arabic numerals may be combined if:

— the individual amounts are not material; or

— combining them facilitates assessment of the profit or loss for the year, although in this case the individual components must be disclosed in the notes to the accounts.

If there is no amount to be shown for a particular heading or sub-heading in either the current or the previous financial year, that heading or sub-heading should not appear in the profit and loss account.

Analysis between headings

8.6 CA 1985 provides definitions of turnover and staff costs but does not provide any guidance on the items that should be included under the other headings in the statutory formats. The headings are broad in nature and this has led to different interpretations being applied in practice. It is not practical to provide definitive guidance on what should be included under each heading, although some indications are given in the following chapters where relevant. The most important point is that the approach decided on by each individual company is applied consistently from year to year. Under FRS 18 'Accounting Policies' a change in the way in which a particular item is presented in the financial statements is a change of accounting policy and must be accounted for as such in the year in which the change takes place. In a group of companies it is important that clear decisions are taken on how expenses are to be categorised and that these are conveyed to those responsible for preparing accounts for each company within the group. This should ensure that a consistent approach is adopted throughout the group in each year, as well as from year to year.

Condensed presentation

8.7 Each item in the profit and loss account formats is given an Arabic number. The presentation on the face of the profit and loss account can therefore be condensed to key figures, with the detail required by the Act being given in the notes to the accounts, if this will help in understanding the results for the period. However, the profit or loss on ordinary activities before taxation must always be shown on the face of the profit and loss account, as must dividends paid and proposed and transfers, or proposed transfers, to and from reserves.

Potential duplication of headings and sub-totals

8.8 Where one or more of the standard headings are not required, because there are no items to be disclosed in either the current or previous year, this may give rise to a potential problem over the heading given to sub-totalled items. For instance, if there is no taxation charge, the sub-total for the profit or loss for the year before taxation will be the same as that for the profit or loss for the year after taxation, and the question arises whether there is any need to disclose both headings. In most cases it is usually simplest to combine the headings.

Example 8.1 – Combining headings

	2002	*2001*
	£'000	*£'000*
Operating profit	675	581
Interest payable	(14)	10)
Profit on ordinary activities before and after taxation	661	571

Similarly, where there are no extraordinary items (and these are now very rare under the requirements of FRS 3 'Reporting Financial Performance') the profit and loss on ordinary activities after taxation will usually be the same as the profit or loss for the financial year and it is usually simplest to combine the headings.

Example 8.2 – Combining headings where there are no extraordinary items

	2002	*2001*
	£'000	*£000*
Profit on ordinary activities before taxation	844	975
Tax on profit on ordinary activities	(250)	(311)
Profit on ordinary activities after taxation and for the financial year	594	664

Comparative figures

8.9 Comparative figures must be given for each item in the profit and loss account. If any item appeared in the previous year but does not appear in the current year, the heading and comparative amount must still be shown in the profit and loss account. Comparative amounts are considered in more detail in **Chapter 5**.

Additional disclosures

8.10 In addition to the items set out in the standard formats, the legislation requires every profit and loss account to show:

— the profit or loss on ordinary activities before taxation;

— the aggregate amount of any dividends paid and proposed;

— the aggregate amount of any proposed dividends, if this is not disclosed in the notes to the accounts;

— any amount transferred, or proposed to be transferred, from the profit and loss account to reserves;

— any amount transferred, or proposed to be transferred, from reserves to the profit and loss account.

The profit and loss account formats also include notes which require additional information or analyses to be given for certain items. These details are usually given in the notes to the accounts, although they may be given on the face of the profit and loss account if this is considered necessary or helpful. Where appropriate these are discussed in the following chapters.

CONTINUING, DISCONTINUED AND ACQUIRED OPERATIONS

Operating profit

8.11 FRS 3 'Reporting Financial Performance' requires each item from turnover through to operating profit to be analysed into amounts relating to continuing, discontinued and newly-acquired operations. The heading 'operating profit' does not appear in the standard formats and is not a term that is used or defined in CA 1985. The standard states that for most companies, operating profit (or loss) will usually be the profit or loss before income from shares in group companies. In the case of Formats 1 and 2 therefore (the most common formats for the profit and loss account), operating profit will usually appear in the following place:

— in Format 1, between 'Other operating income' and 'Income from shares in group undertakings'; and

— in Format 2, between 'Other operating charges' and 'Income from shares in group undertakings'.

As a result of the introduction of this new heading, the reported operating profit or loss has become a key feature of accounts. Before FRS 3, many of the presentation debates centred around whether an individual charge or credit was extraordinary or not. FRS 3 has virtually removed extraordinary items from accounts but to some extent the debate has now transferred to the operating profit heading, the main issue usually being whether a particular charge or credit should be reflected within or below operating profit in the profit and loss account. It is also important to recognise that executive bonus schemes may be related to the operating profit shown in the accounts and the decision on whether a particular charge or credit is taken before or after operating profit may consequently increase or reduce the base figure for bonus payments.

Classification of discontinued operations

8.12 FRS 3 sets out a lengthy definition of discontinued operations. All of the following conditions must be met if an operation is to be classified and disclosed as a discontinued operation under the standard:

- the sale or termination must be completed in the accounting period or before the earlier of:
  - three months after the beginning of the next accounting period, and
  - the date on which the accounts are approved by the directors;
- if the discontinuation is a termination, the former activities must have ceased permanently;
- the sale or termination must have:
  - a material effect on the nature and focus of the reporting entity's operations, and
  - represent a material reduction in its operating facilities, resulting either from withdrawal from a particular market or from a material reduction in turnover in the continuing markets;
- the assets, liabilities, results of operations and activities must be clearly distinguishable - physically, operationally and for financial reporting purposes.

Any operation that is sold or terminated during the year but which does not meet all of these conditions must be classified under continuing operations for financial reporting purposes. The definition of discontinued operations under FRS 3 is therefore quite restrictive and it is clearly intended that only sales and terminations of very significant activities should be reported separately. It is unlikely that many companies will need to disclose information on discontinued operations on a regular basis.

Completion of sale

8.13 No guidance is given in the standard on what constitutes 'completion' in the case of a sale. FRS 2 'Accounting for Subsidiary Undertakings' provides some guidance in the context of changes in group membership and states that: 'The date for accounting for an undertaking ceasing to be a subsidiary undertaking is the date on which its former parent undertaking relinquishes control over that undertaking'. Control is defined as 'the ability of an undertaking to direct the financial and operating policies of another undertaking with a view to gaining economic benefit from its activities'. These sections of FRS 2 can be used as a benchmark for assessing when the sale of an operation has been completed. In straightforward cases, completion will usually be identified with a binding, unconditional contract or the date when consideration actually passes between the parties. However, the terms of a particular contract can be complex and the circumstances of each case must therefore be assessed individually.

Completion of termination

8.14 Where former activities are terminated rather than sold, FRS 3 does provide some guidance on what constitutes completion, by stating that the former activities must have ceased permanently. However, this can also give rise to problems – for instance:

- what is the position if the company is still completing contracts already in progress but is not taking on new work?
- what is the position if the company has completed all contracts and therefore has no ongoing work in this field, but is still committed to warranty or maintenance work under previous contracts?

Once again, each case must be assessed individually and the materiality of any ongoing activities should be taken into account. For instance, in the first example quoted above, it will usually be difficult to argue that operations have ceased permanently if there is a substantial level of activity on the remaining contracts, even though new work is not being accepted. In the second example, the decision may rest on the level of work normally required under warranties or maintenance agreements. If experience has shown that this is minimal, it may be acceptable to say that the operations have to all intents and purposes ceased permanently.

Deadline for completion of sale or termination

8.15 In order to be treated as a discontinued operation in the current year's accounts, the sale or termination must either:

- be completed during the accounting period; or
- be completed by the earlier of:
  - three months from the beginning of the next accounting period, and
  - the date of approval of the accounts.

Example 8.3 – Where date of approval is used

A Ltd prepares its accounts to 31 December each year. The accounts for the year to 31 December 2001 are approved by the board of directors on 27 February 2002. Therefore, if any operations are to be classified as discontinued operations, the sale or termination must have been completed by 27 February 2002 at the latest (i.e. the date of approval of the accounts).

Example 8.4 – Where three months from the beginning of the next accounting period is used

A Ltd prepares its accounts to 31 December each year. The accounts for the year to 31 December 2001 are approved by the board of directors on 24 April 2002. Therefore, if any operations are to be classified as discontinued operations, the sale or termination must have been completed by 31 March 2002 at the latest (i.e. within three months of the start of the next financial year).

Operational effect of a discontinuation

8.16 In order to meet the conditions for a discontinued operation, a sale or termination must:

- have a material effect on the nature and focus of the entity's operations; and
- represent a material reduction in its operating facilities, resulting from:
  - withdrawal from a particular market, or
  - a material reduction in turnover in the continuing markets.

Paragraph 42 of FRS 3 explains that the nature and focus of an entity's operations refers to the positioning of the entity's products or services in the market place and that this includes both quality and location. The standard quotes various examples within the hotel industry to illustrate this.

- If a hotel company operating in the lower end of the general hotel market sells its existing hotels and replaces them with a number of luxury hotels, it will change the nature and focus of its business, even though it will still be operating in the hotel business.
- The same would apply if the company was initially operating hotels in America and decided to sell these and replace them with a chain of hotels in Europe. The nature and focus of the company's operations would change as a result of the completely new geographical location.
- However, the regular sale of individual hotels and their replacement with other hotels in similar markets and locations (i.e. routine changes to a portfolio of properties) would not constitute a change in the nature and focus of the operations.

Material effect on turnover

8.17 The sale or termination must also have a material effect on the company's operating facilities and overall turnover in order to meet the definition of a discontinued operation. It must therefore result in either:

- withdrawal from a particular market – this can be either a class of business or a geographical market; or
- a material reduction of turnover in a market in which the company is continuing to operate.

The explanatory material in FRS 3 goes further than this and emphasises that the reduction in turnover must be the result of a strategic decision by the company either to withdraw from a particular market or to significantly reduce its presence in a continuing market. Therefore, where a strategic decision to improve productivity or reduce costs in one part of the business results, in turn, in the withdrawal from a different market or a reduction in turnover, the latter will not usually meet the conditions set out in the standard for a discontinuation of operations. Any costs resulting from these decisions would therefore be included in the results of continuing operations. The following examples illustrate how this part of the standard might apply in practice.

- A company manufactures the same products in two factories, one in England and one in Wales. Management decide to close the site in England and transfer all production to the newer factory in Wales. By working additional shifts and improving efficiency, they expect to be able to match the present output levels from both factories. The closure of the factory in England will not be classified as a discontinued operation because there has not been any termination of activities. Production levels (and therefore, presumably, turnover) will be unaffected and the company will continue to produce and sell the same number of items to the same customers.
- A company manufactures two completely separate products in two factories, one in England and one in Wales. Demand for the product made in England is falling and management decide to sell the factory. By introducing new plant, working additional shifts and improving efficiency at the factory in Wales, they expect to be able to increase both output and profitability at this site. Products from the factory in England previously represented approximately 25% of the company's turnover. Provided that the other conditions in FRS 3 are also met, the closure of the factory in England will be classified as a discontinued operation, on the basis that:
  - the company has taken a strategic decision to withdraw from a particular market (i.e. the remaining factory has a different product and a different market);
  - products from the factory in England previously contributed 25% of the company's turnover; and
  - the focus of the business will in future be concentrated on one product and one operational unit.

However, decisions on these issues will always be subjective to some degree, and there will be many cases where there is no obviously right or wrong answer.

Separate identification of operation

8.18 The final condition for a discontinued operation is that all of the following must be separately identifiable:

- assets;
- liabilities;
- results of operations;
- activities.

In addition, the clear distinction must apply physically, operationally and for financial reporting purposes. The explanatory material in the standard emphasises that if the assets, liabilities or results of an operation can only be identified by making allocations of material items of income and expenditure in the accounting records, the condition will not be met. Therefore if significant expenses are incurred by the company as a whole and have to be apportioned in some way between the company's various activities in order to establish the individual results of each operation, the operations are not considered to be clearly distinguishable for financial reporting purposes under FRS 3.

Consideration individually or in aggregate?

8.19 One aspect of FRS 3 that is not clear is whether sales and terminations that might potentially be classified as discontinued operations should be considered individually or in aggregate. Individual consideration appears to be more in keeping with the spirit of the standard, unless the sales and terminations effectively form part of one overall transaction. An individual approach may result in a company being involved in a number of smaller sales and terminations, none of which qualify as discontinued operations, but which taken together are significant to the company as a whole. In this situation, it may be necessary to disclose details of these sales and terminations in a note to the accounts, even though they must be included under continuing operations for financial reporting purposes.

Disclosure of continuing, discontinued and acquired activities

8.20 FRS 3 requires each of the standard profit and loss account headings from turnover to operating profit to be analysed into:

- amounts relating to discontinued operations;
- amounts relating to continuing operations, which must be further analysed to show amounts relating to:
  - acquired operations,
  - other continuing operations.

As a minimum, turnover and operating profit for the current year must be analysed in this way on the face of the profit and loss account. The analysis of the other figures and of the comparatives may be given in the notes to the accounts. The purpose of a detailed analysis of results is to enable a user of the accounts to assess the financial performance of various aspects of entity's activities and to provide a more realistic basis for an assessment of future income and results. It also enables a user of the accounts to distinguish organic growth from acquisitive growth. Where an acquisition, sale or termination has a material impact on a major segment of the business, FRS 3 requires this fact to be disclosed and explained in the accounts.

Columnar format

8.21 Companies are free to choose any disclosure format that meets the requirements of the standard, but whatever format is chosen should be used consistently. The appendix to FRS 3 includes illustrative examples setting out how the disclosure requirements might be met and most companies have followed these. The most straightforward presentation is a columnar format across the page with headings for the required categories.

Example 8.5 – Columnar disclosure

	Continuing operations	*Acquisitions*	*Discontinued operations*	*Total 200X*	*Total 200Y*
	£'000	*£'000*	*£'000*	*£'000*	*£'000*
Turnover	5,672	784	591	7,047	6,434
Cost of sales	(3,982)	(660)	(503)	(5,145)	(4,876)
	1,690	124	88	1,902	1,558
Distribution costs	(978)	(58)	(61)	(1,097)	(994)
Administrative expenses	(531)	(21)	(29)	(581)	(476)
	181	45	(2)	224	88
Other operating income	53	20	—	73	42
Operating profit	234	65	(2)	297	130

Where this format is used, the analysis of the comparative figures is usually given in the notes to the accounts.

Alternative presentation

8.22 Although the layout used in **8.21** above is perhaps the clearest presentation from the reader's point of view, it can be difficult to present all the necessary columns on one page and the concentration of figures can sometimes mask the key features. An alternative presentation adopted by a number of companies is to give a sub-analysis under the statutory heading, with only the total being shown in the profit and loss account itself. This can be a useful format where only the minimum disclosure is given on the face of the profit (i.e. the analysis of current year turnover and operating profit).

Example 8.6 – Disclosure under statutory headings

	200X	200X	200Y
	£'000	£'000	£'000
Turnover:			
Continuing operations	5,672		6,434
Acquisitions	784		
	6,456		
Discontinued operations	591		–
		7,047	6,434
Cost of sales		(5,145)	(4,876)
		1,902	1,558
Distribution costs		(1,097)	(994)
Administrative expenses		(581)	(476)
		224	88
Other operating income		73	42
Operating profit:			
Continuing operations	234		
Acquisitions	65		
	299		
Discontinued operations	(2)		
		297	130

The analysis of other headings and the comparatives must be given in the notes to the accounts. Where acquisitions are comparatively small, a further possibility is to include headings for continuing and discontinued operations only, and to disclose the details for acquisitions as part of the heading for continuing operations.

Example 8.7 – Acquisitions disclosed under continuing operations

	200X	200X	200Y
	£'000	£'000	£'000
Turnover:			
Continuing operations (acquisitions 784,000)	6,456		
Discontinued operations	591		
		7,047	6,434
Cost of sales		(5,145)	(4,876)
		1,902	1,558

Distribution costs		(1,097)	(994)
Administrative expenses		(581)	(476)
		224	88
Other operating income		73	42
Operating profit:			
Continuing operations (acquisitions 65,000)	234		
Discontinued operations	(2)		
		297	130

No discontinued operations or acquisitions during the year

8.23 If a company has no material acquisitions and no discontinued operations during the year, there is no formal requirement to state that all the turnover and results relate to continuing operations. However, it is helpful to include a footnote to the profit and loss account or a note to the accounts to clarify this point.

Disclosures in respect of acquisitions

8.24 The standard recognises that it may not always be possible to identify the relevant figures in respect of acquisitions. For instance, an operation may be acquired with the intention that it should be fully integrated with an existing part of the company. Where the post-acquisition results cannot be separately identified, the standard requires the accounts to give an indication of the amount that the acquisition has contributed to turnover and operating profit. If such an indication cannot be given, the accounts must state this fact and explain the reason why the information cannot be provided. Where operations are acquired towards the end of the accounting period, the full impact will not be apparent until the following accounting period. FRS 3 therefore notes that in some circumstances it may be helpful to give separate disclosure of the results of acquired operations for their first full year as part of the reporting entity as well as in the year of acquisition.

Disclosures in respect of discontinued operations

8.25 The column or heading for discontinued operations should only include income and costs relating directly to the operation that has been discontinued. Where, as a result of the sale or termination of an operation, other parts of the business are reorganised or restructured, the costs relating to this must be included under the heading of continuing operations. Where the discontinued operation is sold or terminated in the early part of the following accounting period (as permitted under the standard), the discontinued column or heading in the accounts for the current year must only include the results of the discontinued operation up to the balance sheet date. The results of any trading in the early part of the following accounting period (i.e. up to the date of sale or termination) must be included in the accounts for that year, and may need to be shown separately as discontinued operations if the figures are material.

Sale or termination not yet completed

8.26 Where a sale or termination is in progress but has not been completed within the financial year or the early part of the following accounting period (as defined in the standard), the results of the operation must be included under continuing operations. However, the standard recognises that in some cases, it may be appropriate to provide additional information in the notes to the accounts on operations that are in the process of being discontinued. In these circumstances, it is likely that the sale or termination will meet the conditions for a discontinued operation in the following year, in which case it will be disclosed as such in the accounts for that year under the requirements of FRS 3.

Additional analysis of interest and tax

8.27 The standard only requires analysis of profit and loss account headings from turnover to operating profit. Analysis of the other headings is not encouraged in view of the fact that this will usually involve a high degree of subjectivity, which might cast doubt on the reliability of the figures. If a company chooses to provide additional analyses of the figures for interest and tax, the standard requires the method of allocation and the underlying assumptions to be disclosed in the accounts.

Comparative figures

8.28 Comparative figures must be given for all the disclosures required under FRS 3. However, in the case of the profit and loss account, the comparative figures for continuing operations must reflect only the results of the operations that are still classified as continuing in the current year. The comparative figures will therefore not necessarily be the same as those disclosed in the previous year's accounts. Where discontinued operations are disclosed in the accounts for the current year, the comparative figures will need to be restated to move the results of those activities from continuing to discontinued operations in the previous year. The comparative figures for discontinued operations will therefore comprise:

— the previous year's results of any operations classified as discontinued operations in the previous year; and

— the previous year's results for any operations classified as discontinued activities in the current year.

Example 8.8 – Comparatives for continuing and discontinued operations

A Ltd's accounts for 2001 showed the following analysis for turnover.

		£
Turnover:	Continuing operations	506,100
	Discontinued operations	124,732
		630,832

During 2002 it has discontinued a further operation, which contributed £98,750 to turnover in 2001. In the 2002 accounts, the comparative figure for turnover will therefore need to be restated as follows.

		£
Turnover:	Continuing operations (a)	407,350
	Discontinued operations (b)	223,482
		630,832

(a) £506,100 – £98,750

(b) £124,732 + £98,750

Where this is done the headings to the profit and loss account and the relevant notes to the accounts should indicate that the figures have been restated. There is no requirement to analyse the comparative figures for discontinued activities into those discontinued in the previous year and those discontinued in the current year, although in some circumstances this may be helpful.

ADDITIONAL FORMAT HEADINGS

Requirements of FRS 3 'Reporting Financial Performance'

8.29 FRS 3 introduced three additional headings, to be shown in the profit and loss account after operating profit and before interest:

- profits and losses on the sale or termination of an operation;
- costs of a fundamental reorganisation or restructuring that has a material effect on the nature and focus of the entity's operations;
- profits and losses on the disposal of fixed assets (other than marginal adjustments to depreciation previously charged).

These headings must be used whenever any of the items arise in the current year or in the previous year. There was initially some confusion over whether the headings were only intended to be used for items that met the definition of exceptional items (caused mainly by the fact that the introduction of the headings is covered in the section of FRS 3 headed 'Exceptional items'). However, it is now clear that the headings should be used whenever there are material items to be disclosed in these categories, regardless of whether the items would be classified as exceptional under the definition in FRS 3 (see **8.35** below). The disclosures should cover both actual income and costs during the year, and any provisions in respect of these categories (see **Chapter 29**). Although the headings come below operating profit in the profit and loss account, FRS 3 specifically requires any items disclosed under these headings to be classified as relating to continuing or discontinued operations (see **8.11–8.28** above).

Profits or losses on the sale or termination of an operation

8.30 This disclosure covers all sales and terminations during the year, not just those that are classified as discontinued operations for accounting purposes. It is therefore quite possible for the total figure in this category to be analysed partly to continuing operations and partly to discontinued operations. FRS 3 also sets out specific rules on the timing and content of provisions in respect of a decision to sell or terminate an operation. These rules are considered in **Chapter 29**.

Costs of a fundamental reorganisation or restructuring

8.31 A fundamental reorganisation or restructuring is defined as one which has a material effect on the nature and focus of the entity's operations, but this is not considered further in either the standard or the explanation. However, the phrase 'nature and focus of the entity's operation' is considered in the context of discontinued operations. In practice it is unlikely that many reorganisations will meet this definition and most reorganisation and restructuring costs should therefore be included in arriving at the operating profit or loss for the year. They should be disclosed as exceptional items if they meet the necessary criteria.

Profits and losses on the disposal of fixed assets

8.32 Significant profits and losses on the sale or other disposal of fixed assets should normally be disclosed under this heading. The standard specifies that marginal adjustments to depreciation charged in previous years should not be reported under this heading. Such adjustments should be included as part of the depreciation charge in arriving at the operating profit or loss for the year. The calculation of profits and losses on the disposal of fixed assets under FRS 3 is covered in **Chapter 12**.

Additional disclosure requirements

8.33 The standard also requires disclosure of the tax effect of the items appearing under these additional profit and loss account headings. Further details are given in Chapter 14. Where the net profit or loss on the sale or termination of operations or the disposal of fixed assets is small, but the gross profits and losses making up that figure are material, the standard requires the heading to appear on the face of the profit and loss account with a cross reference to a note to the accounts analysing the relevant profits and losses.

FRS 17 'Retirement Benefits'

8.34 FRS 17 'Retirement Benefits' was published in November 2000 and is fully effective for accounting periods beginning on or after 1 January 2005, although earlier adoption is encouraged. In the case of defined benefit retirement schemes, the standard requires interest cost and the expected return on assets to be presented as a separate item (other finance costs) adjacent to interest in the standard profit and loss account formats. The standard also amends FRS 12 'Provisions, Contingent Liabilities and Contingent Assets' to require the unwinding of any discount in respect of provisions to be included under the same heading.

DISCLOSURE OF EXCEPTIONAL ITEMS

Definition of exceptional

8.35 The tightening of the definitions of ordinary activities and extraordinary items under FRS 3 reduced significantly the number of items disclosed as extraordinary in annual accounts. The converse effect is that many of the items that might once have been classified as extraordinary are now disclosable as exceptional items. FRS 3 includes the following definition of exceptional items.

> 'Material items which derive from events or transactions that fall within the ordinary activities of the reporting entity and which individually or, if of a similar type, in aggregate, need to be disclosed by virtue of their size or incidence if the financial statements are to give a true and fair view.'

Exceptional items are a normal part of business activities and most companies will need to disclose an exceptional charge or credit to the profit and loss account at some point. Depending on the circumstances, exceptional items might include:

- a large bad debt;
- a significant charge to the profit and loss account for redundancy costs;
- the write-down of a fixed asset by a significant amount to recognise a permanent diminution in its value;
- reorganisation costs that do not meet the FRS 3 definition of a fundamental reorganisation.

Presentation of exceptional items

8.36 FRS 3 introduced a significant change to the way in which exceptional items are reported in the accounts. Previously it had become common practice to disclose exceptional items as a separate line within the profit and loss account. Under FRS 3, exceptional items must be included under the statutory profit and loss account heading to which they relate. In most cases, additional detail should then be given in the notes to the accounts, either:

- individually for each exceptional item; or
- where there are a number of items of a similar type, in aggregate by type of exceptional item.

Where it is considered necessary for a true and fair view, exceptional items may be disclosed separately on the face of the profit and loss account but this must still be within the appropriate statutory heading.

Use of columnar format

8.37 Where an individual transaction gives rise to a number of exceptional charges or credits under different statutory headings, some companies have found it useful to present the detail in a columnar format.

Example 8.9 – Columnar disclosure of exceptional items

	Before exceptional items	*Exceptional items (Note xx)*	*Total*
	£'000	*£'000*	*£'000*
Turnover	6,705	—	6,705
Cost of sales	(3,916)	(785)	(4,701)
	2,789	(785)	2,004
Distribution costs	(564)	—	(564)
Administrative expenses	(344)	(213)	(557)
	1,881	(998)	883
Interest receivable	124	—	124
Profit/(loss) on ordinary activities before taxation	2,005	(998)	1,007
Taxation	(346)	145	(201)
Profit on ordinary activities after taxation	1,659	(853)	806

This presentation has the advantage of highlighting the overall effect of the exceptional items. However, the disadvantage is that it can become very complex where there are also details of discontinued and acquired operations to report. It will usually be most suitable where the materiality of the exceptional items requires them to be given the prominence of appearing on the face of the profit and loss account. However there may be situations where a columnar layout in the notes to the accounts could also be useful to indicate the overall impact of an exceptional item on the accounts.

Continuing and discontinued operations

8.38 FRS 3 requires exceptional items to be allocated between continuing and discontinued operations in the same way as any other charge or credit to the profit and loss account. Two items of a similar type should therefore not be combined for disclosure purposes if individually they relate to continuing and to discontinued operations.

DISCLOSURE OF EXTRAORDINARY ITEMS

CA 1985 requirements

8.39 Each of the four standard Formats for the profit and loss account requires separate disclosure of:

— extraordinary income;

— extraordinary charges; and

— tax on extraordinary profit or loss.

In addition, Formats 1 and 2 require disclosure of the extraordinary profit or loss for the year. CA 1985 Sch 4 para 57(2) requires particulars to be given of any extraordinary income or of charges arising in the year. The details can be disclosed on the face of the profit and loss account or in the notes to the accounts. It is normal practice for companies to show the net effect in the profit and loss account under the heading 'Extraordinary items' and disclose the detailed analysis in the notes to the accounts.

Classification of income or expenditure as extraordinary

8.40 Whether a particular item of income or expenditure is extraordinary to an individual company will be a matter of judgement and will depend to a large extent on the nature of the company's activities. CA 1985 does not provide any guidance on what constitutes extraordinary income or expenditure. Extraordinary items are defined in FRS 3 as:

> 'Material items possessing a high degree of abnormality which arise from events or transactions that fall outside the ordinary activities of the reporting entity and which are not expected to recur. They do not include exceptional items nor do they include prior period items merely because they relate to a prior period.'

To appreciate the full impact of this, the FRS 3 definition of ordinary activities must also be considered.

> 'Any activities which are undertaken by a reporting entity as part of its business and such related activities in which the reporting entity engages in furtherance of, incidental to, or arising from, these activities. Ordinary activities include the effects on the reporting entity of any event in the various environments in which it operates, including the political, regulatory, economic and geographical environments, irrespective of the frequency or unusual nature of the event.'

The definition of ordinary activities given in FRS 3 is therefore very broad, and items that were previously classified as extraordinary under its predecessor standard (SSAP 6) are unlikely to meet the definition in the present standard. Extraordinary items now appear only rarely, if at all. In view of the expected rarity of extraordinary items under these requirements, FRS 3 does not give any examples of items that might fall within the definition.

Suggested disclosure

8.41 FRS 3 requires any extraordinary profit or loss to be shown separately on the face of the profit and loss account, below the profit or loss on ordinary activities after taxation and before any appropriation for dividends. In effect, this is the same as the disclosure required by CA 1985. The standard also requires each extraordinary item to be shown separately, either on the face of the profit and loss account or in the notes to the accounts, with a description that enables its nature to be understood. The tax on any extraordinary profit or loss must be shown separately as part of the extraordinary item, either on the face of the profit and loss account or in the notes to the accounts. If the tax on extraordinary items requires adjustment in subsequent years, the adjustment must be disclosed as an extraordinary item in the year in which it is reflected in the accounts. If, in rare circumstances, it is considered necessary to disclose one or more items of income or expenditure as extraordinary, the following layout would meet the requirements of FRS 3:

Example 8.10 – Disclosure of extraordinary items

	200X	*200X*	*200Y*
	£	£	£
Extraordinary income:			
Full description of item a		x	—
Full description of item b		x	—
		x	
Extraordinary expenditure:			
Full description of item c	x		

	200X	*200X*	*200Y*
	£	£	£
Full description of item d	x		
		(x)	–
Extraordinary profit before taxation		x	—
Tax on extraordinary profit		(x)	—
Extraordinary profit after taxation		x	—

LIKELY FUTURE DEVELOPMENTS

FRED 22 'Review of FRS 3: Reporting Financial Performance'

8.42 The ASB published FRED 22 'Revision of FRS 3: Reporting Financial Performance' in December 2000. The exposure draft puts forward some significant changes to current reporting and disclosure requirements and is based on the ASB Discussion Paper 'Reporting Financial Performance: Proposals for Change' published in June 1999. The proposals reflect an agreed international approach to reporting financial performance and the ASB considers them to be a natural progression from the requirements of the present FRS 3, which was a ground-breaking standard when it was introduced in 1992. Under the proposals, the profit and loss account and statement of total recognised gains and losses would be replaced with a single performance statement showing all gains and losses recognised during the reporting period and relating to that period. The format of the proposed performance statement mirrors more closely that of the cash flow statement, and the ASB hopes that this will help users of the accounts to understand the cashflow effects of items shown in the performance statement. In its White Paper 'Modernising Company Law' issued in July 2002, the Government supports the view that the profit and loss account should become a wider performance statement reporting all gains and losses, and notes that current moves to modernise EC Directives include similar proposals. The proposals are now being taken forward as a joint ASB/IASB project and a further exposure draft is expected in the middle of 2003.

Structure of financial performance statement

8.43 The performance statement proposed in FRED 22 is divided into three sections:

- operating;
- financing and treasury; and
- other gains and losses.

An Appendix to the FRED sets out an illustrative example, together with some of the suggested supporting notes. Most gains and losses will be shown in the operating section and this at least will continue to be analysed between acquisitions, continuing operations and discontinuing operations. Only items specified in the revised FRS 3, or in other accounting standards and UITF Abstracts, will be reported in the other two sections of the statement. Where a choice of section is permitted, any plans to change the section in which particular gains and losses are reported should be considered in accordance with the requirements of FRS 18 'Accounting Policies' relating to a change in accounting policy. However, the project to develop a single statement of financial performance is now being influenced by the need for increased convergence with international accounting standards. In the April 2002 edition of its 'Inside Track' newsletter, the ASB reported that a number of possible formats for the performance statement, including that proposed in FRED 22, were currently under consideration. Pensions accounting, and in particular the treatment of actuarial gains and losses in the performance statement, is proving a particularly difficult issue and problems are also being encountered as a result of the varied accounting treatments adopted for fixed assets (especially revalued assets) and depreciation in national accounting regimes.

Financing and treasury section

8.44 The following gains and losses would be recognised in the financing and treasury section of the performance statement:

- interest payable and receivable;
- the unwinding of the discount on long-term items;
- income from investments held as part of treasury activities;
- gains and losses arising on the repurchase or early settlement of debt; and
- any other gains and losses identified for inclusion by other accounting standards or UITF Abstracts.

The total for each of the above headings should be disclosed in the notes to the accounts if the details are not shown separately on the face of the performance statement.

Other gains and losses section

8.45 The following gains and losses would be recognised in the other gains and losses section of the performance statement:

- revaluation gains and losses on fixed assets;
- gains and losses on the disposal of properties in continuing operations;

— actuarial gains and losses arising on defined benefit schemes;

— profits and losses on disposal of discontinuing operations;

— exchange translation differences on foreign currency net investments;

— revaluation gains and losses on investment properties;

— amounts previously recognised in respect of warrants that have lapsed unexercised; and

— any other gains and losses identified for inclusion by other accounting standards or UITF Abstracts.

The total for each of the above headings should be disclosed in the notes to the accounts if the details are not shown separately on the face of the performance statement.

Continuing operations, discontinuing operations and acquisitions

8.46 The aggregate results for each of continuing operations, acquisitions and discontinuing operations should be shown separately for the results of the operating section of the performance statement. The same information should be shown for the other two sections of the statement unless it is impracticable to do so or the resulting information would be misleading. As a minimum, turnover and operating profit must be analysed in this way on the face of the performance statement. The analysis of other items may be given in the notes to the accounts. In the case of financing and treasury items, and other gains and losses, the underlying assumptions used in making any allocations between the categories should be disclosed. The post-acquisition results for the period in which an acquisition occurs should also be disclosed. Where this is impracticable, the financial statements should give an indication of the contribution to turnover and operating profit. If this information cannot be given, that fact and the reasons should be explained.

Discontinuing operations

8.47 The following details should be disclosed for a discontinuing operation in the financial statements in which the initial disclosure event occurs (both discontinuing operation and initial disclosure event are defined in the FRED):

— description of the discontinuing operation;

— business or geographical segment in which it is reported;

— date and nature of the initial disclosure event;

— date or period in which discontinuance is expected to be completed (if known or determinable);

— carrying amounts at the balance sheet date of the total assets and liabilities to be disposed of;

— results of the discontinuing operations for the period;

— amounts of net cash flows attributable to the operating activities of the discontinuing operation in the current reporting period.

If an initial disclosure event occurs after the balance sheet date but before the date of approval of the financial statements, the above disclosures should be given for the period covered by the financial statements. Additional disclosures are required in respect of the disposal of assets and liabilities relating to a discontinuing operation. All disclosures should continue to be given for periods up to and including the period in which the discontinuance is completed.

Prohibition on recycling

8.48 The recycling of gains and losses between the different sections will be prohibited – in other words, once a gain or loss has been shown in one section of the statement, it cannot be shown again in a different section in a future period.

Offsetting

8.49 No change is proposed to the present requirement that gains and losses should generally not be offset when presenting information on financial performance unless:

— they relate to the same event or circumstance; or

— disclosing the gross components is unlikely to be useful in assessing either future results or the effects of past transactions and events.

Taxation

8.50 Two figures will be given for taxation on the face of the performance statement – one for tax attributable to the operating and financing sections (to be shown after the statutory heading 'Profit on ordinary activities before taxation') and one for tax attributable to other gains and losses (to be shown within that section of the performance statement). Any special circumstances that affect the overall tax charge or credit for the reporting period, or that will affect those of future periods, should be disclosed. An optional note is also suggested to show the unusual tax implications of certain gains and losses.

Dividends

8.51 Dividends will not be reported in the performance statement as they represent transactions with owners rather than elements of financial performance. However, the FRED proposes they should be shown as a memorandum item at the foot of the statement. UK companies' legislation currently requires dividends to be reported in the profit and loss account and the ASB is therefore discussing with the DTI the possibility of changing the law.

Earnings per share

8.52 The FRED also proposes that earnings per share is shown as a memorandum item at the foot of the performance statement and reinforces the requirements of FRS 14 'Earnings per Share' on consistency of disclosure where alternative versions are given in addition to the basic earnings per share calculated in accordance with the standard. The ASB has subsequently published FRED 26 'Earnings per share' which proposes the replacement of FRS 14 with a new standard based on a proposed revision of IAS 33 'Earnings per share'. As with FRS 14, the standard will apply only to entities:

- whose ordinary shares or potential ordinary shares are publicly traded;
- who are in the process of issuing ordinary shares or potential ordinary shares in public securities markets; or
- who voluntarily disclose earnings per share (this is rare in practice).

Prior period adjustments

8.53 Prior period adjustments will continue to be accounted for by restating the comparative figures for the preceding period in the primary statements and the supporting notes, and adjusting the opening balance of reserves for the cumulative effect. The FRED also proposes that the cumulative gain or loss arising from a prior period adjustment should be shown as a memorandum item at the foot of the performance statement. The correction of fundamental errors will continue to be accounted for by means of a prior period adjustment.

Notes to the accounts

8.54 The proposals specify comprehensive notes to accompany the performance statement, including a reserves note and a table of exceptional items reported over the last five years. The note of historical cost profits and losses (currently required by FRS 3) becomes an optional disclosure.

Ownership interests

8.55 A reconciliation of ownership interests must be given as a primary statement. This brings together the performance for the period and all other changes in ownership interests, including dividends paid and new capital contributed. It is very similar to the reconciliation of shareholders' funds currently required by FRS 3.

Investment properties

8.56 SSAP 19 'Accounting for Investment Properties' requires changes in the market value of investment properties to be taken to the statement of total recognised gains and losses. FRED 22 follows this approach by requiring them to be reported in the 'Other gains and losses' section of the performance statement, but notes that it may be more logical for such gains and losses to be shown as operating items. The ASB is therefore considering whether SSAP 19 should be revised.

Specialised sectors

8.57 The FRED considers separately how the single performance statement might be adapted for specialised entities such as banking, insurance and investment companies' and notes that the ASB expects these and other sectors to develop the basic format where necessary through relevant Statements of Recommended Practice (SORPs). There are also specific requirements in the FRED for banking companies and groups, insurance companies and groups and investment companies.

Comparatives

8.58 Comparative figures should be given for all items in the primary statements and the notes required by the draft standard. The comparative figures for the continuing category should include only the results of operations that are included in the current period's continuing operations. Where financial statements show a discontinuing operation, the comparatives for preceding periods should be restated to segregate continuing and discontinuing assets, liabilities, income, expenses and cash flows. If a new accounting standard is issued on the basis of the exposure draft, comparative figures in the financial statements for the period in which the new standard is implemented will need to be restated to comply with the new formats and presentational requirements.

Impact on other standards

8.59 The exposure draft includes a substantial number of proposed amendments to other accounting standards and UITF Abstracts to bring these into line with the new requirements. The main changes are:

— references to the profit and loss account are to be read as references to the statement of financial performance;

— where an accounting standard or UITF Abstract requires a gain, loss, revenue or expense to be recognised in the profit and loss account, it should generally be reported in the operating section of the performance statement;

— where an accounting standard or UITF Abstract requires a gain, loss, revenue or expense to be recognised in the statement of total recognised gains and losses, it should generally be reported in the other gains and losses section of the performance statement;

- references to the reconciliation of shareholders' funds are generally to be replaced by reference to the reconciliation of ownership interests.

Appendix

PROFIT AND LOSS ACCOUNT: FORMAT 1

1. Turnover.
2. Cost of sales.
3. Gross profit or loss.
4. Distribution costs.
5. Administrative expenses.
6. Other operating income.
7. Income from shares in group undertakings.
8. Income from participating interests.
9. Income from other fixed asset investments.
10. Other interest receivable and similar income.
11. Amounts written off investments.
12. Interest payable and similar charges.
13. Tax on profit or loss on ordinary activities.
14. Profit or loss on ordinary activities after taxation.
15. Extraordinary income.
16. Extraordinary charges.
17. Extraordinary profit or loss.
18. Tax on extraordinary profit or loss.
19. Other taxes not shown under the above items.
20. Profit or loss for the financial year.

PROFIT AND LOSS ACCOUNT: FORMAT 2

1. Turnover.
2. Change in stocks of finished goods and work in progress.
3. Own work capitalised.
4. Other operating income.
5.
   (a) Raw materials and consumables.
   (b) Other external charges.
6. Staff costs:
   (a) wages and salaries,
   (b) social security costs,
   (c) other pension costs.

7.

(a) Depreciation and other amounts written off tangible and intangible fixed assets.

(b) Exceptional amounts written off current assets.

8. Other operating charges.
9. Income from shares in group undertakings.
10. Income from participating interests.
11. Income from other fixed asset investments.
12. Other interest receivable and similar income.
13. Amounts written off investments.
14. Interest payable and similar charges.
15. Tax on profit or loss on ordinary activities.
16. Profit or loss on ordinary activities after taxation.
17. Extraordinary income.
18. Extraordinary charges.
19. Extraordinary profit or loss.
20. Tax on extraordinary profit or loss.
21. Other taxes not shown under the above items.
22. Profit or loss for the financial year.

PROFIT AND LOSS ACCOUNT: FORMAT 3

A. Charges

1. Cost of sales.
2. Distribution costs.
3. Administrative expenses.
4. Amounts written off investments.
5. Interest payable and similar charges.
6. Tax on profit or loss on ordinary activities.
7. Profit or loss on ordinary activities after taxation.
8. Extraordinary charges.
9. Tax on extraordinary profit or loss.
10. Other taxes not shown under the above items.
11. Profit or loss for the financial year.

B. Income

1. Turnover.
2. Other operating income.
3. Income from shares in group undertakings.
4. Income from participating interests.
5. Income from other fixed asset investments.
6. Other interest receivable and similar income.
7. Profit or loss on ordinary activities after taxation.
8. Extraordinary income.
9. Profit or loss for the financial year.

PROFIT AND LOSS ACCOUNT: FORMAT 4

A. Charges

1. Reduction in stocks of finished goods and work in progress.
2.
   (a) Raw materials and consumables.
   (b) Other external charges.
3. Staff costs:
   (a) wages and salaries,
   (b) social security costs,
   (c) other pension costs.
4.
   (a) Depreciation and other amounts written off tangible and intangible fixed assets.
   (b) Exceptional amounts written off current assets.
5. Other operating charges.
6. Amounts written off investments.
7. Interest payable and similar charges.
8. Tax on profit or loss on ordinary activities.
9. Profit or loss on ordinary activities after taxation.
10. Extraordinary charges.
11. Tax on extraordinary profit or loss.
12. Other taxes not shown under the above items.
13. Profit or loss for the financial year.

B. Income

1. Turnover.
2. Increase in stocks of finished goods and work in progress.
3. Own work capitalised.
4. Other operating income.
5. Income from shares in group undertakings.
6. Income from participating interests.
7. Income from other fixed asset investments.
8. Other interest receivable and similar income.
9. Profit or loss on ordinary activities after taxation.
10. Extraordinary income.
11. Profit or loss for the financial year.

Chapter 9

Turnover

SEGMENTAL ANALYSIS OF TURNOVER

CA 1985 requirements

9.1 If a company has carried on two or more classes of business during the year and, in the opinion of the directors, these classes of business differ substantially from one another, the accounts must include:

— a description of each class of business;

— the amount of turnover attributable to each class of business.

If a company has supplied different geographical markets during the year and, in the opinion of the directors, these markets differ substantially from each other, turnover must also be analysed by geographical market supplied. These requirements only apply in the case of material items. Therefore, where the amounts attributable to a particular class of business or geographical market are not material, they may be combined with the amounts relating to another class or market.

Requirements of SSAP 25 'Segmental reporting'

9.2 SSAP 25 reinforces the segmental disclosure requirements of CA 1985 and also contains additional disclosure requirements which apply to any entity that:

— is a public limited company or has a public limited company as a subsidiary;

— is a banking or insurance company or group (as defined in CA 1985); or;

— exceeds the criteria, multiplied in each case by ten, for defining a medium-sized company under CA 1985 s 247, as amended from time to time by statutory instrument (see **7.107**).

Subsidiary companies that are not public companies or banking or insurance companies are not required to comply with the additional disclosure requirements of SSAP 25 provided that the parent company gives appropriate segmental information in its own accounts, although the CA 1985 disclosure requirements continue to apply. SSAP 25 also requires disclosure of inter-segment sales and transfers where these are material.

Identification of classes of business and geographical markets

9.3 It is for the directors to decide whether the company has carried on different classes of business or supplied differing geographical markets during the year. CA 1985 does not provide any definitions or detailed guidance to assist directors in deciding when classes of business or geographical markets 'differ substantially', although it does require the directors to take account of the way in which the company's activities are organised. For instance, if the company operates through separate divisions, this might provide a suitable basis for the analysis by class of business. The explanatory notes to SSAP 25 do provide some useful guidance on these issues. They explain that the directors should bear in mind the overall purpose of providing segmental information. For instance, a reader or user of the accounts may need to know that the company is operating in business areas or geographical markets that are subject to different degrees of risk, have experienced different growth rates or have different future potential. SSAP 25 suggests that any business or geographical segment that represents 10% or more of total turnover should be regarded as significant and should therefore be treated as a 'reportable segment'.

Separate classes of business

9.4 SSAP 25 defines a separate class of business as a distinguishable part of an entity that provides:

- a separate product or service; or
- a separate group of related products or services.

As well as taking account of the manner in which the company's activities are organised, the directors should consider:

- the nature of the products or services;
- the nature of the production processes;
- the markets in which the products or services are sold;
- the distribution channels for the products;
- any separate legislative framework relating to part of the business.

Geographical segments

9.5 A geographical segment may be an individual country or a group of countries. SSAP 25 suggests that the following factors may be relevant in deciding on suitable reporting segments:

— differing economic climates;
— stable or unstable political regimes;
— exchange control regulations;
— exchange rate fluctuations.

CA 1985 requires turnover to be analysed by geographical market supplied. SSAP 25 also requires analysis by geographical origin (i.e. the area from which goods or services are supplied). If there is no material difference between the two, this can simply be stated in the accounts. A suitable geographical analysis for a company with major activities in the UK and Germany and a smaller level of activity elsewhere might be as follows:

Example 9.1 – Geographical analysis

	Turnover by origin	*Turnover by origin*	*Turnover by destination*	*Turnover by destination*
	2002	*2001*	*2002*	*2001*
United Kingdom				
Germany				
Rest of Europe				
Asia				
Rest of the world				

Redefining reporting segments

9.6 The general requirement for accounting information to be presented on a consistent basis year by year applies equally to segmental disclosure. SSAP 25 requires the directors to redefine the reporting segments where appropriate. This might be necessary where the company diversifies into new activities, acquires a new business or ceases part of its previous activities. If the definitions of segments are changed, the nature of the change should be disclosed in the accounts, with details of the reason for and the effect of the change, and comparative figures should be restated accordingly.

Exemption from segmental disclosure

9.7 If the directors are of the opinion that making the required segmental disclosures would be seriously prejudicial to the interests of the company, the information need not be given, but the fact that disclosure has not been made must be stated in the accounts. The reasons for non-disclosure do not have to be given. Neither the Act nor the standard provides further guidance on this point, but it is usually accepted that the exemption cannot be used simply to avoid disclosing information that competitors may find useful. It is only available when the segmental disclosure could potentially cause serious damage to the company's operations. This is likely to be rare in practice. One example might be the supply of substantial amounts of goods or services to two countries that have significantly different political ideologies. If the future success of the business is heavily dependent on continued trading with both countries, and disclosure of the level of trading with one country might lead to loss of business with the other, disclosure may be considered seriously prejudicial to the company's interests. If the directors believe that it is appropriate to take advantage of this exemption, it would be advisable for them to formally document their reasons for doing so.

Maintaining appropriate records

9.8 It is clear that companies need to maintain detailed records as the year progresses to provide the information for these disclosure requirements. Obtaining information by class of business is usually relatively straightforward, especially as it will often form part of regular management information reports during the year. However, the collation of details by geographical market may require more thought and planning.

Turnover relating to continuing, discontinued and acquired activities

9.9 FRS 3 'Reporting Financial Performance' requires separate disclosure of the results of continuing, acquired and discontinued operations. This analysis must be given for all statutory headings in the profit and loss account from turnover through to operating profit. The requirements are considered in more detail in **Chapter 8**.

ACCOUNTING POLICIES FOR TURNOVER

Profit and loss account formats

9.10 CA 1985 requires a company's profit and loss account to be presented in one of four standard formats prescribed in the Act. More detail on these formats is given in Chapter 8. Turnover is one of the separate items that must be shown, regardless of which format is chosen. Turnover is defined in CA 1985 as the amount derived from the provision of goods and services falling within the company's ordinary activities, after deduction of:

- — trade discounts;
- — value added tax; and
- — any other taxes based on the amounts so derived.

SSAP 5 'Accounting for Value Added Tax' also requires turnover to exclude VAT.

Requirements of FRS 18

9.11 Revenue recognition concerns when revenue is recorded as such in an entity's profit and loss account. FRS 18 'Accounting Policies' requires an entity to adopt accounting policies that enable its financial statements to give a true and fair view and that are consistent with the requirements of accounting standards, UITF Abstracts and companies' legislation. Where more than one accounting policy would satisfy these requirements, the entity should select whichever of those policies is judged the most appropriate to its particular circumstances for the purpose of giving a true and fair view. The standard also requires financial statements (other than cashflow information) to be prepared on the accruals basis of accounting, which it defines as requiring the non-cash effects of transactions and events to be reflected, as far as is possible, in the financial statements for the accounting period in which they occur and not in the period in which any related cash is received or paid. The standard refers to the CA 1985 requirement that only profits realised at the balance sheet date should be included in the profit and loss account, and notes that profits are to be treated as realised for these purposes only when they have been realised in the form of cash or of other assets the ultimate cash realisation of which can be assessed with reasonable certainty. These requirements are to apply unless there are special reasons for departing from them, in which case two additional rules come into effect:

- such 'special reasons' will not exist unless, as a minimum, it is possible to be reasonably certain that an unrealised gain exists and can be measured with sufficient reliability;
- due consideration must be given to whether a departure from the requirements would result in the use of valuation bases or accounting treatments not permitted by companies' legislation and which could therefore only be used if the true and fair override was justified.

Further guidance on the requirements of FRS 18 can be found in **Chapter 1** and **Chapter 4**. The ASB *Statement of Principles for Financial Reporting* also provides guidance on the recognition of transactions and events in financial statements.

Disclosure of accounting policy adopted

9.12 Because there are different methods of recognising income, and because turnover is usually both material and critical to the calculation of the profit or loss for the year, the accounting policy for turnover will usually need to be explained in the notes to the accounts. For many companies a simple statement on turnover will suffice.

Example 9.2 – Simple accounting policy on turnover

Turnover represents the amounts receivable, excluding value added tax, in respect of goods sold and services provided to customers during the year.

Specialised businesses

9.13 More specialised businesses may need to give additional details to enable the reader of the accounts to understand the basis on which turnover is calculated. Some of the issues affecting the following businesses are considered below:

— house-builders;

— computer software developers;

— companies providing extended warranties on goods sold by them; and

— lessors.

Suggestions for turnover accounting policy notes are included in each case. Issues that need to be considered when drafting accounting policy notes for other specialised businesses are considered in 9.21.

House-builders

9.14 In some businesses, the timing of the recognition of a sale is important and therefore needs to be explained in the accounting policy note. For instance, in the case of a house-builder, it may be acceptable to recognise a sale in the accounts when contracts are exchanged, provided that completion is unconditional.

Example 9.3 – Recognition on exchange of contracts

Turnover represents the amounts receivable in respect of houses sold during the year. Sales are recognised when contracts for sale have been exchanged and have become unconditional. All sales related taxes are excluded from turnover.

Some companies recognise sales on the basis of exchange of contracts, but only where completion has taken place by a specified date. This date must be before the date of approval of the accounts and should be the same date each year to meet the requirement for consistency.

Example 9.4 – Recognition on exchange of contract and subsequent completion

Turnover represents the amounts receivable in respect of houses sold during the year. Sales are recognised when contracts for sale have been exchanged, provided that legal completion has taken place by 31 August (i.e. within two months of the balance sheet date). All sales related taxes are excluded from turnover.

However, many house-building companies take a more conservative approach and only recognise a sale in the accounts once legal completion has taken place.

Example 9.5 – Recognition on legal completion

Turnover represents the amounts receivable in respect of houses sold during the year. Sales are recognised at the time of legal completion. All sales related taxes are excluded from turnover.

Computer software developers

9.15 There has been much debate in recent years over the point at which revenue and profit on the sale of computer software programs should be recognised in a set of accounts. Software developers will often have three main sources of income:

— sales of 'off-the-shelf' software, where the customer is given a licence to use the program developed by the software house, sometimes for a specified period only;

— sales of software programs developed specifically for individual customers; and

— sales of software support services, which may relate to either of the above categories.

In the case of 'off-the-shelf' software, sales are usually recognised when the licensing agreement is signed or when the master program is delivered to the customer. The sale of tailor-made programs is a more complex issue. The project will usually be broken down into various phases (e.g. establishing the specification, carrying out the initial design and development work, testing and finally installing the new program). In these circumstances the project may have the nature of a long-term contract and revenue may therefore need to be recognised in line with SSAP 9 'Stocks and long-term contracts' (see 9.22 to 9.26 below and Chapter 23). Software support services are usually provided through a separate maintenance contract and it will normally be appropriate to spread this income over the period of the contract and thus match the income with any related maintenance costs incurred by the software house. A suitable turnover accounting policy note might be as follows.

Example 9.6 – Turnover in the IT industry

Turnover represents the amounts receivable, excluding value added tax, in respect of goods sold and services provided to customers during the year. Non-refundable income in respect of annual licences is recognised at the date of invoicing. Income in respect of systems development contracts is recognised in proportion to the stage of completion of the contract. Once the overall outcome of the contract can be foreseen with reasonable certainty, attributable profit is recognised in proportion to the turnover recognised in the accounts. Provision is made for all foreseeable future losses. Income in respect of software and hardware support is apportioned over the period to which it relates.

Extended warranty contracts

9.16 Where a company sells extended warranty contracts relating to its retail products, the potential costs associated with the warranty will need to be predicted. This is usually done on the basis of historical experience. The usual method of accounting for this type of income is to recognise it at the time of sale and to make provision for any anticipated costs. If income from extended warranties is material, the turnover note should explain the accounting treatment adopted.

Example 9.7 – Income from extended warranty contracts

Income from extended warranty contracts is included in turnover in the period in which the contracts are sold. Full provision is made for the expected liabilities that the company has assumed under these contracts.

Leasing income in the accounts of a lessor

9.17 SSAP 21 'Accounting for Leases and Hire Purchase Contracts' sets out separate requirements on accounting for rental income from operating leases and finance leases, and requires the aggregate rentals from each type of lease to be shown separately in the accounts.

Income from operating leases

9.18 In the case of an operating lease, SSAP 21 requires a lessor to account for rental income on a leased asset on a straight-line basis over the period of the lease, regardless of the actual timing of the rental payments. Another systematic and rational basis may be used to allocate the income if this is more representative of the way in which the benefit from the leased asset is receivable. Any charges for services such as insurance and maintenance of the asset should be treated separately from rental income in the accounts of the lessee. Direct costs incurred in arranging a lease (e.g. commissions, legal fees) may be charged to the profit and loss account as they are incurred, or may be apportioned over the period of the lease on a systematic and rational basis. SSAP 21 requires disclosure of the accounting policy adopted and the following wording may be suitable (although this will depend on the precise treatment adopted):

9.8 – Income from operating leases

Gross earnings from operating leases are recognised in the profit and loss account on a straight-line basis over the period of each lease. The initial direct costs incurred in negotiating and arranging operating leases are charged to the profit and loss account in the period in which they are incurred.

Operating lease incentives

9.19 Incentives offered to encourage a lessee to enter into a lease agreement will usually be structured to give the lessor the market return that he requires, but in a way that meets the cash flow requirements of the lessee. Thus, where a lease agreement includes an incentive (e.g. a cash payment or rent-free period), the level of rental payments will usually be higher than prevailing market rates, even though they may be described in the agreement as being at market rates. A payment or other transfer of value from the lessor to, or for the benefit of, the lessee should be regarded as a lease incentive when that fairly reflects its substance. Under UITF Abstract 28 'Operating Lease Incentives', all incentives for the agreement of a new or renewed operating lease should be recognised as an integral part of the net payment agreed for the use of the leased asset, irrespective of the nature or form of the incentive or the timing of the payments. A lessor should therefore recognise the aggregate cost of incentives as a reduction of rental income and should allocate this cost over the lease term or a shorter period ending on the date from which the prevailing market rental is expected to be payable. The allocation should be on a straight line basis unless another systematic basis is more representative of the time pattern in which the benefit from the leased asset is receivable by the lessee.

Income from finance leases

9.20 In the case of a finance lease, the total gross earnings under the lease should normally be allocated to accounting periods so that each period shows a constant periodic rate of return on the lessor's net cash investment in the lease. The net cash investment in the lease at any one point in time is defined as the amount of funds invested in the lease by the lessor, comprising the cost of the asset, plus or minus the following payments and receipts where relevant:

- grants receivable towards the purchase or use of the asset;
- rentals received;
- tax payments and receipts, including the effect of capital allowances;
- any residual value at the end of the lease term;
- any interest payments;
- any interest received on any cash surplus; and

— any profit taken out of the lease.

The net cash investment in the lease should not be confused with the net investment in the lease which forms the basis for recording the amount due from the lessee in the balance sheet of the lessor (see **Chapter 24**). Rentals received from the lessee represent partly gross income for the lessor and partly a repayment of capital. The rental receipts must therefore be apportioned between these two elements. The guidance in SSAP 21 illustrates in detail two methods of allocating gross earnings to accounting periods in a way that meets the requirements of the standard:

— the actuarial method after tax; and

— the investment period method.

These are the two most commonly used methods, but others may be equally appropriate. Direct costs incurred in arranging a lease (eg commissions, legal fees) may be charged to the profit and loss account as they are incurred, or may be apportioned over the period of the lease on a systematic and rational basis. SSAP 21 requires disclosure of the accounting policy adopted and the following wording may be suitable (although this will depend on the precise treatment adopted):

> **9.9 – Income from finance leases**
>
> Rental payments under finance leases are apportioned between interest, which is credited to the profit and loss account as gross earnings, and repayment of capital which reduces the amount due from the lessees. Gross earnings from finance leases are allocated to accounting periods to give a constant periodic rate of return on the net cash investment in the lease, using the investment period method of allocation. The initial direct costs incurred in negotiating and arranging finance leases are charged to the profit and loss account in the period in which they are incurred.

Issues to consider

9.21 Issues to consider when drafting turnover accounting policy notes for specialised businesses include the following.

— Does the company have more than one income stream? If so, do these income streams need to be considered and explained separately?

— Is the timing of the recognition of income critical? If so, the treatment adopted will need to be explained in the note.

— Are goods supplied on sale or return? If so, the assumptions made in respect of returns may need to be explained.

Reference should also be made to the issues raised in the ASB Discussion Paper 'Revenue Recognition' (see **9.34** to **9.39** below)

LONG-TERM CONTRACTS

Definition of long-term contract

9.22 SSAP 9 'Stocks and Long-term Contracts' considers the accounting treatment of turnover in respect of long-term contracts. A long-term contract is defined in the standard as one which relates to:

(i) the design, manufacture or construction of a single substantial asset, or a combination of assets which together constitute a single project, or

(ii) the provision of a service or a combination of services that together constitute a single project,

where the time taken to complete the work is such that the contract activity falls into more than one accounting period. In other words, it will usually be a contract that runs for more than one year. However, the fact that a contract runs for less than a year does not necessarily mean that it should not be accounted for as a long-term contract. If the contract is material and spans two accounting periods, it will usually be appropriate to account for it as a long-term contract. The identification of long-term contracts is considered in more detail in **Chapter 23**.

Accounting treatment

9.23 If long-term contracts were not accounted for until they were complete, the accounts would not reflect the results of contract activity during the year. Instead they would show the results of contracts completed during the year, which could give a very different picture. It is therefore considered more appropriate to take account of turnover, and the profit or loss earned, as the work proceeds. Calculation of the profit or loss earned to date is considered further in **Chapter 23**.

Calculating turnover

9.24 Each long-term contract should be considered separately. The calculation of the amount of turnover to be included for each contract should take into account:

- the nature of the contract;
- the stage of completion of the work;
- the contractual relationship with the customer.

For instance, in the case of a construction contract, the amount to be included in turnover may be based on a formal valuation of the work completed to date. In the case of other types of contract, the specification may require the work to be analysed into specific stages and these can be used to assess the value of work completed to date.

Variations to original specification

9.25 A common feature of long-term contracts is variations to the original specification, which are often approved as the contract progresses. Where these have been agreed but not yet fully settled, it will usually be appropriate to estimate the amount likely to be received and include this in turnover as the relevant work is completed. However, a prudent approach should be taken in all cases where the final outcome is not known. The final negotiation of claims can often be a protracted exercise and income in respect of claims is usually only included as turnover when negotiations have reached an advanced stage and there is sufficient evidence that eventual receipt is reasonably certain. The accounting treatment of variations and claims is considered in more detail in **Chapter 23**.

Disclosure of method of calculating turnover

9.26 As there are many different ways of calculating turnover for long-term contracts, SSAP 9 is not prescriptive on the method that should be used. It therefore requires disclosure of the method adopted. An example of the type of explanation that should be given in accounting policy notes on long-term contracts is given in **Chapter 23**.

BARTER TRANSACTIONS FOR ADVERTISING

Scope of UITF Abstract 26

9.27 UITF Abstract 26 'Barter transactions for advertising' was issued in November 2000 and considers the accounting treatment that should be adopted when an entity agrees to provide advertising in exchange for advertising services provided by its customer rather than for cash consideration. At the moment, this situation is most likely to arise in the context of commercial websites that display advertising in exchange for advertising their own services on another website. However, the Abstract applies to barter transactions in all media and not just to website transactions. Barter transactions for services other than advertising are not covered, although the UITF notes that the principles in the Abstract may be relevant to such transactions.

Presentational issue

9.28 The accounting treatment of barter transactions for advertising will have no overall effect on the profit or loss for the period, but could affect the amount of turnover and costs recognised in the profit and loss account. Turnover is often regarded as a critical figure, and this is particularly the case with internet companies.

Recognition criteria

9.29 The Abstract refers to the recognition criteria set out in the ASB 'Statement of Principles for Financial Reporting', and notes that a barter transaction provides little or no evidence of the value of the services provided. It therefore concludes that it would not be appropriate to recognise turnover and costs in respect of such transactions unless there is persuasive evidence of the value at which the advertising would have been sold for cash, in a similar transaction, if it had not been the subject of an exchange.

Substance of the transaction

9.30 The Abstract also refers to the requirements of FRS 5 'Reporting the Substance of Transactions' and in particular the requirement that:

— all aspects and implications of a transaction should be identified; and

— greater weight should be given to those aspects that are more likely to have commercial effect in practice.

On this basis, an arrangement should be regarded as a barter transaction where this fairly reflects the substance of the transaction. Consequently, a contract to provide advertising for cash consideration may nevertheless be a barter transaction if it is made on the understanding that a reciprocal arrangement will also be entered into. Arrangements involving a third party may also constitute a barter transaction – for instance, where the purchaser of the advertising agrees to procure advertising services from another party in exchange, rather than providing these services itself.

Accounting treatment

9.31 Turnover and costs in respect of barter transactions for advertising should not be recognised unless there is persuasive evidence of the value at which the advertising, if not exchanged, would have been sold for cash in a similar transaction. This will only be the case where:

— the entity has a history of selling similar advertising for cash; and

— substantially all of the turnover from advertising within the accounting period is represented by cash sales.

Persuasive evidence

9.32 In order to provide persuasive evidence of the value of exchanged advertising, cash sales of advertising must be similar in all material respects – in other words:

— they must relate to advertising space in the same vehicle (e.g. the same website or magazine);

— they must have taken place within a reasonably short period of the exchange transaction (in no case more than six months before or after it); and

— there must be no other factors that would be expected to make the value of the advertising sold for cash significantly different from that exchanged - specific issues to consider here include:

  — circulation, exposure or saturation within an intended market;

  — timing (e.g. time of day, day of week, regularity, season of the year etc)

  — prominence;

  — demographics of readers, viewers or customers;

  — duration (i.e. length of time advertising will be displayed).

Even where similar advertising has been sold for cash, the Abstract notes that due consideration should still be given to whether, in the light of all the available information, there is persuasive evidence of the value at which the exchanged advertising would have been sold. Specific factors to consider here include:

— the entity's practice in setting prices for advertising and the circumstances in which discounts are offered;

— the probability that a cash sale would have taken place if the advertising had not been exchanged; and

— the value to the entity of the advertising received in exchange and whether there is evidence that the entity would have been willing to buy that advertising for cash if it had not obtained it through the exchange transaction.

Disclosure

9.33 Where the stringent conditions set out in the Abstract are met, and both turnover and costs are therefore recognised in the profit and loss account, the notes to the financial statements should disclose the total amount that is included in turnover in respect of barter transactions for advertising. The Abstract also encourages the disclosure of additional information on the volume and type of these transactions, and other forms of barter transactions, irrespective of whether they are included in turnover, but does not specifically require this.

ASB DISCUSSION PAPER 'REVENUE RECOGNITION'

What constitutes revenue?

9.34 The ASB Discussion Paper 'Revenue Recognition' examines revenue measurement and recognition from first principles. The aim is to establish a framework within which consistent solutions can be found to the many and varied practical issues that arise in accounting for revenue. The Paper proposes the following definition of revenue.

> 'In the context of a business operating cycle, revenue is the class of gains, before deduction of associated costs, arising as a result of benefit being transferred to a customer in an exchange transaction (i.e. under a contract).'

An operating cycle is defined in the Paper as 'a sequence of business activities, carried out with a view to profit, which involves the transfer of benefit to customers in exchange for consideration (i.e. payment)'.

How and when benefit is transferred?

9.35 The Paper explores how benefit is transferred to customers in exchange transactions and concludes that benefit is transferred when the seller honours the promises that it has made under the contract – in other words, when it performs its contractual obligations. In particular, the Paper considers whether full performance of a contract is necessary in order for revenue to arise. It concludes that, where contractual performance is incomplete, revenue should be recognised to the extent that the seller has performed and that performance has resulted in a benefit accruing to the customer.

Techniques for applying this general principle

9.36 The ASB recognises that the practical application of this principle is the issue that is most likely to give rise to difficulties. Chapter 3 of the Paper explores issues such as:

- 'unbundling' a contract (i.e. breaking down an overall contract into elements that might otherwise have been contracted for separately);
- assigning values to the individual elements of the contract identified in this exercise; and
- assessing the value accrued to date and the value outstanding.

Impact of customer rights of return

9.37 The Paper identifies two possible approaches to accounting for goods which are transferred together with a right of return:

- the expected sales approach - revenue should be recognised on the transfer of the benefit, with an appropriate adjustment to reflect the risk of return; and
- the accounting policy approach - the entity should select and apply consistently whichever of the following accounting policies is the most appropriate to its circumstances:
  - revenue should be recognised on the transfer of benefit with an appropriate adjustment to reflect the risk of returns; or
  - revenue should be recognised on expiry of the right to return the goods.

Comments were invited on which of these two approaches would be more appropriate.

Measurement principles

9.38 The Paper proposes that revenue should be measured as the change in fair value, arising from the seller's performance, of:

- assets representing rights or other access to consideration; and
- liabilities in respect of consideration received in advance of performance.

This approach prevents the measurement of revenue being distorted by the timing of the related payments. This section of the Paper also includes consideration of barter transactions and options.

Agency agreements

9.39 The Paper also explores the issue of revenue recognition in the context of an agency agreement and concludes that:

- the principal's revenue should reflect the full consideration payable by the customer in respect of the transaction and any commission or other amounts payable to the agent should be treated as an expense rather than as a reduction of revenue;
- the revenue of a disclosed agent should be the amount of commission or other income receivable from the principal; and
- an undisclosed agent should account for revenue in the same way as a principle.

Chapter 10

Staff Costs and Employee Numbers

DISCLOSURE OF STAFF COSTS

CA 1985 disclosure requirements

10.1 CA 1985 Sch 4 para 56 requires details of staff costs to be disclosed each year (with comparatives), analysed into the following aggregate amounts:

— wages and salaries paid or payable in respect of the year to the company's employees;

— social security costs incurred by the company on behalf of its employees;

— other pension costs incurred by the company on behalf of its employees.

A company that has chosen Format 2 or Format 4 for its profit and loss account must disclose staff costs as part of the profit and loss account. The information may be given on the face of the profit and loss account or in the notes to the accounts. A company that has chosen Format 1 or Format 3 must give details of staff costs in the notes to the accounts. Paragraph 56 is not repeated in CA 1985 Sch 8, and a small company preparing shorter form accounts is therefore not required to disclose details of staff costs and the average number of employees in the notes to the accounts (see **Chapter 7**). However, if the company has chosen to use Format 2 or Format 4 for its profit and loss account, details of staff costs must continue to be given as part of the standard profit and loss account format.

Requirements of FRS 3 'Reporting Financial Performance'

10.2 FRS 3 requires all figures from turnover to operating profit or loss to be analysed between continuing, discontinued and newly-acquired activities (see **Chapter 8**). A company using Format 2 or Format 4 for its profit and loss account must therefore give this analysis for staff costs where appropriate. The disclosure may be given on the face of the profit and loss account or in the notes to the accounts. A company using Format 1 or Format 3 for its profit and loss account is not required to analyse staff costs in this way, as the detailed disclosure of staff costs is supplementary to the profit and loss account rather than an integral part of it.

Wages and salaries

10.3 Wages and salaries are defined in CA 1985 Sch 4 para 94(3) as payments made or costs incurred in respect of persons employed by the company (as defined for the purposes of calculating the average number of employees – see **10.8** below) but there is no further guidance on which items should be included. The amount disclosed is usually the gross amount paid in respect of wages and salaries, including amounts such as overtime and bonus payments.

Benefits in kind

10.4 In particular there is no specific reference to the benefits in kind that may be made available to employees (e.g. use of a company car, private health insurance). In the case of directors, the Act states that the estimated money value of benefits in kind must be included as remuneration. The term 'costs incurred' in para 94(3) could be interpreted as including benefits in kind, but it is normal practice at present to exclude benefits from staff costs.

Social security costs

10.5 Social security costs are defined in CA 1985 Sch 4 para 94(1) as contributions by the company to any state social security or pension scheme, fund or arrangement. The amount disclosed under this heading will usually represent the total of employers' national insurance contributions paid or payable by the company during the year. For share options granted after 5 April 1999 under unapproved schemes, this will include employers' national insurance contributions payable on gains made by directors and employees on the exercise of the options.

Pension costs

10.6 Pension costs are defined in to CA 1985 Sch 4 94(2) as including:

— any costs incurred by the company in respect of any pension scheme established for the purpose of providing pensions for current or former employees;

— any sums set aside for the future payment of pensions directly by the company to current or former employees;

— any pensions paid directly to current or former employees without having first been set aside.

The accounting treatment of pension costs is considered in more detail in **Chapter 11**.

CALCULATION OF AVERAGE NUMBER OF EMPLOYEES

CA 1985 disclosure requirements

10.7 All companies are required to disclose the average number of employees during the year, in total and analysed by category. The categories used are to be decided by the directors, taking into account the way in which the company's activities are organised.

Basic rules

10.8 The Act is very specific on how the average number of employees should be calculated. The figure must be calculated by:

(i) ascertaining the number of people employed by the company under contracts of service in each month of the financial year, regardless of whether they were employed for the full month or only for part of it;

(ii) adding up the numbers ascertained in this way for each month of the financial year;

(iii) dividing the resultant total by the number of months in the financial year.

A contract of service (or a contract of employment) is a formal agreement between the employer and employee under which the employee agrees to work for the employer and the employer agrees to pay the employee a wage or salary in respect of that work. All employees should have a formal contract of service or employment.

Contracts for services

10.9 Certain individuals may carry out work for a company under a contract for services, as opposed to a contract of service. In this case, the individual will usually be self-employed (e.g. a consultant, or a contractor) and will be engaged to carry out specific duties. They will not usually be required to work full-time for the company. Individuals who carry out work for the company under a contract for services will not normally be included in the calculation of the average number of employees. Similarly, amounts paid to them should not be included as staff costs. They will usually be disclosed instead as 'other external charges' or 'other operating costs'.

Directors

10.10 Executive directors will often have a contract of service with the company and they should therefore be included in the calculation of the average number of employees, even though separate details of their remuneration must also be given in the accounts (see **Chapter 16**). It is usually helpful to explain that executive directors are included in the figure for the average number of employees, although there is no specific requirement to do so. Non-executive directors will usually have contracts for services and should therefore be excluded from the calculations.

Employees working overseas

10.11 The Act makes no separate mention of employees working wholly or mainly overseas in the context of these disclosures. Overseas employees should therefore be included in the calculation of the average number of employees during the year.

Arrangements which may give rise to problems

10.12 In some situations a strict interpretation of the requirements of the Act could result in misleading details being disclosed. It may therefore be necessary to depart from the strict requirements in order for the accounts to show a true and fair view. In these circumstances, details of the departure, the reasons for it and the effect should be disclosed. Some of the more common situations are considered below.

Temporary or casual employees

10.13 Temporary or casual employees are normally excluded from the calculations on the basis that they do not usually have formal contracts of employment with the company and they will often be used only to cover for existing staff (e.g. to cover absence through illness). In these circumstances, the numbers involved are likely to be relatively low. However, in situations where temporary or casual staff are employed in larger numbers and on a more regular basis (e.g. in the hotel and catering industry, where business is often seasonal and wide use is made of temporary staff as a result) it may be necessary to treat them as employees for the accounts to show a true and fair view.

Staff employed by a different company

10.14 This problem is most likely to arise in a group situation, where staff may have service contracts with one company but carry out work for one or more other companies within the group. They may also be paid by the company employing them rather than by the company or companies for which they actually work. In some cases, the companies for which they work may be recharged with their salary cost, but this is not always done. Examples of these arrangements and suggested disclosures in each case are set out below.

Disclosure in subsidiary company's accounts

10.15 The following treatment and disclosures will usually be appropriate in a situation where staff are employed by the holding company A, but work for its subsidiary company B.

Example 10.1 – Where staff are employed by holding company A but work for subsidiary B

The staff work full-time for B, and B effectively pays the relevant staff salaries and related costs (either directly or by means of a recharge).

- Treat the payments as staff costs in B's accounts.
- Include the staff in the average number of employees in B's accounts.
- Explain in the notes to the accounts that staff are under contracts of employment with A but work full-time for B and that they have therefore been included in the average number of employees and in staff costs.
- Explain that this constitutes a departure from the requirements of the Act but is necessary for the accounts to show a true and fair view.

Example 10.2 – Where staff work for B and B bears a management charge

The staff work full-time for B, and B bears a group management charge, which effectively includes the relevant salary cost but does not separately identify this amount.

The notes to B's accounts should explain that:

- staff are under contracts of employment with A but work full-time for B;
- B is recharged for the cost of these employees by means of a group management charge, but it is not possible to identify separately the element relating to staff costs;
- details of the total number of A's employees and their staff costs are given in the accounts of A.

It may be helpful to give details of the number of staff working for B, but this is not strictly a requirement in this situation.

Example 10.3 – Where staff work for B, but B does not pay their salaries in any way

The staff work full-time for B, but B does not pay their salaries, either directly or indirectly.

The notes to B's accounts should explain that:

- staff are under contracts of employment with A but work full-time for B;

- B is not recharged for the cost of these employees;
- details of the total number of A's employees and their staff costs are given in the accounts of A.

It may be helpful to give details of the number of staff working for B, but this is not strictly a requirement in this situation.

Example 10.4 – Where staff split work between B and another company and B bears relevant costs

The staff work partly for B and partly for other group companies, and B bears an appropriate level of the relevant staff costs.

B's accounts should explain the situation and follow the disclosures in **Example 10.1**.

Example 10.5 – Where staff split work between B and another company but B bears no cost

The staff work partly for B and partly for other group companies, but B does not bear any of the relevant staff costs.

B's accounts should explain the situation and follow the disclosures in **Example 10.3**.

Disclosure in holding company accounts

10.16 In the above examples, if A prepares group accounts, no additional disclosures will usually be required as the staff costs and employee details will cover the group as a whole. However, if A is exempt from preparing group accounts, an explanation of the arrangements and the treatment adopted may also need to be given in A's accounts in order for them to show a true and fair view.

Arrangements involving another group company

10.17 Where arrangements similar to those described above operate through a different structure (e.g. staff employed by another subsidiary within the group rather than by the holding company) the arrangements will usually need to be explained in the accounts of both companies.

Disclosure of number of employees by category

10.18 The Act requires the average number of employees during the year to be disclosed in total and by category. The directors are free to choose how to categorise employees, although they must take account of the way in which the company's activities are organised. Most companies give the analysis of employee numbers by function, for example:

— production;

— sales and distribution;

— management;

— administration.

However, others have chosen categories such as:

— full-time and part-time;

— hourly-paid, weekly-paid and salaried;

— by division (e.g. manufacturing, retail, construction);

— by geographical area.

The analysis can be given in more than one way if this is considered helpful. The number of employees by category should be calculated in the same way as the average number of employees in total.

Link between staff costs and employee numbers

10.19 CA 1985 Sch 4 para 94(3) defines the amount to be shown as wages and salaries and social security costs, within staff costs, as payments made or costs incurred in respect of all persons employed by the company during the year who are taken into account in calculating the average number of employees. There is consequently a direct link between the staff costs and employee numbers disclosures, and the two should therefore be shown on a consistent basis (i.e. if it is appropriate to exclude certain individuals from employee numbers because they do not meet the criteria specified in the Act, payments to those individuals should not be treated as staff costs in the accounts).

EMPLOYEE SHARE SCHEMES

Requirements of UITF Abstract 17

10.20 UITF Abstract 17 'Employee Share Schemes' considers the accounting treatment of shares awarded to employees through annual bonuses or long-term incentive schemes. The requirements apply to all share schemes including:

— those that clearly involve employee remuneration, such as approved profit-sharing schemes under the *Income and Corporation Taxes Act 1988*;

— new types of scheme, such as the all-employee share plan introduced in 2000; and

— where, on the initial listing of a company, employees are given the opportunity to subscribe for shares or rights to shares at a discount to the float price payable by public investors.

The only exception is that the Abstract need not be applied to Inland Revenue approved SAYE schemes and equivalent overseas schemes. Where an entity chooses to take advantage of this exemption, it must disclose in the notes to the accounts that it has done so. The ASB is currently developing proposals for an accounting standard on share-based payments. If adopted, these would represent a radical change to existing accounting practice, and would not include any exemption for SAYE and similar schemes (see **10.48** to **10.56** below).

Recognition of the cost of share awards

10.21 The consensus reached by the UITF on accounting for the award of shares, or rights to shares, to employees is that:

- the cost should be recognised over the period to which the employee's performance relates;
- the amount charged to the profit and loss account should be based on the fair value of the shares at the date they are awarded to the employee;
- the minimum amount to be recognised should be the difference between:
  - the fair value of the shares at the date of the award or, where the shares have been purchased by an ESOP trust and accounted for under UITF Abstract 13, or have been revalued, the book value of the shares that are available for the award; and
  - the amount of any consideration that participants may be required to pay for the shares.

The fair value of the shares at the date they are awarded to the employee reflects the amount that the employer would receive if the shares were issued for cash, and also the value of the award to the employee. The guidance explains that fair value will usually be equivalent to the market value of the shares at the date of issue. UITF Abstract 30 'Date of Award to Employees of Shares and Rights to Shares' clarifies what constitutes the date of the award when:

- the award is subject to approval by the shareholders; or
- the award is conditional on the company's shares becoming publicly traded or on a trade sale taking place.

Need for shareholder approval

10.22 Under CA 1985 s 80, a company will often need authorisation from its shareholders in order to allot shares or rights to shares. In practice, many companies seek advance authorisation from their shareholders at each Annual General Meeting to cover planned share awards during the coming year, but this will not happen in every case. The UITF therefore considered the situation where shares or share options are promised to employees, but the arrangements are subject to shareholder approval. It concluded that the company does not have the power to make the award, or grant the options, until the shareholders have approved the arrangements. In these circumstances, therefore, the date of the award of the shares, or the granting of the options, is the date on which formal shareholder approval is given. Any charge to the profit and loss account will therefore be based on the fair value of the shares at that time rather than at the date when the promise was originally made.

Creation of an obligation

10.23 Where an award of shares or options is subject to shareholder approval, the employer may nevertheless create an obligation to the employee, either explicitly or implicitly. For instance, an explicit obligation will be created if the company agrees to pay a cash bonus to the employee in the event that the share award is not approved by the shareholders. An implicit obligation may arise through the employee having redress against the company for failure to carry out the promise made. The UITF consensus is that, where the company creates an obligation that may involve a future transfer of economic benefits, a charge should be made to the profit and loss account on the date that the arrangement is entered into. The amount charged should be calculated in accordance with UITF Abstract 17 and should take account of any performance criteria relating to the award. Changes in the share price between the date of the arrangement and the date of approval will therefore affect the total amount charged to the profit and loss account. If the shareholders subsequently approve the share award, any charge required by Abstract 17 at the date of the award will be based on the fair value of the shares at the date of approval and should be adjusted for the amount already charged to the profit and loss account in making provision for the obligation. The provision made should be treated as part of the consideration for the share award and should be transferred to shareholders' funds.

Shares becoming publicly traded

10.24 Shares and options may sometimes be awarded to employees in anticipation of the company's shares becoming publicly traded on a stock exchange, or of a trade sale taking place, and the award may be made conditional on such arrangements being put into place. The UITF consensus is that this constitutes a performance condition of the award. The date of the award will therefore be the date on which the condition is satisfied (e.g. the date on which the shares become listed). This ensures that the amount charged to the profit and loss account under Abstract 17 is based on the fair value of the shares after listing and not on a value applying before the shares are publicly traded.

Consideration paid by employee

10.25 Where the employee is required to make some contribution to the cost of the shares awarded under the scheme, this should be deducted from the amount to be charged to the profit and loss account.

Shares purchased by ESOP trust

10.26 Where shares are purchased at fair value by an Employee Share Ownership Plan trust in conjunction with an employee share scheme and the company retains de facto control of the shares held by the trust, the charge to the profit and loss account should be based on the book value of the shares under UITF Abstract 13 'Accounting for ESOP Trusts'. This is normally the fair value of the shares at the date they were acquired by the ESOP. The requirements of Abstract 13 are considered in **Chapter 3**.

Uncertainty over achievement of performance criteria

10.27 In some cases, particularly where the award relates to a long-term incentive scheme, there may be a degree of uncertainty over whether the performance criteria underlying the award will actually be met. Some schemes may also allow for employees to receive a proportion of the award where the performance criteria are partially achieved. UITF Abstract 17 requires the effect of uncertainty to be dealt with by making a reasonable estimation of the number of shares that may be required to be issued under the scheme, based on the extent to which the performance criteria are expected to be met. Therefore, in the case of awards under a long-term incentive scheme:

- the amount initially recognised should be based on a reasonable expectation of the extent to which the relevant performance criteria will be met;
- this amount should be charged to the profit and loss account over the period to which the performance criteria relate, either on a straight line basis or on another basis that more fairly reflects the services received from the employee; and
- subsequent adjustments should be made as necessary to deal with changes in the probability of the performance criteria being met, lapses in conditional awards or purchases of shares at different prices.

Schemes requiring employees to retain shares awarded

10.28 Some schemes may incorporate a requirement, or an encouragement, for employees to retain shares awarded under the scheme for a minimum period. The UITF concluded that the amount charged to the profit and loss account in respect of the share award should not be adjusted in any way to reflect conditions of this nature.

Revision of charge in subsequent years

10.29 Under UITF Abstract 17, the fair value of the shares expected to be awarded should be determined at the time that a conditional award is made. This initial estimate may need to be revised in subsequent years, for instance to reflect:

- changes in the probability of the performance criteria being met, which may change the estimate of the number of shares expected to be issued;
- expected awards which lapse due to the employee leaving the company;
- purchases of shares at different prices (for instance, if the share price falls, the company may be able to use shares purchased at the lower price to fulfil its obligation).

However, no adjustment should be made to reflect increases or decreases in the value of the shares to which employees will become entitled in due course (other than in the third situation noted above).

When should the award be recognised in the accounts?

10.30 The Abstract requires the cost of employee share awards to be recognised over the period to which the employee's performance criteria relates. Where the share award relates to an annual bonus scheme, the award should be recognised in the year to which the bonus relates. In the case of a long-term incentive scheme, the total amount to be recognised should be spread over the period covered by the performance criteria. The amount to be charged to the profit and loss account each year should reflect the service provided by the employee during that period. In most cases, a straight line charge will be appropriate, but an alternative basis should be used if this results in a more appropriate allocation of the costs over the total performance period. The annual charge will also include the effect of any adjustments required to reflect changes in estimates and expectations as explained in **10.29** above. Where no performance criteria are included in the scheme, and it is clear that the share award is not related to past performance, the cost of the award should be spread over the period from the date the award is made to the date when the employee becomes unconditionally entitled to the shares.

Requirement for further period of employment

10.31 Some schemes may include a requirement for an employee to complete an additional period of continued employment before the share award becomes unconditional. This additional period should not normally be included in the period over which the costs are spread. However, if it is clear that the effect of the scheme is to reward services during the additional period as well as the original period, the cost of the award should be spread over the full period (i.e. the original period plus the additional period of continued employment).

Share options

10.32 Where the scheme involves the award of share options, the total amount to be charged to the profit and loss account should be based on the difference between the exercise price of the option and market value at the date of the grant. This cost should be spread over the relevant performance period in the same way as any other share award.

Accounting for share awards in the company's balance sheet

10.33 The amount accrued in the accounts in respect of employee share awards should be included within shareholders' funds in the balance sheet. When the shares are eventually issued, the total amount accrued should be allocated between share capital and reserves. As shares cannot be issued at a discount, the amount allocated to share capital will usually be equal to the par value of the shares. No amount should be allocated to the share premium account, as the UITF has received legal advice that the share premium account is normally only required to reflect cash subscribed for shares. In most cases, the balance will be allocated to the profit and loss account reserve, which should mean that distributable reserves are not affected by the profit and loss account charge in respect of the share award.

Shares held by ESOP trust

10.34 If the shares are held in an ESOP trust before being transferred to participants in the scheme, the shares should be accounted for under UITF Abstract 13 (i.e. they will usually be shown as 'Own shares' within fixed assets, and the amount accrued will reflect a diminution in value of the shares held.) The requirements of Abstract 13 are considered in **Chapter 3**. The UITF had issued proposals for changing this accounting treatment, but subsequently indicated that any amendments will be dealt with as part of a future ASB project on equity rather than by revision of Abstract 13 and Abstract 17. However, the UITF has emphasised that the financial effect of the sale of any own shares treated as an asset of the company should be clearly disclosed in the accounts, noting that disclosure will normally be required under the requirements of FRS 3 'Reporting Financial Performance' relating to exceptional items.

Inclusion in reconciliation of movements in shareholders' funds

10.35 The credit entry for the amount charged to the profit and loss account each year should be reported in the reconciliation of movements in shareholders' funds. This reflects the fact that the amount charged is in effect the proceeds of an issue of shares. It would therefore be inappropriate for the credit entry to be reported in the statement of total recognised gains and losses.

Worked example

10.36 The following example illustrates how the requirements of Abstract 17 might be applied in practice:

Example 10.6 – Accounting for share award to employees

Company A operates a long-term incentive scheme for senior staff. Participants in the scheme are granted a conditional award of up to 1,000 shares on 1 January 2001. The nominal value of each share is £1 and the market price is £8. The shares will be transferred to the participants after a period of 3 years, provided that specific performance targets have been achieved. The scheme provides for a proportion of the shares to be transferred if the targets are only partially met. Participants in the scheme are not required to contribute towards the shares.

The company makes up its accounts to 31 December each year. The expected share transfers to employees at the end of the 3 years, based on the information available at the end of each accounting period, are as follows:

31 December 2001	60% of the maximum award
31 December 2002	80% of the maximum award
31 December 2003	75% of the maximum award (actual award)

750 new shares of £1 were issued on 1 January 2004 and transferred to the scheme participants. The price of the shares on 1 January 2004 was £11.

The accounting treatment over the 3-year period would be:

(i) At 31 December 2001 the company would accrue costs of £1,600 calculated as follows:

Maximum award	1,000 shares x £8 =	£8,000
Expected award of	60% 60% x £8,000 =	£4,800
First year of 3-year period	£4,800 x 1/3 =	£1,600

£1,600 would be charged to the profit and loss account for the year and shown in the reconciliation of movements in shareholders' funds, and £1,600 would be shown within shareholders' funds in the balance sheet.

(ii) At 31 December 2002 the company would accrue a total of £4,267 calculated as follows:

Maximum award	1,000 shares x £8 =	£8,000
Expected award of 80%	80% x £8,000 =	£6,400
Second year of 3-year period	£6,400 x 2/3 =	£4,267

£2,667 would be charged in the profit and loss account for the year (£4,267 – £1,600) and shown in the reconciliation of movements in shareholders' funds and £4,267 would be shown within shareholders' funds in the balance sheet.

(iii) At 31 December 2003 the actual award is known to be £6,000, calculated as follows:

Maximum award	1,000 shares x £8 =	£8,000
Actual award of	75% 75% x £8,000 =	£6,000

£1,733 would be charged in the profit and loss account for the year (£6,000 – £4,267) and shown in the reconciliation of movements in shareholders' funds and £6,000 would be shown within shareholders' funds in the balance sheet.

When the new shares are issued on 1 January 2004, the nominal value of the shares (750 x £1 = £750) will be allocated to share capital and £5,250 (£6,000 – £750) will be allocated to reserves. [NB The price of the shares at the date of issue is not relevant for accounting purposes.]

Other examples

10.37 UITF Abstract 17 also includes a number of illustrative examples, some of which cover situations where shares are acquired at the start of the scheme, or during the scheme, and are then held by an ESOP trust until the date of transfer to participants.

NATIONAL INSURANCE CONTRIBUTIONS ON SHARE OPTION GAINS

Charge to NI

10.38 A charge to national insurance (NI) has been introduced in respect of share options granted to directors and employees after 5 April 1999 under unapproved share option schemes (i.e. schemes that have not been approved by the Inland Revenue). The employer is required to pay NI contributions on any gains on the options made by directors and employees, calculated by reference to the exercise price paid and the market value of the shares at the date of the exercise.

When the liability arises

10.39 UITF Abstract 25 'National Insurance contributions on share option gains' notes that the granting of a share option is an event that gives rise to a present obligation on the employer to pay NI contributions when the option is subsequently exercised. The amount that will be payable is uncertain as it will depend on the share price at the date on which the option is exercised, but it is possible to make a reliable estimate of the liability at each intervening balance sheet date on the basis of the outstanding options that are expected to be exercised and the market price of the shares at that date. Where it is probable that a cash outflow will occur, a provision for the liability should therefore be made in accordance with the requirements of FRS 12 'Provisions, Contingent Liabilities and Contingent Assets'. The provision should be calculated using the latest enacted NI rate applied to the difference between the market value of the underlying shares at the balance sheet date and the option exercise price.

Impact of employee performance criteria

10.40 If the granting of the option is not linked to a performance period, full provision for the NI liability should be made at the time that the option is granted. The liability should then be adjusted at each balance sheet date to take account of any changes in the market value of the shares. A different approach is required if the granting of the option is linked to the performance of services by the employees over a specified period. For instance, the grant may be conditional on the employee meeting certain performance criteria over a specified period or remaining in the reporting entity's employment for an agreed period (or a combination of the two). The employee will therefore not become unconditionally entitled to the option until the performance period has been completed. Where the option is linked to a performance period, the Abstract requires the liability to be accrued systematically over the period from the date of the grant of the option to the end of the performance period. From that date to the date of actual exercise of the option, the calculations should be updated at each balance sheet date to reflect any changes in the market value of the shares and any other changes affecting the expected liability. For instance, assumptions on whether the full entitlement will in fact be exercised may change as a result of employees leaving before the end of the agreed service period or failing to meet some or all of the performance criteria. The charge in each period will therefore represent a combination of:

- the charge for that year; and
- adjustments to the opening accrual in respect of previous years in the performance period to reflect changes in the market price of the shares and any changes in the assumptions on the extent to which the options will be exercised.

Date of grant of the option

10.41 UITF Abstract 30 'Date of Award to Employees of Shares and Rights to Shares' clarifies what constitutes the date of the grant of the option. Where the grant is subject to shareholders' approval, the date of the award is the date on which that approval is given, and the provision for related NI should therefore be accrued from that date.

Worked example

10.42 The following example illustrates the accounting requirements of UITF Abstract in the case of a performance-related option scheme.

Example 10.7 – Calculating and accruing the NI provision on share option gains in a performance-related scheme

A Ltd grants 20,000 share options to its employees on 1 July 2000 at an exercise price of £1 (equivalent to the market value at that date). The options are conditional on the employees meeting agreed performance criteria in the period from 1 July 2000 to 30 June 2002 and remaining in the company's employment for a further year until 30 June 2003. The options are exercisable from 1 July 2003 to 1 July 2004.

The current rate for employer's NI contributions is 12.2%.

The company's accounting date is 31 December.

Year to 31 December 2000

The market price of the shares at 31 December 2000 is £1.50.

The company estimates that the full amount of the options will be exercised.

Market value at 31 December 2000	£1.50
Exercise price	£1.00
Expected gain per share option	£0.50
Total expected gain: 20,000 x £0.50	£10,000
Employers NI: £10,000 x 12.2%	£1,220
Total performance period:	
1 July 2000–30 June 2003	36 months
Provision required at 31 December 2000:	
6/36 x £1,220	£203
Charge for the year	£203

Year to 31 December 2001

The market price of the shares at 31 December 2001 is £2.20.

The company still expects the full amount of the options to be exercised.

Market value at 31 December 2001	£2.20
Exercise price	£1.00
Expected gain per share option	£1.20
Total expected gain: 20,000 x £1.20	£24,000
Employers NI: £24,000 x 12.2%	£2,928

Total performance period:	
1 July 2000–30 June 2003	36 months
Provision required at 31 December 2001:	
18/36 x £2,928	£1,464
Charge for the year: £1,464–£203	£1,261

Year to 31 December 2002

The market price of the shares at 31 December 2002 is £2.70.

The company now expects only 18,000 of the options to be exercised.

Market value at 31 December 2002	£2.70
Exercise price	£1.00
Expected gain per share option	£1.70
Total expected gain: 18,000 x £1.70	£30,600
Employers NI: £30,600 x 12.2%	£3,733
Total performance period:	
1 July 2000–30 June 2003	36 months
Provision required at 31 December 2002:	
30/36 x £3,733	£3,111
Charge for the year: £3,111–£1,464	£1,647

Year to 31 December 2003

17,500 options vested during the year, but none were exercised.

The market price of the shares at 31 December 2003 was £3.00.

Market value at 31 December 2003	£3.00
Exercise price	£1.00
Expected gain per share option	£2.00
Total expected gain: 17,500 x £2.00	£35,000
Employers NI: £35,000 x 12.2%	£4,270
Charge for the year: £4,270–£3,111	£1,159

Year to 31 December 2004

All 17,500 options are exercised on 31 March 2004 when the market value of the shares was £3.20.

Market value at 31 March 2004	£3.20
Exercise price	£1.00
Gain per share option	£2.20

Total gain: 17,500 x £2.20	£38,500
Employers NI: £38,500 x 12.2%	£4,697
Charge for the year: £4,697–£4,270	£427

Recognition in the accounts

10.43 All amounts provided for NI on share option gains should be charged to the profit and loss account as part of staff costs, except where they form part of staff costs capitalised under companies' legislation and accounting standards (e.g. own labour used in the construction of tangible fixed assets).

Reimbursement by employee

10.44 Legislation before Parliament when the Abstract was issued (and which has since been enacted) permits some or all of the NI liability in respect of gains on share options to be transferred from the employer to the employee, where the employee agrees to this. Where there is a formal agreement between the employer and employee, under which the employee agrees to reimburse all or part of the NI, the expected reimbursement should be accounted for by the employer as a separate asset if it is virtually certain to be received. This is in line with the requirements of FRS 12 'Provisions, Contingent Liabilities and Contingent Assets' in respect of any reimbursement expected in relation to a provision. A net presentation is permitted in the profit and loss account.

Transfer of liability to employee

10.45 Where there is a joint election by the employer and the employee under which the NI liability is formally transferred to the employee, the Abstract notes that no provision will be necessary in the accounts of the employer. However, it will be important to determine that the liability has been genuinely transferred in full to the employee before such an accounting treatment can be adopted.

Disclosure

10.46 FRS 12 requires detailed disclosures for each class of provision recognised in the accounts, including an indication of the uncertainties over the timing or amount of the transfer of economic benefits and the main assumptions made concerning future events. UITF Abstract 25 notes that it may be necessary to disclose the share price used in calculating the NI provision, together with the effect of a significant movement in that price.

Other situations

10.47 The Abstract is drafted specifically in the context of NI contributions on share option gains, but the UITF has taken the opportunity to emphasise that the principles apply equally to other analogous situations that give rise to employer NI liabilities.

LIKELY FUTURE DEVELOPMENTS

FRED 31 'Share-based payment

10.48 The ASB published FRED 31 'Share-based Payment' in November 2002. The FRED sets out proposals for a UK accounting standard based on the International Accounting Standards Board's (IASB's) exposure draft ED 2 which was published simultaneously. The draft standards are based on the following principles:

- when an entity receives goods or other services in exchange for a share-based payment, it should recognise an expense;
- that expense should be recognised over the period in which the services involved are rendered or as the goods involved are received;
- the expense should be measured by reference to fair value.

FRED 31 proposes that the standard should apply to all UK entities (both listed and unlisted) and to all share-based payment transactions, including all employee share option schemes, all Save-As-You-Earn (SAYE) plans and similar arrangements, and all share-based payment transactions involving the receipt of goods and non-employee services.

Proposed timing

10.49 In view of the importance and urgency that the ASB attaches to this subject, it is proposing that the standard should be implemented in the UK as soon as possible. Under the IASB's current timetable, the international accounting standard would come into effect for accounting periods beginning on or after 1 January 2004 and the ASB is proposing the same effective date for the UK standard.

Recognition of share-based payments

10.50 When an entity receives or acquires goods or services in a share-based payment transaction, those goods or services should be recognised as they are received. In the case of a cash-settled share-based payment, the entity should recognise a liability. In the case of an equity-settled share-based payment, the entity should recognise a corresponding increase in equity. The goods or services should be recognised as expenses unless they qualify for recognition as assets.

Cash-settled share-based payment transactions

10.51 A cash-settled share-based payment transaction is one where:

- the settlement amount is calculated by reference to the price of an equity instrument of the payee; and
- settlement is made by means of a payment in cash or other assets rather then by the issue of equity instruments.

Goods and services received by means of a cash-settled share-based payment transaction should be measured at the fair value of the liability. Fair value should be remeasured at each reporting date, with any changes recognised in the profit and loss account, until the liability is settled.

Equity-settled share-based transactions

10.52 An equity-settled share-based payment transaction is one where:

- the settlement amount is calculated by reference to the price of an equity instrument of the payee; and
- settlement is made by issuing equity instruments rather than by means of a payment in cash or other assets.

Most employee share option plans and all Inland Revenue approved SAYE plans are equity-settled share-based payment transactions. Where a reporting entity acquires goods or services through such a transaction, both the goods and services and the corresponding increase in equity should be measured:

- either directly at the fair value of the goods or services received at the date that they are received; or
- indirectly by reference to the fair value of the equity instrument granted at the grant date, if this is more readily determinable.

For transactions with parties other than employees, there is a rebuttable presumption that the fair value of the goods or services received is the more readily determinable fair value. Transactions with employees should be measured by reference to the fair value of the equity instrument granted. If the equity instruments vest immediately and unconditionally, the entity should recognise the services received in full, with a corresponding increase in equity. If the instruments do not vest until a specified period of service has been completed, the services should be recognised as they are rendered during the vesting period, with a corresponding increase in equity. The draft standard includes additional guidance on:

- measuring the services received in each period;
- establishing the fair value of the equity instruments granted; and

— dealing with any modifications to the terms and conditions on which equity instruments were granted.

Share-based payment transactions with cash alternatives

10.53 Where either the reporting entity or the other party can choose whether the transaction is settled in cash or by the issue of equity instruments, the entity should account for the transaction (or any relevant components of the transaction) as a cash-settled share-based payment transaction if a liability has been incurred, and as an equity-settled share-based payment transaction if no such liability has been incurred. The draft standard sets out detailed guidance and accounting treatments in each case (i.e. depending on whether the option rests with the reporting entity or with the other party).

Disclosure

10.54 The following minimum disclosures are proposed:

(i) a description of each type of share-based payment arrangement that has existed during the reporting period, including details of:

— whether the rights granted by the entity consisted of rights to shares, share options, other equity instruments, cash or other assets;

— when the rights were granted;

— details of those to whom the rights were granted (eg number and class of employees);

— the contractual life of any options granted;

— whether the exercise price is fixed or variable and, if variable, how it is determined; and

— a description of any vesting requirements;

(ii) the number and weighted average exercise prices of options for options:

— outstanding at the beginning of the period;

— granted during the period;

— forfeited during the period;

— exercised during the period;

— outstanding at the end of the period; and

— exercisable at the end of the period;

(iii) or options exercised during the period, the weighted average share price at the date of exercise;

(iv) for options outstanding at the end of the period, the range of exercise prices and weighted average remaining expected life and contractual life;

(v) if the entity has measured the fair value of goods and services received by reference to the fair value of equity instruments granted:

- the weighted average fair value of options granted during the period and details of how fair value was measured (the draft standard specifies the information that should be included);
- the number and weighted average fair value of any shares or other equity instruments granted during the year, and information on how fair value was measured (the draft standard specifies the information that should be included);
- the weighted average fair value of any rights to cash, or rights to either cash or equity instruments, granted during the year (analysed into debt and equity components where appropriate) and details of how fair values were measured;
- where share-based payment arrangements have been modified during the period, an explanation of the modifications, the incremental fair value granted as a result and details on how this was measured;
- for options, shares and other equity instruments that vested during the period (or would have done so if vesting conditions had been satisfied), a comparison of the percentage or number of equity instruments that vested and the grant date estimate of the percentage or number expected to vest;
- for options exercised during the period, a comparison of actual option life and the grant date estimate of expected life;

(vi) where the fair value of goods and services received during the period has been measured directly, how that fair value was determined;

(vii) where appropriate, an explanation of why the presumption in **10.52** has been rebutted;

(viii) the total expenses recognised for the period arising from share-based payment transactions;

(ix) for cash-settled share-based payment transactions, the portion attributable to the transaction having been measured as a cash-settled rather than an equity-settled transaction.

Additional information must be given where this is necessary to enable users to understand the extent and nature of share-based payment arrangements in the period, how fair values have been determined for share-based payment transactions, and the effect of such transactions on the profit and loss account.

Transitional provisions

10.55 The IASB proposes that the new standard should apply retrospectively, except that it should not apply to share-based payments that vested before 1 January 2004 or to grants of equity-settled share-based payments that were made prior to publication of the standard. However, the ASB outlines certain difficulties arising from this proposal and comments are specifically invited on the issue.

Changes to current UITF Abstracts

10.56 In the preface to FRED 31, the ASB also summarises the effect of the latest proposals on current UITF Abstracts:

- UITF Abstract 13 'Accounting for ESOP trusts' is likely to be withdrawn and the ASB intends to ask the UITF to consider whether a new Abstract should be developed on accounting for ESOP trusts;
- UITF Abstract 17 'Employee share schemes' will be superseded by the new standard;
- no changes are likely to be needed to UITF Abstract 25 'National insurance contributions on share option gains' or UITF Abstract 30 'Date of award to employees of shares or rights to shares'; and
- UITF Abstract 32 'Employee benefit trusts and other intermediate payment arrangements' may need some amendment to ensure its requirements are aligned with any successor to UITF Abstract 13.

Chapter 11

Retirement Benefits

TYPES OF RETIREMENT SCHEME

What are retirement benefits?

11.1 Many employers include the provision of a pension, and possibly other retirement benefits, in the remuneration package that they offer to employees, and retirement benefits can often form a significant element of total staff costs for the year, hence the requirement for separate disclosure of pension costs under CA 1985 (see **Chapter 10**). FRS 17 'Retirement Benefits' defines retirement benefits as:

> 'All forms of consideration given by an employer in exchange for services rendered by employees that are payable after the completion of employment.'

The guidance in the standard emphasises that retirement benefits do not include termination benefits payable on termination of employment before the employee's normal retirement date or where an employee accepts voluntary redundancy in exchange for the benefits. This is on the basis that such benefits are not given in exchange for employee services. The objective of FRS 17 is to ensure that:

- financial statements reflect at fair value the assets and liabilities arising from an employer's retirement benefit obligations and any related funding;
- the operating costs of providing retirement benefits are recognised in the accounting period(s) in which the benefits are earned by the employees, and the related financing costs and other changes in the value of the assets and liabilities are recognised in the accounting periods in which they arise; and
- there is adequate disclosure of the cost of providing retirement benefits and the related assets, liabilities, gains and losses.

Employer commitments

11.2 FRS 17 covers all retirement benefits that an employer is committed to making, regardless of whether the commitment is statutory, contractual or implicit. Each of the following would therefore come within the scope of the standard:

- a commitment to provide pension and other retirement benefits (e.g. medical care) set out in the employee's contract of employment;
- a commitment arising from custom and practice over a period of time (i.e. where the employer has traditionally made retirement arrangements for employees, even though it has no contractual obligation to do so); or
- a commitment arising when an employer makes *ex gratia* or discretionary payments on a case by case basis.

Commitments arising outside the UK are also covered.

Unfunded schemes

11.3 Where an employer operates an unfunded scheme (i.e. benefits are simply paid as they fall due and no payments are made to fund benefits earned during the period), FRS 17 still requires a liability to be recognised in the financial statements as the benefits are earned by the employees, rather than as the actual payments become due.

Defined contribution schemes

11.4 A defined contribution scheme is defined in FRS 17 as:

> 'A pension or other retirement benefit scheme into which an employer pays regular contributions fixed as an amount or as a percentage of pay and will have no legal or constructive obligation to pay further contributions if the scheme does not have sufficient assets to pay all employee benefits relating to employee service in the current and prior periods.'

The definition goes on to explain that the benefits of an individual member are determined by reference to the contributions paid into the scheme in respect of that member, usually increased by an amount based on the investment return on the contributions. Defined contribution schemes may also provide death-in-service benefits, but these are not deemed to relate to employee service in the current and prior reporting periods.

Defined benefit schemes

11.5 A defined benefit scheme is defined in FRS 17 as 'a pension or retirement benefit scheme other than a defined contribution scheme'. The definition goes on to explain that the scheme rules will usually define the benefits independently of the contributions payable, and the benefits will not usually be directly related to the scheme investments. A defined benefit scheme may be funded or unfunded.

Difficulties in accounting for defined benefit schemes

11.6 Under a defined benefit scheme, the benefits paid to an employee on retirement will usually be based in some way on the length of service provided and his/her salary during the period of employment. Benefits may be based on an average salary for the period, but are more commonly based on final salary or an average salary over (say) the last three years of employment. The benefits are therefore not specifically linked to the contributions paid into the scheme and the employer will usually have a commitment to ensure that there are sufficient funds in the scheme to pay the appropriate benefits, and may be required to make good any potential deficit in the funding of the scheme. In the case of a defined benefit scheme, therefore, the full extent of the employer's commitment is more difficult to quantify and to account for. Actuarial calculations must be carried out on a regular basis to establish the overall funding level of the scheme and to assess the level of contributions required to maintain adequate funding of the scheme. One of the particular problems is the very long-term nature of such schemes and the fact that a number of assumptions about future events will need to be made in order to carry out the calculations. Most of the detailed requirements of FRS 17 therefore deal with accounting for defined benefit retirement schemes.

ACCOUNTING FOR DEFINED CONTRIBUTION SCHEMES

Profit and loss account

11.7 FRS 17 notes that the cost of a defined contribution scheme is equal to the contributions payable to the scheme for the accounting period. Where an employer operates a defined contribution scheme, the charge to the profit and loss account each year will therefore represent the contributions payable by the employer in respect of that accounting period. This figure must be calculated on an accruals basis and the amount charged may therefore not be the same as the amount actually paid over to the scheme during the period. As the contributions payable represent the full extent of the employer's commitments under the scheme, this accounting treatment meets the objective of FRS 17. The standard specifies that the cost must be recognised in arriving at operating profit in the profit and loss account.

Disclosure

11.8 The accounts must include the following disclosures:

- the nature of the scheme (i.e. the fact that it is a defined contribution scheme);
- the cost for the period; and
- any outstanding or prepaid contributions at the balance sheet date.

These disclosure requirements might be met as follows:

Example 11.1 – FRS 17 disclosure requirement

The company operates a defined contribution pension scheme which is open to all employees. The assets of the pension scheme are held separately from those of the company in an independently administered fund. The amount payable to the pension scheme during the year in respect of the company's contributions amounted to £35,700 (20XX: £35,400). At the end of the year contributions of £2,540 (20XX: £2,150) had not been paid over to the scheme. These are included in creditors due within one year.

Any unpaid contributions at the end of the accounting period should be shown within creditors due within one year, and any prepaid contributions should be shown within debtors.

Accounting policy

11.9 It will usually also be appropriate to disclose the accounting policy adopted for a defined contribution scheme. Wording along the following lines might be suitable:

Example 11.2 – Accounting policy disclosure (defined contribution scheme)

Retirement benefits

The company operates a defined contribution pension scheme which is open to all employees. In accordance with FRS 17 'Retirement Benefits', the company's contributions to this scheme are charged in arriving at operating profit in the profit and loss account in the year to which they relate. No other retirement benefits are provided.

MULTI-EMPLOYER SCHEMES

Group retirement schemes

11.10 In some cases, more than one employer may participate in the same retirement scheme. This situation is relatively common in groups of companies, where a single retirement scheme is operated for the whole group and each subsidiary participates in the scheme in respect of its own employees.

Defined contribution schemes

11.11 If the scheme is a defined contribution scheme, the multi-employer aspect does not give rise to any particular accounting issues.

Each employer's commitment is limited to the contributions that it is expected to make in respect of its own employees, and the cost in each reporting period will be the contributions due for that period.

Defined benefit schemes

11.12 Where more than one employer participates in a defined benefit scheme, the general requirement under FRS 17 is that each employer should account for the scheme as a defined benefit scheme. However, the standard recognises that this may not be appropriate or practical in every case and two specific exceptions to this general rule are therefore permitted:

- where the employer's contributions are set in relation to the current service period only (i.e. they are not affected by any surplus or deficit in the scheme relating to the past service of its own employees or any other members of the scheme), the scheme should be accounted for as a defined contribution scheme - this treatment should only be adopted where there is clear evidence that the employer cannot be required to pay additional contributions relating to past service, including the existence of a third party which accepts the obligation to fund the pension payments if the scheme's assets should prove to be insufficient;
- where the employer's contributions are affected by a surplus or deficit in the scheme but the employer is unable to identify its share of the underlying assets and liabilities in the scheme on a consistent and reasonable basis, the employer should account for the scheme as a defined contribution scheme but should disclose:
  - the fact that the scheme is a defined benefit scheme but that the employer is unable to identify its share of the underlying assets and liabilities; and
  - any available information on the surplus or deficit in the scheme and the implications for the employer.

In the case of a group scheme, the second exception only enables the individual subsidiaries (and, where appropriate, the parent company in its own individual accounts) to account for the scheme as a defined contribution scheme. However, the scheme must still be accounted for as a defined benefit scheme in the group accounts, as it does not constitute a multi-employer scheme at this level and the impracticality of identifying individual shares of the underlying assets and liabilities is no longer relevant.

ACCOUNTING FOR DEFINED BENEFIT SCHEMES

FRS 17 'Retirement benefits'

11.13 FRS 17 'Retirement Benefits' is fully effective for accounting periods beginning on or after 1 January 2005. The standard makes some very significant changes to the previous accounting practice on accounting for pension and similar costs, bringing UK requirements more into line with international developments, and the ASB has therefore set a long implementation period, although early adoption is encouraged. If the new standard is not adopted early, detailed information calculated on the basis of FRS 17 must be disclosed in the notes to the accounts in the intervening years. Gains and losses arising on the initial recognition of items in the primary statements under FRS 17 should be dealt with as prior period adjustments in accordance with FRS 3 'Reporting Financial Performance'.

Actuarial valuations

11.14 Actuarial valuations provide the actuary's best estimate of the cost to the employer of providing the promised retirement benefits to employees. In carrying out a valuation, a number of assumptions about future events will need to be made and the decisions taken here can have a very significant effect on the level of contributions required from the employer (and, where relevant, the employees). The main assumptions will cover issues such as:

- future pay increases;
- future rates of inflation;
- increases in pension payments;
- changes to the number of employees in the scheme;
- the age profile of employees; and
- expected earnings from scheme investments.

Once decisions have been reached on these factors, the actuary will assess how the scheme should be funded to ensure that adequate resources are available to meet the pension commitments as they fall due. The aim is to ensure that present and future contributions to the scheme will be sufficient to secure payment of the agreed benefits to former employees.

Valuation methods

11.15 Various actuarial methods can be used to determine the liabilities of a defined benefit scheme and thus the level of contributions needed to achieve and maintain adequate funding. The two principal categories of actuarial valuation methods are:

- accrued benefits methods - these are based on the principle that the obligation to provide retirement benefits to an employee will be greater as that employee gets closer to retirement; and
- prospective benefits methods - these are based on the principle that the obligation to provide retirement benefits to an employee accumulates evenly throughout the period of that individual's employment.

FRS 17 requires scheme liabilities to be measured using the projected unit method. This is an accrued benefits valuation method under which allowance is made for projected earnings. Further guidance on this method is given in Guidance Note 26 (GN26) issued by the Faculty and Institute of Actuaries.

Measurement of scheme assets

11.16 Under FRS 17, scheme assets should be measured at their fair value at the balance sheet date. Scheme assets include current assets as well as investments, and any liabilities (such as accrued expenses) should be deducted. The standard includes the following specific guidance on establishing fair value for each category of asset:

- for quoted securities, the mid-market value is to be taken as fair value;
- in the case of unquoted securities, an estimate of fair value should be used;
- for unitised securities, the average of the bid and offer prices should be taken;
- property should be valued at open market value or on another appropriate basis in accordance with the Appraisal and Valuation Manual published by the Royal Institution of Chartered Surveyors (RICS);
- insurance policies that exactly match the amount and timing of some or all of the benefits payable should be measured at the same amount as the related obligations;
- for other insurance policies, the entity should choose the valuation method that gives the best approximation to fair value, given the circumstances of the scheme.

The guidance also notes that notional funding of a pension scheme does not give rise to assets in a scheme for the purpose of the standard.

Measurement of scheme liabilities

11.17 Scheme liabilities are liabilities for outgoings due after the valuation date, reflecting the benefits that the employer is committed to providing for employee services provided up to that date. They should be measured on an actuarial basis using the projected unit method. Scheme liabilities comprise:

- benefits promised under the formal terms of the scheme; and
- any constructive obligations for further benefits where a public statement or past practice by the employer has created a valid expectation in the employees that these benefits will be granted.

Benefits should be attributed to periods of service according to the scheme's benefit formula, except where this attributes a disproportionate share of the benefits to later years of service. In this case, the benefit should be attributed on a straight line basis over the period during which it is earned. Where the scheme rules require a surplus in the scheme to be shared between the employer and the scheme members, or where past practice has established a valid expectation that this will be done, the amount that will be passed to the members should be treated as increasing the scheme liabilities.

Actuarial assumptions

11.18 Actuarial assumptions underlying the valuation of scheme liabilities should be mutually compatible (i.e. they must reflect the underlying economic factors on a consistent basis), and they should lead to the best estimate of the future cash flows that will arise. The directors (or equivalent) have ultimate responsibility for the assumptions, but they should be set on advice given by an actuary. Any assumptions that are affected by economic conditions should reflect market expectations at the balance sheet date. The assumptions should also reflect expected future events that will affect the cost of the benefits to which the employer is committed (either legally or constructively) at the balance sheet date. Depending on the nature of the scheme these will usually include:

- expected cost of living increases - these may be provided for in the scheme rules or may have been established by the past practice of the employer, so that employees have developed a valid expectation of receiving them;
- salary increases (where the pension is to be based on final salary);
- expected early retirement (where the scheme gives this right to employees);
- expected future changes in the cost of retirement health care - the guidance notes that these costs are particularly difficult to estimate and suggests a number of factors that may need to be taken into account, including:
  - advances in medical skills and technologies, which may result in higher treatment costs;
  - a rise in the expectations of prospective patients; and
  - in the light of the above, the possibility of employers and other benefit providers reducing benefits and making the patient pay a proportion of the costs.

Expected future redundancies should not be reflected in the assumptions as the employer is not committed to making them. When the employer does become committed to making redundancies, the impact on the scheme should be treated as a settlement or curtailment. Also, it should not be assumed that benefits will be reduced below those currently promised (e.g. on the grounds that the employer will curtail the scheme at some point in the future).

Discounting of scheme liabilities

11.19 Scheme liabilities should be discounted at a rate reflecting the time value of money and the characteristics of the liability. This should be assumed to be the current rate of return on a high quality (AA) corporate bond of equivalent currency and term to the scheme liabilities. The guidance notes that, if no suitable corporate bond can be identified, the rate of return on appropriate government bonds, together with a margin for assumed credit risk spreads (from the global bond markets), may provide an acceptable alternative.

Frequency of valuations

11.20 Full actuarial valuations by a professionally qualified actuary should be obtained for a defined benefit scheme at intervals not exceeding three years. The actuary should review the valuation at each balance sheet date and update it to reflect current conditions – for instance, the fair values of scheme assets and financial assumptions such as the discount rate may need to be adjusted each year.

Balance sheet recognition of surplus or deficit

11.21 The surplus or deficit in a defined benefit scheme is the excess or shortfall of the value of the scheme assets over or below the present value of the scheme liabilities. The employer should recognise a liability to the extent that it reflects a legal or constructive obligation to make good the deficit. The employer should recognise an asset to the extent that it is able to recover this through reduced contributions or through refunds from the scheme.

Determination of employer's liability

11.22 A legal obligation to make good a deficit in the scheme may arise under the terms of the trust deed. A constructive obligation may arise if the employer has in the past acted to make good such deficits. Where the employees also contribute to the scheme, any deficit should be assumed to be borne by the employer unless the scheme rules specifically require employee contributions to be increased to help fund the deficit. In these circumstances, the present value of the additional employee contributions should be treated as reducing the deficit to be borne by the employer.

Determination of employer's asset

11.23 A scheme surplus will give rise to an asset for the employer to the extent that:

— the employer has control over its use – for instance, the employer can use the surplus to generate future economic benefits, in the form of reduced contributions or a refund from the scheme; and

— that control arises as a result of past events.

Under most schemes, an employer's obligation will be to pay contributions at the level recommended by the actuary to keep the scheme fully funded. There will not usually be any requirement to generate a surplus in the scheme. Where a surplus does arise, it is therefore unlikely that the employer could be required to continue to make contributions to maintain the surplus. Also, the decision on whether the surplus should be used to improve scheme benefits will usually rest with the employer. In most cases, therefore, control over the use of a surplus will rest with the employer.

Asset resulting from reduced contributions

11.24 When determining an asset to be recognised in the balance sheet, the amount that can be recovered through reduced future contributions is the present value of the liability expected to arise from future service by current and future scheme members, less the present value of future employee contributions. No growth in the number of active scheme members should be assumed, but a decline in membership should be reflected if appropriate. The amount that can be recovered should be based on the assumptions used under the accounting standard, rather than on funding assumptions, and the present value of the reduction in future contributions should be determined using the discount rate applied to measure the defined benefit liability.

Refunds from the scheme

11.25 The amount to be recovered from refunds should reflect only refunds agreed by the pension scheme trustees at the balance sheet date.

Improvement in benefits

11.26 Where some or all of the surplus is used to improve members' benefits under the scheme, this should be accounted for as a past service cost at the time that it occurs. It should not be anticipated by reducing the amount recognised as an asset in the balance sheet of the employer.

Balance sheet presentation

11.27 Any unpaid pension contributions at the balance sheet date should be shown within creditors due within one year. The defined benefit asset or liability, net of any related deferred tax balance, should be shown separately on the face of the balance sheet as follows:

- in a balance sheet prepared under Format 1, Companies Act 1985 Sch 4, after item J (Accruals and deferred income) but before item K (Capital and reserves);
- in a balance sheet prepared under Format 2, Companies Act 1985 Sch 4, an asset should be shown after item D (Prepayments and accrued income) in the 'Assets' section and a liability should be shown after item D (Accruals and deferred income) in the 'Liabilities' section.

Appendix I to FRS 17 suggests the following layout for this disclosure:

Example 11.3 – Balance sheet disclosure of pension asset

	20X2	20X1
	£	£
Net assets excluding pension asset	70,400	65,200
Pension asset	3,500	1,450
Net assets including pension asset	73,900	66,650

Where an employer has more than one scheme, the total of any defined benefit assets and the total of any defined benefit liabilities should be shown separately on the face of the balance sheet.

Deferred tax

11.28 The deferred tax relating to the defined benefit asset or liability should be offset against the defined benefit asset or liability and not included with other deferred tax assets or liabilities.

Recognition in performance statements

11.29 The change in the net defined benefit asset or liability (other than changes arising from contributions to the scheme) should be analysed into:

- periodic costs:
  - current service cost;
  - interest cost;
  - expected return on assets;

  — actuarial gains or losses;

— non-periodic costs:

  — past service costs; and

  — gains and losses on settlements and curtailments.

Current service cost

11.30 Current service cost is the increase in the present value of the scheme liabilities expected to arise from employee service in the current period. The current service cost should be based on the most recent actuarial valuation at the beginning of the period, with the financial assumptions updated to reflect conditions at that date. It should be included within operating profit in the profit and loss account, except to the extent that employee remuneration is capitalised in accordance with another accounting standard. Any contributions from employees should be set against the current service cost.

Interest cost

11.31 Interest cost is the expected increase during the period in the present value of scheme liabilities because the benefits are one period closer to settlement. The interest cost should be based on the discount rate and the present value of the scheme liabilities at the beginning of the period. In addition, it should reflect changes in the scheme liabilities during the period. The net of the interest cost and the expected return on assets should be included as other finance costs (or income) adjacent to interest.

Expected return on assets

11.32 The expected rate of return on assets is the average rate of return (both income and changes in fair value), net of scheme expenses, expected over the remaining life of the related obligation on the actual assets held by the scheme. The expected return on assets should be based on long-term expectations at the beginning of the period and is expected to be reasonably stable. For quoted corporate or government bonds, the expected return should be calculated by applying the current redemption yield at the beginning of the period to the market value of the bonds at that date. For other assets, such as equities, the expected return should be calculated by applying the expected long-term rate of return at the beginning of the period to the fair value of the assets held by the scheme at that date. The expected return on assets should also reflect changes in the assets during the period as a result of contributions paid into and benefits paid out of the scheme. The expected rate of return should be set by the directors (or equivalent), based on advice given by an actuary. The net of the expected return on assets and the interest cost should be included as other finance costs (or income) adjacent to interest.

Actuarial gains and losses

11.33 These are changes in actuarial deficits or surpluses that arise because events have not coincided with the actuarial assumptions made at the time of the last valuation (i.e. experience gains and losses), or because the actuarial assumptions have changed. They may arise in relation to both scheme assets and scheme liabilities and comprise:

- differences between the expected and actual returns on scheme assets;
- differences between the actuarial assumptions underlying scheme liabilities and actual experience during the period;
- the effect of changes in the actuarial assumptions underlying the scheme liabilities; and
- any adjustments resulting from the limit on the recognition of a defined benefit asset in the employer's balance sheet.

Actuarial gains and losses arising from a new valuation or from an update of the latest valuation should be recognised in the statement of total recognised gains and losses for the period. Once recognised in this way, the gains and losses should not be recognised again in the profit and loss account in subsequent accounting periods.

Past service costs

11.34 Past service costs are the increase in the present value of the scheme liabilities related to employee service in prior periods arising in the current period as a result of the introduction of new or improved retired benefits. They arise when an employer makes a commitment to provide a higher level of benefit than previously promised (e.g. a new pension benefit for a spouse). This includes improvements made as a result of the scheme being in surplus - this still represents a cost to the employer, because using the surplus to improve benefits means that the employer cannot benefit from it in other ways. However, past service costs do not include increases in the expected costs of benefits that the employer is already committed to provide (e.g. cost of living increases) - these are covered by the actuarial assumptions and differences between the assumptions and actual experience, and the effect of any changes in the assumptions, are actuarial gains and losses and should be accounted for as such. Past service costs should be recognised in the profit and loss account on a straight-line basis over the period in which the increases in benefit vest. Where benefits vest immediately, the past service cost should be recognised immediately. Any unrecognised past service costs should be deducted from the scheme liabilities, and the balance sheet asset or liability should be adjusted accordingly.

Settlements and curtailments

11.35 A settlement is an irrevocable action that relieves the employer (or the defined benefit scheme) of the primary responsibility for a pension obligation and eliminates significant risks relating to the obligation and the assets used to effect the settlement. Settlements include:

— a lump-sum cash payment to scheme members in exchange for their rights to receive specified pension benefits;

— the purchase of an irrevocable annuity contract sufficient to cover vested benefits; and

— the transfer of scheme assets and liabilities relating to a group of employees leaving the scheme.

A curtailment is an event that reduces the expected years of future service of present employees or reduces for a number of employees the accrual of defined benefits for some or all of their future service. Curtailments include:

— early termination of employees' services (e.g. through closure of a factory or discontinuation of a business segment); and

— termination of, or amendment to, the terms of a defined benefit scheme so that some or all future service by current employees will no longer qualify for benefits or will only qualify for reduced benefits.

Where the scheme rules permit employees to retire early or transfer out of the scheme, the related settlements and curtailments will be reflected in the actuarial assumptions - any gains or losses are actuarial gains and losses and should be accounted for as such. However, gains and losses may also arise on a settlement or curtailment that has not been allowed for in the actuarial assumptions - for instance, a reduction in the number of employees as a result of the sale or termination of an operation, or a decision to transfer the accrued benefits of some members into a defined contribution scheme. Losses should be measured at the date on which the employer becomes demonstrably committed to the transaction and should be recognised in the profit and loss account covering that date. Gains should be measured at the date on which all parties whose consent is required are irrevocably committed to the transaction and should be recognised in the profit and loss account in the period covering that date. These gains and losses should be recognised within operating profit unless they relate to an item that is required to be shown separately after operating profit.

Impact of limit on balance sheet asset

11.36 The limit on the amount that can be recognised as a defined benefit asset may result in some part of a defined benefit scheme surplus not being recognised in the balance sheet. In this case, the amounts recognised in the profit and loss account and statement of total recognised gains and losses should be adjusted as follows:

- if any refund is agreed and is covered by the unrecognised surplus, it should be recognised as other finance income adjacent to interest, with separate disclosure in the notes – refunds from schemes where the whole of the surplus is already regarded as recoverable do not give rise to gains, as the cash received (together with any related tax effect) simply reduces the asset shown in the employer's balance sheet;
- next, the unrecognised surplus should be applied to extinguish past service costs or losses on settlements or curtailments that would otherwise be charged in the profit and loss account for the period, and the notes to the accounts should disclose the items and amounts extinguished;
- next, the expected return on assets should be restricted so that it does not exceed the total of the current service cost, interest cost (and any past service costs and losses on settlements and curtailments not covered by the unrecognised surplus) and any increase in the recoverable surplus;
- any further adjustment necessary should be treated as an actuarial gain or loss.

An increase in the recoverable amount of a surplus as a result of an increase in the active membership of the scheme (for instance, due to increased recruitment or the acquisition of another business) should be recognised as an operating gain. In the case of an acquisition, the gain should be accounted for as a post-acquisition operating gain and not as an adjustment to the purchase consideration and related goodwill. A decrease in the recoverable amount of a surplus arising from a fall in the active membership of the scheme should be treated as an actuarial loss unless it arises from an event not covered by the assumptions underlying the amount originally regarded as recoverable (e.g. a settlement or curtailment). In this case, it should be treated as part of the loss arising on that event.

Tax

11.37 Where current tax relief arises on contributions made to the scheme, it should be allocated to the profit and loss account or statement of total recognised gains and losses on the basis that the contribution covers firstly items reported in the profit and loss account and then any actuarial losses recognised in the statement of total recognised gains and losses, unless it is clear that another method of allocation is more appropriate (e.g. tax relief on a special contribution to fund a deficit arising from an actuarial loss should be allocated to the statement of total recognised gains and losses as this is where the actuarial loss itself is recognised). To the extent that the contribution exceeds these items, the current tax relief attributable to the excess should be allocated to the profit and loss account, unless it is clearly more appropriate to allocate it to the statement of recognised gains and losses. FRS 16 'Current Tax' requires disclosure of any current tax recognised in the profit and loss account and statement of total recognised gains and losses.

Death-in-service and incapacity benefits

11.38 A charge should be made to operating profit to reflect the expected cost of providing any death-in-service or incapacity benefits for the period. Any difference between that expected cost and the amounts actually incurred should be treated as an actuarial gain or loss. Where the costs of death-in service or incapacity benefits are insured by the scheme, the expected cost for the accounting period will be the insurance premium payable for that period. If the costs are not insured, the expected cost should take into account the probability of employee deaths or incapacity during service and the benefits that would be payable in these circumstances. UITF Abstract 35 'Death-in-service and incapacity benefits' now clarifies that uninsured benefits should be measured using the projected unit method of valuation in the same way as other scheme liabilities.

Disclosure

11.39 The following disclosures should be given for a defined benefit scheme:

- nature of the scheme;
- date of the most recent full actuarial valuation on which amounts in the financial statements are based;
- if the actuary is an employee or officer of the reporting entity, this fact must be disclosed;
- contributions made in respect of the accounting period and any agreed contribution rates for future years;
- for closed schemes and those in which the age profile of the active membership is rising significantly, the fact that under the projected unit method the current service cost will increase as the members of the scheme approach retirement;
- each of the main financial assumptions used at the beginning of the period and at the balance sheet date, including:
  - inflation assumption;
  - rate of increase in salaries;
  - rate of increase for pensions in payment and deferred pensions; and

    — rate used to discount scheme liabilities.

  These details should be disclosed as separate figures and should not be combined or netted;

- the fair value of the assets held by the scheme at the beginning and end of the period, analysed into the following classes, together with the expected rate of return assumed for each class for the period and the subsequent period:
  - equities;
  - bonds;
  - other (sub analysed if material);
- the following amounts included within operating profit (or capitalised as part of employee remuneration where relevant) should be disclosed in the notes to the financial statements:
  - current service cost;
  - any past service costs;
  - any previously unrecognised surplus deducted from past service costs;
  - gains and losses on any settlements and curtailments; and
  - any previously unrecognised surplus deducted from settlement or curtailment losses;
- any gains and losses on settlements and curtailments (and any previously unrecognised surplus deducted from the losses) included within a separate item after operating profit;
- the following amounts included as other finance costs (or income) should be disclosed separately in the notes to the financial statements:
  - interest cost; and
  - expected return on assets in the scheme;
- the following amounts included within the statement of total recognised gains and losses should be disclosed separately in the notes to the financial statements:
  - difference between the expected and actual return on assets;
  - experience gains and losses arising on scheme liabilities;
  - effects of changes in the demographic and financial assumptions underlying the present value of scheme liabilities.

Reconciliation to the balance sheet

11.40 Where an entity operates a defined benefit scheme, the following amounts should be disclosed in a note to the balance sheet:

— fair value of scheme assets;

— present value of scheme liabilities (based on the accounting assumptions);

— the resulting surplus or deficit; and

— an analysis of the movement in the surplus or deficit during the period.

Where the defined benefit asset or liability in the balance sheet differs from the scheme surplus or deficit shown in the note, an explanation of the difference should be given. Differences will usually arise because of the need to account for deferred tax on the asset or liability, or the need to restrict the amount recognised as an asset.

Five-year summary

11.41 In addition, where an entity operates a defined benefit scheme, the financial statements must include a five-year summary of the following:

— the difference between expected and actual returns on assets, expressed as (a) an amount and (b) a percentage of the scheme assets at the balance sheet date;

— experience gains and losses arising on scheme liabilities expressed as (a) an amount and (b) a percentage of the present value of scheme liabilities at the balance sheet date; and

— the total actuarial gain or loss expressed as (a) an amount and (b) a percentage of the present value of the scheme liabilities at the balance sheet date.

This disclosure is to highlight trends, which will generally be more relevant than gains or losses in one period. For instance, a consistent trend of experience losses may indicate that actuarial assumptions have been over-optimistic and could cast doubt on the reliability of amounts included in the profit and loss account. However, the standard does not require retrospective creation of five-year summaries of amounts recognised in the statement of total recognised gains and losses.

Analysis of reserves

11.42 Where an entity operates a defined benefit scheme, the analysis of reserves in the notes to the financial statements should distinguish the amount relating to the defined benefit asset or liability, net of related deferred tax. Appendix I to FRS 17 suggests the following layout:

Example 11.4 – Analysis of reserves note

	20X2	*20X1*
	£	£
Profit and loss reserve, excluding pension asset	20,500	19,250
Pension reserve	3,500	1,450
Profit and loss reserve	24,000	20,700

Entities with more than one defined benefit scheme

11.43 Where an employer has more than one defined benefit scheme, the required disclosures may be given in total, separately or in such groupings as are felt to be most useful (e.g. by geographical location, or where schemes are subject to significantly different risks). Where the disclosures are given in total, the assumptions should be given in the form of weighted averages or relatively narrow ranges, with separate disclosure of any items outside the range.

Accounting policy

11.44 It will usually also be appropriate to disclose the accounting policy adopted for a defined benefit scheme. Wording along the following lines might be suitable:

Example 11.5 – Accounting policy disclosure (defined benefit scheme)

Retirement benefits

The company operates a defined benefit pension scheme which is open to all employees. The assets of the scheme are held separately from those of the company in an independently administered fund, and pensions payable under the scheme are based on final pensionable salary. In accordance with FRS 17 'Retirement Benefits', the operating costs of providing these benefits are recognised in the profit and loss account in the accounting period in which the benefits are earned by the employees, and related financing and other costs are recognised in the period in which they arise. No other retirement benefits are provided.

ACCOUNTING UNDER SSAP 24

Transitional period

11.45 FRS 17 'Retirement Benefits' is fully effective for accounting periods beginning on or after 1 January 2005, although earlier adoption is encouraged, and supersedes SSAP 24 'Accounting for Pension Costs', UITF Abstract 6 'Accounting for post-retirement benefits other than pensions' and UITF Abstract 18 'Pension costs following the 1997 tax changes in respect of dividend income'. If the new standard is not adopted early, the requirements of SSAP 24, UITF Abstract 6 and UITF Abstract 18 should be followed, with additional disclosures given in the notes to the accounts.

Pension commitments

11.46 The explanatory note to SSAP 24 identifies various forms of pension commitment that may arise for the employer:

- a commitment to provide pension arrangements set out in the employee's contract of employment;
- a commitment arising from custom and practice over a period of time (i.e. where the employer has traditionally made pension arrangements for employees, even though it has no contractual obligation to do so);
- a commitment arising when an employer makes *ex gratia* or discretionary pension payments on a case by case basis.

The requirements of SSAP 24 apply wherever an employer has a commitment to make pension payments in respect of employees, regardless of whether this commitment is contractual or simply implied by past practice. Separate requirements cover the payment of *ex gratia* or discretionary pensions.

The accounting objective of SSAP 24

11.47 The accounting objective of SSAP 24 is based on the fact that from the point of view of:

- the employer, the provision of pension benefits to employees is part of the cost of employing the individuals during their period of service with the company;
- the employee, the provision of pension benefits by the employer effectively represents deferred remuneration (i.e. remuneration which is only paid at a later date).

The accounting objective, therefore, is that an employer should recognise the cost of providing pensions on a systematic basis over the period during which he has the benefit of the employee's services. In the case of a defined benefit scheme, the allocation of costs to each accounting period will depend to a large extent on the actuarial method used and the assumptions made.

Accounting for a defined contribution scheme

11.48 Where an employer operates a defined contribution scheme, the charge to the profit and loss account each year will be the amount of the contributions payable by the employer in respect of that year. This figure must be calculated on an accruals basis and therefore may not be the same as the amount actually paid over to the pension scheme during the year. As the contributions payable represent the full extent of the employer's commitments under the pension scheme, this accounting treatment will meet SSAP 24's accounting objective. The accounts must include the following disclosures:

— the nature of the pension scheme;

— the accounting policy - the following wording might be appropriate:

Example 11.6 – Accounting policy for a defined contributions scheme

Pension arrangements

The company operates a defined contribution pension scheme which is open to all employees. The company's contributions to the scheme are charged to the profit and loss account in the year to which they relate.

— the charge to the profit and loss account in respect of pension costs; and

— any amounts included in the balance sheet in respect of pension arrangements – any contributions due but not paid over to the pension scheme by the company at the end of the financial year or (probably more rarely) any prepaid contributions at the end of the year should therefore be disclosed in the notes to the accounts.

Example 11.7 – Disclosure in notes to the accounts

The company operates a defined contribution pension scheme which is open to all employees. The assets of the pension scheme are held separately from those of the company in an independently administered fund. The amount payable to the pension scheme during the year in respect of the company's contributions amounted to £35,700 (20X1: £35,400). At the end of the year, contributions of £2,540 (20X1: £2,150) had not been paid over to the scheme. These are included in creditors.

Actuarial valuations and funding methods

11.49 In the case of a defined benefit scheme, the pension cost for the year must be calculated by means of an actuarial valuation. This should give the actuary's best estimate of the cost to the employer of providing the promised pension benefits for employees. In carrying out the valuation, the actuary will need to make a number of assumptions, and the decisions that he takes here can have a very significant effect on the level of contributions required from the employer. Various actuarial methods can be used to determine the level of contributions needed to achieve and maintain adequate funding in the scheme. The principal categories of actuarial methods are:

- accrued benefits methods – these are based on the principle that the obligation to provide a pension to an employee will be greater as the relevant employee gets closer to retirement;
- prospective benefits methods – these are based on the principle that the obligation to provide a pension to an employee accumulates evenly throughout the period of the individual's employment.

Under SSAP 24, a method in either of these categories may be used. Having carried out actuarial calculations based on one of these methods, the actuary will recommend a contribution rate (or rates), expressed as a percentage of salary, usually with the intention that this rate will apply for a considerable period of time.

Regular pension cost

11.50 Regular pension cost is defined in SSAP 24 as 'the consistent ongoing cost recognised under the actuarial method used'. Where the actuary has recommended a contribution rate, this should be acceptable as the basis of calculating regular pension cost. Pension costs charged to the profit and loss account on this basis should therefore meet the accounting objective of SSAP 24.

Accounting for variations from regular cost

11.51 Many of the more difficult aspects of pension cost accounting arise from variations from the regular pension cost. These variations arise from:

- experience surpluses or deficiencies;
- changes in the assumptions made;
- changes in the actuarial method used;
- retroactive changes to benefits;
- retroactive changes to the conditions for membership of the scheme;
- increases in pension payments.

Under SSAP 24, the effect of the following variations should normally be spread over the expected remaining service lives of the existing employees who are members of the pension scheme:

- experience surpluses and deficiencies;
- changes in assumptions and valuation method;
- changes to benefits and scheme membership.

The reasoning behind this approach is that short-term changes are inevitable when trying to account for a long-term cost and it would be inappropriate to recognise the effect of such changes in one accounting period. Experience surpluses and deficiencies arise from the ongoing process of comparing actual experience with the original assumptions. Most schemes are subject to a triennial actuarial valuation, sometimes with detailed reviews in the intervening years, and these will highlight areas where actual experience has been different to the assumptions made at the time of the last valuation. As a result, the estimate of the potential liability on the employer may change. Any changes in the assumptions underlying the actuarial valuation, or in the valuation method used, will have a similar effect to experience surpluses and deficiencies and should therefore be accounted for in the same way. Even though retrospective changes to benefits or to the rules governing scheme membership will usually mean that pension cost charges made in the accounts in earlier years will have been under or overstated, the changes arise from decisions taken in the current year. It is therefore not considered appropriate to treat any resulting adjustments to pension costs as a prior year adjustment. The exceptions to the general rule on the treatment of variations from regular cost are considered in **11.55** to **11.56** below.

Spreading the effect of variations

11.52 SSAP 24 does not provide any guidance on how to allocate variations from regular pensions cost over the remaining service lives of current employees and the various methods in use can produce very different results. The most common methods are:

— allocation on a straight-line basis over average remaining service lives;

— allocation as a set percentage of pensionable pay.

The cash effect of these variations will usually be very different from the accounting treatment. For instance, if the employer chooses to take a contributions holiday, to absorb part of the surplus in the pension scheme, no contributions will be paid to the scheme. However, in accounting terms there will still be a charge in the profit and loss account each year in respect of pension costs, because the effect of the 'holiday' has to be spread over the remaining service lives of the employees rather than being recognised as it happens.

Example 11.8 – An example of the difference between accounting treatment and cash effect

An actuarial valuation of D Ltd's pension scheme was carried out at 31 March 199X and revealed a surplus of £70,000. The company's normal contributions are £25,000 per annum. On the recommendation of the actuary, the company proposes to take a contributions holiday for 2 years and then pay reduced contributions of £20,000 for the following 4 years. After this, the company's contributions will revert to £25,000 per annum.

The average remaining service life of employees at 31 March 199X was 20 years.

If the variation is spread on a straight-line basis the annual effect will be £70,000 divided by 20 years i.e. £3,500 per annum. The profit and loss account charge will therefore become £25,000 - £3,500 = £21,500 per annum.

The accounting for the next few years will therefore be as follows.

	Charged to profit and loss account	*Cash paid*	*Balance sheet Cr*
Year 1	21,500	—	21,500
Year 2	21,500	—	43,000
Year 3	21,500	20,000	44,500
Year 4	21,500	20,000	46,000
Year 5	21,500	20,000	47,500
Year 6	21,500	20,000	49,000
Year 7	21,500	25,000	45,500
Year 8	21,500	25,000	42,000
Year 9	21,500	25,000	38,500
Year 10	21,500	25,000	35,000

The remaining provision of £35,000 will continue to be absorbed over the next 10 years at £3,500 per annum (i.e. £25,000 - £21,500).

Increases in pensions

11.53 The actuarial valuation will usually take account of any increases in pensions that are set out in the scheme rules or which are required by law. However, an employer may feel that other discretionary increases need to be made over time, to allow for the changing needs of pensioners or to preserve good relationships between the employer and its employees. Although such increases are discretionary at the time they are awarded, once an increase has been granted it is highly unlikely that it will be withdrawn in the future. The increased pension payments will therefore become part of the employer's pension commitment. The preferred treatment under SSAP 24 is that, where such discretionary increases are likely to be awarded on a regular basis, they should be taken into account in the actuarial assumptions. The effects of any increases will therefore be recognised as part of the regular pension cost. If the actuarial assumptions have not allowed for such increases, SSAP 24 requires the capital cost of an increase to be charged to the profit and loss account in the year in which it is granted. This will not be necessary if the increase is adequately covered by a surplus in the pension scheme.

One-off increase in pensions

11.54 If an increase is awarded with the intention that it will apply only in the current year and will therefore have no impact on future pensions, the cost of the increase should be charged to the profit and loss account in the year in which it is granted. Once again, this will not be necessary if the increase is adequately covered by a surplus in the pension scheme.

Significant changes in normal level of contributions

11.55 The requirement to spread the effect of variations from regular pension cost over the remaining service lives of current employees does not apply where a surplus or deficiency arises from a significant change in the normal level of contributions as a result of a substantial reduction in the number of employees covered by the pension scheme. Such a reduction in members of a pension scheme is most likely to arise where a company implements a major reorganisation programme involving a significant level of redundancies. A major reduction in employee numbers often results in a large surplus arising in the pension scheme, with no prospect of this surplus reversing. In these circumstances it is considered inappropriate to spread the effect of the surplus over the remaining service lives of current employees. If the significant reduction in the number of members of the scheme is related to the sale or termination of an operation (as defined in FRS 3 'Reporting Financial Performance'), the associated pension surplus (or deficit, where appropriate) should be taken into account when assessing any provisions to be made in relation to the sale or termination under FRS 3, para 18. Where, as a result of a significant reduction in the number of employees who are members of the scheme, any of the following occur:

- a refund of a pension scheme surplus;
- a contributions holiday; or
- a reduction in contributions;

the benefit should normally be accounted for as it becomes receivable. The amount receivable should not be anticipated. For instance, if the decision is taken to absorb a surplus by reducing contributions over a period of (say) ten years, the total effect should not be accumulated and reflected in the accounts when the decision is taken. The reduction should be accounted for over the ten-year period during which the reduced contributions are paid. The only exception to this rule is where a refund of a pension scheme surplus is made to the employer in accordance with the *Finance Act 1986* or other equivalent legislation. In these circumstances the refund can be recognised in the accounting period in which it occurs.

Material deficiency in the scheme

11.56 SSAP 24 recognises that there may be very limited circumstances where prudence will require a deficit to be recognised over a shorter period than the remaining service lives of current employees. This is only allowed where:

— the deficit arises as a result of a major transaction or event which is outside the normal scope of the actuarial assumptions and which was therefore not allowed for in the assumptions; and

— significant additional contributions have had to be paid into the pension scheme as a result.

The example given in the standard is a situation where there has been serious mismanagement of the pension scheme, but it is clearly intended that this accounting treatment should only be applied in very rare circumstances. The Urgent Issues Task Force concluded in UITF Abstract 18 'Pension costs following the 1997 tax changes in respect of dividend income' that changes made in the Finance (No 2) Act 1997, which meant that pension funds could no longer reclaim the tax credit on their dividend income, did not come within the scope of this paragraph of SSAP 24. The loss resulting from this tax change was therefore required to be spread forward over the expected remaining service lives of existing employees.

Ex gratia and discretionary pensions

11.57 Where an employer grants *ex gratia* or discretionary pensions to employees, the capital cost should be recognised in the profit and loss account in the year in which the pensions are granted. An appropriate allowance should be made where the pensions are partly covered by a surplus in the pension scheme. If they are fully covered by such a surplus, no charge to the profit and loss account will be required.

Accounts disclosures

11.58 In the case of a defined benefit scheme, SSAP 24 requires the following detailed disclosures in the accounts:

— the nature of the scheme;

— whether it is funded or unfunded;

— the accounting policy (and the funding policy, if different);

— whether costs and provisions in respect of pensions are assessed in accordance with the advice of a qualified actuary (if the actuary is an employee or officer of the company, this must be disclosed);

— the pension cost charge in the profit and loss account and an explanation of any significant change compared with the previous year;

- any amounts in respect of pensions included in the balance sheet;
- the date of the latest formal actuarial valuation (or later formal review);
- an outline of the results of the latest actuarial valuation (or review), including:
  - the actuarial method used,
  - the main actuarial assumptions made,
  - the level of funding, expressed in percentage terms (i.e. the extent to which the projected assets of the scheme are sufficient to cover the expected liabilities in respect of pensions),
  - comments on any major surplus or deficiency in the scheme;
- the amount of any deficiency, indicating the action being taken to deal with it in current and future accounting periods;
- any commitments to make additional payments over a limited number of years;
- details of the expected effects of any major changes in pension arrangements;
- the accounting treatment of a refund subject to tax, if relevant.

Example disclosures

11.59 The following wording might be suitable for an accounting policy in respect of a defined benefit scheme.

Example 11.9 – Accounting policy note for a defined benefit scheme

Pension arrangements

The company operates a defined benefit pension scheme which is open to all employees. Under the scheme pensions are based on final pensionable salary. The company's contributions to the scheme are charged to the profit and loss account so as to spread the cost of pensions over the services lives of the employees who are members of the scheme.

SSAP 24 includes as an appendix two examples of a note to the accounts on pension costs and commitments in respect of a defined benefit scheme operated by a small company and a large group. The actual disclosures will depend on the circumstances of each case, but the following is an indication of how the disclosure requirements (excluding those required by FRS 17) might be met in a relatively straightforward case.

Example 11.10 – Disclosures on pension costs and commitments in a straightforward case

The company operates a pension scheme providing benefits based on final pensionable salary. The assets of the scheme are held separately from those of the company and are invested with insurance companies.

Contributions to the scheme are charged to the profit and loss account so as to spread the cost of pensions over the service lives of employees who are members of the scheme. These contributions are determined by a qualified actuary on the basis of a formal triennial valuation of the scheme, using the projected unit method.

The most recent valuation of the scheme was as at 31 March 200X. The following main assumptions were made:

— investment returns of 6% per annum,

— average salary increases of 4% per annum.

It was also assumed that present and future pensions would increase at 2.5% per annum.

This valuation showed that the market value of the scheme's assets at 31 March 200X was £850,000 and that the actuarial value of those assets represented 105% of the benefits that had accrued to members, after allowing for expected future increases in earnings. It is proposed to maintain company contributions at 7% of earnings and employee contributions at 3% of earnings.

The pension cost charge to the profit and loss account for the year was £26,500 (200Y: £23,400). This includes £4,800 (200Y: £4,200) in respect of experience surpluses that are being recognised over 18 years, the average remaining service lives of current employees.

More than one pension scheme

11.60 If a company has more than one pension scheme, only the combined details for the schemes need to be disclosed, unless individual details for the schemes need to be shown for a proper understanding of the accounts. However, in the case of defined benefit schemes, a deficiency in one scheme should not be off-set against a surplus in another scheme. Any deficiency in funding, and the action being taken to deal with it, should therefore always be disclosed, even if there is a compensating surplus in another company (or group) pension scheme.

Group schemes

11.61 The standard recognises that some groups operate pension schemes covering the employees of all group companies. Where the employees of a subsidiary company are members of a group scheme, the company is exempt from some of the detailed disclosures normally required by SSAP 24, provided that:

- the company's holding company is registered in the UK or the Republic of Ireland;
- the accounts disclose the name of the holding company whose financial statements include full details of the group pension scheme;
- the accounts state that the company is a member of a group scheme;
- the accounts disclose the nature of the group scheme and, where appropriate, indicate that contributions are based on the pension costs of the group as a whole.

The exemptions relate to the disclosures on the amount of any deficiency and action taken to deal with it and the results of the last formal actuarial valuation (or later review). The other disclosure requirements continue to apply where relevant.

Foreign pension schemes

11.62 Where an employer has pension commitments in respect of a foreign operation, the pension costs and commitments should be accounted for in accordance with SSAP 24. In the case of a group, consolidation adjustments may be necessary to bring the relevant costs and commitments into the accounts (e.g. where foreign companies do not account for pension costs in line with SSAP 24). However, the standard recognises that the relevant actuarial information may be difficult to obtain in the case of foreign schemes. In these circumstances the minimum disclosure is:

- the amount charged to the profit and loss account; and
- the basis of the charge.

Transitional disclosures before adoption of FRS 17

11.63 The following transitional disclosure requirements apply where accounts continue to be prepared in accordance with SSAP 24 'Accounting for pension costs' in the period before FRS 17 becomes mandatory:

- financial statements for accounting periods ending on or after 22 June 2001 should give the following additional disclosures for the closing balance sheet only:
  - the contribution made in respect of the accounting period and any agreed contribution rates for future years;
  - for closed schemes and those in which the age profile of the active membership is rising significantly, the fact that under the projected unit method the current service cost will increase as the members of the scheme approach retirement;
  - the fair value of the assets held by the scheme at the end of the period, analysed into the following classes, together with the

expected rate of return assumed for each class for the period and the subsequent period:

(i) equities;

(ii) bonds;

(iii) other (sub-analysed if material);

— the fair value of scheme assets, the present value of scheme liabilities (based on the accounting assumptions) and the resulting surplus or deficit, together with an analysis of movements during the period - where the asset or liability in the balance sheet differs from the scheme surplus or deficit shown in the note, an explanation of the difference should be given; and

— the analysis of reserves in the notes to the financial statements should distinguish the amount relating to the defined benefit asset or liability, net of related deferred tax;

— financial statements for accounting periods ending on or after 22 June 2002 should give the above additional disclosures for both the opening and closing balance sheets and the following details in respect of the performance statements for the current period:

— the following amounts (which will be included within operating profit under FRS 17, or capitalised as part of employee remuneration where relevant):

(i) current service cost;

(ii) any past service costs;

(iii) any previously unrecognised surplus deducted from past service costs;

(iv) gains and losses on any settlements and curtailments; and

(v) any previously unrecognised surplus deducted from settlement or curtailment losses;

— any gains and losses on settlements and curtailments and any previously unrecognised surplus deducted from the losses to be included within a separate item after operating profit under FRS 17;

— the following amounts (which will be included as other finance costs or income under FRS 17):

(i) interest cost; and

(ii) expected return on assets in the scheme;

— the following amounts (which will be included within the statement of total recognised gains and losses under FRS 17):

(i) difference between the expected and actual return on assets;

(ii) experience gains and losses arising on scheme liabilities;

(iii) effects of changes in the demographic and financial assumptions underlying the present value of scheme liabilities;

- the difference between expected and actual returns on assets, expressed as (a) an amount and (b) a percentage of the scheme assets at the balance sheet date;
- experience gains and losses arising on scheme liabilities expressed as (a) an amount and (b) a percentage of the present value of scheme liabilities at the balance sheet date; and
- the total actuarial gain or loss expressed as (a) an amount and (b) a percentage of the present value of the scheme liabilities at the balance sheet date.

- financial statement for accounting periods ending on or after 22 June 2003 should give the above additional disclosures relating to the opening and closing balance sheet and to the performance statements, with comparatives for the previous year, and five-year summary information (the last three items described above) should be disclosed in respect of all accounting periods ending on or after 22 June 2002.

None of the amounts disclosed are required to be recognised in the primary statements. Where an employer has more than one defined benefit scheme, the required disclosures may be given in total, separately or in such groupings as are felt to be most useful (e.g. by geographical location, or where schemes are subject to substantially different risks). Where the disclosures are given in total, the assumptions should be given in the form of weighted averages or relatively narrow ranges, with separate disclosure of any items outside the range.

Chapter 12

Depreciation

NATURE AND METHODS OF DEPRECIATION

Definition of depreciation

12.1 Depreciation is defined in FRS 15 as 'the measure of the cost or revalued amount of the economic benefits of the tangible fixed asset that have been consumed during the period. Consumption includes the wearing out, using up or other reduction in the useful economic life of a tangible fixed asset whether arising from use, effluxion of time or obsolescence through either changes in technology or demand for the goods and services produced by the asset.' Depreciation reflects the fact that most fixed assets have a finite useful economic life within the organisation that has acquired them. Fixed assets are defined in CA 1985 as assets intended for use on a continuing basis in the company's activities. FRS 15 defines tangible fixed assets as 'assets that have physical substance and are held for use in the production or supply of goods or services, for rental to others, or for administrative purposes on a continuing basis in the reporting entities' activities'. FRS 10 'Goodwill and Intangible Assets' sets out detailed requirements on the amortisation of intangible assets and goodwill, determining useful economic lives for these assets and the need to carry out impairment reviews. These requirements and their practical application are considered in more detail in **Chapter 19**.

Fair allocation of cost

12.2 Where an asset is purchased for continuing use in the business over a number of years, it would be inappropriate to charge the full amount of the expenditure on the asset to the profit and loss account in the year of purchase. There should instead be a charge against income for the use of the asset during its useful life and this is done by means of the annual depreciation charge. Depreciation is therefore intended to provide a fair allocation of the cost of the asset to each accounting period during which the company benefits from the use of the asset. FRS 15 emphasises that a charge to operating profit should continue to be made, even if the asset has risen in value or has been revalued. The depreciation charge for each period should be recognised in the profit and loss account unless it is permitted to be included in the carrying amount of another asset.

Key factors

12.3 The assessment of the total amount to be charged over the life of the asset and the allocation of that charge to individual years involves consideration of the following key factors:

- the amount at which the asset is recorded in the accounting records – this will be its original cost, or its value if it has been revalued;
- the expected useful economic life of the asset within the organisation;
- the estimated residual value of the asset once it has reached the end of its useful economic life within the business.

Purchase price or production cost

12.4 CA 1985 sets out specific rules for determining the purchase price or production cost of both fixed and current assets (see **Chapter 1**). Where fixed assets are shown in the accounts at historical cost, the purchase price or production cost will form the basis for the annual depreciation charge in respect of those assets.

Residual value

12.5 Under both CA 1985 and FRS 15, the depreciable amount of an asset is its cost (or revalued amount) less its estimated residual value. This recognises the fact that some assets will still have a value, even though they no longer have a useful life in the company.

Example 12.1 – Calculating the depreciable amount

A Ltd purchases a new car at a cost of £11,350. It intends to keep the car for use in the business for four years, after which a replacement will be purchased. When the replacement is purchased, A Ltd estimates that it will be able to part-exchange the existing car for £2,500.

	£
Purchase price	11,350
Estimated residual value	(2,500)
Depreciable amount	8,850

The depreciable amount of £8,850 should be charged to the profit and loss account on a systematic basis over four years.

The Act provides no guidance on establishing the residual value of an asset, but residual value is defined in FRS 15 as:

> 'the net realisable value of an asset at the end of its useful economic life. Residual values are based on prices prevailing at the date of acquisition (or revaluation) of the asset and do not take account of expected future price changes'.

One of the difficulties in estimating residual value, therefore, is that the assessment must be based on present prices and the potential effect of inflation over the expected life of the asset must be ignored.

Regular review of residual value

12.6 FRS 15 requires residual values to be reviewed at the end of each reporting period and revised where necessary. As far as is practicable, the revised residual value should be stated in terms of the price level that existed when the asset was acquired (or revalued). If this is not possible, the residual value should only be revised to current values where the current residual value is lower than the original estimate of residual value. In other words, residual value should not be increased in these circumstances. The standard also emphasises that events or changes in circumstances that cause residual value to fall may also be indicators that the asset has become impaired, in which case it should be reviewed for impairment in accordance with FRS 11 'Impairment of Fixed Assets and Goodwill'.

Impact of revision of residual value

12.7 Where it is necessary to revise residual values, the change should be accounted for prospectively over the remaining useful economic life of the asset. No adjustment should be made to the depreciation charged in previous years. If the asset is impaired, the impairment will need to be accounted for in accordance with FRS 11. The report published by the Financial Reporting Review Panel in September 2001, following its review of the accounts of Groupe Chez Gerard plc for the period ended 25 June 2000, emphasised that revisions to residual values may result in the depreciation of assets that were previously not depreciated on the grounds of immateriality. In these circumstances, the commencement of depreciation does not represent a change in accounting policy and the carrying amounts of the assets should be depreciated prospectively over their remaining useful economic lives, as in any other case where residual values are revised.

Useful economic life

12.8 CA 1985 also fails to provide any guidance on assessing the useful economic life of an asset. FRS 15 defines the useful economic life of an asset as 'the period over which the entity expects to derive economic benefit from that asset'. The key factor, therefore, is the length of time for which the company expects to use the asset. This will not necessarily be the same as the asset's expected total useful life, although in some cases it may be. For instance, many companies choose to replace motor vehicles on a fairly regular basis (e.g. every three or four years) on the grounds that repair costs may become excessive and the vehicle may not run efficiently if it is retained for a longer period. However, the company will usually be able to sell a three- or four-year old car and it will continue to be used by the new owner (i.e. the car will not have reached the end of its entire useful life when it is sold by the company). For depreciation purposes, the expected useful economic life of the car from the company's point of view will be three or four years (i.e. the period for which it expects to use the car). In the case of items of plant and equipment and furniture and fittings, the company is more likely to retain the asset for the whole of its useful life, or at least a substantial proportion of it. The expected residual value of these assets will usually be much lower. In some cases, the only amount to be recognised, if any, might be the underlying scrap value.

Other factors to take into account

12.9 FRS 15 emphasises that, although the economic benefits embodied in a tangible fixed asset are consumed mainly through use of the asset, other factors may also diminish the benefits that would otherwise have been available. The assessment of the useful economic life and residual value of an asset should therefore also take into account:

- the expected usage of the asset, assessed by reference to expected capacity or physical output;
- the expected physical deterioration of the asset through use or the effluxion of time – this may depend on the repair and maintenance programme for the asset;
- economic or technological obsolescence (e.g. resulting from changes or improvements in production, or changes in market demand for a product or service); and
- legal or similar restrictions on the use of the asset (e.g. the expiry date of a related lease).

These issues may also affect the choice of depreciation method.

Review of asset lives

12.10 FRS 15 requires the useful economic lives of assets to be reviewed at the end of each reporting period. Where necessary, as a result of this review, asset lives should be revised. This should help to ensure that companies do not carry significant amounts of fully depreciated assets in their accounts. The FRRP report on the accounts of Groupe Chez Gerard plc (referred to in **12.7** above) also emphasised that revisions to useful economic lives may result in the depreciation of assets that were previously not depreciated on the grounds of immateriality. Where asset lives need to be revised, the remaining net book values of the relevant assets should be written off over their revised remaining useful economic lives. Changes to asset lives are most likely to be due to changes in circumstances (e.g. technological changes, changes to product lines, changes in the general economic climate) or to the fact that, with the benefit of experience and hindsight, more informed decisions can be made about the expected lives of individual assets. In the case of revalued assets, and in particular those valued at depreciated replacement cost, a reassessment of useful economic life may indicate that a further revaluation of the asset is necessary.

Disclosure of revision of asset lives

12.11 Asset lives (or depreciation rates) are required to be disclosed under FRS 15. Any change to those lives should therefore be disclosed in the accounts in the year of the change. The financial effect of the change in asset lives should also be shown if it is material. However, this situation should arise only rarely if asset lives are reviewed regularly. It is important to recognise that a change in asset lives does not constitute a change in accounting policy. The underlying accounting policy is to depreciate fixed assets over their expected useful economic lives and this has not changed in any way. The assessment of asset lives will always be a matter of judgement and it is right that this assessment should be refined in the light of actual experience to allow the accounting policy to be properly implemented.

Assets purchased under finance lease or hire purchase contract

12.12 In the accounts of a lessee, SSAP 21 'Accounting for Leases and Hire Purchase Contracts' requires an asset purchased under a finance lease to be depreciated over the shorter of the lease term and the useful economic life of the asset. The lease term is defined as the period for which the lessee has contracted to lease the asset and any further term for which he has the option to continue to lease the asset, where it is reasonably certain at the start of the lease that the option will be exercised. An asset purchased under a hire purchase contract should be depreciated over its useful economic life.

Impairment reviews

12.13 FRS 15 requires a tangible fixed asset, other than non-depreciable land, to be reviewed for impairment at the end of any reporting period where its estimated remaining useful economic life is more than 50 years.

Methods of depreciating assets

12.14 Both CA 1985 and FRS 15 require the depreciable amount of an asset to be written off in a fair and systematic way over its useful economic life. There are various ways of achieving a fair and systematic charge for depreciation and a company is free to choose whichever method is considered most appropriate. FRS 15 emphasises that the method chosen should result in a depreciation charge throughout the asset's useful economic life and not just towards the end of that life or when the asset is falling in value. The Financial Reporting Review Panel report following its review of the accounts of Wyevale Garden Centres plc for the year ended 31 December 2000 also emphasised the need for depreciation to be charged from the date of acquisition of the asset rather than from another date (e.g. the start of the next full accounting period). The most common depreciation methods are:

— straight-line;

— reducing balance.

Others are possible (e.g. sum of the digits) but these are used so rarely in practice that they are not covered here.

Straight-line method

12.15 This is probably the easiest and most straightforward method of calculating depreciation and is consequently in common use. It assumes that equal amounts of the asset's economic benefits are consumed in each year of its life and results in a consistent charge for depreciation throughout the life of the individual asset.

Example 12.2 – Using the straight-line method

Using the details of the car in **Example 12.1**.

	£
Purchase price	11,350
Estimated residual value	2,500
Depreciable amount	8,850

The car has an expected useful life in the company of four years and the annual depreciation charge will therefore be the depreciable amount (£8,850) divided by four, giving an annual depreciation charge of £2,212.50.

FRS 15 notes that, when the pattern of the consumption of economic benefits is unclear, the straight-line method of depreciation should usually be adopted. The only potential disadvantage to the straight-line method of depreciation is that the profit and loss account receives the same annual charge when the asset is a few years old as when it was new. In some cases, this may not properly reflect the benefit to the company of using the asset, but in most instances the effect of any such distortion will not be significant.

Reducing balance method

12.16 The alternative method of calculating depreciation, also in common use, is the reducing balance method. This is slightly more complicated and may involve keeping more detailed records to enable the calculations to be carried out. The depreciation charge is based on a constant percentage of the asset's carrying value. Under this method, therefore, the depreciation charge is higher in the early years than towards the end of the asset's life. In some cases, this may give a better reflection of the consumption of benefits. For instance, an asset may provide greater benefits when it is new than when it is older and possibly more prone to breakdown, or less capable of providing a high quality output.

Example 12.3 – Using the reducing balance method

Using the details from **Example 12.1**.

	£
Purchase price	11,350
Estimated residual value	2,500
Depreciable amount	8,850

Using a depreciation rate of 50% the depreciation in years one to four will be calculated as follows.

Year 1	Depreciable amount	8,850.00
	Depreciation at 50%	4,425.00
Year 2	Carrying value	4,425.00
	Depreciation at 50%	2,212.50
Year 3	Carrying value	2,212.50
	Depreciation at 50%	1,106.25
Year 4	Carrying value	1,106.25
	Depreciation at 50%	553.13
		553.12

The potential disadvantages to the reducing balance method of depreciation are:

— the depreciable amount is never fully written off;

— the depreciation charge in the early years is very high;

— it is more complicated to calculate an appropriate rate to ensure the asset is written down, as far as possible, to its residual value by the end of its useful economic life.

Comparison of straight-line and reducing balance methods

12.17 **Examples 12.2** and **12.3** illustrate that the annual depreciation charge and carrying values of the asset are very different over the four years, depending on which depreciation method is used.

Example 12.4 – Comparing the methods

	Straight line	*Reducing balance*
Annual depreciation charge:		
	£	£
Year 1	2,212.50	4,425.00
Year 2	2,212.50	2,212.50
Year 3	2,212.50	1,106.25
Year 4	2,212.50	553.13
Carrying value of asset:		
	£	£
Year 1	6,637.50	4,425.00
Year 2	4,425.00	2,212.50
Year 3	2,212.50	1,106.25
Year 4	0.00	553.12

This highlights the importance of disclosing the depreciation method used.

Change in method of depreciating assets

12.18 A change in the method of providing depreciation is only permitted under FRS 15 where the new method is considered to give a fairer presentation of the company's results and financial position. Where the method is changed, the net book value of the assets should be written off under the new method over their remaining useful economic lives. The following disclosures should be given in the accounts:

— a statement that the method of calculating depreciation has been changed;

— an explanation of why the new method is considered to give a fairer presentation of the company's results and financial position;

— the financial effect of the change on the depreciation charge for the year, if the effect is material.

However, a change in the method of calculating depreciation does not constitute a change in accounting policy.

Assets with two or more major components

12.19 Where a tangible fixed asset has two or more major components with substantially different useful economic lives, FRS 15 requires each component to be treated separately for depreciation purposes. Each component should therefore be depreciated over its individual useful economic life. The standard gives as examples land and buildings, which comprise separable components for accounting purposes (even though they may be purchased together), and the structure of a building and the items within the structure, such as general fittings. The standard notes, however, that it is not appropriate to treat the trading potential associated with a property such as a hotel or public house as a separate component of the asset, if the value and life of the trading potential is inherently inseparable from that of the property.

RENEWALS ACCOUNTING

Conditions

12.20 FRS 15 permits renewals accounting to be used to estimate the depreciation charge on certain assets within an infrastructure system or network. Definable major assets or components within the system or network must always be separately identified and depreciated over their individual useful economic lives. The remaining assets may be treated as one asset and the depreciation estimated using the renewals method where all of the following conditions are met:

- the infrastructure is a system or network that, as a whole, is intended to be maintained at a specified level of service potential by the continuing replacement and refurbishment of its components; and
- the level of annual expenditure required to maintain the operating capacity or service potential of the infrastructure asset is calculated from an asset management plan certified by a person who is both appropriately qualified and independent of the reporting entity; and
- the system or network is in a mature or steady state.

The guidance in the standard suggests that a system or network is in a mature or steady state when the annual cost of maintaining it is relatively constant.

Accounting treatment

12.21 Where renewals accounting is adopted, the accounting treatment is as follows:

- the annual expenditure required to maintain the infrastructure asset (as described in **12.20** above) should be treated as the depreciation charge for the period and deducted from the carrying value of the asset as part of accumulated depreciation;
- the actual expenditure should be capitalised as part of the cost of the asset in the period in which it is incurred; and
- the carrying amount of the parts of the system or network that are replaced or restored by subsequent expenditure should be removed from the carrying value of the asset.

Renewals accounting is an optional accounting treatment where the conditions are met. If it is not adopted, maintenance costs should be charged to the profit and loss account as they are incurred, and depreciation on the remaining infrastructure assets should be calculated in the usual way.

NON-DEPRECIATION OF ASSETS

The general rule

12.22 FRS 15 states categorically that subsequent expenditure on an asset to maintain or enhance its standard of performance does not in itself negate the need to charge depreciation on the asset. The assessment of the useful economic life of the asset will usually take account of the fact that routine expenditure will be incurred to maintain the expected performance standard of the asset (e.g. the routine servicing and overhauling of equipment). If this expenditure was not incurred, the expected useful economic life of the asset would be reduced and the depreciation charge would be higher. Routine maintenance expenditure of this nature should be charged to the profit and loss account as it is incurred.

Enhancement of the asset

12.23 In some cases, subsequent expenditure may:

— enhance the economic benefits of the asset beyond the previously assessed standard of performance;

— restore or replace a component that has been separately depreciated; or

— restore the economic benefits of the asset.

This expenditure may extend the expected useful economic life of the asset but cannot increase it indefinitely and does not negate the need for depreciation to be charged. In these cases, the subsequent expenditure should be capitalised as it is incurred and depreciated over the useful economic life of the asset (or component), or over the period to the next major overhaul.

Where depreciation is immaterial

12.24 Under FRS 15, the only grounds for not charging depreciation on a tangible fixed asset (other than non-depreciable land) are that the depreciation charge and accumulated depreciation are immaterial. FRS 15 acknowledges that the depreciation charge may be immaterial in two situations:

— where the estimated remaining useful economic life of the asset is long; or

— where the estimated residual value of the asset is not materially different from its carrying value.

It is important to remember that the materiality of the depreciation charge must be assessed in terms of both the charge for the year and the accumulated depreciation. The materiality of any uncharged depreciation must also be assessed in aggregate as well as for the individual assets. Where depreciation is omitted from the accounts on the grounds that it is immaterial, the potential depreciation charge will still need to be calculated (and accumulated) to support this view. FRS 15 notes that the depreciation charge for the year and accumulated depreciation are immaterial if they would not reasonably influence the decisions of a user of the accounts. The report published by the Financial Reporting Review Panel in September 2001, following its review of the accounts of Groupe Chez Gerard plc for the year ended 25 June 2000, emphasised that revisions to useful economic lives and residual values may result in the depreciation of assets that were previously not depreciated on the grounds of immateriality. This does not constitute a change in accounting policy and the carrying amounts of the relevant assets should therefore be depreciated prospectively over their remaining useful economic lives in accordance with the normal requirements of FRS 15.

High residual values

12.25 FRS 15 notes that high residual values may occur when:

— an entity has a policy and practice of regular maintenance and repair (the costs of which are charged to the profit and loss account) so that the asset is kept at its previously assessed standard of performance;

— the asset is unlikely to suffer from economic or technological obsolescence; and

— where residual values are material:

  — the entity has a policy and practice of disposing of similar assets well before the end of their economic lives; and

  — the disposal proceeds of similar assets (after excluding the effect of price changes since the date of acquisition or last revaluation) have not been materially lower than their carrying amounts.

It should also be noted that the standard requires residual values to be reviewed at the end of each reporting period.

Annual impairment review

12.26 FRS 15 requires a tangible fixed asset to be reviewed for impairment at the end of each reporting period when either:

— no depreciation has been charged, on the grounds that it is immaterial; or

— the estimated remaining useful economic life of the asset exceeds 50 years.

This does not apply in the case of non-depreciable land. Where an impairment review is required, it should be carried out in accordance with FRS 11 'Impairment of Fixed Assets and Goodwill'. If it is not practicable to carry out an impairment review of an individual asset, the review should be completed for groups of assets as part of income-generating units. Once the first impairment review has been carried out, it can simply be updated in subsequent accounting periods. If expected cash flows and discount rates have not changed significantly, such updates should be relatively straightforward to perform.

Freehold land

12.27 Freehold land does not usually require any regular provision for depreciation. The only exception is where the land is depleted in some way (e.g. a working quarry or mine), in which case depreciation will usually need to be charged. This does not mean that the value of freehold land will not change. The value of land is as susceptible as other assets to external changes and economic factors. Environmental issues in particular can have a significant effect on the value of land. Where the value of freehold land has become impaired, it should be written down in the same way as any other fixed asset.

DEPRECIATION OF REVALUED ASSETS

Alternative accounting rules

12.28 Under the alternative accounting rules, CA 1985 permits certain assets to be included in the accounts at valuation rather than historical cost. These are:

— intangible fixed assets (other than goodwill) which may be included at their current cost; and

— tangible fixed assets which may be included at either market value (as at the date of their last valuation) or current cost.

Further guidance on the operation of the alternative accounting rules is given in **Chapter 1**. CA 1985 makes no reference to the frequency of valuation where the alternative accounting rules are used, but FRS 15 now includes a specific requirement for valuations to be kept up to date once they have been incorporated into the accounts. This requirement is considered in more detail in **Chapter 20**.

Basis of depreciation charge

12.29 Where assets have been revalued, both the Act and FRS 15 require the depreciation in respect of those assets to be based on the valuation figure rather than on original cost. The full amount of this depreciation must be charged to the profit and loss account. If a revaluation has a material effect on the depreciation charge for the year, details should be disclosed in the accounts for the year in which the revaluation takes place. FRS 15 notes that ideally the depreciation charge should be based on the average value of the asset for the period, but in practice either the opening or closing value may be used as the basis for the charge, provided that a consistent approach is adopted in each accounting period and between accounting periods.

Amount charged to the profit and loss account

12.30 CA 1985 permits depreciation on the revalued element of the asset to be disclosed separately, either on the face of the profit and loss account or in the notes to the accounts. The wording of this part of the Act is not particularly clear and it has been suggested in the past that it might permit the depreciation charge in the profit and loss account to be restricted to the depreciation based on historical cost. Even if the Act can be interpreted in this way, FRS 15 ensures that the full amount of depreciation is charged to the profit and loss account.

Transfers between reserves

12.31 There is, however, no reason why the additional depreciation charge relating to the revaluation of an asset should not be debited to the revaluation reserve and credited to the profit and loss account reserve as a reserves movement. Many companies choose to do this. Such a transfer reflects the fact that, under CA 1985, only depreciation charged on the original cost of an asset is regarded as a realised loss for distribution purposes.

Example 12.5 – Reserves transfers in respect of depreciation

B Ltd has freehold land and buildings with an original cost of £70,000. The buildings, which have an original cost of £50,000, are being depreciated over 50 years. B Ltd's accounting date is 31 December.

The land and buildings are professionally valued at £95,000 at 31 December 2001 (£22,000 for the land and £73,000 for the buildings) and this valuation is incorporated in the accounts. The expected useful economic life of the buildings is unchanged and they have a remaining life of 43 years. Depreciation is charged on a straight line basis.

In the 2002 accounts, the depreciation charge will be £1,698 (i.e. the valuation of £73,000 depreciated over the remaining useful life of 43 years). This amount must be charged to the profit and loss account.

> B Ltd can then transfer £698 (i.e. the additional depreciation over and above the £1,000 that would be charged on the original cost of £50,000) from the revaluation reserve to the profit and loss account reserve as a reserves movement.

Such a transfer is specifically permitted under the alternative accounting rules by CA 1985 Sch 4 para 34(3), because the additional depreciation has been charged to the profit and loss account.

Historical cost profits and losses

12.32 FRS 3 'Reporting Financial Performance' requires most accounts to include a separate note of historical cost profits and losses. This also highlights the difference between depreciation based on the historical cost of assets and the actual depreciation charge in the accounts. The note of historical cost profits and losses is considered in detail in **Chapter 35**.

Depreciation in the year of revaluation

12.33 Depreciation should continue to be charged on the original cost of the asset up to the date of the first valuation. There may be a temptation to disregard this depreciation charge in the year of revaluation, but to do so would not comply with the requirements of FRS 15. The effect would be to understate the depreciation charge in the profit and loss account and understate the credit to the revaluation reserve by the same amount. If an asset is revalued part way through the financial year, rather than at the year-end, depreciation should strictly be based on the original cost of the asset up to the date of valuation and on the new valuation for the remainder of the year. When further revaluations take place, the standard permits the charge for the year to be based on either the opening or the closing balance, provided that a consistent approach is taken between accounting periods.

PROFIT OR LOSS ON DISPOSAL OF ASSETS

Measurement rules

12.34 FRS 3 'Reporting Financial Performance' paragraph 21 requires profits and losses on the disposal of assets to be accounted for:

- in the period in which the disposal occurs; and
- as the difference between net sales proceeds and the carrying value of the asset.

This means that, where an asset has been revalued for accounts purposes, any profit or loss on disposal must be based on the revalued figure rather than on historical cost.

Example 12.6 – A loss on disposal

Using the details from Example 12.5:

The land and buildings are sold for £90,000 on 2 January, two years after the valuation was incorporated in the accounts. There have been no additions to the building during this time.

Valuation at 31 December 2001	95,000
Depreciation for two subsequent years at £1,698 each year (see Example 12.5)	(3,396)
Carrying value at date of disposal	91,604
Sales proceeds	90,000
Loss on disposal	1,604

The standard also requires profits and losses on the disposal of fixed assets to be disclosed separately on the face of the profit and loss account, unless they are in effect no more than marginal adjustments to depreciation previously charged (see **Chapter 8**).

Revaluation reserve

12.35 Prior to FRS 3, some companies chose to calculate the profit or loss on disposal as the difference between sales proceeds and historical cost (rather than the valuation figure) by crediting any remaining balance on the revaluation reserve to the profit and loss account. Any remaining balance on the revaluation reserve, relating to the asset that has been disposed of, should now be transferred to the profit and loss account reserve as a reserves movement.

Example 12.7– Remaining balances on revaluation reserve

Using the details from **Examples 12.5** and **12.6**:

	£	£
Revaluation reserve at 1 January 2001 (assumed)		34,500
Surplus on revaluation:		
Original cost	70,000	
Depreciation to 31 December 2001:		
£50,000 x 2% x 7 years	(7,000)	
Carrying value	63,000	
Valuation	95,000	
		32,000
Revaluation reserve at 31 December 2001		66,500
Transfers to profit and loss account reserve in respect of freehold buildings		

	£	£
2 years at £698 (see Example 12.5)		(1,396)
Transfers to profit and loss account in respect of other revalued assets (assumed)		(1,475)
Balance on revaluation reserve immediately prior to disposal of freehold land and buildings		63,629
Transfer to profit and loss account reserve in respect of buildings disposed of (£32,000–£1,396)		(30,604)
Balance remaining on revaluation reserve in respect of other revalued assets		(33,025)

The transfer to the profit and loss account reserve reflects the fact that the surplus recognised at the time of revaluation has now been realised as a result of the disposal of the freehold land and buildings.

Note of historical cost profits and losses

12.36 The amount transferred between reserves in this way also appears within the note of historical cost profits and losses as it is an item that arises from the use of valuation rather than historical cost in accounting for fixed assets. In historical cost terms, this amount represents an additional gain on disposal of the asset. This gain has been recognised in the accounts in previous years (by including the asset at valuation) but is only realised when the asset is disposed of.

ACCOUNTING FOR IMPAIRMENT

Permanent and temporary diminutions in value

12.37 Where a fixed asset suffers a permanent diminution in value, CA 1985 requires a provision to be made for this. The provision must be charged to the profit and loss account and must be shown separately, either on the face of the profit and loss account or in the notes to the accounts. The Act makes no reference to temporary diminutions in value, other than in the case of fixed asset investments, where provision may be made but is not required.

Impact of FRS 11 'Impairment of Fixed Assets and Goodwill'

12.38 The distinction effectively made in CA 1985 between permanent and temporary diminutions in value was the cause of considerable difficulty for many years. Following the publication of FRS 11 'Impairment of Fixed Assets and Goodwill', the requirement to make provision for a permanent diminution in value is encompassed in the requirement under that standard for fixed assets and goodwill to be written down to their recoverable amount when there are indications that impairment has occurred. Appendix

II to FRS 11 notes that the distinction between permanent and temporary diminutions in value is recognised inherently in the standard, in that it requires all impairments that are clearly due to the consumption of economic benefits (and which are therefore clearly permanent) to be charged to the profit and loss account.

The need to carry out an impairment review

12.39 Impairment is defined in FRS 11 as a reduction in the recoverable amount of a fixed asset or goodwill below its carrying amount. Under this standard, an impairment review should be carried out when events or changes in circumstances indicate that the carrying value of a fixed asset (including goodwill) may not be recoverable. A review will therefore not necessarily be required every year – it will usually only need to be carried out when something has happened to the asset or to the economic environment in which the asset is used. The systematic charging of depreciation will usually ensure that the carrying amount of a fixed asset is reduced throughout its useful life to reflect the reduction in the asset's recoverable amount arising from the consumption of economic benefits. FRS 11 therefore notes that, for most assets, impairments should be a relatively infrequent addition to normal depreciation.

Events and changes that might prompt a review

12.40 FRS 11 gives examples of events and changes that may indicate impairment of an asset has occurred. These include:

- a current operating loss or net cash outflow, combined with either similar losses or outflows in the past, or the expected continuation of losses or outflows in the future;
- a significant decline in the market value of an asset;
- physical damage or obsolescence;
- a significant adverse change in the business or market in which the asset is used (e.g. a major new competitor);
- a significant adverse change in the statutory or other regulatory environment in which the business operates;
- a significant adverse change in any indicator (such as turnover) used to measure the fair value of the asset at the time of acquisition;
- a commitment by management to undertake a major reorganisation.

The standard emphasises that the useful economic lives and residual values of the assets affected may also need to be reviewed in these circumstances. Even if the assets are not actually impaired, their expected useful lives and residual values may have changed.

Separate requirements for intangible assets and goodwill

12.41 It is important to note that FRS 10 'Goodwill and Intangible Assets' imposes more specific requirements for impairment reviews in the case of goodwill and intangible assets. Separate requirements apply depending on the period over which the intangible asset or goodwill is being amortised. Goodwill and intangible assets amortised over a finite period of 20 years or less from the date of acquisition should be reviewed for impairment at the end of the first full financial year following acquisition (and the standard permits a less extensive review process to be used for this) and in other periods if events or changes in circumstances indicate that the carrying value of the asset or goodwill may not be recoverable. Goodwill and intangible assets amortised over a period of more than 20 years from the date of acquisition, and any that are not amortised, must be reviewed for impairment at the end of each reporting period. Further details are given in **Chapter 19**.

Recognition of impairment losses

12.42 The general rule is that an impairment loss (i.e. the difference between the carrying amount of a fixed asset or goodwill and its recoverable amount) should be recognised in the profit and loss account of the period. However, a different approach is required in the case of fixed assets that have previously been revalued. If an impairment loss relating to a revalued fixed asset is caused by a clear consumption of economic benefits (for example, physical damage or a deterioration in the quality of service provided by the asset), it should be recognised in the profit and loss account. Other impairments of revalued assets (for instance, those arising from a general fall in prices) should be recognised in the statement of total recognised gains and losses until the carrying amount of the asset reaches its depreciated historical cost. Any further reduction below this amount should be recognised in the profit and loss account. It is important to keep detailed records of where impairment losses are recognised, in case reversals of the losses should need to be recognised in subsequent years.

Presentation of impairment losses

12.43 Impairment losses recognised in the profit and loss account should be included within operating profit under the appropriate statutory heading, which will usually be that for depreciation and diminutions in value. Impairment losses recognised in the profit and loss account should be disclosed as exceptional items where they are material. Impairment losses recognised in the statement of total recognised gains and losses should be disclosed separately on the face of that statement. In the notes to the financial statements for accounting periods after the impairment, the impairment loss should be treated as follows:

— for assets held on a historical cost basis, the impairment loss should be included within cumulative depreciation – the cost of the asset should not be reduced;

- for revalued assets held at market value (e.g. existing use or open market value), the impairment loss should be included within the revalued carrying amount; and
- for revalued assets held at depreciated replacement cost:
  - an impairment loss charged to the profit and loss account should be included within cumulative depreciation (i.e. the carrying amount of the asset should not be reduced); and
  - an impairment loss charged to the statement of total recognised gains and losses should be deducted from the carrying amount of the asset.

Reversal of an impairment loss

12.44 The standard sets out different rules on the recognition of a reversal of an impairment loss for tangible fixed assets and investments, and for intangible assets and goodwill:

- in the case of tangible fixed assets and investments for which an impairment loss has been recognised, if the recoverable amount increases as a result of a change in economic conditions or in the expected use of the asset, the reversal should be recognised to the extent that it increases the carrying amount of the asset up to the amount that it would have been if the original impairment had not occurred;
- in the case of intangible assets and goodwill, the reversal of an impairment loss should only be recognised if:
  - an external event caused the recognition of the impairment loss in previous periods and subsequent external events clearly and demonstrably reverse the effects of that event in a way that was not foreseen in the original impairment calculations; or
  - the impairment loss arose on an intangible asset with a readily ascertainable market value and the net realisable value based on that market value has increased to above the asset's carrying amount.

Recognition of a reversal of an impairment loss

12.45 The reversal of an impairment loss should be recognised in the profit and loss account of the current period, unless it relates to a revalued asset, in which case it should be recognised in the profit and loss account to the extent that the original impairment loss (adjusted for subsequent depreciation) was recognised in the profit and loss account and any additional amount should be recognised in the statement of total recognised gains and losses. It is therefore important to keep detailed records of where impairment losses are recognised, in case reversals of the losses should need to be recognised in subsequent years. In the year in which it is recognised, the accounts should disclose the reason for the reversal of the original impairment loss, including any changes in assumptions upon which the calculation of recoverable amount is based.

Further detail

12.46 The requirements of FRS 11 on the measurement of impairment losses, the recognition of impairment losses in the accounts, the allocation of impairment losses and the recognition of the reversal of an impairment loss are considered in more detail in **Chapter 20**.

Depreciation of impaired assets

12.47 Where an impairment loss is recognised, the remaining useful economic life and residual value of the fixed asset or goodwill should be reviewed and revised where necessary. The revised carrying amount should be depreciated over the revised estimate of the remaining useful economic life. This is consistent with the requirements of FRS 15 on the depreciation of assets following a revision of useful economic life.

TRANSFERS FROM CURRENT TO FIXED ASSETS

Requirements of UITF Abstract 5

12.48 UITF 5 'Transfers from Current Assets to Fixed Assets' tackles the issue of how to account for an asset that was not initially intended for continuing use in the business, but which subsequently becomes a fixed asset. An example might be the case of a property construction company that builds a property initially for sale in the ordinary course of its business, but then decides to use the building as its own office. The Abstract requires the following approach to be adopted:

- assess the net realisable value of the asset at the date of transfer;
- if net realisable value is below cost, the asset must be written down to net realisable value before it is transferred;
- any provision needed to reduce cost to net realisable value must be charged to the profit and loss account, recognising the loss suffered by the company during the time that the asset was held as a current asset;
- the asset is then subject to the normal rules for fixed assets (i.e. those set out in CA 1985 and FRS 15) from the date of transfer, and should be treated as an asset recorded at valuation under the alternative accounting rules of the Act.

Example 12.8 – A transfer from current to fixed assets

C Ltd has constructed a property at a cost of £46,000. It initially intended to sell the property but has decided to use it as the company's head office from 1 January 199X. The net realisable value of the property at 1 January 199X is £39,000. It has an expected useful economic life of 45 years and an expected residual value of £10,000. The company uses the straight-line method of depreciation.

C Ltd must charge the diminution in the value of the property of £7,000 (i.e. £46,000 – £39,000) to the profit and loss account and then record the new office as a fixed asset, shown at a valuation of £39,000. Depreciation of £644 must be charged each year in respect of the property (i.e. £39,000 – £10,000 over 45 years).

DEPRECIATION DISCLOSURES

Disclosure of accounting policy on depreciation

12.49 FRS 18 'Accounting Policies' requires financial statements to include a description of each of the accounting policies that is material in the context of the entity's financial statements and CA 1985 specifically requires disclosure of the policy on depreciation and the diminution of assets. FRS 15 specifies that the disclosure must include:

— the depreciation methods used; and

— the useful economic lives or depreciation rates used.

FRS 15 requires these disclosure to be given for each class of tangible fixed assets. A class of tangible fixed assets is defined in the standard as 'a category of tangible fixed asset having a similar nature, function or use in the business of the entity'. This is considered further in the context of the valuation of assets in **Chapter 20**. The disclosures on economic lives or depreciation rates should normally correspond with the categories of asset shown in the detailed movements table for fixed assets in the notes to the accounts. Some companies choose to disclose asset lives (or depreciation rates) in the fixed asset note rather than as part of the accounting policy on depreciation and this is quite acceptable. The following wordings might be appropriate for the accounting policy note.

Example 12.9 – Depreciation policy note (I)

Depreciation is provided on the straight-line method to write off the cost or valuation of tangible fixed assets, less any estimated residual value, over their expected useful economic lives.

The following asset lives are used:

Freehold buildings	45 years
Leasehold property	The life of the lease; current leases range from 10 to 20 years
Plant and machinery	7 to 10 years
Fixtures and fittings	10 years

No depreciation is provided on freehold land.

Example 12.10 – Depreciation policy note (II)

Depreciation is provided on the reducing balance method to write off the cost or valuation of tangible fixed assets, less any estimated residual value, over their expected useful economic lives.

The following depreciation rates are used:

Plant and machinery	40%
Motor vehicles	50%
Computer equipment	70%

Reasons for non-depreciation of assets

12.50 If certain categories of asset are not depreciated, the accounting policy note should explain why this is considered appropriate. For instance, in a case where depreciation is considered to be immaterial, the following wording might be appropriate.

Example 12.11 – Immaterial depreciation

The estimated residual value of the company's freehold property is approximately equal to its net book value. It is the company's policy to maintain this property to a high standard, so that the estimated residual value will not be impaired over time. The costs of this maintenance are charged to the profit and loss account as they are incurred. The directors are of the opinion that any depreciation in respect of the company's freehold property would be immaterial and consequently no provision is made in the accounts for such depreciation.

As discussed in **12.22–12.27** above, careful consideration must be given to a number of factors before adopting an accounting policy along these lines.

Disclosure when depreciation method is changed

12.51 The effect of any change in the method of providing depreciation must be disclosed in the year of the change, if it is material. This information may be given in the accounting policy note or in the detailed note on fixed assets. The accounting policy note will need to include details of both the previous and the new depreciation method, as the comparative figures will have been calculated under the previous method. The reasoning behind the change of method should also be explained.

Other accounts disclosures

12.52 Other required disclosures are:

- The total depreciation charge for the period - this is usually given as part of the profit and loss account if Format 2 or Format 4 is used and in a note to the accounts if Format 1 or Format 3 is used. A company that has chosen Format 1 or Format 3 for its profit and loss account must include any relevant provisions for depreciation or diminution of assets values in the figures for:

  - cost of sales;
  - distribution costs;
  - administrative expenses.

  FRS 15 also requires the charge for the year to be analysed by class of asset - this is usually covered in the detailed fixed assets movements table in the notes to the accounts.
- Separate disclosure of the depreciation charged in the year in respect of leased assets, as required by SSAP 21 - this is usually given as part of the detailed note to the accounts on fixed assets or within the note that sets out the total depreciation charge for the period;
- The cumulative amount of provisions for depreciation and impairment at the beginning and end of the period (also by class of asset) - this is usually given as part of the detailed note to the accounts on fixed assets;
- The effect on the depreciation charge of any revaluation during the year, if the effect is material - this information is usually given as part of the detailed note on fixed assets or within the note that sets out the total depreciation charge for the period.

LIKELY FUTURE DEVELOPMENTS

FRED 29 'Property, plant and equipment; Borrowing costs'

12.53 The ASB issued FRED 29 'Property, plant and equipment; Borrowing costs' in May 2002 as part of its project to achieve convergence between UK accounting standards and international accounting standards. The Exposure Draft proposes replacing FRS 15 'Tangible fixed assets' with two new standards based on a revised IAS 16 and the existing IAS 23. Much of the content of these two international standards is consistent with current UK requirements. The main differences are in relation to the accounting treatment of revalued assets, in particular the use of a 'fair value' model rather than the UK's present 'value to the business' approach. A separate international group is currently considering the issue of revaluation and whether changes should be made to the present IAS requirements. The ASB is participating in this project and is continuing to press for IAS 16 to incorporate the revaluation principles currently set out in FRS 15. If it is clear at the time that the present proposals to revise IAS 16 are finalised that the revaluation project will result in a further revision of that standard before 2005, the ASB will defer the finalisation of new UK standards. However, if at that time further changes to the international standard seem unlikely, the ASB proposes to issue revised UK standards based on FRED 29. The main changes affecting depreciation would be:

- where residual values need to be revised, the revision should be based on current prices rather than those at the date of acquisition or revaluation;
- there is no guidance on when uncharged depreciation may be regarded as immaterial;
- there is no specific requirement for annual impairment reviews on assets that are not depreciated; and
- there is no reference to renewals accounting, and thus no alternative to the principle that depreciation is determined by reference to the depreciable amount of an asset.

Chapter 13

Other Expenses

FINANCE COSTS OF DEBT

Accounting for debt instrument

13.1 Under the requirements of FRS 4 'Capital Instruments', a debt instrument should be recorded at the time of issue at the amount of the net issue proceeds. The carrying value of the debt will subsequently be:

— increased each year by the finance costs charged to the profit and lost account in respect of the debt; and

— reduced by the payments made by the issuer in respect of the debt.

The classification of capital instruments is considered in **Chapter 25** and accounting for finance costs in respect of non-equity shares is covered in **Chapter 15**.

Finance costs

13.2 The total finance costs of a debt instrument are defined as the difference between:

— the net issue proceeds, after deduction of any direct issue costs; and

— the total amount of the payments or other transfers of economic benefits that the issuer may be required to make in respect of the instrument.

However, payments that are contingent on an uncertain future event (for instance, changes in an index) should only be included in finance costs once the event that gives rise to the payment has actually occurred.

Issue costs

13.3 Issue costs are defined in FRS 4 as the costs that are incurred directly in connection with the issue of a capital instrument – that is, those costs that would not have been incurred had the specific instrument in question not been issued. The Explanatory Notes to the standard set out more detail on the type of costs that should be treated as issue costs. In particular, the definition does not allow the following costs to be treated as issue costs:

— the costs of researching and negotiating finance;
— the costs of ascertaining the suitability or feasibility of particular capital instruments;
— allocations of internal costs which would still have been incurred regardless of whether the instrument was issued (e.g. the remuneration of the individuals involved in the negotiation process);
— costs relating to a financial restructuring or renegotiation.

These costs must be charged to the profit and loss account as they are incurred. A tightly drawn definition of issue costs is necessary, as these costs effectively become part of the finance costs of the instrument and are charged to the profit and loss account over the term of the debt. A wide definition of issue costs would therefore result in the finance cost of the debt being overstated.

Calculation of net issue proceeds

13.4 The net issue proceeds are calculated by deducting the eligible issue costs from the fair value of the consideration received.

Example 13.1 – Net issue proceeds calculation

A Ltd issues a debt instrument on 1 January 20X2 for cash of £5,000.

The direct issue costs amount to £250.

The net issue proceeds are therefore £4,750 (i.e. £5,000 – £250).

Calculation of finance costs

13.5 The finance costs are calculated by comparing the net issue proceeds with the total payments (or other transfers of benefits) that the issuer may be required to make in respect of the debt. Payments that the issuer may be required to make will usually include interest and any amounts payable on redemption of the debt.

Example 13.2 – Finance costs calculation

In 1996, B Ltd issues a 5% bond at its nominal value of £8,000. The bond is redeemable in 2006 at a premium of 10%. The direct issue costs in respect of the bond amount to £750.

The net issue proceeds are £7,250 (i.e. £8,000 – £750).

The total payments required from B Ltd in respect of the bond are:

	£
Interest on £8,000 at 5% = £400 p.a. x ten years	4,000
Repayment of the bond on redemption	8,000
Premium payable on redemption £8,000 at 10%	800
	12,800

The finance costs in respect of the bond are therefore:

Total payments in respect of the bond	12,800
Less: Net issue proceeds	7,250
Finance costs	5,550

Allocation of finance costs over the term of the debt

13.6 The total finance costs of a debt instrument must be allocated over the term of the debt, at a constant rate on its carrying value.

Example 13.3 – Allocation of finance costs

Using the details in **Example 13.2**, the total finance cost of £5,550 should be allocated over ten years at a constant rate on the carrying amount of the debt. The effective rate will therefore be approximately 7.06% and the accounting entries will be as follows.

Date	*Opening carrying amount* £	*Finance costs (P&L account)* £	*Amounts actually paid* £	*Closing carrying amount* £
Year 1	7,250	512	(400)	7,362
Year 2	7,362	520	(400)	7,482
Year 3	7,482	528	(400)	7,610
Year 4	7,610	537	(400)	7,747
Year 5	7,747	547	(400)	7,894
Year 6	7,894	557	(400)	8,051
Year 7	8,051	569	(400)	8,220
Year 8	8,220	580	(400)	8,400
Year 9	8,400	593	(400)	8,593
Year 10	8,593	607	*(9,200)	—
		*Interest	400	
		Redemption premium	800	
		Repayment of bond	8,000	
			9,200	

Convertible debt

13.7 Where the debt is convertible into shares at the option of the investor, it should be accounted for on the basis that it will not be converted, until conversion actually takes place. Therefore, where convertible debt includes a redemption premium that is payable only if conversion does not take place, the premium should be treated as a payment that the issuer may be required to make (i.e. it should be treated as part of the finance costs of the instrument).

Example 13.4 – Finance costs of convertible debt

In 1996, B Ltd issues a 5% convertible bond at its nominal value of £8,000. The bond is convertible to shares between 2004 and 2006 but if it is not converted, it will be redeemed in 2006 at a premium of 10%. The direct issue costs in respect of the bond amount to £750.

The net issue proceeds are £7,250 (i.e. £8,000 – £750).

Assuming that conversion does not take place, the total payments required from B Ltd in respect of the bond will be:

	£
Interest on £8,000 at 5% = £400 pa x 10 years	4,000
Repayment of the bond on redemption	8,000
Premium payable on redemption £8,000 at 10%	800
	12,800
The finance costs in respect of the bond are therefore:	
Total payments in respect of the bond	12,800
Less: Net issue proceeds	7,250
Finance costs	5,550

This will give the same allocation of finance costs as is shown in **Example 13.3** above.

Accounting treatment on subsequent conversion

13.8 If the debt is subsequently converted into shares, the amount recognised as shareholders' funds at the time of conversion will be the amount shown as the liability in respect of the debt at the date of conversion. No gain or loss should be recognised at the time of conversion.

Example 13.5 – Conversion occurs

The details are as in **Example 13.4** above.

If the bond is converted to shares at the end of 2005 (i.e. at the end of Year 9), the carrying value of the bond of £8,593 at that date (see **Example 13.3**) will be recognised as shareholders' funds at the time of conversion.

Gains and losses on repurchase of debt

13.9 Gains and losses on the repurchase or early settlement of debt should be recognised in the profit and loss account in the period in which the repurchase or early settlement takes place. Such gains and losses must be disclosed separately within or adjacent to 'interest payable and similar charges' in the profit and loss account.

Options

13.10 The term of a debt instrument is usually clearly stated, but in some cases either the issuer or the investor may have the option of redeeming the instrument early. The explanatory notes to FRS 4 emphasise that options should be carefully evaluated. Where both parties have the option to redeem the instrument early, the term of the debt should normally be assumed to end on the earliest date on which redemption can take place. The finance costs of the instrument will therefore be spread over the period from the date of issue to the earliest date of redemption. However, this treatment should not be adopted if there is no genuine commercial possibility that the option will be exercised (i.e. the option is artificial). When evaluating options, it should be assumed that each party to the debt instrument will act in their own economic and commercial interest.

Option to extend the term of the debt

13.11 Similarly, if the term of a debt instrument can be extended, the extended period should not be taken into account unless it is virtually certain that extension will take place. The finance costs should therefore normally be allocated over the original term of the debt (i.e. excluding any extension that may, or might not, take place). Once again, it will be necessary to consider whether the extension is a genuine option at the end of the original term of the debt, or whether the arrangement will only make commercial sense if extension actually takes place (i.e. the option for extension is in effect artificial because it will always be exercised).

Options held by the issuer only

13.12 UITF Abstract 11 'Capital Instruments: Issuer Call Options' was issued to clarify the accounting treatment that should be adopted where the issuer of a debt instrument holds an option to redeem the instrument early, but the investor does not hold a similar option. In these circumstances, any additional premium payable by the issuer on exercise of the option should not be treated as part of the finance costs of the instrument but should be charged to the profit and loss account as part of the gain or loss arising on early settlement or repurchase of the debt. However, the term of the debt will continue to end on the earliest date on which redemption can take place (in accordance with FRS 4 – see **13.10** above).

Example 13.6 – Treatment in line with UITF 11

In 1996, B Ltd issues a 5% bond at its nominal value of £8,000. The bond is redeemable in 2011. The direct issue costs in respect of the bond amount to £750. B Ltd has the option of redeeming the bond in 2006 on payment of a premium of £800.

The option is held by the issuer only and the premium payable on early redemption should therefore be ignored when calculating the finance costs.

The finance costs are therefore:

	£
Interest on £8,000 at 5% = £400 p.a. x 10 years	4,000
Repayment of the bond on redemption	8,000
	12,000
Less: Net issue proceeds	7,250
Finance costs	4,750

The finance costs of £4,750 must be allocated over the ten-year term (i.e. to the earliest date of redemption) at a constant rate on the carrying amount of the debt. A rate of approximately 6.29% will achieve this as follows:

Date	*Opening carrying amount* £	*Finance costs (P&L account)* £	*Amounts actually paid* £	*Closing carrying amount* £
Year 1	7,250	456	(400)	7,306
Year 2	7,306	460	(400)	7,366
Year 3	7,366	463	(400)	7,429
Year 4	7,429	467	(400)	7,496
Year 5	7,496	472	(400)	7,568
Year 6	7,568	476	(400)	7,644
Year 7	7,644	481	(400)	7,725
Year 8	7,725	486	(400)	7,811
Year 9	7,811	491	(400)	7,902
Year 10	7,902	498	(400)	8,000

If B Ltd exercises its option to redeem the bond early in 2006 the premium of £800 payable on exercise of the option will be charged to the profit and loss account in that year, as part of the loss on early redemption of the debt.

	£
Amount to be repaid	8,000
Carrying value of the debt (end of year 10)	8,000
	–
Premium payable on early redemption	800
Loss on early redemption	800

If B Ltd decides not to exercise the option, interest of £400 p.a. will continue to be paid (and will be charged to the profit and loss account each year) for the remaining five years of the original term of the debt (i.e. until it is redeemed in 2011).

Premiums payable on redemption of debt

13.13 The above treatment only applies in the case of a redemption premium that is payable by the issuer on exercise of the option that he holds. Any premium that is payable on redemption of the debt is unaffected.

Example 13.7 – Premium payable on redemption of debt

In 1996, B Ltd issues a 5% bond at its nominal value of £8,000. The bond is redeemable in 2011 on payment of a premium of £800. The direct issue costs in respect of the bond amount to £750. B Ltd has the option of redeeming the bond in 2006 on payment of an additional premium of £600.

The total payments required from B Ltd in respect of the bond are:

	£
Interest on £8,000 at 5% = £400 p.a. x 10 years	4,000
Repayment of the bond on redemption	8,000
Premium payable on redemption £8,000 at 10%	800
	12,800

The finance costs in respect of the bond are therefore:

	£
Total payments in respect of the bond	12,800
Less: Net issue proceeds	7,250
Finance costs	5,550

The total finance costs of £5,550 should be allocated over ten years (i.e. to the earliest date of redemption) at a constant rate on the carrying amount of the debt. The effective rate will therefore be approximately 7.06% and the accounting entries will be as follows.

Date	*Opening carrying amount* £	*Finance costs (P&L account)* £	*Amounts actually paid* £	*Closing carrying amount* £
Year 1	7,250	512	(400)	7,362
Year 2	7,362	520	(400)	7,482
Year 3	7,482	528	(400)	7,610
Year 4	7,610	537	(400)	7,747
Year 5	7,747	547	(400)	7,894

Date	*Opening carrying amount* £	*Finance costs (P&L account)* £	*Amounts actually paid* £	*Closing carrying amount* £
Year 6	7,894	557	(400)	8,051
Year 7	8,051	569	(400)	8,220
Year 8	8,220	580	(400)	8,400
Year 9	8,400	593	(400)	8,593
Year 10	8,593	607	(400)	8,800

If B Ltd exercises its option to redeem the bond early in 2006 (i.e. at the end of year 10) the premium of £600 payable on exercise of the option will be charged to the profit and loss account in that year, as part of the loss on early redemption of the debt.

	£
Amount to be repaid	8,800
Carrying value of the debt (end of year 10)	8,800
	–
Premium payable on early redemption	600
Loss on early redemption	600

If B Ltd decides not to exercise the option, interest of £400 p.a. will continue to be paid (and will be charged to the profit and loss account each year) for the remaining five years of the original term of the debt (i.e. until it is redeemed in 2011).

Situations where UITF 11 does not apply

13.14 The accounting treatment set out in UITF Abstract 11 does not apply where:

- the option held by the issuer is not a genuine option – for instance, where it is clear from the terms of the agreement that the issuer will always gain a commercial benefit by exercising the option and there is therefore no question that he will take advantage of the option on the exercise date; or
- the effective rate of interest in respect of the debt increases after the date on which the option is exercisable – in this case, the exercise premium is deemed to compensate the investor for forgoing the additional interest that would have been payable.

In these cases the exercise premium should be treated as a cost that the issuer may be required to pay and should therefore be included as part of the finance costs charged to the profit and loss account in respect of the debt.

Charging of issue expenses to the share premium account

13.15 CA 1985 s 130 permits the share premium account to be used to:

- write-off issue expense relating to shares and debentures;
- provide for a premium payable on the redemption of debentures.

Paragraph 97 of FRS 4 emphasises that the requirements of the standard are not intended to prohibit the subsequent charging of issue costs to the share premium account. However, the costs must first be charged to the profit and loss account (as required by the standard) and then transferred to the share premium account by means of a reserves transfer.

More complex debt instruments

13.16 FRS 4 includes a separate section of Application Notes which consider how the requirements of the standard should be applied to specific types of capital instrument. The items covered in this guidance include:

- capital contribution;
- convertible capital bonds;
- convertible debt with a premium put option;
- convertible debt with enhanced interest;
- debt issued with warrants;
- deep discount bonds;
- index linked loans;
- limited recourse debt;
- perpetual debt;
- repackaged perpetual debt;
- stepped interest bonds;
- subordinated debt.

The guidance includes worked examples to illustrate how the requirements of FRS 4 should be applied in practice to these more complex instruments. They are also useful as a point of reference on how to deal with individual features that may be attached to other debt instruments.

FINANCE CHARGES IN RESPECT OF FINANCE LEASES

Initial recording of asset and liability

13.17 Under SSAP 21 'Accounting for Leases and Hire Purchase Contracts', leases that are classified as finance leases should be recorded in the lessee's balance sheet as an asset and as an obligation to pay future rentals to the lessor. The classification of leases is considered in more detail in **Chapter 20**. At the inception of the lease (which is defined in the standard as the earlier of the date when the asset is brought into use or the date from which rental payments accrue), the amount recorded as an asset and the obligation recorded to the lessor will be the same. Strictly this should be the present value of the minimum lease payments. The minimum lease payments are defined in the standard as the minimum payments over the remaining part of the lease term (excluding charges for services and taxes to be paid by the lessor) and, in the case of the lessee, any residual amounts guaranteed by him or by a party related to him. However, SSAP 21 emphasises that, for practical purposes, the fair value of the leased asset will usually be a sufficiently close approximation to the present value of the minimum lease payments to make the fair value an acceptable figure to use when initially recording the asset and the related obligation to the lessor. Fair value is defined as the price at which an asset could be exchanged in an arm's length transaction less, where applicable, any grants receivable towards the purchase or use of the asset.

Calculating the present value of lease payments

13.18 If the fair value of the asset is not known, or is not considered a suitable figure to use, the present value of the lease payments should be calculated by discounting the minimum payments to be made under the lease at the interest rate implicit in the lease.

Example 13.8 – Present value calculation

F Ltd enters a finance lease in respect of an item of plant. The rental payments under the lease are £2,000 p.a., payable in advance, and the lease is for a term of four years. F Ltd establishes that the implicit rate of interest for such a lease is 8%. The payments are therefore discounted as follows.

Year	*Discount factor* (at 8%)	*Payment*	*Present value*
		—	—
0	1.000	2,000	2,000
1	0.926 (a)	2,000	1,852
2	0.857 (b)	2,000	1,714
3	0.794 (c)	2,000	1,588
		8,000	7,154

(a) = 1.00/1.08
(b) = 0.926/1.08
(c) = 0.857/1.08

The asset and liability should therefore be recorded at the present value of £7,154.

Depreciation of asset

13.19 The leased asset must be depreciated over its expected useful economic life in the same way as any other fixed asset, but the life used should not exceed the lease term. The lease term is defined as:

- the period for which the lessee has contracted to lease the asset; and
- any further terms for which the lessee has the option to continue to lease the asset, with or without further payment, when it is reasonably certain at the inception of the lease that the lessee will exercise this option.

The depreciation of fixed assets is considered in **Chapter 12**.

Analysis of rental payments

13.20 The rental payments made by a lessee under a finance lease will consist of two elements:

- partial repayment of the amount due to the lessor; and
- finance charges in respect of the amount effectively 'borrowed' from the lessor to finance the purchase of the asset.

The rental payments must be analysed between these two elements for accounting purposes. The finance charges will be charged to the profit and loss account, as part of 'interest payable and similar charges' and the amount representing the repayment of 'borrowings' will reduce the balance due to the lessor.

Calculation of total finance charge

13.21 The total finance charge represents the difference between the fair value of the asset at the inception of the lease (or the present value of the minimum lease payments) and the total payments to be made by the lessee under the agreement.

Example 13.9 – Total finance charge

Using the details given in Example 13.8 above, the total finance charge is £846 (i.e. the difference between the total payments of £8,000 and the present value of those payments of £7,154).

Allocation of finance charge

13.22 SSAP 21 requires the total finance charge to be allocated to accounting periods over the term of the lease in a way that produces a constant periodic rate of charge on the balance outstanding in respect of the lessee's obligation to the lessor (or a reasonable approximation of this). There are three common methods of allocating the finance charge:

— the straight-line method;

— the sum of the digits (or rule of 78) method; and

— the actuarial method.

Each of these gives a different degree of accuracy, and the suitability of each method will depend on the materiality of the lease to the reporting entity.

The straight-line method

13.23 This is the least accurate method of allocating the finance charge, but is easy to apply and may be suitable where the amounts involved are small.

Example 13.10 – Allocating the finance charge (straight-line method)

G Ltd leases an asset under a finance lease with a primary term of four years, with the option to continue to lease for as long thereafter as the company wishes on payment of a nominal rental. The rental payments during the primary term of the lease are £3,000 pa, payable in arrears. The cash purchase price of the asset at the inception of the lease was £9,500.

The asset (and the related liability) will therefore be recorded at £9,500. Actual payments during the primary term of the lease will amount to £12,000 (i.e. £3,000 p.a. for four years).

The total finance charge is therefore £2,500 (i.e. £12,000 – £9,500).

If the finance charge is allocated on the straight line method, the annual charge will be £2,500/4 = £625.

The rental payments for each year will therefore be analysed as:

	£
Finance charge	625
Capital repayment	2,375
	3,000

The sum of the digits method

13.24 The sum of the digits (or rule of 78) method provides a reasonable approximation to the actuarial method (which gives the most accurate allocation of the finance charge) provided that:

- the lease term is not too long (e.g. up to five years);
- the interest rate is not very high.

To apply this method, it is necessary to calculate the number of periods over which the finance is to be allocated and assign a weighting to each period. The allocation can be done on a monthly, quarterly or an annual basis. Again this will give differing degrees of accuracy, and the most suitable method will depend on the materiality of the amounts involved.

Example 13.11 – Allocating the finance charge (sum of the digits method)

Using the same details as for **Example 13.10**.

The total finance charge is £2,500

Allocation on an annual basis using sum of the digits:

Year	*Weighting*	*Fraction*	*Finance charge* £
1	4	4/10	1,000
2	3	3/10	750
3	2	2/10	500
4	1	1/10	250
	10		2,500

The analysis of rental payments between capital repayments and finance charges will therefore be:

Year	*Capital repayment* £	*Finance charge* £	*Total rental* £
1	2,000	1,000	3,000
2	2,250	750	3,000
3	2,500	500	3,000
4	2,750	250	3,000
	9,500	2,500	12,000

The actuarial method

13.25 This method is the most complicated method to apply but gives the most accurate result and should always be used where the level and value of finance leases is significant in the context of the company. The appropriate rate of finance charge can be calculated by:

- using a calculator or computer program;
- using a mathematical formula;
- using present value tables;
- trial and error.

Once again, the calculation can be done on a monthly, quarterly or annual basis and the degree of accuracy will vary accordingly.

Example 13.12 – Allocating the finance charge (actuarial method)

Using the same details as for **Example 13.10**.

The total finance charge is £2,500.

Allocation on an annual basis using the actuarial method, with a rate of charge of 10.05%.

Year	*Opening capital sum* £	*Rental payment* £	*Finance charge (10.05%)* £	*Closing capital sum* £
1	9,500	(3,000)	955	7,455
2	7,455	(3,000)	749	5,204
3	5,204	(3,000)	523	2,727
4	2,727	(3,000)	273	—
		12,000	2,500	

The analysis of rental payments between capital repayments and finance charges will therefore be:

Year	*Capital repayment* £	*Finance charge* £	*Total rental* £
1	2,045	955	3,000
2	2,251	749	3,000
3	2,477	523	3,000
4	2,727	273	3,000
	9,500	2,500	12,000

Comparison of results

13.26 The results of the three methods can be compared by considering the finance charge for each year in **Examples 13.10** to **13.12**.

Year	*Straight-line*	*Sum of the digits*	*Actuarial*
	£	£	£
1	625	1,000	955
2	625	750	749
3	625	500	523
4	625	250	273
Total	2,500	2,500	2,500

As the lease is short, the amounts are comparatively low and all of the calculations were carried out on an annual basis, the sum of the digits method gives a similar result to the actuarial method. However, this will not always be the case. Where finance leases are material, it will usually be necessary to use the actuarial method to achieve an accurate result and to use a monthly or quarterly basis (depending on the payment schedule) for the calculations. Where leases are less significant, the sum of the digits method may provide an acceptable alternative as the basis for allocating the finance charge. The straight line method will usually only be acceptable where finance leases are not significant to the company.

Lease payments in advance

13.27 The above examples are calculated on the basis that the rental payments are paid annually in arrears (i.e. at the end of the relevant year). Where payments are made in advance (i.e. at the beginning of the year, quarter or month), the number of periods over which the finance charge is allocated will alter.

Example 13.13 – Allocation of finance charge (payments in advance)

G Ltd leases an asset under a finance lease with a primary term of four years, with the option to continue to lease for as long thereafter as the company wishes on payment of a nominal rental. The rental payments during the primary term of the lease are £3,000 p.a.

(i) If the rental payments are made annually in arrears (i.e. at the end of Years 1 to 4), the finance charge will be allocated over four years.

(ii) If the rental payments are made annually in advance (i.e. at the beginning of Years 1 to 4), the full amount of 'finance' will be repaid at the beginning of Year 4 and it would therefore be inappropriate to allocate a finance charge to Year 4. The finance charge will therefore be allocated over Years 1, 2 and 3 only.

Lease variation clauses

13.28 Lease agreements sometimes include variation clauses which adjust the rental payments:

— by reference to interest rate indicators (e.g. base rate);

— to protect the parties to the lease from the effects of any tax changes that may take place during the term of the lease.

Where the level of rental payments changes as a result of a variation clause in the lease taking effect, the increase or decrease in payments should normally be accounted for as an increase or decrease in the finance charges in the period in which the variation takes place. It will not usually be necessary to rework the finance charge calculations carried out at the start of the lease.

Accounts disclosure

13.29 SSAP 21 also requires the following profit and loss account disclosures in respect of finance leases in the accounts of a lessee:

— the accounting policy for leases (see **Chapter 20**); and

— the aggregate finance charge in respect of finance leases -- this is usually given in the note to the accounts dealing with interest payable and similar charges.

OPERATING LEASE CHARGES IN THE ACCOUNTS OF THE LESSEE

Accounting for rental payments

13.30 In the accounts of a lessee, rental payments under an operating lease should normally be accounted for on a straight line basis over the term of the lease, regardless of the actual timing of the payments. However, another systematic and rational basis of allocating the rental charges may be used if this is more appropriate. For instance, an alternative allocation might be appropriate if the rental charges are related to the amount of use that the lessee makes of the asset. Most operating lease agreements will be relatively straightforward, in that rental charges will usually be paid on a regular basis over the term of the lease. The charge to the profit and loss account for the year will therefore often be equivalent to the amount paid in the year, although some adjustment may be needed to reflect accruals and/or prepayments at the end of each accounting period (e.g. where rental is paid quarterly in advance).

Irregular payments

13.31 In some cases, the rental charges may not be paid systematically over the term of the lease. For instance, there may be a substantial initial payment followed by a number of small monthly, quarterly or annual payments. SSAP 21 'Accounting for Leases and Hire Purchase Contracts' is clear that the timing of the rental payments should not affect the accounting treatment. In this situation, therefore, the total payments over the term of the lease must be calculated and then allocated over the lease term on a straight-line basis.

Example 13.14 Accounting for irregular rental charges

A Ltd takes out a four-year operating lease on an item of equipment. The rental charges are as follows:	
Year 1 – initial charge	£10,000
Year 1 – annual charge	£750
Year 2 – annual charge	£750
Year 3 – annual charge	£750
Year 4 – annual charge	£750
	£13,000

A Ltd must account for the rental payments by charging £3,250 to the profit and loss account each year for Years 1 to 4. The accounts will therefore show a prepayment at the end of Years 1 to 3, as a substantial element of the total rental has been paid in the form of the initial charge in Year 1.

Accounting for incentives

13.32 It has become relatively common in recent years for lessors to include various lease incentives in the arrangements to encourage a lessee to enter into a leasing agreement, particularly in the case of property leases. Such incentives include:

- up-front cash payments by the lessor to the lessee (known as reverse premiums);
- contributions to some of the costs to be incurred by the lessee (for instance, in fitting out the property to meet its own specific needs or in relocating from another site);
- a rent-free period;
- the assumption by the lessor of the lessee's rental commitments under an existing lease.

Incentives of this type were not as common when SSAP 21 was issued and so the accounting treatment is not covered in the standard. The latest guidance is contained in UITF Abstract 28 'Operating Lease Incentives'. This Abstract concludes that most lease agreements that include incentives will have been structured by the lessor to provide the overall market return required, but in a way that meets the cash flow requirements of the lessee. Therefore, where an operating lease agreement includes an incentive such as a cash payment or rent-free period, the level of the rental payments under the lease will usually be higher than would normally be expected under prevailing market rates (even though the rentals may be described in the agreement as being at market rates). Without this, the lessor would not be able to achieve the required rate of return. In these circumstances, application of the accruals concept requires the benefit of the incentive to be matched with the additional costs to the lessee in subsequent years in the form of higher rental payments. The effect of any incentive should therefore be spread over the term of the lease, except where there is provision for the rental payments to be adjusted to market rates during the term of the lease, in which case it will usually be appropriate to spread the incentive over a shorter period.

Review of rental payments

13.33 Where the lease agreement provides for the rental payments to be reviewed during the term of the lease and adjusted to prevailing market rates, it will usually be appropriate to spread the benefit of the incentive over the period to the first review, if it is reasonably expected that the rental payments will be adjusted to genuine market rates at that point.

Method of spreading the incentive

13.34 The benefits of the incentive should usually be spread over the term of the lease (or the period to the first review date) on a straight-line basis. However, the Abstract does permit another systematic allocation method to be used if this will give a more accurate reflection of the time pattern of the benefit that the lessee receives from the use of the asset.

Accounts disclosure

13.35 SSAP 21 requires disclosure of the total operating lease rentals charged to the profit and loss account, analysed between:

— hire of plant and machinery; and
— other operating leases.

The disclosure of commitments under operating leases in **Chapter 32.**

Chapter 14

Taxation

TAX ON THE PROFIT OR LOSS ON ORDINARY ACTIVITIES

Requirement of CA 1985

14.1 Each of the standard formats for the profit and loss account requires separate disclosure of tax on the profit or loss from ordinary activities and tax on any extraordinary profit or loss. The formats also have a further heading for 'other taxes not shown under the above items'. This heading is not generally used in the UK at present. In addition, CA 1985 requires the following details to be disclosed:

- details of any special circumstances which affect the tax liability in respect of profits, income or capital gains for the current year or any future year;
- the amount charged in respect of UK corporation tax;
- the amount that would have been charged for UK corporation tax but for the availability of double tax relief;
- the amount charged in respect of UK income tax;
- the amount of any taxation imposed outside the UK in respect of profits, income and capital gains (so far as these are charged to revenue).

The last four disclosures must be given separately in respect of tax on the profit or loss on ordinary activities and tax on any extraordinary profit or loss. Compliance with the disclosure requirements of FRS 3 'Reporting Financial Performance', FRS 16 'Current tax' and FRS 19 'Deferred tax' will usually be sufficient to ensure compliance with CA 1985.

Current tax

14.2 FRS 16 defines current tax as: 'the amount of tax estimated to be payable or recoverable in respect of the taxable profit or loss for a period, together with adjustments to estimates in respect of previous periods'. The current tax charge or credit on the profit or loss on ordinary activities will usually comprise some or all of the following items:

- a charge or credit in respect of UK corporation tax;

— a charge or credit in respect of foreign tax;

— a charge or credit in respect of group relief payable or receivable;

— adjustments to tax provided in previous years.

Recognition of current tax

14.3 FRS 16 requires all current tax to be recognised in the profit and loss account, except where the gain or loss to which it relates is (or has been) dealt with directly in the statement of total recognised gains and losses. In this case, the attributable tax should also be recognised directly in the statement of total recognised gains and losses. The guidance in the standard notes that where it is difficult to determine the amount of current tax relating to items recognised in the statements of total recognised gains and losses (and this is only expected to happen in exceptional circumstances), tax should be allocated on a pro-rata basis, or using another allocation method that is more appropriate in the circumstances.

Taxable profit or loss

14.4 FRS 16 defines a taxable profit or loss as: 'the profit or loss for the period, determined in accordance with the rules established by the tax authorities, upon which taxes are assessed'. The charge or credit for UK corporation tax will be the estimated tax payable or recoverable as a result of trading profits or losses, capital gains or losses and other income and charges arising during the year, as shown by the draft corporation tax computation.

Tax rate

14.5 FRS 16 requires current tax to be measured at the amounts expected to be paid or recovered, using tax rates and laws that have been enacted, or substantively enacted, by the balance sheet date. Substantively enacted is defined as included in either:

— a Bill that has been passed by the House of Commons and is awaiting only passage through the House of Lords and Royal Assent; or

— a resolution having statutory effect that has been passed under the Provisional Collection of Taxes Act 1968 (this is rarely used in practice).

There is no formal requirement to disclose the tax rate used, but it has become normal practice to do so.

Effect of double tax relief

14.6 In some cases, the charge in respect of corporation tax may be reduced by the availability of double tax relief. In this situation, FRS 16

requires UK tax disclosures to be given both before and after the double tax relief. Appendix 1 to the standard gives the following method of disclosure as an example:

Example 14.1 – Disclosure of double tax relief

	£	£
UK corporation tax:		
Current tax on income for the period	10,500	
Adjustments in respect of prior periods	(345)	
	10,155	
Double tax relief	(625)	
		9,530

Charge or credit for deferred taxation

14.7 FRS 19 'Deferred Tax' requires the deferred tax charge or credit for the accounting period to be recognised in the profit and loss account, except to the extent that it is attributable to a gain or loss that is, or has been, recognised directly in the statement of total recognised gains and losses. In this case, the attributable deferred tax should also be recognised directly in the statement of total recognised gains and losses. The guidance notes that, in exceptional circumstances, it may be difficult to determine the amount of deferred tax relating to gains and losses recognised in the statement of total gains and losses, in which case a reasonable pro-rata or other more appropriate allocation may be used. All deferred tax that is recognised in the profit and loss account must be included in tax on profit or loss on ordinary activities. The recognition and measurement requirements of FRS 19 are considered in **Chapter 30**.

Separate disclosure of deferred tax

14.8 The accounts must show separately:

- the amount of deferred tax charged or credited within tax on profit or loss on ordinary activities; and
- the amount of deferred tax charged or credited in the statement of total recognised gains and losses for the period.

In each case, the deferred tax charge or credit must be analysed into the following components, if the amounts involved are material:

- the origination and reversal of timing differences;
- changes in tax rates and laws;

- adjustments to deferred tax assets arising in previous periods; and
- where relevant, changes in the amount of discount deducted in arriving at the deferred tax balance.

Example 14.2 – Disclosure and analysis of deferred tax

		20X2		*20X1*
		£		*£*
UK corporation tax:				
Current tax on income for the period		7,450		6,321
Adjustments in respect of prior periods		40		(131)
		7,490		6,190
Deferred tax:				
Origination and reversal of timing differences	390		275	
Effect of decrease in tax rate on opening liability	(70)		–	
		320		275
Tax on profit on ordinary activities		7,810		6,465

Reconciliation of tax charge

14.9 As part of the requirement to disclose the circumstances that affect the current and total tax charges and credits for the current period, or might affect those of future periods, FRS 19 requires the notes to the accounts to include a reconciliation of the current tax charge or credit on ordinary activities for the period (i.e. the tax charge or credit before taking into account any deferred tax) to the current tax charge that would result from applying a relevant standard rate of tax to the profit or loss on ordinary activities before tax. Either the monetary amounts or the tax rates can be reconciled – it is anticipated that most companies will choose to use monetary amounts in the reconciliation. The note should also explain the basis on which the standard tax rate has been determined.

Example 14.3 – Reconciliation of current tax charge

Factors affecting the current tax charge for the period:

	20X2	*20X1*
	£	*£*
Profit on ordinary activities before tax	41,350	32,300
Multiplied by standard rate of UK corporation tax for small companies – 20% (20X1: 20%)	8,270	6,460

	20X2 £	*20X1* £
Effects of:		
Expenses not deductible for tax purposes (primarily goodwill amortisation)	3,155	1,634
Capital allowances for period in excess of depreciation	(4,480)	(1,246)
Utilisation of tax losses	—	(527)
Higher tax rates on overseas earnings	505	—
Adjustments to tax charge in respect of prior periods	40	(131)
Current tax charge for period	7,490	6,190

Foreign tax

14.10 If the company has overseas interests and part of the profit or loss for the year is therefore subject to foreign tax, the amount of this tax must be separately disclosed.

Example 14.4 – Separate disclosure of foreign tax

		20X2 £		*20X1* £
UK corporation tax:				
Current tax on income for the period	7,450		6,321	
Adjustments in respect of prior periods	40		(131)	
		7,490		6,190
Foreign tax:				
Current tax on income for the period	80		20	
Adjustments in respect of prior periods	(5)		–	
		75		20
		7,565		6,210
Deferred tax:				
Origination and reversal of timing differences	390		275	
Effect of decrease in tax rate on opening liability	(70)		–	
		320		275
Tax on profit on ordinary activities		7,885		6,485

Tax recognised in the statement of total recognised gains and losses must be similarly analysed.

Withholding tax

14.11 Withholding tax is defined in FRS 16 as: 'tax on dividends or other income that is deducted by the payer of the income and paid to the tax authorities wholly on behalf of the recipient'. Where an entity receives (or is due to receive) dividends, interest or other similar income, the amount shown as income in the profit and loss account should include any amount deducted for withholding tax but should exclude any other taxes and any notional tax. Income received after the deduction of withholding tax should therefore be grossed up for the amount of tax deducted, and this tax should be shown as part of the entity's tax charge for the year.

Example 14.5 – Accounting for income subject to withholding tax

A Ltd has received income of £17,000 from which withholding tax of £3,000 has been deducted. The profit and loss account will therefore show the gross income of £20,000 and £3,000 will be deducted from profit before tax as part of the current tax charge for the year.

Similarly, any outgoing dividends paid by the entity, or any interest or similar payments made, should include the amount of any withholding tax but should exclude any other taxes (e.g. the attributable tax credit on UK dividends). All other income and expenses should be included in pre-tax results on the basis of the amount receivable or payable. No adjustment should be made to reflect a notional amount of tax that would have been paid or relieved in respect of the transaction if it had been taxable or allowable for tax on a different basis.

Dividend income

14.12 The tax credit attributable to UK dividends is not the same as withholding tax. In effect, the tax credit is a notional amount, reflecting the fact that the dividend has been paid out of income that has been taxed, rather than an actual amount of tax deducted from the dividend. UK dividend income should not be grossed up to reflect this notional tax and the amount included in income will therefore be the actual sum received or receivable. Under certain circumstances, companies with overseas interests and activities may be able to pay a dividend under the foreign income dividend (FID) scheme. A dividend paid under this scheme does not carry a tax credit. Where a company receives a dividend which has been paid under the FID scheme, the amount to be recorded as income will be the amount actually received (i.e. with no adjustment for tax).

Transitional arrangements for charities

14.13 Certain non-taxpaying entities (e.g. charities) are entitled to transitional relief following the removal of their right to reclaim tax credits on UK dividends. FRS 16 permits these entities to continue to gross up dividend income for this transitional relief, provided that the nature and amount of the relief is disclosed separately in the accounts.

Group relief

14.14 Where potential tax liabilities are covered by group relief, the company receiving the relief may pay the surrendering company for the relief given. Payment may be made at any amount up to the gross amount of the group relief received, but in most cases the amount paid will be based on the equivalent rate of corporation tax. Particular care should be taken if it is proposed to make payments at a higher or lower rate, or to make no payment for group relief, as this could be considered to be a transaction at undervalue or overvalue between the companies and could give rise to legal difficulties if one of the companies becomes insolvent.

Disclosure of payments for group relief

14.15 Where the payment for group relief is based on the equivalent rate of corporation, the charge (or credit) should be included in the current tax charge or credit on the profit or loss on ordinary activities for the year and should be disclosed separately.

Example 14.6 – Separate disclosure of payment for group relief

		20X2 £		*20X1* £
UK corporation tax:				
Current tax on income for the period	3,250		6,321	
Payment to a fellow subsidiary for group relief (at 30%)	4,200		–	
Current tax for the period	7,450		6,321	
Adjustments in respect of prior periods	40		(131)	
		7,490		6,190
Deferred tax:				
Origination and reversal of timing differences	390		275	
Effect of decrease in tax rate on opening liability	(70)		–	
		320		275
Tax on profit on ordinary activities		7,810		6,465

If, in certain circumstances, it is considered appropriate to make payments at other rates, or to make no payment in respect of group relief, full details should be disclosed in the accounts. Where amounts are paid in excess of or below the rate of corporation tax, the payments are usually disclosed as separate items on the face of the profit and loss account, immediately above the profit or loss before taxation, rather than as part of the tax charge or credit for the year. Additional information will usually need to be given in the notes to explain the transaction.

Adjustments in respect of prior periods

14.16 Tax figures are usually included in the accounts on the basis of draft computations, and adjustments are often needed in the subsequent year (or years) to reflect the final figures. Charges and credits relating to previous years should be shown separately as part of the appropriate element (i.e. current tax, foreign tax, deferred tax) of the tax charge or credit on the profit or loss on ordinary activities. If the adjustments relate to an item that was recognised in the statement of total recognised gains and losses, the tax adjustments should also be recognised in that statement and should be analysed into the various components in the same way as the tax charge or credit in the profit or loss account. If they relate to an item that was classified as extraordinary for accounting purposes, the tax adjustment should also be recognised as an extraordinary item.

Tax on extraordinary items

14.17 Where the accounts include an extraordinary profit or loss, any tax relating to this profit or loss must be shown separately as part of the extraordinary item. The tax element must be analysed into its component parts (e.g. current tax, foreign tax, deferred tax) where relevant. As explained in **Chapter 8**, the stringent requirements of FRS 3 'Reporting Financial Performance' mean that extraordinary items will now appear in accounts only rarely, if at all. FRS 3 sets out rules for calculating the tax effect of an extraordinary item. This is to be done by:

- determining the tax on the profit or loss on ordinary activities as if the extraordinary item did not exist;
- comparing this with the tax charge on the profit or loss for the period, including the extraordinary item.

Any difference in the tax charge or credit (including deferred tax) is the tax to be attributed to the extraordinary item. If there is no difference, then the extraordinary item has no tax effect. It is helpful if this fact is stated in the note to the accounts setting out details of the extraordinary item.

Tax on additional FRS 3 Format headings

14.18 FRS 3 'Reporting Financial Performance' identifies three specific items which it requires to be shown separately on the face of the profit and loss account, after operating profit and before interest:

- profits or losses on the sale or termination of an operation;

— costs of a fundamental reorganisation or restructuring having a material effect on the nature and focus of the reporting entity's operations;

— profits and losses on the disposal of fixed assets (other than marginal adjustments to depreciation previously charged).

The requirements of FRS 3 are considered in more detail in Chapter 8. Where any of these specific items are disclosed in the accounts, FRS 3 also requires information on the tax effect to be given in the notes to the accounts. The tax effect is to be calculated in the same way as for an extraordinary item (see **14.17** above). As a minimum, the tax effect should be disclosed for these items in aggregate, but if the tax effect of individual items is different, further detail should be given to clarify the impact on the accounts. If there is no tax effect, it is helpful to state this in the notes to the accounts.

Special circumstances affecting the tax charge

14.19 FRS 3 'Reporting Financial Performance' requires the accounts to include disclosure of any special circumstances affecting:

— the tax charge or credit for the year;

— the expected tax charge or credit for future years.

This requirement is very broad and the disclosures will inevitably depend on individual circumstances, but the following are examples of some of the issues that might be covered:

— the effect of significant levels of losses brought forward, utilised in the year or carried forward to future years;

— the effect on the tax charge for the year of significant amounts of disallowable expenditure;

— the inclusion in the profit and loss account for the year of other items that do not have a tax effect (e.g. the receipt of a significant tax free grant).

In each case, the individual effects should be quantified. FRS 19 'Deferred Tax' amplifies the disclosure requirement of FRS 3 by requiring the notes to the accounts to include a reconciliation of the current tax charge or credit on ordinary activities for the period to the current tax charge that would result from applying a relevant standard rate of tax to the profit or loss on ordinary activities before tax (see **14.9** above).

Change in the basis of taxation

14.20 If there is a fundamental change in the basis of taxation, the effect of the change should be treated as part of the tax charge or credit for the year on the profit or loss on ordinary activities but should be shown separately on the face of the profit and loss account. Such fundamental changes are likely to be rare in practice. It is important to recognise that a change in the basis of taxation does not constitute a change in accounting policy. The underlying accounting policy is to provide for the amount of taxation that is expected to become payable. The fact that the basis of the taxation charge has altered does not change the underlying accounting policy. The effect is therefore reflected in the accounts in the year that the change takes place, but is separately disclosed because of its significance.

Changes in tax rates and allowances

14.21 Changes in the rates of taxation or in tax allowances will usually affect the provision for deferred taxation. The effect of such changes should be included in the tax charge or credit on the profit or loss on ordinary activities but should be shown separately. Disclosure in the notes to the accounts will usually be sufficient. Once again, there is no change in accounting policy when the underlying rate of taxation changes or when tax allowances are altered. The underlying accounting policy for deferred taxation is to provide for the liability that is expected to crystallise, and provision will be made at the existing rate of tax and on the basis of the existing system of tax allowances if there is no indication that these are expected to change. If changes do subsequently take place, they do not alter the fact that the previous provision was the best estimate on the basis of the information available at the time that the provision was made. Therefore the effect of any change must be reflected in the accounts for the year when the change occurs and should not be treated as a prior year adjustment.

ACCOUNTING FOR RECOVERABLE ADVANCE CORPORATION TAX

Background

14.22 Prior to April 1999, companies paying a dividend to their shareholders were required to pay advance corporation tax (ACT) in respect of the dividend. ACT paid in this way was normally recoverable by being offset against the corporation tax liability on the profits of the year in which the dividend was paid or against the profits of future years, although there were also provisions which allowed ACT to be carried back or surrendered to other group companies. A shadow ACT system continues to operate, allowing companies with unrecovered ACT carried forward after April 1999 to continue to recover this in the same way as if the previous ACT system still existed. Appendix II to FRS 16 sets out transitional arrangements on accounting for ACT that becomes recoverable after April 1999. These arrangements are based on the accounting treatment adopted in SSAP 8 'The Treatment of Taxation under the Imputation System in the Accounts of Companies' which was superseded by FRS 16.

Recoverable ACT

14.23 ACT can be carried forward indefinitely for tax purposes, although the shadow ACT system imposes a restriction on the set-off of ACT so that it is only recoverable to the same extent as under the previous tax system. For accounting purposes, an assessment must be made of the likely recoverability of any ACT that is unrecovered at the balance sheet date. In most cases, its recoverability will be dependent on the level of corporation tax in future years, which in turn will depend on the company's profitability in those years, along with various other factors, such as the level of capital expenditure and any disallowable expenditure in those years. Under the guidance in FRS 16, an amount of ACT previously paid on outgoing dividends is regarded as recoverable when it can be:

- offset against a corporation tax liability on the profits of the current accounting period or of previous accounting periods;
- properly offset against a credit balance on the deferred tax account; or
- expected to be recoverable, taking into account expected profits and dividends - normally those of the next accounting period only.

Offset against deferred tax balance

14.24 If the accounts include a provision for deferred tax, unrecovered ACT can be deducted from the amount provided on the basis that this represents future corporation tax against which the ACT can be recovered. However, the amount offset in this way should not exceed the amount that can actually be recovered against that liability, taking into account the restrictions on recoverability imposed by the tax system.

Future period considered

14.25 Where there is no deferred tax provision, or where the total unrecovered ACT exceeds the amount that can be offset against the deferred tax provision, the recoverability of the remaining ACT needs to be carefully assessed. In considering the recoverability of ACT for accounting purposes, only the immediate and foreseeable future should be taken into account. The guidance in Appendix II to FRS 16 does not impose a formal limit on the future period considered, noting that this will depend on the circumstances of each case, but it suggests that the future period should not extend beyond the next accounting period.

Recognition of recoverable ACT

14.26 Any ACT that is regarded as recoverable under the stringent requirements of the standard should be recognised in the accounts and either:

— deducted from the deferred tax provision, if there is one; or

— shown as a deferred tax asset.

Change in assessment of recoverability

14.27 If ACT that was previously regarded as recoverable becomes irrecoverable, it should be charged in the profit and loss account as a separately disclosed component of the tax charge for the period. Similarly, if ACT that was not previously recognised in the accounts is recovered under the tax system applying after April 1999, it should be credited to the profit and loss account as a separately disclosed component of the tax charge (or credit) for the period.

Chapter 15

Dividends and other Appropriations

DIVIDENDS

Requirements of CA 1985

15.1 The disclosure of the aggregate amount of dividends paid and proposed is not covered in the standard formats but is a separate disclosure requirement of CA 1985 Sch 4. Consequently the Act does not specify where the amount for dividends should be shown, although it does require the aggregate disclosure to be given on the face of the profit and loss account. Additional details may be given in the notes to the accounts.

Appropriations of profit

15.2 FRS 4 'Capital Instruments' requires all dividends to be reported as appropriations of profit. Dividends should therefore be shown in the profit and loss account after arriving at the profit or loss for the financial year. Under the requirements of FRS 16 'Current Tax', outgoing dividends should be recognised in the profit and loss account including the amount of any withholding tax but excluding any other taxes (such as the attributable tax credit on UK dividends) not payable wholly on behalf of the recipient of the dividend. The usual format for the disclosure is therefore as follows.

Example 15.1 – Profit and loss: usual format for disclosure

	20X2	*20X1*
	£	£
Profit or loss for the financial year	362	247
Dividends paid and proposed	(130)	(120)
Retained profit for the year transferred to reserves	232	127

The dividends figure should be cross-referenced to a note showing the amounts of any proposed dividends.

Additional disclosure where there are non-equity shares

15.3 FRS 4 requires separate disclosure of equity and non-equity dividends. This information can be given on the face of the profit and loss account or in the notes to the accounts. Where the analysis of dividends between equity and non-equity shares is not given on the face of the profit and loss account, FRS 4 requires the heading to make clear that amounts relating to non-equity shares are included. The distinction between equity and non-equity shares under FRS 4 is considered in more detail in **Chapter 31**. Examples of two possible disclosures are set out below.

Example 15.2 – Equity and non-equity shares (I)

	20X2	*20X2*	*20X1*	*20X1*
	£	*£*	*£*	*£*
Profit or loss for the financial year		362		247
Dividends paid and proposed:				
Equity shares	(90)		(80)	
Non-equity shares	(40)		(40)	
		(130)		(120)
Retained profit for the year transferred to reserves		232		127

The dividends figure should be cross-referenced to a note showing the amounts of any proposed dividends.

Example 15.3 – Equity and non-equity shares (II)

	20X2	20X1
	£	£
Profit or loss for the financial year	362	247
Dividends paid and proposed on equity and non-equity shares	(130)	(120)
Retained profit for the year transferred to reserves	232	127

In this case, the dividends figure should be cross-referenced to a note to the accounts giving the required analysis between equity and non-equity dividends, as well as separate details of any proposed dividends.

Additional disclosure in the notes to the accounts

15.4 In addition to the aggregate amount of dividends paid and proposed, CA 1985 requires separate disclosure of the aggregate amount of proposed dividends. In most cases this will be the amount proposed to be paid as the final dividend for the year. The disclosure can be given on the face of the profit and loss account or in the notes to the accounts. Usual practice is to give the total figure for dividends on the face of the profit and loss account and the detail in the notes to the accounts. FRS 4 also requires separate disclosure of the aggregate dividend for each class of shares, including the totals for:

— equity dividends;
— participating dividends;
— non-equity dividends.

A participating dividend is defined in FRS 4 as a dividend (or part of a dividend) on a non-equity share that, in accordance with a company's memorandum and articles of association, is always equivalent to a fixed multiple of the dividend payable on an equity share. The most common example of a dividend that would meet this definition, and the one referred to in the Application Notes to the standard, is the dividend on participating preference shares, where the shares carry an entitlement both to a fixed dividend for each accounting period and also to an additional amount based on a proportion of the dividend paid to the holders of equity shares. The analysis required by FRS 4 will usually be given in the notes to the accounts. It can be included on the face of the profit and loss account but the level of detail will usually make this inappropriate. The following example takes the details given in **Examples 15.2** and **15.3** and shows a suggested note disclosure that would meet the basic requirements of CA 1985 and of FRS 4.

Example 15.4 – Disclosure to meet basic requirements of FRS 4 and the Act

Dividends paid and proposed:

	20X2	*20X1*
Equity shares:	£	£
Interim dividend paid during the year	30	20
Proposed final dividend	60	60
	90	80
Non-equity shares:		
Dividend paid during the year	40	40
	130	120

FINANCE COSTS OF NON-EQUITY SHARES

Basic requirement

15.5 FRS 4 requires all finance costs in respect of non-equity shares to be treated as appropriations of profit. Finance costs are to be calculated in the same way as for debt and specifically include:

— dividends payable in respect of the shares;
— any direct issue costs in respect of the shares;
— any other payments made in respect of the shares (e.g. an additional amount payable on redemption of the shares).

The detailed requirements of FRS 4 on the calculation and treatment of finance costs are considered in **Chapter 13**. The total finance costs of non-equity shares are defined as the difference between the net issue proceeds of the shares (i.e. after deduction of any direct issue costs) and the total amount payable in respect of the shares (e.g. dividends and any amounts payable on redemption).

Treatment of issue costs

15.6 The definition of issue costs under FRS 4 is considered in more detail in **Chapter 13**. In the case of non-equity shares, costs that meet the definition must be accounted for initially as a reduction in the proceeds of issue of the shares. Any issue costs that do not meet the definition must be charged to the profit and loss account as they are incurred. The usual accounting treatment is to debit the direct issue costs to the share premium account. The accounting entries at the time of issue of the shares would therefore be as follows.

Example 15.5 – Treatment of issue costs

Issue of 500 4% preference shares of £1 with direct issue costs of £60.

Dr	Cash received	440	
Dr	Share premium account	60	
Cr	Share capital account		500

If there is no balance on the share premium account, or the balance is insufficient to absorb the issue costs, the costs should be debited directly to the profit and loss account reserve.

Issue costs in respect of non-redeemable shares

15.7 If the non-equity shares are not redeemable at a specified future date, there is no obligation for the issuer to make a repayment in respect of the shares. In this case, the finance costs of the shares will simply be the amount of dividend payable each year. Any direct issue costs relating to the shares will remain within shareholders' funds (usually as a reduction of the share premium account) until the shares are redeemed or cancelled, when the issue costs will be taken to the profit and loss account.

Issue costs in respect of redeemable shares

15.8 The definition of finance costs explained in **15.5** above means that any direct issue costs in respect of redeemable non-equity shares are effectively appropriated in the profit and loss account over the life of the shares as part of the annual finance cost.

Example 15.6 – Issue costs of redeemable shares

Issue of 500 4% preference shares of £1 at the beginning of the year with direct issue costs £60. Shares are redeemable at par at the end of five years.

The initial accounting entries would be:

Dr	Cash received	£440	
Dr	Share premium account	£60	
Cr	Share capital account		£500

The total finance costs of the shares are calculated as:

Dividends payable £4% on £500 for five years	£100
Repayment at par at the end of ten years	£500
Total amount payable in respect of the shares	£600
Less: Net issue proceeds	£440
Total finance cost	£160

Share issue expenses charged to share premium account

15.9 CA 1985 s 130 permits the expenses of an issue of shares to be charged to the share premium account. FRS 4 emphasises that the requirements of the standard are not intended to prohibit the subsequent charging of share issue costs to the share premium account. This must be done by means of a reserves transfer. As the share issue costs may well have been debited to the share premium account at the time of the share issue, this means that the issue costs appropriated in the profit and loss account in any one year will effectively be credited to the share premium account at the time of appropriation and then debited again as a reserves transfer.

Example 15.7 – Share issue expenses charged to share premium account

Using the details from **Examples 15.6** and **15.8**.

	Profit and loss reserve	*Share premium*	*Non-equity share capital*
	£	£	£
Opening balance (assumed)	400	100	100
Issue of non-equity shares	—	(60)	500
Year 1 finance costs (appropriated in P&L account)	—	10	—
Retained profit transferred from P&L account	45	—	—
Transfer of issue costs to share premium	10	(10)	—
Closing balance	455	40	600

Allocation of finance costs over the life of the shares

15.10 The total finance costs of the non-equity shares must be allocated over the life of the shares, at a constant rate on the carrying value of the shares.

Example 15.8 – Allocating finance costs over the life of the shares

Using the details in **Example 15.6**, the total finance cost of £160 should be appropriated in the profit and loss account over five years at a constant rate on the carrying amount of the shares. The effective rate will therefore be approximately 6.9% and the accounting entries will be:

Date	*Opening carrying amount*	*Finance costs (P&L account)*	*Amounts actually paid*	*Closing carrying amount*
	£	£	£	£
Year 1	440	30	(20)	450
Year 2	450	31	(20)	461
Year 3	461	32	(20)	473
Year 4	473	33	(20)	486
Year 5	486	34	(520)	—

The profit and loss account disclosure in Year 1 might be as follows (assuming dividends of £35 on equity shares).

	£	£
Profit for the financial year (assumed)		110
Dividends paid and proposed on equity and non-equity shares	(55)	
Other finance costs in respect of non-equity shares	(10)	
		(65)
Retained profit for the year transferred to reserves		45

With a note to the accounts showing the following detail:

Dividends and other appropriations		
Equity shares:		
Interim dividend paid during the year	15	
Proposed final dividend	20	
		35
Non-equity shares:		
Dividend paid during the year	20	
Other finance costs	10	
		30
		65

Insufficient distributable reserves

15.11 FRS 4 requires the full amount of finance costs of non-equity shares to be appropriated from the profit and loss account each year. This includes the amount of any dividend payable and applies even if the company does not have sufficient reserves to pay the relevant dividend. However, in these circumstances it would generally be unacceptable to describe the amount appropriated as a dividend. It will usually be more appropriate to describe such an amount as other finance costs in respect of non-equity shares.

Example 15.9 – Insufficient distributable reserves

Dividend payable on non-equity shares of £40 pa.

Dividend actually paid in 20X1 restricted to £20 due to unavailability of distributable profits.

Dividends and other appropriations.

	20X1	*20X2*
	£	*£*
Non-equity shares:		
Dividend paid	20	40
Other finance costs	20	–
	40	40

The notes to the accounts should explain how the additional finance costs arise in the current year.

Accruals basis for dividends

15.12 FRS 4 emphasises that dividends should normally be accounted for on an accruals basis, except in circumstances where ultimate payment is remote. An example of the latter situation given in the standard is where profits are insufficient to support the declaration and payment of a dividend and the dividend rights are non-cumulative. In practice many non-equity shares will carry cumulative dividend rights. Where dividend rights are cumulative, shareholders retain their right to the dividend, even if distributable reserves are insufficient to pay the dividend. FRS 4's requirements mean that the dividends on cumulative non-equity shares must always be appropriated in the profit and loss account as part of the overall finance costs of the shares, regardless of whether they can be legally declared and paid. Difficulty often arises over where the credit entry for this appropriation should be made. If the dividend cannot be legally declared and paid, it is not appropriate to include it as an amount payable within current liabilities. The credit should usually be taken to the profit and loss account reserve and the arrears of the dividend should be disclosed in the notes on reserves. In the year in which the dividend arrears are paid, the notes to the accounts should disclose the total amount paid in respect of non-equity dividends and the fact that part of this amount was appropriated in the accounts of previous years. The amount shown as dividends paid and proposed in the profit and loss account will be the dividend relating to the current year only, as the amount paid in respect of the previous years will have already been shown as an appropriation in the profit and loss account for those years. The following disclosure might be appropriate.

Example 15.10 – Payment of dividend arrears

Using the details from **Example 15.9** and assuming the dividend arrears are paid in the following year.

Extract from profit and loss account:

		20X2		*20X1*
	£	£	£	£
Profit for the financial year		90		20
Dividends paid and proposed on non-equity shares	(40)		(20)	
Other finance costs in respect of non-equity shares	–		(20)	
		(40)		(40)
Retained profit/(loss) transferred to reserves		50		(20)

Extract from the notes to the accounts:

Dividends and other appropriations

Non-equity shares:				
Dividends paid during the year		60		20
Dividends appropriated in previous year	(20)		–	
Additional finance costs	–		20	
		(20)		20
		40		40

SCRIP DIVIDENDS

Alternative to cash dividends

15.13 Shareholders may sometimes be offered additional shares as an alternative to cash dividends. These are known as scrip dividends. FRS 4 includes specific guidance on accounting for scrip dividends in the accounts of the issuer and requires the value of any shares issued in this way to be taken as the amount that would have been receivable if the shareholder had chosen the cash dividend alternative. The amount appropriated in the profit and loss account should be the value of the shares taken up by shareholders, plus the amount actually paid in cash dividends. The amount appropriated in the profit and loss account will therefore always be the same, irrespective of whether the dividend is payable in cash or in the form of shares.

Bonus issue of shares

15.14 A scrip dividend often takes the legal form of a bonus issue of shares and shareholders who opt to take the share alternative will usually do so before they become entitled to the cash dividend. In this case, the amount appropriated in the profit and loss account in respect of the scrip dividend should be written back as a movement on the profit and loss account reserve and an appropriate amount should be transferred between reserves and share capital to record the capitalisation of reserves. The amount transferred will usually be the nominal value of the shares issued.

Issue of shares for cash

15.15 If the shareholder has not elected to take the share alternative before becoming entitled to the dividend, the legal form of the share issue is slightly different. In this case, the shareholder who takes up additional shares has effectively invested the cash received in the form of a dividend in the additional shares taken up. The amount of the cash dividend therefore represents the issue proceeds of the shares, and if these are greater than the nominal value of the shares, a share premium will need to be recorded in the accounts.

Uncertainty over take-up

15.16 Where there is uncertainty over how many shareholders will elect to take the share alternative, FRS 4 requires the accounts to reflect the dividend on the basis that the full amount will be payable in cash. The full amount will therefore be appropriated as a proposed dividend in the profit and loss account and the liability to pay the dividend in cash will be shown as a creditor in the balance sheet. In the following year, adjustments will have to be made to reserves and share capital to reflect the actual take-up of the share alternative. No adjustment should be required in the profit and loss account, as FRS 4's requirement means that the appropriation will always be based on the full amount of the cash alternative.

DISTRIBUTABLE RESERVES

Significance of distributable reserves

15.17 CA 1985 does not often use the term 'dividend' but refers instead to a 'distribution'. Under the Act, a distribution can only be made if the individual company has sufficient distributable reserves available. This is a highly complex area and only a brief outline of the issues is given here. Legal advice should always be sought in cases where there is any doubt over the potential availability of reserves for distribution. CA 1985 ss 270-274 set out detailed rules on the accounts that must be used as the basis for establishing whether a company has profits available for a distribution.

Definition of distribution

15.18 CA 1985 ss 263(2) defines a distribution as any distribution of a company's assets to its members, in cash or in any other form, except distributions by way of:

- an issue of fully-paid or partly-paid bonus shares;
- the redemption or purchase of the company's own shares out of:
  - capital;
  - the proceeds of a fresh issue of shares; or
  - unrealised profits;

  in accordance with Chapter VII of Part V of the Act;
- the reduction of share capital by:
  - extinguishing the liability of any members in respect of share capital not paid up;
  - reducing the liability of any members in respect of share capital not paid up; or
  - paying off paid up share capital; or
- a distribution of assets to members on the winding up of the company.

Profits available for distribution

15.19 A company may only make a distribution out of profits that are available for that purpose. Profits available for distribution are defined in CA 1985 s 263(3) as:

- accumulated, realised profits, to the extent that these have not been previously distributed or capitalised, less
- accumulated, realised losses to the extent that these have not previously been written off in a reduction or reorganisation of capital.

Separate rules apply in the case of investment companies. These are set out in sections 265 and 266 but are not considered here. Reference should also be made to the company's memorandum and articles of association, as these may contain additional, more restrictive rules on the distribution of the company's profits.

Additional rules for public companies

15.20 Additional rules apply in the case of public companies. A public company may only make a distribution if:

— at the time of the distribution, the amount of its net assets is not less than the aggregate of its called up share capital and undistributable reserves; and

— the distribution does not reduce the amount of its net assets to less than that aggregate.

Again, separate rules apply to investment companies. In this context, net assets is defined as the aggregate of the company's assets less the aggregate of its liabilities. Uncalled share capital cannot be treated as an asset for this purpose and liabilities specifically include any provisions for liabilities and charges. The effect of this section is that a public company must take account of any unrealised losses when establishing profits available for distribution. A private company needs only to consider realised profits and realised losses.

Undistributable reserves

15.21 A company, whether public or private, may not distribute any of the following reserves:

— the share premium account;

— the capital redemption reserve;

— the excess of accumulated, unrealised profits over accumulated, unrealised losses (to the extent that profits have not been previously capitalised and losses have not been previously written off in a reconstruction or reorganisation - in this context, a transfer to the company's capital redemption reserve made on or after 22 December 1980 is not regarded as a capitalisation of reserves);

— any other reserve which the company is prohibited from distributing by its memorandum or articles of association or by any other enactment.

Definition of realised profit and losses

15.22 The interpretation of realised profits and losses is covered by CA 1985 ss 262(3) and 742(2). Realised profits and losses are the profits and losses that fall to be treated as realised, in accordance with the principles generally accepted for determining realised profits and losses for accounting purposes, at the time the accounts are prepared. Additional guidance is given in 'The Determination of Realised Profits and Disclosure of Distributable Profits in the Context of the Companies Act', an Accounting Recommendation issued by the Institute of Chartered Accountants in England and Wales in 1982. This suggests that any interpretation of 'the principles generally accepted' should be based on the principles laid down in CA 1985 Sch 4 and the requirements of accounting standards. However, the concept of a realised profit or loss is affected by changes in accounting practice and in the financial and economic environment, and the guidance set out in the existing technical releases has inevitably become out of date. In July 1999, the ICAEW issued an initial consultation draft of revised guidance reflecting recent developments in business and accounting practice. A further draft was issued in August 2000 (published as ICAEW Technical Release TECH 25/00). FRS 18 'Accounting Policies' also considers the issue of realised profits in the context of the CA 1985 requirements. The guidance in this standard notes that profits are to be treated as realised for these purposes only when they have been realised in the form of cash or of other assets the ultimate cash realisation of which can be assessed with reasonable certainty. These requirements are to apply unless there are special reasons for departing from them, in which case two additional rules come into effect:

- such 'special reasons' will not exist unless, as a minimum, it is possible to be reasonably certain that an unrealised gain exists and can be measured with sufficient reliability;
- due consideration must be given to whether a departure from the requirements would result in the use of valuation bases or accounting treatments not permitted by companies' legislation, and which could therefore only be used if the true and fair override was justified.

Development costs

15.23 Under CA 1985 s 269, any development costs shown as an asset in a company's accounts are to be treated as a realised loss, with the following exceptions:

- if the costs have been revalued, any element that represents an unrealised profit need not be treated as a realised loss;
- if there are special circumstances which justify the directors' decision not to treat the costs as a realised loss, and the note to the accounts on development costs:
  - states that the costs are not to be treated as a realised loss, and
  - explains the circumstances relied on by the directors to justify their decision.

There is no further guidance on these special circumstances in the Act, but it is usually acknowledged that the carry forward of development costs in accordance with SSAP 13 'Accounting for Research and Development' will usually justify a decision by the directors not to treat the costs as a realised loss for distribution purposes.

Revaluation of fixed assets

15.24 Under CA 1985 s 275(1), a provision mentioned in Sch 4 paras 88 and 89 to the Act is to be treated as a realised loss. These paragraphs relate respectively to:

- provisions for depreciation or diminution in value of assets and amounts written off assets; and
- provisions for liabilities and charges.

However, a specific exception is made in the case of a diminution in value of a fixed asset which arises on a revaluation of all of the company's fixed assets (or all of its fixed assets except goodwill). A formal revaluation of all the assets is not necessarily required. CA 1985 s 275(4) states that any consideration by the directors of the value at any particular time of a fixed asset is treated as a revaluation of the asset in determining whether a revaluation of the company's assets has taken place for the purposes of s 275(1). In considering the value of fixed assets in this way, the directors must be satisfied that the aggregate value is not less than the aggregate amount at which the assets are stated in the accounts. In other words, there must not be an overall deficit which has not been recognised in the accounts. Specific disclosures must be given in the notes to the accounts if the directors wish to take advantage of this exception.

Depreciation charged on revalued assets

15.25 As noted in **15.24**, provisions for depreciation are to be regarded as realised losses. However, if an asset has been revalued and depreciation is charged on the revalued amount (in accordance with present accounting requirements), CA 1985 s 275(2) requires the depreciation on the revaluation surplus to be treated as a realised profit. The effect of this is that only depreciation based on the original cost of the asset is treated as a realised loss for distribution purposes. If the original cost of an asset is not readily available, its cost is taken to be the value shown in the earliest available record since acquisition by the company.

Particular problem areas

15.26 The following situations may give rise to particular difficulty in establishing whether profits or losses are realised or unrealised. They are therefore indicative of the type of situation where specific advice should be sought before a distribution is made:

- the purchase and sale of assets between companies in the same group, but where no payment is actually made in respect of the transaction;

- dividends which are declared by subsidiary companies but which are not paid, particularly if the subsidiary does not appear to have adequate resources to make the payment;

- non-monetary transactions, such as asset swaps or share exchanges;

- transactions that include option clauses, particularly if these appear to be in any way artificial or commercially unrealistic;

- transactions between related parties, particularly where these do not appear to be at arm's length or where there are doubts over the commercial viability or purpose of the transaction for one of the parties involved;

- a series of transactions between related parties, particularly if the transactions involve the circulation of cash between the parties - in this case, it will usually be necessary to consider the series of transactions as a whole and assess its overall substance, rather than looking at each part of the arrangement in isolation;

- the inclusion in the profit and loss account of unrealised exchange gains on long-term monetary items, as required by SSAP 20 'Foreign Currency Translation'.

Goodwill

15.27 The impact of the write-off of goodwill on distributable reserves is considered in an Appendix to FRS 10 'Goodwill and intangible assets'. The issues are summarised in **Chapter 19.**

Pension liabilities

15.28 FRS 17 'Retirement Benefits' was published in November 2000 and is fully effective for accounting periods beginning on or after 1 January 2005. Under this standard, a deficit arising in a defined benefit pension scheme will usually need to be included as a liability in the accounts of an employer. This might inhibit the ability of the company to pay a dividend - for instance, where the defined benefit liability is so large that it reduces distributable reserves below the level needed to cover a proposed distribution. Appendix IV to the standard notes that this situation is not expected to arise very often in practice. It was therefore not considered appropriate to deal with it in the standard, and companies who do encounter the problem are advised to discuss the matter with their legal advisors.

LIKELY FUTURE DEVELOPMENTS

Conflicts between CA 1985 and the ASB 'Statement of Principles'

15.29 The ASB's 'Statement of Principles for Financial Reporting' was published in December 1999. Two elements of the principles conflict with current company law requirements:

- under the principles in the Statement, dividends are defined as distributions to owners and, as such, should be reported in the reconciliation of movements in shareholders' funds rather than in the financial performance statement - however, CA 1985 requires the aggregate amount of dividends paid and proposed to be shown on the face of the profit and loss account and this legal requirement currently prevails over the principles in the ASB Statement;
- a proposed dividend does not meet the definition of a liability set out in the Statement - however, CA 1985 effectively requires proposed dividends to be recognised as liabilities in the accounts and this requirement also prevails over the principles in the ASB Statement at present.

As explained below, both of these issues are now under active consideration and changes are likely in the not too distant future.

FRED 22 'Review of FRS 3: Reporting Financial Performance'

15.30 The ASB published FRED 22 'Revision of FRS 3: Reporting Financial Performance' in December 2000. The exposure draft puts forward some significant changes to current reporting and disclosure requirements. Under the proposals, the profit and loss account and statement of total recognised gains and losses would be replaced with a single performance statement showing all gains and losses recognised during the reporting period, and relating to that period. Dividends would not be reported in the performance statement as they represent transactions with owners rather than elements of financial performance, although they could be shown as a memorandum item at the foot of the statement. The ASB is discussing with the DTI the possibility of changing the present company law requirements on the disclosure of dividends. FRED 22 is considered in more detail in **Chapter 8**.

FRED 27 'Events after the balance sheet date'

15.31 The ASB issued FRED 27 'Events after the balance sheet date' in May 2002 as part of its project to achieve convergence between UK accounting standards and international accounting standards. The Exposure Draft proposes replacing SSAP 17 'Accounting for Post Balance Sheet Events' with a new standard based on a proposed revision of IAS 10. FRED 27 states specifically that equity dividends declared after the balance sheet date should not be recognised as liabilities, although it does require them to be disclosed in a note to the accounts. The ASB has asked the DTI to consider changing the present company law requirements in respect of dividends to enable this aspect of the new standard to be implemented.

FRED 30 'Financial instruments: Disclosure and presentation; Recognition and measurement'

15.32 The ASB issued FRED 30 'Financial Instruments: Disclosure and Presentation; Recognition and Measurement' in June 2002 as part of its project to achieve convergence between UK accounting standards and international accounting standards. The Exposure Draft sets out proposals for the implementation in the UK of standards based on proposed revisions of IAS 32 'Financial Instruments: Disclosure and Presentation' and IAS 39 'Financial Instruments: Recognition and Measurement'. These have been published simultaneously by the International Accounting Standards Board (IASB). The implementation of accounting requirements based on FRED 30 could have significant implications for companies with preference shares. Preference shares are currently shown as part of shareholders' funds but under the proposals in FRED 30 many will be treated as liabilities rather than shares, and dividends payable on them will be accounted for as interest. FRED 30 is considered in more detail in **Chapter 25**.

Chapter 16

Directors' Remuneration and Benefits

DETAILED DISCLOSURE REQUIREMENTS

Distinction between quoted and unquoted companies

16.1 The annual accounts of every company must include detailed information on the remuneration paid to, or receivable by, anyone who was a director during the year. The disclosure requirements cover all amounts receivable by the directors in respect of their services as directors of the company (and, where relevant, of its subsidiaries), regardless of who actually makes the payment. The legislation requires basic aggregate disclosures to be given by all companies, and then makes a clear distinction between quoted and unquoted companies in requiring more detailed information to be given. The requirements are broadly similar for accounting periods ending before 31 December 2002, although greater detail is required in the case of quoted companies. However, the Directors' Remuneration Report Regulations 2002 (SI 2002/1986) introduce some significant changes to the disclosure requirements for quoted companies for accounting periods ending on or after 31 December 2002. For these purposes, a quoted company is defined as a company whose equity share capital is:

— included in the Official List of the London Stock Exchange;

— officially listed in an EEA State; or

— admitted to dealing on the New York Stock Exchange or the NASDAQ exchange.

Brief details of the new requirements for quoted companies are given in **16.2** but the rest of this chapter concentrates on the requirements that apply to unquoted companies. If the required information is not disclosed in the accounts, the auditors are required to include it in their audit report, as far as they are reasonably able to do so.

Detailed disclosure by quoted companies

16.2 For accounting periods ending on or after 31 December 2002, the directors of a quoted company are required to prepare a directors' remuneration report containing the detailed information specified in a new CA 1985 Sch 7A. The legislation generally requires this detailed information to be given in tabular form and in a way that links the information to each director by name. Current directors, and those who have served as director in the preceding five years, are given a specific duty to disclose relevant information to the company to enable the report to be prepared. The report must be formally approved by the directors and must be signed on behalf of the board by a director or by the company secretary. A signed copy must be delivered to the registrar as part of the company's annual reports and accounts. The auditors are required to report on the auditable part of the report (which is defined as the part covering the detailed disclosures on remuneration received by the directors) and to include any missing information in their audit report, so far as they are reasonably able to do so. The general meeting at which the annual reports and accounts are laid must include a resolution enabling the shareholders to approve the directors' remuneration report, but the legislation notes that this requirement does not mean that the entitlement of any individual to the remuneration shown in the report is conditional on the resolution being passed.

Emoluments and other benefits

16.3 The following information must be disclosed in the annual accounts of an unquoted company:

- the aggregate amount of emoluments paid to, or receivable by, the directors in respect of qualifying services;
- the aggregate of the following amounts payable under a long-term incentive scheme in respect of qualifying services:
  - money paid to, or receivable by, the directors; and
  - the net value of any assets (other than shares and share options) received or receivable by the directors.
- the number of directors who exercised share options during the year; and
- the number of directors who received shares in the company (or the group) under long-term incentive schemes in respect of qualifying services.

Reduced requirements apply in the case of a company that qualifies as small under CA 1985 (see **Chapter 7**). For the purposes of the disclosure requirements, qualifying services are:

- services as a director of the company;
- whilst a director of the company, services as a director of any of its subsidiary undertakings; and
- services otherwise in connection with the management of the affairs of the company or any of its subsidiary undertakings.

Highest paid director

16.4 Where the aggregate of the amounts required to be disclosed under CA 1985 Sch 6 paras 1(1)(a) and (c) (ie emoluments and amounts receivable under long-term incentive schemes) total £200,000 or more, an unquoted company must disclose the following additional information:

- the total amount attributable to the highest paid director;
- the aggregate company contributions to money purchase pension schemes in respect of that director;
- if the highest paid director is accruing retirement benefits under a defined benefit scheme:
  - the amount of pension accrued at the end of the year; and
  - the amount of any lump sum accrued at the end of the year;
- whether the highest paid director exercised any share options during the year; and
- whether the highest paid director received any shares under a long-term incentive scheme in respect of qualifying services.

A company that qualifies as small under CA 1985 does not have to make these disclosures (see **Chapter 7**).

Pension contributions

16.5 The annual accounts of an unquoted company must disclose:

- the aggregate amount of company contributions to pension schemes in respect of qualifying services where the benefits payable to the directors will be calculated on the basis of the contributions paid;
- the number of directors accruing retirement benefits under money purchase schemes; and
- the number of directors accruing retirement benefits under defined benefit schemes.

Only pension contributions to money purchase (ie defined contribution) schemes are, therefore, disclosable. The amount of any contributions to defined benefit schemes for directors does not have to be shown in the accounts. Slightly reduced requirements apply in the case of a company that qualifies as small under CA 1985 (see **Chapter 7**).

Excess retirement benefits

16.6 An unquoted company must disclose in its annual accounts the aggregate amount of any retirement benefits paid to, or receivable by, directors and former directors that are in excess of the retirement benefits to which they were entitled on 31 March 1997 or the date when benefits first became payable, whichever is the later. However, disclosure is not required where:

— the funding of the scheme allowed the amounts to be paid without recourse to additional contributions; and

— the amounts were paid to, or receivable by, all pensioner members of the scheme on the same basis.

Compensation for loss of office

16.7 The aggregate amount of compensation for loss of office paid to, or receivable by, directors and former directors must be disclosed in the annual accounts of an unquoted company. This includes:

— amounts in respect of loss of office as director of the company or of any of its subsidiary undertakings; and

— amounts in respect of the loss of any other office in connection with the management of the affairs of the company or of any of its subsidiary undertakings.

Payments to third parties

16.8 The accounts must disclose the aggregate amount of any consideration paid to, or receivable by, third parties for making available the services of any person:

— as a director of the company; or

— whilst a director of the company:

  — as a director of any of its subsidiary undertakings; or

  — otherwise in connection with the management of the affairs of the company or any of its subsidiary undertakings.

Voluntary disclosure of detailed information

16.9 CA 1985 provides for a situation where an unquoted company voluntarily discloses detailed information for each director. In this case, aggregate totals need not be given and the highest paid director need not be identified. Similarly, if the aggregate figures or total numbers required by the regulations are readily identifiable from other information in the accounts, they generally do not have to be disclosed again.

Amounts to be included

16.10 The amounts to be disclosed each year are:

- amounts receivable in respect of that year, regardless of when payment is actually made;
- for amounts not receivable in respect of a specific period, the amount paid.

If any amounts are not disclosed on the grounds that the director is liable to account to the company or any of its subsidiary undertakings for the amount received, or that they are expense allowances which are not chargeable to UK income tax and, subsequently, the director's liability to account for the amounts received is partly or wholly released, or the expense allowance is charged to UK income tax, the amounts must be disclosed separately in the first set of accounts in which it is practicable to show them. Where a single amount is paid to a director to cover more than one element of emoluments and similar benefits, and the amount relating to each element is not specified, CA 1985 allows the directors to make an appropriate apportionment of the amount received in order to comply with the disclosure requirements.

Comparative figures

16.11 Comparative figures must be given for all amounts requiring disclosure under CA 1985 Sch 6.

Positioning of note on directors' remuneration

16.12 The disclosures on directors' remuneration are extensive and should be dealt with in a separate note on directors' remuneration within the section of the notes to the accounts relating to profit and loss account items. As explained above, directors' remuneration may include amounts paid by other companies and persons as well as amounts paid by the company itself, and may include estimated values to reflect benefits received in kind. For this reason it is not appropriate to include details of directors' remuneration in the note to the accounts which sets out details of individual items charged or credited in arriving at the operating profit or loss for the year.

Example disclosures

16.13 Examples of the disclosures for an unquoted company and a small company are given in the appendix to this Chapter.

DEFINITION OF EMOLUMENTS

CA 1985 definition

16.14 Emoluments are defined in CA 1985 Sch 6 para 1. In addition to normal salary and bonus payments they include:

- fees and percentages;
- expense allowances, if these are chargeable to UK income tax; and
- the estimated money value of benefits in kind received by a director, otherwise than in cash.

The use of the word 'include' in this paragraph suggests that the list is not intended to be exhaustive and that any other similar amounts paid to, or receivable by, directors will, therefore, be disclosable. Payments to a person in respect of acceptance of office as director of a company are specifically included in emoluments by CA 1985 Sch 6 para 1(6)(b). This was introduced by the Companies Act 1989 to bring 'golden hellos' within the disclosure requirements. Prior to this, companies had avoided disclosure on the grounds that 'golden hellos' were not payments in respect of services as a director of the company. The amounts to be disclosed are the gross figures before any deductions in respect of taxation, employee national insurance contributions or contributions by the director into a pension scheme. The inclusion of bonus payments is considered in more detail below.

Items that are not included

16.15 However, emoluments do not include the following:

- share options;
- any amounts payable under long-term incentive schemes;
- contributions paid into any pension scheme in respect of directors;
- any amounts paid as compensation for loss of office; and
- pension payments.

These items are subject to separate disclosure requirements under CA 1985 and so should not be included in the figure for directors' emoluments. Also, employer's national insurance contributions paid by the company in respect of the directors are not disclosable as directors' emoluments, although they do need to be disclosed as part of staff costs (see **Chapter 10**).

Emoluments in the year of appointment or retirement

16.16 If a director holds office for only part of the year, the disclosures should cover only the period during which he actually held office. For instance, if an existing company employee was appointed as director half-way through the financial year, any remuneration that he received for his services as director during the last six months of the year would be disclosable as directors' emoluments. The salary he received as an employee for the earlier part of the year would not be disclosable.

Accounting periods of more or less than one year

16.17 Where the accounting period is more or less than one year, the disclosures should cover the amounts actually paid or receivable in respect of that period. In this situation, some companies choose to make additional disclosure of the equivalent annual sums. This can be helpful in explaining apparently large movements between the current and previous years which arise only as a result of the differing lengths of the accounting periods. However, the statutory information must still be given – the twelve month details are simply additional information given voluntarily by the company.

BONUS PAYMENTS

When bonus payments become disclosable

16.18 Bonus payments to directors are generally disclosable as emoluments but it may be difficult to establish when they should be included in the disclosures. The difficulties usually arise where the payment is dependent or conditional on some other event – for example, approval by the shareholders or the completion of a specified contract term by the director. Where the payment depends on company performance over a longer period than one year, it will normally constitute a payment under a long-term incentive scheme rather than a bonus, and will be subject to separate disclosure requirements (see **16.28–16.33** below).

Provisions for bonus payments

16.19 In accounting terms, provision for bonus payments will usually need to be made in the period in which the director performs the services that are to be paid for, or rewarded through, the bonus payment. Appropriate accruals should, therefore, be made in the accounts each year to reflect the amount of bonus 'earned' in respect of that year.

Timing of recognition as emoluments

16.20 Under CA 1985, emoluments are disclosable when they are paid to, or receivable by, the director. The director must, therefore, have the right to receive a sum before it becomes disclosable as emoluments. Bonus payments should normally be disclosed as emoluments in the year in which the director becomes entitled to receive payment. This will not always match the timing of the payment. Often, a bonus payment will be based on the profits of a particular financial year but will not be payable until the following financial year. Once the results of the current year are known, the director will become entitled to receive a bonus (assuming that the appropriate level of profitability has been achieved), even though it may not actually be payable until some time later. In this case, the conditions attaching to the bonus will usually have been satisfied by the date the accounts are approved and signed. The accounts should, therefore, include provision for the bonus that is expected to be paid and this should be disclosed within emoluments for the period.

Shareholder approval

16.21 A bonus payment to directors may require approval by the shareholders before the directors are entitled to receive it. In these circumstances, it is usual to treat the bonus as being receivable by the directors (and, therefore, disclosable within emoluments) in the year in which shareholder approval is given.

Bonus contingent on future events

16.22 The payment of a bonus to the directors may be contingent on future events, such as:

- achievement of profit targets over a specified period; or
- completion of a specific length of service.

In this situation the directors will not usually be entitled to receive the bonus until the conditions have been met and, even though it may be necessary to accrue for the bonus payments in each year, the bonus will not become disclosable as emoluments until the full conditions have been met and the directors become entitled to receive the bonus. A scheme where payments are based on performance over a period of more than one year will usually meet the definition of a long-term incentive scheme and the payments will be subject to separate disclosure requirements (see **16.28** below). They should, therefore, not be treated as bonus payments within emoluments.

Exceptional and extraordinary items

16.23 The detailed terms of the bonus scheme will often refer to the bonus being based on 'operating profit' or 'profit before taxation'. The classification of specific costs and credits within the profit and loss account (particularly under the requirements of FRS 3 'Reporting Financial Performance') may, therefore, have a significant effect on the amount of bonus payable to directors (see **Chapter 8**).

BENEFITS IN KIND

Examples of benefits in kind

16.24 Under CA 1985, emoluments includes 'the estimated money value of benefits in kind received by a director otherwise than in cash'. This can be one of the most difficult aspects of remuneration to deal with. The most common benefits in kind are:

- the provision of a company car;
- the provision of free or subsidised accommodation;
- the provision of insurance for the benefit of the director (e.g. private health cover, indemnity insurance, personal accident cover);
- loans at preferential interest rates;
- share options; and
- relocation costs (in some circumstances).

Some of these may also be disclosable as loans or transactions with directors. Share options are now subject to separate disclosure requirements and are, therefore, specifically excluded from the definition of emoluments for disclosure purposes.

Estimated money value

16.25 The main difficulty usually arises in establishing an appropriate and realistic money value for the benefit. CA 1985 does not provide any detailed guidance on this. There are two possible interpretations of 'value' in this context:

- the value of the benefit to the director (or the saving achieved by him as a result of being given the benefit); and
- the cost to the company.

In some cases, it has become common practice to use taxable amounts as an indication of the value of the benefit. For instance, the taxable amount in respect of a company car is often used as the estimated money value of the benefit for disclosure purposes, although this will not always be a realistic assessment of the true value of the benefit. Wherever possible, market value should be used as the basis for valuing the benefit in kind. In some cases, this will be relatively easy to assess. For instance, where the company provides free or subsidised accommodation, it will usually be straightforward to establish the normal rental value. In the case of insurance cover, the premium actually paid by the company is usually used as the value of the benefit. In the case of preferential loans, the value of the benefit is usually established by taking the difference between the interest actually paid and the interest that would be payable at normal commercial rates.

Relocation expenses

16.26 The reimbursement of relocation expenses may constitute a benefit but will not always do so. The key factor is usually whether the director chooses to move of his own accord, or whether he moves at the company's request or insistence. Where a director moves of his own volition, any relocation expenses borne by the company will usually be disclosable as a benefit in kind. If the company instigates the move, the reimbursement of relocation expenses will not usually constitute a benefit. However, if the expenses are paid in the form of an allowance rather than the reimbursement of actual expenses incurred, and the allowance is chargeable to UK income tax, it will fall within the definition of emoluments and must be disclosed.

Contributions by director

16.27 If the director makes any contributions to the company in respect of benefits in kind received by him, these should be deducted from the value of the benefit included in emoluments.

LONG-TERM INCENTIVE SCHEMES

CA 1985 definition

16.28 A long-term incentive scheme is defined as any agreement or arrangement under which money or other assets become receivable by a director, and where one or more of the qualifying conditions relating to service or performance cannot be fulfilled within a single financial year. Bonuses relating to an individual year (which will normally come within 'emoluments'), termination payments and retirement benefits are specifically excluded from the disclosure requirements in respect of long-term incentive schemes.

Provisions for payments under long-term incentive schemes

16.29 In accounting terms, provision for payments under long-term incentive schemes should be made in each period in which the director performs the services that are to be paid for, or rewarded through, the scheme. Appropriate accruals should, therefore, be made in the accounts each year to reflect the amount 'earned' in respect of that year. In complex schemes, where the director has to meet targets over a number of years, this will usually require overall estimates to be made in order to spread the total expected 'cost' of the scheme over the period in question.

Disclosure under CA 1985

16.30 Under CA 1985, amounts payable under long-term incentive schemes are disclosable when they are paid to, or receivable by, the director. The director must, therefore, have the right to receive a sum before it becomes disclosable. Amounts should, therefore, normally be disclosed in the year in which the director becomes entitled to receive payment. In the case of a long-term incentive scheme, the director will not usually be entitled to receive payment until all the specified conditions have been met. Even though it will usually be necessary to accrue for the payments in each accounting year, these sums will not become disclosable until all the relevant conditions have been met and the director becomes entitled to receive payment. As with annual bonuses, this will not always match the actual timing of the payment.

Schemes with a guaranteed minimum payment

16.31 Complex incentive schemes which extend over a number of years will sometimes include the provision of a guaranteed minimum payment to the directors once a specified target has been achieved. In this case, the guaranteed minimum payment will become disclosable in the year in which the target is achieved, as this is when the directors become entitled to the minimum payment.

Payments other than in cash

16.32 Where payments are made in the form of assets rather than cash, the amount to be included for disclosure purposes is the net value of the asset. This is defined in CA 1985 as the value after deducting any money paid or any other value given by the director in respect of that asset.

Payment in the form of shares

16.33 In the case of an unquoted company, the amount to be disclosed specifically excludes any shares in the company (or, in the case of a group, shares in any undertaking within the group) given to the directors as part of the long-term incentive scheme. However, the accounts must still disclose the number of directors receiving shares in this way.

SHARE OPTIONS

Estimated money value

16.34 Share options granted to directors have been a particularly difficult area in terms of assessing the estimated money value of the benefit. It is usually acknowledged that the benefit arises when the option is granted rather than when it is exercised. However, the value of the option is often negligible at the time that it is granted and the true value to the director only arises when the option is exercised. As share option schemes often operate as an incentive to encourage directors and employees to achieve a good company performance, it is appropriate that the value of the option increases with the passage of time. The accounting treatment of shares issued to directors and employees under bonus and long-term incentive schemes, and of employer's national insurance contributions payable on gains made by directors and employees on share options granted to them, is covered in detail in **Chapter 10**. This section looks at the detailed accounts disclosure that must be given in respect of share options granted to directors.

Disclosure under CA 1985

16.35 In the case of an unquoted company, CA 1985 only requires the accounts to show the number of directors who exercised share options during the year (although additional details will usually need to be given in the director' report – see **Chapter 36**). In the case of this disclosure requirement, the legislation makes no reference to qualifying services. Where an individual receives share options before appointment as a director (for instance, as an employee of the company) and exercises them after becoming a director, the relevant disclosures will, therefore, still be required.

UITF Abstract 10

16.36 UITF Abstract 10 was issued in September 1994 in response to concerns that the existing disclosure requirements did not give shareholders full information on the remuneration effectively paid to management through the use of share options schemes. The Abstract recommended extensive disclosures on the granting and exercise of directors' share options, which were intended to apply to all companies. The Abstract remained non-mandatory, although the FSA Listing Rules in effect required quoted companies to comply with its disclosure recommendations. The Abstract has been withdrawn for accounting periods ending on or after 31 December 2002 on the basis that the Directors' Remuneration Report Regulations 2002 have now introduced a legal requirement for quoted companies to prepare a directors' remuneration report, including equivalent disclosures on directors' share options.

EMOLUMENTS AND BENEFITS OF THE HIGHEST PAID DIRECTOR

Detailed disclosures

16.37 Where the aggregate amounts disclosable under CA 1985 in respect of emoluments and payments under long-term incentive schemes total £200,000 or more, the emoluments of the highest paid director must be separately disclosed. This additional disclosure does not apply to a company that qualifies as small. The following details must be shown:

- the aggregate of emoluments and amounts under long-term incentive schemes paid to or receivable by the highest paid director;
- the amount of any company contributions to money purchase retirement schemes for the benefit of that director;
- if that director is accruing retirement benefits under a defined benefit scheme:
  - his accrued pension at the end of the financial year; and
  - any accrued lump sum at the end of the financial year;
- whether the highest paid director exercised any share options during the year; and
- whether the highest paid director received any shares in the company (or the group) during the year under a long-term incentive scheme.

Accrued pension and accrued lump sum

16.38 The accrued pension and accrued lump sum entitlement of the highest paid director at the end of the financial year are defined in CA 1985 as the annual pension and lump sum that would be payable under the scheme on the director attaining normal pension age assuming:

- he had left the company at the end of the year;
- there were no inflationary increases between the end of that year and the date he reached normal pension age;
- no commutation of the pension or inverse commutation of the lump sum; and
- disregarding any amounts attributable to voluntary contributions or to money purchase benefits under the scheme.

The following example illustrates how the accrued pension and accrued lump sum of the highest paid director might be calculated for disclosure purposes:

Example 16.1 - Accrued pension of highest paid director

The highest paid director was 55 at the start of the financial year and 56 at the end. He joined the company pension scheme at the age of 25 and will retire at the age of 60. His maximum pension entitlement is 35/80 of final salary, after 35 years in the scheme. The maximum lump sum payable to him after 35 years in the scheme is 105/80 of final salary. His salary in the previous financial year was £105,000 and in the current year is £110,000.

The following calculations can be made for disclosure purposes:

Accrued pension	— beginning of year	30/80 × £105,000 =	£39,375
	— end of year	31/80 × £110,000 =	£42,625
Accrued lump sum	— beginning of year	90/80 × £105,000 =	£118,125
	— end of year	93/80 × £110,000 =	£127,875

The disclosure will then be made as follows.

> 'The accrued pension of the highest paid director at 31 December 20X2 was £42,625 (20X1 - £39,375) and the accrued lump sum at that date was £127,875 (20X1 - £118,125).'

PENSION ARRANGEMENTS

Disclosure requirements under CA 1985

16.39 CA 1985 sets out various definitions in respect of pensions and pension schemes, and also requires separate disclosure of:

— certain pension contributions for the benefit of directors;

— basic details of pension arrangements for directors; and

— certain pension scheme retirement benefits paid to directors and former directors.

Accounting for retirement benefits generally is considered in more detail in **Chapter 11**. The legislation sets out the following definitions for disclosure purposes:

(i) 'pension scheme' is given the meaning assigned to 'retirement benefit scheme' by ICTA 1988 s 611; and

(ii) 'retirement benefits' is given the meaning assigned to relevant benefits by ICTA 1988 s 612(1).

Pension contributions and arrangements

16.40 All companies must disclose the following details in their accounts:

— the aggregate amount of company contributions to pension schemes in respect of qualifying services where the benefits payable to the directors will be calculated on the basis of the contributions paid;

— the number of directors accruing retirement benefits under money purchase schemes; and

— the number of directors accruing retirement benefits under defined benefit schemes.

Company contributions are defined as any payment (including insurance premiums) made, or treated as made, to a pension scheme in respect of a director by any person other than the director. Contributions to money purchase (defined contribution) schemes are considered to provide a reasonable measure of the benefit to the director and are, therefore, disclosable. This is not necessarily the case with defined benefit schemes, and the level of contributions to such schemes for directors is, therefore, not required to be shown. The number of directors accruing benefits under each type of pension scheme must be disclosed in all cases. A company that qualifies as small may aggregate the amount of company contributions to defined contribution pension schemes with certain other information on directors' remuneration (see **Chapter 7**).

Hybrid pension schemes

16.41 For disclosure purposes, all pension schemes must be classified as either money purchase schemes (in which case contributions in respect of directors are disclosable) or defined benefit schemes (in which case contributions during the year in respect of directors do not need to be disclosed). A money purchase scheme is defined in CA 1985 as a scheme where all the benefits that may become payable to the director are money purchase benefits (ie they are calculated by reference to the contributions made and are not average salary benefits). A defined benefit scheme is defined as a pension scheme that is not a money purchase scheme. A hybrid pension scheme under which a director will be entitled to receive both money purchase benefits and defined benefits will, therefore, be classified as a defined benefit scheme for disclosure purposes. Any death in service benefits should be disregarded when classifying a pension scheme for disclosure purposes.

Pension scheme with an underpin

16.42 CA 1985 also provides specifically for a pension scheme where the benefits payable to, or receivable by, a director will be money purchase benefits or defined benefits, whichever is the greater. In this case, the legislation allows the company to assume for disclosure purposes that the benefits will be either money purchase benefits or defined benefits, whichever appears more likely at the end of the financial year in question.

Disclosure of excess retirement benefits

16.43 CA 1985 requires disclosure of any pension scheme retirement benefits paid to, or receivable by, directors or past directors that are in excess of the retirement benefits to which they were entitled at the date the benefits first became payable, or on 31 March 1997, whichever is the later. However, excess amounts need not be included in this disclosure if:

— the funding of the scheme was sufficient to enable the payments to be made without recourse to additional contributions; and

— the additional amounts were paid to, or receivable by, all pensioner members of the scheme.

For instance, regular inflationary increases that are paid to all pensioners in the scheme will not usually be disclosable. However, any other discretionary increases to the pensions of directors and former directors will normally be disclosable. A company that qualifies as small under CA 1985 is exempt from this additional disclosure requirement (see **Chapter 7**).

Benefits other than in cash

16.44 Where pension benefits include non-cash items, these should be included in the disclosures at their estimated money value and the nature of the benefit must be disclosed. The most common example is where a director continues to be given the use of a company car after he has retired.

COMPENSATION FOR LOSS OF OFFICE

Separate category of payment

16.45 CA 1985 requires disclosure of the aggregate amount of compensation for loss of office paid to, or receivable by, directors and former directors. This constitutes a separate category of payment to directors and should not be included in the figure for directors' emoluments for the period. Under CA 1985 Sch 6 para 8(4)(a), compensation for loss of office specifically includes payments connected with a director's retirement from office. However, this does not include normal pension payments, as these are covered by separate disclosure requirements (see **16.39–16.44** above).

Examples of compensation payments

16.46 The most common examples of compensation payments are:

— *ex gratia* payments made by the company when a director resigns; and

— payments in respect of breach of contract if a director is dismissed by the company before his service contract expires.

Both the nature and the circumstances of such payments need to be considered when deciding whether or not they are disclosable under CA 1985. In particular, payments that are described as *ex gratia* will often have a degree of compensation attached to them and will, therefore, be disclosable. The legislation makes it clear that payments for damages as a result of breach of contract and payments to settle a claim for breach of contract are to be treated as compensation for loss of office for disclosure purposes.

Shareholder approval

16.47 Many compensation payments to directors will also require shareholder approval under CA 1985 ss 312 or 313. This is not, however, usually required for genuine payments in respect of damages for breach of contract or for pensions in respect of past services unless they require approval under the provisions on substantial property transactions.

Pension top-ups

16.48 Compensation might also include pension top-up payments made when a director ceases to hold office. However, if these payments are made simply to make good a deficiency in the pension fund rather than to increase the director's pension, it will usually be more appropriate to treat them as normal pension contributions. This is because the company will usually be liable for making good the deficiency in the pension fund, regardless of whether the director ceases to hold office, and in these circumstances the top-up should not be treated as relating to the director's loss of office.

Benefits other than in cash

16.49 Where compensation payments include non-cash benefits, these should be included in the disclosures at their estimated money value and the nature of the benefit must be disclosed. The most common example is where a director is given his company car as part of the compensation arrangements.

Continuing involvement

16.50 In some cases directors who have officially retired may continue to have an involvement with the company in a part-time or consultancy capacity, or may even continue to receive a normal salary, even though they carry out only minimal duties. Where payments to former directors are in excess of normal market rates for the work that they perform, there may well be an element of compensation for loss of office, in which case the details should be disclosed under the requirements of CA 1985.

Example disclosure

16.51 The disclosure on compensation for loss of office is usually given in narrative form, although a table may be used if this gives a clearer presentation:

Example 16.2 – Compensation for loss of office

Payments of £... (20X1 £...) were made to directors during the year in connection with the termination of their service contracts. One director retained his company car and the payments shown above include the estimated market value of the car at the date on which his service contract was terminated.

PAYMENTS TO AND BY OTHER PARTIES

Payments to third parties

16.52 CA 1985 requires disclosure of the aggregate amount of any consideration paid to, or receivable by, third parties for making available the services of any person:

- as a director of the company; or
- whilst a director of the company:
  - as a director of any of its subsidiary undertakings; or
  - otherwise in connection with the management of the affairs of the company or any of its subsidiary undertakings.

The most common example of this is an arrangement whereby a substantial investor in a company (eg a bank or venture capital company) has the right to appoint a director to the board of the investee company and payment for the services of this director is made to the investor rather than to the director himself. Where payments include non-cash benefits, these should be included in the disclosures at their estimated money value and the nature of the benefit must be disclosed.

Definition of third party

16.53 In this context, the Act defines 'third party' as persons other than:

- the director himself;
- a person connected with the director;
- a body corporate controlled by the director; and
- the company or any of its subsidiary undertakings.

Payments to connected parties

16.54 CA 1985 specifically includes within the remuneration disclosure requirements amounts paid to, or receivable by, a person connected with a director or a body corporate controlled by him. Disclosure of emoluments and other benefits, therefore, cannot be avoided by arranging for the payment to be made to another person. In the case of payments to a company owned by the director, the emoluments' note to the accounts usually includes an explanation that some or all of the payments have been made through the company:

Example 16.3 – Payment to company owned by director

Included within emoluments is £... which was paid to ABC Limited, a company owned by Mr J T Smith, in respect of his services as a director of the company.

Such arrangements may also require disclosure as a transaction in which a director had a material interest. CA 1985 specifies that amounts should not be counted twice under these provisions. Thus, payments to a director's wife would not be treated as emoluments of the director if his wife was also a director of the company and received the emoluments in her own right.

Payments by other parties

16.55 The amounts to be included in the disclosures are all relevant amounts in respect of a director's services paid by, or receivable from:

— the company;

— the company's subsidiary undertakings; and

— any other person.

Payments from a parent undertaking are, therefore, disclosable, but only if they relate to the director's services to the company. However, if a director must in turn account to the company or any of its subsidiary undertakings for the amounts that he has received, those amounts are not disclosable.

Example 16.4 – Amounts paid over to company

M is a director of ABC Limited and also of its subsidiary companies, CDE Limited and EFG Limited. He receives emoluments of £20,000 from ABC Limited in respect of his services as director of that company. He also receives emoluments of £5,000 from CDE Limited, but is required to pay these over to ABC Limited. He also receives emoluments of £4,000 from EFG Limited.

In the accounts of CDE Limited, M's emoluments will be shown as £5,000.

In the accounts of EFG Limited, M's emoluments will be shown as £4,000.

In the accounts of ABC Limited, M's emoluments will be shown as £24,000.

(That is, the £20,000 he receives from ABC Limited plus the £4,000 he receives from EFG Limited. The £5,000 from CDE Limited is excluded as M is required to pay this over to ABC Limited.)

Payments for services to holding company and fellow subsidiaries

16.56 The directors' remuneration disclosures cover all amounts paid to, or receivable by, a director in respect of his services as a director of the company and any of its subsidiaries and in an executive or managerial capacity for any of those companies. However, they do not cover any payments relating to services by the same director to a holding company or to a fellow subsidiary company:

Example 16.5 – Disclosure of emoluments within a group

ABC Limited has two subsidiary undertakings, JKL Limited and MNO Limited. JKL Limited has one subsidiary undertaking, PQR Limited.

Group structure

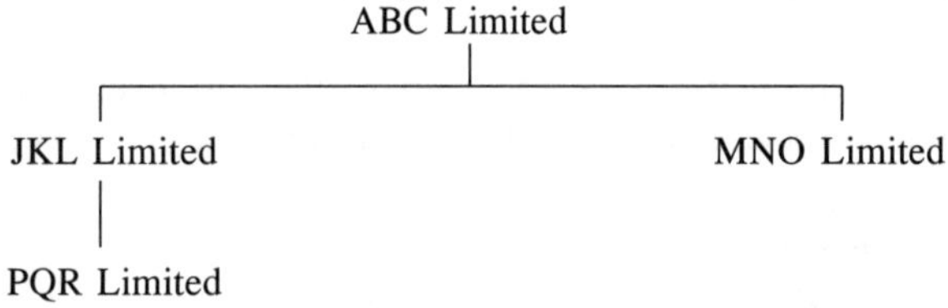

D is a director of JKL Limited, MNO Limited and PQR Limited. He is not a director of the overall holding company, ABC Limited, but he is a manager in that company. In 199X he received the following remuneration.

(i) As director of JKL Limited – £10,000 from JKL Limited.

(ii) As director of MNO Limited – £12,000 from MNO Limited.

(iii) As director of PQR Limited – £5,000 from JKL Limited.

(iv) As a manager of ABC Limited – £20,000 from ABC Limited.

The following amounts are disclosable.

(i) In the accounts of JKL Limited – £15,000 (his remuneration in respect of services to the company and its subsidiary PQR Limited).

(ii) In the accounts of MNO Limited – £12,000 (his remuneration in respect of services to that company only).

(iii) In the accounts of PQR Limited – £5,000 (his remuneration in respect of services to that company only).

(iv) In the accounts of ABC Limited – no disclosure as he is not a director of ABC Limited.

Remuneration paid by the holding company

16.57 In some groups all directors' remuneration is paid by the holding company. Recharges may be made to subsidiary undertakings to reflect the cost of the services of their directors, but this will not always be done. This can cause difficulties over the disclosure of directors' remuneration in the accounts of the holding company and the subsidiaries.

Disclosure by holding company

16.58 Directors' remuneration in the accounts of the holding company will comprise:

- remuneration paid to directors of the holding company in respect of their services to the company and management of the company and group; and
- if any holding company directors are also directors of one or more of the subsidiaries, remuneration paid to them for these services.

Remuneration paid to those who are directors of subsidiaries but who are not directors of the holding company is not disclosable in the accounts of the holding company. The same disclosure requirements apply in the holding company's accounts, regardless of whether some or all of the remuneration costs are recharged to the subsidiaries.

Disclosure by subsidiary where costs are recharged

16.59 Where the holding company recharges the subsidiaries with the cost of remunerating their directors, each subsidiary should disclose as directors' remuneration the amount paid to the holding company in respect of directors' services to the company. In some cases, the holding company may make a global recharge to the subsidiaries to cover general management costs, which will include directors' remuneration but may include other costs as well. If the element for directors' remuneration cannot be separately identified, an appropriate apportionment should be made for disclosure purposes.

Disclosure by subsidiary where costs are not recharged

16.60 Where the holding company does not recharge the subsidiaries with the cost of remunerating their directors, the amounts paid by the holding company for the services of the subsidiary directors are still disclosable as directors' remuneration in the accounts of the subsidiary. It is usually helpful to explain that this cost has been borne by the holding company and has not been recharged to the subsidiary, although this is not a disclosure requirement under CA 1985. It is not acceptable to simply disclose the fact that the directors have been remunerated by the holding company and not quantify the amount that they have received.

No remuneration in respect of services to subsidiary

16.61 Where directors of a subsidiary are also directors or employees of the holding company, it is sometimes argued that the holding company remunerates them only for their services to the holding company and that they receive no remuneration in respect of their services as directors of the subsidiary. The validity of this argument will usually depend on the amount of time that the director or employee devotes to the subsidiary company. If the time is relatively small (eg the role is in effect that of a non-executive director) it may be acceptable that he does not receive remuneration specifically for this role. In this case, an explanation should be included in the subsidiary's accounts.

Example 16.6 – No remuneration as director of subsidiary

The directors of the company are also employees of ABC Limited, the company's ultimate holding company. They do not receive any remuneration specifically in respect of their services as directors of the company.

Appendix

EXAMPLE EMOLUMENTS AND BENEFITS DISCLOSURES FOR A SMALL COMPANY AND AN UNQUOTED COMPANY

Example 1 – Small company with no long-term incentive schemes

	20X2	*20X1*
	£	£
Directors' emoluments and company contributions to money purchase schemes in relation to directors' pensions	108,950	99,760

Two directors are accruing pension benefits under money purchase schemes and two directors are accruing pension benefits under a defined benefit scheme.

Example 2 – Unquoted company with no share options or long-term incentive schemes

	20X2	*20X1*
	£	£
Directors' emoluments	304,900	289,950
Company contributions to money purchase schemes in relation to directors' pensions	11,800	7,500

Two directors are accruing pension benefits under money purchase schemes and one director is accruing pension benefits under a defined benefit scheme.

The above details include the following amounts in respect of the highest paid director:

	20X2	*20X1*
	£	£
Emoluments	103,854	95,677
Company contributions to money purchase pension scheme	5,750	4,250

Example 3 – Unquoted company with share options and long-term incentive schemes

	20X2 £	*20X1* £
Directors' emoluments	304,900	289,950
Company contributions to money purchase schemes in relation to directors' pensions	11,800	7,500
Aggregate amounts receivable by directors in respect of long-term incentive schemes (other than shares and share options)	6,250	10,800

In addition to the above, one director received shares during the year under a long-term incentive scheme.

One director exercised share options during the year.

Two directors are accruing pension benefits under money purchase schemes and one director is accruing pension benefits under a defined benefit scheme.

The above details include the following amounts in respect of the highest paid director:

	20X2 £	*20X1* £
Emoluments and amounts receivable under long-term incentive schemes (other than shares and share options)	103,854	95,677
Company contributions to money purchase pension scheme	5,750	4,250

During the year, this director also received shares under a long-term incentive scheme.

Chapter 17

Other Profit and Loss Account Disclosures

REMUNERATION OF THE AUDITORS AND THEIR ASSOCIATES

CA 1985 disclosure requirements

17.1 CA 1985 requires separate disclosure of the following amounts:

— the remuneration paid to the auditors in respect of their work as auditors, including any amounts in respect of expenses and any benefits in kind; and

— the remuneration paid to the auditors or their associates in respect of non-audit work.

The disclosures should be given in the notes to the accounts. Small and medium-sized companies are not required to disclose details of remuneration for non-audit work, but remuneration for audit services must be disclosed.

Remuneration for services as auditors

17.2 The amount to be disclosed in respect of their work as auditors includes:

— the audit fee;

— any expenses incurred by the auditors which have been reimbursed by the company; and

— the estimated money value of any benefits in kind received by the auditors in respect of their services as auditors and the nature of any such benefit.

In practice, professional and ethical guidelines will usually prevent auditors from accepting benefits in kind from the company. The amount to be disclosed is the audit fee in respect of the current year. This will usually be an estimate of the amount to be charged in respect of the audit and will often be the figure included in accruals. The legislation does not consider a situation where the actual fee in respect of any year is different to the amount provided and disclosed in the accounts for that year. Minor adjustments to the figure are not usually disclosed, but if the audit fee for a particular year has effectively been under or overstated by a material amount, it will usually be appropriate to disclose the adjustment separately in the following year's accounts.

Example 17.1 – Where disclosed audit fee is materially different to actual one

Auditors' remuneration, including expenses:

	20X2	*20X1*
	£	£
Current year	3,100	2,950
Additional fee in respect of previous year	400	—

REMUNERATION FOR OTHER SERVICES

17.3 Remuneration receivable by the auditors and their associates in respect of other services provided to the company might include fees and expenses in respect of:

- accountancy assistance;
- payroll services;
- tax compliance work;
- tax advisory work; and
- consultancy work.

The detailed requirements in respect of these disclosures are set out in SI 1991/2128 The Companies Act 1985 (Disclosure of Remuneration for Non-Audit Work) Regulations 1991, as amended by SI 1995/1520. The figure to be disclosed is the aggregate amount of remuneration in respect of work carried out during the financial year, regardless of whether it has been billed to the company. Comparative information must also be given. Once again, remuneration specifically includes the estimated money value of benefits in kind, although these are likely to be rare in practice, and both the nature and the estimated money value of any such benefits must be disclosed. Where the auditors (or their associates) are also the auditors of any UK subsidiary undertaking of the company (as defined in CA 1985), any amounts in respect of services to the subsidiary must be included in the aggregate remuneration. The auditors have a duty under the Regulations to provide the company with such information as it needs to be able to comply with the disclosure requirements. Where more than one auditor has held office during the year, separate disclosure is required in respect of each auditor and their associates.

Associates of auditors

17.4 The definition of associates is very complex but it broadly includes:

- any partnership in which the auditors are a partner or with which the auditors have a partner in common;
- any body corporate in the same group as the auditors;
- any directors of the auditors; and
- any body corporate in which the auditor, a partner of the auditors or a director of the auditors controls the exercise of 20% or more of the voting rights, or any other body corporate in the same group as such a body corporate.

If such a relationship exists at any time during the financial year, the entity is regarded as an associate of the auditors for that year. Reference should be made to the detail in the Regulations if there is any doubt over whether an entity should be treated as an associate of the auditors. Amendments to the Regulations introduced in 1995 specifically exclude entities that might otherwise have been treated as associates of the auditors as a result of insolvency and receivership appointments.

Proposals for additional disclosure

17.5 Draft guidance on more extensive disclosure of the nature and value of non-audit services provided by auditors was published by the ICAEW in December 2002. The draft is based on EC recommendations and recommends that full and transparent disclosure should be made of all fees due to the audit firm and its network firms in relation to work performed during the period for the audit client and all entities controlled by that client. In the case of joint audits, the same disclosures should be given for each audit firm. The disclosures should cover both the nature and extent of the services provided and the review and approval process followed, and should provide sufficient information to enable a user of the accounts to judge whether the potential for conflicts of interest has been satisfactorily addressed. The draft recommends that fees are analysed into the following categories:

(i) Statutory audit services:
  - Annual audit
  - Regulatory reporting

(ii) Further assurance services (eg advice on accounting matters, non-regulatory reporting on internal controls, due diligence work on acquisitions, environmental audits);

(iii) Tax advisory services;

(iv) Other non-audit services:

- Financial information technology
- Internal audit
- Valuation
- litigation
- Recruitment
- Other services.

Amounts that are not material may be included under 'other services'. Further analysis should be given where the amounts in individual categories are material and differ substantially from one another and narrative explanations should be given where this would be helpful. The non-audit fees disclosure currently required by statute covers only UK entities and, where there are also overseas entities (which are included in the ICAEW disclosure recommendations), the UK element of non-audit fees would therefore need to be shown separately. Fees should be calculated on an accruals basis and should include fees for all services where the substance of the arrangement is that the service has been rendered to the client, even if the fee itself has been paid by another party (eg the client's solicitor in the case of litigation support). Comments on the ICAEW proposals have been requested by 20 March 2003.

RELATED PARTY DISCLOSURES

Requirements of FRS 8 'Related Party Disclosures'

17.6 FRS 8 'Related Party Disclosures' requires disclosure of material transactions undertaken by the reporting entity with a related party, irrespective of whether a price is charged. The disclosures must include:

- the names of the parties involved;
- a description of the relationship between them;
- a description of the transaction (or transactions);
- any additional details of the transaction necessary for an understanding of the financial statements;
- the amounts due to or from related parties at the balance sheet date;
- any provisions for doubtful debts due from related parties; and
- any amounts written off during the year in respect of debts due to or from related parties.

The standard applies to all accounts that are required to give a true and fair view. The disclosure requirements therefore apply to all companies, regardless of their size, and also to non-corporate entities, such as charities, if their accounts are required to show a true and fair view. However, exemptions are granted in a small number of cases as explained in **17.19** below.

Objective of FRS 8

17.7 The primary objective of FRS 8 is 'to draw attention to the possibility that the reported financial position and results may have been affected by the existence of related parties and by material transactions with them'. This recognises that, where a related party relationship exists, transactions between the entities may not be carried out at arm's length – for instance:

- prices may not be freely negotiable between the parties;
- prices may not be based on commercial or market rates;
- the parties may be prepared to enter into transactions with each other that they would not be willing to undertake with an independent third-party; or
- the parties may be prepared to agree terms with each other (eg on payment dates) that they would not accept from an independent third-party.

This should not be taken to imply that all transactions between related parties will be on artificial or uncommercial terms. The aim of the standard is to highlight the possibility that this might be the case so that the potential impact can be borne in mind when considering the results and financial position of the company.

Definition of related party

17.8 Two or more parties are related when:

- one has direct or indirect control of the other;
- both are subject to common control from the same source;
- one has influence over the financial and operating policies of the other to such an extent that the latter may be inhibited from pursuing its own interests; or
- in respect of a particular transaction, both parties are subject to influence from the same source to such an extent that one party subordinates its own interests.

Example 17.2 – Common control and direct control

A Ltd controls both B Ltd and C Ltd

Therefore:

— A Ltd is related to B Ltd.

— A Ltd is related to C Ltd.

— B Ltd is related to C Ltd.

Example 17.3 – Influence

D Ltd controls E Ltd and is able to influence F Ltd.

Therefore:

— D Ltd is related to E Ltd.

— D Ltd is related to F Ltd.

E Ltd and F Ltd are not related parties simply as a result of their relationship with D Ltd, but they might become related in respect of a particular transaction as a result of the influence exercised by D Ltd (eg if D Ltd requires E Ltd to sell goods to F Ltd at cost rather than market price).

Where a related party relationship exists, the disclosure requirements apply to both parties. In the case of the fourth definition above, all transactions between the parties during the year become disclosable, even though the relationship arises as a result of one specific transaction.

Parties that will always be related to the reporting entity

17.9 To avoid doubt, the standard specifies that the following should always be treated as a related party of the reporting entity:

- its ultimate parent, immediate parent, subsidiary undertakings and fellow subsidiary undertakings;
- associates and joint ventures;
- an investor or venturer in respect of which the reporting entity is an associate or joint venture;
- directors of the reporting entity and of any parent (ultimate or intermediate);
- pension funds for the benefit of employees of:
  - the reporting entity,
  - a related party of the reporting entity.

Directors include shadow directors as defined in CA 1985.

Parties that are presumed to be related to the reporting entity

17.10 The following should be presumed to be related parties of the reporting entity unless it can be demonstrated that neither has influenced the financial and operating policies of the other so as to prohibit the pursuit of own interests:

- key management of the reporting entity;
- key management of any parent undertaking;
- a person owning, or able to exercise control over, 20% or more of the voting rights of the reporting entity, whether directly or indirectly;
- each person able to exercise control or influence over the reporting entity by acting in concert;
- an entity managing or managed by the reporting entity under a management contract.

Example 17.4 – Acting in concert

G Ltd, H Ltd and K Ltd, by acting together, are able to control D Ltd.

Therefore:

- G Ltd and D Ltd are related.
- H Ltd and D Ltd are related.
- K Ltd and D Ltd are related.

However, G Ltd, H Ltd and K Ltd will not be related parties simply by virtue of their relationship with D Ltd (although they may be related by some other means).

In addition, the following are also to be presumed to be related parties of the reporting entity, unless it can be demonstrated otherwise:

- members of the close family of any related party referred to in **17.8–17.10** above;
- partnerships, trusts or other entities in which any individual mentioned in **17.8–17.10** above (or any member of their close family) has a controlling interest.

Other related parties

17.11 The standard emphasises that none of these lists is intended to be exhaustive. Parties which do not specifically appear in the lists may, therefore, still be related for the purposes of the standard and, if so, transactions between them will require disclosure.

Definition of control and influence

17.12 Control is defined in the standard as 'the ability to direct the financial and operating policies of an entity with a view to gaining economic benefits from its activities'. Influence is not included in the definitions in the standard but is to be interpreted as the ability to inhibit a party from pursuing, at all times, its own separate interests. Two parties are subject to common control when they are controlled by the same entity. They are also deemed to be subject to common control when they are subject to control from boards which have a controlling nucleus of directors in common.

Close family members

17.13 Close family members are defined as 'family members, or members of the same household, who may be expected to influence, or be influenced by, that person in their dealings with the reporting entity'. This definition is much wider than a director's 'immediate family' under CA 1985 in the context of transactions between the company and its directors.

Disclosure of control

17.14 Where the reporting entity is controlled by another party, FRS 8 requires disclosure of:

— the related party relationship;

— the name of the controlling party; and

— the name of the ultimate controlling party (if different).

These disclosures must be given even if there have been no disclosable transactions between the parties during the year. If details of the controlling party or ultimate controlling party are not known, this fact must be stated in the accounts.

Disclosure of related party transaction

17.15 The disclosure requirement covers all transactions between related parties, not just those that might be considered to be abnormal. The standard defines a related party transaction as 'the transfer of assets or liabilities or the performance of services by, to or for a related party irrespective of whether a price is charged'. Where material transactions with a related party (or parties) have taken place during the year, irrespective of whether a charge has been made or not, the following details must be disclosed:

— the names of the parties involved;

— a description of the relationship between them;

- a description of the transaction (or transactions);
- any additional details of the transaction necessary for an understanding of the financial statements;
- the amounts due to or from related parties at the balance sheet date;
- any provisions for doubtful debts due from related parties; and
- any amounts written off during the year in respect of debts due to or from related parties.

Additional details may need to be given in some cases, depending on the nature of the transaction. For instance, the fact that the sale of a significant asset took place at a value substantially below the normal commercial rate might need to be disclosed. Comparative information should be given for all related party disclosures.

Aggregation of transactions

17.16 In order to avoid excessive detail, the disclosures may be aggregated (ie similar transactions by type of related party) unless individual disclosure of a particular transaction, or a series of connected transactions, is necessary to enable the reader to understand the impact on the financial statements. However, different categories of transaction should not be aggregated. For instance, where a company buys both raw materials and fixed assets from the same related party, these transactions should not be aggregated for disclosure purposes. In the case of transactions involving directors, individual disclosure will usually be required by the provisions of CA 1985.

Examples of related party transactions

17.17 The following are examples of transactions which will require disclosure where they involve related parties:

- the purchase or sale of goods, property or other fixed assets;
- the rendering or receiving of services;
- agency agreements;
- leasing agreements;
- the provision of finance; and
- the provision of guarantees or security.

The Explanatory Notes to the standard include further examples.

Materiality

17.18 In the context of FRS 8, transactions are to be considered material if 'their disclosure might reasonably be expected to influence decisions made by users of general purpose financial statements'. Where a related party transaction involves:

— a director, key manager or other individual in a position to influence, or accountable for stewardship of, the reporting entity; or

— a member of the close family of any individual mentioned above; or

— an entity controlled by any of these individuals,

the materiality of the transaction should be judged in relation to that individual (or party) as well as in terms of its significance to the reporting entity.

Exemptions from disclosure

17.19 The standard allows the following exemptions from the normal disclosure requirements:

— transactions and balances between group companies which have been eliminated on consolidation do not have to be disclosed in the consolidated accounts;

— disclosure of related party transactions is not required in the individual accounts of a parent company, if group accounts are also presented;

— transactions with members of the group or investees of the group do not require disclosure in the accounts of a subsidiary undertaking where 90% or more of the voting rights are controlled within the group, provided that:

  — consolidated accounts, which include the subsidiary, are publicly available, and

  — the subsidiary's accounts state that advantage has been taken of this exemption;

— pension contributions paid to a pension fund do not require disclosure as related party transactions (although they still require disclosure under FRS 17 'Retirement benefits' - see **Chapter 11**);

— emoluments in respect of services as an employee of the reporting entity do not require disclosure as related party transactions.

Confidentiality

17.20 The disclosure requirements do not override any duty of confidentiality that arises through the operation of law. For instance, banks will not be expected to disclose confidential information in respect of customers. However, disclosure of a particular transaction cannot be avoided simply by including a confidentiality clause in a contract.

Identification of disclosable transactions

17.21 One of the main practical difficulties in complying with the standard is establishing systems and procedures to identify related parties and collate details of disclosable transactions as they arise during the year. Identification will usually be particularly difficult where no price is actually charged in respect of the transaction. Statement of Auditing Standards 460 (SAS 460) 'Related Parties', which was issued shortly after FRS 8, includes some useful guidance on the issues to be considered by both management and auditors when considering the identification and disclosure of related party transactions.

Potentially illegal transactions

17.22 Where significant transactions take place between any entities at an undervalue or overvalue, this could give rise to serious legal difficulties. Companies should always take appropriate legal advice before entering into such a transaction.

Likely future developments

17.23 The ASB issued FRED 25 'Related party disclosures' in May 2002 as part of its project to achieve convergence between UK accounting standards and international accounting standards. The Exposure Draft proposes replacing FRS 8 'Related party disclosures' with requirements based on the revised IAS 24, although retaining the present UK requirement for an entity's controlling party to be named.

Changes to exemptions

17.24 A number of changes to the current exemptions are proposed. In particular, the exemption for subsidiaries will in future only be available to wholly-owned subsidiaries, whereas entities that are 90% owned are currently exempt from the disclosure requirements of FRS 8. FRED 25 also gives no exemption for pension contributions paid to a pension fund. FRS 8 currently exempts these amounts from its disclosure requirements, although, in practice, the details have to be given under the requirements of FRS 17 'Retirement Benefits'. FRS 8 also notes that its disclosure requirements do not override a duty of confidentiality arising by law. There is no equivalent exemption in FRED 25, although there will no longer be a requirement to name the transacting parties.

Definition of related party

17.25 The new proposals will change the definitions of related parties. In particular, whilst FRS 8 identifies separately parties that are related parties and those that are presumed to be related parties, all those listed in FRED 25 are considered to be related parties. Otherwise, the lists are broadly equivalent, except that:

- FRED 25 identifies a related party relationship where one party has an interest that gives it significant influence over the other - FRS 8 currently defines in more detail the level of influence that triggers such a relationship;
- there is no reference in FRED 25 to the situation where transacting parties are subject to influence from the same source to such an extent that one subordinates its own separate interests; and
- FRED 25 makes no specific reference to shadow directors, to persons acting in concert to exercise control or influence, or to management of an entity through a management contract.

Disclosure

17.26 When developing FRS 8, the ASB took the view that disclosure of the identity of a controlling party is relevant information for users and it has, therefore, retained this disclosure requirement in FRED 25 even though it is not included in IAS 24. The other disclosure requirements are broadly in line with those currently required, except that under FRED 25:

- there is no requirement to disclose the names of the transacting parties; and
- where amounts are due to or from related parties, the Exposure Draft specifically requires disclosure of the terms and conditions, the nature of the consideration and details of any related guarantees.

Also, under FRED 25, the required disclosures must be given separately for each of the following categories: parent, entities with joint control or significant influence, subsidiaries, associates, joint ventures, key management personnel of the entity or its parent, and other related parties.

GEOGRAPHICAL ANALYSIS OF RESULTS

Scope of SSAP 25 'Segmental Reporting'

17.27 SSAP 25 'Segmental Reporting' repeats some of the segmental disclosure requirements of CA 1985 and also requires certain additional disclosures. These additional disclosure requirements apply to any entity that:

- is a public limited company or has a public limited company as a subsidiary;
- is a banking or insurance company or group; or
- exceeds the CA 1985 criteria, multiplied in each case by ten, for defining a medium-sized company (see **Chapter 7**).

Subsidiary companies that are not public companies or banking or insurance companies are not required to comply with the additional disclosures, provided that the parent company gives appropriate segmental information in its own accounts. All other entities are encouraged to apply the provisions of the standard in accounts that are required to show a true and fair view.

Disclosure requirements

17.28 SSAP 25 requires the following items in the accounts to be analysed by class of business and by geographical segment:

- turnover (see **Chapter 9**);
- the profit or loss before taxation; and
- net assets (see **Chapter 33**).

Comparative information should be provided for all segmental disclosures. The standard sets out detailed guidance on determining classes of business and geographical segments for reporting purposes. This guidance is considered in more detail in **Chapter 9**. If, in the opinion of the directors, the disclosures required by the standard would be seriously prejudicial to the interests of the reporting entity, the information need not be disclosed, but the fact that the disclosures have not been given must be stated in the accounts. This aspect of the standard is also considered in more detail in **Chapter 9**.

Consistency

17.29 The general requirement for accounting information to be presented on a consistent basis year by year applies equally to segmental disclosure. However, SSAP 25 requires the directors to redefine the reporting segments where appropriate. This might be necessary where the company diversifies into new activities, acquires a new business or ceases part of its previous activities. If the definitions of segments are changed, the nature of the change should be disclosed in the accounts, with details of the reason for and the effect of the change, and comparative figures must be restated to reflect the change.

Apportionment of costs

17.30 The geographical analysis of results should normally be based on the areas from which goods or services are supplied. Costs that relate directly to a segment should be allocated to that segment for reporting purposes. Where costs cover a number of segments, rather than relating to one individual segment, the directors should establish an appropriate method of apportioning the costs in order to arrive at the segmental analysis of results. If it would be misleading to apportion the costs in this way, they may be treated as a deduction from the total of the segmental results.

Treatment of interest

17.31 Where the accounts include a segmental analysis of the results for the year, the figure to be analysed should normally be the profit or loss for the year before interest and taxation. This reflects the fact that any interest charged or received will usually result from the overall financial policy of the entity rather than from the activities of an individual segment. However, where all or part of the entity's business is to earn interest, or interest paid or received is central to the business, the segmental analysis should be provided for the profit or loss after interest but before taxation. In this case, interest bearing assets and liabilities should be also included in the net assets analysis to ensure that the analyses of results and net assets are given on a consistent basis (see **Chapter 33**).

Link with profit and loss account

17.32 The total of the amounts disclosed in the segmental analysis should agree with the net result shown in the profit and loss account. If it does not, a reconciliation of the two amounts should also be provided.

EXPENDITURE ON RESEARCH AND DEVELOPMENT

Requirements of SSAP 13 'Accounting for Research and Development'

17.33 SSAP 13 'Accounting for Research and Development' requires disclosure of the amount of research and development expenditure charged in the profit and loss account, analysed between:

- current year expenditure; and
- amounts amortised from deferred expenditure.

However, this disclosure requirement only applies to a company that:

- is a public limited company or has a public limited company as a subsidiary;
- is a banking or insurance company or group; or
- exceeds the CA 1985 criteria, multiplied in each case by ten, for defining a medium-sized company (see **Chapter 7**).

Chapter 18

Balance Sheet Formats

COMPANY LAW REQUIREMENTS

CA 1985 prescribed formats

18.1 CA 1985 prescribes standard formats for the profit and loss account and the balance sheet which must be followed by both individual companies and by groups when preparing their annual accounts. The Act provides a choice of two formats for the balance sheet – these are set out in the Appendix to this Chapter. The directors are free to decide which format to use, but once a particular format has been chosen it must be used consistently year by year unless there are good reasons for changing. If a format is changed, details must be given in the accounts and the reason for the change must be explained. A small company which chooses to prepare shorter form accounts can reduce some of the detailed balance sheet disclosures (see **Chapter 7**).

Vertical or horizontal structure

18.2 Format 1 for the balance sheet presents assets and liabilities in a continuous vertical format and separates creditors into those falling due within one year and those falling due after more than one year. There is no indication where the balance sheet totals should be drawn. The most common practice is to draw the main balance sheet total after item J (Accruals and deferred income) and thus match net assets (or liabilities) with the total of capital and reserves. However, it is also possible to draw the total after item G (Total assets less current liabilities) and match this with the aggregate of creditors falling due after more than one year, provisions for liabilities and charges, accruals and deferred income (where these are shown separately) and capital and reserves. Format 2 discloses similar details but groups together all of the company's assets, followed by all of its liabilities (including capital and reserves). Although the headings are set out vertically in the Act, this format can be used to present a horizontal balance sheet. The two sub-totals for net current assets (or liabilities) and total assets less current liabilities set out in Format 1 are not required (or indeed possible) under Format 2. The other main difference is that creditors are presented in total under Format 2, although for each item within creditors, the following information must be given in the notes to the accounts:

— the amount falling due within one year;

— the amount falling due after more than one year.

The aggregate amounts due within one year and after more than one year must also be shown. In practice, most companies prepare their balance sheet in line with Format 1 and Format 2 is rarely seen.

Change of format

18.3 The directors may only change the format of the balance sheet if, in their opinion, there are special reasons for doing so. It is possible to imagine how changes in a company's activities might justify a change of format for the profit and loss account, but it is more difficult to envisage a situation which might justify a change in the format of the balance sheet, particularly as the two formats present the required information under broadly the same headings. If the format of the balance sheet is changed, the accounts must disclose:

— the fact that a different format has been used;

— the reasons for changing to a different format.

Order of headings and sub-headings

18.4 The balance sheet formats are set out using a hierarchy of letters, Roman numerals and Arabic numerals to prescribe the order in which the individual headings and sub-headings must appear. The letters and numerals do not have to be reproduced in the accounts but are provided so that other sections of the Act can refer to the headings by category. Although the headings and sub-headings should normally follow the order prescribed in the formats, the Act requires the directors to adapt or rearrange the items identified by Arabic numerals if the special nature of the company's business requires this. Items may also be shown in greater detail than required by the formats and additional items may be shown, provided that they are not already covered elsewhere in the standard format. Items identified by Arabic numerals may be combined if:

— the individual amounts are not material; or

— combining them facilitates assessment of the state of the company's affairs (in this case the individual components must be disclosed in the notes to the accounts).

If there is no amount to be shown for a particular heading or sub-heading in either the current or the previous financial year, that heading or sub-heading should not appear in the balance sheet.

Condensed presentation

18.5 The main headings on the balance sheet are prefixed with letters and Roman numerals and must therefore always be disclosed on the face of the balance sheet. However, the more detailed items are given Arabic numerals and disclosure of these items may therefore be given in the notes to the accounts if this results in a clearer presentation of the company's state of affairs. Most companies adopt this approach in practice. Items designated by Arabic numerals may also be combined if the individual amounts that would otherwise be disclosed are not material.

Alternative positions

18.6 The formats allow alternative positions for three items in the balance sheet:

- pre-payments and accrued income may be disclosed as a sub-heading within debtors or may appear as a separate heading on the balance sheet after current assets;
- accruals and deferred income may be disclosed as a sub-heading within creditors (in which case items may need to appear in both amounts falling due within one year and amounts falling due after more than one year) or all accruals and deferred income may be shown under a separate heading on the balance sheet after provisions for liabilities and charges;
- called up share capital not paid may be included as a separate item on the balance sheet, or may be included as a sub-heading within debtors.

The notes to the formats emphasise that these are alternative positions and it is therefore clear that each company should decide which position to use and group together all the relevant items in that position (i.e. the headings should not appear in both positions in the same set of accounts). In the case of pre-payments and accrued income and accruals and deferred income, both forms of presentation are in common usage, although it is probably more usual for pre-payments and accrued income to be included within debtors, and for accruals and deferred income to be included within creditors, than for separate headings for these items to be shown on the balance sheet. By its very nature, called up share capital not paid does not arise frequently in annual accounts. Where it does arise, it is probably more common for the balance to be included within debtors than for it to be treated as a separate heading on the balance sheet.

Changes in presentation

18.7 FRS 18 'Accounting Policies' emphasises that any change in the way in which a particular item is presented in the balance sheet or profit and loss account is a change of accounting policy. However, the presentation of additional information (e.g. analysing a particular heading in more detail than previously) does not constitute a change of accounting policy, although any corresponding figures should be reanalysed so that they are presented in the same amount of detail.

Comparative figures

18.8 Comparative figures must be given for each item in the balance sheet. If any item appeared in the previous year but does not appear in the current year, the heading and comparative amount must still be shown in the balance sheet. Comparative amounts are considered in more detail in **Chapter 5**.

Additional disclosures

18.9 The balance sheet formats include notes which require additional information or analyses to be given for certain items. These details are usually given in the notes to the accounts, although they may be given on the balance sheet if this is considered necessary or helpful. CA 1985 Sch 4 paras 37–51 also set out requirements on the disclosure of information to supplement the balance sheet items or to assist generally in the assessment of the company's state of affairs. Where appropriate these are discussed in the following chapters.

Items which must not be treated as assets

18.10 CA 1985 does not permit the following items to be treated as assets in a company's balance sheet:

(i) preliminary expenses;

(ii) expenses of, and commission on, any issue of shares and debentures;

(iii) costs of research.

The accounting treatment of issue costs in respect of shares and debentures is considered in more detail in **Chapters 13** and **31**. Although research costs cannot be treated as assets, the Act does permit development costs to be treated as an asset in special circumstances. This is considered in conjunction with the requirements of SSAP 13 'Accounting for Research and Development' in **Chapter 19**.

DEFINED BENEFIT ASSETS AND LIABILITIES

Requirements of FRS 17

18.11 FRS 17 'Retirement Benefits' was published in November 2000 and supersedes SSAP 24 'Accounting for Pension Costs' for accounting periods beginning on or after 1 January 2005, although earlier adoption is encouraged. The standard requires the defined benefit asset or liability in respect of retirement benefits, net of any related deferred tax balance, to be shown separately on the face of the balance sheet as follows:

— in a balance sheet prepared under Format 1, after item J (Accruals and deferred income) but before item K (Capital and reserves);

— in a balance sheet prepared under Format 2, an asset should be shown after item D (Prepayments and accrued income) in the 'Assets' section and a liability should be shown after item D (Accruals and deferred income) in the 'Liabilities' section.

Where an employer has more than one scheme, the total of any defined benefit assets and the total of any defined benefit liabilities should be shown separately on the face of the balance sheet. The requirements of FRS 17 are considered in detail in **Chapter 11**.

Appendix 1

BALANCE SHEET: FORMAT 1

A. Called up share capital not paid.

B. Fixed assets.

I Intangible assets.

1 Development costs.

2 Concessions, patents, licences, trade marks and similar rights and assets.

3 Goodwill.

4 Payments on account.

II Tangible assets.

1 Land and buildings.

2 Plant and machinery.

3 Fixtures, fittings, tools and equipment.

4 Payments on account and assets in course of construction.

III Investments.

1 Shares in group undertakings.

2 Loans to group undertakings.

3 Participating interests.

4 Loans to undertakings in which the company has a participating interest.

5 Other investments other than loans.

6 Other loans.

7 Own shares.

C. Current assets.

I Stocks.

1 Raw materials and consumables.

2 Work in progress.

3 Finished goods and goods for resale.

4 Payments on account.

II Debtors.

1 Trade debtors.

2 Amounts owed by group undertakings.

3 Amounts owed by undertakings in which the company has a participating interest.

4 Other debtors.

5 Called up share capital not paid.

6 Pre-payments and accrued income.

III Investments.

1 Shares in group undertakings.

2 Own shares.

3 Other investments.

IV Cash at bank and in hand.

D. Pre-payments and accrued income.

E. Creditors: amounts falling due within one year.

1 Debenture loans.

2 Bank loans and overdrafts.

3 Payments received on account.

4 Trade creditors.

5 Bills of exchange payable.

6 Amounts owed to group undertakings.

7 Amounts owed to undertakings in which the company has a participating interest.

8 Other creditors including taxation and social security.

9 Accruals and deferred income.

F. Net current assets (liabilities).

G. Total assets less current liabilities.

H. Creditors: amounts falling due after more than one year.

1 Debenture loans.

2 Bank loans and overdrafts.

3 Payments received on account.

4 Trade creditors.

5 Bills of exchange payable.

6 Amounts owed to group undertakings.

7 Amounts owed to undertakings in which the company has a participating interest.

8 Other creditors including taxation and social security.

9 Accruals and deferred income.

I. Provisions for liabilities and charges.

1 Pensions and similar obligations.

2 Taxation, including deferred taxation.

3 Other provisions.

J. Accruals and deferred income.

K. Capital and reserves.

- I Called up share capital.
- II Share premium account.
- III Revaluation reserve.
- IV Other reserves.
  - 1 Capital redemption reserve.
  - 2 Reserve for own shares.
  - 3 Reserves provided for by the articles of association.
  - 4 Other reserves.
- V Profit and loss account

Appendix 2

BALANCE SHEET: FORMAT 2

Assets

A. Called up share capital not paid.

B. Fixed assets.

- I Intangible assets.
  - 1 Development costs.
  - 2 Concessions, patents, licences, trade marks and similar rights and assets.
  - 3 Goodwill.
  - 4 Payments on account.
- II Tangible assets.
  - 1 Land and buildings.
  - 2 Plant and machinery.
  - 3 Fixtures, fittings, tools and equipment.
  - 4 Payments on account and assets in course of construction.
- III Investments.
  - 1 Shares in group undertakings.
  - 2 Loans to group undertakings.
  - 3 Participating interests.
  - 4 Loans to undertakings in which the company has a participating interest.
  - 5 Other investments other than loans.
  - 6 Other loans.
  - 7 Own shares.

C. Current assets.

- I Stocks.
  - 1 Raw materials and consumables.
  - 2 Work in progress.
  - 3 Finished goods and goods for resale.
  - 4 Payments on account.
- II Debtors.
  - 1 Trade debtors.
  - 2 Amounts owed by group undertakings.
  - 3 Amounts owed by undertakings in which the company has a participating interest.

4 Other debtors.

5 Called up share capital not paid.

6 Pre-payments and accrued income.

III Investments.

1 Shares in group undertakings.

2 Own shares.

3 Other investments.

IV Cash at bank and in hand.

D. Pre-payments and accrued income.

Liabilities

A. Capital and reserves.

I Called up share capital.

II Share premium account.

III Revaluation reserve.

IV Other reserves.

1 Capital redemption reserve.

2 Reserve for own shares.

3 Reserves provided for by the articles of association.

4 Other reserves.

V Profit and loss account.

B. Provisions for liabilities and charges.

1 Pensions and similar obligations.

2 Taxation, including deferred taxation.

3 Other provisions.

C. Creditors.

1 Debenture loans.

2 Bank loans and overdrafts.

3 Payments received on account.

4 Trade creditors.

5 Bills of exchange payable.

6 Amounts owed to group undertakings.

7 Amounts owed to undertakings in which the company has a participating interest.

8 Other creditors including taxation and social security.

9 Accruals and deferred income.

D. Accruals and deferred income.

Chapter 19

Intangible Fixed Assets

COSTS OF RESEARCH AND DEVELOPMENT

CA 1985 requirements

19.1 CA 1985 sets out separate requirements in respect of research costs and development costs but does not define either of these. The costs of research must not be treated as an asset in a company's balance sheet. Development costs may only be treated as an asset in special circumstances. Where development costs are included in the balance sheet, the accounts must disclose:

— the reasons for capitalising these costs;

— the period over which the costs are being, or are to be, written off.

The carry forward of development costs in accordance with SSAP 13 'Accounting for Research and Development' is usually accepted as complying with the requirements of the Act. The CA 1985 balance sheet formats require disclosure of the total amount of intangible fixed assets, together with the following analysis.

— Development costs.

— Concessions, patents, licences, trade marks and similar rights and assets.

— Goodwill.

— Payments on account (i.e. in respect of the purchase of intangible fixed assets).

The total must be disclosed on the face of the balance sheet but the detailed analysis may be given in the notes to the accounts. The legislation also requires a detailed analysis of movements in the year to be given for each category of intangible fixed asset identified in the balance sheet format. Comparative figures are not required for these disclosures.

Categories of research and development

19.2 SSAP 13 'Accounting for Research and Development' identifies three broad categories of research and development:

- *pure (or basic) research* – this is defined as 'experimental or theoretical work undertaken primarily to acquire new scientific or technical knowledge for its own sake rather than directed towards any specific aim or application';
- *applied research* – this is defined as 'original or critical investigation undertaken in order to gain new scientific or technical knowledge and directed towards a specific practical aim or objective'; and
- *development* – this is defined as the 'use of scientific or technical knowledge in order to produce new or substantially improved materials, devices, products or services, to install new processes or systems prior to the commencement of commercial production or commercial applications, or to improving substantially those already produced or installed'.

The standard sets out some examples of the type of activity that should normally be classed as research and development. These include:

- work aimed at the discovery of new knowledge or the advancement of existing knowledge;
- formulation and design of possible applications for such work;
- testing or evaluation of alternative products, services or processes;
- design, construction and testing of prototypes, models and development batches; and
- design of products, services or processes involving new technology.

The requirement for a substantial element of scientific or technical knowledge was emphasised in an FRRP report, issued in January 2003, following its review of the report and accounts of Finelot Plc for the year ended 31 July 2001. During the year, the company paid a third party £966,000 to carry out pre-production work for a new life-style magazine and capitalised this amount as development costs. The work included concept design and establishing distribution and marketing networks, and in the opinion of the Panel it did not include a substantial element of scientific or technical knowledge in the sense that was intended by SSAP 13. In the Panel's view, therefore, the costs incurred were not for 'development' as defined within SSAP 13, nor did they satisfy the criteria for recognition as an asset under any other relevant accounting standard. Therefore, the costs should have been written off as incurred, as required by UITF Abstract 24, 'Accounting for start-up costs'.

Activities that do not constitute research and development

19.3 Activities that should not usually be classified as research and development include:

- testing for the purposes of quality or quantity control;

- periodic alterations to products, services or processes, even though these may involve some improvement;
- general operational research;
- legal and administrative work connected with patents, licences or litigation; and
- market research.

Research costs

19.4 Both CA 1985 and SSAP 13 require costs relating to research to be written off as they are incurred, irrespective of whether the research is pure or applied. SSAP 13 specifies that these costs should be charged to the profit and loss account. The only exception to this is in the case of fixed assets acquired for use in research work. These assets should be capitalised in the same way as any other fixed asset, and depreciated over their expected useful liives in accordance with the requirements of FRS 15 'Tangible Fixed Assets'.

Development costs

19.5 The main distinction between development and research is that development is an evident precursor to commercial production or application. Development work will not usually be undertaken unless there is a reasonable prospect of commercial success at the end of the development phase. This success may take the form of either increased revenue or reduced costs. FRS 18 'Accounting Policies' requires financial statements (other than cash flow information) to be prepared on the accruals basis of accounting, which it defines as requiring the non-cash effects of transactions and events to be reflected, as far as is possible, in the financial statements for the accounting period in which they occur and not in the period in which any related cash is received or paid. The standard makes a clear link with the definitions of assets and liabilities set out in FRS 5 'Reporting the Substance of Transactions' (and also in the ASB Statement of Principles) and notes that the use of those definitions to determine which items should be recognised as assets and liabilities in the balance sheet is consistent with the accruals concept. Development costs which meet the definition of assets (i.e. rights or other access to future economic benefits controlled by the entity as a result of past transactions or events) can therefore be recognised as such in the balance sheet. However, SSAP 13 does not require development costs to be recognised in this way, even where the conditions set out in the standard appear to be met, and many companies continue to write off such costs as they are incurred, usually because of the high degree of uncertainty over the expected future benefits to which the costs provide access. It should be noted that SSAP 13 was developed before publication of the ASB 'Statement of Principles for Financial Reporting' and of FRS 18 'Accounting Policies' – it therefore does not present the issues in quite the same way as the later documents, although the end result is broadly the same.

Prudent approach

19.6 The conditions set out in SSAP 13 are stringent and many of the related issues will be highly judgmental and surrounded by uncertainties. The standard emphasises the importance of involving a wide spectrum of individuals in assessing the various aspects of the project (i.e. technical, commercial and financial viability) and the expected future benefits, and the need for a prudent view to be taken on all issues. If adequate evidence is not available to support the assumptions, the development costs should not be deferred but should be charged to the profit and loss account as they are incurred.

Conditions for deferral of development costs

19.7 SSAP 13 sets out a number of conditions, all of which must be met if development costs are to be deferred. The costs of any development work which does not meet these conditions must be charged to the profit and loss account as they are incurred. The detailed conditions are as follows:

- there must be a clearly defined project;
- the related expenditure must be separately identifiable;
- the outcome must have been assessed with reasonable certainty and this assessment must cover both:
  - technical feasibility, and
  - ultimate commercial viability;
- there must be a reasonable expectation that future sales or other revenues will exceed the aggregate of:
  - the costs that are being deferred,
  - any further development costs to be incurred on the same project, and
  - the related production, selling and administration costs;
- adequate resources must already exist, or there must be a reasonable expectation that they will be available, to allow the project to be completed and to provide any additional working capital that may be required as a result.

Amortisation of development costs

19.8 Development costs should only be deferred until commercial production or application of the product or service begins. At this point, the costs should start to be amortised on a systematic basis. The standard sets out two methods of allocating the costs to match them with the related revenue:

— by reference to the actual sale or use of the product or service;

— by reference to the period over which the product or service is expected to be used or sold.

The nature of the product or service will usually decide which of these is the most appropriate method of allocation. Whichever allocation method is used, the period over which the costs are to be charged to the profit and loss account should be finite and should be both prudent and realistic. In many cases the period will be relatively short (e.g. three or four years).

Annual review

19.9 At the end of each year, every project in respect of which development costs are carried forward in the accounts must be reviewed so that the expected recoverability of the costs can be reassessed. If circumstances have changed, or if there is any doubt over the assumptions previously made, the related costs should be charged to the profit and loss account to the extent that they are no longer considered recoverable. In carrying out this review, and any related write-off, each project must be considered individually (i.e. potential under-recoveries on one project should not be ignored on the basis that there are significant over-recoveries on other projects).

Consistency of accounting

19.10 Although the standard does not require development costs to be carried forward, even where the conditions are met, it does require a consistent approach to be taken within an individual organisation. Therefore, where a company adopts a policy of deferring development costs, this accounting treatment should be followed for all projects that meet the criteria set out in SSAP 13.

Exceptions to the normal rules

19.11 SSAP 13 does not apply to the following:

— the location and exploitation of oil, gas and mineral deposits (however, the development of new surveying methods and techniques will usually qualify as research and development);

— development work carried out under a contract with a third party, where the expenditure is to be fully reimbursed by the third party;

— work carried out under a contract to develop and manufacture at an agreed price, which is calculated to reimburse the development costs as well as the costs of production.

In the last two cases, any costs that have not been reimbursed at the balance sheet date should be accounted for as contract work in progress (see **Chapter 23**).

Accounts disclosure

19.12 SSAP 13 requires disclosure of the accounting policy on research and development. Where development costs are capitalised, the Act specifically requires disclosure of the reason for this treatment and the period over which they are to be amortised. The following wordings might be suitable to meet both requirements.

Example 19.1 – Disclosure of accounting policy on research and development (I)

Expenditure on research and development is charged to the profit and loss account in the year in which it is incurred.

Example 19.2 – Disclosure of accounting policy on research and development (II)

Expenditure on research is charged to the profit and loss account in the year in which it is incurred. Expenditure on development is charged to the profit and loss account as it is incurred, except where it relates to individual projects. Where the recoverability of expenditure on individual projects is reasonably assured, the expenditure is deferred until the commencement of commercial production and then amortised by reference to sales of the relevant products over a period of four years.

Both CA 1985 and SSAP 13 require disclosure of opening and closing balances in respect of deferred development costs and details of any movements during the year. The following layout will usually be suitable.

Example 19.3 – Layout for disclosing movements

	£
Development costs	
Cost:	
Balance at 1 January 20X2	49,786
Additions during the year	45,670
Balance at 31 December 20X2	95,456
Amortisation:	
Balance at 1 January 20X2	14,561
Amortisation during the year	32,345
Balance at 31 December 20X2	46,906
Net book value at 31 December 20X2	48,550
Net book value at 31 December 20X1	35,225

Amount charged to the profit and loss account

19.13 For larger companies only (see **17.33**), SSAP 13 requires disclosure of the total charged to the profit and loss account in the year in respect of research and development expenditure; this must be analysed between:

— expenditure incurred in the current year;

— amounts amortised from deferred development expenditure.

This disclosure is normally given in the notes to the accounts, usually as part of a note disclosing specific amounts charged or credited in arriving at the operating profit or loss for the year. The amount disclosed as expenditure incurred during the year should include any depreciation charged on fixed assets acquired for use in general research and development work. This amount will also need to be disclosed as depreciation of fixed assets in accordance with FRS 15 'Tangible Fixed Assets'.

Treatment as unrealised loss

19.14 Under CA 1985 s 269, any development costs shown as an asset are to be treated as a realised loss for distribution purposes, unless:

— there are special circumstances which justify the directors' decision not to treat the costs as a realised loss;

— the note to the accounts on development costs states that they are not to be treated as a realised loss and explains the circumstances relied on by the directors to justify their decision.

The Act does not provide any further guidance on these points, but it is usually acknowledged that the carry forward of development costs in accordance with SSAP 13 'Accounting for Research and Development' will usually justify a decision by the directors not to treat the costs as a realised loss for distribution purposes. The following wording might be suitable as a footnote to the note on development costs.

Example 19.4 – Footnote to note on development costs

Development costs represent expenditure on individual development projects. Where the recoverability of such expenditure is reasonably assured, the expenditure is deferred until the commencement of commercial production and then amortised by reference to sales of the relevant products over a period of four years. The directors consider that the development costs deferred on this basis should not be treated as a realised loss.

Directors' report

19.15 The directors' report must give an indication of any activities in the field of research and development. The contents of the directors' report, and the need for consistency between the accounts and the directors' report, are considered in **Chapter 36**.

CONCESSIONS, PATENTS, LICENCES, TRADE MARKS AND SIMILAR INTANGIBLE ASSETS

Capitalisation under company law

19.16 Under CA 1985, a company's balance sheet may only include amounts in respect of concessions, patents, licences, trade marks and similar rights if:

— the assets were acquired for valuable consideration and are not required to be shown under goodwill; or

— the assets were created by the company itself.

Requirements of FRS 10

19.17 Definitive guidance on accounting for intangible assets is set out in FRS 10 'Goodwill and intangible assets'. The standard defines intangible assets as 'non-financial fixed assets that do not have physical substance but are identifiable and are controlled by the entity through custody or legal rights'. Additional guidance is provided on applying this definition in practice:

— an identifiable asset is one that can be disposed of separately without disposing of the business of the entity (UITF Information Sheet No 34 has subsequently clarified that where the terms of a licence make it non-transferable and thus incapable of separate disposal, this does not imply that the licence is no longer an intangible asset - the issue is whether in principle the item could be disposed of separately from the business and any particular circumstances that make a disposal uneconomic or illegal are not relevant);

— an asset that can only be disposed of as part of the revenue-earning activity to which it contributes is regarded as being indistinguishable from the goodwill relating to that activity and is therefore accounted for as part of that goodwill;

— control of an intangible asset is usually secured by legal rights, which either grant access to economic benefits (e.g. through a franchise or licence) or restrict the access of others (e.g. through a patent or trade mark);

— control is more difficult to demonstrate in the absence of legal rights, but may be obtained through custody - however, in the case of assets such as confidential technical or intellectual knowledge, an expectation that the present situation will continue will not usually give the entity sufficient control over the expected future benefits to justify recognition of the item as an asset in the accounts (e.g. a team of skilled staff will not be recognised as an intangible asset because the entity will not usually have custody of, or a legal right to retain, those skills);

- software development costs that are directly attributable to bringing a computer system or other computer-related equipment into working order should be treated as part of the cost of the related hardware.

Certain intangible assets (such as research and development costs and oil and gas exploration and development costs) are excluded from FRS 10 on the basis that they are covered by more specific accounting requirements.

Initial recognition

19.18 FRS 10 sets out separate requirements on initial recognition for intangible assets that are purchased externally and those that are developed internally. Purchased intangible assets are classified further into those acquired as part of a business and those purchased separately. The following requirements apply:

- an internally-developed intangible asset should only be capitalised if it has a readily ascertainable market value;
- an intangible asset purchased separately from a business should be capitalised at cost; and
- an intangible asset acquired as part of a business should be capitalised separately from goodwill if its value can be measured reliably at the time of initial recognition - in other cases the value of the intangible asset should be subsumed within the amount attributed to goodwill.

Readily ascertainable market value

19.19 Readily ascertainable value is defined in FRS 10 as a value established by reference to a market where:

- the asset belongs to a homogeneous population of assets that are equivalent in all material respects; and
- an active market, evidenced by frequent transactions, exists for that population of assets.

The guidance suggests that certain operating licences, franchises and quotas might meet these conditions, but a brand, publishing title or patent would not usually do so as each of these is inevitably unique, even though other similar assets may exist and may be traded from time to time. This point was emphasised in the FRRP report, published in July 2002, on the results of its enquiry into the report and accounts of Equator Group Plc for the year ended 31 December 1999. The matter at issue was the accounting treatment adopted for the purchase of Equator Films Limited in June 1999 and the subsequent accounting for the film libraries acquired. The Panel took the view that:

— although the rights attaching to each film were similar, the films themselves were unique and could not, therefore, belong to a homogenous population of assets that was equivalent in all respects; and

— the market in which film libraries are bought and sold is not an 'active market'.

The Panel therefore concluded that the films did not have a readily ascertainable market value, as defined in FRS 10.

Valuing an intangible asset acquired as part of a business

19.20 An intangible asset acquired as part of a business should initially be recorded at fair value, but where the asset does not have a readily ascertainable market value, the fair value should be restricted to an amount that does not create or increase any negative goodwill arising on the acquisition. This point was also emphasised in the FRRP case referred to in **19.19** above. Fair value should be established in accordance with FRS 7 'Fair Values in Acquisition Accounting'. This requires fair value to be based on replacement cost, which in most cases will be the estimated market value of the asset. The standard also considers fair value in the context of unique intangible assets for which replacement cost or market values may be difficult to determine. In some cases techniques have been developed for estimating the value of such assets (e.g. brands, publishing titles) for the purpose of sale and purchase agreements, and the guidance in the standard notes that these may also be used to establish fair value for initial recognition purposes.

Amortisation

19.21 CA 1985 requires any items capitalised as intangible fixed assets to be amortised over their expected useful economic lives in the same way as any other fixed assets. Under FRS 10, an intangible asset that is regarded as having a limited useful economic life must be amortised on a systematic basis over that life, but an intangible asset that is regarded as having an indefinite useful economic life should not be amortised. Amortisation charged in the year will need to be disclosed as required by the standard profit and loss account formats.

Determining useful economic life

19.22 FRS 10 defines the useful economic life of an intangible asset as 'the period over which the entity expects to derive economic benefit from that asset'. There is a rebuttable presumption that the useful economic life of an intangible asset should be no more than 20 years, and this presumption can only be rebutted if:

— the durability of the intangible asset can be demonstrated and justifies a life of more than 20 years; and

— the intangible asset is capable of continued measurement so that annual impairment reviews can be carried out.

FRS 10 notes that the useful economic lives of intangible assets will often be uncertain, but this does not justify an assumption that the life of a particular intangible asset is 20 years, or that its life is indefinite. Conversely, uncertainty should not be used to justify the adoption of an unrealistically short life. A prudent but realistic estimate of the useful economic life must be made for each intangible asset. The standard also notes that an asset will not be capable of continued measurement where the cost of carrying out the measurement is unjustifiably high - for instance, where the amounts involved are not sufficiently material to justify the detailed procedures needed to carry out an annual impairment review.

Legal rights granted for a finite period

19.23 Legal factors may also influence the useful economic life of an intangible asset, in that they may restrict the period during which the reporting entity has access to the economic benefits associated with the asset. The guidance notes that the useful economic life of an intangible asset is the shorter of:

— the period over which the future benefits are expected to arise; and

— the period over which the reporting entity is expected to have control of those benefits.

Where access to the benefits is granted for a finite period, the useful economic life of the asset will usually be limited to that period. The life of the asset should only be extended beyond this period if, and to the extent that, the legal rights over the asset are renewable and renewal is assured. Any costs that are expected to recur each time the legal rights are renewed should be excluded from the amount treated as having a longer life. The standard gives the following additional guidance on when the renewal of rights may be regarded as being assured:

— if the value of the intangible asset does not reduce as the initial expiry date approaches, or where the value reduces only by an amount reflecting the cost of renewal of the rights;

— where there is evidence that the rights will be renewed, for instance on the basis of past experience; and

— where there is no evidence that the entity has breached any conditions under the terms of the original rights which might otherwise prevent the rights being renewed.

Residual value

19.24 A residual value should only be assigned to an intangible asset if it can be measured reliably. The guidance in the standard notes that the residual value of an intangible asset will usually be insignificant. Residual value is defined as 'the net realisable value of an asset at the end of its useful economic life' and should be based on prices prevailing at the date of acquisition (or revaluation) without taking account of any expected future price changes. The residual value of an intangible asset will generally only be significant and capable of reliable measurement where the entity has a legal or contractual right to receive a certain sum at the end of the period during which it has use of the asset, or where there is a readily ascertainable market value for the residual asset. This point was also emphasised in the FRRP case referred to in **19.19** above.

Method of amortisation

19.25 FRS 10 requires amortisation to be charged on a systematic basis over the useful economic life of the asset, using a method that reflects the expected pattern of depletion of the asset. A straight-line method should be used unless another method can be shown to be more appropriate. For instance, where a licence covers production of a finite quantity of a particular product rather than unlimited production over a period of time, it may be more appropriate to base amortisation on the quantity produced rather than the period of the licence. The ASB has proposed an amendment to FRS 10 to clarify that:

- it is unlikely that there will be circumstances that would support a method of amortisation that is less conservative than straight-line;
- interest rate methods, such as the 'reverse sum of digits' or the annuity method, are not appropriate methods of amortising intangible assets.

Review and revision of economic lives

19.26 The useful economic lives of intangible assets should be reviewed at the end of each accounting period and revised where necessary. Where the useful economic life of an intangible asset is adjusted, the carrying value of the asset should be amortised over its revised remaining useful economic life. UITF Abstract 27 'Revision to estimates of the useful economic life of goodwill and intangible assets' clarifies that this applies equally where the presumption of a 20-year life has previously been rebutted, on the basis that a decision not to rebut the presumption is not a change of accounting policy, but a change in the way in which useful economic life is estimated. If the revision extends the life of the asset to a period of more than 20 years from the date of its acquisition, the additional requirements of FRS 10 on annual impairment reviews automatically come into effect.

Requirement for impairment reviews

19.27 Intangible assets that are amortised over a period of 20 years or less should be reviewed for impairment at the end of the first full financial year following acquisition and in other periods if events or changes in circumstances indicate that the carrying value of an asset may not be fully recoverable. Intangible assets that are amortised over a period of more than 20 years, or are not amortised, should be reviewed for impairment at the end of each accounting period. Impairment is defined in FRS 10 as 'a reduction in the recoverable amount of a fixed asset or goodwill below its carrying value.' Recoverable amount is defined as the higher of:

- net realisable value - which is the amount at which an asset could be disposed of, less any direct selling costs; and
- value in use - which is the present value of the future cash flows obtainable as a result of an asset's continued use, including those resulting from its ultimate disposal.

Impairment reviews should generally be carried out in accordance with the requirements of FRS 11 'Impairment of Fixed Assets and Goodwill'. However, the first year impairment review for intangible assets amortised over 20 years or less may be carried out by comparing post-acquisition performance in the first year with pre-acquisition forecasts used to support the purchase price, and only carrying out a full impairment review if this exercise indicates that post-acquisition performance has failed to meet expectations, or if other factors indicate that the carrying value of the asset may not be fully recoverable.

Accounting for impairment losses

19.28 Impairment losses should be accounted for in accordance with FRS 11. If an impairment loss needs to be recognised, the revised carrying value of the intangible asset should be amortised over the current estimate of the remaining useful economic life of the asset. The reversal of an impairment loss in respect of an intangible asset can only be recognised when:

- the original impairment loss was caused by an external event; and
- subsequent external events clearly and demonstrably reverse the effects of that event in a way that was not foreseen when the original impairment calculations were carried out.

The guidance in the standard emphasises that most reversals will be the result of the internal generation of intangible asset value and should therefore not be recognised in the accounts. Where a reversal is recognised, it should be treated as arising in the current year.

Revaluation of intangible assets

19.29 CA 1985 permits intangible fixed assets (other than goodwill) to be included in the accounts at their current cost, subject to specific disclosure requirements (see **Chapter 1**). Under FRS 10, where an intangible asset has a readily ascertainable market value, as defined in the standard, it may be revalued to market value, provided that all other capitalised intangible assets of the same class are revalued at the same time. The standard defines a class of intangible assets as 'a category of intangible assets having a similar nature, function or use in the business of the entity' and suggests that licences, quotas, patents, copyrights, franchises and trade marks are examples of such classes. The guidance also notes that further subdivision may be appropriate in certain cases, for instance where an entity holds licences with different functions within the business. Intangible assets used in different segments of the business may also be treated as separate classes of intangible assets. The standard does not specify a frequency of revaluation, but states that, once an intangible asset has been revalued, the valuation should be updated sufficiently often to ensure that the carrying value of the asset does not differ materially from its market value at the balance sheet date.

Amortisation of revalued assets

19.30 Where an intangible asset has been revalued, the amortisation charge should be based on the revalued amount and the remaining useful economic life of the asset. Amortisation charged before the revaluation took place should not be written back in the profit and loss account.

Accounts disclosure

19.31 CA 1985 requires disclosure of opening and closing balances in respect of each category of intangible asset identified in the Act, details of any movements during the year and additional details where assets have been included in the accounts at valuation. FRS 10 requires the following detailed disclosures, which effectively encompass those set out in the Act.

- the method used to value intangible assets;
- for each class of intangible asset capitalised on the balance sheet:
  - the cost or revalued amount at the beginning and end of the period;
  - the cumulative provision for amortisation or impairment at the beginning and end of the period;
  - a reconciliation of movements, showing additions, disposals, revaluations, transfers, amortisation, impairment losses, reversals of past impairment losses and negative goodwill written back; and
  - the net carrying amount at the balance sheet date;

— the methods and periods of amortisation of intangible assets and the reasons for choosing those periods;

— where an amortisation period is shortened or extended after a review of remaining useful economic lives, the reasons and the effect if material (i.e. in the year of change only);

— where the amortisation method has been changed, the reasons and the effect if material (i.e. in the year of change only);

— where the amortisation period is more than 20 years from the date of acquisition, or where no amortisation is charged, the grounds for rebutting the 20 year presumption, including specific factors contributing to the durability of the intangible asset;

— where a class of intangible assets has been revalued:

  — the year of valuation, the values and the bases of valuation,

  — the original cost (or fair value) of the assets and the amortisation that would have been recognised if they had continued to be valued at this amount;

— where an asset has been revalued during the year, the name and qualifications of the valuer.

Details of opening and closing balances and movements in the year are usually presented in one note as follows:

Example 19.5 – Disclosure of opening and closing balances and movements in the year

Intangible fixed assets

	Development costs	*Patents*	*Total*
	£	£	£
Cost:			
Balance at 1 January 20X2	49,786	6,500	56,286
Additions during the year	45,670		45,670
Disposals during the year		(3,000)	(3,000)
Balance at 31 December 20X2	95,456	3,500	98,956
Amortisation:			
Balance at 1 January 20X2	14,561	1,250	15,811
Amortisation during the year	32,345	750	33,095
Eliminated in respect of disposals		(900)	(900)
Balance at 31 December 20X2	46,906	1,100	48,006
Net book value at 31 December 20X2	48,550	2,400	50,950
Net book value at 31 December 20X1	35,225	5,250	40,475

The other disclosures required by FRS 10 will usually be given as narrative notes below this table, or included within the accounting policy note where appropriate.

Accounting policy

19.32 Depending on the circumstances, wording along the following lines will usually be suitable for the accounting policy note:

> **Example 19.6 – Accounting policy for intangible assets**
>
> Licences are capitalised at their historical cost and amortised on a straight-line basis over the period of the licence, being the period during which the company expects to have control of the benefits associated with the asset. The licences currently held are being amortised over periods of 4 to 6 years.

GOODWILL

Nature of goodwill

19.33 This section considers the accounting treatment of purchased goodwill in the accounts of an individual company (for instance, on the acquisition of an unincorporated business). FRS 10 'Goodwill and intangible assets' defines purchased goodwill as 'the difference between the cost of an acquired entity and the aggregate of the fair values of that entity's identifiable assets and liabilities'. Identifiable assets and liabilities are defined as 'the assets and liabilities of an entity that are capable of being disposed of or settled separately, without disposing of a business of the entity'. Positive goodwill arises where the cost of acquisition exceeds the aggregate fair values of the identifiable assets and liabilities of the business acquired – in other words, where the value of the business as a whole is considered to be more than the aggregate of the values of its component parts and the purchaser is therefore prepared to pay more than the value of individual assets and liabilities that make up the business. Negative goodwill arises in the converse situation – where the value of the business is considered to be less than the value of the component parts and the aggregate fair values of the identifiable assets and liabilities are therefore more than the cost of acquisition. Negative goodwill is expected to arise only rarely.

Recognition of goodwill

19.34 Neither CA 1985 nor FRS 10 permit internally generated goodwill to be recognised on the balance sheet. Goodwill is therefore only recognised for accounting purposes when the business to which it relates is purchased by another party. Under FRS 10:

— positive purchased goodwill should be capitalised and classified as an asset on the balance sheet;

— any negative goodwill that arises on an acquisition should be recognised in the accounts and shown separately on the face of the balance sheet immediately below the goodwill heading. A sub-total of the net amount of positive and negative goodwill should also be given.

Purchased goodwill arising on a single transaction should not be divided into positive and negative components.

Value of purchased goodwill

19.35 When a business is acquired, the value of the purchased goodwill is established by comparing the fair values of the various assets and liabilities at the time of acquisition with the fair value of the consideration given by the purchaser. Any excess of the consideration over the fair values of the net assets represents the value of the purchased goodwill. Where an intangible asset is acquired as part of the transaction, it should normally be capitalised separately. However, if its value cannot be measured reliably, it should be subsumed within the amount of the purchase price attributed to goodwill.

Value of negative goodwill

19.36 The standard emphasises that, where an acquisition appears to give rise to negative goodwill, the fair values of the assets acquired should be tested for impairment and the fair values of the liabilities acquired should be reviewed carefully to confirm that they have not been understated and that no items have been overlooked. The requirements of FRS 10 in respect of intangible assets require the fair values of certain intangibles to be limited to an amount that does not create or increase any negative goodwill arising on the acquisition (see **19.20** above).

Fair values

19.37 FRS 7 'Fair Values in Acquisition Accounting' provides detailed guidance on establishing the fair values of individual assets and liabilities at the time of acquisition and the fair value of the purchase consideration (which will not necessarily be in the form of cash).

Amortisation

19.38 Under FRS 10:

— where purchased goodwill is regarded as having a limited useful economic life, it should be amortised on a systematic basis over that life;

— where purchased goodwill is considered to have an indefinite useful economic life, it should not be amortised.

CA 1985 requires goodwill to be amortised systematically over a finite period, and an entity following the requirements of FRS 10 in respect of goodwill that is considered to have indefinite life will therefore need to adopt the true and fair override and make appropriate disclosures in the accounts (see **Chapter 2**). No residual value should be attributed to purchased goodwill. The standard requires amortisation to be charged on a systematic basis over the useful economic life of the goodwill, using a method that reflects the expected pattern of depletion. A straight-line method should be used unless another method can be shown to be more appropriate. The guidance notes that, in the case of goodwill, an amortisation method that is less conservative than the straight-line method is unlikely to be justifiable. In particular, interest rate methods, such as the 'reverse sum of digits' or the annuity method, are not appropriate methods of amortising goodwill. Amortisation charged in the year should be disclosed as required by the standard profit and loss account formats.

Determining the useful economic life of goodwill

19.39 FRS 10 defines the useful economic life of purchased goodwill as 'the period over which the value of the underlying business acquired is expected to exceed the values of its identifiable net assets'. The standard also notes that, if purchased goodwill includes intangible assets that have not been recognised separately because their values cannot be measured reliably, the useful economic lives of the intangible assets will need to be taken into account when assessing the useful economic life of the goodwill. There is a rebuttable presumption that the useful economic life of goodwill should be no more than 20 years, and this presumption can only be rebutted if:

- the durability of the acquired business can be demonstrated and justifies a life of more than 20 years; and
- the goodwill is capable of continued measurement so that annual impairment reviews can be carried out.

The guidance in the standard emphasises that it is inappropriate to assume that the premium of an acquired business over its net asset value can be maintained indefinitely. In practice, purchased goodwill will usually be replaced by internally generated goodwill over time and, because internally generated goodwill should not be recognised for accounting purposes, it is important that the write-off period for the purchased goodwill is sufficiently short to allow it to be eliminated from the accounts before it is fully replaced with internally generated goodwill. The standard notes that the useful economic life of goodwill will often be uncertain, but this does not justify an assumption that it has a life of 20 years, or that its life is indefinite. Conversely, uncertainty should not be used to justify the adoption of an unrealistically short life. A prudent but realistic estimate of the useful economic life must be made in each case where goodwill arises.

Durability and continued measurement

19.40 The guidance in the standard emphasises that the durability of a business will vary depending on various factors, including:

— the nature of the business;

— the stability of the industry in which it operates;

— the typical lifespan of the products to which the goodwill relates;

— the extent to which the acquisition overcomes market entry barriers that will continue to exist; and

— the expected impact of competition in future years.

In practice, these are factors that will also need to be considered when determining the useful economic life of goodwill. The standard also notes that the goodwill will not be capable of continued measurement where the cost of carrying out the measurement is unjustifiably high - for instance, where the acquired business is merged with an existing business to such an extent that the acquired goodwill cannot be separately identified and reviewed in future years.

Review and revision of economic life

19.41 The useful economic life of purchased goodwill should be reviewed at the end of each accounting period and revised where necessary. Where the useful economic life is adjusted, the carrying value of the goodwill should be amortised over its revised remaining useful economic life. UITF Abstract 27 'Revision to estimates of the useful economic life of goodwill and intangible assets' clarifies that this applies equally where the presumption of a 20-year life has previously been rebutted, on the basis that a decision not to rebut the presumption is not a change of accounting policy, but a change in the way in which useful economic life is estimated. If the revision extends the life of the goodwill to a period of more than 20 years from the date of its acquisition, the additional requirements of FRS 10 on annual impairment reviews automatically come into effect.

Requirement for impairment reviews

19.42 Goodwill that is amortised over a period of 20 years or less should be reviewed for impairment at the end of the first full financial year following acquisition and in other periods if events or changes in circumstances indicate that its carrying value may not be fully recoverable. Goodwill that is amortised over a period of more than 20 years, or is not amortised, should be reviewed for impairment at the end of each accounting period. Impairment is defined in FRS 10 as 'a reduction in the recoverable amount of a fixed asset or goodwill below its carrying value'. Recoverable amount is defined as the higher of:

— net realisable value – which is the amount at which an asset could be disposed of, less any direct selling costs; and

— value in use – which is the present value of the future cash flows obtainable as a result of an asset's continued use, including those resulting from its ultimate disposal.

Impairment reviews should generally be carried out in accordance with the requirements of FRS 11 'Impairment of Fixed Assets and Goodwill'. However, the first year impairment review for goodwill amortised over 20 years or less may be carried out by comparing post-acquisition performance in the first year with pre-acquisition forecasts used to support the purchase price, and only carrying out a full impairment review if this exercise indicates that post-acquisition performance has failed to meet expectations, or if other factors indicate that the carrying value of the goodwill may not be fully recoverable.

Accounting for impairment losses

19.43 Impairment losses should be accounted for in accordance with FRS 11. If an impairment loss needs to be recognised, the revised carrying value of the goodwill should be amortised over the current estimate of its remaining useful economic life. The guidance in FRS 10 emphasises that:

— the recognition of an impairment loss must be justified by reference to expected future cash flows, in the same way as the absence of an impairment loss;

— the fact that the value of the goodwill may not be capable of continued measurement in future does not necessarily justify writing off the entire balance at the time of the first year impairment review.

The reversal of an impairment loss in respect of goodwill can only be recognised when:

— the original impairment loss was caused by an external event; and

— subsequent external events clearly and demonstrably reverse the effects of that event in a way that was not foreseen when the original impairment calculations were carried out.

The guidance in the standard emphasises that most reversals will be the result of the internal generation of goodwill and should therefore not be recognised in the accounts. Where a reversal is recognised, it should be treated as arising in the current year.

Accounting for negative goodwill

19.44 Negative goodwill up to the fair values of the non-monetary assets acquired should be recognised in the profit and loss account in the period in which those assets are recovered (i.e. through depreciation or on sale of the assets). Any negative goodwill in excess of the fair values of the non-monetary assets acquired should be recognised in the profit and loss account in the periods expected to benefit.

Accounts disclosure

19.45 CA 1985 requires disclosure of opening and closing balances in respect of goodwill, details of any movements during the year, the period of write-off and the reasons for choosing that period. FRS 10 requires the following detailed disclosures, which effectively encompass those set out in the Act:

- separately for positive goodwill and negative goodwill:
  - the cost at the beginning and end of the period;
  - the cumulative provision for amortisation or impairment at the beginning and end of the period;
  - a reconciliation of movements, showing additions, disposals, transfers, amortisation, impairment losses, reversals of past impairment losses and negative goodwill written back in the period; and
  - the net carrying amount at the balance sheet date;
- the profit or loss on each material disposal of a previously acquired business or business segment;
- the methods and periods of amortisation and the reasons for choosing those periods;
- where an amortisation period is shortened or extended after a review of remaining useful economic lives, the reasons and the effect if material (i.e. in the year of change only);
- where the amortisation method has been changed, the reasons and the effect if material (i.e. in the year of change only);
- where the amortisation period is more than 20 years from the date of acquisition, or where no amortisation is charged, the grounds for rebutting the 20 year presumption, including specific factors contributing to the durability of the acquired business;
- where goodwill is not amortised, the true and fair override disclosures (which should incorporate the explanation of the specific factors contributing to the durability of the acquired business);
- the period(s) in which any negative goodwill is being written back in the profit and loss account; and
- where negative goodwill exceeds the fair values of the non-monetary assets acquired, an explanation of the amount and source of the excess and of the period(s) in which it is being written back.

Movements on the goodwill account should be disclosed within the note giving details of all intangible fixed assets. The other disclosures are usually covered in a footnote to the movements table:

Example 19.7 – Goodwill disclosure within intangible assets

Intangible fixed assets:

	Development costs	*Patents*	*Purchased goodwill*	*Total*
	£	£	£	£
Cost:				
Balance at 1 January 20X2	49,786	6,500	25,000	81,286
Additions during the year	45,670	£	12,000	57,670
Disposals during the year	£	(3,000)	£	(3,000)
Balance at 31 December 20X2	95,456	3,500	37,000	135,956
Amortisation:				
Balance at 1 January 20X2	14,561	1,250	10,000	25,811
Amortisation during the year	32,345	750	8,000	41,095
Eliminated in respect of disposals	£	(900)	£	(900)
Balance at 31 December 20X2	46,906	1,100	18,000	66,006
Net book value at 31 December 20X2	48,550	2,400	19,000	69,950
Net book value at 31 December 20X1	35,225	5,250	15,000	55,475

The company acquired an unincorporated business on 1 January 20X2 for consideration of £45,000, which gave rise to purchased goodwill of £12,000. This is being amortised on a straight line basis over its expected useful economic life of 4 years. Goodwill in respect of a business acquired in previous years is being amortised over its expected useful economic life of 5 years. In the opinion of the directors, these periods represents a reasonable and prudent estimate of the time during which the company will derive economic benefit from the goodwill acquired.

Accounting policy

19.46 In a straightforward case of positive goodwill, the following wording will usually be suitable:

Example 19.8 – Accounting policy for purchased goodwill

Purchased goodwill represents the difference between the cost of an acquired business and the aggregate of the fair values of its identifiable assets and liabilities. Purchased goodwill is capitalised and amortised through the profit and loss account on a straight-line basis over its useful economic life.

Transitional arrangements

19.47 The predecessor accounting standard to FRS 10 was SSAP 22 'Accounting for Goodwill' and this allowed two alternative accounting treatments for purchased goodwill: capitalisation and amortisation, or immediate write-off against reserves. FRS 10 notes that any changes in accounting policy necessary to implement its requirements should be applied retrospectively. The preferred treatment, therefore, is for goodwill that has previously been eliminated against reserves to be reinstated to the extent that it would not have been fully written down under the requirements of the new standard. However, the ASB accepted that this would not always be practicable and included certain transitional arrangements in FRS 10.

Reinstatement of goodwill previously eliminated

19.48 Where goodwill previously eliminated against reserves is reinstated on implementing FRS 10:

- any impairment attributed to prior periods must be determined on the basis of reviews performed in accordance with FRS 11;
- the notes to the accounts should disclose:
  - the original cost of the goodwill,
  - the amount attributed to prior period amortisation, and
  - the amount attributed to prior period impairment;
- intangible assets subsumed within the goodwill need not be identified separately.

The reinstatement of the goodwill will therefore give rise to a prior period adjustment (see **Chapter 5**).

Goodwill not reinstated

19.49 Where goodwill that was previously eliminated against reserves is not reinstated on the implementation of FRS 10, the following treatment should be adopted:

- the accounting policy followed in respect of that goodwill should be disclosed;

- the cumulative amounts of positive goodwill eliminated against reserves and negative goodwill added to reserves (net of any goodwill attributable to businesses disposed of before the balance sheet date) should be shown, except that:
  - amounts relating to overseas business need not be given if it would be prejudicial to the business and official agreement has been obtained; and
  - disclosure need not be made for acquisitions before 23 December 1989 if the information is unavailable or cannot be obtained without unreasonable expense or undue delay;

  (the exclusion of these amounts, and the reasons for it, should be explained);
- the eliminated goodwill should be offset against the profit and loss account or another suitable reserve – it should not be shown as a debit balance on a goodwill write-off reserve, nor should the amount by which the profit and loss account or other reserve has been reduced be shown separately on the face of the balance sheet;
- in the reporting period in which the related business is disposed of or closed, the profit or loss on disposal or closure should include any attributable goodwill not already written off in the profit and loss account, and this should be separately disclosed as a component of the profit or loss (if it is not practicable to ascertain the goodwill attributable to a business acquired before 1 January 1989 this fact, and the reasons, should be disclosed).

Impact of goodwill on distributable reserves

19.50 The issue of distributable reserves and realised profits and losses is considered briefly in **Chapter 15**. This is a highly complex area and only an outline of the main issues is given in this book. The potential impact of goodwill on distributable reserves is not an issue where goodwill is accounted for in accordance with FRS 10 'Goodwill and Intangible Assets'. However, where a company follows the transitional arrangements in FRS 10 and does not reinstate goodwill previously eliminated directly against reserves, the impact of this write-off on distributable reserves may still need to be considered. The write-off of purchased goodwill must eventually give rise to a realised loss, and under the requirements of FRS 10 this loss will be recognised as the goodwill is amortised through the profit and loss account. Where a company adopted the policy of writing off purchased goodwill against reserves immediately on acquisition under SSAP 22 'Accounting for Goodwill' and does not reinstate any of this goodwill on implementing FRS 10, the question arises whether the full amount written off should be treated as a realised loss, and thus as a reduction of distributable reserves. This issue was considered in an appendix to SSAP 22 'Accounting for Goodwill', which is reproduced as Appendix V to FRS 10. The guidance concluded that the write-off of goodwill against reserves did not constitute an immediate reduction in the company's realised reserves, unless the goodwill had suffered a permanent diminution in value. This was on the basis that the write-off was usually a matter of accounting policy rather than the recognition of a diminution in value. It was therefore suggested that the company could deem the amount written off not to be an immediate realised loss, and recognise it as being realised on a systematic basis over the useful economic life of the goodwill, giving the same effect on reserves as when goodwill is capitalised and amortised through the profit and loss account over its useful economic life. Where the goodwill was initially written off against an unrealised reserve, it should be transferred to realised reserves on a systematic basis over its useful economic life.

Public companies

19.51 Additional rules apply in the case of public companies. In particular, a public company must take account of unrealised losses when establishing the profits available for distribution. Therefore the immediate write-off of goodwill, even against an unrealised reserve, may have a significant effect on the ability of a public company to pay a dividend.

Negative goodwill

19.52 Although SSAP 22 required negative goodwill to be credited to reserves at the time of acquisition, it should not have been treated immediately as a realised reserve. It should instead have been credited to an unrealised reserve, and should be transferred to realised reserves in line with the depreciation or realisation of the assets acquired.

Need for legal advice

19.53 If a company proposes to pay a dividend at any time when there is any doubt over the availability of sufficient distributable reserves, legal advice should always be taken before proposing and paying the dividend.

Chapter 20

Tangible Fixed Assets

CLASSIFICATION OF ASSETS

Definition of fixed asset

20.1 Under CA 1985, all assets must be categorised as either fixed assets or current assets. There is no flexibility for presenting items outside these two categories. The legislation defines a fixed asset as one which the company intends to use on a continuing basis in its activities. FRS 11 'Impairment of Fixed Assets and Goodwill' and FRS 15 'Tangible Fixed Assets' define tangible fixed assets as: 'Assets that have physical substance and are held for use in the production or supply of goods or services, for rental to others, or for administrative purposes on a continuing basis in the reporting entity's activities.' A current asset is any asset that does not meet the fixed asset definition. The wording of the Act and of the standards suggests that it is the intended use of the asset at the balance sheet date that decides whether a particular asset is fixed or current. This can give rise to difficulties in accounting for fixed assets which the company proposes to sell and for current assets which the company decides to retain.

Proposed sale of fixed asset

20.2 If a company has decided to sell an asset but is still using it at the balance sheet date, and plans to continue to use it until it is actually sold, there seems to be little difficulty in continuing to show the asset as a fixed asset in the account until it is physically disposed of.

Example 20.1 – When a fixed asset is to be sold but is still being used at balance sheet date

A Ltd operates two factories but decides to transfer all production to the newer of the two sites in due course. The older site is, therefore, put on the market but A Ltd proposes to continue to operate from that site until a buyer is found.

Both factories should, therefore, continue to be shown as fixed assets in the accounts.

However, in this situation the carrying value of the asset in the accounts may need further consideration to ensure that it is not overstated in light of the planned disposal. If the company has stopped using the asset that is to be sold, it would seem that the asset ceases to meet the definition of a fixed asset set out in CA 1985.

Example 20.2 – When a fixed asset is to be sold and is not being used

A Ltd operates two factories but decides to transfer all production to the newer of the two sites on 1 June 20X2. The older site is put on the market but is still unsold at 30 September 20X2, the end of the company's financial year.

The older site has, therefore, ceased to meet the definition of a fixed asset set out in CA 1985.

The accounting treatment in this situation is more difficult. It may seem appropriate to transfer the asset from fixed assets to current assets but this is likely to give rise to problems if, for instance:

— the fixed asset is included in the accounts at valuation – a company is permitted to include fixed assets in the accounts at cost or valuation, but current assets must usually be included in the accounts at the lower of cost and net realisable value;

— the asset is significant and disposal may take more than 12 months (eg a major property which is put up for sale when the market is depressed) – the inclusion of such an item in current assets could significantly distort the accounts.

In the light of these difficulties, it has become normal practice to continue to include assets in the course of disposal within fixed assets and to show them separately as 'assets awaiting disposal' or 'assets held for sale', rather than to transfer them to current assets. FRS 15 acknowledges this by setting out a specific valuation basis for properties surplus to requirements where the entity adopts a policy of revaluation. Any profit or loss on the eventual disposal will usually be separately disclosable under the requirements of FRS 3 'Reporting Financial Performance'.

Transfers from current assets to fixed assets

20.3 UITF 5 'Transfers from Current Assets to Fixed Assets' tackles the issue of how to account for an asset that was not initially intended for continuing use in the business, but which subsequently becomes a fixed asset. An example might be where a property construction company builds a property initially for sale in the ordinary course of its business, but then decides to use the building as its own office. The Abstract requires the following approach:

— assess the net realisable value of the asset at the date of transfer;

- if net realisable value is below cost, the asset must be written down to net realisable value before it is transferred;
- any provision needed to reduce cost to net realisable value must be charged to the profit and loss account (this recognises the loss suffered by the company during the time that the asset was held as a current asset);
- the asset is then subject to the normal rules for fixed assets (i.e. those set out in the Act and FRS 15) from the date of transfer, and should be treated as an asset recorded at valuation under the alternative accounting rules of the Act (see **Chapter 1**).

Analysis of tangible fixed assets

20.4 CA 1985 requires tangible fixed assets to be analysed into the following categories.

- Land and buildings.
- Plant and machinery.
- Fixtures, fittings, tools and equipment.
- Payments on account and assets in the course of construction.

This detail is usually given in the notes to the accounts, although it may be given on the face of the balance sheet. Depending on the nature of the company's business, categorising fixed assets into these headings may not always be straightforward.

Class of tangible fixed assets

20.5 FRS 15 defines a class of tangible fixed assets as 'a category of tangible fixed assets having a similar nature, function or use within the business of the entity'. This definition is particularly relevant where the reporting entity adopts a policy of revaluation, because all tangible fixed assets in the same class must be revalued at the same time. The guidance in the standard notes that the categories set out in CA 1985 are broad categories and, for the purposes of valuation, entities may adopt other, narrower categories within the main headings. For instance, land and buildings may be analysed into specialised properties, non-specialised properties and short leasehold properties. However, where narrower classifications are adopted, it should be remembered that the disclosures required under the standard must be given by class of asset, rather than simply by the main categories identified in CA 1985.

Land and buildings

20.6 Land and buildings is probably the most straightforward of the three main categories and will normally comprise freehold, long leasehold and short leasehold properties. A long lease is defined in CA 1985 as a lease that has not less than 50 years remaining at the balance sheet date. All other leases are short leases. The Act requires separate details for each of these headings and this information is usually disclosed in a note to the accounts. The Act is not totally specific as to what is required and refers only to an analysis of 'amounts' relating to freehold and leasehold tenure. The minimum disclosure would, therefore, be an analysis of the net book value of land and buildings.

Example 20.3 – Analysis of land and buildings

The net book value of land and buildings comprises:

	20X2	*20X1*
	£	£
Freehold	239,750	245,600
Long leasehold	35,671	37,849
Short leasehold	25,600	29,780
	301,021	313,229

However, many companies give full details of the movements during the year in respect of each category.

Example 20.4 – Fuller analysis of land and buildings

	Freehold	*Leasehold Long*	*Leasehold Short*	*Total*
	£	£	£	£
Cost:				
Balance at 1 January 20X2	287,733	47,477	34,230	369,440
Additions	—	5,400	—	5,400
Disposals	—	—	(3,250)	(3,250)
Balance at 31 December 20X2	287,733	52,877	30,980	371,590
Depreciation:				
Balance at 1 January 20X2	42,133	9,628	4,450	56,211
Charge for the year	5,850	7,578	3,430	16,858
Eliminated on disposals	—	—	(2,500)	(2,500)
Balance at 31 December 20X2	47,983	17,206	5,380	70,569
Net book value 31 December 20X2	239,750	35,671	25,600	301,021
Net book value 31 December 20X1	245,600	37,849	29,780	313,229

Other asset categories

20.7 In a production company, plant and machinery will usually comprise assets relating to the company's main production activities.

Fixtures, fittings, loose tools and equipment will then cover the remaining assets such as small tools and office furniture and equipment, including computers. Non-production companies will often not hold assets in the plant and machinery category and will therefore classify all of their assets, other than property, under fixtures, fittings, tools and equipment. One common problem in practice is that the headings in CA 1985 do not cater specifically for motor vehicles. The Act permits information to be given in greater detail than is required by the formats and allows additional headings to be included, provided that the items in question are not dealt with elsewhere in the formats. If the value of motor vehicles is significant, it is therefore acceptable:

— to show motor vehicles as a separate category within plant and machinery or within fixtures, fittings, loose tools and equipment as appropriate; or

— to include a separate heading for motor vehicles in the table of fixed assets.

Similar arguments might apply to computer equipment if this is particularly significant in the context of the company's assets. A further point to remember is that FRS 15 also requires disclosure of the asset lives or depreciation rates used (see **Chapter 12**). The categories used for this disclosure should be consistent, as far as possible, with the analysis of fixed assets given in the accounts (eg if motor vehicles are sufficiently material to be shown as a separate category within fixed assets, the depreciation rate for motor vehicles should also be disclosed).

Payments on account and assets in the course of construction

20.8 This category represents payments the company has made in respect of assets that are in the process of construction or installation but which are incomplete at the balance sheet date. It is normal practice to charge depreciation from the date that an asset comes into use. It could, therefore, be misleading to include in the main asset categories significant amounts relating to assets still in the course of construction or development. The payments are, therefore, required to be disclosed separately within fixed assets until the asset is brought into use, at which point the cost should be transferred to the appropriate asset categories.

Example 20.5 – Disclosure of assets in the course of construction

	Plant and machinery £	*Assets in the course of construction* £
Cost:		
Balance at 1 January 20X2	546,780	26,700
Additions during the year	35,660	9,850

	Plant and machinery £	*Assets in the course of construction* £
Disposals during the year	(14,677)	—
Transfer on completion of asset	36,550	(36,550)
Balance at 31 December 20X2	604,313	—

INITIAL MEASUREMENT OF TANGIBLE FIXED ASSETS

Measurement at cost

20.9 Where the historical cost accounting rules are adopted, both CA 1985 and FRS 15 require a tangible fixed asset to be measured initially at cost. In the case of assets that are purchased, the Act defines purchase price as the actual price paid, plus any expenses incidental to the acquisition, and also notes that this includes any consideration given in respect of the asset, regardless of whether it is in cash or some other form. The guidance in FRS 15 explains that any related trade discounts and rebates should be deducted from the cost of the asset.

Cost of production

20.10 The production cost of an asset is calculated by adding together the purchase price of the raw materials and consumables used, and the direct costs of production. In addition, the Act permits the inclusion of a reasonable proportion of indirect production costs and interest on capital borrowed to finance the production of the asset, but in each case only to the extent that the costs relate to the period of production. FRS 15 is more specific than the Act and only allows the inclusion of costs that are directly attributable to bringing the asset into working condition for its intended use. Directly attributable costs are defined as:

- the labour costs of own employees arising from the construction or acquisition of the specific tangible fixed asset (but not more general employee costs); and
- the incremental costs that would have been avoided only if the tangible fixed asset had not been acquired.

Under the standard, therefore, it is not permissible to include an element of general overhead or administration costs in the cost of a fixed asset as these are, by their very nature, costs that would have been incurred regardless of whether the asset was constructed (or acquired) or not.

Examples of directly attributable costs

20.11 The standard sets out examples of directly attributable costs, which include:

- acquisition costs such as stamp duty, import duties and non-refundable purchase taxes (eg irrecoverable VAT);
- costs of site preparation and clearance;
- initial delivery and handling costs;
- installation costs;
- professional fees (eg architects, engineers);
- the estimated cost of dismantling and removing the asset and restoring the site, to the extent that this is recognised as a provision under FRS 12 'Provisions, Contingent Liabilities and Contingent Assets' – these costs can still be capitalised even if they do not become apparent until some time after the asset was acquired (eg where a liability arises as a result of changes in legislation).

Exclusion of abnormal costs

20.12 Abnormal costs, such as those arising from design errors, industrial disputes, idle capacity, wastage and production delays must not be included in the cost of the asset. Similarly, costs such as operating losses resulting from the suspension of a revenue activity whilst a tangible fixed asset is constructed, are not directly attributable costs and should not be included in the cost of the asset.

Cessation of capitalisation of costs

20.13 FRS 15 requires the capitalisation of directly attributable costs to cease as soon as substantially all of the activities necessary to get the asset ready for use have been completed. This applies even though the asset may not actually have been brought into use at that time. The standard notes that an asset is ready for use when its physical construction is complete.

Start-up or commissioning period

20.14 Certain assets require a start-up or commissioning period, during which it is not possible for the asset to operate at normal levels. For instance, machinery may need to be run in, specific equipment may need to be tested, or checks may need to be made to confirm that the plant is functioning properly before actual production begins. Under FRS 15, where an asset is available for use, but not capable of operating at normal levels without such a start-up or commissioning period, the costs associated with that period should be included in the cost of the asset. UITF Abstract 24 'Accounting for Start-up Costs' sets out the accounting treatment that should be applied to start-up costs that do not meet the specific conditions for recognition in FRS 15:

- where similar costs are incurred by the entity as part of its ongoing activities, the start-up costs should be accounted for on a consistent basis with those similar costs;

- where no similar costs are incurred, start-up costs that do not meet the specific conditions for recognition as assets under FRS10 'Goodwill and Intangible Assets', FRS 15 'Tangible Fixed Assets' or SSAP 13 'Accounting for Research and Development', should be recognised as an expense when they are incurred.

Start-up costs that meet the definition of an exceptional item set out in FRS 3 'Reporting Financial Performance' should be disclosed separately in accordance with the requirements of that standard (see **Chapter 8**).

Initial operating period

20.15 FRS 15 makes a clear distinction between a genuine start-up or commissioning period (as described above) and an initial operating period, where the plant or asset is available for use and capable of running at normal levels, but it is operated at a lower level because demand has not yet built up. The standard gives, as examples, a new hotel or retail shop, where reputation and customer demand will only build up over a period of time. The guidance in the standard emphasises that there is no justification for including the costs of such a period in the cost of the asset.

Gifts and donations

20.16 The issue of donated assets arises most frequently in the charity sector. FRS 15 requires assets received by way of gift or donation to be included in the accounts initially at their current value at the date they are received. Current value is defined in the standard as the lower of replacement cost and recoverable amount. However, the guidance acknowledges that there may be circumstances where a conventional approach to valuation is not appropriate (for instance, where the asset cannot be disposed of, or is of particular historical or artistic significance), and also that the significant costs associated with a valuation may make this approach inappropriate. In these situations, the standard permits a different approach to valuation and refers entities to sector-specific guidance and relevant Statements of Recommended Practice (SORPs).

Capitalisation of finance costs

20.17 CA 1985 permits the capitalisation of interest on capital borrowed to finance the production of an asset, but only to the extent that it relates to the period of production. Once again, FRS 15 is more specific on this issue. There is no requirement to capitalise finance costs but, where an entity adopts such a policy, it should be applied consistently to all tangible fixed assets where finance costs fall to be capitalised. Finance costs are defined as the difference between the net proceeds of an instrument and the total amount of payments or other transfers of economic benefits that the issuer may be required to make in respect of the instrument. They include interest on bank overdrafts and loans, the amortisation of discounts or premiums relating to debt and the amortisation of ancillary costs incurred in connection with the arrangement of debt. In the case of leased assets, finance costs should be accounted for in accordance with SSAP 21 'Accounting for Leases and Hire Purchase Contracts'.

Directly attributable finance costs

20.18 Where an entity opts to capitalise finance costs, the finance costs that are directly attributable to the construction of the tangible fixed asset should be capitalised as part of the cost of the asset. However, the total amount of finance costs capitalised during a period should not exceed the total amount of finance costs incurred in that period. Directly attributable finance costs are defined as those that would have been avoided if there had been no expenditure on the asset. For instance, finance costs might have been avoided by not taking out additional borrowings or by using funds expended on the asset to repay existing borrowings. Finance costs should be capitalised gross (i.e. without the deduction of any tax relief arising from them).

Specific and non-specific borrowings

20.19 Where an entity borrows funds specifically to finance the construction of a tangible fixed asset, the relevant finance costs are easily identified. The amount that can be capitalised is limited to the actual costs incurred on the borrowings during the period in which expenditure on the asset has been incurred to date. In some cases, the funds used to finance the construction of a tangible fixed asset may be part of the entity's general borrowings. In this situation, the amount capitalised should be calculated by applying a capitalisation rate to the expenditure incurred on the asset, as follows:

— the capitalisation rate for the accounting period should be based on the weighted average of rates applicable to the general borrowings outstanding during the period; and

— the expenditure on the asset is the weighted average carrying amount of the asset during the period, including any finance costs already capitalised in previous periods.

The objective of this exercise is to make a reasonable estimate of the finance costs that are directly attributable to the construction of the tangible fixed asset. Borrowings should, therefore, exclude any borrowings taken out for specific purposes such as financing other tangible fixed assets or hedging foreign investments. Other adjustments may also need to be made in order to select the borrowings most likely to achieve the objective of the calculation.

Commencement of capitalisation of finance costs

20.20 Where finance costs are capitalised, capitalisation should begin when:

- finance costs are being incurred;
- expenditures for the asset are being incurred; and
- activities that are necessary to get the asset ready for use are in progress.

The activities that are necessary to get an asset ready for use may encompass more than its physical construction. The guidance in the standard gives, as an example, preparatory technical work, such as obtaining necessary permits. However, finance costs should not be capitalised when an asset is simply held for future development (ie when no changes are being made to the condition of the asset). For example, finance costs should not be capitalised on land held for future development, although capitalisation can commence once activities on the site are under way.

Suspension of capitalisation of finance costs

20.21 Capitalisation should be suspended during extended periods in which active development of the tangible fixed asset is interrupted.

Cessation of capitalisation of finance costs

20.22 Capitalisation should cease when substantially all the activities needed to get the tangible fixed asset ready for use are complete. When the construction of a tangible fixed asset is completed in parts, and each part is capable of being used while construction continues on other parts, capitalisation of finance costs relating to a part should cease when substantially all the activities needed to get that part ready for use are complete. The guidance in the standard gives, as an example, the construction of a business park, where each building can be brought into use as soon as it has been completed, even though construction work may still be continuing on other buildings forming part of the site. On the other hand, a major industrial plant such as a steel mill, which involves a number of processes carried out in sequence, cannot be operated until all the relevant parts have been constructed.

Finance costs disclosures

20.23 Where an entity adopts a policy of capitalising finance costs, the financial statements should show:

- the accounting policy adopted;
- the aggregate amount of finance costs included in the cost of tangible fixed assets;

- the amount of finance costs capitalised during the period;
- the amount of finance costs recognised in the profit and loss account in the period; and
- the capitalisation rate used to determine the amount of finance costs capitalised during the period.

These details will usually be given in a narrative note below the fixed assets table.

Write-down to recoverable amount

20.24 The amount recognised under these requirements as the initial purchase or construction cost of a tangible fixed asset may exceed the recoverable amount of the asset. In this case, it should be written down to recoverable amount in accordance with the requirements of FRS 11 'Impairment of Fixed Assets and Goodwill'. However, there is no requirement to carry out an impairment review of a new fixed asset unless there is some indication that impairment has occurred. Further guidance on this is given in FRS 11 (see **20.54**).

Subsequent expenditure on fixed assets

20.25 The accounting treatment adopted for subsequent expenditure on a tangible fixed asset should reflect the circumstances taken into account on initial recognition and in determining useful economic life and residual value for depreciation purposes. Subsequent expenditure to ensure that the asset maintains its previously assessed standard of performance should normally be recognised in the profit and loss account as it is incurred. Routine repair and maintenance expenditure on the asset will usually have been assumed when assessing the useful economic life of the asset for depreciation purposes.

Capitalisation of subsequent expenditure

20.26 There are three circumstances in which subsequent expenditure on an asset should be capitalised:

- where it enhances the economic benefits of the asset beyond the previously assessed standard of performance (for instance, where the asset is modified or upgraded to increase capacity or improve the quality of output);
- where a component of the asset that has been treated separately for depreciation purposes is replaced or restored;
- where it relates to a major inspection or overhaul of the asset that restores the economic benefits that have already been consumed by the entity and have been reflected in depreciation (ie where an amount

equivalent to the cost of the inspection or overhaul has been depreciated over the period up to the date of the inspection or overhaul).

Where tangible fixed assets have not been separated into individual components for depreciation purposes (for instance, because the expected lives of the major components are not substantially different from those of the remaining parts of the asset), or no part of the asset has been depreciated over a different time scale to reflect the cost of a major inspection or overhaul, the costs of replacing, restoring, inspecting or overhauling the asset should be charged to the profit and loss account as they are incurred.

VALUATION OF TANGIBLE FIXED ASSETS

CA 1985 alternative accounting rules

20.27 Under the alternative accounting rules, tangible fixed assets may be included in the accounts at their market value at the date of the last valuation, or at current cost. Further guidance on the operation of the alternative accounting rules is given in **Chapter 1**. In practice, the only widespread use of the alternative accounting rules is the inclusion of freehold and leasehold properties in the accounts at valuation. CA 1985, FRS 15 and the Royal Institute of Chartered Surveyors 'Appraisal and Valuation Manual' all require additional disclosures to be given in the accounts when assets have been included at valuation. These are considered in more detail at **20.51–20.54** below.

Adopting a policy of valuation under FRS 15

20.28 FRS 15 also permits assets to be revalued, but only where the entity adopts a policy of revaluation. Where such a policy is adopted, it must be applied consistently within a class of tangible fixed assets, and all tangible fixed assets in the same class must be revalued at the same time. However, the revaluation policy need not be applied to all classes of tangible fixed assets. Prior to FRS 15, there was no formal guidance on how frequently tangible fixed assets should be revalued once they had been included in the accounts at a valuation. FRS 15 now clarifies the position by stating that, where a tangible fixed asset is subject to a policy of revaluation, its carrying amount in the accounts should be its current value at the balance sheet date. Current value is defined as the lower of replacement cost and recoverable amount. The guidance in FRS 15 outlines the procedures that should be adopted to achieve this, although formal valuations can be carried out more frequently where appropriate. The guidance also notes that the suggested approach may be inappropriate for charities and other not-for-profit organisations because of the cost implications, and refers these bodies to relevant sector-specific guidance and Statements of Recommended Practice (SORPs).

Keeping property valuations up to date

20.29 In the case of properties, there are two acceptable ways of meeting the requirement to show revalued assets at their current value at the balance sheet date without undertaking a full revaluation each year:

- a full valuation should be carried out at least every five years, with an interim valuation:
  - at the end of year three; and
  - at the end of years one, two and four if it is likely that there has been material change in value in those years; or
- for portfolios of non-specialised properties, a full valuation may be performed on a rolling basis designed to cover all the properties over a five-year cycle, with an interim valuation on the remaining four-fifths of the portfolio where it is likely that there has been a material change in value.

The second approach can only be adopted where the portfolio consists of a number of broadly similar properties that are likely to be affected by the same market factors, and the properties in the portfolio can be divided on a continuing basis into five groups of a broadly similar spread. A material change in value is described in the standard as a change in value that would reasonably influence the decisions of a user of the accounts. This assessment should take into account the combined impact of all relevant factors (eg physical deterioration, general market price movements).

Full valuation

20.30 A full valuation will usually involve:

- detailed inspection of the interior and exterior of the property;
- inspection of the locality;
- enquiries of local planning and similar authorities; and
- research into market transactions in similar properties, identification of market trends, and application of these to determine the value of the property.

A full valuation must either be carried out by a qualified external valuer, or carried out by a qualified internal valuer and subject to review by a qualified external valuer. Such a review should involve:

(i) the independent valuation of a sample of properties, representing a genuine cross-section of the entity's property portfolio;

(ii) the comparison of these valuations with those prepared by the qualified internal valuer; and

(iii) the expression of a formal opinion on the overall accuracy of the internal valuation on the basis of the results in (i) and (ii) above.

Qualified valuer

20.31 FRS 15 defines a qualified valuer as a person who:

— holds a recognised and relevant professional qualification; and

— has recent post-qualification experience and sufficient knowledge of the state of the market in the location and category of tangible fixed asset being valued.

An internal valuer is a director, officer or employee of the reporting entity. An external valuer is someone who is not a director, officer or employee of the entity, and who has no significant financial interest in the entity.

Interim valuation

20.32 An interim valuation may be carried out by either a qualified external valuer or a qualified internal valuer and includes:

— research into market transactions in similar properties, identification of market trends and the application of these to determine the value of the property under consideration;

— confirmation that there have been no changes of significance to the physical buildings, legal rights or local planning considerations; and

— inspection of the property or locality by the valuer, to the extent considered professionally necessary after taking into account, for instance, recent changes to the property or locality and the date of the last inspection.

Keeping other asset valuations up to date

20.33 In practice, it is comparatively rare for assets other than property to be included in the accounts at valuation. However, FRS 15 caters for this to be done and suggests that, for certain assets (eg cars), there may be a sufficiently active secondhand market, or appropriate indices, which will enable the directors to establish the asset's value with reasonable reliability. In this case the valuation may be updated annually by the directors. Where indices are used, they must:

— be appropriate to the class of asset being valued and to its location and condition, and take account of technological change;

— have a proven record of publication and use; and

— be expected to continue to be available for the foreseeable future.

For other assets, a valuation should be carried out by a qualified valuer at least every five years, with an update (also by a qualified valuer) in year three. Updates should also be carried out in the intervening years if it is likely that there has been a material change in value. If a qualified internal valuer carries out the five-yearly valuation, it should be reviewed by a qualified external valuer.

Valuation basis – properties

20.34 Where a policy of revaluation is adopted, the following valuation bases should be used for properties that are not impaired:

- non-specialised properties should be valued on the basis of existing use value, with the addition of notional directly attributable acquisition costs where these are material. Where open market value is materially different from existing use value, the open market value and the reasons for the difference should be disclosed in the notes to the accounts;
- specialised properties should be valued on the basis of depreciated replacement cost;
- properties that are surplus to the entity's requirements should be valued on the basis of open market value, after deducting expected directly attributable selling costs where these are material.

The terms 'specialised' and 'non-specialised' have the meaning set out in the RICS 'Appraisal and Valuation Manual'. Broadly, specialised properties are those which, due to their specialised nature, are rarely sold on the open market for single occupation for a continuation of their existing use, other than through sale of the business in occupation. They include:

- oil refineries and chemical works;
- power stations and dock installations;
- schools, colleges and universities;
- hospitals and other specialised health care premises;
- museums and libraries; and
- properties whose construction, arrangement, size, specification or location is such that there is no market for them.

The non-specialised category essentially covers all other properties and would normally include shops, offices, standard industrial buildings and warehouses, public houses, garages and residential property.

Impaired properties

20.35 Where there is an indication that the value of a property is impaired, an impairment review should be carried out in accordance with FRS 11 'Impairment of Fixed Assets and Goodwill' and the property should be written down to the lower of its revalued amount and its recoverable amount.

Notional acquisition costs

20.36 Notional acquisition costs directly attributable to the property are costs such as professional fees, duties and non-recoverable taxes. The guidance in the standard notes that the costs of obtaining planning consent, preparing and clearing sites and making site improvements are not included as they will already be reflected in the existing use value. For practical purposes, notional acquisition costs may be ignored if they are not material.

Non-specialised properties valued as businesses

20.37 Certain non-specialised properties are bought and sold as businesses and, therefore, need to be valued as an operational entity. In this case the existing use value of the property should take into account the trading potential of the property but should exclude any personal goodwill created by the present owner and management, as this may not remain with the business if it is sold.

Adaptation works

20.38 Structural changes or special fittings made to meet the needs of individual businesses usually have a low or nil market value because of their specialised nature. If only the shell of the property (ie excluding the adaptation works) is valued using the existing use value, the adaptation works should be included at depreciated replacement cost or depreciated historical cost.

Specialised properties

20.39 As explained at **20.34**, specialised properties are not usually sold on the open market and consequently do not have a market value. They are, therefore, valued at depreciated replacement cost. This is defined by the RICS as 'the aggregate amount of the value of the land for the existing use or a notional replacement site in the same locality, and the gross replacement cost of the buildings and other site works, from which appropriate deductions may then be made to allow for the age, condition, economic or functional obsolescence, environmental and other factors; all of these might result in the existing property being worth less to the undertaking in occupation than would a new replacement'. The objective of using depreciated replacement cost is to make a reasonable estimate of the current cost of constructing an asset with the same service potential as the existing property.

Valuation basis – other assets

20.40 Tangible fixed assets other than property should be valued using market value, with the addition of notional directly attributable acquisition costs where these are material. Where assets are surplus to requirements, the expected selling costs should be deducted from market value if material. Where market value is not obtainable, the assets should be valued on the basis of depreciated replacement cost. In this case, depreciated replacement cost is defined as 'the cost of replacing an existing tangible fixed asset with an identical or substantially similar new asset having a similar production or service capacity, from which appropriate deductions are made to reflect the value attributable to the remaining portion of the total useful economic life of the asset and the residual value at the end of the asset's useful economic life.' Costs that are directly attributable to bringing the asset into working condition for its intended use (transportation, installation and commissioning costs, irrecoverable taxes etc) should be included in the value, and the deductions should take account of the age, condition and economic and functional obsolescence of the asset, together with any environmental or other relevant factors. Professional assistance from a qualified valuer will usually be needed in valuing assets at depreciated replacement cost.

Consistency within a class of assets

20.41 Where a tangible fixed asset is revalued, all assets in the same class should be revalued. The only exception permitted by the standard is where it is impossible to obtain a reliable valuation of an asset held outside the UK and the Republic of Ireland, but this situation is expected to be rare in practice. If an asset is excluded from the valuation on these grounds, the accounts must disclose the carrying value of the asset and the fact that it has not been revalued.

Accounting entries on revaluation of assets

20.42 Where a tangible fixed asset is to be included in the accounts at valuation rather than historical cost, the following steps should usually be taken:

- compare the valuation figure for the asset in question with its net book value at the date of the valuation to calculate the uplift required;
- adjust both the original cost of the fixed asset and cumulative depreciation to date, so that the cost of the asset becomes the valuation figure and cumulative depreciation to the date of valuation is eliminated; and
- credit the net adjustment to the revaluation reserve.

The important point to note is that the cumulative depreciation to date is not written back to the profit and loss account but forms part of the credit to the revaluation reserve.

Example 20.6 – Incorporating a revaluation of fixed assets

B Ltd has freehold land and buildings with an original cost of £70,000. The buildings, which have an original cost of £50,000 are being depreciated over a life of 50 years.

B Ltd's accounting date is 31 December.

The land and buildings are professionally valued at £95,000 at 31 December 20X2 and this valuation is to be incorporated in the accounts at 31 December 20X2.

The net book value of the land and buildings at 1 January 20X2 was as follows.

Cost:	£
Land	20,000
Buildings	50,000
	70,000
Depreciation:	
Buildings	(6,000)
Net book value at 1 January 20X2	64,000

There have been no movements in land and buildings during the year.

As the valuation is at 31 December 20X2, a full year's depreciation charge must be incorporated for 20X2 (ie £1,000). This will reduce the net book value at 31 December 20X2 to £63,000. The uplift required to incorporate the valuation is therefore £32,000 (ie £95,000 – £63,000). This should be accounted for as follows.

Land and buildings at cost at 1 January 20X2	70,000
Surplus on revaluation	25,000
Land and buildings at valuation at 31 December 20X2	95,000
Depreciation at 1 January 20X2	6,000
Depreciation for 2002	1,000
Adjustment on revaluation	(7,000)
Depreciation at 31 December 20X2	0

The entries in the revaluation reserve will be as follows:

Dr Fixed assets – land and buildings cost	25,000	
Cr Revaluation reserve		25,000
Dr Fixed assets – depreciation	7,000	
Cr Revaluation reserve		7,000

Resulting in a credit balance of £32,000 on the revaluation reserve.

Alternative approach where depreciated replacement cost is used

20.43 FRS 15 allows an alternative approach to be adopted where the valuation is calculated on the basis of depreciated replacement cost. In this case, both the cost (or revalued amount) and the accumulated depreciation at the date of revaluation can be adjusted, so that the net carrying amount of the asset after revaluation equals the revalued amount.

Example 20.7 – Alternative approach

C Ltd has a specialised property with an original cost of £70,000 on which depreciation of £5,000 has been charged to date. The property is revalued at depreciated replacement cost as follows:

	£
Gross replacement cost	120,000
Adjustments	(25,000)
Depreciated replacement cost	95,000

Under the alternative approach this could be incorporated into the accounts as:

	£
Original cost	70,000
Gain on revaluation	50,000
	120,000
Depreciation to date	5,000
Adjustment on revaluation	20,000
	25,000
Net book value	95,000

The net credit to the revaluation reserve is still £30,000 (ie £50,000 less £20,000).

Depreciation in the year of valuation

20.44 Depreciation should continue to be charged in the year in which the valuation takes place, even though it may subsequently be eliminated when the valuation is incorporated into the accounts. This is considered in more detail in **Chapter 12**.

Recognition of revaluation gains

20.45 A revaluation gain should only be recognised in the profit and loss account to the extent that it reverses a revaluation loss already recognised in the profit and loss account. The gain that is recognised in the profit and loss account should be reduced by the amount of depreciation that would have been charged on the asset if the original revaluation loss had not been recognised. All other revaluation gains must be recognised in the statement of total recognised gains and losses.

Example 20.8 – Recognition of revaluation gains

D Ltd has a property with an original cost of £70,000. This was revalued in 20X0 at £65,000. Depreciation is charged at 2% pa. In 20X2 the property is revalued again at £75,000.

The surplus on the second revaluation is accounted for as follows:

	£
Original cost	70,000
Loss on first revaluation	(5,000)
Revalued amount	65,000
Less: 2 years' depreciation at 2% on 65,000	(2,600)
Carrying amount in accounts	62,400
Gain on second revaluation	12,600
	75,000

The amount of the gain recognised in the profit and loss account is:

Loss previously recognised in profit and loss account	5,000
Less: additional depreciation that would have been charged if loss had not been recognised:	
5,000 × 2% for 2 years	(200)
Gain to be recognised in profit and loss account	4,800

The remaining gain of £7,800 (ie £12,600 – £4,800) should be recognised in the statement of total recognised gains and losses.

The amount actually charged to the profit and loss account for the two years is:

Original loss on revaluation	5,000
Actual depreciation for the two years	2,600
Gain subsequently recognised	(4,800)
	2,800

This is equivalent to two years' depreciation on the original cost of £70,000 (ie £70,000 × 2% × 2 years) – the amount that would have been charged if the first revaluation had not taken place.

Recognition of revaluation losses

20.46 All revaluation losses that are caused by a clear consumption of economic benefits (eg physical damage or a deterioration in the quality of service provided by the asset) must be recognised in the profit and loss account. Other revaluation losses (eg those resulting from a general decline in the market) should be recognised in the statement of total recognised gains and losses until the carrying amount of the asset reaches depreciated historical cost. Any further loss should be recognised in the profit and loss account. The only exception permitted by the standard is where the recoverable amount of the asset is demonstrably greater than its revalued amount. In this case, the difference between recoverable amount and revalued amount should be recognised in the statement of total recognised gains and losses, with any further loss recognised in the profit and loss account.

No aggregation of gains and losses

20.47 Material gains and losses on individual assets within a class of assets must not be aggregated when determining the performance statement in which gains and losses should be recognised.

Transitional arrangements under FRS 15

20.48 There may be entities who do not wish to adopt a policy of revaluation of tangible fixed assets under the requirements of FRS 15, but who have revalued certain assets in previous years when the requirements were not as stringent. FRS 15 provides two options to cater for this situation:

- the entity can retain the book amounts (ie the previously revalued amounts) of these assets, subject to the requirement to test for impairment under FRS 11 'Impairment of Fixed Assets and Goodwill', provided that the accounts disclose:
  - the fact that the transitional provisions of FRS 15 are being followed;
  - the fact that the valuation has not been updated; and
  - the date of the last valuation; or
- the entity can restate the carrying amounts of the previously revalued assets to historical cost, less any equivalent accumulated depreciation, as a prior period adjustment arising on a change in accounting policy.

The first of these transitional arrangements can only be used when FRS 15 is first implemented (ie it cannot be used to justify a failure to keep subsequent valuations up to date as required by the standard).

PRINCIPAL ACCOUNTS DISCLOSURES

Movements in the year

20.49 CA 1985 and FRS 15 require considerable detail to be disclosed on the movements in both cost and depreciation during the year. This is usually presented in the form of a table in the notes to the accounts. The Act requires the disclosures to be given separately for the categories of asset identified in the legislation. FRS 15 requires the details to be given for each class of asset, as defined in the standard (see **20.4** and **20.5** above). The specific disclosures required are:

- cost or valuation at the beginning of the year and at the balance sheet date;
- the effect of any revaluation during the year;
- any additions during the year;
- any disposals during the year;
- any transfers during the year;
- the cumulative amount of depreciation at the beginning of the year and at the balance sheet date;
- the amount provided for depreciation during the year;
- any adjustments to depreciation in respect of disposals during the year;
- any other adjustments to depreciation during the year.

Example 20.9 – Movements in cost and depreciation

	Land and buildings	*Plant and machinery*	*Fixtures, fittings, tools and equipment*	*Assets in the course of construction*	*Total*
	£'000	*£'000*	*£'000*	*£'000*	*£'000*
Cost:					
Balance at 1.1.X2	369	547	57	27	1,000
Additions	5	36	9	10	60
Disposals	(3)	(15)	—	—	(18)
Transfers	—	37	—	(37)	—
Revaluation	79	—	—	—	79
Balance at 31.12.X2	450	605	66	—	1,121
Depreciation:					
Balance at 1.1.X2	56	321	27	—	404
Charge for the year	17	82	4	—	103
Eliminated on disposal	(3)	(12)	—	—	(15)

Revaluation	(70)	—	—	—	(70)
Balance at 31.12.X2	—	391	31	—	422
Net book value:					
At 31.12.X2	450	214	35	—	699
At 31.12.X1	313	226	30	27	596

Additional disclosures are required where interest has been capitalised as part of the cost of certain assets (see **20.23** above)

Disclosures in respect of revalued assets

20.50 Where certain assets are included in the accounts at valuation rather than historical cost, the following details must be given by class of revalued asset in each reporting period:

- the name and qualifications of the valuer(s) or the valuer's organisation and a description of its nature;
- the basis (or bases) of valuation, including whether notional directly attributable acquisition costs have been included, or expected selling costs deducted;
- the dates and amounts of the valuations;
- where historical cost records are available, the carrying amount that would have been included in the financial statements if the tangible fixed assets had been included at historical cost less depreciation, and the cumulative figures for depreciation or diminutions in value that would have been included in the accounts under the historical cost accounting rules;
- whether the person (or persons) carrying out the valuation is internal or external to the entity;
- where the directors are not aware of any material change in value and the valuation has therefore not been updated, a statement to that effect;
- where the valuation has not been updated, or is not a full valuation, the date of the last full valuation.

The following details must also be given for revalued properties:

- where properties have been valued as fully-equipped operational entities, having regard to their trading potential, a statement to that effect and the carrying amount of those properties; and
- where material, the total amount of notional directly attributable acquisition costs included in the carrying amount, or the total amount of expected selling costs deducted.

All of this information will usually be set out in a note below the fixed assets table.

Disclosures required by the RICS

20.51 Practice Statement 7 in the RICS 'Appraisal and Valuation Manual' also requires specific disclosures to be given in the accounts. Some of these overlap with the requirements of the Act and FRS 15, but some are additional to those requirements:

- the name and qualification of the valuer or the valuer's organisation and a description of its nature;
- whether the valuer is internal, external or independent;
- the date and basis of the valuation;
- confirmation that the valuation has been made in accordance with the RICS 'Appraisal and Valuation Manual' (or a named alternative where relevant), or the extent of, and reasons for, any departure;
- where valuation figures are given, the valuation basis and full details of any special assumptions adopted;
- where a definition is included, the whole of the definition;
- where the publication includes statements attributed to the valuer on the prospect of future growth in rent and/or capital values, a statement that such growth may not occur and that values can fall as well as rise; and
- where relevant, a statement that the property has been valued as a fully-equipped operational entity and with regard to its trading potential.

Written consent

20.52 The company should obtain written consent from the valuer before including his name in the accounts and the valuer will usually be responsible for ensuring that the disclosures are accurate and adequate and that there is no risk of the reader being misled. The precise wording must, therefore, be discussed and agreed with the valuer in each case.

Example disclosure

20.53 The details disclosed will inevitably vary depending on the circumstances of each case, but wording along the following lines will usually be appropriate:

Example 20.10 – Disclosures for revalued assets

Accounts for the year ended 31 December 20X2

The company's freehold property was professionally valued at £250,000 at 31 December 20X1. The valuation was carried out externally by Messrs

................, Chartered Surveyors, on the basis of open market value for existing use and in accordance with the RICS 'Appraisal and Valuation Manual'. No notional directly attributable acquisition costs were included in the valuation on the grounds that these would not be material.

If the freehold property had been included in the accounts at historical cost, it would have been included at the following amount:

	£
Cost	120,000
Accumulated depreciation	(9,000)
	£111,000

The directors are not aware of any material change in the value of the property since 31 December 20X1 and the valuation has, therefore, not been updated in the current year.

IMPAIRMENT REVIEWS

The need to carry out an impairment review

20.54 Impairment is defined in FRS 11 'Impairment of Fixed Assets and Goodwill' as a reduction in the recoverable amount of a fixed asset or goodwill below its carrying amount. Under this standard, an impairment review should be carried out when events or changes in circumstances indicate that the carrying value of a fixed asset (including goodwill) may not be recoverable. A review will, therefore, not necessarily be required every year – it will usually only need to be carried out when something has happened to the asset or to the economic environment in which the asset is used. The systematic charging of depreciation will usually ensure that the carrying amount of a fixed asset is reduced throughout its useful life to reflect the reduction in the asset's recoverable amount arising from the consumption of economic benefits. FRS 11, therefore, notes that, for most assets, impairments should be a relatively infrequent addition to normal depreciation. However, FRS 15 requires an annual impairment review to be carried out when an asset is not depreciated or when its remaining useful economic life exceeds 50 years.

Events and changes that might prompt a review

20.55 FRS 11 gives examples of events and changes that may indicate impairment of an asset has occurred. These include:

- a current operating loss or net cash outflow, combined with either similar losses or outflows in the past, or the expected continuation of losses or outflows in the future;
- a significant decline in the market value of an asset;

— physical damage or obsolescence;

— a significant adverse change in the business or market in which the asset is used (eg a major new competitor);

— a significant adverse change in the statutory or other regulatory environment in which the business operates;

— a significant adverse change in any indicator (such as turnover) used to measure the fair value of the asset at the time of acquisition;

— a commitment by management to undertake a major reorganisation.

The standard emphasises that the useful economic lives and residual values of the assets affected may also need to be reviewed in these circumstances (see **Chapter 12**). Even if the assets are not actually impaired, their expected useful lives and residual values may have changed.

Separate requirements for intangible assets and goodwill

20.56 FRS 10 'Goodwill and Intangible Assets' imposes more specific requirements for impairment reviews in the case of goodwill and intangible assets. Separate requirements apply depending on the period over which the intangible asset or goodwill is being amortised. Goodwill and intangible assets, amortised over a finite period of 20 years or less from the date of acquisition, should be reviewed for impairment at the end of the first full financial year following acquisition (and the standard permits a less extensive review process to be used for this) and in other periods if events or changes in circumstances indicate that the carrying value of the asset or goodwill may not be recoverable. Goodwill and intangible assets amortised over a period of more than 20 years from the date of acquisition, and any that are not amortised, must be reviewed for impairment at the end of each reporting period. Further details are given in **Chapter 19**.

Fixed assets not held to generate cash flows

20.57 The guidance in FRS 11 notes that, where fixed assets are not held for the purpose of generating cash flows, either individually or in conjunction with other assets (for instance, certain fixed assets held for charitable purposes), it may not be appropriate to write down the asset to recoverable amount on the basis of expected future cash flows. In this case, an alternative measure of service potential may be more appropriate.

Measuring impairment losses

20.58 When an impairment review is required, it should be carried out by comparing the carrying amount of the fixed asset with its recoverable amount. Recoverable amount is defined as the higher of net realisable value and value in use. Net realisable value is the amount at which the asset could be disposed of, less any direct selling costs. Value in use is the present value of the future cash flows obtainable as a result of the asset's continued use, including those resulting from its ultimate disposal. If the carrying value of the asset exceeds its recoverable amount, it is impaired and should be written down to the recoverable amount.

Using net realisable value

20.59 The first stage in an impairment review will usually be to estimate the net realisable value of the asset. If this is higher than the carrying amount, the asset is not impaired and no further work is required. If net realisable value is lower than the carrying amount of the asset, value in use will need to be established to see whether this is higher or lower than net realisable value. Even in this case, detailed value in use calculations will not always be required – a simple estimate will often be sufficient to indicate whether or not value in use is more than the carrying value of the asset (in which case there is no impairment) or less than net realisable value (in which case net realisable value will form the basis for recoverable amount). If value in use is lower than carrying value but higher than net realisable value, the impairment write-down will be based on value in use rather than on net realisable value, and more detailed calculations of value in use will be needed. If it is not possible to make a reliable estimate of net realisable value, the comparison of carrying amount with recoverable amount will need to be based on detailed calculations of value in use.

Impact of taxation

20.60 The guidance in FRS 11 emphasises that, in establishing whether recoverable amounts should be based on net realisable value or value in use, the deferred tax balances that would arise in each case must be taken into account. For example:

Example 20.11 – Impact of tax on recoverable amount

	Net realisable value	*Value in use*
	£	*£*
Asset value	100	110
Tax effect	(30)	(45)
	70	65

Although value in use may appear to be higher than net realisable value, after taking account of the tax effects in this case, it is clear that recoverable amount should be based on net realisable value and not on value in use.

Calculating net realisable value

20.61 Where an asset is traded on an active market, net realisable value should be based on market value. In other cases, it will be necessary to estimate the amount at which the asset could be disposed of. Any direct selling costs relating to the disposal of the asset, such as legal costs and stamp duty, should be deducted in arriving at net realisable value. The guidance in the standard also notes that costs relating to the removal of a sitting tenant are direct costs of selling the relevant building. However, costs that relate to a reduction or reorganisation of the business rather than the sale of the fixed asset are not direct selling costs and should not be taken into account.

Calculating value in use

20.62 The value in use of an asset is the present value of the future cash flows obtainable from the continued use of the asset and from its ultimate disposal. The standard requires value in use to be calculated for individual fixed assets wherever possible. In practice, it will often not be possible to calculate cash flows for an individual fixed asset. Cash flows normally result from the use of a group of assets and liabilities rather than from individual assets. In these circumstances, value in use can only be calculated for each group of assets and liabilities. The standard describes such a group of assets and liabilities as an income-generating unit. However, the guidance does note that only material impairments need to be identified and it may, therefore, be acceptable in certain circumstances to consider a group of income-generating units together rather than individually.

Identifying income-generating units

20.63 An income-generating unit is defined as:

> 'A group of assets, liabilities and associated goodwill that generates income that is largely independent of the reporting entity's other income streams. The assets and liabilities include those directly involved in generating the income and an appropriate proportion of those used to generate more than one income stream.'

Income-generating units should be identified by dividing the total income of the entity into as many largely independent income streams as is reasonably practicable. The individual income streams identified should be capable of being monitored separately and the units should be as small as is reasonably practicable. This approach is consistent with the normal prohibition on portfolio accounting. In practice, the income streams identified will usually reflect the way in which management monitors the business and takes decisions on the continuation or discontinuation of different lines of business. Income-generating units might be identified by reference to major products or services, or by reference to individual intangible assets, such as brands. The standard includes a number of examples showing how income-generating units might be identified in particular circumstances:

- a transport company running a network of trunk routes fed by a number of supporting routes, where decisions on continuing or closing the supporting routes are based on the contribution made to returns generated by the trunk routes - an income-generating unit comprises a trunk route plus the supporting routes associated with it;
- a manufacturer producing a product at a number of sites, not all of which are operating at full capacity so that the manufacturer can choose how much to make at each site, but with insufficient surplus capacity to enable any one site to be closed - the income-generating unit comprises all the sites at which the product can be made;
- a restaurant chain with a large number of restaurants throughout the country, for which cash flows can be individually monitored and to which costs can be allocated sensibly - each restaurant is an income-generating unit, although it may be acceptable to group together restaurants affected by the same economic factors;
- an entity with three stages of production:
  - growing and felling trees, some of the timber being transferred to the second production stage and some being sold externally;
  - creating parts of wooden furniture, all of which are transferred to the final production stage; and
  - assembling the parts into finished goods.

The first production stage forms an income-generating unit, and stages two and three together form a separate income-generating unit. The guidance notes that the cash flows for the two units should be based on market prices for the timber and not on any internal transfer pricing arrangements that may be in place.

Allocation of assets and liabilities

20.64 All of the assets and liabilities of the entity other than taxation, interest-bearing debt, dividends payable and other items relating wholly to financing, should be allocated to, or apportioned between, the income-generating units. The guidance notes that the income stream of a fixed asset that is awaiting disposal will be largely independent of the income streams of other assets and the asset should, therefore, be treated as a separate income-generating unit. Also, if there is any working capital in the balance sheet that will generate cash flows equal to its carrying amount, the guidance allows the carrying amount to be excluded from the value of the income-generating units and the cash flows to be excluded from the value in use calculations.

Allocation of central assets

20.65 In some cases it will be clear that individual assets and liabilities are directly related to the activities of one income-generating unit. In other cases, central assets may need to be apportioned across all the income-generating units on a logical and systematic basis. Central assets might include group and regional head offices and working capital. The total of the carrying amounts of the income-generating units should equal the carrying amount of the net assets (other than financing and taxation) of the entity as a whole. FRS 11 para 30 illustrates how this might work in practice:

Example 20.12 – Allocation of central assets

An entity has three independent income streams with the following directly involved net assets:

A Net assets of 100 million

B Net assets of 150 million

C Net assets of 200 million

In addition, there are head office net assets of £18 million, which are used by the three income streams in the proportion 2:3:4.

The income-generating units are defined as follows:

	A *£m*	*B* *£m*	*C* *£m*	*Total* *£m*
Net assets directly attributable	100	150	200	450
Head office net assets	4	6	8	18
Total	104	156	208	468

If a fixed asset in income-generating unit B was thought to be impaired, the recoverable amount of B should be compared with its carrying value of £156 million and the cash flows of B should include the relevant proportion of any cash outflows resulting from the central overheads.

Central assets that cannot sensibly be allocated

20.66 The standard acknowledges that, in some cases, it will not be possible to allocate certain central assets across the income-generating units in a sensible or logical manner. In this case, it requires the impairment review to be completed in two stages:

— the carrying amount of assets allocated directly to each individual income-generating unit should be compared with the value in use of the unit;

— the central assets should be tested for impairment by comparing the carrying value of all the income-generating units to which the central assets contribute, with the combined value in use of those units.

Example 20.13 – Testing central assets for impairment

Using the details in Example 20.12, but assuming that the central net assets cannot be sensibly allocated between the income-generating units, the first stage would be to compare the recoverable amount of B with its carrying value of £150 million in this case, and the second stage would be to compare the recoverable amount of the entity as a whole with its overall carrying value of £468 million.

Capitalised goodwill

20.67 Goodwill should be allocated to income-generating units in the same way as other assets and liabilities. However, where a number of income-generating units are acquired together as one investment, the units may be combined in order to assess the recoverability of the goodwill. This will also require the impairment review to be carried out in two stages:

— the income-generating units should be reviewed individually to assess the recoverability of tangible fixed assets and any intangible assets that have been capitalised;

— the combined units should then be reviewed to assess the recoverability of the goodwill.

FRS 11 para 35 illustrates this as follows:

Example 20.14 – Combining units to review goodwill

An entity acquires a business with three income-generating units. After five years, the carrying amount of the net assets in the units and the purchased goodwill compares with value in use as follows:

	A	*B*	*C*	*Goodwill*	*Total*
	£m	*£m*	*£m*	*£m*	*£m*
Carrying amount	80	120	140	50	390
Value in use	100	140	120		360

An impairment loss of £20 million should be recognised in respect of unit C to reduce its carrying amount to £120 million. This will reduce the total carrying amount of the entity to £370 million. A further impairment loss of £10 million will need to be recognised in respect of the goodwill to reduce the overall carrying amount of the entity to its value in use of £360 million.

Cash flows

20.68 The value in use of the individual income-generating units is the present value of the future cash flows obtainable as a result of their continued use and ultimate disposal. The standard requires the expected future cash flows, which should include those relating to any central overheads allocated to the units, to be:

- based on reasonable and supportable assumptions; and
- consistent with the most up-to-date budgets and plans already approved by management.

Cash flows for future periods not covered by formal plans and budgets should assume a steady or declining growth rate not exceeding the long-term average growth rate for the country or countries in which the business operates. The guidance notes that higher growth rates may be assumed in exceptional circumstances, for example, where the long-term growth rate for the industry is expected to be significantly higher than the average growth rate for the relevant country, and the business is expected to grow as rapidly as the industry as a whole, after allowing for the likelihood of new competitors. Specific additional disclosures are required in the accounts in any case where:

- the period before a steady or declining long-term growth rate has been assumed extends to more than five years; or
- the long-term growth rate used exceeds the long-term average growth rate for the country or countries in which the business operates.

Newly acquired units

20.69 The general rule is that future cash flows should be estimated for individual assets or income-generating units in their current condition. In particular they should not include:

- future cash outflows or related cost savings (eg reduced staff costs) or benefits expected to arise from a future reorganisation for which provision has not yet been made; or
- future capital expenditure that will improve or enhance the asset or income-generating unit in excess of the originally assessed standard of performance, or the related future benefits of this future expenditure.

However, in the case of a newly acquired income-generating unit (eg a new subsidiary), the standard acknowledges that the purchase price will often reflect the expected opportunities for making more effective use of the assets as a result of the acquisition. In some cases, the purchaser will undertake related capital expenditure, and possibly a reorganisation of the business, in order to maximise the benefits from its investment. In this situation, the standard allows the impairment review to take into account the costs and benefits of capital expenditure and reorganisations anticipated in the period up to the end of the first full year after acquisition, provided that they are consistent with management's budgets and plans at that time. If the capital expenditure or reorganisation does not take place as planned, the costs and benefits should be excluded from the cash flow projections prepared for subsequent impairment reviews. Failure to carry out the planned investment or reorganisation may be an indication that assets have become impaired and thus necessitate an impairment review.

Discount rates

20.70 The standard requires the expected future cash flows of an income-generating unit to be discounted at an estimate of the rate that the market would expect on an equally risky investment. The guidance notes that discount rates may be estimated by reference to:

— the rate implicit in market transactions of similar assets;

— the current weighted average cost of capital of a listed company whose cash flows have similar risk profiles to those of the income-generating unit;

— the weighted average cost of capital for the entity, provided that this is adjusted for the specific risks associated with the income-generating unit under review - the guidance emphasises that, if discount rates were calculated for each individual income-generating unit, the weighted average discount rate should equal the entity's overall weighted average cost of capital.

The standard requires the discount rate to be a pre-tax rate, and guidance is given in Appendix I to the standard on making appropriate adjustments to the weighted average cost of capital (which will be a post-tax rate). If cash flows are expressed in current prices, a real discount rate should be used, but if cash flows use expected future prices, a nominal discount rate will be used. In all cases, the discount rate used should be disclosed in the accounts.

Reflecting risk

20.71 As noted above, the standard requires the discount rate to reflect the risks associated with the cash flows by requiring the discount rate to be equivalent to the rate that the market would expect on an equally risky investment. The guidance explains that, as an alternative, it may be acceptable for the cash flows to be adjusted for risk and then discounted at a risk-free rate. The important point is to ensure that risk is not double-counted, for instance, by adjusting the cash flows for risk and then reflecting risk again in the discount rate that is applied to the adjusted cash flows. Where a risk-free discount rate is used, the accounts should include an indication of the risk adjustments that have been made to the cash flows.

Subsequent monitoring of cash flows

20.72 The standard includes specific measures to prevent abuse of the somewhat subjective and judgmental issues inevitably involved in basing impairment reviews on assessments of value in use. In each case, where an impairment review has involved the calculation of value in use, the actual cash flows must be compared with the projected cash flows for the five years following the review. Where the actual cash flows are significantly different from those forecast, such that a more accurate projection of the cash flows might have required the recognition of an impairment loss, the standard requires the original calculations to be reworked on the basis of the actual cash flows, but without altering other assumptions. Any impairment identified in the exercise must be recognised in the current period. The only exception is where the impairment has subsequently reversed and the recognition of the reversal would have been permitted under the strict requirements set out in the standard. In this case, the original impairment and its subsequent reversal must be disclosed in the accounts.

ACCOUNTING FOR IMPAIRMENT LOSSES

General rule

20.73 The general rule is that an impairment loss (ie the difference between the carrying amount of a fixed asset or goodwill and its recoverable amount) should be recognised in the profit and loss account of the period. However, a different approach is required in the case of fixed assets that have previously been revalued, as explained in **20.74** below.

Revalued fixed assets

20.74 If an impairment loss relating to a revalued fixed asset is caused by a clear consumption of economic benefits (for example, physical damage or a deterioration in the quality of service provided by the asset), it should be recognised in the profit and loss account. Other impairments of revalued assets (for instance, those arising from a general fall in prices) should be recognised in the statement of total recognised gains and losses until the carrying amount of the asset reaches its depreciated historical cost. Any further reduction below this amount should be recognised in the profit and loss account. It is important to keep detailed records of where impairment losses are recognised, in case reversals of the losses should need to be recognised in subsequent years.

Reversal of an impairment loss

20.75 The standard sets out different rules on the recognition of a reversal of an impairment loss for tangible fixed assets and investments, and for intangible assets and goodwill:

- in the case of tangible fixed assets and investments for which an impairment loss has been recognised, if the recoverable amount increases as a result of a change in economic conditions or in the expected use of the asset, the reversal should be recognised to the extent that it increases the carrying amount of the asset up to the amount that it would have been if the original impairment had not occurred;
- in the case of intangible assets and goodwill, the reversal of an impairment loss should only be recognised if:
  - an external event caused the recognition of the impairment loss in previous periods and subsequent external events clearly and demonstrably reverse the effects of that event in a way that was not foreseen in the original impairment calculations; or
  - the impairment loss arose on an intangible asset with a readily ascertainable market value and the net realisable value based on that market value has increased to above the asset's carrying amount.

Tangible fixed assets and investments

20.76 Events and circumstances that indicate an increase in the recoverable amount of an impaired asset are likely to be the reverse of those used in the standard to illustrate when impairment may have occurred. The guidance notes that they might include situations where capital investment or a reorganisation of the business, the benefits of which were excluded from the original calculations, have increased the recoverable amount of existing assets. However, increases in value that arise simply from the passage of time (eg increases in the discounted value of future cash inflows as they become closer) should not be recognised in the accounts. Any reversal recognised should only increase the asset to the value at which it would have been shown in the accounts if the original impairment loss had not been recognised. The recognition of any further increase in value would constitute a revaluation of the asset.

Intangible assets and goodwill

20.77 More stringent requirements apply in the case of intangible assets and goodwill and the approach in FRS 11 is consistent with that in FRS 10 'Goodwill and Intangible Assets'. Once again, where the recognition of a reversal is permitted by the standard, it should only increase the carrying amount of the goodwill or intangible asset to the amount at which it would have been shown if the original impairment loss had not been recognised. The recognition of any further increase in value would constitute a revaluation. FRS 10 specifically prohibits the revaluation of goodwill but permits the revaluation of intangible assets in certain circumstances as described in **Chapter 19**.

Recognition of a reversal of an impairment loss

20.78 The reversal of an impairment loss should be recognised in the profit and loss account of the current period unless it relates to a revalued asset, in which case it should be recognised in the profit and loss account to the extent that the original impairment loss (adjusted for subsequent depreciation) was recognised in the profit and loss account, and any additional amount should be recognised in the statement of total recognised gains and losses. It is, therefore, important to keep detailed records of where impairment losses are recognised, in case reversals of the losses should need to be recognised in subsequent years. In the year in which it is recognised, the accounts should disclose the reason for the reversal of the original impairment loss, including any changes in assumptions upon which the calculation of recoverable amount is based.

Allocation of impairment losses

20.79 The carrying amounts of the income-generating units under review should be calculated as the net of the carrying amounts of the assets, liabilities and goodwill allocated to the unit. To the extent that the carrying amount of the unit exceeds its recoverable amount, the unit is impaired. In the absence of an obvious impairment of specific assets within the unit, the impairment should be allocated in the following order:

- first, to any goodwill in the unit;
- then, to any capitalised intangible asset in the unit (subject to the proviso set out below); and
- finally, to the tangible assets in the unit, on a pro-rata or more appropriate basis (subject to the proviso below).

This allocation aims to write down the assets with the most subjective valuation first. However, no intangible asset with a readily ascertainable market value should be written down below its net realisable value. Similarly, no tangible asset with a net realisable value that can be measured reliably should be written down below its net realisable value. The standard gives the following example of the allocation and reversal of impairment losses:

Example 20.15 – Allocation and reversal of impairment losses

The recoverable amount of an income-generating unit falls to £60 million compared with a carrying amount of £140 million as a result of the product it makes being overtaken by a technologically advanced model produced by a competitor. The impairment loss is allocated as follows:

	Carrying amount £m	*Impairment* £m	*Revised amount* £m
Goodwill	40	(40)	—
Patent (with no market value)	20	(20)	—
Tangible fixed assets	80	(20)	60
	140	(80)	60

After three years, the company makes a technological breakthrough of its own and the recoverable amount of the income-generating unit increases to £90 million. If the impairment had not occurred, the carrying value of the tangible fixed assets would have been £70 million.

The reversal of the impairment loss is recognised to the extent that it increases the carrying amount of the fixed assets to what it would have been if the original impairment had not been recognised – ie £10 million of the impairment loss is reversed to increase the carrying value of tangible fixed assets to £70 million.

No reversal is recognised in respect of the impairment of the goodwill and intangible asset, because the effect of the external event that caused the impairment has not reversed (ie the original product has still been overtaken by a more advanced model).

Goodwill in a merged business

20.80 Where an acquired business is merged with an existing business it will result in an income-generating unit that contains both purchased and internally-generated goodwill (ie goodwill that is not allowed to be recognised for accounts purposes). In this case, a notional adjustment should be made to the carrying amount of the income-generating unit to take account of the goodwill of the existing business at the date of the acquisition so that any future impairment can be apportioned between the two elements of the merged business. The process will, therefore, be as follows:

- the notional carrying amount of the internally-generated goodwill should be estimated by deducting the fair values of the net assets and purchased goodwill within the existing income-generating unit from its estimated value in use before the combination with the acquired business – the notional goodwill should be assumed to be subject to the same pattern of amortisation as the purchased goodwill;
- the notional value of the internally-generated goodwill of the existing business should be added to the carrying amount of the income generating unit for the purposes of performing impairment reviews;
- any impairment of the existing business will have been recognised in the comparison of fair values with value in use in the first stage above – any impairment arising on merging the businesses should, therefore, be allocated solely to the purchased goodwill within the newly-acquired business;

- subsequent impairments should be allocated between the goodwill of the acquired business and that of the existing business, pro rata to their carrying values;
- the impairment allocated to the existing business should be allocated first to the notional internally-generated goodwill; and
- only the impairments allocated to purchased goodwill (and, if necessary, to any recognised intangible or tangible assets) should be recognised in the financial statements.

Paragraph 53 of the standard includes an example of this process. The calculations will need to be carried out whenever an acquisition that gives rise to goodwill is merged with an existing business.

Presentation of impairment losses

20.81 Impairment losses recognised in the profit and loss account should be included within operating profit under the appropriate statutory heading and disclosed as an exceptional item if appropriate. Impairment losses recognised in the statement of total recognised gains and losses should be disclosed separately on the face of that statement. In the notes to the financial statements for accounting periods after the impairment, the impairment loss should be treated as follows:

- for assets held on a historical cost basis, the impairment loss should be included within cumulative depreciation - the cost of the asset should not be reduced;
- for revalued assets held at market value (eg existing use or open market value), the impairment loss should be included within the revalued carrying amount; and
- for revalued assets held at depreciated replacement cost:
  - an impairment loss charged to the profit and loss account should be included within cumulative depreciation (ie the carrying amount of the asset should not be reduced); and
  - an impairment loss charged to the statement of total recognised gains and losses should be deducted from the carrying amount of the asset.

Additional disclosures

20.82 The standard requires the following additional disclosures in the notes to the financial statements:

- if the impairment loss is measured by reference to the value in use of a fixed asset or income-generating unit, the discount rate applied to the cash flows should be disclosed - if a risk-free discount rate is used, some indication of the risk adjustment made to the cash flows should be given;

- where an impairment loss previously recognised is reversed in the current period, the financial statements should disclose the reason for the reversal, including any changes in the assumptions upon which the calculation of recoverable amount is based;
- where an impairment loss would have been recognised in an earlier period if the forecasts of future cash flows had been more accurate, but the impairment has reversed and recognition of the reversal is permitted, the impairment now identified, and its subsequent reversal, should be disclosed;
- where, in measuring value in use, the period before a steady or declining long-term growth rate has been assumed to extend to more than five years, the length of the longer period and the circumstances justifying it should be disclosed;
- where, in measuring value in use, the long-term growth rate used has exceeded the long-term average growth rate for the country or countries in which the business operates, the growth rate assumed and the circumstances justifying it should be disclosed.

INVESTMENT PROPERTIES

Treatment under accounting standards

20.83 The expression 'investment property' is not used in CA 1985 and no distinction is made in the legislation between accounting for investment properties and accounting for other properties shown as tangible fixed assets in the accounts. In contrast, accounting standards require totally different accounting treatments for investment properties and other properties included in tangible fixed assets. FRS 15 'Tangible Fixed Assets' covers all other tangible fixed assets but does not apply to investment properties. SSAP 19 'Accounting for Investment Properties' sets out the accounting treatment to be adopted for this particular category of property. As is usual with accounting standards, the requirements of SSAP 19 need not be applied to immaterial items. The materiality of an investment property should, therefore, be considered in the context of the company's other assets. For instance, if a large manufacturing company with several freehold production sites also holds one relatively small investment property, it will not usually be necessary to apply SSAP 19 to the investment property.

Definition of investment property

20.84 An investment property is defined in SSAP 19 as an interest in land and buildings:

- in respect of which construction work and development have been completed; and

— which is held for its investment potential, any rental income being negotiated at arm's length.

Investment properties may be held by a company specialising in investments, such as an investment trust or a property investment company, or may be held by a company which has a different business as its main activity. However, a property owned and occupied by a company for its own purpose, or let to and occupied by another group company, is specifically excluded from the definition of an investment property.

Need for different treatment

20.85 The introductory note to SSAP 19 explains that a different accounting treatment is considered necessary for such properties because:

— the properties are held for investment rather than consumption, and disposal would not materially affect the trading operations of the entity;

— the current value of the investment, and changes in that value, are of more importance than systematic depreciation.

The only exception to this is in the case of leasehold property with a relatively short term remaining, where annual depreciation should continue to be charged. In practice this is usually taken to be a remaining term of 20 years or less.

Requirements of SSAP 19

20.86 SSAP 19 requires an investment property to be accounted for as follows:

— the property should be included in the balance sheet at its open market value;

— changes in the market value should normally be taken to an investment revaluation reserve, and reflected in the statement of total recognised gains and losses, unless a deficit is considered to be permanent, in which case it should be charged to the profit and loss account;

— the property should not be subject to periodic charges for depreciation.

Separate rules apply in the case of investment companies, property unit trusts, insurance companies and pension funds. These are not dealt with in this manual. Property valuations will sometimes include an element that reflects rent on a lease agreed with a tenant. UITF Abstract 28 'Operating Lease Incentives' emphasises that the value at which an investment property is stated in the balance sheet should not include any amount that is already reported as a separate asset in the same balance sheet. For instance, SSAP 21 'Accounting for Leases and Hire Purchase Contracts' and UITF Abstract 28 require both the rent receivable under a lease and any related incentive to be recognised over the term of the lease (or the period to the first rent review if shorter), usually on a straight-line basis. Where a lease includes an incentive such as an initial rent-free period, the timing of the recognition of the rent receivable will differ from the actual cash flows, and the lessor's balance sheet will, therefore, include a debtor for accrued rent receivable. If the open market value of the investment property includes an element to reflect rent receivable under the lease, the amount already included as a debtor should be deducted from the valuation to prevent any double-counting of this element of the asset.

Departure from the requirements of CA 1985

20.87 Since CA 1985 does not distinguish between investment properties and other properties and, therefore, requires an investment property to be included in the accounts at either cost or valuation and to be depreciated over its useful life in the same way as any other tangible fixed asset, compliance with the requirements of SSAP 19 in respect of investment properties will usually constitute a departure from the requirements of the Act. Compliance with SSAP 19 will, therefore, usually require the use of the true and fair override, unless:

- the estimated residual value of the property (calculated in accordance with FRS 15) is at least equal to its carrying value; or
- the estimated residual value of the property is so close to its carrying value that any depreciation would be immaterial.

Further consideration of both of these issues is set out in **Chapter 12**.

Disclosure of true and fair override

20.88 The use of the true and fair override is considered in more detail in **Chapter 2**, along with the specific disclosures required under FRS 18 'Accounting Policies'. The disclosures normally require the effect of the departure from the Act to be quantified. In the case of investment properties, this would require disclosure of the effect of not depreciating the investment property. However, the calculation of depreciation in respect of an investment property may not always be possible. In 1981 the Department of Trade and Industry recognised this by indicating to the accountancy bodies at the time that inclusion of the following wording in respect of depreciation would meet the disclosure requirements of the Act in this case: 'Depreciation or amortisation is only one of the many factors reflected in the annual valuation and the amount which might otherwise have been shown cannot be separately identified or quantified'. The following is an example of wording that might be appropriate to explain the use of the true and fair override where investment properties are accounted for under SSAP 19.

Example 20.16 – Disclosure to reflect the true and fair view override

In accordance with SSAP 19:

— investment properties are revalued annually and the aggregate surplus or deficit is transferred to a revaluation reserve; and

— no depreciation or amortisation is provided in respect of freehold investment properties and leasehold investment properties with over 20 years to run.

The Companies Act 1985 requires tangible fixed assets to be depreciated systematically over their estimated useful economic lives. However, investment properties are held for investment rather than consumption; the directors therefore consider that depreciation on a systematic basis would not be appropriate in this case and that the accounting policy adopted is necessary for the accounts to give a true and fair view. Depreciation or amortisation is only one of the many factors reflected in the annual valuation and the amount which might otherwise have been shown cannot be separately identified or quantified.

Valuation of investment properties

20.89 SSAP 19 does not require the annual valuation to be carried out independently of the company or by professional or qualified valuers. However, where investment properties represent a substantial proportion of total assets, and the company is a major enterprise, the notes suggest that:

— the annual valuation should normally be carried out by persons holding a recognised professional qualification and with appropriate recent experience of the relevant locality and the type of property being valued;

— the valuation should be carried out by an external valuer at least every five years.

Accounts disclosures

20.90 SSAP 19 requires the following details to be given in the accounts:

— the names of the valuers, or details of their qualifications;

— the bases of valuation used;

— if the valuer is an employee or officer of the company, this fact must also be disclosed.

The standard also requires the carrying value of investment properties and the investment revaluation reserve to be displayed prominently in the annual accounts. Additional disclosures may be needed under RICS requirements (see **20.51** above).

Historical cost of investment properties

20.91 The historical cost of investment properties will continue to require disclosure under CA 1985 (because investment properties are fixed assets included in the accounts at valuation under the alternative accounting rules – see **Chapter 1**), but there will be no related cumulative depreciation to disclose.

Accounting policy

20.92 SSAP 19 does not specifically require disclosure of the accounting policy adopted in respect of investment properties, but where they are sufficiently material to be accounted for in accordance with the standard, disclosure will normally be necessary under the requirements of FRS 18 'Accounting Policies'. Normal practice would be to include the explanation of the accounting policy and the use of the true and fair override in the section of the accounts setting out the detailed accounting policies (see **20.87** above).

Tangible fixed asset or investment?

20.93 Neither the Act, nor SSAP 19, provides any guidance on whether investment properties should be included in the balance sheet under tangible fixed assets or under investments. Arguments can be put forward for disclosure in either category and the main issue, therefore, is for each individual company to be consistent in its approach.

ACCOUNTING FOR LEASED ASSETS

Distinction between leases and hire purchase agreements

20.94 Under a lease agreement, a company usually obtains the right to use an asset, but title to the leased asset does not usually pass to the lessee under the agreement. Hire purchase contracts are similar to leases, but in this case legal title will usually pass at the end of the agreement, sometimes on the exercise of an option by the purchaser. Hire purchase contracts which are similar in characteristics to finance leases should be accounted for in the same way as finance leases.

Definition of a finance lease

20.95 Under SSAP 21 'Accounting for Leases and Hire Purchase Contracts', both lessees and lessors must classify all leasing agreements as finance leases or operating leases and apply different accounting treatments, depending on the nature of the lease. A finance lease is defined in SSAP 21 as a lease that transfers substantially all the risks and rewards of ownership of an asset to the lessee. Under a finance lease, the lessee will usually pay the full cost of the asset, together with a return to the lessor in respect of the finance that has effectively been provided. A lease should normally be presumed to be a finance lease when, at the inception of the lease, the present value of the minimum lease payments, including any initial payment, amounts to substantially all of the fair value of the leased asset. 'Substantially all' is defined as normally 90% or more. However, this presumption will not apply if it is clear that the lease does not transfer substantially all the risks and rewards to the lessee, even if the 90% condition is met. Any lease that does not qualify as a finance lease is an operating lease.

Asset value at end of lease term

20.96 The expected value of the asset at the end of the lease term, and who benefits from this, can also help to establish whether the lease is a finance lease. If the value of the asset is likely to be insignificant, the lease will usually be a finance lease. If the value of the asset is significant and the benefit will rest with the lessee, this will also usually indicate that the lease is a finance lease. For instance, a lease agreement will often include a clause preventing the lessee from purchasing the asset at the end of the agreement but, if the lessee has the right to any sales proceeds relating to the asset, or has a right to a guaranteed residual value at the end of the agreement, the benefit to the lessee will be similar to that of having title to the asset at the end of the agreement.

Impact of FRS 5 'Accounting for the Substance of Transactions'

20.97 The classification of leases can be a highly complex issue, especially as agreements sometimes include clauses which are intended to ensure that the lease fails the 90% test in SSAP 21, or which appear to leave most of the risks with the lessor (although, in some cases, the actual risk retained by the lessor through these clauses may be minimal). Such clauses are intended to enable the lessee to justify not bringing the lease and the related obligation onto the balance sheet. Although the detailed requirements of SSAP 21 still stand, the more general requirements of FRS 5 'Accounting for the Substance of Transactions' apply equally to leasing transactions (see **Chapter 3**). Where the substance of a lease agreement is that of a finance lease, it will have to be accounted for as such, even though the specific tests in SSAP 21 may not be met.

Guidance notes on SSAP 21

20.98 The guidance notes on SSAP 21 set out in considerable detail the practical issues relating to both lessee and lessor accounting, and as well as considering some of the general problem areas associated with lease accounting, provide guidance on accounting for some of the particularly complex leasing transactions such as:

— sale and leaseback arrangements;

— sub-leases and back-to-back leases;

— leasing by manufacturers and dealers.

Initial recording of asset and liability by lessee

20.99 Under SSAP 21, leases that are classified as finance leases should be recorded in the lessee's balance sheet as an asset and as an obligation to pay future rentals to the lessor. At the inception of the lease (which is defined in the standard as the earlier of the date when the asset is brought into use or the date from which rental payments accrue), the amount recorded as an asset and the obligation recorded to the lessor will be the same. Strictly this should be the present value of the minimum lease payments. The minimum lease payments are defined in the standard as:

> 'the minimum payments over the remaining part of the lease term (excluding charges for services and taxes to be paid by the lessor) and, in the case of the lessee, any residual amounts guaranteed by him or by a party related to him.'

This should include any initial payment made by the lessee under the agreement. However, the standard emphasises that, for practical purposes, the fair value of the leased asset will usually be a sufficiently close approximation to the present value of the minimum lease payments to make the fair value an acceptable figure to use when initially recording the asset and the related obligation to the lessor. Fair value is defined as 'the price at which an asset could be exchanged in an arm's length transaction less, where applicable, any grants receivable towards the purchase or use of the asset'. An example of the calculation of the present value of the minimum lease payments is given in **Chapter 13**, along with examples of accounting for finance charges in respect of leased assets.

Depreciation of asset by lessee

20.100 The leased asset must be depreciated over its expected useful economic life in the same way as any other fixed asset, but the life used should not exceed the lease term. The lease term is defined in SSAP 21 as:

— the period for which the lessee has contracted to lease the asset; and

— any further terms for which the lessee has the option to continue to lease the asset, with or without further payment, when it is reasonably certain at the inception of the lease that the lessee will exercise this option.

Consideration of whether an option is likely to be exercised will usually include:

— how the lessee has dealt with similar lease options in the past;

— whether there are any penalties for not extending the lease, which might, therefore, encourage the lessee to exercise the option;

— whether the terms of the option are commercially realistic (ie is the option genuine, or will the agreement only make commercial sense if the lessee exercises the option?).

The depreciation of fixed assets is considered in more detail in **Chapter 12**.

Accounts disclosures by lessee

20.101 The policies adopted for accounting for operating leases and finance leases must be disclosed in the accounts of the lessee. Wording along with following lines will usually be appropriate:

Example 20.17 – Disclosure of accounting policies

Finance leases

Where the company enters into a lease which transfers substantially all the risks and rewards of ownership of the asset to the company, the lease is accounted for as a finance lease. The leased asset is included in tangible fixed assets at its fair value at the inception of the lease and the company's obligation to the lessor is recorded at the same amount. The asset is depreciated on the straight-line basis over the shorter of the lease term and the expected useful economic life of the asset. Rental payments are apportioned between the finance charge, which is charged to the profit and loss account, and the capital repayment element, which reduces the outstanding obligation, so that the finance charge for each accounting period represents a constant percentage of the capital sum outstanding.

Operating leases

Other leases are accounted for as operating leases, and the rental payments are charged to the profit and loss account on a straight-line basis over the term of the lease.

Where assets under finance leases (or hire purchase contracts similar to finance leases) are included in fixed assets, SSAP 21 also requires the following disclosures in the accounts:

— the gross amounts of assets held under finance leases and the related accumulated depreciation by each major class of asset; or

— where leased assets are integrated with other fixed assets, the net amount of assets held under finance leases, together with the depreciation for the period in respect of leased assets.

There are two alternative methods of meeting the disclosure requirements in respect of assets under finance leases within tangible fixed assets, both of which are in common use:

- a separate column (or columns, if the assets fall into more than one main category) can be included in the fixed assets table, headed 'Assets under finance leases' – in this case, all movements during the year in respect of the leased assets will be disclosed; or
- the net book value of leased assets can be included as a footnote to the table and the depreciation charge in respect of leased assets can be disclosed as part of this note or as part of the profit and loss account disclosures on depreciation for the year.

Example 20.18 – Footnote disclosures for leased assets

The above net book values include the following amounts in respect of assets held under finance leases.

	20X2	*20X1*
	£	£
Plant and machinery	125,460	89,670
Fixtures, fittings, tools and equipment	85,673	56,799
	211,133	146,469

Depreciation of £40,561 (20X1: £23,557) was charged in the year in respect of these assets.

Assets held by lessor for use in operating leases

20.102 In the accounts of a lessor, assets held for use in operating leases must be recorded as fixed assets and depreciated over their expected useful economic lives. The assets should, therefore, be capitalised in accordance with the normal requirements of CA 1985 (ie usually at purchase price or production cost) and depreciated in accordance with the requirements of FRS 15 'Tangible Fixed Assets'. Within fixed assets, the gross amount of assets held for use in operating leases must be disclosed, along with the related accumulated depreciation. This disclosure requirement is usually met by including these assets in a separate column in the fixed assets table, and thus disclosing all movements during the year, including depreciation. The policies adopted for accounting for operating leases and finance leases must also be disclosed in the accounts of the lessor including, in detail, the policy for accounting for finance lease income. The following wording may be suitable, but this will, of course, depend on the exact policies followed.

Example 20.19 – Disclosures of policies for operating leases and finance leases

Assets held for use in operating leases are included in tangible fixed assets at cost and are depreciated on the straight-line method over their expected useful economic lives. The following asset lives are used:

.... years

.... years

Gross earnings from operating leases are recognised in the profit and loss account on a straight-line basis over the period of each lease. The initial direct costs incurred in negotiating and arranging operating leases are charged to the profit and loss account in the period in which they are incurred.

Amounts due from lessees in respect of assets held under finance leases are included in debtors at the amount of the net investment in the lease.

Rental payments under finance leases are apportioned between interest, which is credited to the profit and loss account as gross earnings, and repayment of capital, which reduces the amount due from the lessee. Gross earnings from finance leases are allocated to accounting periods to give a constant periodic rate of return on the net cash investment in the lease, using the investment period method of allocation. The initial direct costs incurred in negotiating and arranging finance leases are charged to the profit and loss account in the period in which they are incurred.

Classification of property leases

20.103 SSAP 21's requirements apply to property leases in the same way as to leases involving other assets. Both lessees and lessors must, therefore, classify each property lease as either a finance lease or an operating lease and the normal accounting and disclosure requirements will apply. Short-term leases will generally be operating leases, as the lessor will usually retain the long-term benefits of ownership of the property, although the position may be different if the property is very specialised. In general, long-term leases are more likely to be finance leases, although the specific terms of the lease agreement, and the length of the agreement, may mean that the lease qualifies as an operating lease.

Sale and leaseback arrangements

20.104 Particular care is required in accounting for sale and leaseback transactions involving property. Many of these will be financing arrangements rather than genuine sales and, if so, should be accounted for as finance leases under the requirements of both SSAP 21 and FRS 5. Sale and leaseback arrangements are considered in detail in the guidance notes attached to SSAP 21 and, in effect, are also covered by Application Note B of FRS 5. Where a sale and leaseback arrangement results in a finance lease, SSAP 21 requires any difference between the selling price and the previous carrying value to be deferred and amortised in the accounts of the seller/lessee over the shorter of the lease term or the useful life of the asset. Where a sale and leaseback arrangement results in an operating lease, SSAP 21 requires the following treatment of any profit or loss on the sale:

— if it is clear that the transaction is at fair value, the profit or loss should be recognised immediately;

— if the selling price is below fair value, any profit or loss should be recognised immediately, except where the apparent loss is compensated for by future rentals that are below market price - in this case, the loss should be deferred and amortised over the remainder of the lease term (or the period during which the reduced rentals apply, if this is shorter);

— if the selling price is above fair value, the excess over fair value should be deferred and amortised over the remainder of the lease term (or the period to the next rent review, if this is shorter).

ACCOUNTING FOR COSTS RELATING TO THE INTRODUCTION OF THE EURO

The basic issues

20.105 UITF Abstract 21 'Accounting Issues Arising from the Proposed Introduction of the Euro' notes that entities may incur a variety of costs associated with the introduction of the euro. Depending on individual circumstances, these might include:

— administrative and planning costs;

— staff training;

— the provision of relevant information to customers;

— software modification costs; and

— the adaptation of relevant hardware (vending machines, cash registers etc).

There may also be implications for accounting for foreign currency translation. The issues considered by the UITF included:

— whether costs incurred in connection with the introduction of the euro should be charged as an expense or capitalised as an asset, and what disclosure should be given in the accounts;

— the impact that the irrevocable locking of the national currencies of participating Member States will have on cumulative foreign exchange differences recognised in periods before the introduction of the euro; and

— the impact that the irrevocable locking of the national currencies of participating Member States will have on anticipatory hedging instruments existing at the date of introduction of the euro in respect of future transactions.

Accounting for modification of assets

20.106 The consensus on accounting for costs arising from the introduction of the euro is that the costs of modifying or adapting assets to deal with the introduction of the euro should generally be written off to the profit and loss account. The only exception is where the entity already has an accounting policy for capitalising assets of the relevant type and the expenditure clearly results in an enhancement of economic benefits by extending the service potential of an asset beyond that originally assessed, rather than merely maintaining its current service potential. Costs that do not give rise to assets should be charged to the profit and loss account as they are incurred.

When provision should be made

20.107 Under the requirements of FRS 12 'Provisions, Contingent Liabilities and Contingent Assets', a mere intention or even the necessity to undertake future expenditure will not necessarily give rise to a liability. Costs associated with the introduction of the euro should, therefore, be recognised in the accounting period in which the work is actually carried out and no provision should be made in earlier accounting periods for estimated future costs.

Disclosure

20.108 In some cases, costs associated with the introduction of the euro may require disclosure as exceptional items under the requirements of FRS 3 'Reporting Financial Performance' and significant commitments in respect of modification costs may need to be disclosed under the requirements of CA 1985. The Abstract also recommends that additional information is given where the potential impact for the reporting entity is likely to be significant. The additional disclosures should include an indication of the total costs likely to be incurred and can be given in the directors' report, an operating and financial review or any other statement published as part of the annual report.

ACCOUNTING FOR WEBSITE DEVELOPMENT COSTS

Categories of development cost

20.109 Websites are now used for a wide range of business purposes and companies frequently incur significant costs in developing their websites. UITF Abstract 29 'Website Development Costs' was issued in February 2001 and is effective for accounting periods ending on or after 23 March 2001, although earlier adoption is encouraged. The Abstract analyses website development costs into four principle categories:

- planning costs;
- application and infrastructure costs;
- design costs; and
- content costs.

Planning costs

20.110 Planning costs include the costs of undertaking a feasibility study, determining the objectives of the website, exploring ways of achieving those objectives, identifying appropriate hardware and software and choosing suitable suppliers and consultants. The Abstract notes that planning costs do not in themselves give rise to future economic benefits controlled by the entity and should, therefore, not be recognised as assets in the financial statements. All website planning costs should be charged to the profit and loss account as they are incurred.

Application and infrastructure costs

20.111 Application and infrastructure costs include the costs of obtaining and registering a domain name, and buying or developing appropriate hardware and operating software. These costs will usually give rise to an asset and should therefore be capitalised. The UITF specifically considered whether such costs should be capitalised as tangible or intangible assets and concluded that, although websites do not fit either classification perfectly, it is most appropriate for the costs to be capitalised as tangible fixed assets. This is mainly on the basis of FRS 10 'Goodwill and Intangible Assets' para 2 which states that:

> 'Software development costs that are directly attributable to bringing a computer system or other computer-operated machinery into working condition for its intended use within the business are treated as part of the cost of the related hardware rather than as a separate intangible asset.'

The guidance in the Abstract notes that this treatment should be adopted irrespective of whether the reporting entity owns the related hardware.

Design and content costs

20.112 Website design and content costs are considered together in the Abstract. They include costs to develop the design and appearance of individual website pages and preparing and posting the website content. As there is often uncertainty over the viability, value and useful economic life of a website, the UITF took the view that website design and content costs should be capitalised only to the extent that they lead to the creation of an enduring asset that delivers benefits at least as great as the amount capitalised. This will only apply where:

- the expenditure is separately identifiable;
- the technical feasibility and commercial viability of the website have been assessed with reasonable certainty;
- the website will generate sales or other revenues directly (eg orders placed via the website, amounts paid by subscribers for access to information on the website, revenues from selling advertising space on the website), and the expenditure makes an enduring contribution to the development of the revenue-generating capabilities of the website – where the website is used only for advertising or promotion, it will not usually be possible to demonstrate that sales or revenue are generated directly from the website;
- there is a reasonable expectation that the present value of future cash flows to be generated by the website will be no less than the amounts capitalised in respect of the revenue-generating activity; and
- adequate resources exist, or are reasonably expected to be available, to enable the website project to be completed and to provide any consequential increases in working capital.

If there is insufficient evidence on which to base reasonable estimates of the economic benefits to be generated, website design and content costs should be charged to the profit and loss account as they are incurred.

Capitalisation of costs

20.113 The UITF concluded that it would be difficult to separate website development costs into tangible and intangible assets, and that to do so would serve no practical purpose. Therefore, where capitalisation of website design and content costs is justified:

- they should be capitalised as tangible fixed assets, together with the related application and infrastructure costs, in accordance with the requirements of FRS 15 'Tangible Fixed Assets';
- the asset should be amortised over its estimated useful economic life which, given the rapid rate of technological development, is likely to be short – the useful life should be reviewed at the end of each accounting period and revised where necessary;
- where the design or content of a website requires more frequent replacement than the website as a whole, it may be appropriate to select a shorter depreciation period for the design and content costs than for the remaining elements of the asset;
- the asset should be reviewed for impairment if events or changes in circumstances indicate that the carrying amount may not be recoverable.

Accounting for subsequent costs

20.114 Expenditure to maintain or operate a website once it has been developed should be charged to the profit and loss account as incurred, in accordance with the requirements of FRS 15 'Tangible Fixed Assets'.

LIKELY FUTURE DEVELOPMENTS

ASB Discussion Paper 'Leases: Implementation of a New Approach'

20.115 The ASB Discussion Paper 'Leases: Implementation of a New Approach' was issued in December 1999. This document represents a Position Paper developed by the G4+1 group of accounting standard-setters and reflects an agreed international approach to the treatment of leases in financial reporting. In particular it proposes removing the sometimes arbitrary distinction between operating and finance leases and applying the same accounting treatment to all leases. The proposals affect both lessee and lessor accounting. The Discussion Paper is a very detailed document and only the key points raised are summarised here.

Potential impact in the UK

20.116 The Board notes that it does not agree with all of the views expressed in the Paper, but it does consider that there is a strong case for change and that the approach set out in the Paper merits serious consideration. In particular, it notes that the present distinction between operating and finance leases is unsatisfactory and that the comparability and usefulness of financial statements would be improved by introducing a single accounting treatment for all leases. The foreword to the document highlights the following aspects where the Board may wish to adopt a slightly different approach to that put forward in the Paper:

- the Paper suggests that, where property leases provide for rent reviews to reflect price changes, those changes should be reflected in the assets and liabilities recorded on inception of the lease – the ASB prefers the alternative approach, where only existing rentals are recorded on inception and adjustments are made when a rent review actually takes place;
- at present, lessors are required to adopt the net cash investment method in accounting for leases although, in practice, the net investment method may often be used on the grounds that it does not result in materially different amounts – the ASB would wish to retain this approach.

Structure of the Paper

20.117 The Paper deals with the following issues:

- **Introduction and scope**: This section reviews the current arrangements on accounting for leases, highlights the difficulties that arise and summarises the approach taken in the present Paper. A separate chapter looks in detail at the characteristics of leases and the rights and obligations that they create, and compares leases with other forms of contract.
- **Leases in the financial statements of lessees**: This section looks in detail at the assets and liabilities of lessees and how these should be measured for accounting purposes. It also considers the impact of optional features of a lease (eg renewal or purchase options), the role of probability in determining the assets and liabilities that arise from the lease contract and dealing with any residual interests that may be conveyed to the lessee. Separate chapters consider discounting and discount rates, and sale and leaseback transactions.
- **Leases in the financial statements of lessors**: This section analyses the assets that arise for lessors under a lease contract and considers how these should be measured and presented in financial statements. Separate chapters cover leases with optional features and subsequent remeasurement in the financial statements.
- **Other issues**: This section covers property leases and issues relating to fair value.

Proposals on leases put forward by the G4+1 group in 1996 were criticised on the grounds that, for consistency, the suggested approach would also need to be applied to executory contracts. The current Paper draws a distinction between leases and executory contracts and emphasises that the proposals are not intended to apply to any form of executory contracts including, for instance, take-or-pay contracts or service contracts.

Accounting by lessees

20.118 The Paper proposes that, for all leases, the objective should be to record, at the beginning of the lease term, the fair value of the rights and obligations conveyed by the lease. Fair value is measured by the fair value of the consideration given by the lessee, including any liabilities incurred, except where the fair value of the asset received is clearly more evident. The fair value of the rights obtained by the lessee cannot be less than the present value of the minimum lease payments required by the lease, assuming that the lease is negotiated on an arm's-length basis. The Paper identifies the following amounts that should be included in, or excluded from, the assets and liabilities at the beginning of the lease.

- Included in initial assets and liabilities:
  - minimum payments required by lease;

  - amounts payable in respect of obtaining renewal options;
  - contingent rentals representing consideration for the fair value of rights conveyed by the lease; and
  - fair value of residual value guarantees.
- Excluded from initial assets and liabilities:
  - rentals relating to optional renewal periods;
  - contingent rentals relating to optional additional usage; and
  - residual values guaranteed where transfer of economic benefits in settlement is not probable.

Operating leases

20.119 Leases that are currently accounted for as operating leases and are, therefore, not included in the balance sheet still give rise to assets and liabilities, but only to the extent of the rights and obligations conveyed by the lease. The general effect of the proposed approach would be to recognise varying amounts of assets and liabilities depending on the nature of the lease. The different financial obligations and the financial flexibility resulting from operating leases would, therefore, be reflected in the amounts shown in the financial statements.

Discount rates

20.120 The discount rate to be applied by lessees to the rental payments should be:

- an estimate of the lessee's incremental borrowing rate for a loan of similar term and with the same security as is provided by the lease; or
- the rate implicit in the lease when it is known by the lessee and represents a reasonable approximation for the rate referred to above.

Accounting by lessors

20.121 The Paper concludes that a lessor's interest in a leased asset has two distinct elements: the amounts receivable from the lessee, and the residual interest in the leased asset. As these two assets are subject to very different risks, it proposes that they should be reported separately in the lessor's balance sheet. The amounts receivable from the lessee should be recorded initially at fair value, representing the fair value of the consideration that the lessee has agreed to pay and should be recorded as a financial asset. The fair value of the rights conveyed by the lease cannot be less than the present value of the minimum lease payments required by the lease, assuming that it is negotiated on an arm's-length basis. Residual interests, both guaranteed and unguaranteed, should be shown as non-financial assets, and information should be provided to enable users to understand the lessor's residual value exposures. This should include information on the existence of residual guarantees and similar agreements.

FRED 29 'Property, plant and equipment; Borrowing costs'

20.122 The ASB issued FRED 29 'Property, plant and equipment; Borrowing costs' in May 2002 as part of its project to achieve convergence between UK accounting standards and international accounting standards. The Exposure Draft proposes replacing FRS 15 'Tangible fixed assets' with two new standards based on a revised IAS 16 and the existing IAS 23. Much of the content of these two international standards is consistent with current UK requirements. The main differences are in relation to the accounting treatment of revalued assets, in particular the use of a 'fair value' model rather than the UK's present 'value to the business' approach. A separate international group is currently considering the issue of revaluation and whether changes should be made to the present IAS requirements. The ASB is participating in this project and is continuing to press for IAS 16 to incorporate the revaluation principles currently set out in FRS 15. If it is clear at the time that the present proposals to revise IAS 16 are finalised, that the revaluation project will result in a further revision of that standard before 2005, the ASB will defer the finalisation of new UK standards. However, if at that time further changes to the international standard seem unlikely, the ASB proposes to issue revised UK standards based on FRED 29.

Proposed changes in respect of revaluations

20.123 If the proposals in FRED 29 are implemented, the main changes in respect of revalued assets will be:

- FRED 29 requires revaluation to fair value, whereas FRS 15 requires revaluation to current value - in particular, FRED 29 states that the fair value of property, plant and equipment is usually its market value, whilst FRS 15 requires valuation on the basis of existing use value for non-specialised properties, depreciated replacement cost for specialised properties and open market value for properties that are surplus to the entity's requirements;
- FRED 29 requires valuations to be kept up to date but does not specify a maximum period between valuations, although it indicates that annual revaluation may be needed for assets that experience significant and volatile changes in value and that revaluation every three to five years will usually be sufficient for other assets - FRS 15 requires a full valuation at least every five years with interim updates in the intervening period;
- the basis of valuations is covered in less detail in FRED 29 - for instance:

  - there is no requirement to use an external valuer at least every five years (although FRED 29 does note that property valuations should normally be undertaken by qualified valuers);
  - the detailed guidance in FRS 15 on full and interim valuations is not repeated in FRED 29;
  - there is no guidance on the use of appropriate indices to value plant and machinery;
  - there is no reference to notional directly attributable acquisition or selling costs;
- FRED 29 proposes that any revaluation loss that exceeds an existing revaluation surplus, in respect of the same asset, should be recognised as an expense in the profit and loss account - FRS 15 requires recognition in the profit and loss account only to the extent that the asset is impaired;
- FRED 29 requires a revaluation loss to be recognised in the statement of total recognised gains and losses to the extent that there is a revaluation surplus in respect of the same asset - FRS 15 requires any element that is caused by impairment to be recognised in the profit and loss account.

The ASB notes that it proposes to retain, as a transitional measure, the special treatment given in FRS 15 to gains and losses on the revaluation of assets held by insurance companies and groups as part of their insurance operations, even though this is not included in IAS 16.

Other changes proposed

20.124 The other main changes to current UK accounting practice proposed in FRED 29 are:

- there is a new requirement for an item of property, plant or equipment acquired in exchange for another item of property, plant or equipment to be measured at fair value, based on the fair value of the asset given up or, if more clearly evident, the fair value of the asset received - however, if fair value cannot be determined reliably, the acquired asset should be measured at the carrying value of the asset given up;
- there is no reference to accounting for donated assets received by charities;
- where residual values need to be revised, the revision should be based on current prices rather than those at the date of acquisition or revaluation;
- there is no guidance on when uncharged depreciation may be regarded as immaterial;
- there is no specific requirement for annual impairment reviews on assets that are not depreciated; and

— there is no reference to renewals accounting and, thus, no alternative to the principle that depreciation is determined by reference to the depreciable amount of an asset.

Borrowing costs

20.125 The capitalisation of borrowing costs would continue to be optional under the proposals in FRED 29. The definition of borrowing costs in IAS 23 allows certain exchange differences to be capitalised as borrowing costs, but the ASB does not intend to incorporate this element into UK accounting standards. The main differences from present UK accounting requirements are:

— the scope of the international standard is wider than that of FRS 15 and, its requirements consequently apply to certain inventories as well as to tangible fixed assets;

— under the proposals in FRED 29, if specific borrowings are taken out to fund a qualifying asset, the borrowing costs eligible for capitalisation are the actual costs less any investment income received from the temporary reinvestment of unused borrowings - under FRS 15 only interest on borrowings actually spent on the asset to date can be capitalised (any investment income on surplus borrowings must be recognised in the profit and loss account);

— two disclosures required under FRS 15 are not repeated in FRED 29:

  — the aggregate amount of finance costs included in the cost of tangible fixed assets - this disclosure is also required by CA 1985; and

  — the amount of finance costs recognised in the profit and loss account for the period.

Transitional arrangements

20.126 FRS 15 includes special transitional arrangements for entities who had previously revalued tangible fixed assets but did not wish to adopt a policy of revaluation when implementing FRS 15 for the first time. IAS 16 does not include such a provision, but the ASB states in FRED 29 that it proposes to include in any new UK standard a transitional arrangement equivalent to that in FRS 15 to enable entities who have taken advantage of the existing provision to continue their present accounting treatment.

Chapter 21

Investments

CLASSIFICATION AS FIXED OR CURRENT ASSETS

Balance sheet disclosure

21.1 Depending on their nature, investments may be classified in the balance sheet as fixed assets or current assets. In both cases, the heading is given a Roman numeral in the formats and the totals for fixed asset investments and current asset investments must therefore be shown on the face of the balance sheet. The balance sheet formats require the following analysis of investments:

- investments classified as fixed assets:
  - shares in group undertakings;
  - loans to group undertakings;
  - participating interests;
  - loans to undertakings in which the company has a participating interest;
  - other investments other than loans;
  - other loans; and
  - own shares;
- investments classified as current assets:
  - shares in group undertakings; and
  - own shares;
  - other investments.

These sub-headings are given Arabic numerals in the formats. The details may therefore be given in the notes to the accounts and the figures may be combined if the individual amounts are not material.

Definition of fixed asset investment

21.2 The usual CA 1985 definitions of fixed asset and current asset apply equally to investments. A fixed asset investment is therefore an investment which the company intends to retain and use on a continuing basis in its activities. All other investments should be classified as current assets. Although the balance sheet formats allow for the inclusion of shares in group undertakings under current assets, most group shareholdings will meet the definition of fixed assets and should therefore be accounted for under this heading.

Loans to group undertakings

21.3 Particular care is needed over the treatment of loans to group undertakings. In this case, the classification will normally depend on whether the loan is seen as providing long-term financing to another group undertaking (in which case it will usually be a fixed asset investment) or whether it is more in the nature of an inter-company account, in which case it may be more appropriate to disclose the balance in debtors. The treatment and disclosure of group loans should be consistent between companies within the group. For instance, it will not usually be appropriate for the lender to treat a group loan as a fixed asset investment and for the borrower to treat the same loan as being payable within one year. Proper documentation of the terms of the loan should help to establish the appropriate treatment in the accounts of both companies.

Disclosure of movements in the year

21.4 The general disclosure requirements of CA 1985 in respect of fixed assets apply equally to any investments shown as fixed assets. The accounts must therefore show for each category of fixed asset investment set out above:

- cost or valuation at the beginning of the year and at the balance sheet date;
- the effect of any revaluation during the year;
- any additions during the year;
- any disposals during the year;
- any transfers during the year;
- the cumulative amount provided for any diminution in value at the beginning of the year and at the balance sheet date;
- the amount provided for any diminution in value during the year;
- any adjustments to such provisions in respect of disposals during the year;
- any other adjustments to such provisions during the year.

Comparative figures are not required for these disclosures.

Current asset investments

21.5 Although the balance sheet formats allow for three categories of current asset investments, in practice, investments which are held as current assets will usually comprise items such as:

- listed investments;
- unlisted investments;
- certain bank and building society deposit accounts (although this will depend very much on the nature and purpose of the account).

All of these would come under the category of 'other investments'.

GROUP INVESTMENTS

Definition of group undertaking

21.6 Under CA 1985, the following are defined as group undertakings:

- a parent undertaking or a subsidiary undertaking; and
- a subsidiary undertaking of any parent undertaking of that undertaking.

An undertaking is defined as a body corporate or partnership, or an unincorporated association carrying on a trade or business, with or without a view to profit. Entities other than companies are therefore encompassed although, in practice, most group undertakings will be other companies. The disclosure for shares in and loans to group undertakings will therefore cover:

- any parent undertaking of the company (i.e. not just the company's immediate parent, but also any intermediate or ultimate parent);
- any subsidiary of the company;
- any fellow subsidiary – this might be another subsidiary of the company's immediate parent, or a subsidiary of another parent undertaking in a wider group.

In practice, any shareholdings will usually relate only to a company's own subsidiaries. However, loans may involve a wider range of group companies.

Straightforward presentation of information

21.7 The most appropriate way of presenting the required information will depend on the complexity of the investments, the level of detail disclosed on the face of the balance sheet and whether there have been any (or many) movements during the year. If there are no (or few) movements to report, the following format is usually the most straightforward:

Example 21.1 – Shares in and loans to group undertakings

Fixed asset investments

Investments in group undertakings

	20X2	*20X1*
	£	£
Shares in group undertakings	452,000	452,000
Loans to group undertakings	66,500	88,500
Total investments in group undertakings	518,500	540,500
Movements during the year on loans to group undertakings were as follows:		
At 1 January 20X2		88,500
Loans advanced		10,000
Loans repaid		(32,000)
At 31 December 20X2		66,500

Where movements during the year are more complicated, a full movements table may be required, as shown for other investments in **Example 21.4** (see **21.48** below). CA 1985 Sch 5 also requires the disclosure of detailed information in respect of a company's subsidiary undertakings.

Definition of participating interest

21.8 A participating interest is defined in CA 1985 as an interest held by an undertaking in the shares of another undertaking which it holds on a long-term basis for the purpose of securing a contribution to its activities by the exercise of control or influence arising from, or related to, that interest. The expression 'shares' includes an interest which is convertible into shares and an option to acquire shares or to acquire an interest in shares, regardless of whether the shares are issued or unissued at the time. A holding of 20% or more of the shares of another undertaking is presumed to be a participating interest, unless it can be demonstrated that this is not the case. In this case, interests which are convertible into shares and options to acquire shares or interests do not have to be taken into account. No minimum holding is laid down in CA 1985, and it is therefore possible that a holding of less than 20% could still qualify as a participating interest if the other conditions are fulfilled. The legislation notes specifically that, in the case of the balance sheet and profit and loss account formats, a participating interest does not include an interest in a group undertaking. Any interests in group undertakings must therefore be shown under that heading in the accounts and not as participating interests.

Associated undertakings

21.9 An associated undertaking is defined in CA 1985, in the context of group accounts, as an undertaking in which an undertaking included in the consolidation has a participating interest and over whose operating and financial policy it exercises a significant influence, and which is not a subsidiary undertaking of the parent company, or a joint venture included in the accounts by proportional consolidation. FRS 9 'Associates and Joint Ventures' defines:

- an associate as an entity (other than a subsidiary) in which another entity (the investor) has a participating interest and over whose operating and financial policies the investor exercises a significant influence; and
- a joint venture as an entity in which the reporting entity holds an interest on a long-term basis and which is jointly controlled by the reporting entity and one or more other venturers under a contractual arrangement.

It follows from these definitions that an associated undertaking (or an associate) will invariably qualify as a participating interest under CA 1985, but a participating interest will not necessarily meet the definition of an associated undertaking or of an associate under FRS 9. Accounting for associates is considered in more detail in **21.30** below.

Holding of own shares

21.10 The formats allow for the inclusion of 'own shares' under fixed asset investments or current asset investments, but these headings are rarely used in practice. The purchase by a company of its own shares is strictly controlled by CA 1985 and, where purchase or acquisition is possible, the company is usually required to cancel the shares at the time of purchase. The only situations where a company may be able to hold its own shares for a period of time are where the shares are acquired by forfeiture, or where the shares are surrendered in lieu of forfeiture, for failure to pay any sum payable in respect of the shares. The accounting treatment required by UITF 13 'Accounting for ESOP Trusts' may also result in shares in the company being recorded as 'own shares' in either fixed or current assets. The requirements of UITF 13 are considered in **Chapter 3**. Under CA 1985, the nominal value of any own shares held must also be disclosed in the accounts.

JOINT ARRANGEMENTS THAT ARE NOT ENTITIES

What is an entity?

21.11 In the course of their activities, businesses enter into a variety of agreements with other entities, but these agreements do not always result in the formation of another wholly separate entity. FRS 9 defines an entity as 'a body corporate, partnership or unincorporated association carrying on a trade or business with or without a view to profit. The reference to carrying on a trade or business means a trade or business of its own and not just a part of the trades or businesses of entities that have interests in it.'

Carrying on a trade or business

21.12 The explanatory material in FRS 9 considers some of the factors to be taken into account when deciding whether or not an arrangement results in a separate trade or business. The following features will usually indicate that the joint arrangement has a separate trade or business:

— it has some independence in following its own commercial strategy (i.e. in buying and selling); and

— it has access to the market in its own right for its main inputs and outputs or, if it buys from or sells to the participants, it does so on terms that are generally the same as those available in the market.

The following features will usually indicate that the joint arrangement does not have a separate trade or business:

— the participants benefit from the products or services by taking them in kind rather than by receiving a share of trading results (this does not necessarily preclude receiving the benefit of a product in cash); or

— each participant's share of the output or result is determined by its supply of key inputs to the joint activity that produces the output or result.

Definition of joint arrangement that is not an entity

21.13 FRS 9 defines a joint arrangement that is not an entity as follows:

> 'A contractual arrangement under which the participants engage in joint activities that do not create an entity because it would not be carrying on a trade or business of its own. A contractual arrangement where all significant matters of operating and financial policy are predetermined does not create an entity because the policies are those of its participants, not of a separate entity.'

In practice, joint activities that are not entities are likely to involve some element of cost-sharing or risk-sharing in carrying out a process that forms part of the business activities of the participants. The standard gives the following examples:

— a joint marketing or distribution network; and

— a shared production facility.

Joint arrangement to carry out a single project

21.14 The standard also emphasises that carrying on a trade or activity implies some continuity and repetition in the activity of buying and selling. Where a joint arrangement is set up to carry out one specific project, there is no continuing activity and the arrangement therefore will not usually constitute a separate trade or business. For instance, it is relatively common in the construction industry for two or more entities to collaborate on a single project without any ongoing arrangement between them once the project has been completed. In the past, this type of collaboration has often been referred to as a joint venture, but it does not constitute a joint venture under FRS 9.

Separate accounting treatment

21.15 FRS 9 defines a joint venture as:

> 'An entity in which the reporting entity holds an interest on a long-term basis and which is jointly controlled by the reporting entity and one or more other venturers under a contractual arrangement.'

Consequently, where two or more parties set up a joint arrangement that is not an entity, this will not constitute a joint venture under the standard, even though the various parties to the agreement may have a long-term interest and may have joint control under the terms of the agreement. The standard therefore sets out separate requirements on accounting for joint arrangements that are not entities, under which the participants are required to account for their own share of the assets, liabilities and cash flows of the joint arrangement. These should be measured according to the terms of the overall agreement that sets up the joint arrangement. The same treatment applies in both individual and consolidated accounts.

Change in the nature of the arrangement

21.16 The standard notes that the nature of a joint arrangement may change over time. For example, an initial agreement to establish and operate a pipeline to provide a service for the participants (i.e. a joint arrangement) may subsequently develop into a pipeline business providing services to third parties as well (i.e. a joint venture). In these circumstances, the accounting treatment should be amended in the year of the change to reflect the new nature of the joint activities.

IDENTIFICATION OF JOINT VENTURES

Joint control

21.17 A joint venture is an entity in which the reporting entity has a long-term interest and which is jointly controlled by the participants under a contractual arrangement. The FRS 9 definition of joint control incorporates two key elements:

- none of the participants alone can control the entity but all together can do so; and
- decisions on financial and operating policy essential to the activities, economic performance and financial position of the entity require the consent of each participant.

Practical implications

21.18 The explanatory material in the standard makes the following points in respect of joint control:

- the participants in the venture exercise joint control for their mutual benefit and each participant conducts its part of the arrangement with a view to its own benefit; and
- each venturer should play an active part in setting the operating and financial policies of the joint venture, at a strategic level at least.

The contractual arrangement may give one participant overall responsibility for the management of the joint venture, but this should not preclude a situation of joint control. If the arrangement provides for all the participants to be involved in reaching a collective agreement on the policies to be followed and gives them the power to ensure that the agreed policies are followed, this will usually constitute joint control.

Right of veto

21.19 An important aspect of the FRS 9 definition of joint control is that each venturer is in effect able to veto decisions on operating and financial policy. Without this veto the venture would be subject to majority rule rather than joint control. The standard emphasises that there is no need for this aspect to be set out in a formal agreement - it is the way that the venture operates in practice that establishes whether or not it meets the definition of a joint venture.

Long-term factors

21.20 Another significant feature of a joint venture is that the interest is held on a long-term basis. An interest held on a long-term basis is defined as an interest held other than exclusively with a view to subsequent resale (which is defined as in FRS 2). The conclusion on whether or not an entity qualifies as a joint venture should be based on long-term factors, and the guidance notes that once an entity has been classified as a joint venture, temporary or minor changes in the relationship between the investor and investee should not change its status as a joint venture for accounting purposes. The guidance in FRS 9 also emphasises that the classification of an entity as a joint venture should not change according to whether it is profitable or loss-making, or has net assets or net liabilities. Similarly, once an investment has been classified and accounted for as a joint venture, its status will not change simply because the investor intends to dispose of the investment.

Joint venture where an investor does not share control

21.21 It is possible for an investor to have an interest in an entity that is a joint venture without sharing control. In these circumstances, the entity will not be a joint venture as far as that investor is concerned and the interest should be accounted for simply as an investment. If the other investors share control of the entity, it will be a joint venture for them and they will account for it as such.

Joint venture that qualifies as a subsidiary of a participant

21.22 A joint venture is sometimes set up so that one investor holds a majority of voting rights and is therefore technically the 'parent'. However, the contractual arrangements with the other investors will usually create severe long-term restrictions that hinder the exercise of the parent's rights. The venture will therefore be excluded from the 'parent's' consolidated accounts under FRS 2 'Accounting for Subsidiary Undertakings' and should be accounted for under FRS 9 instead.

IDENTIFICATION OF ASSOCIATES

Definition of associate

21.23 FRS 9 defines an associate as an entity other than a subsidiary in which the investor has a participating interest and over whose operating and financial policies the investor exercises a significant influence. This is consistent with the definition of an associated undertaking under CA 1985 (see **21.9** above). The emphasis in FRS 9 is very much on the actual relationship in practice between investor and investee.

Participating interest

21.24 A participating interest is defined as an interest in the shares of another entity, held on a long-term basis, for the purpose of securing a contribution to the investor's activities by the exercise of control or influence arising from or relating to that interest. The following points are made in the standard:

- the reference to shares includes:
  - allotted shares in an entity with share capital;

- rights to share in the capital of an entity with capital but no share capital; and
- in the case of entity without capital, interests conferring any right to share in profits, imposing a liability to contribute to losses or giving an obligation to contribute to debts or expenses in a winding up;

— an interest in shares includes an interest that is convertible into an interest in shares, or an option to acquire shares;

— the investor's interest must be beneficial and the expected benefits must be linked to the exercise of its significant influence over the operating and financial policies of the investee; and

— the benefits may be obtained in various ways (eg dividends, fees based on performance etc).

The standard refers to the provision in CA 1985 that a holding of 20% or more of the shares in another entity is presumed to constitute a participating interest unless the contrary can be shown, and emphasises that the presumption will be rebutted if the interest is not long-term or is not beneficial.

Long-term factors

21.25 For an investment to qualify as an associate, the interest must be held on a long-term basis and the conclusion should therefore be based on long-term factors. An interest held on a long-term basis is defined as an interest held other than exclusively with a view to subsequent resale (which is defined as in FRS 2). The guidance notes that once an entity has been classified as an associate, temporary or minor, changes in the relationship between the investor and investee should not change its status for accounting purposes. Also, once the relationship has been established and the investor has been treated as exercising significant influence, that relationship should be regarded as continuing until an event or transaction changes the circumstances and removes the investor's ability to exercise the appropriate degree of influence. The guidance in FRS 9 also emphasises that:

— the classification of an entity as an associate should not change according to whether it is profitable or loss-making, or has net assets or net liabilities; and

— once an investment has been classified and accounted for as an associate, its status will not change simply because the investor intends to dispose of the investment.

Exercise of significant influence

21.26 For an investment to qualify as an associate, the investor must exercise significant influence over the operating and financial policies of the investee. In order to meet this condition the investor must be both actively involved and influential in the direction of the investee through participation in policy decisions on issues relevant to the investor. The guidance notes that this includes decisions on strategic issues and gives the following examples:

- the expansion or contraction of the business;
- participation in other entities;
- changes in products, markets and activities; and
- determination of the balance between dividends and reinvestment.

In effect, the investor will use the associate as a medium through which to conduct part of its business, although this does not mean that the associate must necessarily be involved in the same field of activity as the investor. The fact that the investor's interest must be long-term should mean that the investor will not necessarily look only for high dividends, but will also support a degree of reinvestment by the investee.

Development of policies of the investee

21.27 The guidance notes that, over time, an associate will usually implement policies that are consistent with those of the investor and avoid implementing policies that conflict with those of the investor. If the investee is able to continually pursue policies that are contrary to the strategy of the investor, this will usually indicate that the investor does not exercise significant influence.

Board participation

21.28 An investor will usually exercise its influence over the associate by being actively involved on the board of directors (or any equivalent body), but this is not a requirement. A different arrangement may still allow the investor to be actively involved in policy-setting decisions. The guidance emphasises that it is the practical, day-to-day relationship between the investor and investee that will decide whether or not significant influence is exercised, not any formal structure that may be put in place.

Level of interest in voting rights

21.29 Where the investor's interest in another entity represents 20% or more of the equity voting rights this suggests, but does not necessarily ensure, that the investor will be able to exercise significant influence over the investee. Conversely, where an investor's interest in another entity represents less than 20% of the equity voting rights, this will usually suggest that the investing company is not able to exercise significant influence over the entity. It may, however, be possible to demonstrate that the investor still has the appropriate level of influence without holding a substantial basis of voting power. In most cases, this would require a formal statement from the investee, acknowledging that the investor is able to exercise such influence.

ACCOUNTING FOR ASSOCIATES AND JOINT VENTURES

FRS 9 'Associates and Joint Ventures'

21.30 FRS 9 'Associates and Joint Ventures' deals mainly with the accounting treatment of an associate or joint venture in the context of group accounts, but there are also separate requirements on the treatment to be adopted in the investing company's individual accounts. Additional disclosures are required where the investor does not prepare group accounts, unless it is exempt from preparing group accounts, or would be exempt if it had subsidiaries. Exemption from the preparation of group accounts essentially applies to wholly-owned subsidiaries whose results and assets are included in groups accounts which are delivered to the registrar, and to certain small and medium-sized groups.

Accounting treatment in the individual accounts of the investor

21.31 In the individual accounts of the investor, FRS 9 requires an interest in an associate or joint venture to be accounted for as a fixed asset investment and shown at either cost, less amounts written off, or at valuation. Income from the associate or joint venture should be brought into the accounts on the basis of the amounts received or receivable during the year. The basic treatment of an associate or joint venture in the investor's individual accounts is therefore the same as for any other fixed asset investment. In consolidated accounts, an associate should be accounted for using the equity method of accounting and a joint venture should be accounted for using the gross equity method of accounting.

Joint venture with little commonality of interest

21.32 It is possible to set up a structure that appears to be a joint venture, but where the participants are simply using the structure as a means of carrying out their own business and there is little commonality of interest between them. In these circumstances, FRS 9 requires each participant to account for its own share of the assets, liabilities and cash flows within the structure rather than treating it as a joint venture.

Non-corporate associate or joint ventures

21.33 Where an investor holds an interest in a non-corporate associate or joint venture it is particularly important to ensure that all of the investor's liabilities in relation to the investment are properly reflected in the accounts. For instance, in a case of joint and several liability, a liability could arise in excess of the investor's share of the entity's net assets. This may need to be reported as a contingent liability or, where necessary, provided for in the accounts.

Additional accounts disclosures

21.34 Unless it is exempt from preparing group accounts, or would be exempt if it had subsidiaries, an investor that does not prepare consolidated financial statements must present the relevant amounts for associates and joint ventures in its own accounts. Two alternative forms of presentation are offered:

- the investor can prepare a separate set of financial statements to include the associate or joint venture; or
- the investor can show the relevant amounts, together with the effects of including them, as additional information to its own financial statements.

The use of a pro forma profit and loss account and balance sheet will usually be the clearest way of presenting the required information. If the alternative approach is used (ie supplementary details are included in the company's statutory profit and loss account and balance sheet), particular care will be required to ensure that the results of the associate or joint venture do not appear to be reported as realised profits of the investor. The standard also requires the following disclosures in respect of each principal associate or joint venture:

- its name;
- the proportion of the issued shares in each class held by the investing company or group, together with an indication of any special rights or constraints attaching to them;
- the accounting period or date of the financial statements used, if these differ from those of the investing company or group; and
- an indication of the nature of its business.

Accounting period and date of associates and joint ventures

21.35 Wherever possible, the information included in the investor's accounts should be based on financial statements for the associate or joint venture made up to the accounting date of the investor. Where this is not practicable, the associate or joint venture may be included on the basis of accounts prepared for a period ending not more than three months before the accounting date of the investor. If this would result in the release of restricted, price-sensitive information, accounts for a period ending not more than six months before the accounting date of the investor may be used. Where different accounting dates are used, changes between the accounting date of the associate or joint venture and the accounting date of the investor should be adjusted for if they materially affect the view given by the investor's accounts.

Becoming or ceasing to be an associate

21.36 An investment becomes an associate on the date on which the investor begins to fulfil the two essential elements of the definition of an associate:

- the holding of a participating interest; and
- the exercise of significant influence.

An investment ceases to be an associate on the date on which the investor ceases to fulfil either of these two essential elements. If an investment in an associate is acquired or disposed of in stages, a similar process to that required for subsidiaries under FRS 2 'Accounting for Subsidiary Undertakings' should be followed.

Becoming or ceasing to be a joint venture

21.37 An investment becomes a joint venture on the date on which the investor begins to control the entity jointly with the other venturers, provided that its interest is long-term. An investment ceases to be a joint venture on the date on which the investor ceases to have joint control with the other venturers. If an investment in a joint venture is acquired or disposed of in stages, a similar process to that required for subsidiaries under FRS 2 'Accounting for Subsidiary Undertakings' should be followed.

Disclosure of decision not to treat as an associate

21.38 Where an investor holds 20% or more of the shares in another entity but is deemed not to have a participating interest in the entity, the reasons must be explained in a note to the accounts. Similarly, where the investor holds 20% or more of the voting rights but is deemed not to exercise significant influence over the entity, the reasons should be explained.

Notes on contingent liabilities and commitments

21.39 Where the notes to the associate's or joint venture's accounts include matters that are material to understanding the effect of the investment on the investor, or if the notes would have included such matters if the investor's accounting policies had been followed, details should also be disclosed in the investor's accounts. These disclosures should include in particular:

- the investor's share in contingent liabilities incurred jointly with other investors; and
- the investor's share of the capital commitments of associates and joint ventures.

Significant restrictions on ability to distribute reserves

21.40 Where the ability of an associate or joint venture to distribute its reserves is significantly restricted as a result of statutory, contractual or exchange control requirements, the extent of the restriction should be indicated in the accounts of the investor. This does not apply to reserves that are shown as non-distributable in the accounts of the associate or joint venture.

Amounts owed to or by associates and joint venture

21.41 Any amounts owed to or by associates or joint ventures should be analysed into:

- amounts relating to loans; and
- amounts relating to trading balances.

This disclosure may be combined with the disclosures required under FRS 8 'Related Party Disclosures' (see **Chapter 17**).

Significant associates and joint ventures

21.42 Additional disclosures are required when certain thresholds in respect of:

- gross assets;
- gross liabilities;
- turnover; and
- operating results (on a three-year average),

are exceeded. The thresholds are applied by comparing the relevant figures for the investor (excluding any amounts included for associates and joint ventures under the equity method of accounting) with the investor's share of the equivalent figures for associates in aggregate, joint ventures in aggregate and for individual associates and joint ventures.

Disclosures where an aggregate threshold of 15% is exceeded

21.43 Where the share relating to associates or to joint ventures exceeds 15% of the relevant figure for the investor, the accounts should disclose the investor's share (in aggregate) of the following for associates or joint ventures as appropriate:

- turnover (unless this is already included as a memorandum item);
- fixed assets;
- current assets;
- liabilities due within one year; and
- liabilities due after more than one year.

Disclosures where an individual threshold of 25% is exceeded

21.44 Where the investor's share in any individual associate or joint venture exceeds 25% of the relevant figure for the investor, the accounts should disclose the name of the associate or joint venture and the investor's share of the following:

- turnover;
- profit before tax;
- taxation;
- profit after tax;
- fixed assets;
- current assets;
- liabilities due within one year; and
- liabilities due after more than one year.

Further analysis should be given where this is necessary for an understanding of the nature of the total amounts involved. However, where an individual associate or joint venture accounts for nearly all of the amounts included for that class of investment, only the aggregate amounts need to be given, provided that this is explained and the name of the individual associate or joint venture is disclosed.

ACCOUNTING POLICIES

Historical cost accounting rules

21.45 Under the historical cost accounting rules, fixed assets investments should be included in the accounts at their purchase price. Under CA 1985, provision must be made for any permanent diminution in value and may be made for any temporary diminution in value. Such provisions should be charged to the profit and loss account and shown separately, either on the face of the profit and loss account or in the notes to the accounts. Provisions should be written back in the same way to the extent that they are no longer necessary. Current asset investments should be included in the accounts at the lower of purchase price and net realisable value. Once again, any provision to write down a current asset investment to its net realisable value should be written back to the extent that it is no longer necessary. There is no specific requirement for the accounting policy in respect of investments to be disclosed in the accounts, but where investments are significant it is usual to give a brief description of the accounting treatment.

Example 21.2 – Disclosure of accounting policy on investments

Investments held as fixed assets are included in the accounts at cost, less any provisions for impairment. Investments held as current assets are included in the accounts at the lower of cost and net realisable value.

Alternative accounting rules

21.46 Under the alternative accounting rules, fixed asset investments may be included in the accounts at:

- market value as at the date of their last valuation; or
- at a value determined on any basis which the directors consider to be appropriate in the company's circumstances.

Current asset investments may be included at their current cost.

Example 21.3 – Alternative accounting rules (disclosure of policy for accounting for investments)

Listed investments held as fixed assets are included in the accounts at their market value at the balance sheet date. Investments held as current assets are included in the accounts at their current cost at the balance sheet date.

The option to value fixed asset investments on a basis considered appropriate by the directors could be used to value an unlisted investment on an earnings basis or a net asset basis. Whenever this approach is used, the notes to the accounts must disclose details of the valuation method adopted and the reasons for choosing this method. It is not sufficient simply to state that the investments have been valued by the directors. The use of the alternative accounting rules, and the disclosures that are required when they are adopted, are considered in more detail in **Chapter 1**. In the case of fixed asset investments other than listed investments, the following details must also be given:

- the years and amounts of the valuations; and
- for assets revalued during the year, the names or qualifications of the valuer(s) and the valuation bases used.

Impairment of investments

21.47 Investments in subsidiary undertakings, associates and joint ventures are specifically included within the scope of FRS 11 'Impairment of Fixed Assets and Goodwill'. The standard requires fixed assets and goodwill to be reviewed for impairment if events or changes in circumstances indicate that the carrying amount of the asset or goodwill may not be recoverable. To the extent that the carrying amount exceeds the recoverable amount, the fixed asset or goodwill is impaired and should be written down. The requirements of FRS 11 are considered in more detail in **Chapter 20**.

OTHER ACCOUNTS DISCLOSURE

Fixed asset investments

21.48 In the case of fixed asset investments, CA 1985 requires considerable detail to be given in respect of opening and closing balances and movements during the year. This is usually presented in the form of a table, but other forms of presentation may be more appropriate depending on how many categories of investment need to be included and the complexity of the movements during the year.

Example 21.4 – Table detailing fixed asset movements

	Participating interests		*Other*	*Total*
	Shares	*Loans*	*Investments*	
Cost	£	£	£	£
At 1 January 20X2	556	150	75	781
Additions	—	—	10	10
Disposals	—	—	(20)	(20)
At 31 December 20X2	556	150	65	771
Provisions				
At 1 January 20X2	—	50	—	50
Charged in the year	—	—	7	7
Written back in the year	—	(30)	—	(30)
At 31 December 20X2	—	20	7	27
Net book value				
At 31 December 20X2	556	130	58	744
At 31 December 20X1	556	100	75	731

Current asset investments

21.49 In the case of current asset investments, movements during the year do not have to be disclosed. The only disclosure will therefore be the analysis by category for each year and the information on listed investments discussed in **21.52** to **21.55** below.

Listed investments

21.50 For any item shown in the accounts as investments (in either fixed assets or current assets), CA 1985 requires separate disclosure of:

- the amount relating to listed investments;
- the aggregate market value of the listed investments, if this is different to the amount included in the accounts; and
- both the market value and the stock exchange value of the listed investments, where the market value is taken as being higher than the stock exchange value for accounts purposes.

Most listed investments will be disclosed as 'other' investments within fixed assets or current assets. However, it is possible that shares in group undertakings or in participating interests will include listed investments, in which case the analysis will need to be given for these categories as well.

Definition of listed investment

21.51 CA 1985 defines a listed investment as 'an investment as respects which there has been granted a listing on a recognised investment exchange other than an overseas investment exchange within the meaning of the Finance Act 1986 or on any stock exchange of repute outside Great Britain'. In the case of the UK, only companies which are listed on the London Stock Exchange are covered by this disclosure requirement at the moment. Investments in companies traded on other UK markets should be classified as unlisted investments. In the case of companies listed on overseas stock exchanges, what constitutes a stock exchange of repute will to some extent be a matter of judgment, but investments listed on well recognised foreign exchanges should be treated as listed investments for disclosure purposes.

Example disclosures

21.52 The disclosure requirements might therefore be met by the following presentation in the case of fixed asset investments.

Example 21.5 – Analysis of other fixed asset investments to show details of listed investments

	Listed in the UK	*Unlisted*	*Total*
Cost	£	£	£
At 1 January 20X2	61	14	75
Additions	10	—	10
Disposals	(18)	(2)	(20)
At 31 December 20X2	53	12	65
Provisions			
At 1 January 20X2	—	—	—
Charged in the year	—	7	7
At 31 December 20X2	—	7	7
Net book value			
At 31 December 20X2	53	5	58
At 31 December 20X1	61	14	75

The aggregate market value of the listed investments at 31 December 20X2 was £89,000 (20X1: £97,000).

In the case of current asset investments, the disclosure is less detailed, as movements during the year do not have to be disclosed. The following will therefore usually be sufficient.

Example 21.6 – Disclosure of listed investments within current assets

	20X2	*20X1*
	£	£
Listed investments	76	59
Unlisted investments	13	12
	89	71

The aggregate market value of the listed investments at 31 December 20X2 was £93,000 (20X1: £67,000).

Separate disclosure of stock exchange value

21.53 The requirement to disclose both the market value and the stock exchange value of the listed investments (where the market value is taken as being higher than the stock exchange value for accounts purposes) will not often arise in practice. It might be necessary where, for instance, the shareholding represents a controlling interest. Where disclosure is required, wording along the following lines will usually satisfy the requirement.

Example 21.7 – Where market value is higher than stock exchange value

The aggregate market value of the listed investments at 31 December 20X2 was £89,000 (20X1: £97,000). This market value includes certain investments for which market value is considered to be higher than their stock exchange value. The market value of these investments at 31 December 20X2 was £47,000 and their stock exchange value at that date was £41,000.

Details of significant shareholdings

21.54 CA 1985 requires additional details in respect of any investment where:

— the company's shareholding amounts to 20% or more of the nominal value of any class of shares in that undertaking; or

— the amount of the investment (as shown in the company's accounts) represents more than one-fifth of the company's net assets.

A shareholding of this level will usually mean that the undertaking is an associate, and the accounting requirements of FRS 9 will therefore also apply (see **21.30** to **21.44** above). An investment in a subsidiary undertaking is not covered by these disclosure requirements, as separate disclosures in respect of subsidiaries are set out in CA 1985 Sch 5. The following details must be given for significant shareholdings other than subsidiaries:

— the name of the undertaking;

— its country of incorporation, if this is outside Great Britain;

— if it is unincorporated, the address of its principal place of business;

— the identity of each class of shares held by the company; and

— the proportion of the nominal value of shares in that class held by the company.

The information is usually given in narrative form, as part of the notes on investments. The disclosures apply to both fixed asset and current asset investments.

Example 21.8 – Narrative disclosure of significant share holdings

The total for investments listed in the UK includes an interest of 21.4% in the preference shares of .... plc and the total for unlisted investments includes a 24% interest in the ordinary shares of B Limited.

Where the company needs to disclose information in respect of a number of other entities, presentation in a table might be more appropriate.

Example 21.9 – Where information on a number of entities is needed

Name	*Country of incorporation*	*Class of shares held*	*Percentage held*
Listed investments:			
A plc		Preference	21.4%
Unlisted investments:			
B Limited		Ordinary	24.0%
C Limited	Ireland	Ordinary	32.2%

Financial information in respect of significant investments

21.55 Where the company has one or more significant shareholdings (as defined in **21.56** above), the following details must also be disclosed:

— the aggregate amount of the capital and reserves of the undertaking at the end of its relevant financial year; and

— its profit or loss for that year.

This additional information does not have to be given if:

— the information is immaterial;

— the company is exempt from preparing group accounts under CA 1985 s 228 (ie it is part of a larger group) and the company's investment in all such undertakings is shown in aggregate in the notes to the accounts by way of the equity method of valuation (ie the company's share of the net assets of the undertakings); or

— the investment is in an undertaking that is not required by CA 1985 to deliver a copy of its balance sheet to the registrar and does not otherwise publish its balance sheet in Great Britain, and the company's shareholding is less than 50% of the nominal value of the shares in the undertaking.

Also, the information normally required in relation to significant shareholdings need not be given in respect of an undertaking which is established under the law of a country outside the UK or carries on business outside the UK if:

— in the opinion of the directors, the disclosure would be seriously prejudicial to the business of that undertaking, or to the company or any of its subsidiaries; and

— the Secretary of State agrees that the information need not be disclosed.

In this case, the fact that the company has taken advantage of the exemption must be stated in the notes to the accounts.

Avoiding a disclosure of excessive length

21.56 CA 1985 s 231(5)allows some restriction of the detailed information where the disclosures in respect of subsidiaries and other significant investments would otherwise be of excessive length because of the number of entities involved. The accounts must state that information is only given in respect of the undertakings specified in CA 1985 s 231(5) and that full information will be attached to the next annual return. The information included with the annual return must cover the undertakings that were disclosed in the accounts as well as those that were not.

Chapter 22

Stocks

GENERAL PRINCIPLES OF STOCK VALUATION

Accruals concept under FRS 18

22.1 FRS 18 specifically requires financial statements (other than cash flow information) to be prepared on the accruals basis of accounting, which it defines as requiring the non-cash effects of transactions and events to be reflected, as far as is possible, in the financial statements for the accounting period in which they occur and not in the period in which any related cash is received or paid. The standard makes a clear link with the definitions of assets and liabilities set out in FRS 5 'Reporting the Substance of Transactions' (and also in the Statement of Principles), and notes that the use of those definitions to determine which items should be recognised as assets and liabilities in the balance sheet is consistent with the accruals concept. Where an entity has unused or unsold stocks at the end of an accounting period, it will usually expect to use or sell those items in the following accounting period or, in some cases, in a future accounting period (eg where stocks require time to mature before they can be sold). The company will therefore have incurred costs in buying or producing the stock items in anticipation of earning revenues from them at some time in the future. Consequently, the stock items meet the definition of assets (rights or other access to future economic benefits owned by an entity as a result of past transactions or events) and it is therefore appropriate to carry them forward in the balance sheet.

'Cost' of stocks

22.2 The value carried forward for stocks should represent the expenditure incurred in the normal course of business in purchasing the goods or producing the goods (ie bringing them to their present location and condition). However, in most cases it will not be possible to identify the precise purchase price or production cost for each item held in stock at the end of the year, and in practice an element of averaging, costing and allocation of overheads will usually be required in order to calculate the 'cost' of the stock.

Sensitivity of stock valuation

22.3 The value of closing stocks will be adjusted for when calculating the charge to the profit and loss account in respect of cost of sales (or, where Format 2 is used for the profit and loss account, the charge in respect of raw materials and consumables and the adjustment for the change in stocks of finished goods and work in progress). Consequently, if the value carried forward for stocks at the end of an accounting period is overstated or understated, this will have a direct impact on the operating profit or loss that is reported for the period. The value of stocks is therefore a highly sensitive figure in the accounts, but also one of the most difficult figures to calculate in view of the degree of judgment that will usually be required in the valuation process.

Historical cost accounting rules

22.4 Stocks are classified as current assets in the balance sheet formats and, under the historical cost accounting rules, should therefore be shown at the lower of:

- purchase price or production cost; and
- net realisable value.

The historical cost accounting rules and the rules on determining purchase price and production cost are covered in **Chapter 1**. However, CA 1985 allows a company to apply special rules in the case of stocks and fungible assets. Fungible assets are defined as assets of any description that are substantially indistinguishable from one another. CA 1985 allows stocks and fungible assets to be valued for accounts purposes by one of the following methods, rather than requiring them to be included at actual purchase price or production cost:

- first in, first out (FIFO);
- last in, first out (LIFO);
- a weighted average price; and
- any other method similar to the above methods.

However, not all of these methods are generally acceptable for the purpose of valuing stocks under SSAP 9 'Stocks and Long-term Contracts'. Where stocks are included in the accounts on the basis of one of these methods any material difference between the amount shown in the accounts and the replacement cost of the stocks must be disclosed in the accounts.

Alternative accounting rules

22.5 Under the alternative accounting rules (see **Chapter 1**), stocks may be included in the accounts at their current cost. However, this treatment is rarely adopted in practice as it does not generally comply with the accounting requirements of SSAP 9 'Stocks and Long-term Contracts'.

CA 1985 rules on purchase price and production cost

22.6 CA 1985 sets out specific rules on the calculation of purchase price or production cost. These apply to all assets and are considered here in the context of stocks. The more general application of these rules is covered in **Chapter 1**. The purchase price of an asset is the actual price paid plus any expenses incidental to its acquisition. Incidental expenses include the cost of getting the asset to its present location and into its present condition. The production cost of an asset is to be calculated by adding together:

- the purchase price of the raw materials and consumables used; and
- the direct costs of production.

In addition, CA 1985 permits the following items to be included in production cost:

- a reasonable proportion of indirect production costs, but only to the extent that they relate to the period of production; and
- interest on capital borrowed to finance the production of the asset, but again only to the extent that it relates to the period of production.

Where interest is included in production cost, the notes to the accounts must disclose the fact that interest has been included and the amount of interest involved. In the case of stocks (and other current assets), CA 1985 specifically prohibits the inclusion of distribution costs in production cost.

Requirements of SSAP 9 'Stocks and Long-term Contracts'

22.7 SSAP 9 'Stocks and Long-term Contracts' recognises that it will not usually be possible to identify the exact purchase price or production cost of each item held in stock at the end of the period, particularly where stocks consist of a large number of comparatively small items. There will often be a variety of methods that could potentially be used to allocate costs to stocks and the standard therefore states that the methods used should be 'selected with a view to providing the fairest possible approximation to the expenditure actually incurred in bringing the product to its present location and condition'. The guidance notes set out some of the practical considerations relating to the allocation of costs.

Definition of 'cost'

22.8 SSAP 9 defines 'cost' as 'that expenditure which has been incurred in the normal course of business in bringing the product or service to its present location and condition'. It identifies two elements to cost – cost of purchase and cost of conversion. Cost of purchase is defined as 'purchase price, including import duties, transport and handling costs and any other directly attributable costs, less trade discounts, rebates and subsidies'. Therefore, any costs relating directly to the purchase and transport of items held in stocks should be included in the stock valuation. However, where trade discounts and rebates are reflected in the accounts in relation to these purchases, they must also be adjusted for when valuing the stock, in order to arrive at the closest approximation to the price actually paid for the goods. Costs of conversion are defined as:

— costs which are specifically attributable to units of production, e.g. direct labour, direct expenses and sub-contracted work;
— production overheads (which are separately defined); and
— other overheads, if any, attributable in the particular circumstances of the business to bringing the product or service to its present location and condition.

This is consistent with the requirements set out in CA 1985 on the inclusion of overheads in production cost.

Production overheads

22.9 Production overheads are defined as 'overheads incurred in respect of materials, labour or services for production, based on the normal level of activity, taking one year with another'. A crucial point here is that the allocation of production overheads must be based on a normal level of activity, so that the costs of any inefficiency, excessive wastage or idle time is written off in the year in which it is incurred and is not carried forward to future years within the stock valuation. This is considered further in **22.17.** to **22.19.**

Net realisable value

22.10 Net realisable value is defined in SSAP 9 as the actual or estimated selling price (net of trade but before settlement discounts) less:

— all further costs to completion; and
— all costs to be incurred in marketing, selling and distributing.

Therefore, although selling and distribution costs must not be included in production cost, they should be taken into account when assessing the net realisable value of stocks and the need for any provisions to reduce the cost of stocks to net realisable value. SSAP 9 also reinforces the requirement under CA 1985 that stocks should be stated at the lower of cost and net realisable value, and specifies that the comparison of cost and net realisable value should be made for each individual stock item, or by groups or categories of similar items where individual consideration is not possible. If this comparison was only carried out on a total basis, it might result in unacceptable offsetting of potential losses against potential profits. The SSAP 9 requirement is therefore consistent with the requirement in CA 1985 that individual components of assets and liabilities should be considered separately when calculating the aggregate value of an asset or liability.

ACCEPTABLE COSTING METHODS

Principal types of costing system

22.11 Most companies will need to make use of some form of costing system to gather together the direct costs of purchasing or producing goods or of providing services. At a basic level, they will need this information to enable them to price their products and services effectively (ie by taking account of all raw material costs, time spent on producing goods or performing services, an allowance for related overheads and the margin of profit that they expect to achieve). The more usual types of costing system are:

- job costing;
- batch costing;
- process costing; and
- standard costing.

The most appropriate system will depend on the nature of the company's product or services and the volume of goods produced. A job costing system or process costing system might be appropriate for a production activity that results in a small number of large products, such as the manufacture of machines. A batch costing system may well be more appropriate if the production activity involves producing a large quantity of small items in each production run, for instance the manufacture of items such as bearings or nuts and bolts. Under a standard costing system, management estimates the expected cost of producing each item, usually based on experience to date, and accounts for production on the basis of these standard costs. To be effective the system requires actual cost to be compared with standard cost on a regular basis, with a detailed analysis and review of any variances.

Costing in the services sector

22.12 In the services sector, the major cost will be the time of the staff involved on each project or assignment, and costs will usually be accumulated by recording the time spent by each individual and costing this at standard rates, usually depending on the degree of experience or knowledge required and calculated to recover salary costs and other overheads.

Valuation of stocks

22.13 Any of these methods will usually provide an appropriate basis for valuing items included in stocks at the end of the accounting period. In a manufacturing company the costs to be included will often vary depending on the stage of completion of the product. Raw materials for use in the process will be valued at purchase price; finished goods will include all the costs of raw materials, labour and other production overheads; work-in-progress will include some raw materials, labour and overhead costs, but not all, the amount included being dependent on the stage of production that has been reached for each item. However, in all cases care must be taken to exclude any inappropriate overheads or any profit margin that may be built into the costing system.

Purchase or production cost of identical items

22.14 Another factor that needs to be taken into account where large volumes of similar goods are purchased or produced, and the purchase price or production cost varies, is a method for deciding how to establish the cost of the items remaining in stock at the end of the accounting period. A common approach is to use the FIFO (first in, first out) method of allocating costs. This assumes that the goods that were purchased or produced first will have been used first, and that those remaining in stock at the end of the period will therefore have come from the latest purchases or production run.

Example 22.1 – Remaining stock calculated using FIFO

A Ltd has made the following purchases of the same raw material for use in production:

Date	*Quantity*	*Price per tonne*
16 January	50 tonnes	£23.45
5 February	65 tonnes	£25.60
29 March	44 tonnes	£23.78
23 April	52 tonnes	£27.45
18 May	60 tonnes	£22.95

At the end of the accounting period on 31 May, A Ltd has 127 tonnes of this raw material in stock. Using a FIFO basis, the year-end stocks will be assumed to relate to the last three purchases and stock will therefore be valued as follows:

60	tonnes at £22.95	£1,377
52	tonnes at £27.45	£1,427
15	tonnes at £23.78	£356
127		£3,160

Another method in fairly common usage is to calculate an average cost over a suitable period of time and apply this to the quantity in stock at the end of the period.

Example 22.2 – Remaining stock calculated using average cost

The details are as for **Example 22.1**.

Date	*Quantity*	*Price per tonne*	*Total cost*
16 January	50 tonnes	£23.45	£1,173
5 February	65 tonnes	£25.60	£1,664
29 March	44 tonnes	£23.78	£1,046
23 April	52 tonnes	£27.45	£1,427
18 May	60 tonnes	£22.95	£1,377

Based on normal stock-holding and usage patterns, the company uses an average cost over a three-month period to value stocks. The average cost for year-end purposes will therefore be based on:

44	tonnes at 23.78	£1,046
52	tonnes at 27.45	£1,427
60	tonnes at 22.95	£1,377
156		£3,850

The average cost is therefore £3,850/156 = £24.68 per tonne and the year-end stocks will be valued at £3,134 (ie 127 tonnes at £24.68).

A further averaging method permitted under the CA 1985 is LIFO. This takes the opposite approach to FIFO, and assumes that the latest purchases or production are used first and that the oldest items therefore remain in stock. Base stock is a method that applies a fixed unit value to a specified stock quantity. Any stocks in excess of this quantity are valued on a different basis. Neither LIFO nor base stock will usually be an acceptable method of valuing stocks under SSAP 9, because these methods give little weight to the recent cost of acquiring or producing the goods that are held in stock at the end of the accounting period. They will therefore not meet the SSAP 9 requirement that the valuation gives the fairest approximation to actual cost, and they can give rise to serious distortions in the accounts, particularly when prices are increasing.

Use of estimation techniques

22.15 Under FRS 18 'Accounting Policies', where estimation techniques are needed to enable the adopted accounting policies to be applied, the techniques chosen should enable the financial statements to give a true and fair view and should be consistent with the requirements of accounting standards, UITF Abstracts and companies' legislation. Where it is necessary to choose between estimation techniques that satisfy these conditions, the entity should select the technique that is judged to be the most appropriate to its particular circumstances for the purpose of giving a true and fair view. Estimation techniques are considered in more detail in **Chapter 4**. The guidance in FRS 18 also notes that specific accounting requirements for fungible assets (which the standard defines as assets that are substantially indistinguishable from one another in economic terms) may be set out in accounting standards, UITF Abstracts and companies' legislation. Where fungible assets are recorded at historical cost, the accounting policy may require cost to be determined on an asset-by-asset basis or may consider such assets in aggregate by using a measurement basis such as weighted average historical cost, or historical cost measured on a first in, first out (FIFO basis). The guidance notes that an accounting policy that considers fungible assets in aggregate will be more consistent with the objective of comparability.

Inclusion of raw materials and consumables at a fixed amount

22.16 CA 1985 permits raw materials and consumables to be included at a fixed quantity and value, provided that:

- they are assets of a kind that are constantly being replaced;
- their overall value is not material; and
- their quantity, value and composition do not vary materially.

As with all accounting standards, SSAP 9 need not be applied to immaterial items, and there is consequently nothing in the standard to prohibit this approach being used for items that are not material. It can be a useful and convenient means of accounting for minor consumable items such as screws, nuts, bolts, etc.

ALLOCATION OF OVERHEADS

Overheads to be included

22.17 The allocation of overheads cannot be a precise exercise and will inevitably involve a degree of subjectivity and judgment. There are two key aspects to the allocation:

- only production-related overheads should be included; and

— the allocation should be based on the company's normal level of activity.

In order to carry out the appropriate allocation, all of the company's overheads must be analysed by function, the normal analysis being:

— production;

— marketing, selling and distribution; and

— general administration.

Certain overheads will fall clearly into one category, and will either be included in or excluded from the stock valuation accordingly. The main difficulty relates to those overheads that cover more than one function. In this case, the proportion of the overhead relating to production needs to be established, so that this can be included in the stock valuation. For instance, the apportionment may be based on space (eg to establish the proportion of rent and rates relating to the factory) or on time (eg to allocate the salary cost of an individual who carries out work for more than one function). SSAP 9 makes the point that overheads should not be excluded from the stock valuation on the grounds of prudence. Whilst it is right that a prudent approach should be taken to the valuation of stock, this should be dealt with by the review of net realisable values and not by excluding certain costs from the valuation of stock items.

Management costs

22.18 Where members of management have functional responsibility (eg a production director), their salary and related costs can be charged to that function, and in smaller businesses, where individuals might have more than one responsibility, an appropriate apportionment may be made. However, the principle in SSAP 9 is that other general management costs should not be carried forward within the stock valuation.

Normal level of activity

22.19 SSAP 9 requires overheads to be allocated to production units on the basis of the company's normal level of activity, taking one year with another. The main purpose of this is to ensure that avoidable costs, such as those arising from inefficiencies, excessive wastage (eg due to problems or faults with production plant) and idle time are charged to the profit and loss account in the year in which they are incurred and are not carried forward to future periods in the stock valuation. The factors to be considered when assessing the company's normal level of activity will usually include:

— the volume of production that the facilities should normally achieve – among other things, this will depend on the working conditions that management set for the year under review (eg whether the factory operates for one shift, two shifts or 24 hours a day etc);

- the budgeted level of activity for the current year and for the next year;
- the level of activity actually achieved during the current year and during the previous year.

A normal level of activity will usually be established for a period of more than a year, and certain temporary variations may be acceptable without amendment to the overall calculations, but the level of activity should nevertheless be reviewed each year and, if it is clear that variances are recurring each year and are expected to continue, the normal level of activity for overhead allocation purposes will usually need to be revised.

ASSESSING NET REALISABLE VALUE

Situations where provision may be needed

22.20 Having valued stock at purchase price or production cost, including any relevant overheads, an assessment needs to be made of whether the stocks will realise at least this value when sold. The assessment must be made by individual item or, where individual consideration is not practical, by groups or categories of similar items. Any stock items that are not expected to realise the value attributed to them must be written down to their net realisable value. Many companies need to make provision against stock values in this way, some of the more common reasons being:

- general obsolescence of the product (eg as a result of advances in technology or changes in the market);
- a slow-moving market for individual products;
- physical deterioration in the goods – particular attention is required where goods have a limited shelf life (eg certain chemical or medical products);
- management decisions to sell certain products at a loss (eg as part of a marketing strategy);
- increases in costs; and
- reductions in selling prices (eg as a result competitive pricing).

Provisions on a formula basis

22.21 In some companies, initial provision is made on the basis of an agreed formula, developed on the basis of actual experience in previous years. This can be a useful method of calculating a provision in order to recognise the fact that certain goods are moving slowly.

Example 22.3 – Formula for calculating a provision for slow-moving goods

On the basis of experience in recent years B Ltd calculates that the following provision is required in respect of slow-moving goods:

Last recorded movement	*Provision*
Goods that have moved in the last 6 months	Nil
Goods that last moved 6–12 months ago	35%
Goods that last moved 12–18 months ago	70%
Goods that last moved over 18 months ago	100%

Depending on the nature of the goods and the company's activity, formula provisions can also be based on:

— the age of the products;

— firm orders over the coming months;

— expected future sales.

However, this type of provision alone is unlikely to be adequate to cover all cases where net realisable value may be lower than cost and more detailed reviews of individual items will be required as well to cover the other factors outlined in **22.19** above.

Calculating net realisable value

22.22 Net realisable value is the expected selling price of the goods, less:

— any trade discounts likely to be given (but not settlement discounts);

— any further costs to complete the product; and

— all costs to be incurred in marketing, selling and distributing the product.

Overheads relating to marketing, selling and distribution will need to be identified on a similar basis to production overheads, to enable the comparison of net realisable value and cost to be carried out. It is important to recognise that a straight comparison of cost with expected selling price (net of trade discounts) will not necessarily be sufficient to meet the requirements of SSAP 9, although it may be adequate as a first step. If this initial comparison indicates that there is a substantial margin between cost and selling price, further work will not usually be necessary. However, if selling price is above cost, but only marginally so, further investigation will usually be required, as the impact of any costs to complete, and marketing, selling and distribution expenses, may well erode and reverse a small margin.

Provisions against raw material stocks

22.23 Where net realisable value provisions need to be made against finished goods, this may cast doubt on the stock value of any raw materials or other parts that are used in the production of these items and additional provisions may therefore be needed against the value of raw material stocks or even work-in-progress. When assessing the value of raw material stocks, it is usually necessary to look at the expected realisable value of the end product, not just the realisable value of the raw materials. For instance, if the price of a raw material has fallen, but calculations show that the product in which the raw material is to be used will still be sold at a profit (ie with the raw material included in the calculation at cost rather than realisable value), no provision against the stock value of raw material will usually be required. The situations when provision may be required against raw material stocks are:

— if the end product has a net realisable value below cost;

— if the raw material stocks are likely to be sold rather than used in production (eg because the end product is no longer viable).

ACCOUNTS DISCLOSURES

Analysis of stocks

22.24 The balance sheet formats set out in CA 1985 require separate disclosure of stocks, analysed into the following categories:

— raw materials and consumables;

— work in progress;

— finished goods and goods for resale; and

— payments on accounts.

The heading for stocks is given a Roman numeral and must therefore be shown on the face of the balance sheet. The sub-headings are given Arabic numerals and the detailed analysis of stocks may therefore be given in the notes to the accounts. The figures may also be combined if the individual amounts are not material. The 'payments on account' sub-heading is intended to be used to disclose payments made by the company on account of stock items, but is rarely seen in practice. The accounting treatment of payments on account received from customers in respect of contract work is considered in **Chapter 23**. SSAP 9 requires a similar analysis of stocks by category.

Disclosure of accounting policy

22.25 SSAP 9 requires disclosure of the accounting policy adopted in respect of stocks. The level of detail required will depend on the nature of the stocks and the variety of stock categories held. The following wording may be suitable in a straightforward case.

Example 22.4 – Disclosure of accounting policy on stock

Stocks are included at the lower of cost and net realisable value. In the case of raw materials, consumables and goods purchased for resale, stocks are valued at purchase price using the first in, first out method. In the case of work in progress and manufactured goods, stocks are valued at production cost to the relevant stage of manufacture; production cost consists of direct material and labour costs, together with an appropriate proportion of production overheads.

Replacement cost of stocks

22.26 Where stocks have been valued on the basis of one of the averaging methods permitted by CA 1985, any material difference between this value and the replacement cost of the stocks must be disclosed in the accounts. Where the actual purchase price or production cost of stock items has been calculated on an individual basis (ie without the need for one of the methods set out in CA 1985), this disclosure need not be given. Replacement cost will usually be the amount that would need to be paid to replace the stocks at their current cost. However, CA 1985 permits the disclosure to be based on the most recent purchase price or production cost, but only if this will give a more appropriate standard of comparison for the class of items in question. The disclosure is usually given in a narrative footnote to the analysis of stocks.

Example 22.5 – Disclosure on replacement cost

Stocks	*20X2*	*20X1*
	£	£
Raw materials and consumables	546	481
Work in progress	143	128
Finished goods	322	279
	1,011	888

The current replacement cost of stocks is £1,250,000 (20X1: £925,000).

There is no specific requirement in CA 1985 for a statement where the difference is not considered material, but it is good practice to include this where appropriate.

Example 22.6 – Where difference is not material

There is no material difference between the replacement cost of stocks and the value included in the balance sheet.

CONSIGNMENT STOCKS

Nature of consignment stocks

22.27 The requirements of FRS 5 'Reporting the Substance of Transactions' are considered in **Chapter 3**. Consignment stocks are one of the items potentially affected by this accounting standard and accounting for consignment stocks is specifically considered in the Application Notes to FRS 5. Consignment stocks are particularly common in the motor dealership trade, but may arise in a number of businesses. Essentially consignment stock is held for sale by one party but legally owned by another party. In the case of motor dealerships, the stock is usually held by the dealer but is legally owned by the manufacturer. The dealer is given the right to sell the stock in the normal course of business, with the option of returning unsold stock to the manufacturer, usually within a specified time limit. In most cases, the stock will be physically held at the dealer's business premises. The discussion below uses a motor dealership as an example, but the principles apply equally to other types of consignment stocks.

Transfer of legal title

22.28 Under most consignment stock arrangements for motor dealerships, legal title remains with the manufacturer until:

- the dealer sells the car to a third party;
- the dealer elects to take the car as a demonstration model; or
- a specified time period elapses, after which the dealer must formally acquire the goods (unless he has previously exercised the option to return them to the manufacturer).

Legal title passes to the dealer when one of these events takes place and at that point he is required to pay the manufacturer for the goods.

Deposit arrangements

22.29 Under some agreements the dealer is required to pay a deposit to the manufacturer. This may be a fixed amount or may vary over a period of time and may or may not be interest free. In some cases, the deposit may be arranged through a financing institution (sometimes linked to the manufacturer) which makes the payment direct to the manufacturer but charges interest to the dealer.

On or off balance sheet?

22.30 The issue here is: does the dealer have an asset (usually vehicle stocks) and a liability (the equivalent finance effectively provided by the manufacturer) which should be recorded on his balance sheet? This must be assessed by considering the access that the dealer has to the benefits of the stock and the exposure that he has to any inherent risks associated with the benefit. The solution will depend on the precise terms of the agreement between the dealer and the manufacturer and the impact of the following issues will often be relevant:

— whether the dealer is protected against increases in the manufacturer's price for the cars;

— whether the dealer bears the risk of holding slow-moving or obsolete stock and having to sell this at reduced prices; and

— the potential financing arrangements, including any deposit and any interest charges which the dealer may be required to pay.

An assessment of each factor will not necessarily lead to the same conclusion, and it may therefore be necessary to weigh up which are the most important factors for each particular situation.

Dealer's protection against price increases

22.31 As explained in **22.28** above, legal title will usually pass to the dealer on the occurrence of a particular event (eg the sale of the car to a third party) and at this point the dealer will be required to pay the manufacturer for the car. The key issue here will usually be the basis of the payment, which may be:

— a price fixed at the date that the dealer took delivery of the car; or

— the manufacturer's list price at the date that legal title passes.

The first situation indicates that the car became an asset of the dealer at the date of delivery (ie because the price was fixed at that date and the manufacturer is unable to pass on any subsequent price increases). The second situation indicates that the car is an asset of the manufacturer until the date when legal title passes, because the dealer has no protection against price increases between the date of delivery and the date that title passes.

Right to return the car to the manufacturer

22.32 Under some agreements the dealer will have the right to return the car to the manufacturer (usually within a specified time limit) without any penalty. In this case, the dealer does not bear any risk of the stock being slow-moving or becoming obsolete. This suggests that the stock is an asset of the manufacturer rather than the dealer (ie because the manufacturer bears the risk). If the dealer does not have the right to return the car without payment of a penalty this suggests that the car is an asset of the dealer, because he bears the risk of having to sell at a reduced price if the car proves to be slow-moving or becomes obsolete. In some situations it will be necessary to look at the actual practice in respect of the return of cars to the manufacturer, as well as the rights of each party under the agreement. If the dealer has the right to return cars within a specified time but rarely does so, this indicates that the cars are his stock because he is accepting the potential commercial risk of holding them. Conversely, if the manufacturer introduces incentives to encourage the dealer not to return the cars (eg by extending the consignment period at no financial detriment to the dealer), the fact that the dealer retains the cars will not necessarily indicate that they are his stock, because he may not be taking any additional risk by not returning them to the manufacturer.

Right of manufacturer to require return of the car

22.33 The manufacturer may retain the right to require the dealer to return the car, or to transfer the car to another dealer. Where the dealer receives no compensation, and cars are frequently removed in this way in practice, this would indicate that the stock belongs to the manufacturer rather than the dealer. If the dealer receives compensation from the manufacturer for such returns, or transfers are not actually requested in practice, the stock is more likely to be considered to belong to the dealer.

Accounting treatment – asset of the dealer

22.34 Where the substance of the arrangement is that the consignment stock is effectively an asset of the dealer, the stock should be brought onto the balance sheet, along with the corresponding liability to pay the manufacturer. Where the dealer has paid a deposit to the manufacturer, this should normally be deducted from the liability. The notes to the accounts will need to include:

- an explanation of the arrangement;
- the principal terms; and
- the amount of consignment stock included in the balance sheet.

Accounting treatment – asset of the manufacturer

22.35 Where the substance of the arrangement is that the consignment stock remains an asset of the manufacturer, stock items will only be included in the dealer's balance sheet when legal title has effectively passed (eg the consignment period has expired and the dealer has not elected to return the car). Where the dealer has paid a deposit to the manufacturer, this should normally be included in debtors, as no liability to the manufacturer will be recorded in the balance sheet. The notes to the accounts will need to include:

— an explanation of the arrangement;

— the principal terms; and

— the amount of consignment stock held at the year-end.

SALE AND REPURCHASE AGREEMENTS

Nature of a sale and repurchase agreement

22.36 Sale and repurchase agreements are another type of transaction potentially affected by FRS 5 'Reporting the Substance of Transactions' and the Application Notes to the standard specifically cover the accounting treatment of such agreements. The requirements of FRS 5 are considered in detail in **Chapter 3**. The paragraphs below only consider sale and repurchase agreements which might have an impact on stocks. A sale and repurchase agreement is an agreement under which one party agrees to sell an asset to a second party but where the terms of the agreement provide for the first party to repurchase the asset at some point in the future. The issue is whether the original sale should be recorded as such, or whether the terms of the agreement effectively mean that the asset was not sold, but rather that finance was provided by the second party, effectively secured on the asset. This type of agreement has been particularly common in situations where stock is required to be held for a considerable period of time before it can be sold to customers.

Example 22.7 – Sale and repurchase in practice

An often quoted example is that of a whisky distiller, who 'sells' whisky stock to a bank, with the option to repurchase at a higher price in (say) ten years (ie when the stock has matured). In most cases such an agreement will effectively be a loan from the bank to the distiller, secured on the whisky stock, with the difference between the original selling price and the higher repurchase price representing the interest charge on the loan.

Benefits and risks

22.37 In order to assess the commercial reality of the transaction, it is necessary to consider:

— which party benefits from the use, development or ultimate sale of the asset; and

— which party bears the potential risks of decreases in value of the asset.

In the case of a sale and repurchase agreement, the key features which will decide the commercial effect of the transaction, and thus how it should be accounted for, will usually be:

- the original selling price;
- the repurchase price; and
- the nature of the repurchase part of the agreement, which may take the form of:
  - an option for the seller to repurchase,
  - an option for the buyer to resell,
  - a combination of these options, or
  - an unconditional commitment for both parties.

Original selling price

22.38 Where the selling price is not equivalent to market value at the date of the transaction, there is a strong indication that the seller is in effect retaining some of the benefits and risks relating to the asset. He will therefore still retain an asset (which may or may not be the original asset) and a potential liability to the buyer.

Unconditional commitment to repurchase

22.39 Where the seller has an unconditional commitment to repurchase the asset, there is no question that he has both a liability to the buyer and an asset (ie continued access to the benefits of the original asset), both of which should be recorded on the seller's balance sheet. It is important to recognise that a commercial commitment may exist even if a legal commitment does not, for instance where the asset is essential to the seller's future business or there is an unwritten agreement that repurchase will take place. Returning to the example of the whisky stocks above (**Example 22.7** above), the distiller will undoubtedly repurchase the stocks because he will need them to continue in business. Equally, the transaction would make little commercial sense for the bank if it was not on the understanding that the distiller would repurchase the stocks.

Options to repurchase and resell

22.40 Options must also be viewed from the point of view of commercial sense. If it is inevitable that the option will be exercised (ie because the transaction would not make sense for one, or both, parties if this did not happen), the option is effectively artificial and the situation is not really any different to an unconditional commitment. The terms of an option may make it inevitable that one party will exercise it. However, if there is a genuine commercial possibility that an option will not be exercised, this may strengthen the argument that the seller does not have an asset and liability that should be reflected on his balance sheet. In this case the other terms of the agreement may well be the deciding factors.

Accounting treatment

22.41 Where the substance of the sale and repurchase agreement is that the transaction is a secured loan, the asset should remain on the seller's balance sheet and the proceeds should be shown as a liability. The liability should be treated in the same way as any other loan, and if interest is effectively chargeable, it should be accrued over the period of the loan. If the value of the asset decreases, an appropriate provision should be made in the accounts. The notes to the accounts should include an explanation of:

- the main features of the agreement;
- the status of the asset; and
- the relationship between the asset and the liability.

Where the substance of the agreement is that the original asset has been sold, but the seller has an option to repurchase the asset, the new asset (eg the option to repurchase) and the contingent liability should be accounted for prudently and in the same way as any other contingencies (ie in accordance with FRS 12 'Provisions, Contingent Liabilities and Contingent Assets'). Therefore:

- any unconditional commitment should be included on the balance sheet;
- provision should be made for any expected loss; and
- contingent assets and gains should only be recognised when realised.

In this case, the notes to the accounts should include:

- an explanation of the main features of the agreement;
- an explanation of the status of the asset;
- an explanation of the relationship between the asset and the liability;
- the terms of any provision for repurchase; and
- details of any guarantees under the arrangement.

Chapter 23

Long-term Contracts

IDENTIFICATION OF LONG-TERM CONTRACTS

Definition of long-term contract

23.1 Long-term contracts are considered separately within SSAP 9 'Stocks and Long-Term Contracts'. The standard defines a long-term contract as:

> 'A contract entered into for the design, manufacture or construction of a single substantial asset or the provision of a service (or of a combination of assets or services which together constitute a single project) where the time taken substantially to complete the contract is such that the contract activity falls into different accounting periods.'

The key factors therefore are that the contract relates to a single project and that the time taken to complete the work spans at least two accounting periods. Long-term contracts arise mainly within activities such as construction or engineering (e.g. the construction of an office block, the construction of a road, the installation of major plant and equipment, the installation of a public address system in a large complex) but they can easily occur in other businesses as well.

Accounting treatment to avoid distortion

23.2 Under normal accounting requirements, sales are usually recognised as turnover when delivery or completion has taken place. However, if this approach is adopted in the case of long-term contracts, the accounts might not give a fair view of the activity that has taken place during the year (i.e. the accounts would show the results of contracts completed during the year rather than work undertaken during the year). SSAP 9 therefore requires turnover and profits (or losses) in respect of long-term contracts to be recognised as the work proceeds, subject to the following stringent conditions:

- the amount of turnover recognised must be appropriate to the stage of completion of the contract;
- attributable profit should be recognised only where the outcome of the contract can be assessed with reasonable certainty;

— attributable profit must be calculated on a prudent basis;

— expected losses must be provided for in full as soon as they are foreseen.

Contracts lasting more or less than one year

23.3 SSAP 9 explains that a long-term contract will usually extend for a period of more than one year, but this is not an essential feature of a long-term contract. Contracts lasting less than 12 months may therefore meet the definition of a long-term contract if:

— they satisfy the criteria set out in the standard; and

— they are sufficiently material that failure to account for them as long-term contracts could distort the turnover and profits disclosed in the accounts.

Need for consistency

23.4 The definition of a long-term contract in SSAP 9 allows companies a degree of flexibility in establishing which transactions should be accounted for as long-term contracts and it specifically requires the assessment to take account of the company's business and the industry within which it operates. It is quite possible under SSAP 9 for one company to classify a contract as short-term whilst a second company classifies a very similar contract as long-term. One of the most important points, therefore, is that each company should adopt a consistent approach year by year. To achieve this, a company potentially involved in long-term contracts should:

— develop its own precise definition for a long-term contract, following the guidance set out in SSAP 9 and the related notes;

— apply this definition consistently year by year to the contracts in which it is involved;

— explain clearly in the accounting policy note how it defines a long-term contract for accounting purposes.

Contracts with separable parts

23.5 In some long-term contracts, the overall project is broken down into clearly defined parts, for which sales values are agreed and invoiced. SSAP 9 requires these contracts to be accounted for by matching costs and revenues for each separate part of the contract (i.e. by effectively treating each separate part of the contract as a contract in its own right). However, an overall assessment of the project will still be required (i.e. expected future revenues compared with expected future costs for the project as a whole) to establish whether any provision is required in respect of foreseeable losses.

Changing circumstances

23.6 Where a contract extends over several accounting periods, the estimated outcome of the contract may vary quite substantially over the period of the contract. This may be as a result of unforeseen difficulties over the work, variations to the contract whilst the work is in progress, or the incidence of claims and counter-claims relating to the contract. At the end of each accounting period, the profit and loss account and balance sheet should reflect the best estimate of the expected outcome of the contract at that point in time. The results shown in the profit and loss account for each year will therefore reflect the profit or loss in respect of work completed during the year, and also the impact of any changes in circumstances that have arisen during that year, which result in changes to the estimated outcome of the contract as a whole.

RECOGNITION OF TURNOVER

Individual consideration of contracts

23.7 In assessing and recognising turnover and attributable profit for accounts purposes, the standard requires each long-term contract to be considered individually. Carrying out the assessment on a total basis might result in unacceptable off-setting of potential losses against potential profits. SSAP 9's requirement is consistent with the requirement in CA 1985 that individual components of assets and liabilities should be considered separately when calculating the aggregate value of an asset or liability.

Ascertaining turnover

23.8 The turnover recognised in the profit and loss account for each contract should reflect the value of work carried out and SSAP 9 requires the assessment of turnover to take account of:

- the stage of completion of the work;
- the company's business; and
- the industry in which it operates.

For example, in the case of long-term construction work, turnover will often be based on internal, or in some cases independent, valuations of work completed by the balance sheet date. In other contracts, there may be specific points during the work where sales values can be established with reasonable accuracy (e.g. where the customer has taken delivery), so that only work completed since that point needs to be assessed and valued.

Disclosure of method used

23.9 SSAP 9 recognises that there are different ways of establishing turnover, any of which might meet its requirements, and therefore does not prescribe how turnover should be calculated. As a result, the accounting policy note is required to explain the method used to ascertain turnover in respect of long-term contracts for inclusion in the accounts.

CALCULATION OF ATTRIBUTABLE PROFIT

Definition of attributable profit

23.10 SSAP 9 defines attributable profit as:

> 'That part of the total profit currently estimated to arise over the duration of the contract, after allowing for estimated remedial and maintenance costs and increases in costs so far as not recoverable under the terms of the contract, that fairly reflects the profit attributable to that part of the work performed at the accounting date. (There can be no attributable profit until the profitable outcome of the contract can be assessed with reasonable certainty)'.

The amount of attributable profit must be calculated on a prudent basis.

Contract outcome assessed with reasonable certainty

23.11 The first stage, before any profit is recognised in the accounts, is that the company must be able to assess the likely outcome of the contract and be reasonably certain of the level of profit that will be achieved. SSAP 9 does not provide any further guidance on this point, although the notes to the standard state that, for each contract, the company should define the point before which no profit will be recognised. In the early stages of a contract it will usually be difficult to assess the end result with the appropriate degree of certainty. In practice, many companies take the view that profit should not be recognised until the contract is at least 50% complete. History and experience will usually indicate the appropriate percentage to use. Although it will not usually be acceptable to recognise profit in the early stages of a contract, it may nevertheless be appropriate to recognise as turnover the value of the work completed up to the balance sheet date and to include costs up to this level in the profit and loss account (unless an overall loss is anticipated, in which case full provision for this will need to be made – see **23.15** below).

Costs to be included

23.12 The overall profitability of each contract is assessed by comparing expected future revenues with projected costs, including:

— costs actually incurred to date;

— estimated costs to be incurred in completing the work;

— the estimated costs of any rectification work, or any work that might be required under guarantees given in respect of the contract - these can be difficult to assess and some companies provide for them on the basis of a percentage of total contract costs, the percentage being based on past experience on similar contracts; and

— the costs of any other future work to be undertaken under the terms of the contract.

The estimates for future costs should take into account:

— likely increases in wages and salaries;

— increases in the price of raw materials; and

— the effect of inflation on general overheads,

unless it is clear that the contract provides for these increases to be passed on to the customer.

Profit earned to date

23.13 Where the comparison of expected revenues and projected costs for the contract as a whole indicates that a profit is likely to be achieved, and the contract is sufficiently far advanced for this assessment to be reasonably certain, the total profit on the contract must be apportioned between the element earned to date (which will be recognised in the accounts) and the element to be earned in the remaining part of the contract. The notes to SSAP 9 require the recognition of profits in the accounts to be:

— on a prudent basis, and

— based on a method that is applied consistently from year to year.

For instance, profit may be apportioned on the basis of the stage of completion of the contract as at the balance sheet date, the proportion of total costs incurred to that date or on the basis of the work that has been valued and accepted by the customer at the balance sheet date (on major contracts, inspection and valuation by the customer is usually carried out at specific stages during the contract). In the same way that the method of ascertaining turnover must be disclosed, SSAP 9 requires the accounting policy note to explain the method of ascertaining attributable profit.

Accounting entries

23.14 Once attributable profit has been calculated for each contract, the appropriate element of costs to date should be transferred from total costs incurred on the contract to cost of sales in the profit and loss account (or to the appropriate profit and loss account headings where Format 2 is used):

Example 23.1 – Calculating attributable profit

Contract 1	£
Value of work done to date	245,000
Total costs incurred to date	267,000
Total contract value	320,000
Expected total costs	307,000
Expected profit	13,000
Attributable profit to be recognised in accounts: 245/320 x 13,000	9,950
Turnover recognised in accounts	245,000
Attributable profit	(9,950)
Cost of sales to be recognised	235,050
Total costs incurred to date	267,000
Transferred to cost of sales	(235,050)
Costs carried forward	31,950

ESTIMATION OF FORESEEABLE LOSSES

Provision for projected loss

23.15 Where, on the basis of the costs set out in 23.12 above, a contract is projected to result in an overall loss, SSAP 9 requires full provision to be made in the accounts as soon as the loss is foreseen. This should be done irrespective of:

— whether or not work has yet commenced on the contract;

— the proportion of work carried out by the balance sheet date;

— the amount of profits expected to arise on other contracts.

Example 23.2 – Recognising an estimated loss

Contract 2	£
Value of work done to date	245,000
Total costs incurred to date	267,000
Total contract value	320,000

Contract 2	£
Expected total costs	327,900
Expected loss	(7,900)
Turnover recognised to date	245,000
Projected loss recognised in full	7,900
Costs of sales to be recognised	252,900
Total costs to date	267,000
Transferred to cost of sales	252,900
Costs carried forward	14,100

The provision for the loss should normally be treated as part of the overall charge to the profit and loss account in respect of costs relating to the turnover recognised in the accounts.

Cost of sales greater than costs incurred to date

23.16 Where the provision for the loss results in a cost of sales charge that is greater than the amount of costs incurred to date, the excess should be shown in the accounts as a provision or accrual for a future loss.

Example 23.3 – Cost of sales greater than costs incurred to date

Contract 3	£
Value of work done to date	245,000
Total costs incurred to date	247,000
Total contract value	320,000
Expected total costs	327,900
Expected loss	(7,900)
Turnover recognised to date	245,000
Projected loss recognised in full	7,900
Cost of sales to be recognised	252,900
Total costs to date	247,000
Transferred to cost of sales	(252,900)
Provision/accrual for future loss	(5,900)

Treatment of loss as provision or accrual

23.17 SSAP 9 requires a provision or accrual for a foreseeable loss to be included within provisions for liabilities and charges or within creditors, as appropriate. However, it is singularly unhelpful in explaining the distinction between a provision and an accrual in these circumstances. CA 1985 defines a provision as:

> 'any amount retained as reasonably necessary for the purpose of providing for any liability or loss which is either likely to be incurred, or certain to be incurred but uncertain as to the amount or as to the date on which it will arise.'

It would therefore seem that a provision for a foreseeable loss on a long-term contract should be included under provisions for liabilities and charges if there is a degree of uncertainty over the eventual amount or expected timing of the loss. If the loss can be established with certainty, it should be treated as an accrual and included with creditors (or under the separate heading for accruals and deferred income where this is used).

ACCOUNTING FOR CONTRACT VARIATIONS AND CLAIMS

Impact of variations and claims

23.18 Two of the most complex aspects of long-term contracts are the agreement of variations which arise whilst the contract is in progress and the settlement of claims relating to the contract (e.g. where the customer claims penalties for delays or late completion of the work). The situation can become even more complicated where the contractor issues counter-claims against the customer or where sub-contractors are involved and the main contractor issues equivalent claims for penalties against the sub-contractors.

Contract variations

23.19 If significant variations to the contract have been approved during the course of the work, but the additional sums to be paid for these variations have not been agreed, a reasonable but prudent estimate of the likely value of the additional work should be made and should be included as part of the total sales value of the contract (i.e. when carrying out assessments of overall revenue, costs and profitability).

Claims

23.20 In the case of claims, or unapproved variations, the situation will usually be much more uncertain, even if negotiations are in progress. On larger contracts, negotiations can be very protracted and can themselves extend over more than a year. Claims and unapproved variations should generally only be recognised in the accounts when negotiations have reached an advanced stage. In particular there should be:

— evidence that the customer is prepared to accept the claim (or unapproved variation) in principle; and

— a clear indication of the amount that is likely to be paid.

ACCOUNTS DISCLOSURES

Location of disclosures

23.21 Depending on the individual circumstances of each contract, disclosures may be required on the balance sheet within:

- stocks;
- debtors;
- creditors; or
- provisions for liabilities and charges.

The following paragraphs consider the detailed disclosure requirements and the related accounting entries.

Inclusion of long-term contracts in stocks

23.22 The value of long-term contracts in progress should be shown as a separate item (long-term contract balances) within stocks. Each individual contract should be shown at total costs incurred to date, less:

- amounts transferred to cost of sales;
- provisions for foreseeable losses;
- payments on account not matched with turnover.

Separate disclosure should be made of:

- net costs, less foreseeable losses; and
- payments on account.

Example 23.4 – Long-term contracts included in stocks

Contract 1	£
Value of work done to date	245,000
Total costs incurred to date	267,000
Payments received on account	215,000
Total contract value	320,000
Expected total costs	307,000
Expected profit	13,000
Attributable profit to be recognised in accounts: 245/320 x 13,000	9,950
Turnover recognised in accounts	245,000

Contract 1	£
Attributable profit	(9,950)
Cost of sales to be recognised	235,050

The amount included in stocks in respect of this contract will be:

	£
Total costs incurred to date	267,000
Transferred to cost of sales	(235,050)
Included in long-term contract balances	31,950

Contract 2	£
Value of work done to date	245,000
Total costs incurred to date	267,000
Total contract value	320,000
Expected total costs	327,900
Expected loss	(7,900)
Turnover recognised to date	245,000
Projected loss recognised in full	7,900
Cost of sales to be recognised	252,900

The amount to be included in stocks in respect of this contract will be:

	£
Total costs incurred to date	267,000
Transferred to cost of sales (including loss provision)	(252,900)
Included in long-term contract balances	14,100

Inclusion of amounts recoverable on contracts within debtors

23.23 Where the amount recognised as turnover exceeds payments received on account, the excess should be shown separately within debtors as 'amounts recoverable on contracts'.

Example 23.5 – Excess turnover shown within debtors

Contract 1	£
Value of work done to date	245,000
Total costs incurred to date	267,000
Payments received on account	215,000
Amount recognised as turnover	245,000

Contract 1	£
Payments on accounts	215,000
Amounts recoverable on contracts	30,000
(included as a separate heading in debtors)	

This treatment reflects the fact that once the value of work done has been recognised in the profit and loss account as turnover, it is not appropriate to continue to show it under stocks in the balance sheet. It is therefore disclosed as an amount recoverable from the customer even though it may not have been invoiced at the balance sheet date.

Inclusion of payments on account in creditors

23.24 Where payments on account received from the customer exceed:

- the amounts matched with turnover; and
- the amounts off-set against long-term contract balances,

the excess should be shown separately under creditors as payments on account.

Example 23.6

Contract 4	£
Value of work done	105,000
Total costs incurred to date	124,000
Payments on account	118,000
Total expected revenue	130,000
Total expected costs	144,000
Foreseeable loss	(14,000)
Amount recognised as turnover	105,000
Amount recognised as cost of sales	(119,000)
Loss recognised in the accounts	(14,000)
The amount to be recognised in the balance sheet is therefore:	
Turnover	105,000
Payments on account received	(118,000)
Excess payments on account	(13,000)
The amount recognised as long-term contract balances is:	
Total costs incurred to date	124,000
Transferred to cost of sales	(119,000)
	5,000

Therefore, £5,000 of the excess payments on account should be off-set against this balance; the remaining £8,000 should be included in creditors as payments on account.

The note to the accounts on long-term contracts should show separately:

	£
Net costs, less foreseeable losses	5,000
Payments on account	(5,000)
	—

Excess provision for foreseeable losses

23.25 If the provision or accrual for foreseeable losses exceeds the costs incurred (after adjusting for transfers to cost of sales), the excess should be included under provisions for liabilities and charges or under accruals. This is illustrated in **Example 23.3** above.

Summary of disclosures

23.26 The appendix to this chapter draws together the details from **Examples 23.3** to **23.6** to illustrate the overall disclosures that should be given in the accounts if these four contracts were in progress within one company.

Accounting policy

23.27 SSAP 9 requires disclosure of the accounting policy that has been applied in respect of long-term contracts, and in particular the method of calculating turnover and attributable profit. The wording of the policy in each individual company will vary, depending on the exact policies adopted, but **Example 23.7** illustrates the type of explanation that should be given.

Example 23.7 – Disclosure of accounting policy for long-term contracts

The company classifies as long-term those contracts which relate to the construction of a single asset, where the contract activity extends over more than one accounting period. The length of these contracts usually exceeds 12 months.

The amount recognised as turnover represents the value of work carried out during the period. Where the outcome of a contract can be assessed with reasonable certainty, attributable profit is recognised in proportion to the amount of turnover recognised in the accounts. No profit is recognised in respect of contracts that are less than 50% complete at the balance sheet date. Full provision is made for any foreseeable losses.

Long-term contract balances are included in the balance sheet at net cost, less foreseeable losses, and after deduction of any related payments on account. Where the amount recognised as turnover exceeds the payments on account in respect of that contract, the balance is included in debtors under amounts recoverable on contracts.

Inclusion of interest in the cost of long-term contracts

23.28 CA 1985 allows the production cost of an asset (including stock) to include interest on capital borrowed to finance production, but only to the extent that it relates to the period of production. The notes to SSAP 9 emphasise that it will not usually be appropriate to include interest payable on borrowings as part of the cost of long-term contracts (or, indeed, of other stock items). If, in exceptional circumstances, it is considered appropriate to include interest (i.e. where specific borrowings can be identified as financing individual long-term contracts) the notes to the accounts should disclose the fact that interest has been included and the amount involved. This is consistent with the disclosure requirements of the Act.

LIKELY FUTURE DEVELOPMENTS

FRED 28 – 'Inventories; Construction and service contracts'

23.29 The ASB issued FRED 28 'Inventories; Construction and service contracts' in May 2002 as part of its project to achieve convergence between UK accounting standards and international accounting standards. The Exposure Draft sets out the proposed text of two new accounting standards intended to replace SSAP 9 'Stocks and long-term contracts' with requirements based on a proposed revision of IAS 2 and the existing IAS 11. The aspects of IAS 18 'Revenue' that deal with service contracts are also incorporated into FRED 28. No major changes to UK requirements are proposed, but the following differences in respect of the accounting treatment to be applied to contract costs and revenue will have some effect:

- FRED 28 proposes that contract revenue and related costs should be recognised when the outcome of a contract can be 'estimated reliably' – this is more consistent with FRS 18 'Accounting policies' and the ASB Statement of Principles than the SSAP 9 references to prudence and outcomes that can be assessed with 'reasonable certainty';
- FRED 28 proposes that any amounts received from a customer before work is performed should be recognised as a separate liability, but that any remaining balance sheet amount should be presented as a single asset or liability – SSAP 9 currently requires a more detailed analysis, potentially involving debtors, creditors, stock and provisions; and

- FRED 28 notes that its requirements may be applied to separately identifiable components of a single contract or to a group of contracts together, if this reflects the substance of the transaction – the ASB considers that the practical effect of this will be no different to applying the present SSAP 9 within the context of FRS 5 'Reporting the substance of transactions'.

Appendix

SUMMARY OF DISCLOSURES

Profit and loss account	*Contract 1* (Example 23.4) (Example 23.5)	*Contract 2* (Example 23.4)	*Contract 3* (Example 23.3)	*Contract 4* (Example 23.6)	*Total*
Turnover – value of work done	245,000	245,000	245,000	105,000	840,000
Cost of sales	(235,050)	(252,900)	(252,900)	(119,000)	(859,850)
Recorded profit/(loss)	9,950	(7,900)	(7,900)	(14,000)	(19,850)
Balance sheet					
Long-term contract balances:					
Net costs, less foreseeable losses	31,950	14,100	—	5,000	51,050
Payments on account	—	—	—	(5,000)	(5,000)
	31,950	14,100	—	—	46,050
Debtors – amounts recoverable on contracts	30,000	—	—	—	30,000
Creditors/provisions – provisions for future loss	—	—	(5,900)	—	(5,900)
Creditors – payments on account	—	—	—	(8,000)	(8,000)
Cash: Paid (i.e. costs incurred to date)	(267,000)	(267,000)	(247,000)	(124,000)	(905,000)
Received (i.e. payments on accounts)*	215,000	245,000	245,000	118,000	823,000
	9,950	(7,900)	(7,900)	(14,000)	(19,850)

*In contracts 2 and 3, payments on account are assumed to equal turnover (i.e. the value of work done).

Chapter 24

Debtors, Prepayments and Accrued Income

TRADE DEBTORS

Sales ledger balances

24.1 Trade debtors will normally comprise the aggregate of the outstanding balances shown on the company's sales ledger at the end of the accounting period. As debtors are shown within current assets, they must be stated at the lower of purchase price and net realisable value. The definition of purchase price in the Act effectively allows debtors to be stated at an amount that includes the profit element to be earned by the company, but if the net realisable value of debtors is lower than the amount recorded in the company's books, appropriate provision must be made. Provisions made against the balances recorded in the sales ledger will normally comprise provisions:

- for bad and doubtful debts;
- for credit notes due to be issued;
- in respect of settlement discount to be allowed.

Bad and doubtful debts

24.2 All debts shown on the ledger at the end of the accounts period should be reviewed for expected recoverability, with particular attention being paid to amounts that are outstanding for more than the credit period normally granted by the company. Where payment seems unlikely to be received, or may not be received in full, provision should be made. A bad debt provision may be totally specific (i.e. relating entirely to known problem debtors) or may be partly general. General provisions can be particularly useful where there are a large number of relatively small balances on the ledger. The general provision reflects the fact that a proportion of these balances may not be paid, even though it may not be possible to identify individual bad debts at the balance sheet date. General provisions are usually calculated as a set percentage of the total amount outstanding in respect of unprovided debts. Where possible, this percentage should be based on past experience of bad debts. Although a prudent approach should be taken when assessing the recoverability of debts, provisions should nevertheless be reasonable (i.e. the best estimate of the likely outcome) rather than excessively pessimistic.

Credit notes

24.3 Provision should also be made where credit notes have been issued after the year-end in respect of invoices included in the year-end balances, or where it is known that such credit notes will be issued (e.g. because a price amendment has recently been agreed with the customer). Once again, this recognises that, in these cases, the full amount of the debt shown at the end of the year will not actually be paid by the customer.

Settlement discounts

24.4 Where a company gives discounts for early settlement of invoices, the full amount of the sales value is usually invoiced to the customer. The appropriate discount is then deducted by the customer when making payment. The availability of settlement discounts will therefore mean that the full amount of the balances shown on the sales ledger may not be paid in cash. Settlement discounts are normally only given for prompt payment (e.g. within 7 or 14 days of the invoice date) and in most cases, there will be little difficulty in establishing the amount of discount actually taken in respect of balances which were outstanding at the end of the accounting period. For accounts purposes, year-end trade debtors should be reduced by the amount of discount actually granted by the company in respect of those balances (i.e. the discount should be treated as a cost in the year in which the sale was recorded). In exceptional circumstances (e.g. where the accounts need to be finalised very quickly after the end of the accounting period) it may be necessary to estimate the amount of settlement discount that will be taken by customers. It will usually be possible to calculate the proportion of customers who take advantage of the discount, based on past experience and apply this to those balances that are still within the discount period, to arrive at an appropriate provision for accounts purposes (e.g. where discount is allowed for payment within 21 days, invoices outstanding for more than 21 days should not be included in the calculations, as customers will not be entitled to settlement discount in respect of these items).

Credit balances

24.5 Small credit balances arising on the sales ledger can usually be ignored on the grounds that they are immaterial, but if a material credit balance arises on a debtor account (e.g. as a result of the customer paying an invoice twice by mistake), the credit balance should normally be transferred from debtors to creditors. This is particularly relevant if the company is likely to make a cash payment to the customer to clear the balance.

Uninvoiced sales

24.6 There is no guidance on how to classify any uninvoiced sales arising around the year-end date. In many cases, the sales ledger will be held open for a day or two after the year-end to allow invoices in respect of sales made on the last day (or days) to be processed. In this case, they will form part of the year-end sales ledger and will automatically be included in trade debtors for accounts purposes. Where this does not happen, an adjustment will need to be made to incorporate the sales values of any items delivered in the accounting period but not invoiced at the balance sheet date. Such items should normally be shown as part of trade debtors as they relate to turnover. However, if the amounts involved are not material, they are sometimes included under one of the other headings (e.g. other debtors or accrued income).

LESSOR'S NET INVESTMENT IN FINANCE LEASES

Nature of a finance lease

24.7 When a lessor enters into a finance lease with a lessee, the lessor retains legal title to the asset, but transfers substantially all the risks and rewards of ownership of the asset to the lessee. In return for this, the lessor receives an income stream in the form of lease rentals. The underlying substance of the transaction, therefore, is that the lessor provides finance to the lessee to enable the latter to have access to, and use of, the asset, and that the lessor expects a return from the lessee on the finance provided. SSAP 21 'Accounting for Leases and Hire Purchase Contracts' requires a finance lease to be recorded in the accounts of a lessor based on the underlying substance of the agreement. As a finance lease is similar in character to a loan from the lessor to the lessee, SSAP 21 requires it to be:

- shown within debtors in the lessor's balance sheet;
- included at the amount of the lessor's net investment in the lease.

Net investment in the lease

24.8 At the beginning of the lease agreement, the lessor's net investment in the lease will be the cost of the asset to the lessor, less any grants receivable by him in respect of the asset. In other words, it will be the fair value of the asset at the beginning of the lease agreement.

Payments during the period of the lease

24.9 The lease rentals received from the lessee during the period of the lease must be apportioned between repayment of the 'capital' element of the lease and interest charges on the amount outstanding. During the course of the lease agreement, therefore, the original value of the lessor's net investment in the lease will be reduced by those elements of the lease rentals that are identified as being repayment of the 'capital' effectively advanced to the lessee. The apportionment of lease rentals in the accounts of the lessor is considered in more detail in **Chapter 13**.

Balance sheet disclosure

24.10 The net investment in respect of finance leases must be shown separately within debtors as 'amounts receivable under finance leases'. Where the lessor has also entered into hire purchase agreements with customers, the amount receivable under these agreements must also be disclosed as a separate sub-heading. In effect, the amount disclosed each year will represent:

- the total of the remaining payments due from lessees under the agreements *plus*
- any residual values in respect of the assets (net of any rental rebates that are payable to the lessee in respect of residual value) *less*
- the earnings to be allocated to future accounting periods.

Finance leases and hire purchase agreements will usually extend for more than 12 months, and the amounts receivable in respect of these agreements must therefore be analysed between amounts due within one year of the balance sheet date and those due more than one year after this date.

Provision for bad and doubtful debts

24.11 As with any other debtor, the amount recorded in the balance sheet must be the amount that is expected to be recovered. At the end of the accounting period, the lessor must therefore review the expected recoverability of the amount receivable under each agreement and make appropriate provisions for bad and doubtful debts where necessary.

OTHER DEBTORS

Items normally included

24.12 CA 1985 provides no guidance on how individual items should be classified within the main heading of debtors, but 'other debtors' will usually comprise non-trading amounts receivable, such as sundry loans (e.g. loans advanced to employees), sales proceeds in respect of fixed assets, and other similar items that meet the criteria for recognition as assets.

Tax balances

24.13 Other debtors might also include items such as:

- corporation tax recoverable;
- advance corporation tax recoverable;
- VAT repayment due from Customs and Excise.

There is no requirement under CA 1985 to show tax balances separately when they appear within debtors, although tax creditors do require separate disclosure. If the amounts involved are material, it will usually be advisable to show them separately in the analysis, especially where this will help a reader of the accounts to understand the cash flows relating to tax shown in the cash flow statement.

PREPAYMENTS AND ACCRUED INCOME

Prepayments

24.14 Prepayments will generally comprise pre-paid elements of general overhead expenses, such as rent and rates, insurance, maintenance agreements and vehicle licences. In most cases the amounts involved will not be significant. One significant item that might be included is a prepayment in respect of pension contributions under SSAP 24 'Accounting for pension costs'. SSAP 24 requires an employer to recognise the cost of providing pension benefits on a systematic and rational basis over the period during which the company benefits from the services of the relevant employees. As a result, the accounting treatment of pension costs in respect of defined benefit schemes can be very different to the related cash payments, giving rise to either a prepayment or a liability in the employer's accounts. For accounting periods beginning on or after 1 January 2005, SSAP 24 is superseded by FRS 17 'Retirement Benefits' which requires a different balance sheet presentation in respect of the defined benefit asset or liability (see **Chapter 11**). However, any prepaid contributions at the end of the accounting period should continue to be shown within debtors or prepayments.

Accrued income

24.15 The amounts included as accrued income will vary depending on the nature of the company's activities. Items which might be shown under this heading include:

- amounts receivable in respect of insurance claims
- grants receivable;
- rents receivable; and
- sundry sales income (i.e. sales not relating to the main trading activity).

Rent receivable under an operating lease

24.16 Where an asset, including property, is rented out under an operating lease, SSAP 21 and UITF Abstract 28 'Operating Lease Incentives' require both the rent receivable under the lease and any related incentive offered to the lessee to be recognised over the term of the lease (or the period to the first rent review if shorter), usually on a straight-line basis. The timing of the recognition of the rent receivable may therefore differ from the actual cash flows, and the lessor's balance sheet will include a debtor for accrued rent receivable For instance where an operating lease includes an incentive such as an initial rent free period, no rental will be received during this period but rental income will need to be reflected in the profit and loss account.

Example 24.1 – Accrued rent receivable

A property is rented out for five years under an operating lease. The first year is rent-free. Rent is payable at £5,000 pa for the remaining four years. Total rental income is therefore £20,000 which should be recognised in the lessor's profit and loss account at £4,000 per year for the five years of the lease.

Year 1	Income per accounts	4,000
	Cash received	–
	Debtor	4,000
Year 2	Income per accounts	4,000
	Cash received	5,000
		(1,000)
	Debtor b/fwd	4,000
	Debtor c/fwd	3,000
Year 3	Income per accounts	4,000
	Cash received	5,000
		(1,000)
	Debtor b/fwd	3,000
	Debtor c/fwd	2,000
Year 4	Income per accounts	4,000
	Cash received	5,000
		(1,000)
	Debtor b/fwd	2,000
	Debtor c/fwd	1,000
Year 5	Income per accounts	4,000
	Cash received	5,000
		(1,000)
	Debtor b/fwd	1,000
	Debtor c/fwd	–

UITF Abstract 28 makes two points in relation to the accrued rent receivable carried forward each year:

— where a building is accounted for as an investment property, the value at which it is stated in the balance sheet should exclude any amount that is reported as a separate asset, such as accrued rent receivable; and

— in accordance with normal accounting practice, an amount recognised as a debtor in respect of an operating lease incentive should be written down to the extent that it is not expected to be recoverable.

ACCOUNTING FOR FACTORED DEBTS

Main reasons for factoring debts

24.17 The factoring of debts has become increasingly common as a means of:

— raising finance, by converting debts into cash more quickly than might otherwise be the case;

— providing a degree of protection against the risks of slow payment and bad debts (depending on the nature of the agreement).

In some cases, the factor may also manage the company's sales ledger, but this is usually a completely separate arrangement and will not normally have any impact on the accounting treatment of the debts.

Impact of FRS 5

24.18 The treatment of factored debts is considered in the Application Notes to FRS 5 'Reporting the Substance of Transactions'. The following sections consider only the issues relating specifically to factored debts. The wider impact of FRS 5 is considered in more detail in **Chapter 3**. The principles set out in FRS 5 and the Application Notes apply equally to other arrangements similar to factoring, such as invoice discounting and export financing arrangements.

Importance of reviewing precise terms and conditions

24.19 Factoring agreements take many different forms, and different accounting treatments will be required, depending on the precise terms of each agreement. A thorough understanding of the terms and conditions is therefore necessary in order to establish which of the three possible accounting treatments is appropriate. This should include an understanding and assessment of the commercial and practical effect of the terms and conditions, as well as the theoretical detail.

Usual features of factoring agreements

24.20 Some of the more common features of factoring agreements are as follows:

- The company sells or assigns specific debts to the factor.
- The factor will provide finance to the company usually based on a fixed percentage of the face value of the debts transferred. This may be a non-returnable amount (in which case it will usually be based on a lower percentage of total debts), but in many cases it will be repayable by the company from the amounts actually collected from the relevant debtors.
- The factor will make a charge for the factoring services. This may be a fixed amount, or may vary depending on the amounts actually collected from debtors. The timing of payment may also vary.
- The factor may offer credit protection or insurance cover in respect of unpaid debts, subject to a separate charge usually based on the gross value of factored debts. This will limit the company's potential exposure in respect of slow payment and bad debts.
- The factor may administer the company's sales ledger and thus assume responsibility for the collection of debts and following up non-payment. This is usually subject to a separate arm's length agreement and will not normally affect the accounting treatment of the factored debts.

Possible accounting treatments

24.21 Depending on the precise circumstances of the arrangements, there are three possible accounting treatments in respect of factored debts:

- derecognition;
- separate presentation;
- linked presentation.

The main features of these treatments are considered in the following paragraphs.

Derecognition

24.22 In this case the debts are completely removed from the balance sheet and no liability to the factor is recorded. This treatment is only available where the company does not retain any benefits or risks in connection with the factored debts. This will usually require:

- an outright sale of the debts to the factor at an arm's length price;

- receipt by the company of a fixed, non-returnable payment from the factor in respect of the debts sold;
- no recourse whatsoever to the company in respect of slow payment or non-payment of the debts; and
- no benefit to the company if the debtors pay more promptly than had been anticipated.

Very few factoring agreements will meet all of these requirements. If the conditions are fulfilled, the company will need to record a profit or loss (invariably a loss) on disposal of the debts, representing the difference between the face value of the debts and the fixed payment received from the factor.

Separate presentation

24.23 Under this accounting treatment, the company must continue to show the value of the factored debts on the balance sheet (as part of debtors) and record a liability to the factor (within creditors), representing the finance effectively provided by him in respect of the debts. This approach should be followed where the company has retained significant benefits and risks in relation to the factored debts. The factor's charges should be accrued, and the interest element should be included as part of the interest charge for the year in the profit and loss account. The value of factored debts outstanding at the balance sheet date should be disclosed in the notes to the accounts.

Linked presentation

24.24 Under the linked presentation, the factored debts continue to be shown within debtors but the amount included is reduced by the value of the non-returnable proceeds received by the company from the factor; both amounts must be disclosed separately on the face of the balance sheet. This form of presentation should only be used where the company has retained significant benefits and risks in respect of the factored debts, but the level of its exposure is limited to a specific amount. The interest element of the factor's charges should be included as part of the interest charge for the year in the profit and loss account. The following details should be disclosed in the notes to the accounts:

- the principal terms of the factoring arrangement;
- the gross amount of factored debts outstanding at the balance sheet date;
- the factoring charges recognised in the period, analysed between interest and other charges;
- a statement by the directors that the company is not obliged to support any losses in respect of the debts, nor does it intend to do so;

— a statement that the factor has agreed in writing that it will not require repayment of the amount paid and will not seek recourse from the company in any other form.

Assessment of benefits and risks

24.25 In order to decide which of these three presentations should be used, the benefits and risks retained by the company under the agreement must be assessed. The benefits will usually comprise the future cash flows arising from payments by the debtors. The risks will usually be the risk of slow payment and non-payment (i.e. bad debts). Of these two elements, the risks retained by the company will usually be more critical in the assessment of the transaction for accounting purposes.

Benefits retained by the company

24.26 Under many factoring agreements, the benefits of future cash flows in respect of the debts will appear to rest with the factor (e.g. cash collected in respect of the factored debts will usually be paid into a separate bank account or direct to the factor). However, this may not be the true effect in practice. For instance, where the company is committed to repaying the sums advanced by the factor on or before a specified date (regardless of the level of payment received from the debtors during the period), it will usually be the company that benefits from the cash received from the debtors (i.e. this cash will form a source of funds from which the company can repay the factor). Equally, the company bears the risks of the debtors not making payment before the date when it is committed to repaying the factor. In this case the company will have to use other funds to make the repayment.

Benefits resting with the factor

24.27 However, if the company receives a non-returnable payment from the factor and is then responsible for passing on all sums received from the debtors, as and when payments are made, the benefit of receiving payment from the debtors will usually rest with the factor, as will the risks relating to the slow payment and non-payment of the debts.

The risk of slow payment

24.28 The basis of the factoring charges will often be a key factor in the assessment of who bears the risk of slow payment. Where charges are raised for a fixed sum, agreed at the time that the debts are transferred, the factor will usually bear the risk of slow payment. Where the factoring charges are variable, depending on the level of payment received from debtors, the risk will usually remain with the company (i.e. if the debtors are slow in paying, the company will bear higher factoring costs). In assessing the risks, it is important to consider the commercial implications of all clauses in the factoring agreement. For instance, the inclusion of bonus payments for early settlement, or retrospective changes to the amounts paid in respect of the debts may alter the overall assessment of risk.

The risk of bad debts

24.29 In some cases the factor may retain all the risk in respect of bad debts. Other agreements may provide for debts that remain uncollected after a specified period (e.g. 90 days) to be transferred back to the company. In this case, the company will retain all the risk of bad debts arising. This may also indicate that the company bears some risk in respect of slow payment, in that a bad debt may be the end result of slow payment.

Practical application

24.30 The application of these requirements may be illustrated by the following basic examples, which consider only the main features of a factoring agreement (in practice, the detailed terms of most factoring agreements will be much more complex).

Example 24.2 – Debt factoring: three scenarios

X Ltd factors debts of £100,000 for:

(A) an initial non-returnable payment from the factor of £75,000, plus further deferred sums, based on the amounts actually collected from the debtors,

(B) a fixed sum of £80,000, with no further amount payable by the factor, and no recourse to the company in respect of bad debts,

(C) a sum of £85,000, which is repayable to the factor in three months' time, at which point any unpaid debts will be transferred back to X Ltd.

Situation A

In this case, X Ltd retains:

— some of the benefits of future payments from debtors, because further sums will be receivable from the factor, depending on the level of payment by the debtors;

— some of the risks of non-payment by the debtors (e.g. if payments do not reach a specified level, no further sums will be paid by the factor). However, X Ltd has limited its potential exposure to the risk of slow payment or bad debts to £25,000 (i.e. proceeds of £75,000 are guaranteed as this sum is non-returnable).

The company should therefore adopt a linked presentation on its balance sheet:

	£	£
Current assets:		
Stocks		233
Debtors:		
Gross debtors factored without recourse	100	
Less: Non-returnable proceeds	(75)	
	25	
Other debtors	124	
		149
Cash at bank and in hand		50
		432

The disclosures outlined in paragraph 24.24 above will also need to be given.

Situation B

In this case, X Ltd has sold the debts outright for a fixed sum and therefore does not retain any benefits from the actual payments made by the debtors. Equally the company does not bear any further risk in relation to the debts.

The company should therefore adopt the derecognition treatment in respect of these debts and will record an overall loss of £20,000 in respect of the factored debts.

Situation C

In this case, X Ltd has retained all the benefits and risks in relation to the debts:

- if the debtors are slow in paying, the company will have to find other funds to repay the factor in three months' time – conversely, if the debtors pay promptly, the company will have the benefit of this;
- all potential bad debts revert to the company after three months – conversely if all the debtors pay in full, the company retains the benefit of this.

In effect, the factor has lent X Ltd £85,000 for a period of three months. The company should therefore adopt separate presentation in its balance sheet. It will record:

- debtors of £100,000;
- a liability to the factor of £85,000.

The value of factored debts will need to be disclosed in the accounts.

In both (A) and (C), the recoverability of the amount included in debtors would need to be considered and provision made where necessary.

ACCOUNTING FOR PRE-CONTRACT COSTS

UITF Abstract 34

24.31 Early in 2002, the UITF considered the accounting treatment to be adopted for pre-contract costs. Some entities incur significant costs in bidding for and securing contracts and the issue had therefore arisen whether pre-contract costs should be recognised as an asset and charged as expenses during the period of the contract and, if so, how such an asset should be measured. The Abstract applies to costs incurred by a supplier in respect of tendering for or securing contracts for:

— the design, construction, manufacture or operation of assets;

— the provision of services; or

— the provision of a combination of assets and services.

It does not apply to costs that are subject to more specific requirements set out in accounting standards (such as FRS 10 'Goodwill and intangible assets', FRS 15 'Tangible fixed assets' or SSAP 13 'Accounting for research and development') or to costs incurred by insurers in acquiring insurance policies.

Whether pre-contract costs are an asset

24.32 An asset is defined in the ASB's 'Statement of Principles' as 'rights or other access to future economic benefits controlled by an entity as a result of past transactions or events'. The Abstract notes that the right to bid for a contract, and the bidding process itself, do not necessarily give rise to rights or access to future economic benefits that are controlled by the entity – if it is possible that a contract will be awarded there may well be an expectation that benefits will accrue to the supplier, but the supplier has no control over the benefits at that stage. The supplier is therefore not in a position to recognise an asset in respect of the potential contract. Expenditure that is invested in tendering for a contract before the supplier obtains control over the future benefits should therefore be charged as an expense as it is incurred.

When an asset is created

24.33 The UITF took the view that, in the context of bidding for contracts, control over the future economic benefits does not arise until it is virtually certain that the contract will be awarded to the supplier – prior to that point there will not be sufficient evidence that an asset has been created. The point at which the awarding of the contract becomes virtually certain will depend on the particular circumstances of each case. Only one bidder can recognise an asset reflecting access to the future benefits from a particular contract – an asset can therefore only be created if there are no other bidders in competition. However, whilst it is essential that there are no other bidders in order for the award of a contract to be virtually certain, this situation will not in itself mean that the supplier is in a position to recognise an asset (for instance, the customer may not accept the sole bidder's proposals and may decide to re-tender). The Abstract also emphasises that:

- the actual award of the contract should be expected within a reasonable timescale;
- the proposed contractual arrangements should have been specified in sufficient detail to provide evidence that any pre-contract costs to be recognised as an asset will be recovered from the contract's net cash inflows (ie future revenues less attributable costs); and
- virtually certainty will not have been achieved if the award of the contract is subject to uncertainties that are not wholly within the control of the supplier – the Abstract quotes the example of the need for regulatory approval, or the likelihood of legal challenge.

Measuring the asset

24.34 The UITF considered various options for measuring the asset that arises when the recognition criteria are met. It concluded that only directly attributable pre-contract costs incurred from the date on which the recognition criteria are met should be recognised as an asset. Any pre-contract costs incurred before this point (for instance, during the competitive tendering stage) should be recognised as expenses as they are incurred and should not be reinstated at the time that the asset recognition criteria are met. Directly attributable costs are defined in the Abstract as costs that relate directly to securing the specific contract after the asset recognition criteria are met, provided that they can be separately identified and measured reliably.

Consortium members

24.35 The Abstract notes that a consortium of bidders will sometimes establish a special-purpose entity (for instance, an associate or joint venture) to undertake the contract and that the consortium members may transfer pre-contract costs to that entity once the contract has been awarded. The amount recovered by a consortium member in this way may exceed the amount of pre-contract costs recognised as an asset under the requirements of the Abstract. The UITF emphasises that the accounting treatment adopted by consortium members for the recovery of pre-contract costs from the special-purpose entity should reflect the principles set out in the Abstract and, in particular, that costs written off as an expense before the recognition criteria are met should not subsequently be reinstated as an asset. The UITF also notes that, where the special-purpose entity is an associate or joint venture, the recovery of an amount in excess of the pre-contract costs recognised as an asset does not result in an immediate gain in the consolidated accounts of a consortium member to the extent that the transaction is in substance a financing arrangement.

ACCOUNTS DISCLOSURES

Analysis of debtors

24.36 When the requirements of accounting standards are taken into accounts, the analysis of debtors set out in the CA 1985 balance sheet formats is expanded as follows:

- Trade debtors (see **24.1–24.6** above).
- Amounts recoverable on contracts (see **Chapter 23**).
- Amounts owed by group undertakings.
- Amounts owed by undertakings in which the group has a participating interest.
- Amounts receivable in respect of finance leases (see **24.7–24.11** above).
- Amounts receivable in respect of hire purchase contracts.
- Other debtors (see **24.12–24.13** above).
- Called up share capital not paid.
- Pre-payments and accrued income (see **24.14–24.16** above).

Each sub-heading need only be used where there are material items to be disclosed in that category. The heading for debtors is given a Roman numeral and must therefore be shown on the face of the balance sheet. The sub-headings are given Arabic numerals and the detailed analysis of debtors may therefore be given in the notes to the accounts. The figures may also be combined if the individual amounts are not material. Called up share capital not paid can be shown as a separate heading before fixed assets, and pre-payments and accrued income can be shown as a separate heading after current assets. These are alternative positions (i.e. in each case, amounts should only be shown in one of the positions). Each company should therefore choose which position to use and then adopt this presentation consistently from year to year. Whichever presentation method is used, prepayments and accrued income must always be taken into account in calculating net current assets or liabilities.

Separate disclosures of amounts due after more than one year

24.37 For each item included within debtors, CA 1985 requires separate disclosure of the amount falling due after more than one year. In most cases this detail will be given in the notes to the accounts. Where called up share capital not paid and pre-payments and accrued income are shown as sub-headings within debtors, any amounts due after more than one year must therefore be shown separately, although there is no specific requirement in the Act for the analysis to be given where these items are shown as main headings on the balance sheet. In assessing whether an amount is due within, or after more than, one year, it is normal practice to take the earliest date on which payment is expected to be made. Various forms of presentation are possible, and the most appropriate one will usually depend on the level of detail requiring disclosure.

Example 24.3 – Amounts due after more than one year disclosed as a narrative footnote

Debtors	*20X2*	*20X1*
	£	£
Trade debtors	344	298
Amounts recoverable on contracts	199	143
Other debtors	24	36
Pre-payments and accrued income	56	44
	623	521

Amounts recoverable on contracts includes £54,000 (20X1: £37,000) in respect of retentions, which are due after more than one year.

Example 24.4 – Columnar disclosure

Debtors	*20X2* Due within 1 year	*20X2* Due after more than 1 year	*20X1* Due within 1 year	*20X1* Due after more than 1 year
	£	£	£	£
Trade debtors	344	–	298	–
Amounts recoverable on contracts	145	54	106	37
Amounts due from group undertakings	211	100	254	100
Other debtors	20	4	30	6
Pre-payments	56	–	44	–
	776	158	732	143

Example 24.5 – Disclosure as a footnote giving details by category of debtor

Debtors	*20X2*	*20X1*
	£	£
Trade debtors	344	298
Amounts recoverable on contracts	199	143
Amounts due from group undertakings	311	354
Other debtors	24	36
Pre-payments and accrued income	56	44
	934	875

These figures include the following amounts which are due after more than one year:

	20X2	*20X1*
	£	£
Amounts recoverable on contracts	54	37
Amounts due from group undertakings	100	100
Other debtors	4	6
	158	143

Where all the amounts included within debtors are due within one year, there is no requirement to state this fact in the accounts, but it is good practice to do so.

Disclosure as current assets

24.38 Even where amounts included in debtors are due after more than one year, they must still be shown as current assets on the balance sheet to comply with the requirements of CA 1985. Under the Act, all assets must be classified as either fixed assets or current assets. A fixed asset is defined as an asset held for continuing use in the business, and any asset that does not meet this description must be classified as a current asset. UITF 4 'Presentation of Long-Term Debtors in Current Assets' confirms that in most cases, disclosure in the notes to the accounts will be sufficient. However, where an amount included in debtors and due after more than one year is so material that failure to disclose it on the balance sheet could cause readers to misinterpret the accounts, UITF 4 requires the disclosure to be given on the face of the balance sheet. It quotes the following examples of items that will usually be due after more than one year and which might be material to the accounts:

— a significant pension fund surplus included in pre-payments (and therefore in the calculation of net current assets or liabilities) which may not actually be recovered for a number of years;

— amounts due under finance leases (in the accounts of a lessor);

— deferred consideration in respect of the sale of a fixed asset or an investment.

Presentation on the balance sheet

24.39 Where an item due after more than one year is so material that it needs to be shown on the face of the balance sheet, it must nevertheless still be shown under current assets. UITF 4 does not provide an example of a suitable presentation, but the following will usually meet the requirements of both the Act and the Abstract.

Example 24.6 – Where disclosure of amounts due after more than one year is required on the face of the balance sheet

Extract from balance sheet.

		20X2		*20X1*
	£	*£*	*£*	*£*
Current assets:				
Stocks		133		157
Debtors:				
Due within 1 year	126		143	
Due after more than 1 year	75		50	
		201		193
Cash at bank and in hand		34		27
		368		377

Additional detail on the amounts due after more than one year would need to be given in the notes to the accounts. More information could be shown on the face of the balance sheet if preferred.

Deciding on the form of presentation

24.40 The key points to remember when deciding on the form of presentation to use in this situation are:

— the balance sheet format prescribed by CA 1985 must be preserved;

— the total for debtors (i.e. amounts due within and after one year) must still appear on the face of the balance sheet;

— the total for debtors must be shown within current assets.

LIKELY FUTURE DEVELOPMENTS

ASB Discussion Paper – 'Leases: Implementation of a New Approach'

24.41 The ASB Discussion Paper 'Leases: Implementation of a New Approach' was issued in December 1999. This document represents a Position Paper developed by the G4+1 group of accounting standard setters and reflects an agreed international approach to the accounting treatment of leases in financial reporting. In particular it proposes removing the sometimes arbitrary distinction between operating and finance leases and applying the same accounting treatment to all leases. The proposals would affect both lessee and lessor accounting. Brief details of the contents of the Discussion Paper are given in **Chapter 20**.

Chapter 25

Debenture Loans

CLASSIFICATION OF CAPITAL INSTRUMENTS

Definition of debenture

25.1 The CA 1985 definition of a debenture is very broad. The Act does not specify the precise terms and conditions that identify a debenture, but simply states that it includes stocks, bonds and any other securities, regardless of whether they include a charge over the assets of the company. A debenture loan is usually considered to be a loan involving formal acknowledgement of the amount borrowed and of the fact that interest is payable at regular intervals on the sum borrowed. Therefore, any loan that is the subject of a formal loan agreement will normally be a debenture loan. Bank loans will normally meet this interpretation of a debenture loan. However, bank loans should always be shown within creditors under the heading 'bank loans and overdrafts' rather than as debenture loans.

Definition of capital instruments under FRS 4

25.2 FRS 4 'Capital Instruments' requires capital instruments to be included in the accounts of an individual company as either liabilities or shareholders' funds. No other form of disclosure is permitted. The definition of capital instruments given in FRS 4 encompasses all types of shares and debt instruments, including options and warrants to obtain those instruments. Shares must always be included within shareholders' funds. The standard identifies two types of other capital instrument:

— those that include an obligation on the issuer to transfer economic benefits; and

— those that do not include an obligation to transfer economic benefits.

Capital instruments in the first category should be accounted for as liabilities (and will therefore be included in creditors on the balance sheet). However, capital instruments in the second category (e.g. warrants) should be included in shareholders' funds. Capital instruments that are required by FRS 4 to be accounted for as liabilities are covered by the general description of 'debt' for the purposes of the standard.

The transfer of economic benefits

25.3 An obligation to transfer economic benefits will usually involve an obligation to:

— make cash payments to the holder of the capital instrument - these might take the form of regular interest payments or might involve a payment at the time of redemption of the instrument; or

— transfer other assets to the holder of the capital instrument.

A contingent obligation to transfer economic benefits will also be sufficient to classify the instrument as a liability; for instance, an instrument that gives the holder the option to require a cash payment or the issue of shares will be classified as a liability for accounting purposes, because the issuer may be required to make a cash payment under the terms of the instrument. However, the following contingent obligations should not be taken into account when classifying capital instruments:

— those that would arise only if the issuer became insolvent - taking account of these obligations would not be consistent with the preparation of accounts on a going concern basis; and

— those that would only apply if covenants in respect of the loan were breached - provided that the issuer is expected to be able to meet the requirements set out in the covenants, these obligations should not be taken into consideration.

Shareholders' funds or liabilities?

25.4 UITF Abstract 33 'Obligations in Capital Instruments' sets out detailed requirements on accounting for more complex capital instruments and in particular those which include an obligation that may be settled either by the transfer of economic benefits or by issuing equity shares, at the discretion of the issuer. The Abstract notes specifically that it does not deal with capital instruments issued as part of the contingent purchase consideration for a business combination. The general rule is that a capital instrument should be reported within shareholders' funds only if it is a share, or if it does not contain an obligation to transfer economic benefits. All other capital instruments should be treated as liabilities, even if the obligation to transfer economic benefits does not go beyond that normally contained in a share. An obligation to transfer economic benefits should be ignored only if it would not be considered in accordance with the going concern concept (i.e. if the obligation would only arise on the insolvency of the issuer). A capital instrument other than a share should also be treated as a liability if it includes an obligation to issue another capital instrument and that instrument includes an obligation to transfer economic benefits.

Options at the discretion of the issuer

25.6 If a capital instrument other than a share includes an obligation that can be settled either by the transfer of economic benefits or by issuing equity shares, at the discretion of the issuer, it should be treated as a liability if the number of equity shares that would need to be issued to settle the obligation will vary with changes in the fair value of the shares, so that the total fair value of the shares issued will always be equal to the amount of the obligation. An obligation to issue shares can be expressed either as an obligation to issue a specified number of shares, or as an obligation to issue shares to the value of a specified amount or an amount determined by reference to the value of another item. In the first instance, both the issuer and the holder of the capital instrument are exposed to fluctuations in the price of the shares and the instrument therefore has the essential attributes of shareholders' funds. In the second case, the issuer still has the exposure but the holder does not, so the instrument no longer has the attributes of shareholders' funds and it is therefore required by the Abstract to be treated as a liability.

Options without commercial substance

25.7 In line with the requirements of FRS 5 'Reporting the Substance of Transactions' (see **Chapter 3**), greater weight should be attached to those aspects of the arrangement that are more likely to have a practical commercial effect. Options that have no genuine commercial substance should therefore be ignored in the assessment of whether the reporting entity has an obligation to transfer economic benefits. Therefore:

- if there is no genuine commercial possibility that the option to issue shares will be exercised, the capital instrument should be treated as giving rise to an obligation to transfer economic benefits and should be reported as a liability;
- if there is no genuine commercial possibility that the option to transfer economic benefits will be exercised, the capital instrument should be treated as giving rise to an obligation that can only be settled by issuing equity shares and should therefore be reported as part of shareholders' funds.

Power to issue appropriate number of shares

25.8 Where the classification of the instrument takes into account the reporting entity's option to settle the obligation by issuing shares, consideration must also be given to whether the entity has the unconditional right and ability to issue the number of shares needed to make full settlement of the obligation. Company law generally prohibits a company from issuing shares unless the allotment is authorised by the company in general meeting or by the company's articles of association. If, at the balance sheet date, the company does not have authority to issue sufficient shares to meet the obligation in full on the settlement date, UITF Abstract 33 requires the option to issue shares to be ignored, even though there is no actual requirement for the issuer to settle the obligation at the balance sheet date. In these circumstances, the instrument must always be accounted for as a liability. Where there is uncertainty over the number of shares that will need to be issued to settle the obligation, the Abstract requires the assessment to be based on the maximum number of shares that may need to be issued.

Shares issued by a subsidiary

25.9 Additional considerations apply under UITF Abstract 33 where shares issued by a subsidiary company create an obligation for the group as a whole to transfer economic benefits.

ACCOUNTING TREATMENT UNDER FRS 4

Initial recording of debt

25.10 At the time of issue, FRS 4 'Capital Instruments' requires a debt instrument to be recorded in the accounts at the net issue proceeds. The net issue proceeds are defined as the fair value of the consideration received, less any costs that meet the stringent definition of issue costs. Net issue proceeds and issue costs in respect of debt are considered in more detail in **Chapter 13**.

Finance costs

25.11 Finance costs relating to the instrument must be allocated over the term of the debt at a constant rate on the carrying amount. This is considered in more detail in **Chapter 13**, which includes practical examples of the calculation and allocation of finance costs and consideration of the impact of options. Finance costs include any premiums payable on redemption, as well as accrued interest in respect of the debt instrument, and the accounting treatment required by FRS 4 ensures that provision for a redemption premium is made over the term of the instrument. UITF 11 'Capital Instruments: Issuer Call Options' clarifies the accounting treatment required under FRS 4 where the issuer of an instrument (but not the investor) has an option to redeem the instrument early, usually on payment of a premium. Under the Abstract, a premium payable on the exercise of an issuer option should not be treated as part of the finance cost of the instrument. However the requirements of the Abstract do not apply where:

— the option is artificial in that the issuer will be commercially obliged to exercise it; or

— the effective rate of interest increases after the date on which the option is exercisable – in this case the exercise price is deemed to compensate the investor for forgoing the increased interest.

The requirements of UITF Abstract 11 are considered in more detail in **Chapter 13**.

Carrying value of debt

25.12 Although the initial carrying value of the debt is the amount of the net issue proceeds, in subsequent accounting periods, this figure must be increased by the finance costs charged to the profit and loss account in that period, and reduced by any payments made in respect of the debt (e.g. interest payments made during the period). **Example 3** in **Chapter 13** illustrates this process. The accounting treatment required by FRS 4 ensures that the total amount payable on redemption of the debt is built up on a consistent basis over the life of the instrument.

Accrued finance costs

25.13 Where finance costs have accrued in one accounting period and will be paid in cash in the following accounting period (e.g. interest due but not actually paid at the end of the accounting period), FRS 4 permits the accrued costs to be disclosed as accruals in the accounts rather than being included in the carrying value of the debt. However, any such accrued costs should be taken into account when calculating finance costs or any gain or loss arising on early redemption of the debt.

More complex debt instruments

25.14 FRS 4 includes a separate section of Application Notes which consider how the requirements of the standard should be applied to specific types of capital instrument. The items covered in this guidance include:

- capital contribution;
- convertible capital bonds;
- convertible debt with a premium put option;
- convertible debt with enhanced interest;
- debt issued with warrants;
- deep discount bonds;
- index linked loans;
- limited recourse debt;
- perpetual debt;
- repackaged perpetual debt;
- stepped interest bonds;
- subordinated debt.

The guidance includes worked examples to illustrate how the requirements of FRS 4 should be applied in practice to these more complex instruments. They are also useful as a point of reference on how to deal with individual features that may be attached to other debt instruments.

ACCOUNTS DISCLOSURES

General disclosure requirements

25.15 Both CA 1985 and FRS 4 require specific disclosures in respect of debenture loans or debt instruments. A number of these overlap, but certain disclosures are required only by the Act or only by the accounting standard. Taking the requirements of the Act and FRS 4 together, the following details must be disclosed in respect of this category of borrowing:

- the total amount outstanding at the end of the accounting period, which is due for payment within one year (including any amounts payable on demand);
- the total amount outstanding at the end of the accounting period which is due for payment after more than one year, analysed as follows:
  - the amount falling due for payment in more than one year but not more than two years after the balance sheet date,
  - the amount falling due for payment in more than two years but not more than five years after the balance sheet date,
  - the amount falling due for payment in more than five years;
- where any loans are wholly or partly payable after more than five years, the accounts must also show:
  - the aggregate amounts payable or repayable by instalments,
  - the aggregate amounts which are payable or repayable otherwise than by instalments,
  - details of payment or repayment terms,
  - details of interest rates;
- the aggregate amount of secured borrowings and an indication of the nature of the security given.

The original wording of FRS 4 was updated by paragraph 77 of FRS 13 'Derivatives and Other Financial Instruments: Disclosures' to change the disclosure of amounts due exactly five years after the balance sheet date. Previously such amounts would have been shown in the final band, which covered amounts due after five years or more. The revised wording may also affect the disclosure of amounts due exactly two years after the balance sheet date, depending on how the original wording ('amounts due between one and two years' and 'amounts due between two and five years') was interpreted.

Maturity of debt

25.16 CA 1985 does not provide any detailed guidance on assessing the maturity of debt. FRS 4 requires the maturity date to be assessed on the basis of the earliest date on which the lender can demand repayment. However, if the same lender has granted other facilities to the borrower before the balance sheet date, these may also be taken into account. For instance, if a loan is due for repayment shortly after the balance sheet date, but the lender has formally agreed, before the balance sheet date, to advance another loan of the same amount for a period of (say) three years, the loan can be disclosed as falling due between two and five years after the balance sheet date, rather than within the next 12 months. For this treatment to be available, all of the following conditions must be met:

— the debt and the facility must be available under a single agreement or course of dealing with the same lender (or group of lenders);

— the finance costs of the new debt must not be significantly higher than those of the existing debt;

— the obligations of the lender must be firm (i.e. the lender should not be able to withdraw from providing the new funds, except in circumstances which can be shown to be remote);

— there must be an expectation that the lender will be able to fulfil its obligations in respect of the new facility.

Where the maturity of debt has been assessed in this way, the accounts must disclose the amounts of debt involved, analysed by the earliest date on which the lender could demand repayment if the facilities were not available.

Example disclosures

25.17 The disclosure requirements will usually be met by providing the required analysis as a footnote to the creditors note and supplementing this with the other details in narrative form.

Example 25.1 – Disclosure in respect of debenture loans or debt instruments

	20X2	*20X1*
Creditors: amounts due within one year	£000	£000
Debenture loans	125	50
Bank loans and overdrafts	45	37

	20X2	*20X1*
Trade creditors	98	85
Accruals and deferred income	14	17
	282	189
Creditors: amounts due after more than one year		
Debenture loans	225	223

None of the debenture loans are repayable by instalment. The amounts due after more than one year are repayable as follows:

In two to five years	100	100
After more than five years	125	123
	225	223

The debenture loan of £125,000 (20X1: £123,000) is repayable in 20X9, at a premium of £10,000; the loan bears interest at a fixed rate of 7% per annum and is secured on the company's freehold property.

The other debenture loans are unsecured.

Convertible debt

25.18 Convertible debt is debt that can be converted into shares at some point in the future. Conversion may be at the option of the holder or of the issuer, or both. FRS 4 requires convertible debt to be accounted for on the basis that conversion will not take place. Within the headings for creditors, CA 1985 requires any convertible debentures to be shown separately from debentures that are not convertible. FRS 4 also requires convertible debt to be shown separately from other liabilities, and requires this detail to be given on the face of the balance sheet if it is material. If the detail is not considered material, and the analysis is therefore given in the notes to the accounts, the balance sheet heading must state that convertible debt is included. Disclosure might therefore be made in the following ways:

Example 25.2 – Disclosure of convertible debt on the face of the balance sheet

Extract of balance sheet:

	20X2	*20X1*
	£000	*£000*
Net current assets	761	699

		20X2		*20X1*
		£000		*£000*
Creditors: amounts falling due after more than one year:				
Convertible debt	75		75	
Other creditors	120		118	
		(195)		(193)
Provisions for liabilities and charges		(65)		(58)
		501		448

Example 25.3 – Disclosure of convertible debt in a note

Extract of balance sheet:

	20X2	*20X1*
	£000	*£000*
Net current assets	761	699
Creditors: amounts falling due after more than one year (including convertible debt)	(195)	(193)
Provisions for liabilities and charges	(65)	(58)
	501	448

In this case, a note to the accounts would need to give the required analysis between convertible and non-convertible debt.

FRS 4 also requires the following details to be disclosed in the accounts:

- the dates of redemption;
- the amount payable on redemption;
- the number and class of shares into which the debt may be converted;
- the dates at, or periods within, which the conversion may take place;
- whether conversion is at the option of the issuer (i.e. the company) or the holder of the debt.

These details will usually be given as narrative footnotes to the main disclosures.

Example 25.4 – Convertible debt – additional disclosures in a narrative footnote

Creditors: amounts falling due after more than one year:

	20X2	*20X1*
	£000	*£000*
Convertible debt	75	75
Other debenture loans	120	118
	195	193

None of the above amounts are repayable by instalments. The amounts are payable as follows:

Between two and five years	75	75
After more than five years	120	118
	195	193

The convertible debt is convertible into 'B' ordinary shares of £10 each on 30 June 20X5, at the option of the company, on the basis of one share for each £100 of debt. If the debt is not converted into shares it will be repaid at par on 30 June 20X5.

The debenture loan of £120,000 (20X1: £118,000) is repayable in 20X9, at a premium of £6,000; the loan bears interest at a fixed rate of 7% per annum and is secured on the company's freehold property.

If the debt is subsequently converted into shares, the amount recognised as shareholders' funds at the time of conversion will be the amount shown as the liability in respect of the debt at the date of conversion. No gain or loss should be recognised at the time of conversion. This is considered in more detail in **Chapter 13**, which includes a practical example.

Additional disclosures under FRS 4

25.19 FRS 4 requires further disclosures in two situations that should arise only rarely in practice:

- where the legal nature of any instrument that has been accounted for as debt is different from that normally associated with debt, brief details should be given in the accounts;
- where the amount shown in the accounts is significantly different to the amount actually payable, or the claim that would arise on a winding up, details of the amounts payable or claimable should be given - this information may be given in summary form for all relevant instruments (i.e. individual details are not required).

Where necessary, these disclosures will usually be given as short narrative footnotes to the main disclosures. Also, if the brief summaries required by paragraphs 62 or 63 of the standard cannot provide adequate information for the commercial effect of the instrument to be understood, this fact should be stated and details should be given of where the relevant information can be obtained. However, the principal features of the instrument should always be disclosed.

Issue of debentures during the year

25.20 Where new debentures have been issued during the year, CA 1985 requires the following information to be given in the accounts:

- the class of debentures issued; and
- for each class of debentures issued, the amount issued and the consideration received by the company.

Debentures held by nominee or trustee

25.21 If any of the company's debentures are held by a nominee of, or trustee for, the company, CA 1985 requires the accounts to show:

- the nominal value of the debentures; and
- the amount at which they are stated in the company's accounting records.

LIKELY FUTURE DEVELOPMENTS

FRED 30 'Financial Instruments: Disclosure and Presentation; Recognition and Measurement'

25.22 The ASB issued FRED 30 'Financial Instruments: Disclosure and Presentation; Recognition and Measurement' in June 2002 as part of its project to achieve convergence between UK accounting standards and international accounting standards. The Exposure Draft sets out proposals for the implementation in the UK of standards based on proposed revisions of IAS 32 'Financial Instruments: Disclosure and Presentation' and IAS 39 'Financial Instruments: Recognition and Measurement'. These were published simultaneously by the International Accounting Standards Board (IASB). The implementation of accounting requirements based on FRED 30 could have significant implications for companies with preference shares. Preference shares are currently shown as part of shareholders' funds but under the proposals in FRED 30 many will be treated as liabilities rather than shares, and dividends payable on them will be accounted for as interest. However, the ASB notes in the Exposure Draft that it has some concerns about the IAS 32 approach to the classification of capital instruments into liabilities and equity and it has asked the IASB to carry out a comprehensive review of this issue.

Proposed implementation

25.23 FRED 30 proposes that, with effect from 1 January 2004:

— entities should be required to comply with IAS 32's presentation requirements (including its requirements on the treatment of preference shares) - FRS 4 'Capital Instruments' would therefore be withdrawn;

— all listed entities and banks should be required to comply with IAS 32's disclosure requirements - FRS 13 'Derivatives and Other Financial Instruments: Disclosure' would therefore also be withdrawn (the ASB has specifically invited comments on whether the disclosure requirements should be extended to other entities - for example, to unlisted insurance companies, or even to all unlisted entities); and

— any entity that chooses to adopt fair value accounting should be required to adopt IAS 39's measurement and hedge accounting requirements.

The ASB is not yet proposing UK implementation of the part of IAS 39 dealing with the recognition and derecognition of financial instruments. The proposed effective date of 1 January 2004 assumes that:

— the Government will by then have effected various changes to companies legislation needed to implement the standards; and

— the IASB does not propose to make further changes to IAS 32 and IAS 39 during 2004.

Financial instruments: Disclosure and presentation

25.24 There are a number of significant changes to present accounting practice under the presentation proposals set out in FRED 30:

— capital instruments would have to be classified as either liabilities or equity (rather than liabilities or shareholders' funds as under FRS 4 'Capital Instruments'), depending on the substance of the underlying contractual arrangement - the practical effect of this will be that some instruments that are currently treated as shareholders' funds (for instance, preference shares that have the substance of liabilities) would in future be classified and accounted for as liabilities;

— only income payments on instruments that are classified as equity would be treated as dividends - payments on instruments that are classified as liabilities would have to be recognised as interest payments in the profit and loss account;

- 'split accounting' should be applied to instruments, such as convertible debt, that comprise both an equity element and a liability element, so that the equity element is accounted for as equity and the liability element as a liability;
- the provisions on offsetting in FRS 5 'Reporting the substance of transactions' would be replaced with new provisions that would generally allow balance sheet debits and credits to be offset more often than at present.

The disclosure proposals broadly mirror those currently required by FRS 13 'Derivative and other financial instruments: Disclosure' although they are less detailed and would therefore give reporting entities more flexibility in how to present the required information. This aspect of FRED 30 is not considered further here as the current proposal is that the disclosure requirements should continue to apply only to listed entities and banks.

Financial instruments: Recognition and measurement

25.25 IAS 39 deals with:

- when financial assets and financial liabilities should first be shown on the balance sheet, in what form they should be shown, and when they should cease to be shown;
- the amount at which financial assets and financial liabilities should be shown on the balance sheet;
- the use of hedge accounting techniques to defer recognition in the profit and loss account of certain gains and losses.

The ASB does not propose to incorporate the recognition requirements of IAS 39 into UK accounting standards at this stage and they are therefore not considered further here. The ASB understands that, by 1 January 2004, CA 1985 will have been amended to permit companies to adopt new fair value accounting rules - these will enable them to measure certain financial assets and financial liabilities at fair value and to recognise changes in those fair values in the profit and loss account. Under the ASB's current approach, the measurement proposals in FRED 30 will apply only to entities who chose to adopt the fair value accounting rules, or who are required to do so by other regulations - the proposals will have no direct effect on other entities. FRED 30 also includes requirements on hedge accounting that are additional to those currently proposed in FRED 23 'Hedge accounting'. These additional requirements will also apply only to entities who adopt fair value accounting.

Chapter 26

Bank Loans and Overdrafts

BANK LOANS

Analysis of bank loans

26.1 For disclosure purposes, bank loans must be separated into amounts that are repayable by instalment over a period of time and those that are repayable in one sum at the end of the term of the loan. Where a bank loan is repayable in instalments, the amount outstanding at the balance sheet date must be analysed into:

— the amounts falling due within the next year;

— the amounts falling due after more than one year.

The amounts due to be paid within the next year will be included under creditors due within one year, and the balance will be included in creditors due after more than one year. If the company has loans where any of the instalments fall due for payment more than five years after the balance sheet date (described in CA 1985 Sch 4 para 48(1) as the 'period of five years, beginning with the day next following the end of the financial year'), the accounts must show separately the aggregate amount due in respect of those loans. Where loans are not repayable in instalments, the Act requires separate disclosure of the aggregate amount repayable after five years. The following example illustrates these disclosure requirements.

Example 26.1 - Disclosure of bank loans, including those payable in instalments

At 31 December 20X2, D Ltd has the following bank loans:

Loan A	A remaining balance of £125,000 which is payable in quarterly instalments of £25,000 on 31 March, 30 June, 30 September and 31 December each year.
Loan B	A loan of £300,000 which is payable as follows: — on 30 June 20X4: £100,000 — on 30 June 20X6: £100,000 — on 30 June 20X8: £100,000

Loan C A loan of £175,000 repayable in full on 31 December 20X8

The company also has a bank overdraft of £54,679 at 31 December 20X2 which is repayable to the bank on demand. The analysis of the loans and overdraft at 31 December 20X2 is therefore:

	Due within one year	*Due after one year*
	£	£
Bank overdraft	54,679	—
Loan A	100,000	25,000
Loan B	—	300,000
Loan C	—	175,000
	154,679	500,000

The accounts will therefore show £154,679 under creditors due within one year and £500,000 under creditors due after more than one year, along with the following additional details.

Amounts repayable by instalment:	
Loan not wholly repayable within five years	300,000
Amounts not repayable by instalment:	
Loan repayable after more than five years	175,000

Repayment date of loans

26.2 In assessing whether loans are repayable within, or after more than one year or, within, or after more than, five years, a loan (or an instalment) is to be taken as falling due for repayment or payment on the earliest date on which the lender could require repayment or payment, if he exercised all the options and rights available to him.

Payment terms and interest rates

26.3 CA 1985 also requires disclosure of the payment or repayment terms and interest rates for each bank loan that is wholly or partly repayable after five years. Details should be disclosed individually for each loan, unless this would result in disclosures of excessive length, in which case a general indication of payment terms and interest rates can be given instead.

Example 26.2 – Disclosure of payment/repayment terms and interest rates

Using the details from **Example 26.1**, details will need to be given for Loan B and Loan C as both of these involve some repayment after more than five years. No additional disclosures are required in the case of Loan A as this is wholly repayable within 15 months.

Amounts repayable by instalment:

Loan not wholly repayable within five years	300,000

The loan is repayable in three instalments of £100,000 which fall due in June 20X4, 20X6 and 20X8 respectively. Interest is charged on this loan at 2% above base rate.

Amounts not repayable by instalment:

Loan wholly repayable within five years	175,000

The loan is repayable in full on 31 December 20X8. Interest is charged on this loan at a fixed rate of 6%.

Secured loans and overdrafts

26.4 Where any bank loan or overdraft is secured, CA 1985 requires disclosure of the fact that security has been given and an indication of the nature of that security. In this case, the disclosures apply to all bank loans and overdrafts, not just those that are wholly or partly repayable after more than five years.

Example 26.3 – Disclosure where security has been given

Using the details from **Example 26.1** (and assuming Loan A is unsecured):

Amounts repayable by instalment:

Loan not wholly repayable within five years	300,000

The loan is repayable in three instalments of £100,000 which fall due in June 20X4, 20X6 and 20X8 respectively. Interest is charged on this loan at 2% above base rate. The loan is secured by a fixed charge on the company's freehold property.

Amounts not repayable by instalment:

Loan repayable after more than five years	175,000

The loan is repayable in full on 31 December 20X8. Interest is charged on this loan at a fixed rate of 6%. The loan is secured by a fixed charge on the company's leasehold property.

The company's bank overdraft is secured by a fixed and floating charge over the company's assets. The amount outstanding at 31 December 20X2 was £54,679 (20X1: £70,142).

BANK OVERDRAFTS

Source of the figure for bank overdrafts

26.5 The amount shown as cash at bank or bank overdrafts in the accounts is traditionally the balance shown in the company's accounting records at the end of the financial year. In most cases, this will not be the same as the balance shown on the bank statements. The reconciliation of the balance shown in the cash records with that shown on the bank statements is a standard internal control that should be carried out on a regular basis and which will identify any amounts included in the cash records which have not been processed by the bank at the financial reporting date (ie unpresented cheques and uncleared lodgements). By including the balance shown in the accounting records, debtors and creditors are stated on the assumption that all outstanding lodgements and cheque payments will be accepted by the bank. Debtors are therefore reduced by the amount of cash received but not yet processed and creditors are reduced by the amount of cheques issued but not yet presented. This treatment of payments is justified as, once the cheques have been issued, the company is no longer in a position to control the funds that will be absorbed when the cheques are cleared.

Strictly, the position is not quite the same where the cheques have been prepared but not actually issued to creditors at the balance sheet date. In this case, the company could be considered to retain control over the funds (ie it can decide whether or not to send out the cheques). If the value of cheques drawn but not despatched at the balance sheet date is material, it will usually be appropriate to add this total back to the bank balance and reinstate the creditors.

Use of bank statement balance

26.6 Some companies choose to include the balance shown on the bank statements as the bank overdraft or cash at bank, at the year-end. The accounts are therefore presented on the basis that cash payments and receipts are not recognised until they have been accepted and processed by the bank. Adjustments will need to be made to reflect the unprocessed items in the accounts, usually by reinstating the relevant debtors and creditors. An alternative approach is to include a separate sub-heading within creditors (or debtors where appropriate) for uncleared banking items, usually with an analysis showing how this figure is made up.

Example 26.4 Alternative disclosure of uncleared banking items

	20X2	*20X1*
	£000	£000
Creditors due within one year:		
Bank overdraft	20	10
Uncleared banking items	54	29
Trade creditors	212	207
Accruals and deferred income	56	49
	342	295

	20X2	*20X1*
	£000	£000
Uncleared banking items comprise:		
Cheques issued but not presented	67	34
Lodgements awaiting clearance by the bank	(13)	(5)
	54	29

Even if the uncleared items are not shown as a separate sub-heading, the amounts involved are usually disclosed. As the use of the bank statement figure is not the normal method of presentation, the accounting policies should explain the method that has been adopted. The treatment should also be applied consistently from year to year and, where there is more than one bank account, all accounts should be treated in the same way. If there is a change in the method of presentation, the figures for the previous year will need to be restated and the change in policy explained (see **Chapter 5**).

Repayment date

26.7 In the case of bank overdrafts, the bank will usually retain the right to request immediate repayment. Where an overdraft is technically repayable on demand, it should be shown as being due within one year. This approach should normally be adopted irrespective of the date of the next formal review of the overdraft facility (which may be more than 12 months after the balance sheet date).

Combined disclosure with loans due within one year

26.8 There is no requirement to make separate disclosure in respect of bank overdrafts. The amount outstanding at the balance sheet date should therefore be aggregated with the amount of any other bank loans due within one year of that date (see **Example 26.1**).

Off-setting

26.9 Under FRS 5 'Reporting the Substance of Transactions':

- assets and liabilities should not be off-set;
- debit and credit balances should only be aggregated into a single net item where they do not constitute separate assets and liabilities – specific conditions set out in FRS 5 must be met for this to apply.

This reinforces the general prohibition in the *Companies Act 1985* on the off-setting of assets and liabilities. The off-setting of bank overdrafts against credit balances on other bank accounts is considered in more detail in **Chapter 33**.

Window dressing

26.10 SSAP 17 'Accounting for Post Balance Sheet Events' requires disclosure in the accounts of the reversal or maturity after the balance sheet date of any transactions entered into before the end of the accounting period, where the primary substance of the transaction was to alter the company's balance sheet. These requirements cover changes to the balance sheet commonly known as 'window dressing', many of which have an impact on the figures shown for bank loans and overdrafts in the accounts. The requirements of SSAP 17 are considered in more detail in **Chapter 33**.

Secured overdrafts

26.11 Where any bank loan or overdraft is secured, CA 1985 requires disclosure of the fact that security has been given and an indication of the nature of that security (see **26.4** above).

Chapter 27

Leasing and Hire Purchase Liabilities

CALCULATION OF LIABILITIES UNDER FINANCE LEASES

Initial recording of liability

27.1 Under SSAP 21 'Accounting for Leases and Hire Purchase Contracts', leases that are classified as finance leases should be recorded in the lessee's balance sheet as an asset and as an obligation to pay future rentals to the lessor. The distinction between leases and hire purchase contracts and the classification of individual leasing agreements as finance leases or operating leases is considered in **Chapter 20**. At the inception of a finance lease (which is defined in SSAP 21 as the earlier of the date when the asset is brought into use or the date from which rental payments accrue), the amount recorded as an asset and the obligation recorded to the lessor will be the same. Strictly this should be the present value of the minimum lease payments. The minimum lease payments are defined in SSAP 21 as:

> 'the minimum payments over the remaining part of the lease term (excluding charges for services and taxes to be paid by the lessor) and, in the case of the lessee, any residual amounts guaranteed by him or by a party related to him.'

They should include any initial payment made by the lessee under the agreement. An example of the calculation of the present value of minimum lease payments is given in **Chapter 13**. However, SSAP 21 emphasises that, for practical purposes, the fair value of the asset at the inception of the lease will usually be an acceptable figure to use when initially recording the asset and the related obligation to the lessor.

Analysis of rental payments

27.2 The rental payments made by a lessee under a finance lease will consist of two elements:

- partial repayment of the amount due to the lessor; and
- finance charges in respect of the amount effectively 'borrowed' from the lessor to finance the purchase of the asset.

The rental payments must be analysed between these two elements for accounting purposes:

- the finance charges will be charged to the profit and loss account, as part of 'interest payable and similar charges';
- the amount representing the repayment of 'borrowings' will reduce the balance due to the lessor.

The calculation of finance charges and the allocation of the charge over the term of the lease is considered in **Chapter 13**.

Reduction of liability to lessor

27.3 Once the finance charge has been calculated and allocated over the term of the lease, the annual repayment of the effective 'borrowings' under the lease can be calculated.

Example 27.1 – Calculation of the annual repayment of the effective borrowings

G Ltd leases an asset under a finance lease with a primary term of four years, with the option to continue to lease for as long thereafter as the company wishes on payment of a nominal rental. The rental payments during the primary term of the lease are £3,000 per annum, payable in arrears. The cash purchase price of the asset at the inception of the lease was £9,500.

The asset (and the related liability) will therefore be recorded at £9,500. Actual payments during the primary term of the lease will amount to £12,000 (ie £3,000 p.a. for four years). The total finance charge is therefore £2,500 (ie £12,000 – £9,500).

Allocation of the finance charge on an annual basis using the actuarial method, with a rate of charge of 10.05% gives the following result.

Year	*Opening capital sum*	*Rental payment*	*Finance charge (10.05%)*	*Closing capital sum*
	£	£	£	£
1	9,500	(3,000)	955	7,455
2	7,455	(3,000)	749	5,204
3	5,204	(3,000)	523	2,727
4	2,727	(3,000)	273	—
		12,000	2,500	

The analysis of rental payments between capital repayments and finance charges will therefore be:

Year	*Capital repayment*	*Finance charge*	*Total rental*
	£	£	£
1	2,045	955	3,000
2	2,251	749	3,000

Year	*Capital repayment*	*Finance charge*	*Total rental*
	£	£	£
3	2,477	523	3,000
4	2,727	273	3,000
	9,500	2,500	12,000

The liability under the lease will therefore be recorded in G Ltd's accounting records as follows:

	£
Initial liability at the inception of the lease	9,500
Repayment of capital in Year 1	(2,045)
Creditor at the end of Year 1	7,455
Repayment of capital in Year 2	(2,251)
Creditor at the end of Year 2	5,204
Repayment of capital in Year 3	(2,477)
Creditor at the end of Year 3	2,727
Repayment of capital in Year 4	(2,727)
Balance at the end of Year 4	–

Accounting policies

27.4 The accounting policies adopted for finance leases and operating leases should also be disclosed in the accounts. This is considered in more detail in **Chapter 20**.

SEPARATE DISCLOSURE OF LEASING OBLIGATIONS

Additional sub-heading within creditors

27.5 CA 1985 makes no specific reference to leasing and hire purchase liabilities. However, it does permit items to be shown in greater detail than is required by the formats and also allows additional items to be included, provided that they are not already shown elsewhere in the standard formats. Therefore, where a company has liabilities under a finance lease or hire purchase agreement, an additional sub-heading will usually be introduced within creditors to meet the disclosure requirements of SSAP 21. The standard requires obligations in respect of finance leases and hire purchase agreements to be shown separately from other obligations, either on the face of the balance sheet or in the notes to the accounts. As leasing commitments are similar in nature to borrowings, the additional sub-heading is usually included between bank loans and overdrafts and trade creditors.

Example 27.2 – Separate disclosure of leasing obligations

Creditors due within one year:	*20X2*	*20X1*
	£	£
Debenture loans	125	125
Bank loans and overdrafts	95	84
Obligations under finance leases and hire purchase contracts	30	42
Trade creditors	112	115
Corporation tax	22	15
Other creditors	45	39
Accruals and deferred income	31	35
	460	455

A similar analysis would need to be given for creditors due after more than one year. In the accounts of a lessor, SSAP 21 requires separate disclosure of amounts receivable under finance leases and amounts receivable under hire purchase contracts. No distinction is made in the case of lessees, and only the aggregate amount due in respect of finance leases and similar hire purchase contracts needs to be disclosed.

Alternative disclosure

27.6 The requirements of SSAP 21 can be met by including leasing and hire purchase liabilities under one of the other headings in the format (eg other creditors) and then providing separate details as a footnote to the analysis.

Example 27.3 – Alternative disclosure using a footnote

Creditors due within one year:	*20X2*	*20X1*
	£	£
Debenture loans	125	125
Bank loans and overdrafts	95	84
Trade creditors	112	115
Corporation tax	22	15
Other creditors	75	81
Accruals and deferred income	31	35
	460	455
Other creditors includes the following amounts in respect of obligations under finance leases and hire purchase contracts	30	42

However, where leasing and hire purchase obligations are material, disclosure as a separate sub-heading will usually be more appropriate.

Security in respect of leasing obligations

27.7 CA 1985 requires details of any secured items under creditors, along with an indication of the nature of the security given. Liabilities under finance leases and hire purchase agreements will usually be secured on the related assets. The following note will usually be sufficient, as details of the assets will be shown separately within fixed assets.

Example 27.4 – Disclosure of security

Obligations under finance leases and hire purchase agreements are secured on the related assets.

This note could be cross-referenced to the fixed assets note to indicate where details of the related assets can be found.

Disclosure of future commitments

27.8 Where a company has entered into a finance lease or hire purchase agreement at the balance sheet date, but inception has not yet taken place, SSAP 21 requires disclosure of the company's commitment under the agreement. Inception of the lease is defined in the standard as the earlier of the date when the asset is brought into use or the date from which rental payments accrue. The disclosure of commitments generally is considered in **Chapter 32**.

ANALYSIS OF LEASING LIABILITIES

Requirements under CA 1985

27.9 CA 1985 requires separate disclosure of creditors due after more than one year and also additional disclosure in respect of liabilities that are wholly or partly repayable after five years. As most leasing and hire purchase agreements will involve payment by instalments, the accounts will need to show the aggregate liability under those finance leases or hire purchase agreements where one (or more) of the instalments fall due more than five years after the balance sheet date.

Requirements under SSAP 21

27.10 SSAP 21 requires the following analysis of leasing and hire purchase liabilities:

(i) amounts payable in the next year;

(ii) amounts payable in the second to fifth years (inclusive) from the balance sheet date;

(iii) the aggregate amounts payable after five years.

The disclosures required under the standard are therefore more extensive and apply to all leasing and similar liabilities, not just those that are wholly or partly payable after more than five years. Using the details in **Example 27.1**, the following disclosures would be given at the end of Year 1.

Example 27.5 – Disclosures at the end of Year 1

	20X2 *(ie Year 1)*	*20X1* *(ie Year 2)*
	£	£
Creditors due within one year:		
Bank loans and overdrafts	9,786	7,899
Obligations under leasing and hire purchase contracts	2,251	—
Trade creditors	22,114	20,198
Accruals and deferred income	5,677	6,713
	39,828	34,810
Creditors due after more than one year:		
Bank loans	10,000	10,000
Obligations under leasing and hire purchase contracts	5,204	—
	15,204	10,000
Obligations under finance leases and hire purchase contracts:		
Amounts payable within two to five years	5,204	—

The requirement under SSAP 21 to disclose the amount payable within one year is already covered by the requirement under CA 1985 to separate creditors due within one year from those due after more than one year.

Disclosure using gross obligations

27.11 As an alternative under SSAP 21, the lessee may analyse the gross obligations under finance leases and hire purchase agreements and show future finance charges as a deduction from the total.

Example 27.6 – Alternative disclosure at the end of Year 1

Using the details in **Example 27.1**, the disclosure under this approach would be:

	20X2	*20X1*
	(ie Year 1)	*(ie Year 0)*
	£	*£*
Obligations under finance leases and hire purchase contracts:		
Gross amounts payable within one year	3,000	–
Gross amounts payable within two to five years	6,000	–
	9,000	–
Less: Finance changes allocated to future periods	(1,545)	–
Net obligations	7,455	–

Details of finance charges

27.12 Where any of the payments in respect of finance leases or hire purchase agreements fall due after more than five years, CA 1985 requires disclosure of the payment terms and finance charges. Although the information is strictly required for each individual liability, the Act does permit a general indication to be given if the disclosures would otherwise be excessive, and this approach will usually be adopted for any disclosures required in respect of finance leases and hire purchase agreements.

Example 27.7 – Disclosure of payment terms and finance charges

	20X2	*20X1*
	£	*£*
Obligations under finance leases and hire purchase contracts:		
Amounts payable within two to five years	23,750	22,456
Amounts payable after five years	5,675	6,005
	29,425	28,461

Obligations under those finance leases and hire purchase agreements where instalments fall due after more than five years are payable in quarterly instalments and bear finance charges at rates ranging from 8.6% to 10.05% per annum. The aggregate amount due in respect of these leases and agreements at 31 March 20X2 was £24,570 (20X1: £22,961).

LIKELY FUTURE DEVELOPMENTS

ASB Discussion Paper 'Leases: Implementation of a New Approach'

27.13 The ASB Discussion Paper 'Leases: Implementation of a New Approach' was issued in December 1999. This document represents a Position Paper developed by the G4+1 group of accounting standard-setters and reflects an agreed international approach to the treatment of leases in financial reporting. In particular it proposes removing the sometimes arbitrary distinction between operating and finance leases and applying the same accounting treatment to all leases. The proposals would affect both lessee and lessor accounting. Brief details of the contents of the Discussion Paper are given in **Chapter 20**.

Chapter 28

Other Creditors, Accruals and Deferred Income

PAYMENTS RECEIVED ON ACCOUNT

Items to be included

28.1 The sub-heading for payments on account within the CA 1985 balance sheet formats is intended to be used for any payments received in advance from customers (e.g. where payment, or part payment, is requested along with the order), which are not treated as deductions from stocks (e.g. as in the case of progress payments on long-term contracts). The company will usually be liable to refund such amounts if the order is not fulfilled and such sums are therefore required to be shown separately within creditors.

Payments on account in respect of long-term contracts

28.2 In practice, the sub-heading is most likely to be used by companies involved in long-term contracts. Under the requirements of SSAP 9 'Stocks and Long-Term Contracts', where the total payments received on account in respect of a contract exceed:

— the amounts matched with turnover; and

— the amounts off-set against long-term contract balances,

the excess must be shown separately within creditors as payments on account. This is considered in more detail in **Chapter 23** along with practical examples of accounting for long-term contracts.

TRADE CREDITORS

Purchase ledger balances

28.3 Trade creditors will normally comprise the aggregate of the outstanding balances shown on the company's purchase ledger at the end of the accounting period. There is no guidance in CA 1985 on how to classify receipts of goods and services around the year-end date which are not invoiced until after the year-end. These amounts must clearly be included in purchases, and the liability recognised, for consistency (ie on the basis that the goods will be included in stocks if they were received before the balance sheet date). In many cases, the purchase ledger will be held open for a short period after the year-end to allow invoices in respect of such goods and services to be processed. In this case, they will form part of the year-end purchase ledger and will automatically be included in trade creditors for accounts purposes. This approach requires careful separation of invoices relating to the old and the new financial years to ensure that the cut off between the two accounting periods is accurate.

Adjustment for unprocessed items

28.4 Where invoices relating to items received before the financial year-end are not included within purchase ledger balances, an adjustment will need to be made to recognise the company's liability. Unprocessed items should normally be shown as part of trade creditors, particularly where they relate to cost of sales items. However, if the amounts involved are not material, they are sometimes included under one of the other headings (e.g. accruals and deferred income). As with other aspects of the accounts, the important point is for the figures to be presented on a consistent basis year by year. Even where the purchase ledger has been held open for a period, an adjustment may still be required in order to capture invoices received after the close-down of the ledger but which relate to the previous accounting period.

Credit notes due

28.5 Where credit notes have been issued by suppliers after the year-end in respect of invoices included in the year-end balances, or where it is certain that such credit notes will be issued (e.g. because a price reduction has been formally agreed with the supplier), it will usually be appropriate to adjust for these, so that the balance for trade creditors represents the amount that the company will actually pay in respect of the goods and services received during the year. If the goods are in stock at the balance sheet date, the price reduction should also be reflected in the stock valuation.

Settlement discounts

28.6 Similarly, some of the company's suppliers may offer settlement discounts for early payment of the invoice. The availability of settlement discounts will therefore mean that the full amount of the invoices received from suppliers may not be paid in cash. Settlement discounts are normally only given for prompt payment (e.g. payment within 7 or 14 days of the invoice date) and in most cases, there will be little difficulty in establishing the amount of discount actually taken by the company in respect of balances which were outstanding at the end of the accounting period. For accounts purposes, year-end trade creditors should be reduced by the amount of discount actually taken by the company in respect of those balances (i.e. the accounts should reflect the benefit of the discount taken on purchases made during the year).

Debit balances

28.7 If the company's accounting procedures operate efficiently, debit balances should not arise on the purchase ledger. Any small debit balances that arise from time to time can usually be ignored on the grounds that they are immaterial, but if a material debit balance arises on a purchase ledger account (e.g. as a result of the company making a duplicate payment by mistake), the debit balance should normally be transferred from creditors to debtors. However, the recoverability of the amount included in debtors as a result of the transfer will need to be carefully assessed.

TAXATION, SOCIAL SECURITY AND OTHER CREDITORS

Disclosure under CA 1985

28.8 The balance sheet formats include a sub-heading for other creditors including taxation and social security, but within this heading, the Act requires separate disclosure of the aggregate amounts relating to taxation and social security. Amounts included in respect of taxation might comprise:

— corporation tax payable;

— VAT payable to Customs and Excise;

— PAYE deducted from wages and salaries, not yet paid over to the Inland Revenue;

— excise duties payable (depending on the nature of the company's business).

Social security balances will normally comprise national insurance contributions not yet paid over to the Collector of Taxes. These will include both the employer's contributions and the employees' contributions deducted from gross wages and salaries. However, NI contributions due on potential share option gains (see **Chapter 10**) should normally be treated as a provision rather than as creditors, because the NI due cannot be established with certainty until the option has been exercised. Once exercise has taken place, and the NI consequently becomes payable, any amounts not paid over at the balance sheet date should be included in creditors.

Corporation tax payable

28.9 Although CA 1985 only requires disclosure of the aggregate amount for taxation and social security, Accounting standards previously required the amount due in respect of corporation tax to be shown separately. FRS 16 'Current Tax' includes detailed disclosure requirements in respect of the profit and loss account and statement of total recognised gains and losses, but makes no specific reference to disclosure of current tax in the balance sheet. However, separate disclosure of the amount due in respect of corporation tax can be helpful in enabling a user of the accounts to understand the movements in respect of taxation during the year (e.g. it should be possible to reconcile the opening tax liability with the closing tax liability by adjusting for taxation charged during the year and the payments and receipts shown in the cashflow statement for the year). The accounting treatment of current tax in the profit and loss account and statement of total recognised gains and losses is considered in more detail in **Chapter 14**.

Other creditors

28.10 There is no guidance in CA 1985 on what should be included under 'other creditors'. Basically, it covers items not disclosable elsewhere and might include liabilities such as:

- proposed dividends (which must currently be identified separately in the accounts – see **Chapter 15**);
- sundry loans (eg a loan from a director);
- quantity rebates due to customers (i.e. rebates based on the quantity purchased over a specific period of time, rather than relating to an individual purchase or liability).

As with so many issues, the most important point is to adopt a consistent basis of disclosure year by year (e.g. in the allocation of items between other creditors and accruals and deferred income).

Example disclosure

28.11 The following example illustrates the disclosure points discussed in **28.8–28.10** above.

Example 28.1 – Taxation and social security and other creditors

Creditors due within one year:

	20X2	*20X1*
	£	£
Bank loans and overdrafts	125	137

		20X2		*20X1*
		£		£
Obligations under finance leases		87		70
Trade creditors		359		344
Other creditors including taxation and social security:				
Corporation tax payable	63		54	
Other taxes and social security	38		34	
	101		88	
Proposed dividend	28		20	
Other creditors	36		32	
		165		140
Accruals and deferred income		44		39
		780		730

ACCRUALS AND DEFERRED INCOME

Disclosure under CA 1985

28.12 The balance sheet formats set out in CA 1985 require separate disclosure of the amount included in the accounts in respect of accruals and deferred income but offer two alternative methods of presentation:

- as a separate sub-heading within creditors (with separate disclosure of the amounts due within and after more than one year);
- as a main heading on the balance sheet after current assets.

Each company must choose which position to use and should then use this method of presentation consistently year by year. In practice, many companies include accruals and deferred income within creditors, but the alternative treatment is also in fairly common use.

Items normally included

28.13 There is no guidance in CA 1985 on the items that should be included in accruals and deferred income. FRS 12 'Provisions, Contingent Liabilities and Contingent Assets' describes accruals as liabilities to pay for goods and services that have been received or supplied (including services provided by employees), but which have not yet been paid, invoiced or formally agreed with the supplier. The guidance in the standard emphasises that it may sometimes be necessary to estimate the amount or timing of accruals, but the degree of uncertainty in this case will usually be considerably lower than in the case of a provision. It also notes that accruals are often reported as part of trade and other creditors in the accounts (see **28.3–28.4** above). As with many accounts disclosures, the important point is that a consistent approach should be adopted year by year on which items are included under this heading, and in particular the allocation of items between other creditors and accruals and deferred income.

Accruals

28.14 Accruals will generally comprise the accrued element of general overhead expenses such as:

- heat, light and power costs (eg electricity charges);
- telephone charges;
- legal and professional fees;
- interest payable and similar finance charges.

This is to ensure that the full charge for the year in respect of these costs is reflected in the profit and loss account. The individual amounts involved will not usually be significant.

Deferred income

28.15 The amounts included under deferred income will vary depending on the nature of the company's activities. Examples of items which might be included under this heading are:

- the amount of grants received which has been deferred to future years;
- sundry deposits received from customers (i.e. which will become part of sales income in the following year);
- rental income received in advance (e.g. where the tenant makes rental payments quarterly in advance);
- rental income from operating leases in the accounts of a lessor (i.e. where the timing of the actual payments is not in line with the accounting requirement under SSAP 21 'Leases and Hire Purchase Contracts' for income to be recognised on a straight-line basis over the period of the lease);
- sundry income received in advance of the related costs being incurred (i.e. where the costs will arise in the following, or a subsequent, financial period).

Disclosure of amounts due after more than one year

28.16 For each item included within creditors, CA 1985 requires separate disclosure of the amount falling due after more than one year. Where accruals and deferred income is shown as a sub-heading within creditors, the amount due after more than one year must therefore be disclosed in the notes to the accounts. In practice, items included under accruals will generally be due within one year. However, certain items included under deferred income may be recognised over a period of more than one year (e.g. grants in respect of fixed assets), in which case the amount included within creditors should be analysed accordingly. There is no specific requirement in the Act for amounts due after more than one year to be shown separately where accruals and deferred income is shown as a main heading on the balance sheet. However, disclosure may sometimes be necessary for the accounts to show a true and fair view (e.g. where a material item within accruals and deferred income is due after more than one year).

ACCOUNTING FOR GOVERNMENT GRANTS

Type of grants covered by SSAP 4

28.17 Although SSAP 4 'Accounting for Government Grants' may at first sight appear to cover a relatively narrow category of grants, the definitions within the standard are broad and government is defined as including 'government and inter-governmental agencies and similar bodies, whether local, national or international'. The explanatory note to SSAP 4 also emphasises that 'government' includes:

- national government;
- all of the various tiers of local and regional government of any country;
- government agencies;
- non-departmental public bodies (ie quangos);
- the Commission of the European Community;
- other EC bodies;
- international bodies and agencies.

Grants from any of these bodies are therefore covered by the accounting requirements of SSAP 4.

What are government grants?

28.18 Government grants are defined as 'assistance by government in the form of cash or transfers of assets to an enterprise in return for past or future compliance with certain conditions relating to the operating activities of the enterprise'. The explanatory note to SSAP 4 also states that the requirements of SSAP 4 should be seen as indicative of best practice for accounting for grants and similar assistance from other sources.

General rules on recognition of grants

28.19 Grants should not be recognised for accounts purposes until:

— all conditions for receipt of the grant have been satisfied;

— there is reasonable assurance that the grant will be received.

This is consistent with the need for prudence and also with the requirement under the CA 1985 that only realised profits should be included in the profit and loss account. However, the requirements of SSAP 4 do not mean that grants must be received in cash (or other assets) before they can be recognised in the accounts. In many cases, the grant-making body will confirm that an application has been accepted and will then require claims to be made at specified intervals or after specific costs have been incurred. It is usually acceptable to include any amounts claimed but not yet received in debtors, and account for the grant claimed in accordance with SSAP 4 (i.e. by matching it with the related expenditure), provided it is clear that:

— the application for grant has been accepted;

— any conditions attaching to the grant have been met;

— a claim has been submitted;

— any costs in respect of the amount claimed have actually been incurred; and

— there is no reason to believe that the submitted claim will not be accepted.

Example 28.2 – Recognition of grants

A Ltd has applied for a grant of £75,000 in respect of the installation of a new equipment costing £250,000 and has received confirmation that the application has been accepted. Claims can be submitted quarterly, based on the relevant proportion of costs incurred. Work on the new plant commenced on 1 July 20X2. A Ltd's financial year end is 30 September.

Costs in the period 1 July – 30 September 20X2 amounted to £54,000 and A Ltd claimed £16,200 of the grant in October 20X2 (i.e. 54/250 x 75); the amount claimed was received in December 20X2.

£16,200 should therefore be recorded in debtors as a grant receivable at 30 September 20X2 and also included in deferred income. Whether any of this income is recognised in the profit and loss account for the year to 30 September 20X2 will depend on whether any of the related costs are charged to the profit and loss account in the same period.

Accruals concept

28.20 FRS 18 'Accounting Policies' requires financial statements (other than cash flow information) to be prepared on the accruals basis of accounting, which it defines as requiring the non-cash effects of transactions and events to be reflected, as far as is possible, in the financial statements for the accounting period in which they occur and not in the period in which any related cash is received or paid. The standard makes a clear link with the definitions of assets and liabilities set out in FRS 5 'Reporting the Substance of Transactions' (and also in the Statement of Principles), and notes that the use of those definitions to determine which items should be recognised as assets and liabilities in the balance sheet is consistent with the accruals concept. SSAP 4 requires government grants to be matched with the expenditure towards which they are intended to contribute and, if there is no persuasive evidence otherwise, requires a grant to be presumed to contribute towards the expenditure that forms the basis of the grant payment.

Grants in respect of fixed assets

28.21 Grants in respect of fixed assets are relatively straightforward to account for, in that it will be clear that the grant relates to a specific item or items. The standard offers two alternative treatments for accounting for grants in respect of fixed assets:

- record the asset at cost and record the grant as deferred income - the grant is then released to the profit and loss account over the expected useful economic life of the asset (i.e. at the same rate as the cost of the asset is depreciated); or
- deduct the amount of the grant from the cost of the asset, so that only the net amount is depreciated over the expected useful economic life of the asset.

In the case of a company, the second treatment is not acceptable under CA 1985 Sch 4 paras 17–26, which require fixed assets to be recorded at purchase price or production cost, and also Sch 4 para 5, which prohibits the off-setting of assets and liabilities and income and expenditure. Companies must therefore treat a grant in respect of a fixed asset as deferred income and release it to the profit and loss account in line with the depreciation charged on the related asset. Other entities may follow the alternative treatment under SSAP 4 if they wish.

Example 28.3 – Accounting for fixed asset grants in corporate and non-corporate entities

B Ltd receives a grant of £14,000 in respect of a fixed asset costing £70,000. The expected useful economic life of the asset is seven years. Depreciation is charged on a straight-line basis.

The asset should be recorded at a cost of £70,000.

Depreciation will be charged at £10,000 each year for seven years.

The grant of £14,000 should be included in deferred income and should be released to the profit and loss account at £2,000 each year for seven years.

If B is not a company, it may be acceptable to record the asset at £56,000 (ie £70,000 - £14,000) and charge depreciation at £8,000 each year for seven years.

Grants in respect of non-depreciated assets

28.22 In exceptional circumstances, an asset may not need to be depreciated (eg because it has a finite useful economic life, or because it has a residual value close to its book value and depreciation would therefore be immaterial). These issues are considered in detail in **Chapter 12**. If a grant is received in respect of an asset that is not depreciated, the grant will not be recognised in the profit and loss account (unless the asset is disposed of) because there will be no expenditure in the profit and loss account with which to match the grant. If deferred income includes a material amount that is not being released to the profit and loss account for this reason, it will usually be advisable to explain this in the notes to the accounts, and possibly to show that element of deferred income separately from other grants.

Revenue-related grants

28.23 It can be more difficult to establish the appropriate accounting treatment for grants that relate to revenue costs (as opposed to fixed assets). The over-riding principle remains that the grant should be recognised in the profit and loss account at the same time as the related expenditure. Where the grant relates to a specific cost (or costs), the matching of the income with the related expenditure should be straightforward. The difficulties arise where grants are less specific in nature and relate (for instance) to the creation of jobs or to assistance with a broader scale project, or where there are both capital and revenue aspects (eg the purchase of new plant, coupled with the creation of new jobs). A suitable method of allocating the grant therefore needs to be found.

Relating the grant to expenditure

28.24 The first step will usually be to consider whether the grant can be linked to any specific items of expenditure. For instance, it may be that instalments of the grant can only be claimed when certain costs have been incurred. In this case, it will usually be appropriate to link the grant with those items of expenditure for matching purposes.

Relating the grant to an event

28.25 Alternatively, the grant may be linked to the achievement of an objective that is not wholly financial in nature (e.g. the creation of a specific number of new jobs, and the maintenance of those jobs for a specified period). In this case, it will usually be necessary to establish the costs associated with achieving the objective and match the grant with these. Where one of the conditions of the grant is that the new jobs are maintained for a period of (say) at least three years, the costs of providing the jobs over that period will need to be taken into account. However, this does not necessarily mean that the grant must be released evenly over such a period. The costs of creating the jobs may well be higher than the costs of maintaining them (e.g. as the result of initial training programmes and other start-up costs). This may justify releasing a higher proportion of the grant in the early years to match the higher costs.

Relating the grant to other expenditure

28.26 A grant should normally be presumed to relate to the expenditure that forms the basis of the grant. Where there is persuasive evidence that the grant should be related to other expenditure, SSAP 4 allows a different approach and recognises that this will usually be more appropriate in such circumstances. Evidence linking the grant with other expenditure might be included in:

— the original application for the grant;

— correspondence between the applicant and the grant-making body.

The notes to SSAP 4 quote an example of a grant being made to assist with a project, where instalments are paid once expenditure has been incurred on a specific item of equipment, but where it is clear from the underlying paperwork that the grant is intended to contribute to other related revenue costs, such as the costs of training staff to use the new equipment.

Grants to reimburse previous expenditure

28.27 Occasionally grants may be paid to reimburse an entity for expenditure that has already been incurred. Where the related expenditure has already been charged to the profit and loss account, the grant should be credited to the profit and loss account in full when it becomes receivable (i.e. when it is clear that the application has been accepted and that payment will be made).

Grants to finance general activities or to provide compensation

28.28 Certain grants may be very unspecific in nature (e.g. to support the general activities of an entity over a certain period) or may be paid to provide some element of compensation for losses incurred or to be incurred over a specified period (e.g. subsidy payments). These grants should be recognised in the profit and loss account over the period in respect of which they are paid. If the grants are not linked to a specific period, they should usually be accounted for in the period during which they become receivable.

Grants in forms other than cash

28.29 A grant may occasionally take the form of a transfer of non-monetary assets, although this is relatively rare in practice. Where such a transfer does arise, SSAP 4 requires the grant to be recorded as the fair value of the assets transferred. Fair value is usually taken to be the price at which the asset could be exchanged in an arm's length transaction.

Repayment of grants

28.30 Certain grants, or part of them, may become repayable if conditions laid down by the grant-making body are subsequently breached by the entity which has received the grant or on the occurrence of other events (e.g. in the case of grants in respect of fixed assets, part of the grant may become repayable if the asset is sold within (say) four years). Provision for repayment of a grant should only be made where it is probable that repayment will be necessary. In most cases, no such provision will be required. However, a review should be carried out at the end of each financial year to establish whether any repayment is likely to be required and whether provision should therefore be made for this. In some cases where provision for repayment is not required, it may nevertheless be necessary to disclose a contingent liability, unless the possibility of repayment being required is remote. The requirements of CA 1985 and of FRS 12 'Provisions, Contingent Liabilities and Contingent Assets' are considered in more detail in **Chapter 32**.

Tax treatment of grants

28.31 Grants received from government and other sources may be treated in different ways for tax purposes. Some may be completely free of tax whilst others may be taxed in full at the time when they are received. The tax treatment of a grant should not affect the accounting treatment under SSAP 4. In particular, a grant should not be credited to the profit and loss account in full in the year of receipt simply on the basis that it is taxable in that year. Where the tax treatment of the grant differs from the accounting treatment (eg the grant is taxable in full on receipt but it is credited to the profit and loss account over a number of years under SSAP 4), material timing differences should be accounted for in accordance with FRS 19 'Deferred Tax'. Deferred tax is considered in detail in **Chapter 30**.

Accounts disclosure

28.32 SSAP 4 requires the following disclosures in the accounts:

— the accounting policy for government grants;

— the effects of grants on the results for the period and/or the financial position of the entity (if material);

— where the results are materially affected by the receipt of government assistance in other forms, the nature of the assistance and, where practicable, an estimate of the financial effect.

Accounting policy

28.33 The disclosure of the accounting policy should make clear the method (or methods) that have been adopted in accounting for government grants. The period or periods over which grants are being credited to the profit and loss account should be disclosed, although it is recognised that, where the grants are numerous and varied, detailed disclosure will not be practicable. In this case a broad indication of the future periods in which grants already received will be recognised will usually be sufficient. Wording along the following lines will usually be appropriate to cover a straightforward case.

Example 28.4 – Disclosure of accounting policy

Government grants in respect of fixed assets are treated as deferred income and credited to the profit and loss account over the expected useful economic life of the relevant assets. Grants received to date relate primarily to plant and machinery and are therefore being credited to the profit and loss account over periods of seven to ten years.

Grants relating to revenue costs are credited to the profit and loss account in line with the relevant costs. Grants to be matched with expected future costs are carried forward as deferred income. Grants carried forward in this way at 31 December 1995 are expected to be credited to the profit and loss account in 1996.

Effect of grants on the results and financial position

28.34 If the inclusion of grants has a material effect on the results and financial position of the recipient, or will have a material effect in future years, the effect must be disclosed in the accounts. Disclosure of the amount credited to the profit and loss account during the year in respect of grants will usually meet the requirement to disclose the effect on the results for the year. Where necessary, this information will usually be given in the note to the accounts setting out details of individual amounts charged or credited in arriving at the operating profit or loss for the year. The disclosure of a material effect on the financial position and on the accounts for future years can usually be met by disclosing the amount carried forward as deferred income in respect of grants. Using this in conjunction with the disclosure in the accounting policy of the future periods that are expected to benefit from the grants carried forward, a reader should be able to evaluate the effect on future years of the grants already received. Where the figures are particularly significant, it may be appropriate to analyse the balance for deferred grants into its major components (e.g. grants for buildings, grants for plant and machinery, grants in respect of revenue items). Where a capital grant is treated as a deduction from the cost of the asset rather than as deferred income (see **28.21** above) and the amount involved is significant, further details will usually need to be given in the notes to the accounts in order to meet this disclosure requirement.

Other forms of assistance

28.35 Where the results are materially affected by the receipt of government assistance in other forms, the nature of the assistance and, where practicable, an estimate of the financial effect should be disclosed in the accounts. This is intended to cover assistance such as:

- consultancy and advisory services;
- subsidised loans; and
- credit guarantees.

A brief narrative explanation of the assistance received during the year will usually be sufficient.

RETENTION OF TITLE

Recommended accounts disclosures

28.36 Companies may sometimes supply goods that are subject to reservation of title (i.e. the supplier retains title to the goods until the related invoice is paid by the customer). The purpose of this is to attempt to provide the supplier with a degree of protection if the customer proves to be unable to meet the liability. An Accounting Recommendation issued by the Institute of Chartered Accountants in England and Wales in 1976 (but still in issue) recommends that the following disclosures are included in the accounts:

- where the accounts are materially affected by the accounting treatment adopted in respect of purchases that are subject to retention of title, the treatment adopted should be disclosed in the accounting policies;
- where material amounts outstanding at the balance sheet date (i.e. amounts included within creditors) are subject to retention of title clauses, this fact and, where practicable, the amount involved should be disclosed in the notes to the accounts.

Practical difficulties

28.37 The statement recognises that it will not always be practicable to quantify the amount of creditors which are subject to retention of title clauses. This will depend on the number of purchases entered into by the company which are usually covered by such clauses. For instance, if a company has purchased a major piece of equipment which is subject to reservation of title and the payment is outstanding at the balance sheet date, this should be relatively straightforward to identify and disclose. If, on the other hand, the company frequently trades with a variety of raw material suppliers, many of whom supply goods subject to retention of title, it may be a much more time-consuming exercise to quantify the total outstanding at the balance sheet date which is subject to retention of title. In some cases it may also be unclear whether the clause is legally enforceable. The statement therefore suggests that where quantification is not practicable, the notes to the accounts should explain the position and give an indication of the extent to which creditors are protected in this way.

Application in practice

28.38 In practice, few companies include such disclosures in their accounts. Provided that it is evident that the company is a going concern, the existence of retention of title clauses should have little impact. However, where there are doubts over the company's ability to continue trading and going concern is therefore an issue, additional attention will usually need to be paid to retention of title clauses and the disclosures should normally be included in the accounts where appropriate. The disclosure can usually be covered by a short statement beneath the analysis of creditors.

Example 28.5 – Where retention of title disclosures are appropriate

Trade creditors includes £45,690 in respect of goods which have been supplied subject to retention of title.

Chapter 29

Provisions for Liabilities and Charges

IDENTIFYING PROVISIONS

Definition of provision

29.1 CA 1985 defines provisions for liabilities and charges as:

> 'any amount retained as reasonably necessary for the purpose of providing for any liability or loss which is either likely to be incurred, or certain to be incurred but uncertain as to amount or as to the date on which it will arise.'

FRS 12 'Provisions, Contingent Liabilities and Contingent Assets' defines a provision as a liability that is of uncertain timing or amount, and defines liabilities as the obligations of an entity to transfer economic benefits as a result of past transactions or events. The standard expands on these definitions by requiring a provision to be recognised when:

- an entity has a present obligation (legal or constructive) as a result of a past event;
- it is probable that a transfer of economic benefits will be required to settle the obligation; and
- a reliable estimate can be made of the amount of the obligation (cases where this is not possible are expected to be rare).

These requirements are considered in more detail in **29.6–29.16** below.

Distinction between creditors and provisions

29.2 A key distinction between creditors (including accruals) and provisions is that a creditor will usually represent a legal or contractual obligation to pay a known sum to another party at a given time, whilst a provision will be the best estimate of a known or expected liability that has not yet crystallised and where there is some uncertainty about either the timing or the amount of the payment that will eventually be required. FRS 12 makes the point that:

- trade creditors are liabilities to pay for goods and services that have been received or supplied, and that have been invoiced or formally agreed with the supplier; and

- accruals are liabilities to pay for goods and services that have been received or supplied (including services provided by employees), but which have not yet been paid, invoiced or formally agreed with the supplier.

The guidance emphasises that it may sometimes be necessary to estimate the amount or timing of accruals, but the degree of uncertainty in this case will usually be considerably lower than in the case of a provision.

Other types of provision

29.3 The term 'provision' is sometimes used in other contexts as well, such as provisions for depreciation and impairment in asset values, and provisions for bad and doubtful debts. Strictly, these are adjustments to the carrying value of the related assets rather than provisions as such. It is therefore more appropriate to treat them as a reduction of the asset values than to record them separately as provisions. FRS 12 notes specifically that they are not covered by its requirements.

Distinction between provisions and contingent liabilities

29.4 The guidance also considers the distinction between provisions and contingent liabilities. Provisions are recognised as liabilities because they represent a present obligation where it is probable that a transfer of economic benefits will be required to settle the obligation. Contingent liabilities are either:

- possible obligations – ie it is not yet certain that the entity has an obligation that will require a transfer of economic benefits; or
- present obligations which are not recognised as provisions because:
  - it is not probable that a transfer of economic benefits will be required; or
  - a sufficiently reliable estimate cannot be made of the amount involved (this is expected to be rare in practice).

Accounting for contingent liabilities under FRS 12 is considered in more detail in **Chapter 32**.

Items commonly treated as provisions for liabilities and charges

29.5 Within the heading 'provisions for liabilities and charges', the balance sheet formats require separate disclosure of provisions in respect of pension commitments (and similar obligations) and taxation, but group together any remaining provisions under the subheading 'other', although the Act does require individual details to be given for any material items. FRS 12 now requires separate disclosure for each class of provision. The identification of a class for this purpose is considered in more detail in **29.44**. The following are examples of some of the categories that may be included within the provisions heading:

— product warranties;

— product claims (e.g. where a general fault has been identified);

— reorganisation or restructuring programmes;

— dilapidation or restoration (e.g. the costs of restoring land after mining or quarrying);

— environmental issues (e.g. provisions for clean-up costs).

Separate requirements on pensions apply under FRS 17 'Retirement Benefits' for accounting periods beginning on or after 1 January 2005 (see **29.49–29.53** below).

RECOGNISING PROVISIONS

Scope of FRS 12

29.6 FRS 12 'Provisions, Contingent Liabilities and Contingent Assets' covers the recognition and measurement of all provisions other than those:

— resulting from financial instruments carried at fair value;

— resulting from executory contracts, except where the contract is onerous;

— arising in insurance entities from contracts with policy holders;

— covered by another SSAP or FRS.

The guidance notes that any financial instruments (including guarantees) not carried at fair value and any provisions, contingent liabilities and contingent assets of insurance entities other than those relating to contracts with policy holders are included within the scope of the standard. Executory contracts are defined as those under which neither party has performed any of its obligations or both parties have partially performed their obligations to an equal extent. The issue of onerous contracts is considered in **29.12** below. Current SSAPs and FRSs that deal more specifically with certain types of provisions, contingent liabilities and contingent assets include:

— SSAP 9 'Stocks and long-term contracts';

— SSAP 21 'Accounting for leases and hire purchase contracts';

— FRS 17 'Retirement Benefits'; and

— FRS 19 'Deferred Tax'.

Recognition criteria

29.7 FRS 12 requires a provision to be recognised when:

- an entity has a present obligation (legal or constructive) as a result of a past event;
- it is probable that a transfer of economic benefits will be required to settle the obligation; and
- a reliable estimate can be made of the amount of the obligation (situations where this cannot be done are expected to be very rare in practice).

If these three conditions are not met, no provision should be recognised.

Present obligation

29.8 In most cases it will be clear whether or not a past event has given rise to a present obligation. Where the situation is not clear (the guidance in FRS 12 uses as an example a lawsuit where there is a dispute over whether certain events occurred or whether they have resulted in an obligation), the standard requires the entity to consider all the available evidence, including expert opinions where appropriate, and to recognise a provision if it is more likely than not that a present obligation exists at the balance sheet date. Conversely, if it is more likely that no present obligation exists at the balance sheet date, no provision should be recognised. In this case, it will usually be necessary to disclose a contingent liability (unless the transfer of economic benefits is remote). In its Information Sheet No 35, issued in February 2000, the UITF emphasises that no liability will generally arise at the balance sheet date where a regulated industry is required to reduce its prices in future years as a result of the profit levels achieved in the current year. The only exception to this is where the entity has a binding obligation at the balance sheet date to repay amounts to customers, rather than simply to adjust prices for future years.

Obligating events

29.9 The standard defines an obligating event as 'an event that creates a legal or constructive obligation that results in an entity having no realistic alternative to settling that obligation'. A legal obligation is one that derives from a contract (through either explicit or implicit terms), legislation or otherwise through the operation of the law. A constructive obligation arises where an entity creates a valid expectation on the part of other parties that it accepts and will discharge certain responsibilities. The obligation might arise from an established pattern of past practice, published policies or a specific statement by the entity. For instance, an entity with a widely published policy on environmental issues, and a history of honouring its commitment to clean up any contamination that it causes, will usually have a constructive obligation to clean up any future contamination.

Future operating costs

29.10 The guidance emphasises that financial statements deal with the position of the entity at the end of the reporting period and that no provision should be made for costs that need to be incurred to enable it to continue to operate in the future. Only liabilities that exist at the balance sheet date should be recognised in the accounts. For instance, a factory that is required by law to fit smoke filters by 30 June 2003 will not have a liability to do so at 31 December 2002 (unless it has arranged for the work to be completed by that date). No provision for the cost of fitting the filters should therefore be recognised in the accounts at 31 December 2002. If the filters are still not fitted by 31 December 2003, there is still no obligation to be recognised in the accounts in respect of the fitting of the filters. However, in this case it may be necessary to make provision for any fines for non-compliance payable under the legislation.

Future operating losses

29.11 The standard also specifically prohibits the recognition of a provision for future operating losses, on the basis that such losses do not meet the recognition criteria for provisions. However, where future operating losses are anticipated, any related fixed assets may need to be reviewed for impairment in accordance with the requirements of FRS 11 'Impairment of Fixed Assets and Goodwill'.

Onerous contracts

29.12 An onerous contract is defined as 'a contract in which the unavoidable costs of meeting the obligation under it exceed the economic benefits expected to be received under it'. A common example is a continuing lease on a property that the entity has vacated. The standard requires the present obligation under an onerous contract to be recognised and measured as a provision. The unavoidable costs are the lower of the cost of fulfilling the contract (i.e. in the above example, the cost of continuing to lease the property) and the cost of any penalties or compensation that would be due on a failure to fulfil it. In other words, the unavoidable costs represent the least net cost of exiting from the contract. Before setting up a separate provision for an onerous contract, the entity should carry out an impairment review of any assets dedicated to the contract and account for any impairment losses in accordance with FRS 11 'Impairment of Fixed Assets and Goodwill' (see **Chapter 20**).

Identity of third parties

29.13 Although a legal or constructive obligation will always involve a third party (ie the party to whom the obligation is owed), it is not necessary for the purposes of FRS 12 to know the identity of the third party. However, the guidance emphasises that a board or management decision does not give rise to an obligation at the balance sheet date unless the decision has been communicated to those affected in a way that raises a valid expectation that the entity will discharge its responsibilities. This point is considered further in **29.33** and **29.34** in the context of restructuring provisions.

Future events that create an obligation

29.14 Although an event may not immediately give rise to an obligation, future events or changes in circumstances may do so and may therefore require a provision to be recognised at a later stage. For instance, a company may have no obligation to rectify environmental damage at the time that it is caused, but this situation could be changed by:

- the introduction of legislation that requires the entity to rectify the damage previously caused; or
- a public statement in which the entity accepts responsibility for rectifying the damage previously caused.

Each of these would give rise to an obligation. A provision would therefore need to be recognised in the accounts in the year in which the event that creates the obligation takes place. In the case of new legislation, the guidance notes that an obligation will only arise when the legislation is virtually certain to be enacted as drafted and emphasises that, in many cases, this will not happen until the law is actually enacted.

Probable transfer of economic benefits

29.15 Under the guidance in FRS 12, a transfer of economic benefits, or any other event, is regarded as being probable if the probability that it will occur is greater than the probability that it will not. The degree of probability decides whether an obligation gives rise to a provision or to a contingent liability. Where there are a number of similar obligations (for instance, where an entity has given product warranties) the probability that a transfer of economic benefits will be required should be considered for the class of obligations as a whole.

Reliable estimate

29.16 Some degree of estimation is often required in accounting matters, and the inherent uncertainty surrounding provisions means that estimates are more likely to be needed here than in the case of certain other balance sheet items. FRS 12 requires a reliable estimate to be made of the amount of an obligation before a provision can be recognised, but the guidance notes that situations where this is not possible are expected to be extremely rare. Difficulty in calculating the amount should therefore not be used as a reason for not making provision. Even in some of the most difficult cases, it will usually be possible to determine a range of possible outcomes and assess the likelihood of each arising. The guidance notes that this will usually result in an estimate that is sufficiently reliable for the purposes of recognising a provision. If it is genuinely impossible to make a reliable estimate of the amount required, the obligation will be disclosable as a contingent liability. Calculating the best estimate is considered in more detail in **29.20–29.23** below.

Subsequent changes to provisions

29.17 The standard requires all provisions to be reviewed at each balance sheet date and adjusted to reflect the current best estimate of the liability. If it is no longer probable that a transfer of economic benefits will be required, the recognition criteria are no longer met and the provision should be reversed. Where a provision has been discounted, the amount carried in the balance sheet will change each year as the discount unwinds. This is considered in more detail in **29.24** below. The standard also only allows a provision to be used for the purpose for which it was originally established. This is consistent with the general prohibition on off-setting in accounts.

Recognition of an asset

29.18 In most cases, the setting up of a provision should be charged directly to the profit and loss account in the year in which the provision is recognised, and subsequent movements (eg adjustments to the current best estimate at each balance sheet date) will also be dealt with in the profit and loss account. The only exception is where the entity incurs the obligation in order to gain access to future economic benefits which will arise over more than one accounting period. For instance, a quarrying business will usually incur an obligation to restore the site of a quarry once activities have ceased there – it is prepared to incur this obligation in order to gain access to the materials that it wants to quarry. In these circumstances, an asset (representing the access to future economic benefits gained by incurring the obligation) should be recognised at the same time as the provision.

Further examples

29.19 Appendix III to FRS 12 sets out some useful examples in the form of case studies illustrating how the recognition rules might be applied in practice. These cover:

— warranties;

— contaminated land – legal obligation and constructive obligation;

— offshore oilfield – decommissioning costs;

— refunds policy in a retail outlet;

- closure of a division;
- legal requirement to fit smoke filters;
- staff retraining;
- an onerous contract (lease on vacant premises);
- a single guarantee;
- a court case;
- repairs and maintenance (involving major refits or refurbishment at specified intervals);
- self-insurance.

MEASURING PROVISIONS

Calculating the best estimate

29.20 FRS 12 requires the amount recognised as a provision to be the best estimate of expenditure required to settle the obligation at the balance sheet date. This is described as the amount that the entity would rationally pay to achieve settlement at the balance sheet date or to transfer the obligation to a third party at that time. The guidance notes that in many cases it would be prohibitively expensive, or indeed impossible, to actually settle or transfer the obligation at the balance sheet date, but this approach gives the best estimate of the liability at that date. Establishing the best estimate of an obligation will often involve a degree of judgement by those who are familiar with the business and the actual issues under consideration. Other sources of evidence might include past experience of similar issues and, in some cases, reports from independent experts. Post balance sheet events may also help to provide evidence of the position at the balance sheet date.

Dealing with uncertainty

29.21 FRS 12 requires uncertainty to be taken into account in establishing provisions. The approach to dealing with uncertainty will depend on the circumstances of each case. In the case of a single obligation, the most likely outcome may provide the best estimate of the liability, but it may sometimes be necessary to consider a variety of possible outcomes and to adjust the calculations to reflect this. Where the provision relates to a large population of items, the obligation will usually be estimated by identifying the various possible outcomes and their probabilities and weighting the possible outcomes accordingly. The guidance in FRS 12 gives the following example:

Example 29.1 – Dealing with uncertainty

An entity sells goods with a warranty under which defects that become apparent in the six months after purchase are repaired free of charge. The entity has projected the following total repair costs:

If minor defects are detected in all products	£1 million
If major defects are detected in all products	£4 million

Past experience and future expectations indicate the following probabilities:

75% of goods sold will have no defects

20% of goods sold will have minor defects

5% of goods sold will have major defects

The provision for expected repair costs is therefore calculated as:

	£
20% x £1 million	200,000
5% x £4 million	200,000
	£400,000

In practice, the most difficult aspect of these calculations will usually be identifying the probability of the various outcomes. This may be easier if there is a past history on which to base the assessments, but can be extremely difficult in the case of a new business or new product lines. It may also occasionally be necessary to consider the potential impact of the repair not being carried out successfully, with the result that further work is needed.

Adopting a cautious approach

29.22 FRS 12 also requires risk to be taken into account in reaching the best estimate of a liability. The guidance emphasises that caution is needed in dealing with any items involving judgement, to ensure that profits and assets are not overstated and expenses and liabilities are not understated. However, it also states unequivocally that uncertainty should not be used to justify excessive provisions or a deliberate overstatement of liabilities. Care should be taken not to double count risk and uncertainty. Where the provision is discounted, risk may also be taken into account in the discount rate, and care is also needed here to ensure that the risk adjustment is not in effect duplicated (i.e. by being taken into account in both the estimate of the liability and in the discounting process).

Impact of taxation

29.23 Provisions should always be measured before tax and any tax effects should be accounted for in accordance with FRS 19 'Deferred Tax' (see **Chapter 30**).

Discounting provisions

29.24 Where the effect is material, FRS 12 requires the amount of a provision to be discounted to arrive at the present value of the obligation at the balance sheet date. This reflects the fact that cash outflows that arise soon after the balance sheet date are more onerous than those that arise at a later date. A pre-tax discount rate should normally be used, reflecting the current market assessment of the time value of money and the risks specific to the liability. It may also be acceptable to use a risk-free discount rate, provided that the cash flows have been appropriately adjusted for risk. As noted above, the guidance emphasises that the same risk should not be duplicated by being taken into account in both the cash flow estimates and the discount rate. It is also important to consider the basis of the cash flows used to estimate the liability. If these are expressed in current prices, a real discount rate will need to be used, but if the cash flows already reflect expected changes in prices, a nominal discount rate should be used to avoid duplicating the effects of inflation.

Unwinding the discount

29.25 Where a provision is discounted, some of the discount will unwind each year, reflecting the fact that the obligation is closer than at the end of the previous reporting period. FRS 12 requires the effect of this unwinding to be shown as other finance costs adjacent to interest in the profit and loss account.

Taking account of future events

29.26 In some cases, the best estimate of the liability may be affected by anticipated future changes, such as:

- advances in technology;
- reduced costs as a result of the increased experience in applying existing technology; or
- reduced costs as a result of applying existing technology to larger operations than previously.

For instance, one or more of these changes might enable the cost of carrying out clean-up or restoration work to be reduced. The standard allows such changes to be taken into account in the calculations if there is sufficient objective evidence that they will happen, but emphasises that the development of completely new technology should not be anticipated without appropriate evidence.

Expected disposal of assets

29.27 When measuring provisions under FRS 12, no account should be taken of gains that the entity expects to realise on the disposal of assets, even if the disposal is closely linked to the event that triggers recognition of the provision. This changes the requirements previously set out in FRS 3 'Reporting Financial Performance' in relation to provisions on the sale or termination of an operation (see **29.36–29.42** below).

Expected reimbursement of costs

29.28 In some cases, the entity may expect to receive reimbursement for some or all of the costs that give rise to a provision. For instance, some or all of the liability may be covered by insurance arrangements or indemnity clauses in a contract. Under FRS 12, the reimbursement should only be recognised when it is virtually certain that it will be received if the entity settles the obligation that gives rise to the provision. Where it is appropriate to recognise the reimbursement, it should be treated as a separate asset and not as a reduction of the provision. In no circumstances should the reimbursement that is recognised exceed the provision. In this context, reimbursement includes a situation where the third party meets some of the entity's liability directly. Although the provision and the reimbursement must be treated separately on the balance sheet, the standard permits a net disclosure in the profit and loss account.

Reimbursement that reduces liability

29.29 In most cases where reimbursement applies, the entity will remain liable for the settlement of the full amount of the liability. In exceptional cases, where the entity is not liable for the full amount (i.e. if the third party fails to pay, the entity has no liability to meet that element of the costs), the provision should reflect only the entity's actual liability. Contingent liability disclosures may be needed if the entity has joint and several liability with other parties.

PROVISIONS FOR RESTRUCTURING

Definition of restructuring

29.30 As provisions for costs of restructuring have been a particular problem area in the past, FRS 12 includes a separate section on how the recognition and measurement rules apply in this case. Restructuring is defined as 'a programme that is planned and controlled by management, and materially changes either the scope of a business undertaken by the entity, or the manner in which that business is conducted'. The guidance notes that the following events may fall within the definition of restructuring:

- the sale or termination of a line of business;
- the closure of business locations in a country or region;

- the relocation of business activities from one country or region to another;
- changes in the management structure, for instance by eliminating a layer of management; and
- fundamental reorganisations that have a material effect on the nature and focus of the entity's operations.

Where a restructuring meets the definition of a discontinued operation, the disclosure requirements of FRS 3 'Reporting Financial Performance' will also apply (see **Chapter 8**).

When a constructive obligation arises

29.31 A constructive obligation to restructure only arises when the entity:

- has a detailed formal plan for the restructuring, identifying as a minimum:
  - the business or part of the business concerned;
  - the principal locations affected;
  - the location, function and approximate number of employees who will be compensated for terminating their services;
  - the expenditures that will be undertaken; and
  - when the plan will be implemented;

  AND
- has raised a valid expectation in those affected that it will carry out the restructuring, either by starting to implement that plan, or by announcing its main features to those affected by it.

The guidance in FRS 12 notes that evidence of implementation of the plan might include dismantling plant, selling assets or making a public announcement of the main features of the plan.

Public announcement of the plan

29.32 Public announcement of the plan will only create a constructive obligation to proceed with the restructuring if:

- the announcement is sufficiently detailed to raise a valid expectation amongst suppliers, customers and employees (or their representatives) that the restructuring will be carried out as stated;
- implementation is planned to begin as soon as possible; and
- the restructuring is planned to be completed in a timescale that makes significant changes to the plan unlikely.

The guidance notes that a significant delay in implementation, or an abnormally long timescale for the restructuring, will indicate that the entity is not committed to the plan because it will have adequate opportunity to make changes should it so wish.

Management decisions

29.33 The guidance makes it clear that a management or board decision before the balance sheet date will not give rise to an obligation at that date unless the entity has already:

(i) started to implement the plan; or

(ii) announced the main features of the plan as explained in **29.31** and **29.32** above.

These actions must have been taken before the balance sheet date in order to create a constructive obligation at that date. If the management or board decision was taken before the balance sheet date but implementation begins or an announcement is made after that date, disclosure may be needed under the requirements of SSAP 17 'Accounting for Post Balance Sheet Events' (see **Chapter 33**) but no provision will be recognised in the accounts under FRS 12. However, the guidance notes that, in some cases, board membership may include representatives of interests other than management (e.g. employees) and in these circumstances a board decision might give rise to a constructive obligation, because the decision will have been communicated to these representatives.

Management decision confirming earlier events

29.34 In some cases, a management decision before the balance sheet date may provide formal confirmation of events that took place before that date. For instance, termination payments for employees may have been the subject of negotiations with their representative bodies for some time previously. In this case formal approval of the arrangements by management, and communication of this decision to the other parties, will give rise to a constructive obligation, provided that the other conditions set out in FRS 12 are met.

Costs to be included

29.35 Where a provision needs to be recognised for restructuring, only direct expenditures arising from the restructuring should be included – these are defined as costs that are both necessarily entailed by the restructuring and not associated with the ongoing activities of the entity. In particular, the provision should not include the costs of retraining or relocating staff, marketing activities, investment in new systems and distribution networks, future operating losses or expected gains on the disposal of assets.

PROVISIONS ON THE SALE OR TERMINATION OF AN OPERATION

Consequences of a decision to sell or terminate

29.36 Requirements on the recognition and measurement of provisions arising on the sale or termination of an operation are set out in FRS 3 'Reporting Financial Performance' rather than FRS 12. However, some small amendments to FRS 3 have been made to achieve consistency with the more extensive requirements now set out in FRS 12 'Provisions, Contingent Liabilities and Contingent Assets'. Where the decision has been taken to sell or terminate an operation, FRS 3 requires any provisions made as a result of this decision to reflect the obligations that have actually been incurred and that are not expected to be covered by the future profits of the operation (ie up to the time of sale or termination). The requirements apply regardless of whether the sale or termination is classed as a discontinued operation under FRS 3.

Entity to be demonstrably committed to the sale or termination

29.37 For an obligation to have been incurred, the standard requires the entity to be demonstrably committed to the sale or termination. If this degree of commitment does not exist, provision cannot be justified as there is no obligation to incur the related costs, even though there may be an intention to do so. The introduction of this requirement represented a significant change to general accounting practice. Prior to this, provisions were usually made on the basis of when the decision to pursue a particular course of action was taken by the board. This was justified on the basis that provision for the related costs was in accordance with the need for accounts to be prepared on a prudent basis. However, concern developed over the extensive use of provisioning and the fact that this could both distort profit trends and also result in certain costs being 'lost' within substantial provisions. The ASB has therefore moved clearly towards accounting on the basis of commitments rather than decisions, as is further evidenced by the detailed requirements now set out in FRS 12.

Evidence of demonstrable commitment

29.38 In order for an entity to be demonstrably committed to a sale or termination, FRS 3 requires:

- in the case of a sale, a binding sale agreement; and
- in the case of a termination, a detailed formal plan from which the entity cannot realistically withdraw.

The only additional guidance on these points given in FRS 3 is that the evidence might include:

- the public announcement of specific plans;
- the commencement of implementation; or
- other circumstances effectively obliging the entity to complete the sale or termination.

FRS 12 now reinforces the point that, in the case of the sale of an operation, no obligation arises until a binding sale agreement is in place and also provides further guidance on evidence of implementation and when public announcements will create a constructive obligation to proceed. These are considered above in the context of provisions for restructuring costs. Where the sale is part of a restructuring programme, a constructive obligation for the other parts may arise before a binding sale agreement is in place for the part of the business to be sold.

Commitment at the balance sheet date or subsequently?

29.39 FRS 3 does not make clear whether the demonstrable commitment to the sale or termination must exist at the balance sheet date. For instance, it does not consider the position where a management decision is taken before the balance sheet date, and implementation or announcement takes place after the balance sheet date but before the date of approval of the accounts. FRS 12 has now clarified that the obligation to proceed must exist at the balance sheet date for a provision to be recognised. Implementation or announcement after the balance sheet date but before the date of approval of the accounts may require disclosure as a post balance sheet event but will not justify provision in the accounts.

Costs included in the provision

29.40 Where a provision can justifiably be made, it should only include:

- the direct costs of the sale or termination; and
- any operating losses of the operation up to the date of sale or termination.

In each case, FRS 3 also requires any aggregate future profit from the activities of the operation (ie the profit that will be recognised in the profit and loss account up to the date of sale or termination) to be taken into account in calculating the provision. FRS 3 originally required profits on the disposal of assets to be taken into account as well, but this requirement has now been withdrawn to achieve consistency with FRS 12. The requirement in FRS 3 for operating losses to be taken into account appears to conflict with the prohibition in FRS 12 on making provision for future operating losses. However, this aspect of FRS 3 was not amended by FRS 12 and the requirement to adopt this approach in the case of a provision for the sale or termination of an operation still stands. It could be argued that FRS 3 is the more specific standard in these circumstances and that its requirements therefore override those in FRS 12.

Impairment of assets

29.41 Where an entity takes the decision to sell or terminate an operation, this may reflect the fact that the assets relating to that operation have become impaired. In this case, the carrying value of the assets in the entity's balances should be written down. The fact that the entity is not demonstrably committed to the sale or termination of the operation at the balance sheet date (and that provision for any direct costs or operating losses is therefore not permitted under FRS 3) does not remove the need for the carrying value of the operation's assets to be reviewed and written down where necessary.

Disclosure in the accounts

29.42 FRS 3 also requires specific disclosures to be given in the accounts when provision is made for the sale or termination of an operation. These affect both the current and subsequent years and are considered in detail in **29.47–29.48** below.

ACCOUNTS DISCLOSURE

Principal disclosure requirements

29.43 Within the heading 'provisions for liabilities and charges', the CA 1985 balance sheet formats require separate disclosure of provisions in respect of pension commitments (and similar obligations) and taxation, but group together any remaining provisions under the sub-heading 'other', although the Act does require individual details to be given for any material items. FRS 12 now requires separate disclosure of the following for each class of provision (see **29.44** below):

- opening and closing balances, additional provisions made in the period, amounts used and amounts reversed;
- where relevant, the increase in the discounted amount arising from the passage of time, and the effect of any change in the discount rate;
- a brief description of the nature of the obligation and the expected timing of any resulting transfers of economic benefits;
- an indication of the uncertainties over the amount or timing of those transfers, including where necessary disclosure of the main assumptions made concerning future events; and
- the amount of any expected reimbursement and the amount of any asset that has been recognised for that reimbursement.

Comparative information is not required for the first two items. The principal disclosure requirements are usually dealt with in a summary movements table in the notes to the accounts. The number of columns required will depend on how many separate items need to be disclosed. The following layout will usually be suitable:

Example 29.2 – Summary of movements

	Warranties	*Pensions*	*Deferred taxation*	*Other*	*Total*
	£000	*£000*	*£000*	*£000*	*£000*
Balance at 1 January 20X2	56	34	66	9	165
Utilised during the year	(7)	—	(14)	—	(21)
Reversed during the year	(3)	(3)			
Charge for the year in the profit and loss account	15	4	—	—	19
Balance at 31 December 20X2	61	38	52	9	160

Appendix IV to FRS 12 gives illustrative examples of suitable narrative disclosures in the case of warranties and decommissioning costs.

What constitutes a class of provision

29.44 The guidance notes that in identifying a class of provision, it will be necessary to consider whether the nature of individual items is sufficiently similar for a single statement to meet the narrative disclosure requirements of FRS 12 set out in **29.43** above. For instance, it suggests that it might be appropriate to treat warranty provisions for different products as a single class of provision, but to separate out amounts that arise under normal warranty arrangements and any that arise from legal proceedings.

Provisions linked with contingent liabilities

29.45 Where a provision and a contingent liability arise from the same set of circumstances, the disclosures should be made in a way that clarifies and explains the link between them. For instance, an entity may have joint and several liability with other parties and this may result in a provision being recognised for its own obligation, with separate disclosure of the contingent liability representing the obligation that is expected to be met by the other parties. The disclosures for the provision and the contingent liability should make clear that these obligations arise from the same transaction or arrangement.

Restriction of the disclosures

29.46 Some of the disclosures may be restricted if full disclosure would seriously prejudice the entity's position in a dispute relating to the subject of the provision, although this situation is expected to arise only very rarely. In this case, the general nature of the dispute should be disclosed along with an explanation of why the detailed disclosures have not been given. Appendix IV to FRS 12 gives an illustrative example of how this might be dealt with. The exemption does not apply if disclosure is required by law.

Sale or termination of an operation

29.47 Any provisions for costs and operating losses, and any write-down in asset values, relating to the sale or termination of an operation should be included in the results of continuing operations, unless the sale or termination meets the definition of a discontinued operation under FRS 3 (see **Chapter 8**). Separate disclosure will usually be required under paragraph 20 of FRS 3.

Utilisation of provisions in subsequent year

29.48 If the sale or termination does not qualify as a discontinued operation in the current year, but does so in the following year, any provisions carried forward should be offset against the results of the discontinued operation in the accounts for that year. This should be done by including the results of the operation under the appropriate statutory heading and then showing the utilisation of the provision by disclosing the amounts relating to the operating loss and the loss on sale or termination on the face of the profit and loss account, immediately below the relevant headings:

Example 29.3 – Showing the utilisation of provisions

	Continuing operations	*Acquisitions*	*Discontinued operations*	*Total 20X2*	*Total 20X1*
	£000	*£000*	*£000*	*£000*	*£000*
Turnover	5,672	784	591	7,047	6,434
Cost of sales	(3,982)	(660)	(503)	(5,145)	(4,876)
	1,690	124	88	1,902	1,558
Distribution costs	(978)	(58)	(61)	(1,097)	(994)

	Continuing operations	*Acquisitions*	*Discontinued operations*	*Total*	*Total*
				20X2	*20X1*
	£000	*£000*	*£000*	*£000*	*£000*
Administrative expenses	(531)	(21)	(39)	(591)	(476)
	181	45	(12)	214	88
Other operating income	53	20	—	73	42
Operating profit/(loss)	234	65	(12)	287	130
Utilisation of provision made in earlier years	—	—	10	10	—
	234	65	(2)	297	130
Loss on termination of operations	—	—	(10)	(10)	—
Utilisation of provision made in earlier years	—	—	7	7	—
	234	65	(5)	294	130

If the sale or termination does not qualify as a discontinued operation in the following year, the utilisation of any material provisions made in the previous year should still be disclosed in the accounts. This is now a requirement of FRS 12 as well as FRS 3.

PENSION AND SIMILAR COMMITMENTS

Nature of pension and similar commitments

29.49 FRS 17 'Retirement Benefits' defines retirement benefits as: 'All forms of consideration given by an employer in exchange for services rendered by employees that are payable after the completion of employment.' The standard therefore covers all retirement benefits that an employer is committed to making, regardless of whether the commitment is statutory, contractual or implicit. Each of the following would therefore come within the scope of the standard:

- a commitment to provide pension and other retirement benefits (e.g. medical care) set out in the employee's contract of employment;
- a commitment arising from custom and practice over a period of time (i.e. where the employer has traditionally made retirement

arrangements for employees, even though it has no contractual obligation to do so); or

— a commitment arising when an employer makes *ex gratia* or discretionary payments on a case by case basis.

Commitments arising outside the UK are also covered. The requirements of FRS 17 are considered in more detail in **Chapter 11**.

Unfunded schemes

29.50 Where an employer operates an unfunded scheme (ie benefits are simply paid as they fall due and no payments are made to fund benefits earned during the period), FRS 17 still requires a liability to be recognised in the financial statements as the benefits are earned by the employees, rather than as the actual payments become due.

Balance sheet presentation

29.51 FRS 17 requires a defined benefit asset or liability, net of any related deferred tax balance, to be shown separately on the face of the balance sheet as follows:

— in a balance sheet prepared under Format 1, CA 1985 Sch 4, after item J (Accruals and deferred income) but before item K (Capital and reserves);

— in a balance sheet prepared under Format 2, CA 1985 Sch 4, an asset should be shown after item D (Prepayments and accrued income) in the 'Assets' section and a liability should be shown after item D (Accruals and deferred income) in the 'Liabilities' section.

Under this standard, therefore, pension commitments are shown as a separate item on the balance sheet rather than within provisions for liabilities and charges. An example is given in **Chapter 11**.

Disclosure requirements

29.52 FRS 17 sets out detailed disclosure requirements in respect of both defined contribution and defined benefit retirement schemes. These are explained in **Chapter 11**. CA 1985 requires separate disclosure of any provisions included in the balance sheet in respect of pension commitments – this will be more than covered by the requirements of FRS 17. The Act also requires separate disclosure of any provisions in respect of pensions payable to past directors. This can usually be dealt with in a narrative footnote to the main pension disclosures:

Example 29.4 – Pensions payable to former directors

Included in the above provision for pensions is £……… (20X1 £…..) in respect of pensions payable to former directors.

However, in the case of a defined benefit asset or liability recognised as a separate item in the balance sheet in accordance with FRS 17, it may not be possible to identify the amounts relating to former directors – in these circumstances, it would be advisable to explain this fact in a brief note.

Pension commitments not provided for

29.53 The disclosure requirements in respect of any pensions commitments that have not been provided for are covered in **Chapter 32**.

Chapter 30

Deferred Taxation

THE NATURE OF DEFERRED TAX

Differences between taxable profit and accounting profit

30.1 The profit or loss for the year shown in a company's accounts can often be very different to the taxable profit or loss that forms the basis of the tax charge for the year. As a result, the tax payable in respect of a particular accounting period may have little relationship with the accounting profit or loss shown for that period. Differences arise mainly for the following reasons:

- certain categories of income recognised in the accounts may be tax-free;
- certain categories of expenditure shown in the accounts may be disallowable for tax purposes;
- occasionally, tax allowances or charges may arise with no corresponding income or expenditure in the profit and loss account; and
- certain items of income or expenditure may be recognised in the accounts in one period, but be chargeable to, or allowable for, tax in a different period.

Some of these are classified as permanent differences because they will never become taxable or allowable for tax (or, in the case of the third category above, there will never be corresponding income or expenditure for accounting purposes). Others are classified as timing differences because the tax effect will arise in an earlier or later accounting period than the accounting effect.

Permanent difference

30.2 Permanent differences are defined in FRS 19 'Deferred Tax' as:

> 'Differences between an entity's taxable profits and its results as stated in the financial statements that arise because certain types of income and expenditure are non-taxable or disallowable, or because certain tax charges or allowances have no corresponding amount in the financial statements.'

Permanent differences include items such as:

- most expenditure on entertaining;
- tax-free government grants;
- interest on tax repayments.

Permanent differences result in the tax charge or credit for the accounting period being more or less than tax at the standard rate on the profit or loss shown in the accounts.

Example 30.1 – Effect of permanent differences

A Ltd's profit before tax is £42,000. The profit and loss account includes the following items:

	£
Tax-free grant received	10,500
Entertaining expenses	3,200
The rate of tax is 20%	
A Ltd's taxable profits will be:	
Profit before tax per accounts	42,000
Less: Tax-free grant	(10,500)
Add back: Disallowable expenditure	3,200
	34,700

The tax charge will therefore be £34,700 x 20% = £6,940 rather than tax at the standard rate on the profit shown in the accounts (i.e. £42,000 x 20% = £8,400).

Timing differences

30.3 Timing differences are defined in FRS 19 as:

> 'Differences between an entity's taxable profits and its results as stated in the financial statements that arise from the inclusion of gains and losses in tax assessments in periods different from those in which they are recognised in financial statements. Timing differences originate in one period and are capable of reversal in one or more subsequent periods.

Examples of timing differences include:

- tax deductions for the cost of a fixed asset (e.g. capital allowances) which are received before or after the cost of the asset is recognised in the profit and loss account (e.g. in the form of depreciation);

- pension liabilities which are accrued in financial statements in accordance with FRS 17 'Retirement Benefits' but which are only allowable for tax purposes when paid or contributed at a later date;
- interest charges or development costs which are capitalised in the balance sheet but are treated as revenue expenditure for tax purposes and are therefore allowed at the time that they are incurred;
- the gain recognised in the financial statements when an asset is revalued for accounting purposes, but which only becomes chargeable to tax if and when the asset is sold;
- general bad debt provisions made for accounting purposes, but which do not become allowable for tax purposes until they have been identified with specific debts.

Some timing differences will be short-term and will reverse in the next accounting period, whereas others may take a substantial time to reverse (e.g. timing differences relating to pensions).

Deferred tax

30.4 Deferred tax is defined in FRS 19 as:

> 'Estimated future tax consequences of transactions and events recognised in the financial statements of the current and previous periods.'

The recognition of deferred tax in financial statements is therefore an attempt to eliminate the effect of timing differences between the accounting and taxable profits at each balance sheet date, by reflecting in the accounts the tax effects of those timing differences that have arisen up to that date and which will reverse at some point in the future.

METHODS OF PROVIDING FOR DEFERRED TAX

Three alternatives

30.5 There are three methods of providing for deferred tax in financial statements:

- flow-through (or 'nil provision');
- full provision; and
- partial provision

Each of these is considered briefly below.

Flow-through method

30.6 As the alternative name for this method suggests, no provision is made for deferred tax. Under this method, therefore, the accounts reflect only the tax liability arising on the taxable profit (or loss) for the period. The main advantage of the flow-through method is that it is straightforward to apply. The main disadvantages are that it can result in large fluctuations in the tax charge year by year and that it does not match tax reliefs and charges with the related costs and income in the accounts.

Full provision

30.7 Under this method, the tax effects of all gains and losses recorded in the accounts are provided for in full. As with the flow-through method, full provision is relatively straightforward to apply and can be based on reasonably precise information. The main disadvantage is that it can result in large liabilities being included in the balance sheet, some of which will only arise far into the future, and which even then may be dependent on some future event or transaction before they actually crystallise.

Partial provision

30.8 Under this method, provision is made in the accounts for those tax liabilities that are actually expected to arise as a result of the reversal of timing differences. Liabilities that are not expected to crystallise are not provided for in the accounts. In effect, this method recognises that, if the company maintains a similar level of activity and investment, it will often have a hard core of timing differences that, for all practical purposes, will not reverse. The advantage of this method is that the accounts reflect only those liabilities that are expected to arise. However, one of the main disadvantages of partial provision is that it can involve complex calculations and a high degree of subjectivity, particularly as provision is effectively made on the basis of financial projections and capital expenditure plans covering a number of years in the future.

The UK position

30.9 For many years, the UK accounting treatment for deferred tax was based on SSAP 15 'Accounting for Deferred Tax' (issued in 1978) which required the partial provision method to be used. The ASB reconsidered this accounting treatment in the light of developments in international accounting practice and concluded that:

- SSAP 15 was developed in the context of a very generous corporation tax system operating at that time, which enabled many companies to postpone indefinitely some or all of their deferred tax;
- the recognition rules of SSAP were very subjective and the need to

anticipate future events was inconsistent with the principles underlying other aspects of financial reporting;

- the partial provision method was not appropriate for dealing with long-term deferred assets, such as those associated with provisions for retirement benefits - an amendment had already been made to SSAP 15 to allow these assets to be accounted for on a full provision basis;
- there were considerable variations in the way in which SSAP 15 was applied in practice, which had a detrimental effect on the comparability of financial statements; and
- the partial provision method was increasingly being rejected by standard-setters in other countries.

FRS 19 'Deferred Tax' was therefore published in December 2000 to supersede SSAP 15 for accounting periods ending on or after 23 January 2002. FRS 19 requires deferred tax to be accounted for on a full provision basis, subject to some specific exceptions set out in the standard.

Methods of computing deferred tax

30.10 There are two methods of computing deferred tax:

(i) the deferral method; and

(ii) the liability method.

Under the deferral method, the provision for deferred tax is calculated at the rates of taxation in force when the differences arise and no adjustments are made if rates subsequently change. When the timing differences reverse, the tax effect is again calculated at the rate in force when the differences originally arose. Under this method, therefore, the provision for deferred tax does not necessarily reflect the amount that is expected to be paid. Under the liability method, deferred tax is provided for at the rate that is expected to apply when the timing differences reverse. Therefore, the provision reflects the amount of tax that is expected to be paid. FRS 19 requires the use of the liability method, as did its predecessor standard SSAP 15. Changes in tax rates are not often known in advance and therefore, in practice, the current rate of tax will normally be used to calculate deferred tax. If a change of rate is announced in advance, the new rate should be used to calculate the provision. In addition, under the liability method it will usually be appropriate to provide for deferred tax at the small company rate if this is expected to apply at the time that the timing differences reverse. If tax rates subsequently change, the deferred tax provided in previous years will need to be revised to reflect the fact that timing differences reversing in subsequent years will do so at the new rate. The effect of a change in tax rates should be included as part of the tax charge for the period in which the change is reflected in the accounts, and should be separately disclosed.

RECOGNITION OF DEFERRED TAX UNDER FRS 19

General requirement

30.11 Under FRS 19, deferred tax should be recognised in respect of all timing differences that have originated but have not reversed at the balance sheet date, except in the situations described below. Deferred tax should not be recognised on permanent differences.

Capital allowances

30.12 Deferred tax should be recognised when allowances for the cost of a fixed asset are received before or after the cost of the asset is recognised in the profit and loss account. If capital allowances are received on an asset that is not depreciated and has not otherwise been written down to a carrying value less than cost (for instance, to reflect an impairment), the timing difference will be equivalent to the amount of capital allowances received. Most capital allowances are repayable in the form of a balancing charge if the related asset is sold for more than its tax written-down value, but in some cases (e.g. industrial buildings) the allowances are only repayable if the asset is sold within a specified period. If that period has elapsed and the asset has not been sold, any deferred tax that has been recognised on the excess of the allowances over the related depreciation should be reversed as there is no longer a timing difference to be accounted for (in other words, the difference between the allowances and the related depreciation has become a permanent difference).

Non-monetary assets

30.13 Deferred tax should be recognised on timing differences that arise when a non-monetary asset is continuously revalued to fair value, and changes in fair value are recognised in the profit and loss account - for instance, where investments are 'marked to market'. Most gains and losses on these assets will be subject to current tax when they arise and will therefore not give rise to any deferred tax. Deferred tax will only be an issue if the gains and losses are taxed when they are actually realised rather than when they are recognised for accounts purposes. Deferred tax should not be recognised on timing differences arising when other non-monetary assets are revalued unless the entity has, by the balance sheet date:

— entered into a binding agreement to sell the revalued asset; and

— recognised the gain or loss that is expected to arise on the sale.

Even where these conditions are met, deferred tax may not need to be recognised if it is likely that a resulting gain will be rolled over. The guidance in the standard emphasises that the fact that assets such as stocks have been purchased with a view to resale does not mean that the entity has entered into a binding agreement to sell those assets.

Roll-over of taxable gain

30.14 Deferred tax should not be recognised on timing differences arising when non-monetary assets are revalued or sold if, on the basis of all available evidence, it is more likely than not that the taxable gain will be rolled over and will only be charged to tax if and when the asset(s) into which the gain has been rolled over are sold, or are deemed to have been sold for tax purposes. Where holdover relief applies, the taxation of the gain is only postponed for a finite period, and the conclusion on whether the gain is more likely than not to be rolled over will need to take into account all the evidence available at the time (including any provided by events since the balance sheet date) and to be continually reassessed. Any adjustment to recognise or release a deferred tax provision is a change in estimate – it should therefore be charged or credited as part of the tax charge for the period (in the profit and loss account or statement of total recognised gains and losses, as appropriate) and not accounted as a prior period adjustment.

Unremitted earnings

30.15 Tax that could be payable (after allowing for any double taxation relief) on the future remittance of past earnings of a subsidiary, associate or joint venture should be provided for only to the extent that, at the balance sheet date:

- dividends have been accrued as receivable; or
- the subsidiary, associate or joint venture has entered into a binding agreement to distribute the past earnings in the future – this situation is expected to be rare in practice.

Deferred tax assets

30.16 Deferred tax assets should be recognised to the extent that they are regarded as recoverable – that is, to the extent that, on the basis of all available evidence, it is more likely than not that there will be suitable taxable profits from which the future reversal of the underlying timing differences can be deducted. Where the entity also has deferred tax liabilities, it can be assumed that these will give rise to future taxable profits and, if these constitute suitable profits, the deferred tax asset can be regarded as recoverable. Where there are no deferred tax liabilities, or the liabilities are insufficient to cover the deferred tax assets or unsuitable for this purpose, the likelihood of other suitable taxable profits being available will need to be assessed. Under FRS 19, suitable taxable profits are those:

- generated in the same taxable entity (or in another entity whose profits are available through group relief) and assessed by the same tax authority;

— generated in the period in which the deferred tax is expected to reverse, or in a period to which a tax loss arising from the reversal of a deferred tax asset may be carried back or forward; and

— of a type from which the reversal of the timing difference may be deducted under normal tax rules.

Factors to be taken into account

30.17 The assessment of whether a deferred tax asset is recoverable can take account of actions that the entity might take to generate suitable taxable profits (e.g. by deferring claims for capital allowances or changing from tax-free to taxable investments). The guidance in FRS 19 also notes that:

— historical information about the entity's financial performance and position may provide the most objective evidence;

— the existence of unrelieved tax losses at the balance sheet date provides strong evidence that there may not be suitable taxable profits in future against which the losses and other deferred tax assets can be recovered, unless there is other persuasive and reliable evidence to the contrary (for instance, where the losses result from an identifiable and non-recurring cause and the entity has otherwise been consistently profitable over a long period); and

— in the case of an unrelieved capital loss, there is only likely to be persuasive and reliable evidence of suitable taxable gains against which the loss can be relieved if plans are in place to sell assets which will generate a chargeable gain that has not already been recognised as a deferred tax liability, and the unrelieved loss will be offset against this gain.

If existing tax losses are likely to take some time to be relieved, the recoverability of the deferred tax asset is likely to be relatively uncertain and recognition may therefore not be appropriate.

Subsequent adjustments to a deferred tax asset

30.18 The amount recognised as a deferred tax asset may need to be adjusted in subsequent years as a result of changes in circumstances which affect the extent to which the asset is regarded as recoverable – for instance, an improved trading position or the acquisition of a new subsidiary. These adjustments are changes in estimates and should therefore be reflected in the results for the period in which the changes take place – they should not be accounted for as prior period adjustments.

MEASUREMENT OF DEFERRED TAX UNDER FRS 19

General requirement

30.19 Deferred tax should be measured at the average tax rates that are expected to apply in the periods in which the timing differences are expected to reverse, based on tax rates and laws that have been enacted, or substantively enacted, by the balance sheet date. A tax rate is regarded as substantively enacted if it is included in a Bill that has been passed by the House of Commons and is awaiting only passage through the House of Lords and Royal Assent, or in a resolution having statutory effect that has been passed under the Provisional Collection of Taxes Act 1968 (this is rarely used in practice).

Average tax rates

30.20 The guidance in the standard emphasises that the requirement to measure deferred tax at the average rates expected to apply should not be read as a requirement to average the rates applying to individual types of taxable profits, or to taxable profits arising in different jurisdictions. The rate used should reflect the nature of the individual timing differences and the tax jurisdiction in which they are expected to arise. Average rates will usually only need to be calculated if the enacted tax rates are graduated (i.e. different rates apply to different levels of taxable income).

Discounting

30.21 Deferred tax assets and liabilities may be discounted to reflect the time value of money, but there is no requirement to do so. The decision on whether to discount or not is a matter of accounting policy. Where an entity considers it appropriate to adopt a policy of discounting, all deferred tax balances measured by reference to undiscounted cash flows, and for which the impact of discounting is material, should be discounted. The standard includes guidance on factors that are likely to be relevant to the consideration of whether a policy of discounting is appropriate - these include:

- how material the impact of discounting would be to the overall results and financial position of the entity;
- whether the benefits outweigh the cost of collating the information and carrying out the calculations; and
- whether discounting is an established industry practice, and comparability would therefore be enhanced by the entity also adopting this policy.

Certain timing differences, in particular those arising in respect of provisions for pension liabilities and investments in finance leases in the accounts of a lessor, will have already been measured by reference to discounted cash flows. Related deferred tax provisions should therefore not be discounted further, and they should be disclosed in the accounts as undiscounted deferred tax balances. Discounting may be appropriate in the case of deferred tax balances arising from accelerated capital allowances, revaluation gains and losses and unrelieved tax losses carried forward.

Discounting method

30.22 Where deferred tax balances are discounted, the discount period(s) should be the number of years between the balance sheet date and the date(s) on which it is estimated that the underlying timing differences will reverse. Assumptions made when estimating reversal dates should be consistent with those made elsewhere in the financial statements - for instance, assumptions on depreciation charges and residual values should be consistent with those adopted in accounting for tangible fixed assets in the financial statements. The remaining tax effects of transactions already reflected in the financial statements should be taken into account, but no account should be taken of

— other timing differences expected to arise on future transactions; or

— the potential impact of expected future tax losses.

In the case of fixed assets, therefore, the calculations should take account of future capital allowances and depreciation on assets already held at the balance sheet date, but should ignore any capital allowances and depreciation on assets that the entity expects to purchase in future years. The guidance in FRS 19 notes that it may be possible to use approximations or averages to simplify the calculations without introducing material errors. There may be uncertainty over both the amount of tax payable and the timing of the payment, and estimates and judgements may therefore need to be made. Illustrative examples of the discounting calculations are given in paragraph 49 of, and Appendix I to, the standard.

Discount rates

30.23 The discount rates used should be the post-tax yields to maturity that could be obtained at the balance sheet date on government bonds with similar maturity dates and in similar currencies to those of the deferred tax assets or liabilities. Details of yields to maturity can be obtained from published sources, and the post-tax figure is calculated by deducting tax at the rate at which it would be paid by an entity holding the bond, once again based on enacted or substantively enacted tax rates and legislation (see **30.19** above). In theory a different discount rate should be established for each year in which a timing difference is expected to reverse and, where different tax jurisdictions are involved, for each tax jurisdiction. However, the guidance in FRS 19 notes that it may be possible to use approximations or averages to simplify the calculations without introducing material errors. An illustrative example of the calculations is given in Appendix I to the standard.

PRESENTATION OF DEFERRED TAX IN FINANCIAL STATEMENTS

Performance statements

30.24 Deferred tax should be recognised in the profit and loss account for the period, except to the extent that it is attributable to a gain or loss that is or has been recognised directly in the statement of total recognised gains and losses. In this case, the attributable deferred tax should also be recognised directly in the statement of total recognised gains and losses. The guidance in FRS 19 notes that, in exceptional circumstances, it may be difficult to determine the amount of deferred tax relating to gains and losses recognised in the statement of total gains and losses, in which case a reasonable pro-rata or other more appropriate allocation of the deferred tax charge or credit may be used. All deferred tax recognised in the profit and loss account should be included in tax on profit or loss on ordinary activities. The presentation of both current and deferred tax in performance statements is considered in more detail in **Chapter 14**.

Balance sheet

30.25 With the exception of deferred tax relating to a defined benefit asset or liability recognised under FRS 17 'Retirement Benefits' (see **Chapter 11**):

- net deferred tax liabilities should be classified as provisions for liabilities and charges; and
- net deferred tax assets should be classified as debtors (using a separate sub-heading where material).

Deferred tax assets and liabilities should be shown separately on the face of the balance sheet where the amounts are so material in the context of total net current assets or net assets that readers may misinterpret the financial statements if separate disclosure is not given.

Offset of debit and credit balances

30.26 Deferred tax debit and credit balances should be offset within these balance sheet headings only to the extent that they:

- relate to taxes levied by the same authority; and
- arise in the same taxable entity or in a group of taxable entities where the tax losses of one entity can reduce the taxable profits of another.

A company will therefore usually be able to offset deferred tax balances and this may also be possible where the companies in a group come within the same tax jurisdiction.

DISCLOSURE OF DEFERRED TAX

Performance statements

30.27 The following disclosures should be given in the notes to the financial statements:

- the amount of deferred tax charged or credited within tax on ordinary activities in the profit and loss account, showing separately, where material, amounts relating to:
  - the origination and reversal of timing differences;
  - changes in tax rates and laws;
  - adjustments to deferred tax assets arising in previous periods; and
  - where relevant, changes in the amount of discount deducted in arriving at the deferred tax balance;
- the amount of deferred tax charged or credited in the statement of total recognised gains and losses or the period, with a similar analysis of material components.

Disclosure of both current and deferred tax in the performance statements is considered in more detail in **Chapter 14**.

Balance sheet

30.28 CA 1985 requires the amount provided in respect of deferred tax to be shown separately from any other provisions for taxation and a detailed analysis of movements in the year, as for all provisions. Under FRS 19, the notes to the balance sheet must disclose:

- the total deferred tax balance (before discounting, where relevant) showing separately the amount recognised for each significant type of timing difference;
- where relevant, the impact of discounting on, and the discounted amount of, the deferred tax balance;
- the movements between opening and closing deferred tax balances, showing separately:
  - the amount charged or credited in the profit and loss account;
  - the amount charged or credited directly in the statement of total recognised gains and losses; and

— movements arising from the acquisition or disposal of businesses.

Deferred tax assets

30.29 Where an entity has recognised deferred tax assets, the notes to the accounts should explain the amount and the nature of the evidence supporting this treatment if:

— recoverability is dependent on future taxable profits in excess of those arising from the reversal of deferred tax liabilities; and

— the reporting entity has suffered a loss in either the current or the previous period in the tax jurisdiction to which the deferred tax asset relates.

The guidance in the standard notes that the disclosure should set out the specific circumstances that make it reasonable to forecast the existence of suitable taxable profits against which the deferred tax assets can be recovered.

Other circumstances

30.30 The notes to the accounts should also disclose the circumstances that affect the current and total tax charges and credits for the current period or may affect the current and total tax charges or credits in future periods. This disclosure should include the following:

— a reconciliation of the current tax charge or credit on ordinary activities for the period to the current tax charge that would result from applying a relevant standard rate of tax to the profit on ordinary activities before tax - either the monetary amounts or the rates may be reconciled and the basis on which the standard rate has been determined should be disclosed (an example of this disclosure is given in **Chapter 14**);

— if assets have been revalued without deferred tax being recognised, or if their market value is disclosed in a note, an estimate of the amount of deferred tax that would become payable (or recoverable) if the assets were sold at those values, the circumstances in which tax would be payable (or recoverable) and an indication of the amount that may become payable (or recoverable) in the foreseeable future;

— if the entity has sold (or entered into a binding agreement to sell) an asset but has not recognised deferred tax on a taxable gain because it expects this to be rolled over, the conditions that will have to be met to obtain the rollover relief and an estimate of the tax that would become payable if those conditions were not met;

— if a deferred tax asset has not been recognised on the grounds that there is insufficient evidence of recoverability, the amount that has not been recognised and the circumstances in which the asset would be recovered;

— the nature of any other deferred tax not recognised, the circumstances in which the tax would become payable or recoverable and an indication of the amount that may become payable or recoverable in the foreseeable future.

Accounting policy

30.31 It will also usually be appropriate to disclose the accounting policy adopted for deferred tax. In line with the guidance in FRS 8 'Accounting Policies' this disclosure may be relatively brief if the policy adopted is in line with the detailed requirements set out in FRS 19.

Chapter 31

Share Capital and Reserves

AUTHORISED, ALLOTTED AND CALLED UP SHARE CAPITAL

CA 1985 disclosure requirements

31.1 The company's authorised share capital must be stated in the accounts and the standard balance sheet formats set out in CA 1985 require separate disclosure of the company's called up share capital and share premium account. Both headings are given Roman numerals and must therefore be shown on the face of the balance sheet. The notes to the balance sheet formats requires separate disclosure of:

(i) the company's allotted share capital; and

(ii) the amount of called up share capital that has been paid.

This information is usually given in the notes to the accounts, but may be given on the face of the balance sheet. The amount of called up share capital not paid also requires disclosure under the formats, either as a separate balance sheet heading or as a sub-heading within debtors. In many cases, all the capital that has been allotted will also have been called up and will be fully paid, in which case the required disclosures can be given as follows:

Example 31.1 – Where capital has been allotted, called up and fully paid

	20X2	*20X1*
	£	*£*
Authorised:		
5,000 ordinary shares of £1 each	5,000	5,000
Allotted, called up and fully paid:		
3,200 ordinary shares of £1 each	3,200	3,200

The disclosure is usually given in the notes to the accounts. The authorised share capital can be disclosed on the face of the balance sheet instead, but care is needed in the presentation to make it clear that the figure for authorised share capital is not included in the balance sheet totals.

Disclosure where shares are not fully paid

31.2 If the allotted shares have not been fully paid, separate disclosure is required of the amount paid.

Example 31.2 – Where shares have not been fully paid

A Ltd has an authorised share capital of 5,000 ordinary shares of £1, of which 3,200 have been allotted. The following calls have been made in respect of these shares:

— 1 July 20X2 – 50p per share

— 1 December 20X2 – 30p per share

At 31 December 20X2, A Ltd's accounting date, holders of 500 shares had not yet paid the second call of 30p per share. The accounts will therefore disclose:

	£
Authorised: 5,000 ordinary shares of £1 each	5,000
Allotted and called up:	
3,200 ordinary shares of £1 each	3,200

At 31 December 20X2, £3,050 had been paid in respect of the shares allotted and called up at that date.

The balance sheet will show share capital of £3,200 and the unpaid balance of £150 (ie 500 shares at 30p per share) will be included within debtors or as a separate heading on the face of the balance sheet.

Different classes of share

31.3 Where a company has allotted shares of more than one class, both CA 1985 and FRS 4 'Capital Instruments' require details to be disclosed for every class of shares in issue. FRS 4 also requires the same details in respect of any class of shares which is not yet in issue but which may be issued as a result of the conversion of debt or warrants that are issued. Shares can be issued in many different forms. Some of the more common types of shares are as follows.

— *Ordinary shares* – these usually give the shareholder the residual rights in the company (ie rights which have not been granted to other classes of shareholder) and often carry the main voting powers of the company.

— *Preference shares* – these give the shareholder some preferential right (eg a right to receive a fixed cumulative dividend, or a right to receive a proportion of capital in a winding up) and they often carry limited voting rights, but there is no reason why the voting rights attached to preference shares should not be as great as, or even greater than, those attached to ordinary shares. Equally, in some cases preference shares will not carry any voting rights.

— *Redeemable shares* – these are shares that may be redeemed at some point in the future, either at a specified time or at the option of the shareholder, or of the company, or of both. Both ordinary and preference shares can be redeemable.

The features of each type of share can be combined in various ways. The type of shares that an individual company can issue will usually be governed by its articles of association.

Accounts disclosure by class of share

31.4 Taking the requirements of the CA 1985 and of FRS 4 together, the following details must be disclosed for each class of share:

— the number of shares allotted;

— the aggregate nominal value of the shares allotted;

— rights to dividends;

— dates of redemption and amounts payable on redemption;

— priority and amounts receivable on a winding up;

— voting rights;

— any additional information necessary to clarify why the shares have been classified as equity or non-equity;

— where rights vary depending on circumstances, an explanation of both the circumstances and the variations.

The FRS 4 disclosure requirements do not apply in the case of equity shares with all of the following features:

— no rights to dividends other than those recommended by the directors;

— no redemption rights;

— an unlimited right to share in the surplus remaining on a winding up after all other liabilities and participation rights have been satisfied; and

— one vote per share.

However, the number of shares allotted and the aggregate nominal value must be given for all shares to comply with the disclosure requirements of the Act. If the brief summaries required by FRS 4, cannot provide adequate information for the commercial effect of the instrument to be understood, this fact should be stated and details should be given of where the relevant information can be obtained. The principal features of each instrument should always be disclosed.

Example disclosure

31.5 In the case of a company which only has one class of ordinary shares in issue, the disclosure in **Example 31.1** would meet the requirements of CA 1985. In a more complex case, disclosure along the following lines will usually meet the requirements of both the standard and the Act.

Example 31.3 – Disclosures relating to different classes of share

	20X2	*20X1*
	£	£
Authorised:		
2,000 'A' ordinary shares of £1 each	2,000	2,000
2,000 'B' ordinary shares of 50p each	1,000	1,000
2,000 6% cumulative preference shares of £1 each	2,000	2,000
	5,000	5,000
Allotted, called up and fully paid:		
1,000 'A' ordinary shares of £1 each	1,000	1,000
1,000 6% cumulative preference shares of £1 each	1,000	1,000
	2,000	2,000

The 'A' ordinary shares are not redeemable and carry no rights to dividends other than those recommended by the directors. These shares rank last for payment in a winding up but carry an unlimited right to share in any remaining assets after all other liabilities and participation rights have been satisfied.

The preference shares are non-voting and carry the right to a 6% cumulative dividend. They are redeemable at par on or after 1 January 20X8 at the option of the company. In a winding up, the preference shares rank ahead of the ordinary shares and are repayable at par.

If the holders of the convertible debt exercise their conversion rights they will be issued with 'B' ordinary shares. These shares are non-voting and carry the right to an annual cumulative dividend of 5p per share. In a winding up, the 'B' ordinary shares rank after the preference shares but ahead of the 'A' ordinary shares and are repayable at par.

Although details of the 'A' ordinary shares are not strictly required under FRS 4, it can be helpful to give this information for completeness, especially where it helps to clarify some of the rights attaching to the other shares.

Disclosure of share issue during the year

31.6 Where shares have been allotted during the year, CA 1985 requires disclosure of the following information:

— the class of shares allotted;

— for each class of shares:

  — the number allotted,

  — the aggregate nominal value of the shares allotted,

  — the consideration received by the company.

This detail will usually be given in the notes to the accounts. In most cases a narrative footnote to the share capital note will suffice, but a table could be used if there were a number of share issues during the period.

Example 31.4 – Issue of shares

	20X2	*20X1*
	£	£
Authorised:		
2,000 'A' ordinary shares of £1 each	2,000	2,000
2,000 'B' ordinary shares of 50p each	1,000	1,000
2,000 6% cumulative preference shares of £1 each	2,000	2,000
	5,000	5,000
Allotted, called up and fully paid:		
1,000 'A' ordinary shares of £1 each	1,000	1,000
1,000 (20X1: 500) 6% cumulative preference shares of £1 each	1,000	500
	2,000	1,500

500 6% preference shares of £1 each were issued on 31 March 20X2, at a cash price of £6.50 per share.

The share premium account would show a premium of £2,750 on shares issued during the period (ie 500 shares at a premium of £5.50 each):

	£
Balance at 1 January 20X2	1,500
Premium on shares issued during the year	2,750
Balance at 31 December 20X2	4,250

Share awards to employees

31.7 UITF Abstract 17 'Employee Share Schemes' considers the accounting treatment of shares awarded to employees through annual bonuses or long-term incentive schemes, and requires the cost of share awards to employees to be charged to the profit and loss account over the period to which the employee's performance relates. Where new shares are issued under an employee share scheme, the amount accrued should be included within shareholders' funds in the balance sheet. The credit entry for the charge to the profit and loss account each year should be reported in the reconciliation of movements in shareholders' funds, not in the statement of total recognised gains and losses. This reflects the fact that the amount recognised represents proceeds from the issue of an equity instrument. When the shares are issued, the total amount accrued should be allocated between share capital and reserves. The requirements of Abstract 17 are considered in more detail in **Chapter 10**, together with the requirements of UITF Abstract 30 'Date of Award to Employees of Shares and Right to Shares'.

SHARE PREMIUM ACCOUNT

Creation of share premium account

31.8 Where a company issues shares at a premium, for cash or otherwise, CA 1985 requires a sum equal to the aggregate amount or value of the premiums on the shares to be transferred to the share premium account. Relief from this requirement ('merger relief') is granted in limited cases, provided that specific conditions set out in ss 131–132 of the Act are met.

Use of the share premium account

31.9 The share premium account may be applied as follows:

- in paying up unissued shares to be allotted to members as fully paid bonus shares;
- in writing off the company's preliminary expenses;
- in writing off the expenses of any issue of shares or debentures;
- in writing off any commission paid, or discount allowed, on any issue of shares or debentures;
- in providing for the premium payable on redemption of debentures of the company.

Apart from this, the share premium account must be treated as if it were paid up share capital (i.e. it can only be reduced under the specific conditions laid down in the Act for a reduction of capital). Under certain circumstances, a private company may be able to use the share premium account to purchase or redeem its own shares.

Transfers to and from share premium account

31.10 The share premium account is treated as a reserve for disclosure purposes. Therefore, where any amount is transferred to or from the share premium account, CA 1985 requires disclosure of the amounts transferred, and the source or application of those amounts, together with the balance on the share premium account at the beginning and end of the year. Comparative figures are not required for these disclosures. **Example 31.12** below includes disclosure of movements on the share premium account.

EQUITY AND NON-EQUITY SHARES

Definition of equity share capital under CA 1985

31.11 CA 1985 defines equity share capital as 'issued share capital, excluding any part of that capital which, neither as respects dividends nor as respects capital, carries any right to participate beyond a specified amount in a distribution'. Therefore, in order to qualify as an equity share under the Act, a share must carry the right to participate, without restriction to a set amount, in:

— dividends; or

— a return of capital; or

— both dividends and a return of capital.

For instance, a preference share which carries the right to a fixed cumulative dividend and the right to a fixed proportion of capital on a winding up will not be an equity share under the Act. However, a preference share which carries the right to a fixed cumulative dividend but also carries the right to participate beyond a set amount in a winding up will usually meet the definition of an equity share set out in the Act.

Non-equity and equity shares under FRS 4

31.12 FRS 4 defines non-equity shares as shares which have any of the following characteristics:

— any rights to receive payments, in respect of dividends, redemption or otherwise, are for a limited amount that is not calculated by reference to the company's assets, profits or the dividends on any class of equity share;

— any rights to participate in a surplus in a winding up are limited to a specific amount that is not calculated by reference to the company's assets or profits, and this limitation had a commercial effect in practice at the time that the shares were issued or, if later, at the time that the limitation was introduced;

— the shares are redeemable either according to their terms or because the holder, or any party other than the issuer, can require their redemption.

This definition is widely drawn and in effect ensures that any share which carries a limited right to a dividend, or a limited right to any payment on redemption, will be classed as a non-equity share. This applies irrespective of any other rights that might be attached to the shares. Any other share is an equity share.

Interaction with the definition in the Act

31.13 FRS 4 acknowledges that, in rare circumstances, this definition could result in a share being classified as a non-equity share for the purposes of FRS 4, whilst meeting the definition of an equity share under the Act. In this situation, the accounts would need to disclose sufficient information to explain the position.

Disclosure of equity and non-equity shares

31.14 FRS 4 requires total shareholders' funds to be shown on the face of the balance sheet and to be analysed between equity and non-equity interests. Where the impact of this analysis is material, it should be given on the face of the balance sheet. In other cases, the details may be given in the notes to the accounts, but where this treatment is adopted, the caption on the balance sheet must state that non-equity interests are included. The individual components of shareholders' funds (e.g. share capital, revaluation reserve, profit and loss account etc.) do not have to be analysed.

Example 31.5 – Disclosure of equity and non-equity shares

Using the details from **Example 31.3**, the 'A' ordinary shares are equity shares, and the 'B' ordinary shares and the preference shares are non-equity shares (because their right to receive a dividend is limited and is not based on assets, profits or equity dividends). The information might therefore be presented on the balance sheet as follows.

		20X2		*20X1*
	£	£	£	£
Capital and reserves:				
Called up share capital		2,000		2,000
Revaluation reserve		125		140
Profit and loss account		1,860		1,443
Shareholders' funds:				
Equity	2,985		2,583	
Non-equity	1,000		1,000	
		3,985		3,583

The alternative presentation would be:

	20X2 £	*20X1* £
Capital and reserves:		
Called up share capital	2,000	2,000
Revaluation reserve	125	140
Profit and loss account	1,860	1,443
Shareholders' funds (including non-equity interests)	3,985	3,583

There would also be a cross-reference to a note to the accounts providing the required analysis of shareholders' funds between equity and non-equity interests.

Amounts attributable to non-equity interests

31.15 The amount attributable to non-equity interests will be the net proceeds of the issue(s), plus finance costs to date, less any dividends or other payments made to date. The amount attributable to equity interests is the balancing figure. **Example 31.5** assumes that the finance cost of the non-equity shares is equivalent to the dividends paid, but this will not always be the case. The accounting treatment of finance costs and dividends in respect of non-equity shares is covered in **Chapter 15**.

Analysis of non-equity shareholders' funds

31.16 FRS 4 requires non-equity shareholders' funds to be analysed further into the amount relating to each class of non-equity shares and each series of warrants for non-equity shares (see **31.21–31.26** below). This detail will usually be given in the notes to the accounts.

Debt or equity?

31.17 UITF Abstract 33 'Obligations in Capital Instruments' considers how the principles set out in FRS 4 and FRS 5 'Reporting the Substance of Transactions' should be applied in the context of complex capital instruments that have characteristics of both debt and equity, and how various types of capital instrument issued as a means of raising finance should be reported in the balance sheet (ie whether they should be shown as liabilities or shareholders' funds or, in the case of consolidated financial statements, as minority interests). The Abstract notes specifically that it does not deal with capital instruments issued as part of the contingent purchase consideration for a business combination. The general rule is that a capital instrument should be reported within shareholders' funds only if it is a share, or if it does not contain an obligation to transfer economic benefits. All other capital instruments should be treated as liabilities, even if the obligation to transfer economic benefits does not go beyond that normally contained in a share. The requirements of Abstract 33 are considered in more detail in **Chapter 25**.

REDEEMABLE SHARES

General disclosure requirement

31.18 Where shares are redeemable, CA 1985 requires the following disclosures in the accounts:

— the earliest date on which the company can redeem the shares;

— the latest date on which the company can redeem the shares;

— whether the shares must be redeemed in any event, or whether they are liable to be redeemed at the option of the company or of the shareholder;

— whether any premium is payable on redemption and, if so, the premium that is payable.

These overlap with some of the detailed disclosures required by FRS 4. The other disclosures required by FRS 4 also continue to apply. **Example 31.3** shows the required disclosures in the case of preference shares that are redeemable at par. The following wordings might be suitable for shares redeemable at a premium. The precise wording will obviously vary depending on the underlying nature of the shares.

Example 31.6 – Shares redeemable at a premium (I)

The preference shares are non-voting and carry the right to a 5% cumulative dividend. They are redeemable on 1 January 20X9 at a premium of 4%. In a winding up, the preference shares rank ahead of the ordinary shares and are repayable at par.

Example 31.7 – Shares redeemable at a premium (II)

The 'B' ordinary shares carry one vote per share. They are redeemable between 1 January 20X4 and 31 December 20X4, at the option of either the company or the shareholder, at a premium of 4%. In a winding up, the 'B' ordinary shares rank ahead of the 'A' ordinary shares and are repayable at par.

Accounting for finance costs and dividends

31.19 The accounting treatment of finance costs and dividends in respect of redeemable shares is considered in **Chapter 15**.

Accounting for redemption

31.20 When the shares are redeemed, shareholders' funds should be reduced by the value of the consideration given. This will usually be the amount recorded in shareholders' funds in respect of the shares. **Example 15.8** in **Chapter 15** illustrates how this balance is built up over the life of the shares.

CONVERTIBLE INSTRUMENTS, SHARE OPTIONS AND SIMILAR RIGHTS

Convertible debt

31.21 Where a company has issued debt that is convertible into shares, FRS 4 requires it to be reported within liabilities and the finance cost to be calculated on the assumption that the debt will not be converted. The disclosure of convertible debt is considered in **Chapter 25** and the accounting treatment of the finance costs is considered in **Chapter 13**.

Warrants

31.22 A warrant is defined in FRS 4 as 'an instrument that requires the issuer to issue shares (whether contingently or not) and contains no obligation for the issuer to transfer economic benefits'. A warrant is therefore similar to a share option, but warrants will often be transferable, whilst options will usually be specific to an individual. Warrants issued to employees under employee share schemes are not covered by FRS 4. Where a company issues warrants, any proceeds relating to the warrants should be credited directly to a warrant reserves within shareholders' funds in the year of issue and should be reported in the reconciliation of movements in shareholders' funds. The amount credited to the warrant reserve should not be adjusted subsequently to reflect any changes in the value of the instruments. The balance on the warrant reserve must be analysed into warrants relating to equity shares and warrants relating to non-equity shares, for inclusion in the disclosure of equity and non-equity shareholders' funds (see **31.11–31.17** above).

Composite transactions

31.23 Instruments that are issued at the same time as part of a composite transaction should be considered together under FRS 4 and accounted for as a single instrument unless they can be transferred, cancelled or redeemed independently of each other.

Example 31.8 – A composite transaction?

C Ltd issues a debt instrument and a warrant on 1 January 20X2.

(a) At the date of issue, the fair value of the debt instrument is £1,800 and the fair value of the warrant is £200.

As a fair value can be attributed to the warrant, it must be capable of being separately transferred and redeemed and should therefore be treated as a separate instrument. £200 will therefore be credited to a warrant reserve, which will be non-distributable and will form part of shareholders' funds. The proceeds of £200 will also be reported in the reconciliation of movements in shareholders' funds.

(b) The warrant cannot be separately transferred or redeemed and the fair value of the debt instrument and the warrant together at the date of issue is £2,000.

As the warrant cannot be separately transferred or redeemed, the debt and warrant should be accounted for as one instrument. In effect, the instrument is debt that is convertible into shares and should be accounted for as a liability in the accounts of the issuer. No value will be attributed to the warrant (i.e. no warrant reserve will be created in this instance).

Exercise of warrant

31.24 When a warrant is exercised (i.e. the related shares are issued), FRS 4 requires any amount previously recognised in the accounts in respect of the warrant to be included in the net proceeds of the shares issued (eg for the purpose of calculating finance costs). However, there are different interpretations at present of whether this requires the warrant reserve to be transferred to share capital (and, where appropriate, the share premium account) or whether it should remain as a warrant reserve within shareholders' funds.

Lapse of warrant

31.25 If a warrant lapses because it has not been exercised within the specified time, any amount previously recorded on the warrant reserve becomes distributable and should be transferred from the warrant reserve to the profit and loss account as a reserves movement. It will also be reported as a gain in the statement of total recognised gains and losses for the year. If the warrant related to non-equity shares, the reserve will in effect be transferred from non-equity shareholders' funds to equity shareholders' funds.

Disclosure requirements

31.26 The disclosures required by CA 1985 where a company has granted options or similar rights to subscribe for shares are set out in **31.27** below. These disclosure requirements apply in respect of any instrument which is convertible into shares at some point in the future. Where warrants are convertible into a class of shares that is not yet in issue, the same details must be given in respect of these shares as are required under FRS 4 for each class of shares already in issue (see **31.4** above).

Share options and similar rights

31.27 Where a company has granted options to subscribe for shares, or any other similar rights to require the allotment of shares, CA 1985 requires the accounts to show:

— the number, description and amount of shares involved;

— the period during which the option or right is exercisable;

— the price to be paid for the shares allotted.

This information is usually given as part of the note on share capital. Depending on the complexity of the information to be disclosed, it may be given in a narrative note or in table form.

Example 31.9 – Option disclosure: narrative note

The company has granted options in respect of 1,500 ordinary shares of £1 each which are exercisable between 1 January 20X5 and 31 December 20X5 at £2.50 per share.

Example 31.10 – Option disclosure: table form

The company has granted options in respect of 1,500 ordinary shares of £1 each which are exercisable as follows.

Number of shares	*Exercise dates*	*Exercise price*
500	1 January 20X4 to 31 December 20X4	£2.00
500	1 January 20X5 to 31 December 20X5	£2.50
500	1 January 20X6 to 31 December 20X6	£2.50
1,500		

Specific accounting and disclosure requirements apply where share options are granted to employees – these are considered in **Chapter 10**. Additional disclosures are also required where options or other rights to subscribe for shares are granted to directors – these are considered in more detail in **Chapter 36**.

REVALUATION RESERVE

Use of the alternative accounting rules

31.28 Wherever a company makes use of the alternative accounting rules (see **Chapter 1**), the surplus or deficit arising on revaluation of the asset to market value or current cost must be transferred to the revaluation reserve. The only widespread use of the alternative accounting rules at present is to allow land and buildings to be included in the accounts at valuation rather than historical cost. Most revaluation reserves therefore arise when land and buildings are revalued for accounts purposes. Consequently, the examples in the following sections discuss the issues in the context of the revaluation of tangible fixed assets. **Chapter 20** includes a practical example showing the accounting entries where a fixed asset is revalued for accounting purposes and gives examples of the detailed disclosures that are required both in the year of valuation and in subsequent years. In accordance with the normal rules under CA 1985, when a number of assets are revalued, each item must be considered individually and surpluses and deficits should generally not be off-set against each other.

Surplus or deficit on initial revaluation

31.29 Where the initial revaluation of a fixed asset gives rise to a surplus, the accounting in the year of valuation is reasonably straightforward and the surplus results in a credit balance on the revaluation reserve. Details of the accounting entries and a practical example are given in **Chapter 20**. In the past considerable confusion arose over accounting for deficits arising on the first revaluation of a fixed asset. CA 1985 is clear that any provision for a permanent diminution in the value of a fixed asset must be charged to the profit and loss account. If the initial revaluation of an asset gives rise to a deficit when compared to the cost or book value of the asset, and the diminution in value is considered to be permanent, the deficit must therefore be charged to the profit and loss account. However, the Act is less clear on the treatment of diminutions in value that are not considered to be permanent and a particular problem under these provisions for many years was the distinction between permanent and temporary diminutions in value. FRS 11 'Impairment of Fixed Assets and Goodwill' has attempted to overcome these difficulties by setting out new rules on when and how assets should be reviewed for impairment and on the recognition of impairment losses in the accounts.

Debit balance on revaluation reserve

31.30 Prior to the issue of FRS 11, where an initial revaluation of a fixed asset gave rise to a diminution in value when compared to the cost or book value of the asset, but this diminution was considered to be temporary, it was possible to argue that the deficit was only being recognised in the accounts because the alternative accounting rules were being applied. Under these rules, all adjustments relating to the revaluation of assets, both surpluses and deficits, should be transferred to the revaluation reserve. If the only revaluation adjustment was a deficit, this resulted in a debit balance on the revaluation reserve. Nothing in CA 1985 appears to prevent a debit balance being shown on the revaluation reserve. However, in accounting terms, the need to adopt a prudent approach would normally required such a debit balance to be written off against the profit and loss account.

Impact of FRS 11

31.31 FRS 11 'Impairment of Fixed Assets and Goodwill' requires fixed assets and goodwill to be reviewed for impairment if events or changes in circumstances indicate that the carrying amount of the asset or goodwill may not be recoverable. To the extent that the carrying amount exceeds the recoverable amount, the fixed asset or goodwill is impaired and should be written down. The general rule is that an impairment loss (i.e. the difference between the carrying amount of a fixed asset or goodwill and its recoverable amount) should be recognised in the profit and loss account of the period, although different requirements apply in the case of assets that have previously been revalued (see **31.32** below). An impairment loss arising on an asset that has not previously been revalued must therefore always be charged to the profit and loss account, regardless of whether the diminution in value is considered to be temporary or permanent.

Impairment of previously revalued assets

31.32 In the case of assets that have previously been revalued, an impairment loss caused by a clear consumption of economic benefits should be recognised in the profit and loss account. Appendix II to FRS 11 notes that this is consistent with the requirement under CA 1985 for all permanent diminutions in value to be charged to the profit and loss account. Other impairment losses on revalued assets (for instance, those relating to general reductions in property prices) should be recognised in the statement of total recognised gains and losses until the carrying amount of the asset reaches its depreciated historical cost, and any further reduction below this amount should be recognised in the profit and loss account. The impairment of a revalued asset in this case will therefore be treated as a reduction of the revaluation reserve until the full amount of any previous surplus relating to the asset has been reversed. The requirements of FRS 11 on the measurement and recognition of impairment losses, and the reversal of impairment losses, are considered in more detail in **Chapter 20**.

Movements on the revaluation reserve

31.33 Once the revaluation reserve has been created, any of the following movements might arise in subsequent years:

- adjustments for subsequent changes in the value of assets that have already been revalued;
- surpluses on the initial revaluation of further assets;
- transfers to the profit and loss account reserve in respect of the additional depreciation charged on the revalued assets under the requirements of FRS 15 'Tangible Fixed Assets';
- transfers to the profit and loss account reserve in respect of revaluation surpluses that have become realised when the relevant asset is disposed of; and
- transfers in respect of taxation relating to revalued assets.

Transfer in respect of depreciation on revalued assets

31.34 FRS 15 'Tangible Fixed Assets' requires the depreciation charge for the year to be based on the carrying value of assets rather than on their historical cost. However, the additional depreciation on the revalued element of the asset may be debited to the revaluation reserve and credited to the profit and loss account reserve each year as a movement on reserves, to reflect the fact that only depreciation on the original cost of an asset is regarded as a realised loss for distribution purposes under the Act. This issue is considered in more detail in **Chapter 12**.

Transfer on disposal of a revalued asset

31.35 When an asset that has been revalued is disposed of, any remaining balance in the revaluation reserve relating to that asset should be transferred to the profit and loss account reserve as a reserves movement. This reflects the fact that the revaluation surplus has been realised as a result of the disposal of the asset, and ensures compliance with the requirement under the Act that amounts no longer necessary for the valuation method used should be removed from the revaluation reserve. This is considered in more detail in **Chapter 12**, along with a practical example.

Accounts disclosure

31.36 The balance sheet formats set out in CA 1985 require separate disclosure of the amount carried forward on the revaluation reserve at the balance sheet date. The heading for the revaluation reserve is given a Roman numeral and it must therefore be shown on the face of the balance sheet. Under other provisions in the Act, the reserve need not be called a revaluation reserve in the accounts, but in practice it is preferable for companies to continue to use this description. CA 1985 also requires disclosure of all movements on the revaluation reserve during the year. This can be given as part of a single note setting out movements on all reserves (see **Example 31.12**) or can be given in a separate note covering only the revaluation reserve.

Example 31.11 – Separate note covering only the revaluation reserve

	£000
Balance at 1 January 20X2	145
Write-down of previously revalued asset	(15)
Transfer to profit and loss account reserve in respect of depreciation charged on revalued assets	(12)
Transfer to profit and loss account reserve in respect of revalued assets sold during the year	(20)
Balance at 31 December 20X2	98

Tax implications of revaluations

31.37 CA 1985 also requires disclosure of the treatment for tax purposes of any amounts credited or debited to the revaluation reserve. This means that the tax implications of any revaluations must be explained. FRS 19 'Deferred Tax' also includes accounting and disclosure requirements on the tax implications of asset revaluations. These are considered in **Chapter 30**. Compliance with the requirements of FRS 19 will usually be sufficient to ensure compliance with the Act.

Use of the revaluation reserve

31.38 CA 1985 permits the revaluation reserve to be used to pay up unissued shares in the company which are to be allotted to members of the company as fully or partly paid shares. It does not permit the revaluation reserve to be used for any other purpose. In particular, the revaluation reserve cannot be used to write off goodwill. This was clarified by the *Companies Act 1989*, which inserted paragraph 34(3B) into CA 1985 Sch 4. Prior to this, it was not clear that goodwill could not be written off against the revaluation reserve, and companies which made such a write-off in accounting periods beginning before 23 December 1989 were not required to reinstate the amount written off as a result of the clarification. Certain companies may therefore still show revaluation reserves which have been reduced by goodwill, but this treatment should not be adopted in any other cases.

OTHER RESERVES

Analysis of other reserves

31.39 The balance sheet formats require the following analysis of other reserves:

— capital redemption reserve;

— reserve for own shares;

— reserves provided for by the articles of association;

— other reserves.

The total must be shown separately on the face of the balance sheet, but the analysis may be given in the notes to the accounts. The sub-headings for 'reserve for own shares' and 'reserves provided for by the articles of association' are rarely used in practice. A capital redemption reserve will usually need to be created where a company purchases or redeems its own shares out of distributable profits. A transfer from distributable profits to the capital redemption reserve will normally be required to ensure that the appropriate level of capital is maintained. The capital redemption reserve is non-distributable, but it may be used in paying up unissued shares of the company to be allotted to members of the company as fully paid bonus shares. The sub-heading 'other reserves' - as its name suggests - covers any items not dealt with under any of the specific reserves headings. Generally, there will be little to disclose under this sub-heading, but if material amounts are classified as other reserves it will usually be appropriate to give a brief description of them in the accounts.

Profit and loss account reserve

31.40 The profit and loss account reserve is the accumulation of retained profits and losses reported in the profit and loss account. The reserve must be shown separately on the face of the balance sheet. In some circumstances it may be appropriate to transfer amounts to the profit and loss account reserve from other reserves, and vice versa. The following examples are considered elsewhere in this book:

— transfers between the revaluation reserve and the profit and loss account reserve in respect of depreciation on revalued assets (**Chapter 12**).

— transfers between the profit and loss account and share premium account in respect of issue costs (**Chapter 13** and **Chapter 15**).

Chapter 6 also considers a specific situation where exchange gains and losses in respect of foreign currency borrowings and foreign currency investments may be taken directly to the profit and loss account reserve (ie without passing through the profit and loss account).

Disclosure of movements on reserves

31.41 Where any amount is transferred to or from any reserve during the year, CA 1985 requires disclosure of the following:

— the amount of the reserve at the beginning of the year;

— any amounts transferred to or from the reserve during the year;

- the source and application (respectively) of the amounts transferred; and
- the amount of the reserve at the end of the year.

This disclosure requirement is usually dealt with by presenting a movements table for reserves in the notes to the accounts. Depending on the level of detail requiring disclosure, it may be possible to combine the disclosures for all reserves including the share premium account and revaluation reserve, in one note.

Example 31.12 – Disclosure for all reserves in one note

	Share premium	*Revaluation reserve*	*Other reserves*	*Profit and loss account*
	£000	*£000*	*£000*	*£000*
Balance at 1 January 20X2	35	—	4	65
Premium on shares issued during the year	10	—	—	—
Surplus on revaluation of property during the year	—	55	—	—
Retained profit for the year	—	—	—	40
Balance at 31 December 20X2	45	55	4	105

Comparative figures are not required for movements on reserves.

OTHER DISCLOSURE REQUIREMENTS

Disclosure of non-distributable reserves

31.42 There is no requirement under CA 1985 to distinguish between distributable and non-distributable reserves in the accounts (or between realised and unrealised reserves). However, if a substantial element of reserves is non-distributable it is usually advisable to disclose this fact in a narrative footnote to the reserves table.

Example 31.13 – Disclosure where substantial element of reserves is non-distributable

Of the total reserves shown above, £100,000 is not available for distribution.

A brief outline of the issues relating to distributable and non-distributable reserves is given in **Chapter 15**.

Dividend arrears

31.43 Where a company has issued shares carrying a fixed cumulative dividend, and these dividends are in arrears (ie because there are insufficient distributable reserves to pay the dividends), CA 1985 requires the accounts to disclose:

- the amount of the arrears; and
- the period for which the dividends are in arrears (if more than one class of shares is affected, details must be given for each class of share affected).

The disclosure will usually be covered in a narrative note, which will normally form part of the reserves note, but could be included elsewhere in the accounts (e.g. in the share capital note, which provides details of each class of shares in issue).

Example 31.14 – Disclosure of dividend arrears

No dividends have been paid in respect of the 5% cumulative preference shares since 20X1; total dividend arrears at 31 December 20X3 amount to £9,000.

The accounting treatment of fixed cumulative dividends under the requirements of FRS 4 'Capital Instruments' is considered in **Chapter 15**.

LIKELY FUTURE DEVELOPMENTS

FRED 30 'Financial instruments: Disclosure and presentation; Recognition and measurement'

31.44 The ASB issued FRED 30 'Financial Instruments: Disclosure and Presentation; Recognition and Measurement' in June 2002 as part of its project to achieve convergence between UK accounting standards and international accounting standards. The Exposure Draft sets out proposals for the implementation in the UK of standards based on proposed revisions of IAS 32 'Financial Instruments: Disclosure and Presentation' and IAS 39 'Financial Instruments: Recognition and Measurement'. These have been published simultaneously by the International Accounting Standards Board (IASB). The implementation of accounting requirements based on FRED 30 could have significant implications for companies with preference shares. Preference shares are currently shown as part of shareholders' funds but under the proposals in FRED 30 many will be treated as liabilities rather than shares, and dividends payable on them will be accounted for as interest. However, the ASB notes in the Exposure Draft that it has some concerns about the IAS 32 approach to the classification of capital instruments into liabilities and equity and it has asked the IASB to carry out a comprehensive review of the issue. Nevertheless, the proposal set out in FRED 30 is that, with effect from 1 January 2004:

- all entities should be required to comply with IAS 32's presentation requirements (including its requirements on the treatment of preference shares) - FRS 4 'Capital instruments' would therefore be withdrawn;
- all listed entities and banks should be required to comply with IAS 32's disclosure requirements - FRS 13 'Derivatives and other financial instruments: Disclosure' would therefore also be withdrawn; and
- any entity that chooses to adopt fair value accounting should be required to adopt IAS 39's measurement and hedge accounting requirements.

The ASB is not yet proposing UK implementation of the part of IAS 39 dealing with the recognition and derecognition of financial instruments. The proposed effective date of 1 January 2004 assumes that:

- the Government will by then have effected the various changes to companies legislation needed to implement the standards; and
- the IASB does not propose to make further changes to IAS 32 and IAS 39 during 2004.

The proposals in FRED 30 are summarised in **Chapter 25**.

FRED 31 'Share-based Payment'.

31.45 FRED 31 'Share-based Payment' was issued in November 2002 and sets out proposals for a UK accounting standard based on the IASB's exposure draft ED 2 which has been published simultaneously. The draft standards are based on the following principles:

- when an entity receives goods or other services in exchange for a share-based payment, it should recognise an expense;
- that expense should be recognised over the period in which the services involved are rendered or as the goods involved are received; and
- the expense should be measured by reference to fair value.

FRED 31 proposes that the standard should apply to all UK entities (both listed and unlisted) and to all share-based payment transactions, including all employee share option schemes, all Save-As-You-Earn (SAYE) plans and similar arrangements, and all share-based payment transactions involving the receipt of goods and non-employee services. In view of the importance and urgency that the ASB attaches to this subject, it is proposing that the standard should be implemented in the UK as soon as possible. Under the IASB's current timetable, the international accounting standard would come into effect for accounting periods beginning on or after 1 January 2004 and the ASB is proposing the same effective date for the UK standard.

Further details are given in **Chapter 10**.

Chapter 32

Commitments and Contingencies

CONTINGENT LIABILITIES

Definition of contingent liability

32.1 FRS 12 'Provisions, Contingent Liabilities and Contingent Assets' defines a contingent liability as:

- a possible obligation that arises from past events and whose existence will be confirmed only by the occurrence of one or more uncertain future events not wholly within the entity's control; or
- a present obligation that arises from past events but is not recognised because:
  - it is not probable that a transfer of economic benefits will be required to settle the obligation; or
  - the amount of the obligation cannot be measured with sufficient reliability.

Distinction between provisions and contingent liabilities

32.2 FRS 12 also considers the distinction between provisions and contingent liabilities. A provision is defined as a liability that is of uncertain timing or amount, and liabilities are defined as the obligations of an entity to transfer economic benefits as a result of past events. The standard requires a provision to be recognised when:

- an entity has a present obligation (legal or constructive) as a result of a past event;
- it is probable that a transfer of economic benefits will be required to settle the obligation; and
- a reliable estimate can be made of the amount of the obligation (situations where this is not possible are expected to be rare in practice).

The principal distinctions between provisions and contingent liabilities are, therefore:

- whether the obligation is present or possible at the balance sheet date; and

— in the case of a present obligation, the likelihood of a transfer of economic benefits being required to settle the obligation (ie whether such a transfer is probable or not).

These issues are considered in more detail in **Chapter 29**.

Items commonly identified as contingent liabilities

32.3 A wide variety of items might come into the category of contingent liabilities, depending on the circumstances in each case. Some of the more common ones include:

- outstanding claims and litigation;
- performance bonds;
- guarantees;
- forward foreign exchange contracts;
  - warranties and indemnities;
  - deferred consideration (eg in respect of an acquisition).

Accounting treatment

32.4 Under FRS 12, a contingent liability should not be recognised in the accounts, but should be disclosed unless the possibility of a transfer of economic benefits is remote. For instance, a situation where the possibility of the transfer of economic benefits is remote might arise where an entity assigns a lease to another tenant and signs an authorised guarantee agreement in respect of the performance of the assignee. The entity would continue to have a liability to the landlord if the assignee defaults on the lease, but if there is no evidence to suggest that the assignee is unlikely to meet the rental payments, the possibility of the liability crystallising will usually be sufficiently remote to justify non-disclosure.

Regular review

32.5 The guidance in FRS 12 emphasises the need for contingent liabilities to be assessed continually to determine whether a transfer of economic benefits has become probable. If such a transfer becomes probable in respect of an item previously disclosed as a contingent liability, a provision should be recognised in the accounts of the period in which the change in probability occurs (assuming that all of the recognition criteria are met).

Joint and several liability

32.6 Where an entity has joint and several liability with other entities for a present obligation at the balance sheet date, the liability will usually need to be considered in two parts. Where it is probable that a transfer of economic benefits will be required for the entity to settle its part of the obligation and a reliable estimate of this can be made (ie the recognition criteria set out in FRS 12 are met), the entity should recognise a provision for its own part of the obligation. The obligation that is expected to be met by the other parties will normally be treated as a contingent liability. A different approach will be required if it is apparent that one or more of the other entities may not be able to meet their part of the obligation. In this case there will usually be a higher degree of probability that the entity will need to make an additional transfer of economic benefits and this may therefore need to be recognised as a provision in the accounts.

Detailed disclosures

32.7 CA 1985 requires the following details to be given in respect of any contingent liability that is not provided for in the accounts:

— the amount (or estimated amount) of the liability;

— its legal nature;

— whether any valuable security has been provided by the company and, if so, what.

For each class of contingent liability, FRS 12 requires the accounts to give a brief description of the nature of the liability at the balance sheet date and, where practicable, the following additional information:

— an estimate of the financial effect, measured in accordance with the criteria set out in paragraphs 36 to 55 of FRS 12 (ie those applying to the measurement of provisions - see **Chapter 29**);

— an indication of the uncertainties relating to the amount or timing of any outflow; and

— the possibility of any reimbursement.

In determining a class of liability for these purposes, the guidance notes that it will be necessary to consider whether the nature of the items is sufficiently similar for a single statement about them to meet the disclosure requirements set out in the first two categories above. If any of the required information is not disclosed because it is not practicable to do so, this fact must be stated.

Provisions linked with contingent liabilities

32.8 Where a provision and a contingent liability arise from the same set of circumstances, the disclosures should be made in a way that clarifies and explains the link between them. For instance, an entity may have joint and several liability with other parties and this may result in a provision being recognised for its own obligation, with separate disclosure of the contingent liability representing the obligation that is expected to be met by the other parties. The disclosures for the provision and the contingent liability should make clear that these obligations arise from the same transaction or arrangement.

Restriction of the disclosures

32.9 Some of the disclosures may be restricted if full disclosure would seriously prejudice the entity's position in a dispute relating to the subject of the provision, although this situation is expected to arise only very rarely. In this case, the general nature of the dispute should be disclosed along with an explanation of why the detailed disclosures have not been given. Appendix IV to FRS 12 gives an illustrative example of how this might be dealt with in the context of a provision – the same approach would be appropriate in the case of a contingent liability. The exemption does not apply if disclosure is required by law.

Example disclosure

32.10 Standard disclosure cannot be provided, as the details will inevitably vary depending on the precise circumstances of each case, but the information is often disclosed along the following lines:

Example 32.1 – Contingent liability disclosure

The company is the defendant in proceedings which began in June 20X2 as a result of a claim by a customer that the company was negligent in the performance of contract work carried out in 20X1. The customer is claiming damages of £100,000. This claim is being vigourously defended and the directors are confident that the company will be successful in its defence of the claim. Full provision has been made in the accounts for legal costs of £15,000 incurred to date in defending the claim. It is not practicable at this stage to quantify any additional costs that may be incurred.

CONTINGENT ASSETS

Definition of contingent asset

32.11 FRS 12 defines a contingent asset as 'a possible asset that arises from past events and whose existence will be confirmed only by the occurrence of one or more uncertain future events not wholly within the entity's control.' Contingent assets usually result from unexpected or unplanned events, and the guidance in the standard quotes as an example a claim that is being pursued through the legal system, where the outcome is uncertain.

Accounting treatment

32.12 Under FRS 12, an entity should not recognise a contingent asset in the accounts. To do so would mean recognising a profit that might not actually be realised. However, the guidance notes that, where realisation of the profit is virtually certain, the related asset is no longer contingent (ie it does not meet the definition in **32.11** above) and it should therefore be recognised in the accounts. A contingent asset should only be disclosed in the accounts where an inflow of economic benefits is probable. This is to prevent the accounts giving a misleading impression of the likelihood of future profits arising from contingent assets.

Regular review

32.13 As with contingent liabilities, the standard requires contingent assets to be assessed continually. Where an inflow of economic benefits becomes virtually certain, the asset and the related profit should be recognised in the accounts in the year in which the change in circumstances takes place. If an inflow of economic benefits becomes probable, the contingent asset should be disclosed in the accounts. Under the guidance in paragraph 23 of FRS 12, a transfer of economic benefits, or any other event, is regarded as being probable if the probability that it will occur is greater than the probability that it will not.

Detailed disclosures

32.14 Where an inflow of economic benefits is probable, the accounts should disclose a brief description of the contingent asset at the balance sheet date and, where practicable, an estimate of the financial effect, measured using the principles set out in paragraphs 36 to 55 of FRS 12 (ie those applying to the measurement of provisions – see **Chapter 29**). In drafting these disclosures, care should be taken to avoid giving a misleading indication of the likelihood of future profits arising from a contingent asset.

Restriction of the disclosures

32.15 Some of the disclosures may be restricted if full disclosure would seriously prejudice the entity's position in a dispute relating to the subject of the provision, although this situation is expected to arise only very rarely. In this case, the general nature of the dispute should be disclosed along with an explanation of why the detailed disclosures have not been given. The exemption does not apply if disclosure is required by law. If any of the required disclosures are not given because it is not practicable to do so, the standard requires this fact to be stated in the accounts.

GUARANTEES

Disclosure under CA 1985

32.16 CA 1985 also requires disclosure of any other financial commitments which have not been provided for in the accounts and which are relevant to an assessment of the company's state of affairs. Where any disclosable commitments are undertaken on behalf of any parent, fellow subsidiary or subsidiary undertaking, these commitments must be shown separately (see **32.19** below).

Disclosure of amount outstanding and maximum liability

32.17 A commitment or contingent liability that frequently requires disclosure, especially in the accounts of companies which are members of a group, is the existence of guarantees in respect of borrowings taken out by other members of the group. Where the company has given a guarantee in respect of a loan to another company, the amount outstanding at the end of the year should be disclosed as part of the contingent liability note. In the case of a guarantee relating to an overdraft facility, the maximum amount covered by the guarantee should be stated as well as the amount outstanding at the balance sheet date. The same principle would apply to a guarantee of a loan where the amount could vary (eg where the guarantee covers a facility up to a specified level, but the full amount has not been drawn down at the balance sheet date).

Example 32.2 – Disclosure of a loan/overdraft guarantee

The company has guaranteed an unsecured bank loan of £25,000 to a fellow subsidiary. This loan is repayable in full in June 20X4.

The company has also guaranteed the bank overdraft of its parent company; the maximum amount available under this facility is £100,000 and the amount outstanding at the balance sheet date was £45,678 (20X1: £51,332). No security has been provided by the company.

Aggregate disclosure

32.18 Where the company has guaranteed the overdrafts of more than one company within the group, the aggregate amount outstanding on these accounts at the end of the year should be disclosed, along with the maximum potential liability. Where the bank accounts of some of these companies are in credit at the end of the year, the precise terms of the agreement will need to be reviewed to establish whether the company's liability is for the aggregate amount of the overdrafts outstanding at the balance sheet date or for the net amount outstanding (ie the aggregate of all the relevant accounts, regardless of whether they are in credit or overdraft). The amount (or amounts) disclosed in the contingent liabilities note should reflect the company's actual liability under the guarantee arrangements.

Separate disclosure of group items

32.19 CA 1985 requires financial commitments and contingencies undertaken on behalf of other group companies to be shown separately from other commitments and contingencies. Group items must be analysed into two categories:

- those involving any parent undertaking or any fellow subsidiary undertaking (ie any member of a wider group of which the company is a part); and
- those involving any subsidiary undertaking (ie any member of a group headed by the company).

Charge on the company's assets

32.20 If a guarantee or any other financial commitment involves a charge over the company's assets, details of the security given must also be disclosed under the requirements of CA 1985.

Example 32.3 – Where a charge over the company's assets is included

The company has guaranteed an unsecured bank loan of £25,000 to a fellow subsidiary; this loan is repayable in full in June 20X4.

The company has also guaranteed the bank overdraft of its parent company; the maximum amount available under this facility is £100,000 and the amount outstanding at the balance sheet date was £45,678 (20X1: £51,332). The amount outstanding at any time (up to a maximum of £100,000) is secured on the company's freehold property.

CAPITAL COMMITMENTS

Disclosure under CA 1985

32.21 CA 1985 requires separate disclosure of commitments in respect of capital expenditure contracts entered into by the balance sheet date. The disclosure relates only to contracts for which no provision has been made in the accounts (for instance because work has not been started before the balance sheet date). The disclosures can be given in either table or narrative form.

Example 32.4 – Tabular disclosure; capital commitments

The following capital expenditure has been authorised but has not been provided for in the accounts.

	20X2	*20X1*
	£	£
Capital expenditure contracted for	345	114

Example 32.5 – Narrative form: capital commitments

At 30 September 20X2, the company had contracted for capital expenditure amounting to £345,000 (20X1: £114,000) which is not provided for in these accounts.

No capital commitments

32.22 Where there are no capital commitments at the balance sheet date, there is no formal requirement to state this fact, but it is good practice to do so.

Example 32.6 – Where there are no capital commitments

The company had no unprovided commitments in respect of capital expenditure contracted for at either 30 September 20X2 or 30 September 20X1.

PENSION COMMITMENTS

Disclosure of amounts not provided

32.23 Both the Act and FRS 17 'Retirement Benefits' (or, for accounting periods beginning before 1 January 2005, its predecessor standard, SSAP 24 'Accounting for Pension Costs') require disclosure of the amounts provided in respect of pension commitments. These requirements are considered in detail in **Chapter 10** and **Chapter 29**. In addition, CA 1985 requires separate disclosure of any pension commitments that have not been provided for in the accounts, with separate details of any amounts relating to pensions payable to past directors. Whilst FRS 17 (or, where appropriate, SSAP 24) does not specifically refer to this, it does require extensive disclosures on the funding and valuation of pension schemes, as well as requiring appropriate provision to be made in the accounts for all pension obligations, whether contractual or implied. Compliance with the accounting and disclosure requirements of the accounting standard will usually ensure that all the requirements of the Act in respect of pensions commitments are adequately met.

LEASING COMMITMENTS

Lessee commitments under finance leases

32.24 Where a company has entered into a finance lease or hire purchase agreement at the balance sheet date, but inception has not yet taken place, SSAP 21 'Accounting for Leases and Hire Purchase Contracts' requires disclosure of the company's commitment under the agreement. Inception of a lease is defined in SSAP 21 as the earlier of the date when the asset is brought into use or the date from which rental payments accrue.

Example 32.7 – Agreement entered into, but inception has not taken place

At the balance sheet date, the company had entered into commitments amounting to £35,000 (20X1: £46,000) in respect of a finance lease, the inception of which took place after the balance sheet date.

Further detail on accounting for finance leases under SSAP 21 can be found in **Chapter 20**.

Lessee commitments under operating leases

32.25 SSAP 21 also requires disclosure of the payments that the lessee is committed to make during the next year in respect of operating leases. Separate details must be given for leases of land and buildings and other leases. The leases must be analysed into those which expire:

- within the next year;
- in years two to five (inclusive); and
- more than five years after the balance sheet date.

The requirement for this analysis sometimes gives rise to confusion. The figure to be disclosed is the total amount payable during the next year in respect of operating leases, analysed into the above categories. The accounts are not required to show the amount payable in one year, in two to five years and after more than five years (ie the disclosure requirement in respect of operating lease commitments should not be confused with the requirement – also in SSAP 21 – for leasing and hire purchase creditors to be analysed into amounts payable within one year, in two to five years and after five years).

Example

32.26 In most cases, the clearest method of disclosure will be to set out the required information in table form.

Example 32.8 – Tabular disclosure for operating lease commitments

The following amounts are payable in the next twelve months under non-cancellable operating leases:

	20X2	*20X2*	*20X1*	*20X1*
	Land and buildings	*Other*	*Land buildings*	*Other*
	£	*£*	*£*	*£*
Operating leases which expire:				
Within one year	—	10	—	12
In two to five years (inclusive)	34	20	30	15
Over five years	76	—	76	—
	110	30	106	27

However, if there is only a small amount of detail to disclose, a narrative note may suffice.

Example 32.9 – Narrative disclosure for operating lease commitments

In the next twelve months, the company is committed to paying £51,500 (20X1: £47,800) under a non-cancellable operating lease in respect of land and buildings. This lease expires after more than five years. The company has no other operating lease commitments.

Chapter 33

Post Balance Sheet Events and Other Disclosures

ADJUSTING EVENTS

Definition of post balance sheet events

33.1 SSAP 17 'Accounting for Post Balance Sheet Events' defines post balance sheet events as 'those events, both favourable and unfavourable, which occur between the balance sheet date and the date on which the financial statements are approved by the board of directors'. Events which arise after the date of approval of the accounts are not covered by SSAP 17, although it is noted that the directors may need to consider publishing relevant information in respect of material events in this category.

Definition of adjusting events

33.2 SSAP 17 defines adjusting events as 'post balance sheet events which provide additional evidence of conditions existing at the balance sheet date. They include events which because of statutory or conventional requirements are reflected in financial statements'. As adjusting events provide additional evidence of the situation at the balance sheet date, and it is this situation that must form the basis for the accounts, the effect of an adjusting event should be reflected in the accounts if it is material.

Examples of adjusting events

33.3 The appendix to SSAP 17 lists a number of events that would normally need to be classified as adjusting events, and that would therefore usually result in adjustments being made to the accounts. The examples include:

— the subsequent finalisation of the purchase price of a fixed asset purchased before the year-end - the agreed price should be used as the purchase price of the asset;

— the finalisation of the selling price for an asset sold before the year-end - the agreed price should be used for the sales proceeds of the asset;

— a property valuation that provides evidence of an impairment in value - the carrying amount of the property at the balance sheet date should be written down to its recoverable amount;

— the receipt of a copy of the accounts or other information in respect of an unlisted company that provides evidence of an impairment in the value of a long-term investment - the investment should be written down to its recoverable amount;

— the receipt of sales proceeds after the end of the year which indicates that the net realisable value of certain stocks at the balance sheet date is lower than cost - the value of the stocks would therefore need to be reduced to net realisable value;

— the insolvency of a debtor - in this case, provision will usually need to be made against the balance outstanding at the end of the year;

— the receipt of a sum due in respect of an insurance claim which was under negotiation at the balance sheet date - the agreed amount should therefore be reflected in debtors at the balance sheet date.

Events which impact on the use of the going concern concept

33.4 Certain events which occur after the balance sheet date may indicate the need to reconsider whether it is still appropriate to prepare accounts on the going concern basis (see **Chapter 1**). Such events will usually be rare, but might include:

— a serious deterioration in operating results and financial position;

— the loss of business with a major customer (ie business on which the company is dependent for its future viability);

— an adverse judgement in respect of major litigation which puts into question the company's ability to continue trading.

If, as a result of such an event, it is no longer considered appropriate to prepare accounts on a going concern basis, the event will usually need to be treated as an adjusting event (ie the basis of the accounts will need to be adjusted).

NON-ADJUSTING EVENTS

Definition of non-adjusting events

33.5 SSAP 17 defines non-adjusting events as 'post balance sheet events which concern conditions which did not exist at the balance sheet date'. As the accounts must be based on conditions in existence at the balance sheet date, it would usually be inappropriate to adjust the accounts for such events. However, where such an event is material, details should be disclosed in the accounts to ensure that they are not misleading.

Examples of non-adjusting events

33.6 The appendix to SSAP 17 lists a number of events that would normally be classified as non-adjusting events, and that would therefore usually require disclosure in the accounts (if the effect is material) but which would not normally result in adjustments to the figures shown in the accounts. The examples include:

- the issue of shares or debentures;
- the purchase of a major fixed asset;
- the disposal of a major fixed asset;
- the loss of stock (or other assets) as a result of a fire or flood;
- the commencement of new trading activities or a major extension of the existing activities;
- the closure of a significant trading activity;
- a decline in the value of a property or investment, where it can be clearly demonstrated that the reduction in value took place after the year-end;
- changes in foreign exchange rates;
- increases in pensions benefits.

Exceptional circumstances

33.7 Although these events will normally be classified as non-adjusting events, in exceptional circumstances, it may be necessary to reclassify such an event as an adjusting event and make the necessary changes to the accounts. This situation is likely to be rare in practice, but if it does arise, full details of any adjustments made would need to be disclosed in the accounts.

Window dressing

33.8 SSAP 17 also requires disclosure of the reversal or maturity after the year-end of a transaction entered into before the balance sheet date, where the main substance of the transaction was to alter the appearance of the balance sheet. This disclosure covers adjustments to the balance sheet that are commonly referred to as 'window dressing'. Such transactions will usually (but not always) involve the movement of cash, the aim usually being to show a bank balance that is higher than normal or a bank overdraft that is lower than normal, or to remove a loan from the balance sheet. The transaction may be as simple as delaying a purchase ledger payment run that is normally made at the end of the month and making the payments at the beginning of the following month (ie in the new accounting year) instead. Creditors at the year-end will therefore be higher than is usually the case, but the bank position will be improved (eg it might become a bank balance rather than a bank overdraft). Other arrangements might be more complex, for instance a company may be able to arrange:

— to repay a loan immediately prior to the balance sheet date, and then take out a similar loan with the same lender a few days later - the balance sheet will therefore show lower borrowings than is normally the case;

— for a loan to become unsecured immediately prior to the balance sheet date, and then grant security again a few days into the new accounting year - the accounts would show unsecured borrowings at the balance sheet date, even though, in practice, the lender has security over some of the company's assets.

Where any transaction along these lines has a material impact on the accounts, details should be disclosed under SSAP 17.

DISCLOSURE OF POST BALANCE SHEET EVENTS

Details to be disclosed

33.9 CA 1985 requires the directors' report to include particulars of any important events affecting the company (and, where relevant, its subsidiaries) which have occurred since the end of the financial year. The Act does not specify the details that should be disclosed in respect of a post balance sheet event, requiring only 'particulars' to be given. SSAP 17 requires disclosure of:

— the nature of the event; and

— an estimate of the financial effect.

Where it is not practicable to estimate the financial effect, this fact must be stated. The tax implications of the financial effect must also be explained separately where necessary to enable a user of the accounts to understand the financial position shown in the accounts. The details are usually disclosed in a separate note to the accounts.

Example 33.1 - Possible wording for a post balance sheet event disclosure I

On 10 October 20X2 the company disposed of a freehold property which is included in the accounts at 30 June 20X2 at a value of £134,750. This transaction gave rise to a profit on disposal of £25,400.

Example 33.2 - Possible wording for a post balance sheet event disclosure II

On 13 December 20X2 the company issued 5,000 £1 ordinary shares at £3.50 per share.

Distinctions between SSAP 17 and CA 1985

33.10 There are two major distinctions between SSAP 17 and CA 1985 in respect of the disclosure of post balance sheet events:

- SSAP 17 requires details of non-adjusting post balance sheet events and 'window dressing' transactions to be disclosed in the accounts, whilst the Act requires disclosure in the directors' report; and
- SSAP 17 does not require disclosure of adjusting events as these will have been reflected in the accounts - as the Act does not distinguish between adjusting and non-adjusting events, the directors' report may need to give brief details of any major adjusting events and explain how these have been dealt with in the accounts although, in practice, such events will not usually be sufficiently material to warrant this treatment.

Location of the disclosures

33.11 To avoid an unnecessary duplication of information, it will usually be acceptable to give the detailed disclosures in either the notes to the accounts or the directors' report only (preferably in the notes to the accounts, although there is no firm rule on this) and include a cross- reference in the other location to show where the details can be found. Disclosure in the directors' report alone will not be sufficient to meet the requirements of SSAP 17. If details of a post balance sheet event are disclosed separately in both the directors' report and the notes to the accounts it is important that the information given in each location is consistent.

DATE OF APPROVAL OF ACCOUNTS

Importance of date of approval of accounts

33.12 Post balance sheet events are defined in SSAP 17 as events arising between the date of the balance sheet and the date on which the accounts are approved by the directors. The accounts must therefore reflect the effects of any adjusting events up to the date of formal approval by the directors.

Finalisation process

33.13 Individual companies will adopt different procedures for finalising their statutory accounts, but formal approval by the directors will always be required at some stage and this will normally be given at a board meeting. In some cases this will be the meeting at which the final accounts are discussed in detail, in other cases it may be a meeting at which final accounts are approved, having been discussed in detail at a draft stage (ie earlier in the finalisation process). Where changes are needed to the accounts after consideration by the board, formal approval will usually need to be given at a later stage (ie when the final version of the accounts is available).

Disclosure of the date of approval of the accounts

33.14 As the date on which the accounts were approved is so significant, SSAP 17 requires this date to be disclosed in the accounts. This can be done in one of two ways. The date of approval of the accounts can be shown on the face of the balance sheet, linked with the signature of the director (or directors).

Example 33.3 – Date of approval on the face of the balance sheet

These accounts were approved by the board of directors on 12 December 1996 and signed on its behalf by:

....

AJ Jones, Director

Alternatively, the date of approval of the accounts can be disclosed in a separate note to the accounts.

Example 33.4 – Date of approval in a note

The accounts were approved by the board of directors on 12 December 1996.

Both methods of disclosure are in common use.

DISCLOSURES IN RESPECT OF PARENT UNDERTAKINGS

Disclosures required by CA 1985

33.15 In the case of a subsidiary company, the Act requires details to be disclosed in the accounts in respect of:

— the parent company of the smallest group for which group accounts are prepared and which include the company;

— the parent company of the largest group for which group accounts are prepared and which include the company.

The following details must be given in the company's accounts in respect of each of the above:

— the name of the parent undertaking;

- if it is incorporated outside Great Britain, the country in which it is incorporated;
- if it is unincorporated, the address of its principal place of business;
- if the relevant group accounts are available to the public, the address from which copies can be obtained.

In most cases, this disclosure will be straightforward and will usually be given in a separate note to the accounts.

Example 33.5 – Disclosure of details on parent company

The company's immediate parent company is G Ltd. The group accounts of G Ltd can be obtained from [Address]. The ultimate parent undertaking is X AG, a company incorporated in Germany. The group accounts of X AG can be obtained from [Address].

Ultimate parent company/controlling party

33.16 CA 1985 also requires disclosure of the name of the company's ultimate parent company, if this is different (for instance, where the ultimate parent company does not prepare group accounts) and the country in which it is incorporated, if this is outside Great Britain and if the information is known to the directors. FRS 8 'Related Party Disclosures' requires disclosure of the controlling party and ultimate controlling party (if different). In many cases, these will be the same as the parent and ultimate parent. The disclosure requirements of FRS 8 are considered in **Chapter 17**.

SEGMENTAL REPORTING OF NET ASSETS

Analysis of net assets

33.17 The segmental reporting of net assets is one of the additional disclosures required by SSAP 25 'Segmental Reporting'. It is not required by CA 1985 and therefore only applies to public and larger private companies (see **Chapter 17** for precise details of the scope of SSAP 25). Normally only operating assets and liabilities that are non-interest bearing will need to be analysed. However, the segmental analysis of net assets should be consistent with the analysis of results. In certain circumstances the standard requires interest to be included in the analysis of results, and in these cases the analysis of net assets should include the corresponding interest bearing assets and liabilities. The approach to segmental analysis is considered in more detail in **Chapter 17**.

Apportionment of operating assets and liabilities

33.18 Where some of the operating assets and liabilities relate jointly to more than one segment, they should be allocated between the relevant segments on a reasonable basis.

Link with balance sheet

33.19 The total of the amounts disclosed in the segmental analysis of net assets should agree with the total shown in the balance sheet. If it does not, a reconciliation of the two amounts should also be provided.

Comparative information

33.20 SSAP 25 requires comparative information to be provided for all segmental disclosures.

OTHER BALANCE SHEET DISCLOSURES

Financial assistance for the purchase of own shares

33.21 Where any item in the balance sheet includes outstanding loans made under CA 1985 s 153(4)(b), (bb) or (c) or s 155 (all of which deal with financial assistance for the purchase of own shares), the aggregate amount of the loans must be disclosed for each balance sheet item affected.

Dormant companies acting as agents

33.22 The Companies Act 1985 (Audit Exemption) (Amendment) Regulations 2000 introduced a new disclosure requirement for dormant companies which act as agent for another party. Where the directors take advantage of the exemption from audit conferred by CA 1985 s 249AA and the company has acted as agent for another party during the year, the accounts are required to disclose this fact. CA 1985 Schs 4, 8 and 8A were all amended to incorporate this disclosure requirement. The disclosure must therefore also be given in abbreviated accounts where the company chooses to prepare these for filing purposes.

FRS 13 'Derivatives and Other Financial Instruments: Disclosures'

33.23 FRS 13 'Derivatives and Other Financial Instruments: Disclosures' requires entities within its scope to give narrative statements on their objectives and policies in using financial instruments to manage risk, and numerical information on issues such as interest rate risk, currency risk, liquidity and fair values. At present, the standard applies only to entities with publicly traded capital instruments (although insurance companies are specifically excluded) and to banks and similar financial institutions. The disclosures are therefore not considered further here. FRED 30 'Financial instruments: Disclosure and presentation; Recognition and measurement' proposes the replacement of FRS 13 with requirements based on international accounting standards (see **31.44**) but there is no firm intention at present to extend the disclosure requirements to entities other than listed companies and banks.

LIKELY FUTURE DEVELOPMENTS

FRED 27 'Events after the balance sheet date'

33.24 The ASB issued FRED 27 'Events after the balance sheet date' in May 2002 as part of its project to achieve convergence between UK accounting standards and international accounting standards. The Exposure Draft proposes replacing SSAP 17 'Accounting for post balance sheet events' with a new standard based on a proposed revision of IAS 10. The main changes from current UK requirements are:

- FRED 27 states specifically that equity dividends declared after the balance sheet date should not be recognised as liabilities, although it does require them to be disclosed in a note to the accounts – the ASB has asked the DTI to consider changing the present company law requirements in respect of dividends to enable this aspect of the new standard to be implemented;
- SSAP 17 currently permits a parent company to recognise as an asset a dividend declared after the balance sheet date by a subsidiary or associate if it relates to a period before that date – this will be classified as a non-adjusting event under FRED 27; and
- the Appendix to SSAP 17 permits a non-adjusting event to be reclassified as an adjusting event in exceptional circumstances, but this will not be allowed under FRED 27.

Chapter 34

Cash Flow Statement

REQUIREMENT TO PREPARE A CASH FLOW STATEMENT

Nature of the statement

34.1 There is no specific requirement in company law for accounts to include a cash flow statement. However, the general requirement for accounts to comply with applicable accounting standards means that the requirements of FRS 1 'Cash Flow Statements' are effectively brought within the law. The cash flow statement is a primary statement within the accounts, along with the profit and loss account, balance sheet and statement of total recognised gains and losses. Although FRS 1 'Cash Flow Statements' does not prescribe the positioning of the cash flow statement it is usually presented as a separate page of the accounts, immediately after the profit and loss account and balance sheet.

Prescribed structure

34.2 The inclusion of a cash flow statement in the accounts ensures that an entity reports its cash generation and absorption during the period and provides users of the accounts with information to help them assess the liquidity, solvency and financial adaptability of the business. The use of standard headings and a prescribed structure for the statement is intended to highlight the key components of cash flow during the period and aid comparison between businesses. The accounting standard sets out the required structure for the cash flow statement and the minimum level of disclosure.

Exemption for small companies

34.3 Companies which meet the CA 1985 criteria for a small company (see **Chapter 7**) are exempt from the requirement to include a cash flow statement in their accounts. In line with the other CA 1985 provisions for small companies, the exemption is not available to the following, even if they meet the size criteria:

- public companies;
- banking companies, insurance companies and other entities with permission under Part 4 of FSMA 2000 to carry on one or more regulated activities; and

— members of a group containing any of the above entities.

Unincorporated entities which meet the small company size criteria set out in CA 1985 are also exempt from the requirement to include a cash flow statement in their accounts. Despite the exemption in FRS 1, the Financial Reporting Standards for Smaller Entities (FRSSE) encourages the inclusion of a cash flow statement in the accounts of a small company, although it does not formally require this (see **7.32**).

Exemption for subsidiary undertakings

34.4 The original FRS 1 included an exemption for wholly-owned subsidiaries, subject to stringent requirements set out in the standard. When the standard was revised in 1996, the exemption was widened and the conditions simplified. A subsidiary undertaking is now exempt from the requirement to include a cash flow statement in its accounts provided that:

— 90% or more of the voting rights in the subsidiary are controlled within the group; and

— consolidated financial statements including the subsidiary are publicly available.

Exemption for specialised businesses

34.5 Certain specialised businesses, such as mutual assurance companies, pension funds and open-ended investment funds (subject to certain conditions) are also exempt from the requirements of FRS 1.

Statement on availability of exemption

34.6 Where a company is exempt from the requirement to include a cash flow statement in its annual accounts, there is no requirement in the standard for this fact to be disclosed. However, it is best practice to include a brief note explaining the position. This is usually included in the note on accounting policies.

Example 34.1 – Exemption statement: small company

The company is exempt from the requirement to prepare a cash flow statement under FRS 1 as it meets the qualifying conditions for a small company set out in CA 1985 ss 246, 247.

Example 34.2 – Exemption statement: subsidiary undertaking

The company is exempt from the requirement to prepare a cash flow statement under FRS 1 as it is a subsidiary undertaking and 90% or more of its voting rights are controlled within the group. The company is included in the consolidated financial statements of ABC Limited.

No cash flow transactions

34.7 Most companies with no cash flow transactions will be entitled to one of the exemptions set out in the standard (i.e. as a small company or as a subsidiary undertaking where 90% or more of the voting rights are controlled within the group). If this is not the case, the requirement to present a cash flow statement still stands and should be covered by an explanatory note:

Example 34.3 – No cash flow transactions

There were no transactions giving rise to a cash flow in either the current year or the previous year. A cash flow statement is therefore not included in these accounts.

STRUCTURE OF A CASH FLOW STATEMENT

Definitions

34.8 The standard sets out definitions of cash flow, cash, overdraft, liquid resources, and net debt for the purposes of FRS 1. A clear understanding of these definitions is important to ensure the correct treatment of items in the cash flow statement, especially where more complex financial arrangements (e.g. multi-option facilities) are involved.

— *Cash flow*: Cash flow is defined as an increase or decrease in an amount of cash.

— *Cash:* Cash is defined as cash in hand and deposits repayable on demand with any qualifying financial institution, less overdrafts from any qualifying financial institution repayable on demand. A qualifying financial institution is defined as an entity that as part of its business receives deposits or other repayable funds and grants credit for its own account.

— *Deposits*: The definition of cash goes on to clarify that deposits should be regarded as repayable on demand if:

  — they can be withdrawn at any time without notice and without penalty; or

  — if a maturity or period of notice of not more than 24 hours or one working day has been agreed.

Deposits must be genuinely repayable on demand in order to fall within this definition. Deposit accounts that require a period of notice of more than 24 hours or one working day before withdrawal is possible will constitute investments rather than cash, and will usually be treated as liquid resources in the cash flow statement. The standard emphasises that no investments, however liquid or close to maturity, can be treated as cash. In the case of deposits which have a fixed maturity date but which may be redeemed early if required, and which may therefore appear to be repayable on demand, it will usually be necessary to review the detailed terms of the arrangement. If penalties of any sort are incurred as a result of early redemption, the balance will not meet the FRS 1 definition of a deposit.

- *Foreign currency:* The definition also clarifies that cash includes cash in hand and any relevant deposits denominated in foreign currencies.
- *Overdraft:* An overdraft is defined as a borrowing facility repayable on demand that is used by drawing on a current account with a qualifying financial institution.
- *Liquid resources:* Liquid resources are current asset investments held as readily disposable stores of value. The definition goes on to define a readily disposable investment as one that can be disposed of by the reporting entity without curtailing or disrupting its business and which is:
  - readily convertible into known amounts of cash at or close to its carrying amount; or
  - traded in an active market (which is defined in the standard as 'a market of sufficient depth to absorb the investment held without a significant effect on the price.

Depending on the circumstances, items such as short-term deposits, loan stock, equity investments and government securities might all be classed as liquid resources.

The standard requires each entity to explain in the accounts which items it treats as liquid resources in the cash flow statement, and also any changes in its policy. FRS 4 'Capital instruments' includes an explanatory section on the maturity of debt (see **25.16**), which may be helpful in assessing the maturity date of more complex financial arrangements and thus in establishing the appropriate treatment of these transactions within the cash flow statement.

Standard headings

34.9 The cash flow statement should show inflows and outflows of cash, analysed under the following standard headings:

- operating activities;
- dividends from joint ventures and associates;
- returns on investments and servicing of finance;
- taxation;

— capital expenditure and financial investment;
— acquisitions and disposals;
— equity dividends paid;
— management of liquid resources; and
— financing.

The first seven headings must be shown in the order set out above. Cash flows relating to the management of liquid resources and financing can be combined under one heading provided that:

— the cash flows relating to the management of liquid resources and financing are shown separately; and
— separate sub-totals for each are given in the cash flow statement.

Analysis of each heading

34.10 Only the total for each heading needs to be given on the face of the cash flow statement. The standard specifies which items should be included under each heading and a more detailed analysis of the individual categories of cash inflows and outflows within each heading should be given in the notes to the cash flow statement. The analysis of each heading may be given in more detail than is suggested in the standard and any items not specifically covered in the standard should be included under the most appropriate heading.

Reporting of cash inflows and outflows

34.11 The standard requires the cash flow statement to cover all the cash inflows and outflows of the reporting entity. Conversely, transactions which do not result in a flow of cash (for instance, the inception of a finance lease) should not be reported in the cash flow statement but may nevertheless require disclosure in the notes. The classification of cash flows in the statement should reflect the underlying substance of the transaction that gives rise to the cash flow.

Gross or net disclosure?

34.12 Cash inflows and outflows should normally be shown gross, except in the case of cash flows relating to operating activities. Certain cash flows relating to the management of liquid resources or financing may be netted against each other where:

— they relate in substance to a single financing transaction (which is defined as a transaction that fulfils the conditions set out in paragraph 35 of FRS 4 'Capital Instruments'); or
— they arise from rollover or reissue facilities.

Continuing and discontinued operations

34.13 Where the profit and loss account includes an analysis between continuing, discontinued and acquired operations in accordance with the requirements of FRS 3 'Reporting Financial Performance' (see **Chapter 8**), it will usually be appropriate for the cash flow in respect of operating activities to be analysed in a similar way. However, this analysis is not a specific requirement of either FRS 1 or FRS 3, although FRS 1 encourages the disclosure where appropriate. Some of the illustrative examples in FRS 1 show the separate presentation of cash flows relating to continuing and discontinued operations.

Exceptional items and cash flows

34.14 Cash flows relating to exceptional items should be shown under the appropriate standard heading, but where necessary additional information should be given in a note to enable a reader of the accounts to understand the cash effect of any exceptional items. The disclosure should also explain the relationship between the cash flows and the exceptional item shown in the profit and loss account or related notes. The same principal applies in the case of extraordinary items, but in practice these are now very rare under the requirements of FRS 3 'Reporting Financial Performance'. If an exceptional cash flow arises during the year but there is no related exceptional item requiring disclosure in the profit and loss account or related notes, sufficient detail should be given to explain the nature and cause of the exceptional cash flow.

Totals

34.15 Provided that the prescribed order of headings is followed, totals and sub-totals can be drawn at any point in the cash flow statement. All of the examples given in FRS 1 show the increase or decrease in cash as the residual value on the cash flow statement, but sub-totals are drawn at various points within the statement.

Reconciliations

34.16 The following reconciliations with profit and loss account and balance sheet figures must be given in the notes to the accounts:

- operating profit (which will usually be profit before interest) must be reconciled with the net cash flow from operating activities; and
- the movement in cash during the period must be reconciled with the movement in net debt, and changes in net debt during the period should be analysed in sufficient detail to allow the components of net debt to be identified in the opening and closing balance sheets.

These reconciliations are considered in more detail in **34.35–34.40** below.

The reconciliations can be presented adjoining the cash flow statement or in the notes to the accounts. However, the reconciliations are not part of the cash flow statement and, where one or both of the reconciliations are presented alongside the statement, the standard requires each reconciliation to be clearly headed and separated from the cash flow statement itself.

Need to present comparatives

34.17 Comparative figures are required for each item within the cash flow statement and the related notes, except for the note analysing changes in the balances making up net debt and certain disclosures required in group accounts. Headings will also be needed for any items which appeared in the previous year's statement but which do not feature in the current year. If there are no cash flows in the current year, but cash flows arose in the previous year, a full cash flow statement will be required to present the information for the previous year. If there are no cash flows in either the current year or the previous year, the requirements of FRS 1 can be met by a narrative note as explained in **34.7** above.

Material non-cash transactions

34.18 Material transactions during the year which have no cash flow effect should be disclosed in a note to the cash flow statement if this is necessary to enable a reader of the accounts to understand the underlying transaction. For instance, this might include:

- the issue of shares as part of the purchase consideration in an acquisition;
- the inception of a significant finance lease (SSAP 21 'Accounting for leases and hire purchase contracts' requires a finance lease to be accounted for by recording a 'loan' from the lessor and the purchase of the asset, but these aspects of the transaction do not give rise to an actual cash flow – the only cash flows for the lessee are the rental payments under the lease); and
- a major asset exchange.

Illustrative examples

34.19 The standard includes four illustrative examples of cash flow statements and the related reconciliations, covering the following entities:

- an individual company;
- a group;
- a bank; and
- an insurance company.

The example for an individual company illustrates the presentation of both reconciliations adjoining the cash flow statement. The example for a group presents the reconciliation of net cash flow to movement in net debt adjoining the cash flow statement, but gives the reconciliation of operating profit to operating cash flow in the notes. Appendix III to the FRSSE includes an example of a cash flow statement for a small company (see also **7.32**).

NET CASH FLOW FROM OPERATING ACTIVITIES

Alternative disclosure methods

34.20 Cash flows from operating activities are the cash effects of all the transactions that arise from or relate to the company's operating and trading activities. The results of these activities will be included within operating profit in the profit and loss account. The standard permits operating cash flows to be shown on the direct or the indirect method. The direct method shows the following cash receipts and cash payments relating to operating activities:

- receipts from customers;
- payments to suppliers;
- payments to and on behalf of employees; and
- other cash payments

resulting in an aggregate net cash flow from operating activities. Very few companies choose to present operating cash flow information in this way, probably because of the increased work and analysis required to obtain the relevant details. The reconciliation of operating profit to operating cash flow must still be given. The indirect method is by far the most common presentation, beginning with operating profit and adjusting for non-cash charges and credits to the profit and loss account, to arrive at the net cash flow from operating activities.

Provisions

34.21 The standard emphasises that operating item cash flows which relate to provisions should be included in operating cash flow, even if the provision was not originally charged against operating profit. For example, the costs of a fundamental restructuring are required by paragraph 20 of FRS 3 'Reporting Financial Performance' to be charged in the profit and loss account below operating profit - when the payments are subsequently made, the cash outflows in respect of operating items (e.g. redundancy payments) will need to be reported within cash flow from operating activities, even though the related redundancy costs were not charged against operating profit.

VAT and similar taxes

34.22 In most cases, cash flows will be shown net of VAT in the cash flow statement. The net movement in the amount payable to or receivable from Customs and Excise in respect of VAT should normally be included as part of the cash flow from operating activities, unless another classification is more appropriate (this is likely to be rare in practice). If the VAT is irrecoverable, cash flows should be shown gross (i.e. including the related VAT). If this is impractical for any reason (and it is difficult to think of a situation where this would be the case), the irrecoverable VAT should be included under the most appropriate standard heading. Other sales taxes should be treated in the same way as VAT.

RETURNS ON INVESTMENTS AND SERVICING OF FINANCE

Items to be included

34.23 Returns on investments are cash receipts resulting from the ownership of investments. Servicing of finance represents payments to providers of finance, including non-equity shareholders and minority interests, but excludes the repayment of capital and other items required by the standard to be included under other headings. The most common items in this category are:

- interest paid (including any withholding tax deducted);
- dividends paid on non-equity shares;
- dividends paid to minority interests;
- cash flows in respect of other finance costs (as defined in FRS 4 'Capital Instruments');
- interest received (including any related tax recovered); and
- dividends received (net of any tax credits).

Interest paid

34.24 The standard specifically requires all interest paid to be reported in this section of the cash flow statement, even if some of it has been capitalised for accounting purposes. The interest element of any payments under finance leases should be included and, if material, may need to be shown separately. Where relevant, interest paid should be shown gross (i.e. it should include the amount of any tax deducted and paid over to the relevant tax authority). The figure required is the interest actually paid during the year. The charge in the profit and loss account will therefore need to be adjusted for any interest prepaid or accrued (i.e. included in debtors or creditors) at the end of the current and previous year.

Dividends paid

34.25 Only dividends paid to non-equity shareholders and to minority interests should be included in this section of the cash flow statement. Dividends paid to equity shareholders were previously included here as well, but the standard now requires them to be shown under a separate heading. The figure for dividends paid should exclude any tax credit. Adjustment should be made for any proposed dividends included within creditors at the end of the current or previous year, to arrive at the amount actually paid during the year.

Other finance costs

34.26 Cash flows relating to other finance costs of debt and non-equity shares should also be included under this heading. For instance, this would include items such as issue costs and redemption premiums relating to debt and non-equity shares.

Interest received

34.27 Interest received should include any related withholding tax. Once again, adjustment should be made for any amounts receivable or prepaid at the end of the current and previous year, to arrive at the figure for interest actually received during the year.

Dividends received

34.28 Dividends received should be shown net of any related tax credits. Scrip dividends do not have any cash flow effect and should therefore not be included as dividends received in the cash flow statement. Adjustment should be made for any amounts receivable at the end of the current or previous year, to arrive at the amount actually received during the year.

OTHER SECTIONS OF THE STATEMENT

Joint ventures and associates

34.29 Where a company holds an investment in an associate or joint venture, only actual cash flows between the investing company and the associate or joint venture should be included in the cash flow statement. The most common item will usually be dividends paid by the associate or joint venture and the original requirements of FRS 1 on the disclosure of these items were updated by FRS 9 'Associates and Joint Ventures'. Dividends from associates and joint ventures must now be shown as a separate item in the cash flow statement between operating activities and returns on investment and the servicing of finance. Any other cash flows between the investing company and the associate or joint venture (e.g. advances or repayment of loans) should be shown under the appropriate cash flow heading.

Taxation

34.30 This section of cash flow statement covers cash paid to and received from the relevant tax authorities in respect of the company's revenue and capital profits. It specifically *excludes*:

— any payments and receipts relating to VAT or other sales taxes (these are discussed in **34.22** above); and

— payments to the tax authorities in respect of income tax deducted from wages and salaries paid to employees – the gross cost of wages and salaries (i.e. before deduction of tax) is included within operating profit and operating cash flow.

The following items should be included:

— payments in respect of corporation tax and capital gains, including purchases of certificates of tax deposit;

— receipts from the Inland Revenue in the form of rebates or returns of overpayments, again relating to corporation tax and capital gains; and

— in the case of group companies, any payments or receipts in respect of group relief.

Where relevant, it may be appropriate to show separately the amounts relating to UK and overseas taxation, although this is not a specific requirement under the standard.

Capital expenditure and financial investment

34.31 This section of the cash flow statement deals with cash flows relating to the acquisition or disposal of:

— any fixed assets held by the company, other than those required by the standard to be included under the heading 'Acquisitions and disposals'; and

— any current asset investments held by the company, other than those classified as liquid resources.

If there are no cash flows relating to investments, the heading can be shortened to 'Capital expenditure'. The following items will usually appear in this category:

— cash paid to acquire property, plant or equipment;

- cash received from the sale or disposal of property, plant or equipment;
- loans made by the company to other entities;
- cash received in repayment of loans made by the company to other entities;
- cash paid by the company to acquire debt instruments of other entities (other than payments forming part of an acquisition or disposal, or relating to a movement in liquid resources);
- cash received by the company from the sale of debt instruments of other entities (other than receipts forming part of an acquisition or disposal, or relating to a movement in liquid resources); and
- cash flows relating to any development costs that have been capitalised.

The amounts included should represent cash actually paid or received during the period - any amounts accrued in respect of fixed asset or investment purchases and any amounts included in debtors in respect of fixed assets and investments sold should therefore be excluded from the amounts shown in the cash flow statement. Adjustments will also need to be made to the figure for fixed asset additions during the year, as shown in the accounts, to exclude any assets acquired under finance leases or similar hire purchase arrangements. The capital element of any finance lease payments is dealt with under 'Financing' (see **34.33** below). Cash flows relating to the acquisition or disposal of:

- any trade or business; or
- an investment in any entity that is, or, as a result of the transaction, becomes, or ceases to be, a subsidiary, associate or joint venture of the reporting entity
- should be shown within the 'Acquisitions and Disposals' section of the cash flow statement.

Equity dividends paid

34.32 The amount actually paid during the year to equity shareholders in the form of dividends is now required to be shown under a separate heading in the cash flow statement. This figure should exclude any related tax credit.

Management of liquid resources

34.33 As explained in **34.8** above, each entity is required to explain what it treats as liquid resources and also any changes in its policy. Cash flows relating to liquid resources will usually include:

— payments into short-term deposits (other than those that meet the definition of cash);

— withdrawals from short-term deposits (other than those that meet the definition of cash);

— receipts from the disposal or redemption of any investments classified as liquid resources; and

— payments to acquire any investments classified as liquid resources.

Cash flows relating to the management of liquid resources can be shown under a single heading with the disclosures required under 'Financing' provided that separate sub-totals for each are given.

Financing

34.34 Financing cash flows comprise:

— receipts of principal from external providers of finance; and

— payments to external providers of finance in respect of the repayment of principal amounts of finance.

External providers of finance include shareholders. The most common items to appear here will be:

— cash received on the issue of shares or any other equity instruments;

— cash received on the issue of debentures;

— cash received on taking out loans and other long-term or short-term borrowings (other than overdrafts);

— the repayment of the amounts borrowed (other than overdrafts);

— expenses or commissions on the issue of equity shares;

— payments to acquire or redeem the company's own shares; and

— the capital element of payments under finance leases.

In the case of shares, only the proceeds of shares issued for cash should be included in the cash flow statement. Shares issued as consideration for the purchase of another business have no cash flow effect and therefore do not appear in the cash flow statement. They may, however, require disclosure as a material non-cash transaction (see **34.18** above). Only issue costs relating to equity shares will be included in this section of the cash flow statement. Issue costs relating to non-equity shares and debt instruments will normally be accounted for as finance costs under the requirements of FRS 4 'Capital Instruments'. They will therefore be shown in the cash flow statement under the heading 'Returns on investments and servicing of finance'.

RECONCILIATION OF OPERATING PROFIT TO NET CASH FLOW FROM OPERATING ACTIVITIES

Items to be shown

34.35 Regardless of whether the direct or indirect method is used, the notes to the accounts should include a reconciliation of operating profit to net cash flow from operating activities. The reconciliation should show separately the movements in stocks, debtors and creditors relating to operating activities, and any other differences between operating cash flows and profits.

Debtors and creditors

34.36 When calculating the amounts to be included for debtors and creditors it is important to exclude items within these figures that do not relate to operating activities, as these will be dealt with elsewhere in the cash flow statement. The most common items are:

- interest accruals and prepayments;
- accruals for expenditure on fixed assets;
- anticipated proceeds from the sale of fixed assets, included within debtors; and
- corporation tax payable or recoverable.

Debtors and creditors for the current and previous year therefore require careful analysis to ensure that all non-operating items are identified and excluded.

Other common reconciling items

34.37 In addition to movements in stocks, debtors and creditors, the more common reconciling items are likely to be:

- depreciation charges;
- profits or losses on the sale of fixed assets; and
- certain foreign exchange items (as discussed in **34.41** below).

The aim is to adjust for all items charged or credited to the profit and loss account that have not resulted in a cash flow.

RECONCILIATION OF NET CASH FLOW TO MOVEMENT IN NET DEBT

Purpose of the reconciliation

34.38 The accounts should include a reconciliation of the movement in cash during the period with the movement in net debt. This can be presented in the notes or adjoining the cash flow statement, provided that it is clearly headed and separated from the statement itself. The main purpose of the reconciliation is to provide additional information to assist in the assessment of the entity's liquidity, solvency and financial adaptability.

Definition of net debt

34.39 Net debt is defined in the standard as:

- the borrowings of the reporting entity, which comprise:
  - debt as defined in paragraph 6 of FRS 4 'Capital Instruments'(see **25.2**);
  - related derivatives; and
  - obligations under finance leases,

  less
- cash and liquid resources.

If cash and liquid resources exceed borrowings, the reconciliation should refer to 'net funds' rather than 'net debt'.

Analysis of changes in net debt

34.40 The notes to the accounts should also provide an analysis of the changes in net debt during the year. Changes arising from the following should be shown separately where they are material:

- the cash flows of the entity;
- the acquisition or disposal of subsidiary undertakings;
- other non-cash changes; and
- the recognition of changes in market value and movements in exchange rates.

Sufficient detail must be given to enable a user of the accounts to identify the individual components of net debt in the opening and closing balance sheets. Possible formats for these disclosures are illustrated in the examples in FRS 1 and in the Appendix to this chapter.

FOREIGN CURRENCY TRANSLATION

Exchange differences

34.41 The treatment of foreign exchange translation differences will depend on the nature and status of the underlying transaction and where the differences have been charged or credited in the accounts. Exchange gains and losses relating to transactions settled during the period should be reflected in the cash flow statement. Exchange gains and losses relating to transactions that are unsettled at the balance sheet date should not be reflected in the cash flow statement because they will not have had a cash flow effect during the year in question. In most cases, exchange differences will be charged or credited in arriving at operating profit. If any of these exchange differences relate to non-operating items they will therefore need to be eliminated from operating cash flow and will appear as reconciling items in the reconciliation of operating profit with operating cash flow. Conversely, if exchange differences have been dealt with elsewhere in the profit and loss account, an adjustment will need to be made to bring those differences which relate to operating activities into operating cash flow. This will also be shown in the reconciliation of operating profit with operating cash flow.

Settled transactions relating to operating activities

34.42 Exchange differences that relate to operating transactions which have been settled during the period should be included in operating cash flow. If the differences have been charged or credited in arriving at operating profit, no further adjustment will be required. If the differences have not been included in operating profit, they will need to be included in the reconciliation of operating profit to operating cash flow as explained in **34.41** above.

Unsettled transactions relating to operating activities

34.43 Exchange differences that relate to operating activities but which are still outstanding at the end of the period should be excluded from operating cash flow. If these exchange differences have been charged or credited in arriving at operating profit, the unrealised element will automatically be eliminated from operating cash flow by the trade debtors and trade creditors adjustments which form part of the reconciliation between operating profit and operating cash flow. If these exchange differences have not been included in operating profit, they will need to be brought into the reconciliation of operating profit to operating cash flow (as explained in **34.41** above) so that they effectively cancel out with the trade debtors and creditors adjustments.

Interest on foreign currency borrowings

34.44 Exchange gains and losses in respect of foreign currency borrowings may be included as part of the interest charge in the profit and loss account. In calculating interest paid during the year, the normal adjustments for interest accrued or prepaid should automatically eliminate the effect of any unrealised exchange gains and losses in respect of interest. However, a separate adjustment will be needed to remove any unrealised exchange gains or losses relating to the loan itself.

Liquid resources, financing items and cash

34.45 Exchange differences that arise on the translation of liquid resources, financing items or cash should be excluded from the cash flow statement. They should be shown as movements during the year in the note reconciling the opening and closing balances of the individual components of net debt.

Hedging transactions

34.46 Cash flows that arise from hedging transactions should be reported in the same section of the cash flow statement as the transaction that is being hedged.

Appendix

WORKED EXAMPLE OF A CASH FLOW STATEMENT

A1 The profit and loss account of A Ltd for the year ended 31 March 20X2

		20X2
		£
Turnover		565,750
Cost of sales		(432,500)
Gross profit		133,250
Distribution costs		(46,700)
Administrative expenses		(37,250)
Operating profit		49,300
Interest receivable		5,600
Interest payable		(13,400)
Profit on ordinary activities before tax		41,500
Taxation		(9,400)
Profit after tax for the financial year		32,100
Dividends paid and proposed:		
Equity	10,000	
Non-equity	2,000	(12,000)
Retained profit for the financial year		20,100

A2 The balance sheets of A Ltd at 31 March 20X2 and 20X1

	31 March 20X2	31 March 20X1
	£	£
Fixed assets:		
Tangible assets	130,600	110,700
Investments	36,000	10,000
	166,000	120,700

Current assets:				
Stocks	99,500		79,300	
Debtors	65,850		59,200	
Short-term deposits	3,000		1,750	
Cash at bank	7,300		3,450	
	175,650		143,700	
Creditors: due within 1 year	(164,600)		(134,250)	
		11,050		9,450
		177,650		130,150
Creditors: due after more than 1 year		(85,000)		(65,000)
Provisions for liabilities and charges		(12,000)		(10,000)
Net assets		80,650		55,150
Called up share capital		29,000		25,000
Share premium account		6,000		4,600
Profit and loss account		45,650		25,550
		80,650		55,150

The following details are also relevant.

A3 Tangible fixed assets

Movements in tangible fixed assets during the year were as follows:

	£
Cost:	
Balance at 1 April 20X1	179,900
Additions in 20X1/20X2	39,300
Disposals in 20X1/20X2	(13,000)
Balance at 31 March 200X2	206,200
Depreciation:	
Balance at 1 April 20X1	69,200
Charge for 20X1/20X2	15,400
Applicable to disposals	(9,000)
Balance at 31 March 20X2	75,600
Net book value 31 March 20X2	130,600
Net book value 31 March 20X1	110,700

Additions includes an asset held under a finance lease, which was acquired at a cost of £15,350 (see A8 below).

Details of the fixed asset disposal are as follows:

	£
Cost of asset	13,000
Depreciation to date of sale	(9,000)
Net book value at date of sale	4,000
Sales proceeds	7,000
Profit on disposal	3,000

A4 Investments

On 1 September 20X1, A Ltd acquired a 15% shareholding in B Ltd at a cost of £26,000 which was paid in cash.

A5 Debtors

Debtors is made up as follows:

	20X2	*20X1*
	£	£
Trade debtors	54,700	51,150
Accrued interest receivable	2,250	1,700
Pre-payments	8,900	6,350
	65,850	59,200

A6 Short term deposits

	£
Movements during the year are as follows:	
Balance on deposit at 1 April 20X1	1,750
Additional amounts placed on deposit	5,500
Amounts withdrawn from deposit	(4,250)
Balance on deposit at 31 March 20X2	3,000

A7 Creditors due within one year

Creditors due within one year is made up as follows:

		20X2	*20X1*
		£	£
Bank overdraft		20,500	18,700
Obligations under finance leases		9,950	7,200
Trade creditors		70,300	69,550
Corporation tax		8,900	8,430
Accruals:	Interest payable		2,150
	Fixed assets		20,200
	Other		25,600
Proposed dividend (equity shares)		7,000	5,000
		164,600	134,250

A8 Creditors due after more than one year

Creditors due after more than one year is made up as follows:

	20X2	*20X1*
	£	£
Bank loans	69,400	53,900
Obligations under finance leases	15,600	11,100
	85,000	65,000

The movement on bank loans during the year was as follows:

	£
Loans taken at 1 April 1996	53,900
New loan taken out 1996/97	15,500
Loans at 31 March 1997	69,400

Movements on finance leases during the year were as follows:

	Due within 1 year	*Due after 1 year*	*Total*
	£	£	£
Balance at 1 April 20X1	7,200	11,100	18,300
Repayments during 20X1/20X2	(8,100)	—	(8,100)
New lease of fixed asset	3,350	12,000	15,350
Transfer between categories	7,500	(7,500)	—
	9,950	15,600	25,550

A9 Provisions for liabilities and charges

Provisions for liabilities and charges is made up as follows:

	20X2	*20X1*
	£	£
Deferred taxation	5,000	3,500
Pensions	7,000	6,500
	12,000	10,000

Movements during the year were as follows:

	Deferred tax	*Pensions*
	£	£
Balance at 1 April 20X1	3,500	6,500
Charged to the profit and loss account for 20X1/20X2	1,500	500
Balance at 31 March 20X2	5,000	7,000

A10 Called up share capital and share premium

Called up share capital is made up as follows:

	20X2	*20X1*
	£	£
At 31 March 1997:		
29,000 £1 ordinary shares	29,000	
At 31 March 1996:		
25,000 £1 ordinary shares		25,000

4,000 £1 ordinary shares were issued on 1 January 20X2 at a premium of 35p per share. The movement on the share premium account was therefore:

	£
Balance at 1 April 20X1	4,600
4,000 shares at a premium of 35p per share	1,400
Balance at 31 March 20X2	6,000

Cash flow statement – working sheet

Balance sheet	*20X2*	*20X1*	*Movement*	*Operating profit*	*Ret on inv/ serv of fin*	*Taxation*	*Cap exp & fin'l invest*	*Equity dividends*	*Liquid resources*	*Financing*	*Cash*	*Total*
Tangible fixed assets	130,600	110,700	19,900	15,400			(39,600)					0
				(3,000)			7,000					
Investments	36,000	10,000	26,000				(26,000)					0
Stocks	99,500	79,300	20,200	(20,200)								0
Trade debtors	54,700	51,150	3,550	(3,550)								0
Accrued interest	2,250	1,700	550		(550)							0
Pre-payments	8,900	6,350	2,550	(2,550)								0
Short-term deposits	3,000	1,750	1,250						(1,250)			0
Cash at bank	7,300	3,450	3,850								(3,850)	0
Bank overdraft	(20,500)	(18,700)	(1,800)								1,800	0
Finance leases	(25,550)	(18,300)	(7,250)				15,350			(8,100)		0
Trade creditors	(70,300)	(69,550)	(750)	750								0
Corporation tax	(8,900)	(8,430)	(470)			470						0
Accrued interest	(2,150)	(1,970)	(180)		180							0
Fixed asset accruals	(20,200)	0	(20,200)				20,200					0
Other accruals	(25,600)	(23,400)	(2,200)	2,200								0
Proposed equity dividend	(7,000)	(5,000)	(2,000)					2,000				0
Bank loans	(69,400)	(53,900)	(15,500)							15,500		0
Deferred tax	(5,000)	(3,500)	(1,500)			1,500						0
Pension provisions	(7,000)	(6,500)	(500)	500								0
Share capital	(29,000)	(25,000)	(4,000)							4,000		0
Share premium	(6,000)	(4,600)	(1,400)							1,400		0
Profit and loss	(46,650)	(25,550)	(20,100)									(20,100)
Carried forward	0	0	0	(10,450)	(370)	1,970	(22,750)	2,000	(1,250)	12,800	(2,050)	(20,100)

Profit and loss account

Balance sheet	*20X2*	*20X1*	*Movement*	*Operating profit*	*Ret on inv/ serv of fin*	*Taxation*	*Cap exp & fin'l invest*	*Equity dividends*	*Liquid resources*	*Financing*	*Cash*	*Total*
Brought forward	0	0	0	(10,450)	(370)	1,970	(22,750)	2,000	(1,250)	12,800	(2,050)	(20,100)
Profit and loss account:												
Operating profit		49,300		49,300								49,300
Interest receivable		5,600			5,600							5,600
Interest payable		(13,400)			(13,400)							(13,400)
Taxation		(9,400)				(9,400)						(9,400)
Dividends:												
Equity		(10,000)						(10,000)				(10,000)
Non-equity		(2,000)			(2,000)							(2,000)
		20,100		38,850	(10,170)	(7,430)	(22,750)	(8,000)	(1,250)	12,800	(2,050)	0

Cash Flow Statement

Cash flow statement for the year ended 31 March 20X2

	£
Net cash inflow from operating activities (Note 1)	38,850
Returns on investment and servicing of finance (Note 2)	(10,170)
Taxation (Note 2)	(7,430)
Capital expenditure and financial investment (Note 2)	(22,750)
Equity dividends paid	(8,000)
	(9,500)
Management of liquid resources (Note 2)	(1,250)
Financing (Note 2)	12,800
Increase in cash during the period	2,050

Reconciliation of net cash flow to movement in net debt (note 3)

	£	£
Increase in cash during the period	2,050	
Cash inflow from new bank loan	(15,500)	
Cash outflow in respect of finance leases	8,100	
Cash outflow from increase liquid resources	1,250	
Change in net debt resulting from cash flows		(4,100)
New finance lease		(15,350)
Movement in net debt during the period		(19,450)
Net debt at 1 April 20X1		(85,700)
Net debt at 31 March 20X2		(105,150)

NOTES TO THE CASH FLOW STATEMENT

1 Reconciliation of operating profit to net cash flow

	£
Operating profit	49,300
Depreciation charge	15,400
Profit on sale of fixed assets	(3,000)
Increase in stocks	(20,200)
Increase in debtors (a)	(6,100)
Increase in creditors (b)	2,950
Increase in provisions	500
Net cash flow from operating activities	38,850

(a) Trade debtors £3,550 + pre-payments £2,550

(b) Trade creditors £750 + 'other' accruals £2,200

2 Gross cash flows

	£	£
Returns on investments and servicing of finance:		
Interest received	5,050	
Interest paid	(13,220)	
Non-equity dividends paid	(2,000)	
		(10,170)
Taxation:		
Corporation tax paid		(7,430)
Management of liquid resources:*		
Amounts placed on deposit	(5,500)	
Amounts withdrawn from deposit	4,250	
		(1,250)
Financing:		
Issue of ordinary share capital	5,400	
New long-term bank loan	15,500	
Repayment of capital element of finance leases	(8,100)	
		12,800

* The company classifies amounts held on short term deposit as liquid resources.

3 Analysis of changes in net debt

	1 April 20X1	*Cash flows*	*Other changes*	*31 March 20X2*
	£	£	£	£
Cash at bank	3,450	3,850	—	7,300
Bank overdraft	(18,700)	(1,800)	—	(20,500)
	(15,250)	2,050	—	(13,200)
Debt due after 1 year	(53,900)	(15,500)	—	(69,400)
Finance leases	(18,300)	8,100	(15,350)	(25,550)
Short-term deposits	1,750	1,250	—	3,000
Total	(85,700)	(4,100)	(15,350)	(105,150)

4 Major non-cash transactions

During the year the company entered into a finance lease arrangement in respect of an asset with a capital value of £15,350 at the inception of the lease.

ADDITIONAL WORKING NOTES

B1 Interest received

	£
Accrued interest at 31 March 20X1 (see A5)	1,700
Interest receivable per profit and loss account	5,600
Accrued interest at 31 March 20X2 (see A5)	(2,250)
Interest actually received in 20X1/20X2	5,050

B2 Interest paid

	£
Accrued interest at 31 March 20X1 (see A7)	1,970
Interest receivable per profit and loss account	13,400
Accrued interest at 31 March 20X2 (see A7)	(2,150)
Interest actually received in 20X1/20X2	13,220

B3 Dividends paid

	Equity	*Non-equity*
	£	£
Proposed dividend at 31 March 20X1 (see A7)	5,000	—
Dividends per profit and loss account	10,000	2,000
Proposed dividend at 31 March 20X2 (see A7)	(7,000)	—
Dividends actually paid in 20X1/20X2	8,000	2,000

B4 Corporation tax

	£	£
Tax payable at 31 March 20X1 (see A7)		8,430
Charge in profit and loss account	9,400	
Less: element relating to deferred tax (see A9)	(1,500)	
		7,900
Tax payable at 31 March 20X2 (see A7)		(8,900)
Tax actually paid in 20X1/20X2		7,430

B5 Purchase of tangible fixed assets

Fixed asset accruals at 31 March 20X1 (see A7)	—
Additions in 20X1/20X2 per fixed asset table (see A3)	39,300
Less: asset acquired under finance lease (see A3 and A8)	(15,350)
Fixed asset accruals at 31 March 20X2 (see A7)	(20,200)
Payments in 20X1/20X2 in respect of fixed asset purchases	3,750

Chapter 35

Other Statements

STATEMENT OF TOTAL RECOGNISED GAINS AND LOSSES

Nature and purpose of the statement

35.1 Although CA 1985 requires movements on individual reserves to be disclosed each year, there is no specific requirement in company law for accounts to include a statement of total gains and losses recognised during the year. However, the general requirement for accounts to comply with applicable accounting standards means that the requirement in FRS 3 'Reporting Financial Performance' for such a statement to be presented in the accounts is effectively brought within the law. Although the major part of a company's performance is reflected in the profit and loss account, certain gains and losses are currently permitted or required to be taken directly to reserves. The most common item in this category is an unrealised gain arising on the revaluation of a fixed asset which must be taken directly to the revaluation reserve. The main purpose of the statement of total recognised gains and losses is to draw together all the gains and losses recognised in the accounts and show the total effect of these items on shareholders' funds. The statement is an additional primary statement and must be presented with the same prominence as the other primary statements (ie the profit and loss account, balance sheet and cash flow statement). It is usually presented on a separate page, alongside the profit and loss account, balance sheet and cash flow statement.

Requirement to prepare

35.2 A statement of total gains and losses must be given in every set of accounts intended to show a true and fair view of an entity's financial position and profit or loss (or income and expenditure) for the year. There is no exemption from this requirement for smaller companies. Where there are no recognised gains and losses, in either the current year or the previous year, other than those recorded in the profit and loss account, the standard requires a statement to this effect to be given immediately below the profit and loss account.

Example 35.1 – Where there are no recognised gains or losses

There were no recognised gains and losses in either the current year or the previous year, other than the profit for the year as shown in the profit and loss account.

This statement is not required if the Financial Statement for Smaller Entities (FRSSE) has been adopted (see **Chapter 7**).

Main items

35.3 The main items featuring in the statement will usually be:

- profit or loss for the financial year;
- gains and losses on the revaluation of fixed assets during the year;
- certain impairment losses arising on fixed assets and goodwill;
- unrealised translation differences on foreign currency net investments; and
- tax relating to any items recognised directly in the statement of total recognised gains and losses.

Profit for the financial year

35.4 The statement will include the profit or loss for the financial year, as shown in the profit and loss account. This is the figure before dividends.

Gains and losses

35.5 The same gains and losses should not be recognised twice in the accounts. For instance, a surplus on the revaluation of a fixed asset, which is recognised in the accounts at the time of the revaluation, should not be recognised a second time when the asset is sold. Any profit or loss on disposal is therefore measured by reference to the revalued amount and not to original cost. Gains and losses are interpreted in line with the definitions in the ASB's 'Statement of Principles': gains are increases in ownership interest, other than those relating to contributions from owners and losses are decreases in ownership interest, other than those relating to distributions to owners'. The statement of total recognised gains and losses should therefore exclude any amounts arising from transactions with shareholders (e.g. the proceeds of share issues and dividends payable to shareholders). These are dealt with separately in the reconciliation of movements in shareholders' funds (see **35.16** below).

Goodwill

35.6 Goodwill adjustments should only be recorded as recognised gains and losses when they are reflected in the profit and loss account. This will happen where:

— goodwill is amortised over its useful economic life;

— an impairment loss is recognised in respect of the goodwill; or

— the reporting entity closes or disposes of a previously acquired business, in which case the profit or loss on closure or disposal will include any goodwill not yet amortised through the profit and loss account.

Where goodwill is accounted for in accordance with FRS 10 'Goodwill and Intangible Assets', amortisation is charged to the profit and loss account over the useful economic life of the goodwill. The goodwill is therefore treated as a recognised loss as it is amortised through the profit and loss account. The predecessor accounting standard to FRS 10 (SSAP 22 'Accounting for Goodwill') allowed two alternative accounting treatments for purchased goodwill: capitalisation and amortisation, or immediate write-off against reserves. The preferred treatment on implementing FRS 10 is for goodwill that has previously been eliminated against reserves to be reinstated to the extent that it would not have been fully written down under the requirements of the new standard. However, the ASB accepted that this would not always be practicable and included certain transitional arrangements in FRS 10, which allow the option of not reinstating the goodwill. Where a company does not reinstate goodwill and subsequently closes or disposes of a business that was previously acquired, the profit or loss on closure or disposal should include the full amount of the related goodwill, on the basis that it has not yet been amortised through the profit and loss account. The goodwill will therefore be recognised in the year of closure or disposal. The impact on reserves of goodwill that is not reinstated on implementing FRS 10 is considered in more detail in **Chapter 19**.

Gains and losses on revalued fixed assets

35.7 FRS 15 'Tangible Fixed Assets' requires certain gains and losses arising on the revaluation of tangible fixed assets to be recognised in the statement of total recognised gains and losses rather than in the profit and loss account. Further details of these requirements are given in **Chapter 20**.

Impairment of fixed assets and goodwill

35.8 FRS 11 'Impairment of Fixed Assets and Goodwill' requires certain impairment losses in respect of previously revalued assets to be recognised in the statement of total recognised gains and losses. A similar treatment applies to the reversal of such an impairment loss, provided that recognition of the reversal is permitted by the standard. The requirements of FRS 11 are considered in detail in **Chapter 20**.

Taxation

35.9 FRS 16 'Current Tax' requires current tax to be recognised in the profit and loss account for the period, except to the extent that it is attributable to a gain or loss that is, or has been, recognised directly in the statement of total recognised gains and losses, in which case the tax attributable should also be recognised directly in that statement. Any tax expense (or income) for the period shown in the statement of total recognised gains and losses should be analysed into:

— UK tax; and

— foreign tax.

Each of these should be analysed to distinguish tax estimated for the current period from any adjustments recognised in respect of prior periods. Similarly, FRS 19 'Deferred Tax' requires deferred tax to be recognised in the profit and loss account for the period, except to the extent that it is attributable to a gain or loss that is or has been recognised directly in the statement of total recognised gains and losses. In this case, the attributable deferred tax should also be recognised directly in the statement of total recognised gains and losses. The amount of deferred tax recognised directly in the statement of total recognised gains and losses should be disclosed, showing separately material amounts such as:

— the origination and reversal of timing differences;

— changes in tax rates and laws;

— adjustments to deferred tax assets arising in previous periods; and

— where relevant, changes in the amount of discount deducted in arriving at the deferred tax balance.

The requirements of FRS 16 and FRS 19, including the calculation the tax attributable to an item recognised in the statement of total recognised gains and losses, are considered in more detail in **Chapter 14** and **Chapter 30**.

Share issue costs

35.10 The treatment of share issue costs is dealt with in FRS 4 'Capital Instruments' rather than FRS 3. On the face of it, these costs may appear to be a recognised loss in the year of the share issue. However, share issue costs relate directly to a transaction with shareholders and should therefore be reflected in the reconciliation of movements in shareholders' funds rather than the statement of total recognised gains and losses. This is done by including the net proceeds of the share issue (ie after deduction of the issue costs) in the reconciliation of movements in shareholders' funds.

Amounts attributable to different classes of shareholder

35.11 Where there are different classes of shareholder and the accounts recognise a material movement between the amounts attributable to each class which has no effect on total shareholders' funds, this movement will not be reflected as a gain or loss in the statement of total recognised gains and losses. FRS 3 suggests that an explanatory footnote to the statement may be appropriate in these circumstances. This situation is likely to be rare in practice.

Worked example

35.12 The following is an example of how the statement might be presented.

Example 35.2 – Statement of total recognised gains and losses

	20X2	*20X1*
	£	£
Profit for the financial year	32	61
Unrealised surplus on revaluation of properties (a)	—	8
Currency translation differences on foreign currency net investments (b)	7	(6)
Total gains and losses recognised since the last annual accounts	39	63

(a) This figure will represent the amount credited to the revaluation reserve in respect of revaluations undertaken during the year.

(b) This figure will represent the unrealised gain or loss arising during the year on the translation of foreign currency net investments to Sterling at the appropriate exchange rate at the end of each year.

Comparative figures

35.13 Comparative figures should be given for each item in the statement of total recognised gains and losses. Headings will also be needed for any items which appeared in the previous year's statement but which do not feature in the current year movements.

Prior period adjustments

35.14 Where a prior period adjustment is required in the accounts, the gains and losses for the previous period will need to be adjusted where appropriate. The total effect of the adjustments should also be noted at the end of the statement of total recognised gains and losses for the current year. This is because the adjustments represent gains and losses recognised in the current period even though they relate to previous periods.

Example 35.3 – Where there is a prior period adjustment

Using details from **Example 35.2**	*20X2*	*20X1*
	£	£
		(restated)
Profit for the financial year	32	61
Unrealised surplus on revaluation of properties	—	8
Currency translation differences on foreign currency net investments	7	(6)
Total recognised gains and losses relating to the year	39	63
Prior period adjustment (as explained in note 1)	(13)	
Total gains and losses recognised since the last annual accounts	26	

Full details of the prior period adjustment will need to be given elsewhere in the accounts.

Likely future developments

35.15 The ASB published FRED 22 'Revision of FRS 3: Reporting Financial Performance' in December 2000. The exposure draft puts forward some significant changes to current reporting and disclosure requirements, and reflects an agreed international approach to reporting financial performance. Under the proposals, the profit and loss account and statement of total recognised gains and losses would be replaced with a single performance statement showing all gains and losses recognised during the reporting period and relating to that period. The proposed performance statement is divided into three sections:

— operating;

— financing and treasury; and

— other gains and losses.

Most gains and losses will be shown in the operating section, but items that are currently required to be shown in the statement of total recognised gains and losses will generally be reported in the other sections of the financial performance statement. FRED 22 is considered in more detail in **Chapter 8**.

RECONCILIATION OF MOVEMENTS IN SHAREHOLDERS' FUNDS

Changes in shareholders' funds

35.16 Although CA 1985 requires movements on share capital and individual reserves to be disclosed each year, there is no specific requirement in company law for accounts to include a reconciliation of the overall movements in shareholders' funds during the year. However, the general requirement for accounts to comply with applicable accounting standards means that the requirement in FRS 3 'Reporting Financial Performance' for such a reconciliation to be presented in the accounts is effectively brought within the law. A company's profit and loss account and statement of total recognised gains and losses summarise its performance during the year. However, there may be other changes in shareholders' funds which, because of their nature, are not required to be shown in these two statements but which might nevertheless be important in helping an accounts user understand changes in the company's financial position. The main purpose of the reconciliation of movements in shareholders' funds is to summarise and draw attention to these other changes. The note effectively pulls together the company's performance, as reflected in the profit and loss account and statement of total recognised gains and losses, and any other changes in shareholders' funds during the year. The reconciliation must be given whenever there have been movements in shareholders' funds during the year, although it is not required in accounts prepared under the FRSSE (see **Chapter 7**).

Presentation

35.17 The reconciliation is not one of the primary statements in the accounts, but it is intrinsically linked with the primary statements, in particular the profit and loss account and statement of total recognised gains and losses. It is therefore often presented alongside the primary statements. Alternatively it can be given within the notes to the accounts, usually alongside the notes on share capital and reserves. The standard emphasises that where the note is presented with the primary statements, it must be shown separately from the statement of total recognised gains and losses (ie the movements cannot be summarised into one statement).

Negative statement

35.18 Where there are no movements in shareholders' funds in either the current year or the previous year (for instance, because the company is dormant), there is no requirement in the standard for this fact to be disclosed in the accounts. However, a statement on the following lines is generally helpful to a user of the accounts.

Example 35.4 – Where there are no movements in the year

There were no movements in shareholders' funds in either the current year or the previous year. Consequently a reconciliation of movements in shareholders' funds is not presented as part of these accounts.

Reconciling items

35.19 The main items featuring in the reconciliation will be:

— the profit or loss for the financial year;

— other gains and losses recognised during the year; and

— other changes in shareholders' funds during the year.

The reconciliation will include the profit or loss for the financial year, as shown in the profit and loss account. This is the figure before dividends. Other gains and losses recognised during the year will be disclosed in detail in the statement of total recognised gains and losses. They therefore need only be shown in summarised form in the reconciliation of movements in shareholders' funds. It may be helpful to show separately in the reconciliation any particularly large items that arise only occasionally (e.g. a significant transfer to or from revaluation reserve on revaluation of a company's properties), but there is no requirement in the standard for this to be done.

Other changes in shareholders' funds

35.20 Apart from the profit for the financial year and other gains and losses shown in detail in the statement of total recognised gains and losses, the most common items to feature in the reconciliation will be transactions with shareholders, for example:

— new share capital issued during the year;

— share issue costs; and

— dividends.

FRS 4 'Capital Instruments' specifically requires share issue costs to be reflected in the reconciliation of movements in shareholders' funds rather than in the statement of total recognised gains and losses.

Shares issued under employee share schemes

3.21 UITF Abstract 17 considers the accounting treatment of shares awarded to employees through annual bonuses or long-term incentive schemes, and requires the cost of share awards to employees to be charged to the profit and loss account over the period to which the employee's performance relates. Where new shares are issued under an employee share scheme, the credit entry for the charge to the profit and loss account should be reported in the reconciliation of movements in shareholders' funds, not in the statement of total recognised gains and losses. This reflects the fact that the amount recognised represents proceeds from the issue of an equity instrument. The requirements of Abstract 17 are considered in more detail in **Chapter 10**.

Worked example

35.22 The following is an example of how the reconciliation might be presented.

Example 35.5 – Reconciliation of movements in shareholders' funds (I)

	20X2	*20X1*
	£	£
Profit for the financial year	32	61
Dividends (a)	(10)	(15)
	22	46
Other recognised gains and losses (net)	3	2
New share capital subscribed (b)	10	—
Net addition to shareholders funds	35	48
Opening shareholders funds	375	327
Closing shareholders funds	410	375

(a) This figure will represent the net effect of all gains and losses, other than the profit for the financial year, shown individually in the statement of total recognised gains and losses.

(b) This figure will represent the net proceeds of shares issued during the year, including any amount credited to the share premium account and after deducting any share issue costs.

Example 35.5 follows the presentation used in the illustrative example in FRS 3. However, it is equally acceptable to present the information in the following way.

Example 35.6 – Reconciliation of movements in shareholders' funds (II)

	20X2	*20X1*
	£	£
Opening shareholders funds	375	327
Profit for the financial year	32	61
Dividends	(10)	(15)
Other recognised gains and losses (net)	3	2
New share capital subscribed	10	—
Closing shareholders funds	410	375

Comparative figures

35.23 Comparative figures should be given for each item in the reconciliation of movements in shareholders' funds. Headings will also be needed for any items which appeared in the previous year's reconciliation but which do not feature in the current year movements.

Prior period adjustments

35.24 Where a prior period adjustment is required, the opening balance for shareholders' funds for the previous year will need to be adjusted for the cumulative effect of the prior period adjustment up to that date and other comparative figures within the reconciliation may need to be restated. The illustrative example in FRS 3 suggests that the adjustment to the opening balance could be dealt with in narrative form within the note.

Example 35.7– Prior period adjustment (I)

Extract from **Example 35.6**	*20X2*	*20X1*
	£	£
		(restated)
Net addition to shareholders funds	35	48
Opening shareholders funds (originally 340,000 for 20X1, before prior period adjustment of 13,000)	375	327
Closing shareholders funds	410	375

Alternatively, this could be shown in columnar form.

Example 35.7 – Prior period adjustment (II)

Extract from **Example 35.6**

	20X2		***20X1***
	£	*£*	*£*
			(restated)
Net addition to shareholders funds	35		48
Opening shareholders funds:			
As previously reported		340	
Prior period adjustment		(13)	
	375		327
Closing shareholders funds	410		375

Full details of the prior period adjustment will need to be given elsewhere in the accounts.

Likely future developments

35.25 The ASB published FRED 22 'Revision of FRS 3: Reporting Financial Performance' in December 2000. The exposure draft puts forward some significant changes to current reporting and disclosure requirements, and reflects an agreed international approach to reporting financial performance. Under the proposals, the profit and loss account, and statement of total recognised gains and losses would be replaced with a single performance statement showing all gains and losses recognised during the reporting period and relating to that period. The proposed changes include the following two points:

— dividends will not be reported in the performance statement as they represent transactions with owners rather than elements of financial performance (although the exposure draft does propose that they should be shown as a memorandum item at the foot of the statement) - UK companies' legislation currently requires dividends to be reported in the profit and loss account and the ASB is therefore discussing with the DTI the possibility of changing the law; and

— a reconciliation of ownership interests must be given as a primary statement - this brings together the performance for the period and all other changes in ownership interests, including dividends paid and new capital contributed, and is very similar to the reconciliation of shareholders' funds currently required by FRS 3.

FRED 22 is considered in more detail in **Chapter 8**.

NOTE OF HISTORICAL COST PROFITS AND LOSSES

Nature and purpose of the note

35.26 There is no specific requirement in company law for a set of accounts to include a note of historical cost profits and losses. However, the general requirement for accounts to comply with applicable accounting standards means that the requirement in FRS 3 'Reporting Financial Performance' for a note of historical cost profits and losses is effectively brought within the law. FRS 3 explains that the note of historical cost profits and losses is intended to be a memorandum item which has two main purposes:

— to aid comparison between companies who are carrying assets at revalued amounts and those who are showing all assets at historical cost; and

— to enable users of the accounts to identify the profit or loss on disposal of assets on the basis of historical cost.

FRS 3 requires the note to be given whenever there is a material difference between the results shown in the profit and loss account and the results that would have been shown if historical cost accounting had been adopted throughout the accounts, although it is not required in accounts prepared under the FRSSE (see **Chapter 7**). The note must be given immediately below the profit and loss account or immediately below the statement of total recognised gains and losses.

Detailed disclosures

35.27 The standard requires the note to reconcile the reported profit or loss on ordinary activities before taxation to the equivalent amount under historical cost accounting, and to show the retained profit or loss for the year on the historical cost basis. In practice, the most common reconciling items will be:

— the realisation during the year of revaluation gains or losses reflected in the accounts in previous years (ie where assets revalued in previous years have been disposed of during the current year); and

— the difference between depreciation charged in the year on revalued assets and the depreciation that would have been charged if the assets had been included at historical cost.

The standard identifies two particular accounting treatments that are not to be regarded as departures from historical cost accounting for the purpose of the note on historical cost profits and losses:

— adjustments made to reflect the impact of hyper-inflation on foreign operations (dealt with in UITF 9 'Accounting for Operations in Hyper-Inflationary Economies');

— the marking of investments to market where this is established industry practice (eg in the accounts of market makers and investment dealers).

Including fixed assets at valuation

35.28 CA 1985 and accounting practice allow (but do not require) companies to include fixed assets in their accounts at valuation rather than historical cost (see **Chapter 1** and **Chapter 20**). The result is that some companies make no use of valuations whilst others may show certain assets at valuation and others at cost. The requirement for companies who have made use of valuations in their accounts to make separate disclosure of what their results would have been if they had included all assets at historical cost is intended to make direct comparisons between companies easier.

Profits and losses on disposal of assets

35.29 Paragraph 21 of FRS 3 'Reporting Financial Performance' requires profits and losses on the disposal of assets to be accounted for:

— in the period in which the disposal occurs; and

— as the difference between net sales proceeds and the carrying value of the asset.

This means that, where an asset has been revalued for accounts purposes, any profit or loss on disposal must be based on the revalued figure rather than on historical cost. Prior to FRS 3, some companies chose to calculate the profit or loss on disposal as the difference between sales proceeds and historical cost (rather than the valuation figure) by crediting any remaining balance on the revaluation reserve to the profit and loss account. Under FRS 3, any remaining balance on the revaluation reserve, relating to the asset that has been disposed of, is transferred to the profit and loss account reserve as a reserves movement. The amount transferred between reserves in this way also appears within the note of historical cost profits and losses as it is an item that arises from the use of valuation rather than historical cost in accounting for fixed assets. In historical cost terms, this amount represents an additional gain on disposal of the asset. This gain has been recognised in the accounts in previous years (by including the asset at valuation) but is only realised when the asset is disposed of. If the relevant historical cost figures are unavailable or cannot be obtained without unreasonable expense or undue delay, FRS 3 permits the use of the earliest available values in place of actual historical cost.

Negative statement

35.30 Where there is no material difference between the actual results and the results that would have been shown on the historical cost basis, there is no requirement in the standard for this fact to be disclosed in the accounts. However, a statement on the following lines is generally helpful to a user of the accounts.

Example 35.8 – Where there is no material difference

There is no material difference between the results as disclosed in the profit and loss account and the results that would have been shown on an unmodified historical cost basis.

Where such a statement is given, it should be positioned immediately below the profit and loss account or immediately below the statement of total recognised gains and losses (ie in the same place as the note would have been given under FRS 3).

Worked example

35.31 The following is an example of how the note might be presented:

Example 35.9 – Note of historical cost profits and losses

Profit and loss account for the year ended 31 December 20X2

	20X2	***20X1***
	'000	***'000***
Turnover	820	715
Cost of sales	(727)	(595)
Gross profit	93	120
Distribution costs	(21)	(16)
Administration expenses	(20)	(18)
Operating profit	52	86
Interest payable	(7)	(6)
Profit on ordinary activities before taxation	45	80
Tax on profit on ordinary activities	(13)	(19)
Profit for the financial year	32	61
Dividends	(10)	(15)
Retained profit for the financial year	22	46

Note of historical cost profits and losses

Reported profit on ordinary activities before taxation (a)	45	80
Realisation of property revaluation gains recognised in previous years (b)	14	9
Difference between historical cost depreciation charge and actual depreciation charge based on revalued amounts (c)	5	4
Historical cost profit on ordinary activities before taxation	64	93
Historical cost retained profit for the financial year (d)	41	59

(a) Profit on ordinary activities before taxation as shown in the profit and loss account.

(b) This figure represents the balance transferred from the revaluation reserve to the profit and loss account reserve in respect of assets disposed of during the year – details have not been given for the purpose of this illustration.

(c) This needs to be calculated separately – details have not been given for the purpose of this illustration. The example assumes that assets have increased in value as a result of the revaluation; the depreciation charge on the historical cost basis will therefore be lower than the actual charge and this reconciling item increases the profit for the year as a result.

(d) Calculated as:

Historical cost profit as shown at the end of the reconciliation	64	93
Less:		
Taxation (per profit and loss account)	(13)	(19)
Dividends (per profit and loss account)	(10)	(15)
	41	59

Comparative figures

35.32 Comparative figures should be given for each item in the note on historical cost profit and losses.

Prior period adjustments

35.33 Where a prior period adjustment is required, the figures in the previous note of historical cost profits and losses will need to be restated where appropriate.

Likely future developments

35.34 The ASB published FRED 22 'Revision of FRS: Reporting Financial Performance' in December 2000. The exposure draft puts forward some significant changes to current reporting and disclosure requirements, and reflects an agreed international approach to reporting financial performance. Under the proposals, the note of historical cost profits and losses currently required by FRS 3 becomes an optional disclosure. FRED 22 is considered in more detail in **Chapter 8**.

Chapter 36

Directors' Report

REQUIREMENT TO PREPARE A DIRECTORS' REPORT

Company law requirements

36.1 Under CA 1985 s 234, the directors of a company are required to prepare a report for each financial year and to file this with the registrar. The report must be approved by the board of directors and signed on behalf of the board by a director or by the company secretary. The name of the signatory must also be clearly stated on the report. This is usually done by typing the relevant name under the actual signature. The copy filed with the registrar must include a manuscript signature. There are penalties for failure to comply with these requirements. A small company is permitted to prepare and file a modified directors' report - this is considered in more detail in **Chapter 7**.

Detailed contents of the report

36.2 The following information must be given in the directors' report each year:

- a fair review of the development of the business of the company (and any subsidiaries) during the year and the position at the end of the year;
- the amount recommended by the directors to be paid as dividend;
- the principal activities of the company (and any subsidiaries) during the course of the year and any significant changes in activities;
- an indication of likely future developments in the business;
- an indication of any activities in the field of research and development;
- an indication of the existence of any branches of the company outside the UK;
- particulars of any important events affecting the company (and any subsidiaries) which have occurred since the end of the financial year;
- details of any substantial difference between the market values and the balance sheet values of interests in land held by the company or its subsidiaries;

- the names of all those who were directors of the company at any time during the year;
- the interests (ie the number or amount) held by each director (or a member of his immediate family) in the shares or debentures of the company or of any other body corporate in the same group – the details to be given are:
  - all interests held at the end of the financial year;
  - for each director with interests at the end of the year, his interests at the beginning of the year or at the time of his appointment if this took place during the year;
- the number or amount of any rights to subscribe for shares or debentures in the company or another body corporate in the same group which were granted to or exercised by each director (or a member of his immediate family) during the year;
- where the company has made any donation to a registered party or to any other EU political organisation or incurred any EU political expenditure and the aggregate of all such donations and expenditure exceeded £200, the directors' report must include:
  - the name of each registered party or other political organisation to whom a donation was made;
  - the total amount donated to each party or organisation during the financial year; and
  - the total amount of any other EU political expenditure during the financial year;

  (wholly-owned subsidiaries of a company incorporated in Great Britain are exempt from this disclosure requirement);
- if the company has made any contribution to a non-EU political party, the directors' report must state the amount of the contribution or, where relevant, the total amount of the contributions made during the financial year (wholly-owned subsidiaries of a company incorporated in Great Britain are exempt from this disclosure requirement);
- if the company has given more than £200 for charitable purposes, the directors' report must state the amount given during the financial year for each charitable purpose (wholly-owned subsidiaries of a company incorporated in Great Britain are exempt from this disclosure requirement);
- where the average number of employees exceeds 250, a statement on the company's policy on employment, training, career development and promotion of disabled persons;
- where the average number of employees exceeds 250, a statement on the action taken during the year to introduce, maintain or develop arrangements to:
  - provide employees with relevant information;

  - consult employees or their representatives on a regular basis;
  - encourage employee involvement in the company's performance; and
  - achieve a common awareness among employees of financial and economic factors affecting the company's performance;
- in the case of a company that was at any time during the year a public company or a member of a group headed by a public company, and did not qualify as small or medium-sized in relation to that year, details of the company's policy and practice on payment of creditors.

Additional disclosures in respect of shares

36.3 Where shares in the company have been:

- purchased by the company;
- acquired by the company by forfeiture or surrender in lieu of forfeiture;
- acquired by the company otherwise than for valuable consideration under CA 1985 s 143(3);
- acquired by another person with financial assistance from the company, and the company has a beneficial interest in the shares;
- acquired by a nominee of the company without direct or indirect financial assistance from the company, and the company has a beneficial interest in the shares; and
- made subject to lien or charge taken by the company under CA 1985 s 150 or Companies Consolidation (Consequential Provisions) Act 1985 s 6(3),

the following disclosures must be given in the directors' report for that year:

- the number and nominal value of shares purchased, the aggregate amount of consideration paid and the reasons for the purchase;
- the number and nominal value of shares acquired or charged during the year in the way explained above;
- the maximum number and nominal value of shares held by the company or the other person during the year, having been acquired or charged in the way explained above;
- the number and nominal value of shares disposed of by the company or by the other person, or cancelled by the company during the year, having been acquired or charged as explained above;
- where shares have been disposed of as set out above, the amount or value of the consideration;

- in each of these cases, the percentage of the called-up share capital represented by the shares in question; and
- where shares have been charged, the amount of the charge in each case.

Consistency with accounts

36.4 A number of the disclosures in the directors' report relate to information that also has to be given within the accounts. Care must be taken to ensure that details disclosed in the report are consistent with any related information given in the accounts. The following sections in this chapter include consideration of the areas where problems are most likely to arise. Auditors are specifically required to consider whether the directors' report is consistent with the accounts and to report on any inconsistencies in the audit report.

DEVELOPMENT OF THE BUSINESS AND THE POSITION AT THE YEAR-END

Purpose of the review

36.5 CA 1985 requires the directors' report to include a review of the development of the business during the year but does not specify a format or indicate what should be covered in the review. Directors are therefore free to decide how to present their review. The main purpose of this section of the report is to provide additional information to explain the details shown in the profit and loss account and balance sheet and help the reader to understand both the results for the year and the year-end position. It should therefore identify any significant features or changes during the year that should be drawn to the attention of the members.

Possible contents

36.6 It is impossible to give a standard list of items to include in the review as the contents must inevitably vary by year and business by business. The impact of certain events will also be different, depending on the circumstances of the company. However, the following is an indication of the type of issue that might require explanation:

- particularly significant changes in income or expenditure compared with the previous year;
- particularly significant changes in balance sheet headings compared with the previous year;
- a major restructuring or reorganisation that has taken place during the year;

— significant changes in employee levels during the year;

— major changes in economic or market conditions during the year;

— major changes in the company's products or services during the year; and

— any major impact of foreign currency exchange gains or losses.

CA 1985 requires the review to be 'fair', and the wording and tone of the commentary should be consistent with the result shown in the profit and loss account. For instance, it will usually be inappropriate to present a very positive statement about the success of the business in the year if the profit and loss account shows reduced turnover and a loss for the year. The report should also be balanced and cover both good and bad aspects of the year.

Use of a separate report

36.7 The relevant information may be set out in a separate section of the annual accounts (eg in a chairman's statement or a separate operating and financial review statement). This is acceptable, provided that the directors' report includes a cross-reference to show where the detailed information is presented.

ASB Statement 'Operating and Financial Review'

36.8 The ASB Statement 'Operating and Financial Review' (OFR), which was revised in January 2003, is non-mandatory and is intended to formulate and develop best practice. It sets out recommendations for the annual accounts of listed companies to include formal discussion and interpretation of the business, its particular strengths and weaknesses, the uncertainties that underlie it and the structure of its financing. To some extent, these recommendations overlap with a number of the CA 1985 requirements in respect of the directors' report. Whilst the ASB recommendations are intended primarily for major enterprises, the Statement can provide useful guidance on issues that may need to be discussed in the directors' report. The revised Statement provides a broader framework for the discussion of business performance and sets out six principles that should be applied by the directors when preparing an OFR, together with detailed guidance on the practical application of those principles. In particular, the Statement includes:

— guidance on describing the business, its objectives and its strategy in order to put the directors' discussion of performance and financial position into context;

— a recognition that business objectives and performance may encompass both financial and non-financial measures (eg corporate social responsibility);

— a recommendation that the directors explain the strengths and resources of the business, especially any which are not reflected in the balance sheet, together with action taken to enhance future performance;

— a proposal that the OFR should highlight the accounting policies which are key to understanding the entity's performance and financial position, focusing in particular on any policies to which the results are particularly sensitive; and

— in the light of an increasing use of *pro forma* figures, a recommendation that where information from the financial statements has been adjusted for inclusion in the OFR, this fact should be highlighted and a reconciliation provided.

PROPOSED DIVIDEND

Consistency with accounts

36.9 The amount the directors recommend to be paid as dividend must be stated in the directors' report. This figure will also appear in the profit and loss account or in the notes to the accounts and the details given in the directors' report must therefore be consistent with the details shown in the accounts. Strictly it is only the proposed dividend that needs to be disclosed. In practice, details are usually given for both the interim dividend paid during the year and the proposed final dividend, making up the total dividend for the year as shown in the profit and loss account. Details are usually given for both the dividend per share and the total amount payable in respect of the dividend.

Example 36.1

An interim dividend of … p per share amounting to £ … was paid on [date]. The directors propose a final dividend of … p per share amounting to £ … , making a total dividend for the year of … p per share amounting to £ … .

If the directors do not recommend payment of a dividend, it is best practice to state this fact in the directors' report.

PRINCIPAL ACTIVITIES

Statement on activities

36.10 CA 1985 requires a statement on the principal activities of the company and any subsidiaries during the year, and also on any changes in activities that have taken place during the year. The wording of the Act suggests that information on subsidiaries is required even if the company is exempt from the requirement to prepare group accounts.

Consistency with accounts

36.11 The principal activities identified in the directors' report disclosures should normally be consistent with any segmental information given in the accounts under CA 1985 or under SSAP 25 'Segmental Reporting' (see **Chapter 17**). Similarly, any changes in principal activities during the year disclosed in the directors' report should normally be consistent with the disclosures on continuing, acquired and discontinued operations, as required by FRS 3 'Reporting Financial Performance' (see **Chapter 8**). It is, however, possible that the sale or cessation of part of the business may need to be disclosed as a change in activities in the directors' report, even though it does not meet the FRS 3 criteria for a discontinued operation.

LIKELY FUTURE DEVELOPMENTS

Form and contents

36.12 CA 1985 requires the directors to give an indication of the likely future developments of the company and, where relevant, any subsidiaries. Once again, information on subsidiaries appears to be required even if the company does not have to prepare group accounts. As with the business review, the Act provides no detailed guidance on the form that this statement should take or the type of issue that should be covered and directors are therefore free to decide how best to present the information. UITF Abstract 21 'Accounting Issues Arising from the Proposed Introduction of the Euro' recommends that, where the potential impact of the introduction of the euro is likely to be significant to the reporting entity, additional information should be disclosed in the annual report and accounts. This should include an indication of the total costs likely to be incurred. The disclosures may be given in the directors' report, an operating and financial review or any other statement published as part of the annual report. Smaller entities who adopt the Financial Reporting Standard for Smaller Entities (FRSSE) are exempt from the detailed requirements of Abstract 21 but they are nevertheless encouraged to consider the potential issues and make disclosures where appropriate.

Guidance on wording

36.13 It is usually advisable to keep the statement fairly general in nature. The wording of the statement is a particular problem area for listed companies and those quoted on similar markets as they need to ensure that comments made by the directors cannot later be deemed to constitute a profit forecast. Whilst this is not such a problem for private companies, it is still advisable to refer only to general issues such as:

— expected economic and trading conditions in the next period;

- broad indication of expected level of activity in the next period compared with the current year;
- broad indication of management plans to deal with any expected problem areas.

It is also advisable to keep the statement relatively brief.

RESEARCH AND DEVELOPMENT

Nature of disclosures

36.14 CA 1985 requires the directors to give an indication of activities (if any) in the field of research and development. The disclosure should cover both the company and any subsidiaries, regardless of whether group accounts are prepared. The disclosures required in the directors' report should not be confused with the separate accounts disclosures under SSAP 13 'Research and Development' (see **Chapter 19**). The accounting standard requires the disclosure of the accounting policy adopted in respect of research and development costs, expenditure during the year and movements on any deferred development costs. The directors' report should not repeat this information, but should discuss the commercial aspects of the company's research and development activity rather than the accounting treatment adopted.

Consistency with accounts

36.15 However, it is clear that any discussion on research and development should be consistent with the accounts. On a basic level, if research and development costs are disclosed in the accounts, a discussion of the general activities would be expected in the directors' report. Similarly, if research and development activities are discussed in the directors' report, it will usually be appropriate for an accounting policy on research and development expenditure to be included in the accounts.

Form and content

36.16 CA 1985 does not give any guidance on the information to be included and the level of disclosure will clearly vary depending on the extent of the company's activities and also on how central research and development is to its overall business. For instance, more extensive disclosures would usually be expected from a pharmaceutical company than from a construction company. The discussion might include:

- broad indication of the level and nature of research and development activity;
- explanation of any changes in the level or nature of activity during the year;

- brief comment on any specific projects undertaken during the year;
- brief comment on any particular area of expertise;
- indication of any major contacts or joint projects with other research bodies.

Research and development activities in certain fields can be particularly sensitive areas and companies will often be reluctant to make too much detail available to competitors. As CA 1985 does not specify any minimum level of disclosure, a broad indication of the work being undertaken in the field of research and development should be sufficient to meet the disclosure requirement.

POST BALANCE SHEET EVENTS

Interaction with SSAP 17 'Accounting for Post Balance Sheet Events'

36.17 The directors are required to give particulars of any important events affecting the company or its subsidiaries which have occurred since the end of the financial year. SSAP 17 'Accounting for Post Balance Sheet Events' identifies two categories of post balance sheet event:

- adjusting events, which, if material, require an adjustment to be made to the figures in the accounts; and
- non-adjusting events, which do not require an adjustment to be made to the accounts, but which, if material, require disclosure in the notes to the accounts.

Consequently, there appears to be some duplication with the requirement under CA 1985 for information on material post balance sheet events to be given in the directors' report. The distinction between adjusting and non-adjusting events is discussed in more detail in **Chapter 33**.

Disclosure of adjusting events

36.18 SSAP 17 does not require disclosure of adjusting events as these will have been reflected in the accounts, although disclosure as an exceptional item may be necessary if the effect on the accounts is sufficiently material. As CA 1985 does not distinguish between adjusting and non-adjusting events, the directors' report may need to give brief details of any major adjusting events and explain how these have been dealt with in the accounts. In practice, this situation is likely to be rare as most adjusting events arise from additional evidence on the value of assets and liabilities as at the year-end date and they will not usually be sufficiently material to warrant separate disclosure in the directors' report.

Disclosure of non-adjusting events

36.19 There is a major distinction between the accounting standard and CA 1985, in that SSAP 17 requires details of non-adjusting events to be disclosed in the accounts. Disclosure in the directors' report alone is not sufficient to comply with the standard. To avoid the unnecessary duplication of information it is acceptable to give the detailed disclosures in one location only (preferably the notes to the accounts) and include a cross-reference in the other location to show where the details can be found. If details of a post balance sheet event are disclosed separately in both the directors' report and the notes to the accounts it is important that the information given in each location is consistent.

FIXED ASSETS

Market value of land and buildings

36.20 The directors' report must include details of any material difference between the book value and the market value of any interest in land held by the company (or, where relevant, the group). Disclosure of a substantial difference between the market value and the book value of land and buildings is required if, in the opinion of the directors, the difference is of such significance that it should be drawn to the attention of the members or debenture-holders. In practice, it is advisable to disclose any material difference that arises. CA 1985 requires the difference to be stated 'with such degree of precision as is practicable'. In practice, the disclosure will often be based on a recent professional valuation of the property, although there is no formal requirement for this. Where an entity chooses to adopt a policy of valuation for some of its fixed assets, FRS 15 'Tangible Fixed Assets' now requires the valuations to be kept up to date and any significant valuation gains or losses should therefore be incorporated into the accounts, unless the transitional rules have been adopted (see **Chapter 20**).

Need for additional explanation

36.21 If land and buildings are included in the accounts at depreciated historical cost and the market value of the properties is significantly higher than book value, no further comment will usually be needed as there is no requirement at present for fixed assets to be included in the accounts at valuation. However, if market value is significantly lower than book value, but the directors have decided that no write-down is necessary, some additional comment will usually be required to explain why this approach is justified.

DIRECTORS AND THEIR INTERESTS

Names of directors

36.22 The requirement under CA 1985 is for the directors' report to give the names of all those who were directors of the company at any time during the year. It is usual to indicate the dates of any resignations, retirements and appointments that have taken place during the year.

Example 36.2

The following directors have held office during the year:

— A D Evans

— C B Jones (resigned 3 September 20X2)

— E L Wright (appointed 16 September 20X2)

— J T Smith

It is also usual to give details of any appointments, resignations or retirements between the year-end date and the date on which the accounts and directors' report are approved and signed, although this is not a requirement. These changes should also be noted in the following year's report as they will actually take place in the year covered by that report.

Directors' share interests

36.23 The disclosure requirements on directors' share interests are extremely complex and only the more common problem areas are considered here. In more unusual situations, reference should be made to company law publications to establish whether a particular item constitutes a disclosable interest. In certain cases, specific legal advice may be needed as the wording or meaning of CA 1985 is not always clear and opinions and interpretations may vary. The details may be given either in the directors' report or in the notes to the accounts, but most commonly they are set out in the directors' report. If the details are given in the notes to the accounts, it is helpful to include a cross-reference in the directors' report. The required information must be given for each individual director and must cover all those who were directors at the end of the year. For the purpose of these disclosure requirements, the term 'director' includes shadow directors. A shadow director is defined in CA 1985 as a person in accordance with whose directions or instructions the directors of the company are accustomed to act. However, a person will not be deemed to be a shadow director where the directors act only on advice given by him/her in a professional capacity.

Definition of 'interest'

36.24 An 'interest' in shares or debentures for the purpose of these disclosures is given the very broad definition set out in CA 1985 Sch 13 para 1, which also applies for the purposes of the duty of directors to disclose shareholdings to the company. In general terms, any interest, of any kind whatsoever, in shares and debentures constitutes a notifiable and therefore a disclosable interest for the purposes of CA 1985.

Interests at the end of the year

36.25 For each person who was a director at the end of the financial year, the directors' report or accounts must state:

- whether, at the year-end date, he/she was interested in the shares or debentures of the company; and
- whether, at the year-end date, he/she was interested in the shares or debentures of another body corporate in the same group.

The wording of the legislation requires a negative statement to be given for any individuals who were directors at the end of the financial year but did not hold interests in shares or debentures of the company, or any other company in the group. Disclosable interests are those recorded in the register of directors' interests under the requirements of CA 1985 and include interests held by a director's immediate family. In this context, a body corporate in the same group as the company means a holding company, a subsidiary company or a fellow subsidiary company. However, under the Companies (Disclosure of Directors' Interests) (Exceptions) Regulations 1985, SI 1985/802, where a company is wholly-owned by a body corporate incorporated outside Great Britain, interests in the shares or debentures of that body corporate, or any other body corporate incorporated outside Great Britain, are not notifiable or disclosable.

Interests at the beginning of the year

36.26 For each director who had disclosable interests at the end of the year, the following details must also be given:

- the name of the company (or companies) in which he/she had an interest at the end of the year;
- the number of shares in each company held at the end of the year;
- the amount of debentures of each company held at the end of the year;
- if he/she was also a director at the beginning of the year, the same details for any interests held at that time; and
- if he/she was appointed as a director during the year, the same details for any interests held at the date of appointment.

If a director is appointed on more than one occasion during a financial year, the disclosable interest is that at the time of his/her first appointment. The wording of the legislation means that there is no requirement to disclose interests held at the beginning of the year (or at the date of appointment) by a director who did not have disclosable interests at the end of the year. However, this information is often given voluntarily for completeness.

Interests held by director's immediate family

36.27 The disclosure requirements specifically cover interests in shares and debentures held by the director's immediate family. For disclosure purposes, these are deemed to be interests held by the director. In this context 'immediate family' means the director's spouse, infant children and infant step-children (ie those under the age of 18). It therefore does not include the director's parents, brothers, sisters or children over the age of 18. If any members of a director's immediate family are also directors of the company, their interests are separately disclosable and are therefore not treated as interests of the director.

Change of holding company during the year

36.28 The disclosures can be particularly complicated where there is a change of holding company during the year and the directors of a subsidiary company have disclosable interests in the shares of one or both of the holding companies. The details that need to be disclosed under CA 1985 are:

- interests in the new holding company at the end of the year for all those who are directors at the end of the year; and
- for the directors who have disclosable interests in the new holding company at the end of the year, the interests that they held in the former holding company at the beginning of the year or at the date of their appointment if this took place during the year.

It may be appropriate to disclose additional information to clarify the interests in different companies and any movements in those interests, but this is not strictly a requirement of CA 1985. The normal disclosure requirements apply in respect of any interests held by the directors in the shares or debentures of the subsidiary company itself. The same approach would apply to any disclosable interests in the shares or debentures of other group companies if these also change as a result of the change in holding company.

Beneficial and non-beneficial interests

36.29 It is common practice to show separately the beneficial and non-beneficial interests held by the directors, but this is not a requirement of CA 1985.

Options to subscribe for shares or debentures

36.30 The directors' report or notes to the accounts must also disclose details of directors' rights to subscribe for shares in or debentures of the company or any other company in the group. Rights to subscribe are notifiable interests for the purpose of the register of directors' shareholdings. As with interests in shares and debentures, options held by the director's immediate family must also be included. The following details must be given individually for each person who was a director at the end of the financial year:

- whether during the year he/she was granted any rights to subscribe for shares in or debentures of the company or any other company in the group; and
- whether during the year he exercised any rights to subscribe for shares in and debentures of the company or any other company in the group.

For each director who had disclosable interests in options at the end of the year, the following details must be given:

- the name of the company (or companies) in which he/she was granted or exercised a right to subscribe;
- the number of shares in each company in respect of which he/she was granted or exercised a right to subscribe; and
- the amount of debentures of each company in respect of which he/she was granted or exercised a right to subscribe.

The wording of the legislation requires a negative statement to be given for any directors at the end of the financial year who did not hold rights to subscribe for shares in or debentures of the company, or any other company in the group. The disclosure requirements on directors' remuneration also include certain details of options (see **Chapter 16**).

Cumulative details of options held

36.31 The disclosure requirements in respect of options relate solely to options granted and exercised during the year. There is no specific requirement to disclose details of total options held. There is an argument that options are covered by the broad definition of an 'interest' in shares and debentures but the wording of CA 1985 is very confusing on this point. Options to subscribe for shares and debentures may also be disclosable under the provisions of CA 1985 on arrangements in which a director has a material interest. If so, details of unexercised options granted to date would need to be disclosed in addition to options granted and exercised during the year. UITF Abstract 10 'Disclosure of Directors' Share Options' set out detailed recommendations for disclosing information on options held, granted and exercised by directors, but the Abstract has been withdrawn for accounting periods ending on or after 31 December 2002 because quoted companies are now required by law to provide similar disclosures in their accounts (see **Chapter 16**).

Directors of wholly-owned subsidiaries

36.32 Where a director of a wholly-owned subsidiary is also a director of its holding company, and his interests in the shares and debentures of companies within the group (including options) will be disclosed in the directors' report of the holding company, the information is not required to be given in the directors' report of the subsidiary. In this case, it is usual to explain the situation in the directors' report of the subsidiary company.

Example 36.3

A D Evans is also a director of … Ltd, the company's ultimate holding company, and his interests in the shares and debentures of group companies are disclosed in the directors' report of that company.

POLITICAL DONATIONS AND EXPENDITURE

Political Parties, Elections and Referendums Act 2000

36.33 Significant changes to the rules on political donations were introduced by the *Political Parties, Elections and Referendums Act 2000*, which came into effect on 16 February 2001. The new legislation is complex and wide-ranging. In the context of political donations by companies it inserts a new Part XA into CA 1985 and also amends Sch 7 paras 3–5. The new legislation broadly requires:

- prior shareholder approval for political expenditure within the EU and for aggregate donations to EU political organisations of more than £5,000 by a company and its subsidiaries in any twelve-month period beginning with the company's 'relevant date' (see **36.34**);
- disclosure of the individual recipients, and the amounts given, where the aggregate amount of political expenditure and political donations in the EU by a company or group exceeds £200; and
- disclosure of the aggregate amount paid or donated to non-EU political parties by a company or group (in this case there is no *de minimis* amount).

Where a payment or donation is to be made by a subsidiary, prior approval must also be obtained from the shareholders of the holding company. This is to prevent a company circumventing the approval provisions by making payments through a subsidiary. Wholly-owned subsidiaries of UK parent companies are exempt from the disclosure requirements, on the basis that the details will be given in the parent company's accounts. If the new approval requirements are not followed the directors will be personally liable to make good the amount paid or donated and to pay damages for any loss suffered by the company. In the case of non-compliance by a subsidiary, the directors of the holding company will also be personally liable.

Relevant date

36.34 A company's relevant date is the earlier of:

— the date of its AGM, if one is held within 12 months of 16 February 2001; or

— 16 February 2002.

Shareholder approval must be in place for any payments or donations made after the relevant date and the new disclosures must be given in the directors' report for financial years starting on or after the first anniversary of the relevant date.

Example 36.4 – Impact of relevant date

Financial year-end	31 December
Date of AGM	1 August 2001
Relevant date (earlier of 1 August 2001 and 16 February 2002)	1 August 2001

Prior shareholder approval must therefore be obtained for all political payments and donations made after 1 August 2001.

First anniversary of relevant date	1 August 2002
First financial period beginning after this date	y/e 31 December 2003

The new disclosure requirements will therefore apply for the directors' report for the year ending 31 December 2003.

Definition of EU political expenditure

36.35 The legislation defines EU political expenditure as any expenditure incurred by the company in respect of:

— the preparation, publication or dissemination of any advertising or other promotional or publicity material, of whatever nature and however published or otherwise disseminated, that at the time of publication or dissemination can reasonably be regarded as intended to affect public support for any EU political organisation;

- any activities that can reasonably be regarded as intended to affect public support for any EU political organisation; and
- any activities which can reasonably be regarded as intended to influence voters in any national or regional referendum held under the law of any EU member state.

An EU political organisation is any party registered under Political Parties, Elections and Referendums Act 2000 Pt II, any other political party participating in any elections to public office in an EU member state other than the UK, or any independent candidates at any such elections.

Definition of donations

36.36 A donation to a registered party is given a very broad definition in the legislation, covering:

- any gift of money or other property;
- any sponsorship provided;
- any subscription or fee paid for affiliation to, or membership of, the party;
- any money spent (otherwise than by or on behalf of the party) in paying for any expenses incurred directly or indirectly by the party;
- any money lent to the party, other than on commercial terms; and
- the provision of any property, services or facilities to the party (including the services of any persons) other than on commercial terms.

A subscription for membership of an EU trade association is specifically excluded from the definition of a donation. However, payments made to finance any particular activity of the association are not considered to be subscriptions.

Gifts

36.37 A gift is defined as including:

- any money or other property transferred to the party in a transaction or arrangement where the monetary value of any consideration provided by or on behalf of the party is less than the value of the money or the market value of the property transferred;
- anything that is given or transferred indirectly through a third person; and
- a bequest.

Also, anything given or transferred to any officer, member, trustee or agent of a registered party in his capacity as such (i.e. not for his own use or benefit) is to be treated as if it had been given or transferred to the party. The value of a gift is its market value or, where appropriate, the difference between its market value and the total monetary value of any consideration provided by or on behalf of the party.

Sponsorship

36.38 Sponsorship is provided to a registered party if any money or other property is transferred to the party, or to any person for the benefit of the party, and the purpose (or one of the purposes) is or can reasonably be assumed to be:

- to meet, or help the party to meet, any defined expenses incurred or to be incurred by or on behalf of the party; or
- to secure to any extent that such expenses are not incurred.

Defined expenses are those connected with:

- any conference, meeting or event organised by or on behalf of the party;
- the preparation, production or dissemination of any publication by or on behalf of the party; or
- any study or research organised by or on behalf of the party.

The following are specifically excluded from the definition of sponsorship in the legislation:

- payment of any charge for admission to a conference, meeting or event;
- payment of the purchase price of any publication (or similar charge for access to it); and
- payment for the inclusion of an advertisement in any publication, provided that this is made at the appropriate commercial rate.

The value of any sponsorship provided is the value of the money provided or, where relevant, the market value of the property transferred. The monetary value of any benefit conferred on the person providing the sponsorship is to be disregarded. Where the sponsorship provides the party with an enduring benefit that lasts for two or more financial periods of the donor company, the amount to be disclosed in the directors' report is the amount accruing to the period covered by the report – the total value donated will therefore need to be apportioned between the reporting periods covered.

Loans, services and facilities provided

36.39 The value of a donation provided in the form of a loan or of other services and facilities is the difference between:

- the total monetary value of the consideration that would have had to be provided by or on behalf of the party if the loan, services or facilities had been provided on commercial terms; and
- the total monetary value of any consideration actually provided by or on behalf of the party.

In determining whether a transaction has been undertaken on commercial terms, the legislation requires the assessment to take into account the total value, in monetary terms, of any consideration provided by or on behalf of the party in respect of the transaction.

Contributions to non-EU political parties

36.40 The legislation requires disclosure of the total amount contributed to non-EU political parties - there is no *de minimis* amount in this case. A non-EU political party is any political party whose activities are carried on wholly outside the member states of the EU. The legislation defines a contribution as:

- any gift of money to the organisation, whether made directly or indirectly;
- any subscription or other fee paid for affiliation or membership of the organisation; and
- any money spent (other than by or on behalf of the organisation) in paying any expenses incurred directly or indirectly by the organisation.

CHARITABLE DONATIONS

Donations for charitable purposes

36.41 The directors' report must disclose the total amount given for charitable purposes by the company (and, where relevant, the group) during the financial year, unless the total given is £200 or less. Where amounts have been given for more than one charitable purpose during the year, the amount given for each purpose must be shown. The same threshold applies to both companies and groups. Wholly-owned subsidiaries of a company incorporated in Great Britain are exempt from the disclosure on the basis that the information will be shown in the directors' report of the parent company. The legislation states that the expression 'charitable purposes' means purposes that are exclusively charitable. In this case, therefore, sponsorship payments will not usually be covered by the disclosure requirements as there will usually be an element of advertising or marketing connected with them, and there will consequently be a fairly evident commercial element to the transaction. Similarly, any payments to a charity that are of a direct commercial nature (e.g. payments for services provided by the charity) will not be disclosable. Money given for charitable purposes to a person who was ordinarily resident outside the UK at the time that the gift was made, is also specifically excluded from the disclosure requirements by the legislation.

Payments via a charitable trust

36.42 Some companies make payments to a company trust, which then has discretion to make donations to individual charities. In this case the amount paid to the trust will usually be disclosable, together with brief details of its objectives.

EMPLOYEE DISCLOSURES

Scope of the disclosure requirements

36.43 The disclosure requirements on disabled persons and employee involvement apply only to companies where the average number of employees in each week of the financial year exceeds 250. Other companies are free to give the information voluntarily if they wish. CA 1985 is very specific on how the average number of employees should be calculated in order to establish whether the disclosure requirements apply. The figure must be calculated by:

- ascertaining the number of people employed by the company under contracts of service in each week of the financial year, regardless of whether they were employed for the full week or only for part of it;
- adding up the numbers ascertained in this way for each week of the financial year; and
- dividing the resultant total by the number of weeks in the financial year.

People employed to work wholly or mainly outside the UK should be excluded from the calculation.

Disabled persons

36.44 The directors' report must include a statement on the company's policy during the financial year for:

- giving full and fair consideration to applications for employment made by disabled persons, having regard to their particular aptitudes and abilities;

- continuing the employment of, and arranging appropriate training for, any employees who have become disabled during the period when they were employed by the company;
- the training, career development and promotion of disabled persons employed by the company.

The information is usually given in a short narrative statement on the issues specifically required to be covered by CA 1985. The note might usefully include discussion of the following:

- contacts with local organisations for disabled persons;
- specific actions to encourage applications from disabled persons;
- adaptations to buildings to allow easier access for disabled persons; and
- training programmes offered to disabled persons and whether these are identical to those offered to other employees.

Employee involvement

36.45 The directors' report must include a statement on the action taken during the year to introduce, maintain and develop arrangements for:

- providing employees with information on matters of concern to them as employees;
- consulting employees or their representatives on a regular basis so that their views can be taken into account in making decisions likely to affect their interests;
- encouraging the involvement of employees in the company's performance;
- achieving a common awareness on the part of all employees of the financial and economic factors affecting the performance of the company.

The information is usually given in a narrative statement, which often includes discussion of the following:

- use of internal seminars and training programmes to provide appropriate information to employees;
- use of in-house newsletters and information bulletins;
- relationship with recognised trade unions and other employee groups or bodies;

- arrangements for regular meetings between employee representatives and management;
- details of employee share schemes;
- details of profit-related pay schemes; and
- action to promote equal opportunities.

PAYMENT OF CREDITORS

Scope of the disclosure requirements

36.46 Disclosures on the company's policy and practice on the payment of creditors are only required in the accounts of a company that:

- is a public company at any time during the year; or
- was at any time during the year a member of a group headed by a public company, and did not qualify as small or medium-sized in relation to that year.

Detailed disclosures

36.47 A company that comes within this definition must disclose in its directors' report:

- whether it is the company's policy to follow any code or standard on payment practice for some or all of its suppliers and, if so:
  - the name of the code or standard; and
  - details of the place where information about and copies of the code or standard can be obtained;
- whether it is the company's policy:
  - to settle terms of payment with some or all of its suppliers when agreeing the terms of each transaction;
  - to make those suppliers aware of the terms of payment; and
  - to abide by those terms of payment;
- where the company's policy in respect of some or all of its suppliers differs from either of the above, its actual policy on payment of those suppliers must be stated;
  - if the company has different policies for different suppliers (or classes of suppliers), the suppliers (or classes of suppliers) to which the different policies apply; and
  - the number of days' purchases outstanding at the end of the period, which should be calculated by dividing the amount owed

to trade creditors at the end of the period by the average daily amount invoiced to the company by its suppliers during the accounting period.

Suppliers are defined as any person whose claim on the reporting company in respect of goods and services supplied would be included under 'trade creditors' within 'Creditors: amounts falling due within one year' in a balance sheet drawn up in accordance with balance sheet Format 1 under CA 1985 Sch 4 (see **Chapter 18**).

STATEMENT OF DIRECTORS' RESPONSIBILITIES

Requirement to include a statement

36.48 Statement of Auditing Standards 600 (SAS 600) 'Auditors' Reports on Financial Statements' requires auditors to refer in their report to a description of the responsibilities of the directors in respect of the accounts and to distinguish the responsibilities of the auditors from those of the directors. The statement must therefore be given whenever the accounts are subject to audit. It is preferable for the directors to make their own statement of their responsibilities and it is usual practice for this to be set out on a separate page of the accounts, immediately preceding the audit report. However, it is also acceptable to include the statement within the directors' report. If a statement of the directors' responsibilities is not given in the accounts or directors' report, or if the statement given is not adequate, the auditors are required to include an appropriate description of the directors' responsibilities in their audit report.

Matters to be covered

36.49 The following matters should be covered in the statement:

- the company law requirement for directors to prepare annual accounts giving a true and fair view of the profit or loss for the year and of the state of affairs at the end of the year;
- in preparing those accounts, the requirement for the directors to:
  - select suitable accounting policies;
  - apply those accounting policies on a consistent basis;
  - make judgments and estimates that are prudent and reasonable;
  - state whether applicable accounting standards have been followed, subject to any material departures disclosed and explained in the accounts; and
  - prepare the accounts on a going concern basis unless it is not appropriate to presume that the company will continue in business;

— the requirement for the directors to:

  — keep proper accounting records;

  — safeguard the assets of the company; and

  — take reasonable steps to prevent and detect fraud and other irregularities.

Small and medium-sized companies are not required to state whether their accounts have been prepared in accordance with applicable accounting standards. SAS 600 therefore recognises that it would be inappropriate for a comment on this to be included in the directors' responsibilities statement for small and medium-sized companies. The statement on applicable accounting standards is therefore only required where the company does not qualify as small or medium-sized under CA 1985.

Example wording

36.50 SAS 600 suggests the following wording for the statement in the case of a company.

Example 36.5 – Statement of directors' responsibilities

Company law requires the directors to prepare financial statements for each financial year which give a true and fair view of the state of affairs of the company and of the profit and loss of the company for that period. In preparing those financial statements, the directors are required to:

— select suitable accounting policies and then apply them consistently;

— make judgments and estimates that are reasonable and prudent;

— state whether applicable accounting standards have been followed, subject to any material departures disclosed and explained in the financial statements*; and

— prepare the financial statements on the going concern basis unless it is inappropriate to presume that the company will continue in business.

The directors are responsible for keeping proper accounting records which disclose with reasonable accuracy at any time the financial position of the company and to enable them to ensure that the financial statements comply with CA 1985. They are also responsible for safeguarding the assets of the company and hence for taking reasonable steps for the prevention and detection of fraud and other irregularities.

* Not required for companies that qualify as small or medium-sized under CA 1985.

Audit exemption

36.51 In the case of a small company which is eligible for audit exemption under the provisions of CA 1985, a different statement of responsibilities is required from the directors. In this case, the legislation requires the directors to state that:

- for the year in question, the company is entitled to the exemption under CA 1985 s 249A(1) or (2);
- no notice has been deposited under CA 1985 s 249B(2) requiring an audit for that year;
- they acknowledge their responsibilities for:
  - ensuring that the company maintains accounting records which comply with CA 1985 s 221; and
  - preparing accounts which give a true and fair view of the state of affairs of the company at the end of the financial year and of the profit or loss for that year in accordance with CA 1985 s 226, and which comply with the relevant accounting requirements of CA 1985.

This statement must be positioned above the director's signature on the balance sheet. Where the company also prepares shorter form accounts, the statement is usually combined with the directors' formal statement on those accounts (see **Chapter 7**).

Specialised businesses and unincorporated entities

36.52 SAS 600 applies to all audit reports. The wording of the statement of directors' responsibilities may need to be amended to reflect the specific requirements applying to specialised businesses (e.g. banks, insurance companies). In the case of unincorporated entities (e.g. charities, pension funds) the responsibilities of the directors, managers or trustees may not be so clearly defined and may vary quite considerably between apparently similar entities. Care must be taken to ensure that the statement properly reflects the responsibilities actually in place under the relevant constitution or trust deed.

LIKELY FUTURE DEVELOPMENTS

Government proposals for change

36.53 Following the recent company law review, the Government White Paper 'Modernising Company Law' published in July 2002 proposes removing the present requirement for a narrative directors' report and replacing it with a requirement for the directors to provide a short supplementary statement, to meet the EU requirement for a 'fair review' and provide a location for other necessary disclosures not covered in the accounts. The precise contents of the supplementary statement will be established by Parliament. The detailed reporting by the directors of small companies will be limited to this supplementary statement. Larger companies will be required to prepare an Operating and Financial Review in addition to the supplementary statement. The Government proposes to adopt the company law review recommendations in establishing the initial regime for this. The requirement for an OFR will therefore apply to companies who meet two out of the three following criteria:

	Public companies	*Private companies*
Turnover more than	£50 million	£500 million
Balance sheet total more than	£25 million	£250 million
Number of employees more than	500	5,000

Auditors will be required to report on the adequacy of the preparation process and compliance with applicable rules. The intention is that the new legislation will prescribe the contents of the OFR in general terms, but that detailed requirements will be developed by the new Standards Board (the proposed successor to the ASB). The White Paper notes that the Government welcomes the updating of the ASB Statement 'Operating and Financial Review' (see **36.8**) and it therefore seems likely that the revised Statement will form the basis for any new reporting requirements.

Index

Introduction. The index covers Chapters 1 to 36. Index entries are generally to paragraph numbers in the form 12.2, indicating paragraph 2 of Chapter 12, but the Appendices are indexed in the form 18.App, indicating the Appendix to Chapter 18. Alphabetical arrangement is word-by-word, where a group of letters followed by a space is filed before the same group of letters followed by a letter, eg 'Own shares' will appear before 'Ownership interests'.